The New
Penguin Cookery
Book

The New Penguin Cookery Book

JILL NORMAN

MICHAEL JOSEPH
an imprint of
PENGUIN BOOKS

MICHAEL JOSEPH

Published by the Penguin Group
Penguin Books Ltd, 80 Strand, London WC2R ORL, England
Penguin Putnam Inc., 375 Hudson Street, New York, New York 10014, USA
Penguin Books Australia Ltd, 250 Camberwell Road, Camberwell, Victoria 3124, Australia
Penguin Books Canada Ltd, 10 Alcorn Avenue, Toronto, Ontario, Canada M4V 3B2
Penguin Books India (P) Ltd, 11 Community Centre, Panchsheel Park, New Delhi – 110 017, India
Penguin Books (NZ) Ltd, Cnr Rosedale and Airborne Roads, Albany, Auckland, New Zealand
Penguin Books (South Africa) (Pty) Ltd, 24 Sturdee Avenue, Rosebank 2196, South Africa

Penguin Books Ltd, Registered Offices: 80 Strand, London WC2R ORL, England

www.penguin.com

First published 2001
1

Set in 10.5/14.5 pt Minion
Typeset by Rowland Phototypesetting Ltd,
Bury St Edmunds, Suffolk
Printed in Great Britain by The Bath Press, Bath

A CIP catalogue record for this book is available from the British Library

ISBN 0–718–14350–7

For Paul, with love,
and in memory of Elizabeth David and Richard Olney

Words in the text which are followed by an * indicate an entry in the Glossary.

Contents

Introduction

The original *Penguin Cookery Book* was published half a century ago and has remained in print, with only one major revision in the 1970s, until now. The book was strong on techniques and explanations, which is why it lasted. Like all good cookery books, it also reflected the eating patterns of its time – a past when people wanted to know what vegetables went best with different roast meats, when macaroni cheese and spaghetti with meat sauce were the only common pasta dishes, when greengrocers sold marrows but not courgettes, and when fish-and-chips were practically our only take-away food.

Food has never been a significant part of our culture, as it is in France or Italy and in many oriental countries. This means that we readily borrow or 'interpret' dishes that we have come to know, either from our ever more distant holiday travels, or because in the last fifty years our society has become multicultural – even if the strands are more often parallel than interwoven. We can eat the food of many different countries in local restaurants and from take-aways and we have come to cook in different ways. Meat and two veg may still survive as Sunday lunch, but British food is now just as likely to be a pasta dish, a Chinese stir-fry, Thai curry or Middle Eastern kebabs.

We are becoming more aware of the importance of a healthy balanced diet and of using good-quality ingredients. Large helpings of meat and rich cream-based sauces and desserts are being replaced by lighter dishes using fish, vegetables and fruit. Rice, pasta and couscous have become familiar staples alongside potatoes and bread. Vegetarians are no longer seen as odd but are catered for as a matter of course in most restaurants and on the food-to-go shelves of supermarkets. A huge amount of money may be spent on ready-meals and on sauces to add to a home-cooked dish, but shops and supermarkets sell increasingly wide ranges of herbs and spices and of fresh and often organically grown or reared foods.

Yet, in spite of the abundance of good ingredients, the number of cookery articles written every week and cookery books published every month, the plethora of cooking programmes on television, we do not always eat well. There is a knowledge gap. Cooking and nutrition are still largely absent from the school curriculum, and few young people learn to cook at home. If agricultural disasters are to be prevented, the ways in which animals and crops are reared and grown must be understood more widely and, where necessary, improved. If we are to avoid becoming an obese nation prone to heart disease, we must develop an awareness and appreciation of food, its place in our lives and the ways in which we can make it not just sustain but enhance life. The cult of the chef and the television personality may have somewhat glamorized food but cooking as a spectator sport is no substitute for the real thing.

I learned to cook from books, and essentially from developing the Penguin cookery list and publishing Elizabeth David, Jane Grigson, Claudia Roden and many others. The writer-cooks who have influenced me most are Elizabeth David and Richard Olney. Both were gifted cooks with enquiring minds, intent on understanding fully a method or a dish and always aware that simplicity is often best. They were a delight to work with; to eat their food, to cook with them and eventually to cook for them was always a rewarding experience.

The means I developed for judging the merits of a submitted typescript was to try the recipes that looked most interesting and those that looked most unlikely. My family ate their way, mostly uncomplaining, through weeks of Indian, Chinese, Mexican, Hungarian, Spanish, Middle Eastern and Caribbean food, depending on the book I was working on. In this way I learned in some depth the techniques, ingredients and preparations of very different cuisines. I came to understand that techniques are the key to all cooking, that if you have mastered those you can turn out a dish without necessarily having to follow a recipe to the letter. I also acquired a great curiosity about the foods of the world and started travelling to discover more.

Eating well starts with shopping well, buying the best available ingredients – good unsalted butter, a wild salmon, seasonal fruit and vegetables, whole spices rather than ground ones – and treating them carefully and with respect. Good fresh ingredients can be expensive, but a small amount of something costly can usually be balanced by other, cheaper ingredients. Cooking need not be time-consuming either: many dishes can be prepared and put on the table in half an hour or less, others require the same amount of time in preparation and can then look after themselves as they simmer or stew.

In writing the *New Penguin Cookery Book* I have tried to interpret the diversity of eating habits in present-day Britain. Most chapters start with the techniques that can be applied to the principal ingredients, and then illustrate their use in recipes. Most recipes are capable of variation, but that variation should be thoughtful, respecting the idea of the dish. Gaining an understanding of flavours and textures, and learning how to create harmonious combinations, is one of the pleasures of cooking. Sybille Bedford's maxim, interpreting Escoffier, '*faites simple* does not mean *faites slapdash*' says it all.

London, July 2001

Acknowledgements

Thanks are due first to my husband, Paul Breman, who contributed recipes, some- xi
times cooked and certainly ate his way through the book, offering advice and
encouragement. He also compiled the index with his customary care. Thanks too to
our daughters, Sasha and Elinor, who provided ideas and cooked several of the dishes.

Friends gave information, contributed recipes or allowed me to use recipes from
their own books: thanks go to Lynda Brown, Marion Burdenuik, Sally Clarke, Carol
Field, Nevin Halici, Simon Hopkinson, Jenny Kruss, the Lancellotti family, Prue
Leith, Christine Manfield, Lulu Peyraud, Francesco Radaeli, Claudia Roden, Julie
Sahni, Maria José Sevilla, Ann and Franco Taruschio, Tiziana and Anselmo Zeri.
Clare Marriage of Doves Farm provided material on flours; Eileen MacPhee of the
Sea Fish Industry Authority sent information on fish. Foods From Spain lent videos
on Spanish rice production and its use in traditional dishes. Marion Burdenuik and
Tom Smith made cakes and desserts. Barbara Kafka generously allowed me to use
timings for cooking fish and vegetables from *Microwave Gourmet*.

Many recipes are from the books of authors now dead. I have drawn on the
work of Eliza Acton, Elizabeth David, Jane Grigson, Nika Hazelton, Richard Olney,
Edouard de Pomiane, Mme St-Ange and Alice B. Toklas. The other recipes have
evolved, often originally adapted from other books or cookery articles, sometimes
from ideas picked up on my travels, to become occasional or regular dishes in our
household.

Special thanks to Jenny Dereham for her patience and unflagging support, and for
her thorough and meticulous editing. Thanks to Craig Burgess for his imaginative
approach to finding the right design for a long and complex book and to Suzanne
Olding for the illustrations.

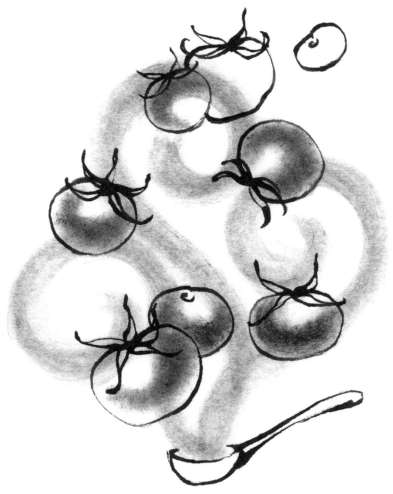

Soups

Soup is restorative and sustaining, a pot simmering on the
stove fills the kitchen with inviting aromas which lift the
spirit, and a bowl of soup on the table induces a sense of
well-being. Soups range from sparkling clear liquids to creamy purées and hearty chowders,
gumbos and pots au feu. The principal ingredients are meat,
fish and vegetables, but fruits also make good soups, especially
cold soups which are so refreshing in hot weather.

Stock

Although some soups are best made with water to keep the pure flavours of the main ingredients, stock is the basis of most soup making. It also forms the basis of many sauces and stews. To make stock is not difficult, but it requires time. Vegetables, meat, poultry or fish, together with aromatic ingredients, are simmered gently in water to extract their flavour, the liquid is strained and any fat removed. Cheap cuts of meat, bones, chicken wings, a cooked chicken carcass, fish bones, some vegetable trimmings can all be used. However, a stock is only as good as the ingredients you put into it, so don't use the stock pot as a dustbin.

It is important for food safety to cool stock quickly once it is made, and to strain it before storing. Make sure the liquid is properly cold before putting it into the refrigerator and don't keep stock there for more than 3 days. Stock freezes well for up to 3 months. It can be boiled down, in an open pan, by a third or a half to make a concentrated stock. Concentrated stock can be diluted later by adding water.

Supermarkets and delicatessens now keep ready-made stocks in their chilled food cabinets; although expensive compared with homemade stock, they are better than stock cubes with their strong synthetic flavours. If you do use stock cubes the Just Bouillon range is better than most. Telma chicken and beef soup mix won't distort the flavour of your dish too much, and for vegetable stock the best product is Marigold granules.

Garnishes and embellishments

The simplest and quickest garnish is a scattering of chopped herbs. Parsley, coriander, chives, fennel, dill, mint or lovage will enhance most soups. A chiffonade* of spinach or sorrel can be softened for a minute or two in the simmering soup before serving. Julienne* strips of firm vegetables such as carrot, turnip, celery or celeriac should be blanched for a minute in boiling water to soften them a little before being added to the soup. Cubes of peeled and seeded tomato or cucumber can be added raw, as can avocado, finely sliced mushrooms or spring onions. Grated citrus peel, slivers of fresh ginger or lemon grass provide a clean, sharp note.

Fine noodles, tortellini, ravioli, won-tons and rice will add substance. The pasta needs pre-cooking: noodles for a couple of minutes, filled pasta for 4–5 minutes. Rice can be cooked in the soup.

A knob of butter, plain or flavoured (p. 385), a swirl of olive oil (use a good one), cream or yogurt will provide enrichment. Egg yolks lightly whisked with a little stock or cream and stirred into simmering soup just before serving will thicken it, improve the texture and give the soup a sheen, but the soup must not boil or the egg will curdle. A poached egg is often added to clear soup in Spain and Italy, particularly to give richness to simple soups of water, garlic and vegetables.

Croûtons and croûtes are easy traditional accompaniments. Croûtes can be put in the bottom of soup bowls, floated on the soup or served separately. Bread is sometimes used to thicken soup too (*see* gazpacho p. 21).

To make toasted croûtons

Cut slices of day-old bread 1cm thick into cubes, discarding crusts, and bake at 180°C, 350°F, gas 4, for 10–12 minutes, turning the cubes frequently, until crisp and lightly browned. If you wish, rub the bread with a cut clove of garlic before baking.

To make fried croûtons

Cut the bread as above and fry in 5mm oil over gentle heat. Stir to ensure the croûtons brown evenly. Drain on kitchen paper. Croûtons, fried or toasted, stored in an airtight container in a cool, dry place, will keep for up to 2 weeks.

To make cheese croûtes

For 4 slices of french bread, mix together 30g grated cheese with 10g butter and season well with mustard, pepper and cayenne. Under the grill, toast the bread lightly on one side, spread the cheese mixture on the other and toast quickly to golden brown. Cheddar, Parmesan and Gruyère are good for croûtes, although Gruyère will become slightly stringy.

To make olive oil and garlic croûtes

Under the grill, toast 4 slices of french bread lightly on one side. Rub the other side with a cut clove of garlic and drizzle olive oil over it. A little mashed anchovy can be good too. Toast until brown.

Stocks

Vegetable stock

Makes about 2 litres	2 stalks celery with leaves, chopped	4 thyme sprigs or 1 tsp dried thyme
3 onions, peeled and chopped	trimmings from any of the following: broccoli, cabbage, lettuce, mushrooms, watercress	1 bay leaf
3 leeks, cleaned and chopped		10 black peppercorns
3 carrots, peeled and chopped		salt
1 head fennel, chopped	a few stalks of flat-leaf parsley, chopped	2 litres cold water

Put everything into a large pan and bring slowly to the boil. Skim off any scum that rises to the surface, lower the heat and simmer for 45 minutes. Strain the stock and check the seasoning.

Chicken stock

Boiling fowls are scarcer than caviare these days, but you should be able to order one from your butcher. If your butcher cuts his own chicken joints he may let you have a couple of raw carcasses to add substance to a stock made from chicken wings.

Makes about 2.25 litres	2 stalks celery with leaves, chopped	2 bay leaves
1 boiling fowl or 2kg wings and uncooked bones	2 carrots, peeled and chopped	1 sprig thyme or ¼ tsp dried thyme
1 large onion, peeled and chopped	2.5 litres water	10 black peppercorns
	10 parsley stalks, chopped	salt

Remove excess fat from the boiling fowl. Put it or the chicken pieces into a large pan with the onion, celery and carrot. Cover with cold water and bring very slowly to the boil. Skim off the scum that rises to the surface; take the time to do this meticulously and you will have a clear stock. Now add the herbs and seasonings, partly cover the pan and simmer very gently for at least 2 hours. The less the pot bubbles, the cleaner the stock will be.

Lift out the chicken and use it later in a soup (p. 7 or p. 11), or pastel de choclo (p. 163), or for a pilaf or for sandwiches. Strain the stock through a sieve or colander lined with damp muslin (p. 528). Adjust the seasoning if necessary. When the stock has cooled use a wad of kitchen paper to blot up the fat from the surface; an alternative and easier method is to refrigerate the cold stock and then lift off the fat once it has hardened. If you are going to freeze the stock make sure to remove any fat first.

Variations

Light chicken stock You can make a lighter chicken stock using the carcass of a roast chicken together with any bits of skin and vegetables and flavourings as above. Simmer for 1½ hours, strain and degrease.

Meat stock 1kg shin of beef and 1kg chicken wings together with a chicken carcass or a veal knuckle, plus the vegetables and flavourings above will make a richer, more gelatinous stock. Simmer for at least 4 hours; strain and degrease.

Court-bouillon

Fish and shellfish are poached in an aromatic broth made with wine, water, vegetables and herbs, called a court-bouillon. Once you've poached your fish, you have a more strongly flavoured stock which can be used for making soups and sauces.

Makes about 1.7 litres	1 carrot, peeled and sliced	6 parsley stalks
½ bottle dry white wine		1 bay leaf
1½ litres water	white part of 1 leek, cleaned and sliced	6 black peppercorns
1 stalk celery, sliced	2 sprigs of thyme or ½ tsp dried thyme	4 coriander seeds
1 medium onion, peeled and chopped		salt

Bring all the ingredients to the boil, lower the heat and simmer for 15 minutes, then strain and the court-bouillon is ready for use.

Variations

• Dry cider can be used in place of wine, or replace it with 120ml wine vinegar and add more water. Herbs can be varied to suit the fish to be cooked – tarragon, dill, fennel are all good additional flavourings, as are 2–3 slices of lemon or a crushed clove of garlic.

Fish stock

A fishmonger will often provide bones or heads to make stock. If you buy a whole fish and have it filleted, make sure to ask for the bones. A small inexpensive fish such as a whiting can be used instead of bones. Crab, lobster and prawn shells make excellent stock.

6

Makes about 1.5 litres	1 leek, white part only, cleaned and sliced	1 bay leaf
1kg white fish bones and trimmings	100ml dry white wine	10 black peppercorns
1 stalk celery, sliced	1½ litres water	salt
1 medium onion, peeled and chopped	2 sprigs of thyme or ½ tsp dried thyme	
1 carrot, peeled and sliced	3–4 parsley stalks	

Break the bones into manageable pieces and put all the ingredients into a large pan. Bring to the boil over medium heat and skim off any scum that rises to the surface. Simmer for 20–25 minutes. Strain and it is ready for use, or when cool can be refrigerated or frozen.

Fish fumet

Make the stock as above, and when strained, reduce it by half at a steady boil. Use the fumet as the base for sauces to accompany fish.

Clear soups

The clear soups that follow have an unthickened or barely thickened broth with solid ingredients cut up and added to the liquid.

Chicken, sweetcorn and mushroom soup

Simple and satisfying, this soup can be made in no more than 10 minutes.

For 4	150g cooked chicken, diced	salt and freshly ground pepper
250g mushrooms, chopped	150g sweetcorn kernels (frozen or canned)	lemon juice (optional)
20g butter		2 tbs chopped dill or chervil
1 litre chicken stock (p. 4)	2 spring onions	

Sauté the mushrooms in the butter. Bring the stock to the boil and add the mushrooms, chicken and sweetcorn. Simmer for 5 minutes, then add the spring onions, sliced, and season. If the taste isn't quite sharp enough add a little lemon juice. Garnish with the dill or chervil.

Chinese hot and sour soup

This soup comes from Sichuan in western China where chillies play an important part in the cooking. It is a clear soup, rich and full of flavour, and very warming in winter. It takes a little time to cut up all the ingredients, but the soup cooks very quickly. Most of the ingredients can be found in a supermarket but you may have to go to an oriental shop for dried Chinese shiitake mushrooms and tofu, or to a health food shop for the latter.

For 4	60g bamboo shoots, cut in matchsticks	2 tsp chilli oil
3 dried Chinese shiitake mushrooms	125g firm tofu, shredded	1 tbs cornflour
900ml chicken stock (p. 4)	1 tbs soy sauce	1 egg
		2 tsp sesame oil
100g lean pork, cut in slivers	3 tbs rice or wine vinegar	2 spring onions, sliced finely

Soak the dried mushrooms in warm water for 20 minutes, then drain, remove the stalks and slice the caps finely. Bring the chicken stock to a simmer in a large pan and add the pork, mushrooms and bamboo shoots. Cover and simmer for 10 minutes. Add the tofu, soy sauce, vinegar and chilli oil. Mix the cornflour with 1 tbs water and when the soup starts bubbling again, stir it in. Simmer over very low heat for 1–2 minutes to thicken the soup. Beat the egg lightly and pour it into the soup through the tines of a fork or a strainer so that it sets in light strands. Add the sesame oil and spring onions and serve at once.

Dutch mussel soup

This recipe is from the Dutch island province of Zeeland, traditionally the best local source of seafood – especially the wonderful small Dutch shrimps. Use small mussels for preference: they look nicer in the soup.

The soup tastes good even without the mussels – their cooking liquid has sufficient flavour. You could just put a few mussels into the soup and use the rest for a separate small dish for 2 people: heat them in snail butter (p. 385) to be served with french bread, or heat them in cream with a dash of Pernod and chopped fennel or dill.

For 6		
1kg mussels	2 carrots, peeled and sliced	40g butter
1.5 litres water or 1 litre water and 500ml fish stock (p. 6)	2 leeks, cleaned and thinly sliced	salt and freshly ground pepper
2 slices celeriac	1 large onion, peeled and chopped finely	1 tbs chopped parsley

Scrub the mussels and remove the beards. Discard any that are broken or gaping open. Put the mussels in a large pan with 100ml of the water, cover and steam, shaking the pan from time to time, until the shells open (discard any that don't). Drain them into a colander set over a large bowl – the liquid will be used later.

Cut 2 slices from the celeriac, peel them and dice the flesh. (To store the rest, *see* p. 122.) Stew it gently with the other vegetables in the butter for 15 minutes in a large pan. Strain the mussel liquid over the vegetables, using a fine sieve and leaving behind any bits of grit in the bowl. Add the remaining water and stock and bring to the boil. Reduce to a simmer and add the shelled mussels to the soup. Taste and season. Let the mussels warm through, then sprinkle over the parsley and serve.

Onion soup

This recipe, from the south-west of France, bears little resemblance to the standard restaurant version served inedibly hot with sticky melted cheese. The amount of garlic varies from a whole head to a couple of cloves. It is sometimes made with milk instead of water.

For 4	8 garlic cloves, peeled and sliced finely	3 egg yolks
2 large onions, peeled and sliced finely	1 litre boiling water	1 tbs wine vinegar
2 tbs olive oil	salt and freshly ground pepper	4 slices of day-old French bread, or bread dried in the oven

Stew the onions gently in the oil, stirring regularly until they are soft and golden. Add the sliced garlic and water and season with salt and a little pepper. Simmer, covered, for 20 minutes. Just before serving, whisk the egg yolks lightly with the vinegar and pour over them a ladleful of the hot soup. Stir well. Remove the pan from the heat and stir in the egg mixture. Serve over the slices of bread.

Thai prawn soup (Tom yam kung)

This seems to be one of the most popular dishes in Thai restaurants, and it is certainly one of the easiest to make. *Tom yam pla* – fish soup – is made by simmering pieces of fish in water or stock and then adding the other ingredients. You could also use mussels, and use the strained liquid from opening them (*see* opposite) as part of the stock. To make the soup more substantial, or to reduce the amount of seafood or fish, add canned straw mushrooms or cellophane (beansprout) noodles, which only need soaking rather than cooking. Straw mushrooms come in cans and are tiny mushrooms which are used in tropical Asian cooking. These days the ingredients for making a Thai broth can be found in most supermarkets, but you might have to go to an oriental shop for the mushrooms and noodles.

For 6–8	1.5 litres chicken or fish stock (p. 4, p. 6)	½ can straw mushrooms (optional)
12–18 large raw prawns	1–4 small red chillies	100g cellophane noodles (optional)
3 stalks lemon grass*	2–3 tbs fish sauce (p. 520)	3–4 tbs chopped coriander
6 slices galangal* or peeled ginger	3–4 tbs lime juice	
6 lime leaves*	1–2 tbs sugar	

Peel the prawns, leaving on the tails, and remove the black vein from the back. Remove outer skin and top two-thirds from the lemon grass, cut the lower part in 5cm pieces. Bruise the lemon grass and galangal or ginger by bashing with a pestle or the back of a heavy knife. Put the lemon grass, galangal and lime leaves into a pot with the stock, bring to the boil and simmer gently for 10 minutes to infuse the flavours. If you don't want to pick bits out of your soup, you could strain the broth at this point, but you will lose something in flavour and in authenticity.

Add chillies, fish sauce, lime juice and sugar according to your taste. Keep the soup simmering and keep trying it; it should taste fresh and clean from the lemon grass, lime leaves and galangal, but it should also take on a different dimension – hot, salty, sour and sweet – from the new additions. When you are happy with it, add the mushrooms and noodles if you are using them. When the soup comes back to the simmer, add the prawns and cook until they turn pink. Serve hot in individual bowls, garnished with the coriander.

Tomato and rice soup

For 4	1 bay leaf	¼ tsp paprika
500g ripe tomatoes, chopped	2 sprigs fresh thyme or ½ tsp dried	800ml water or light stock
1 large onion, peeled and chopped finely	2 garlic cloves, peeled	80g long grain rice
3 tbs olive oil	salt and freshly ground pepper	1 large tomato, peeled, seeded and diced

Sauté the tomatoes and onion in the olive oil for 5–6 minutes, then add the bay leaf and thyme, the garlic first crushed with a little salt in a pestle and mortar, the pepper and paprika and the water or stock. Pour boiling water over the rice and leave to soak. Stir and simmer the soup for 10 minutes, then sieve it into a clean pan to get rid of the tomato skin and seeds and the herbs. Bring to a simmer, then strain the rice, rinse under the cold tap and add to the soup. Cook until the rice is done, about 10–12 minutes. Depending on the amount of liquid the rice absorbs, you may need to add a little more water or stock. Serve garnished with the tomato dice.

Winter vegetable soup

The vegetables for this soup can be varied but do keep the saffron which gives it a warm, rich flavour and a beautiful colour.

For 4–5	1 large carrot, peeled and diced	salt and freshly ground pepper
50g butter or 3 tbs olive oil	2 small white turnips, peeled and diced	50g soup pasta or vermicelli
1 large onion, peeled and chopped	1 medium potato, peeled and diced	¼ tsp powdered saffron or to taste
2 slices celeriac, peeled and diced (to store the rest, *see* p. 122)	1 litre vegetable, chicken or meat stock (pp. 4–5)	

Heat the butter or oil in a large pan and fry the onion until soft and turning golden. Add the other vegetables and stir for 2–3 minutes so that they take up some of the fat. Pour over the stock, season with salt and pepper, bring to the boil and then simmer for 15 minutes. The vegetables should be almost ready. Add the pasta and cook for 4–5 minutes more. Taste for seasoning and to see that the pasta and vegetables are cooked. Dissolve the saffron in 1 tbs warm water and stir it into the soup. Serve.

Puréed soups

Puréed soups are blended, whizzed in a food processor or passed through a sieve to achieve a fairly thick uniform consistency.

Chicken and almond soup

The Spanish make a lightly spiced soup with chicken stock and almonds, thickened with bread, and seem to have taken the idea to Mexico where a richer version is made, thickened with almonds and chicken.

For 6–8	2 tbs oil	1.5 litres chicken stock (p. 4)
60g blanched almonds	200g cooked chicken breast, diced	small bunch coriander, leaves chopped
2 garlic cloves, peeled and crushed	salt and freshly ground pepper	
1 onion, peeled and chopped	¼ tsp cumin	

Lightly fry the almonds, garlic and onion in the oil. Purée them in a food processor with half the chicken, the salt and spices and enough of the stock to make a smooth purée. Stir the purée into the rest of the stock in a pan and cook over low heat for 10 minutes with the remaining chicken. Stir in the coriander and serve.

Jerusalem artichoke soup

Jerusalem artichokes are a much underrated vegetable, perhaps because they are a bore to peel. Persevere though, and you can make a delicately flavoured creamy soup – one of the best. Once peeled, put the artichokes into water acidulated with a little lemon juice or vinegar because they discolour instantly.

For 6	1.2 litres water, vegetable or chicken stock (p. 4)	150ml single cream
80g butter		croûtons or bits of crisply fried streaky bacon to garnish
4 shallots, peeled and chopped	salt and freshly ground pepper	
850g Jerusalem artichokes, peeled and sliced thickly	grated nutmeg	

Heat 60g butter and sweat* the shallots and artichokes in a covered pan over low heat for 8–10 minutes, stirring frequently. Add the water or stock and season. Bring to the boil and simmer until the vegetables are soft, about 10 minutes. Blend the soup, stir in the cream and reheat gently. Whisk in the last knob of butter and serve at once with the croûtons or bacon.

Variations

- Other vegetable soups can be made on the same principle, using butter or olive oil to soften shallots or onions and the chosen vegetable. Add seasonings: ground coriander and orange zest are good with carrot; ground cumin or curry powder with parsnip; sorrel or a fresh tasting herb like chervil or parsley with broad beans; nutmeg with spinach and cauliflower. Don't overdo the flavourings, add a little, taste and add more if necessary. 1–1½ tsp of most spices is about right for a soup using 1 litre of liquid. Use nutmeg and chilli more sparingly; sturdy herbs like mint, tarragon, marjoram, parsley or sage can be cooked in the soup, whereas the more delicate basil, chervil and dill are best added towards the end.
- Soured cream or crème fraîche can replace the cream.

Leek and potato soup

Leek and potato soup is one of those foods that sets you to rights with the world, restores energy and well-being. Easy and quick to make, it can be served as a simple vegetable soup or enriched with cream or yogurt.

For 6	1.5 litres water or light stock	chopped chives to garnish
500g potatoes, peeled	salt and freshly ground pepper	
400g leeks, cleaned		
60g butter	150ml single cream	

Dice the potatoes and slice the white part of the leeks thinly. Stew them gently in the butter in a covered pan. Stir occasionally. When the vegetables have softened, add the water or stock and season. Bring to the boil and simmer until the vegetables are cooked, about 15 minutes. Purée through a sieve. Don't use a food processor or the potato will develop a glue-like texture. Stir in the cream, reheat gently and serve garnished with the chives.

Variations

- Substitute yogurt for the cream. Heat the soup, pour a ladleful into the yogurt and stir well, then pour the yogurt into the pan of soup. Mix it in and serve at once. Don't let it boil or the yogurt may curdle.

Rocket, leek and potato soup Use only 300g leeks and add 150g roughly chopped rocket to the soup with the cream, simmer briefly and serve. This version is also good chilled.

Vichyssoise. See p. 22

Watercress, leek and potato soup Use only 300g leeks and add the chopped leaves of a bunch of watercress at the same time as the cream. Simmer for a minute or two and serve. Also good chilled.

Lentil and lemon soup

You can use any type of lentil for this soup; the little orange ones will disintegrate in cooking, the large brown ones or the small dark Puy lentils will remain whole.

For 6–8	2 stalks celery, strings removed, then sliced finely	2 onions, peeled and sliced finely
2 carrots, peeled and diced	salt and freshly ground pepper	3 garlic cloves, peeled and crushed
350g lentils	juice of 1–2 lemons	1 tsp ground cumin (optional)
2 litres water, vegetable or chicken stock (p. 4)	3 tbs olive or sunflower oil	

Parboil the carrots in a little water. Wash the lentils and put them in a large pan with the water or stock. Bring slowly to the boil and add the carrot and celery to the pot. Cover and simmer gently until the lentils are soft; they will take 20–40 minutes, depending on the type and how old they are. Season with salt and pepper. If the lentils haven't disintegrated, blend or push the soup through a sieve. Keep back a ladleful or so if you like more texture in the soup. Add more hot water or stock if the soup is too thick.

A few minutes before serving, stir in lemon juice to sharpen the taste and keep the soup on a very low heat. Heat the oil in a frying pan and fry the onions until they are lightly browned, then stir in the garlic and, if you like a spicy note, the cumin. Fry for a little longer, then pour the contents of the pan into the soup and serve.

Pea soup

This is one of the best summer soups, especially when made with peas straight from the garden or allotment. If the peas are really fresh and sweet tasting, make the soup with water, otherwise use vegetable stock. You could make this soup with frozen peas if fresh aren't in season, or if you're in a great hurry.

For 6	500g peas, fresh or frozen (shelled weight)	salt and freshly ground pepper
2 leeks, cleaned and finely sliced	1 sprig mint or basil	150ml double cream or crème fraîche
½ small cos or other firm lettuce, shredded	1.2 litres water or vegetable stock (p. 4)	chopped mint or basil to serve
60g butter		

Stew the leeks and lettuce gently in the butter in a large pan. When the lettuce is wilted add the peas and the mint or basil. Stir and pour over the water or stock. Season and simmer until the peas are tender: 10 to 15 minutes for fresh, depending on the age of the peas; frozen peas will be ready in 5–6 minutes. Blend the soup and then reheat it slowly, but don't bring it to the boil. Stir in most of the cream. Taste and adjust the seasoning if necessary.

Serve hot with a swirl of the remaining cream in each bowl and a scattering of chopped mint or basil.

This soup is also good chilled.

Pumpkin and Gruyère soup

This is a version of a soup made by Raymond Blanc when he opened the first Les Quat' Saisons in Oxford in the seventies. I ate it there with Elizabeth David, who developed a version using Fontina cheese. For this recipe I have kept the original Gruyère, but both work well – as indeed does any cheese which melts readily. I have also added a pinch of mace and cloves which I find give depth to the pumpkin flavour.

For 4	pinch of ground cloves	salt and freshly ground pepper
600g pumpkin flesh, cubed	600ml vegetable or light chicken stock (p. 4, p. 5)	150ml double cream
600ml water		100g Gruyère
¼ tsp ground mace		

Simmer the pumpkin in the water until soft enough to push through a fine sieve. Discard the fibrous bits left in the sieve, season the purée with the mace and cloves and reheat with the stock. Taste and season, remembering that the cheese will be somewhat salty. Add the cream.

While the soup is heating (do not let it boil), put on the oven at 180°C, 350°F, gas 4. Cut the cheese into small cubes and distribute them into 4 ovenproof soup bowls. Put these into the oven until the cheese begins to melt. Pour the pumpkin soup onto the cheese and return the bowls to the oven for a few minutes until the cheese starts to form threads. Do not leave the bowls in the oven for too long or the contrast between the sticky cheese and the creamy soup will be lost. Serve straight away.

Hearty soups

A satisfying soup-stew makes an uncomplicated, well-flavoured lunch or supper at any time of the year, followed, if you wish, by cheese, fruit or dessert.

Fish chowder

This classic New England fisherman's soup-cum-stew is easy and very satisfying. Cod and haddock are the fish most often used. To smarten it up, you could add some prawns just before serving the chowder.

For 8	1 onion, peeled and thinly sliced	salt and white pepper
1kg cod, plus bones		300g cooked prawns in their shells (optional)
50g butter	4 medium potatoes, peeled and diced	
100g salt pork or streaky bacon, cubed	1 litre milk	

Simmer the fish with the bones in lightly salted water to cover. Depending on thickness and size it will take about 15–20 minutes to be almost cooked. Lift out the fish, strain and reserve the cooking liquid. Remove skin and bones and cut the fish into small fingers.

Heat the butter in a large pan and fry the salt pork or bacon until crisp. Remove the pork from the pan, put in the onion and brown lightly. Add the potatoes, the fish liquor and enough water to cover the potatoes. Boil until the potatoes are almost tender, about 8–10 minutes. Heat the milk, then add the salt pork, the fish and the hot milk to the soup and season to taste. Simmer for 3–4 minutes. If you are including the prawns, peel them and add them for the last minute so they heat through.

Variation

Smoked haddock chowder Replace the fish cooking liquor by 500ml fish stock and use 1kg smoked haddock, skinned and cut into fingers instead of the cod. Smoked haddock needs virtually no cooking, so make the soup as above, putting in the haddock to heat through for the last 5 minutes. The prawns go well in this chowder, too.

Harira

This thick, creamy Moroccan soup is traditionally eaten at sunset during the month of Ramadan to break the fast. It is the time when people stir themselves and start to think about the night-time celebrations. Like all traditional soups it has many versions: with lentils or dried broad beans instead of chick peas; with rice instead of vermicelli; the variations can be regional, urban, rustic or vegetarian.

For 6–8	½ tsp ground cumin	4 large tomatoes, peeled, seeded and chopped
400g shoulder or leg of lamb, cubed	½ tsp ground ginger	
	½ tsp freshly ground pepper	4 tbs chopped parsley
2 large onions, peeled and chopped	salt	4 tbs chopped coriander
150g chick peas, soaked overnight	1.5 litres water	100g soup vermicelli
1 tsp turmeric	60g butter	lemon quarters

Put the lamb, onion, chick peas and spices into a large pan and pour over the water. Bring slowly to the boil and skim off all the scum that rises to the surface. Add half the butter, cover and simmer for 1–1½ hours. Check the water from time to time and add more if necessary. Add salt to taste towards the end of the cooking time.

Heat the remaining butter in another pan and cook the tomatoes and herbs, seasoned with salt and pepper, to a loose purée. Check that the lamb and chick peas are cooked, then pour in the tomato mixture and add the vermicelli. Simmer for a little longer until the vermicelli is ready. Taste for seasoning and serve the harira with lemon quarters.

Roman bean soup

Small beans are best for this soup. The Italians are fond of mottled, brown borlotti beans, available in most supermarkets as well as Italian groceries. If you can't find them use white haricots. Pick up a pot of red pepper flakes from the spice stand or use chilli powder.

For 4	1 carrot, peeled and chopped finely	4–5 fresh sage leaves, shredded
250g borlotti or haricot beans	2 stalks celery, strings removed, then sliced finely	salt and freshly ground pepper
1 litre water		¼ tsp red pepper flakes
1 bay leaf	3 large tomatoes, peeled, seeded and chopped	2 tbs chopped parsley
4 tbs olive oil		olive oil
60g pancetta* or salt pork, chopped finely	2 cloves garlic, chopped finely	
1 large onion, peeled and chopped finely		

Soak the beans for several hours or overnight. Drain and put them into a large pan, cover with the water, add the bay leaf, cover and bring to the boil. Skim off any scum that rises to the surface, lower the heat and simmer for about 45 minutes.

Heat half the oil in a heavy pan and sweat* the pancetta, onion, carrot and celery. Don't let the vegetables brown. When they are soft add the tomatoes, garlic and sage, season and add the red pepper flakes. Cover and simmer for 10 minutes.

Stir the vegetable mixture into the beans and simmer until the beans are tender. It will take anything from 45 minutes to 1¼ hours, depending on the age of the beans. Stir in the parsley 10 minutes before the soup is ready. If it is too thick, add more hot water. Remove the bay leaf and serve with a little olive oil drizzled over the top.

Soupe au pistou

This summer meal-in-a-bowl is similar to minestrone but comes from Provence and is served with pistou, the local version of Genoese pesto. The vegetables can be varied, but beans, a squash or pumpkin and some root vegetables are always used. The soup can be made ahead of time, but make the pistou at the last moment.

For 6–8	150g haricot beans, soaked for several hours and cooked for 20 minutes	2 or 3 small courgettes, diced
2 litres water		90g short macaroni
1 onion, peeled and chopped finely	100g peas, fresh or frozen (shelled weight)	250g tomatoes, peeled, seeded and diced
2 carrots, peeled and diced	bouquet garni* of bay leaves, thyme and parsley	**For the pistou**
3 potatoes, peeled and diced		3 garlic cloves, peeled
250g pumpkin flesh, diced	salt and freshly ground pepper	large handful of basil leaves
3 stalks celery, strings removed, then chopped	150g green beans, cut into short lengths	75g grated Parmesan
		100ml olive oil

Bring the water to the boil and add the onion, carrots, potatoes, pumpkin, celery, haricot beans, peas and bouquet garni. Salt lightly, season well with pepper, cover and simmer for about 30 minutes until the vegetables begin to soften. Add the green beans, courgettes, macaroni and tomatoes and simmer for a further 15 minutes, until the macaroni is cooked.

To make the pistou, pound the garlic and basil to a paste in a mortar with a little salt. Add the Parmesan gradually, alternating with spoonfuls of olive oil to make a thick paste. It may be easier to mix with a large fork at this stage rather than the pestle. Alternatively, use a food processor or blender.

Check the seasoning of the soup and remove the bouquet. Do not heat the pistou, but serve it as an accompaniment at room temperature. Stir it well as the oil has a tendency to separate from the sauce.

Summer vegetable soup

This recipe was given to me many years ago by an old friend, the American cookery writer Nika Hazelton. It makes good use of fresh summer vegetables and produces a thick stew with very pure flavours.

For 6		
2 large tomatoes, peeled and sliced	1 medium cos lettuce, shredded	300g broad beans, fresh or frozen (shelled weight)
2 medium onions, peeled and thinly sliced	300g peas, fresh or frozen (shelled weight)	100ml olive oil
1 garlic clove, peeled and chopped	large handful of chopped parsley	salt and freshly ground pepper
3 medium courgettes, thinly sliced	3 tbs chopped basil	freshly grated Parmesan (optional)

Make the soup in a deep pan. Put the sliced tomatoes on the bottom and top with the onions and garlic. Put the courgettes on top of the onions, followed by the lettuce and then the peas. Sprinkle half the parsley and the basil over the peas and add the broad beans. Sprinkle the remaining parsley and the olive oil over everything. Be sure to follow this order and do not stir or mix the vegetables.

Cook, covered, over moderate heat for 10 minutes or until the vegetables at the bottom of the pan release their juices. Season with salt and pepper. Now stir the vegetables and mix well. Cover the pan again and simmer over low heat, stirring frequently, for about 30 minutes, until the beans are tender. Do not overcook. Do not add water: the vegetables have enough moisture of their own to make a thick soup. Serve hot or lukewarm, with Parmesan cheese.

Cold soups

We often think of soups as warming and sustaining dishes for cold weather or as soothing foods when we aren't well, but soups have their place in warm weather as well. Cold soups are refreshing and undemanding on a hot day.

Apple and watercress soup

For 4	1 tsp curry powder	2 egg yolks
30g butter	800ml vegetable or chicken stock (p. 4)	150ml double cream
1 onion, peeled and chopped	salt and freshly ground pepper	2 crisp eating apples
1 bunch watercress		juice of ½ lemon

Melt the butter and soften the chopped onion. Reserve a few small watercress leaves for the garnish and chop the rest of the leaves and the stalks. Stir them into the onion and add the curry powder. Pour in the stock, season, bring to the boil and simmer gently for 8 minutes. Remove the soup from the heat.

Whisk the egg yolks, heat the cream gently and pour it over the yolks together with a ladleful of the soup. Whisk everything well together, then pour the egg mixture into the cooling soup. Peel, core and slice one apple, add it to the soup which then whirl in the blender. When the texture is smooth, check the seasoning and chill for 2 hours or more. Peel, core and dice the other apple and toss it in the lemon juice. Garnish the soup with the apple and the reserved watercress.

Chilled avocado soup

Avocado soup is quick and simple to make and needs no cooking, but allow time to chill it.

For 6	1 litre chicken or vegetable stock (p. 4)	salt and freshly ground pepper
3 large ripe avocados	300ml single cream	2 tbs chopped coriander
juice of 1 lemon or lime	Tabasco or other chilli sauce to taste	

Peel the avocados and remove the stones. Put aside one half avocado for the garnish, rubbing it well with lemon juice to avoid discolouration. Mash the remaining avocados with a fork and add the rest of the lemon juice. Blend the purée with the stock and most of the cream. Season with chilli sauce, salt and pepper, remembering that flavours are less pronounced when cold. Chill the soup for 2 hours or more. Serve with a swirl of cream, the reserved avocado cut into fine dice and the chopped coriander.

Chilled pea soup

Follow the recipe for pea soup on p. 14, then chill thoroughly before serving.

Chilled red pepper soup

For 6	3 tbs olive oil	salt and freshly ground pepper
6 red peppers	1 litre vegetable stock (p. 4)	150ml crème fraîche or soured cream
2 leeks, white part only, cleaned and sliced	3 large tomatoes, chopped	2 tbs chopped basil or coriander
2 stalks celery, strings removed, then sliced	½ red chilli, chopped or ½ tsp chilli sauce	

Roast and peel the peppers as described on p. 151. Remove all the charred skin, the core and seeds and cut them into pieces.

Sweat* the leeks and celery in the olive oil over low heat, covered, for 15 minutes. Add the stock, tomatoes, chilli and peppers. Season and simmer for 20 minutes. Purée the soup in the blender, then pass through a sieve. Taste for seasoning, remembering that flavours are less pronounced when cold. Chill for at least 2 hours. To serve, add a dollop of crème fraîche and chopped basil or coriander to each bowl.

Gazpacho

This popular Spanish soup is only worth making if you have really ripe tomatoes.

For 4–6	2 garlic cloves, peeled and crushed	salt and freshly ground pepper
3 slices day-old bread, crusts removed	60ml olive oil	½ tsp paprika
4 tbs sherry vinegar or wine vinegar	300 ml water	1 small cucumber
750g ripe tomatoes	300ml tomato juice (canned or bottled)	1 small onion
		1 green pepper

Soak the bread in the vinegar. Peel and chop the tomatoes roughly. Put them into a blender with the bread, garlic, olive oil, water and tomato juice. Season with salt, pepper and paprika and blend until smooth. Chill the soup for several hours. Add more water if the gazpacho seems too thick and taste for seasoning when you are ready to serve.

Seed and dice the cucumber, peel and chop the onion finely and chop the pepper, discarding the seeds and white membranes. Put the vegetables into small bowls and let everyone take some to garnish the soup. Ice cubes may be added at the last moment too.

Hungarian cherry soup

One of the best chilled soups ever. The recipe was given to me by Victor Sassie, the original owner of Soho's famous Hungarian restaurant, the Gay Hussar, where it was always on the menu in summer.

Dark morello cherries are acid, not sweet, and are available in July and August. Canned morellos can be used, but *see* the note below. If you want to make the soup with sweet cherries, omit the sugar and add more lemon juice.

For 6	60g sugar	small glass brandy
500g morello cherries	2 unwaxed lemons	500ml soured cream
1 bottle Riesling	½ tsp cinnamon	

Remove the stalks and stone the cherries. Put the stalks and stones into a pan with the Riesling, sugar and the juice of 2 lemons and the grated rind of 1. Simmer for 5 minutes and leave to infuse for 15–20 minutes. Strain into a clean pan, add the cinnamon and the cherries with all their juice and bring slowly to the boil. Remove the pan from the heat and when the soup has cooled a little, stir in the brandy. Pour the soured cream into a large bowl and gradually pour in the soup, stirring to mix thoroughly. Chill for at least 2 hours.

Note

You can make the soup with cans or jars of morello cherries, but the flavour is less good. Simmer the cherries and their juices for 5 minutes with all the other ingredients except the cream, and finish the soup as above.

Vichyssoise

Follow the recipe for leek and potato soup (p. 12), but replace the single cream by 250ml double cream and chill thoroughly before serving.

Yogurt and cucumber soup

You find versions of this refreshing soup all over the Middle East. In some places it is finished with fried chopped garlic and crumbled dried mint, elsewhere with chopped fresh mint and coriander. Walnuts are used in southern Turkey. Use low fat or full milk yogurt depending on how rich you want the soup to be.

For 4	2 cucumbers	salt and freshly ground pepper
500ml yogurt	4 spring onions, chopped	
300ml water		3 tbs chopped walnuts
	3 tbs chopped mint	

Stir the yogurt until smooth, then add the water. Peel the cucumbers, remove the seeds and grate or chop the flesh finely. Add the cucumber, onion and mint to the yogurt and season. Chill the soup for at least 2 hours and stir in the walnuts just before serving.

First courses and light dishes

This chapter has a variety of dishes that are suitable as a
first course or a light meal, either alone or with a salad.
But the choice of light dishes is by no means limited to the recipes here; vegetable
tarts, stuffed vegetables, gratins and tians, risotto, pasta and noodles as well as most
egg dishes and, of course, soups can make an
excellent start to a meal or a meal in themselves.

Dips and purées

Dips and purées to be eaten with bread, a platter of raw or cooked vegetables, hard-boiled eggs, maybe some olives and a bowl of fresh herb sprigs to nibble at, make an easy start to a meal. In addition to the suggestions below, the garlic sauces (aïoli, skorthalia and tarator, pp. 363–4) and the salsas, chutneys and relishes (pp. 380–3) can also be eaten as dips. One dip with bread will whet the appetite of 2 or 3 people. Three or four dips served together with bread and vegetables will feed several people. As an accompaniment to a main dish, a dip may be treated as a sauce; use it sparingly for several helpings, or serve it more generously to fewer people.

Aubergine purée (Baba ghanoush)

Grilling gives the aubergines an attractive smoky flavour, but you can bake them in the oven or microwave if you wish.

For 4–6		
3 aubergines	salt	1 tbs finely chopped mint or parsley
80–100ml tahini*	juice of 1 lemon	1 tbs olive oil
2 garlic cloves, peeled	½ tsp paprika	

Prick the aubergines with a fork in a few places and grill over a gas flame or under a grill, turning them frequently, until blackened and soft, about 20–25 minutes. Peel the aubergines, cooling them and your fingers as necessary under the cold tap and squeeze gently to get rid of the juices. Chop the aubergines coarsely and put the flesh into a food processor with some of the tahini, the garlic crushed with salt, and blend. Add the lemon juice and some of the paprika and taste. It may need more tahini, salt or lemon juice. Turn the aubergine purée into a bowl. Just before serving, sprinkle the remaining paprika and the herbs over the surface and drizzle over a little olive oil. Serve with pitta or other bread.

Variations
· If you don't like the strong taste of tahini, make an aubergine purée without it, but add 3–4 tbs olive oil at the end.

Aubergine purée with yogurt Make the version with olive oil instead of tahini and add 150–200ml thick yogurt at the end.

Hummus

One of the staples of Middle Eastern mezze, it is now sold in every supermarket. Most bought hummus can be improved by adding more olive oil, tahina and lemon juice. It is easy, however, to make your own; even using canned chick peas it will have a nuttier, richer flavour.

For 6–8	250g tahini*	1 tsp paprika
300g chick peas or 2 × 400g cans	3 garlic cloves, peeled and crushed	1–2 tbs olive oil
juice of 3 lemons or to taste	salt	1 tbs chopped parsley

Soak the chick peas overnight in plenty of water; they will double in volume. Drain and rinse them, put them in a pan well covered with unsalted cold water and bring to the boil. Lower the heat, cover the pan and cook at a fast simmer for 1–2 hours, until the chick peas are very tender. Drain them, keeping some of the cooking liquid for thinning the purée. If you use canned chick peas, drain and rinse them.

Put the chick peas in a food processor with a little of the lemon juice and cooking water and process to a coarse paste. Add more lemon juice and some of the tahini, the garlic and salt to taste. Keep tasting as you add the lemon juice and tahini; the chick peas can absorb quite a lot of both, so find the balance that suits you. The purée should be creamy. If it is too thick add a little cooking liquid or plain water.

Turn the hummus into a flat dish. Stir the paprika into the olive oil and drizzle over the hummus. Sprinkle the parsley on top and serve with pitta or as a dip for raw vegetables.

Cucumber and yogurt dip (Cacik)

This is one version of a summer salad popular throughout the Middle East. Use a low fat yogurt if you prefer, but a Greek-style yogurt will give a better consistency.

For 4	½ small onion or 1 shallot, peeled and finely chopped	salt and freshly ground pepper
250ml plain yogurt		
1 cucumber, peeled, seeded and chopped or grated	2 tbs chopped mint or dill	

Combine all the ingredients, taste for seasoning and chill before serving with bread or as a dip for vegetables.

Variation
Avocado and yogurt dip Replace the cucumber by a mashed avocado and add a little lime or lemon juice to the dip.

Red pepper, walnut and pomegranate dip (Muhamara)

This Middle Eastern dip is as good as *Baba ghanoush* and hummus, but not nearly as well known. For a refined version, roast and peel the peppers before removing the seeds and chopping the flesh. The softened peppers can then be added to the nut paste at the end of the recipe.

Pomegranate molasses is a thick tangy syrup with a tart edge that is used widely in Middle Eastern cooking, and is especially good with fish and with lamb and pork. It is available from Middle Eastern shops and delicatessens.

For 4–6		
5 red peppers	2 tbs pomegranate molasses	50–75ml olive oil
75g fresh breadcrumbs	1 tsp ground cumin	1 tbs dry-roasted* pine nuts
180g walnuts	salt	
2 tbs lemon juice	2 tsp harissa* or other chilli paste, or chilli powder	

Cut the peppers coarsely, removing white ribs and seeds, and chop them finely in a food processor. Set them aside. Soak the breadcrumbs in a tablespoon or two of water for a few minutes. Put them into the food processor with the walnuts, lemon juice, pomegranate molasses, cumin, salt and chilli. Blend to a coarse paste, then add the peppers and pulse a few times until all the ingredients are well amalgamated. Add olive oil through the feed tube to make a creamy paste. If it appears too thick, add a little more oil or water.

Turn the *muhamara* into a bowl, drizzle over a little olive oil and decorate with the pine nuts.

Guacamole

Guacamole is probably the best known Mexican dish. It should have a rough texture so don't be tempted to make it in a food processor.

For 4–5	4 tbs finely chopped coriander	juice of 1–2 limes
5 ripe but firm tomatoes, seeded and cubed	1–2 jalapeño or other green chillies, seeded and chopped finely	2 ripe avocados
1 onion, peeled and chopped finely	salt and freshly ground pepper	

Put the tomatoes, onion, coriander and chillies into a serving bowl, season to taste and mix in the juice of 1 lime. Cover and refrigerate for at least 30 minutes to allow the flavours to blend. Just before serving, mash the avocado flesh and stir it into the mixture. Taste and add more lime juice if needed. Serve at once before the avocado discolours, with corn chips or tacos, or as a side dish to accompany grilled fish.

Anchoïade

This dip from the south of France is usually made with salted anchovies, which need to be soaked for about 30 minutes to remove excess salt, and then filleted. Tinned anchovy fillets in oil can be used straight away.

For 3–4	2 garlic cloves	freshly ground pepper
10 anchovy fillets or 5 salted anchovies	150ml olive oil	

Pound the anchovies and garlic to a paste or blend them in a food processor. Add the oil, a little at a time, as if making mayonnaise, to produce an emulsion. Season with pepper and serve with raw vegetables, hard-boiled eggs and chunks of bread.

Tapenade

This olive and anchovy paste derives its name from *tapéno*, the provençal word for caper. It is excellent with tomatoes or hardboiled eggs, or just spread on toast or bruschetta. This version comes from Lulu Peyraud of Domaine Tempier in Bandol who also serves it to accompany roast lamb.

For 4–6

250g large black olives, stoned

4 anchovy fillets or 2 salted anchovies, rinsed and filleted

3 tbs capers

1 garlic clove, peeled and crushed

pinch of cayenne

1 tsp chopped fresh savory leaves or a pinch of crumbled dried leaves

4 tbs olive oil

Reduce the olives, anchovies, capers, garlic, cayenne and savory to a coarse purée in a food processor. Add the olive oil and pulse a couple of times, until the mixture is well blended.

Bruschetta

Here are a few suggestions for bruschetta, mostly using toppings for which there are recipes elsewhere in the book. It is easy to devise your own bread-based starters using the resources of a delicatessen and other ideas in this book, such as the dips or purées above. It is essential to use good bread that toasts well.

Bruschetta with goat's cheese

Lightly toast slices of country bread, spread with soft goat's cheese, then return the bruschetta to the grill until the cheese starts to melt. Scatter with chopped walnuts.

Bruschetta with broad bean purée

Lightly toast slices of country bread, brush with olive oil and top with broad bean purée (p. 111) and chopped dill.

Bruschetta with Tuscan beans

Lightly toast slices of country bread, brush with olive oil and top with warm crushed Tuscan beans (p. 113) sprinkled with coarse salt and chopped parsley.

Bruschetta with roasted peppers

Lightly toast slices of country bread or ciabatta, brush with olive oil, top with strips of roasted peppers (p. 151) and a few shredded basil leaves.

Bruschetta with tomatoes and anchovies

Mix diced ripe tomatoes with chopped anchovies, a few chopped capers and some chopped parsley. Season with freshly ground pepper and a little olive oil. Toast slices of country bread or ciabatta lightly, brush with olive oil and top with the tomato mixture. Sprinkle over a little more parsley.

Garlic and tomato bread

This is not Italian but a rustic and utterly simple Catalan way of serving bread. Crush 2 or 3 cloves of garlic to a cream with a little salt and combine this with a few tablespoons of olive oil. Lightly toast slices of country bread or long pieces of french bread. Brush on both sides with the garlic and oil. Cut 1 or 2 large ripe tomatoes in half and rub the bread thoroughly with the tomato. Put the bread under the grill again for a few seconds and serve warm.

Add more garlic if you wish, or if you like a lot of tomato, chop some and whiz with the garlic in a food processor before mixing with the oil.

Garlic and tomato bread is sometimes served with small pieces of Serrano ham and Manchego cheese.

Pizza

The pizza may well have conquered the world, but what the world has done to it in the process has often made it unrecognisable. 'It's a pity. Those who treat the pizza as a dustbin miss the joy of fresh hot dough, well-risen and spongy, with an onion and tomato mixture, aromatic and pungent, seeping into the air pockets to form a delicious whole.' Thus Elizabeth David, who is on record elsewhere saying this tomato and anchovy version was her personal favourite.

Tomato and anchovy pizza

For 4		
bread dough made as for focaccia (p. 454), but using half the quantities	4 garlic cloves, peeled and crushed	1 tsp sugar
	400g tomatoes, peeled and chopped	2 tbs basil, shredded
olive oil	1 tsp dried oregano	50g anchovy fillets
	salt and freshly ground pepper	

Make the pizza base following the instructions for making focaccia. While the dough is proving, make the pizza filling. Heat 2 tbs olive oil in a heavy pan over low heat and lightly sauté the garlic for a minute, then add the tomatoes. Turn up the heat, stir the oregano, seasonings and sugar into the tomatoes and cook until the tomatoes have almost reduced to a thick sauce. Stir in the basil.

Oil a 28–30cm tart tin or earthenware plate. When the dough has risen, knock it back, sprinkle your hands with flour and put the dough in the middle of the tin. Spread it with your hands to fill the tin. Spoon over the tomato filling, leaving a rim of dough 2cm wide around the edge. Drizzle over olive oil. Cover with cling film and leave to rise for 10–15 minutes. Heat the oven to 200°C, 400°F, gas 6. Bake the pizza for 15 minutes, take it from the oven and arrange the anchovy fillets, roughly torn into smaller pieces, over the top. Return the pizza to the oven and cook for a further 10 minutes or until the crust is golden.

Variations

Pizza alla romana Finely slice 8 peeled garlic cloves and chop the leaves from 3 sprigs of rosemary. Brush the dough generously with olive oil and scatter over it the garlic and rosemary. Sprinkle with coarse salt and freshly ground pepper. Drizzle with more olive oil, leave to rise for 10–15 minutes, and bake for 20–25 minutes.

Provençal pissaladière Replace the tomato filling with 600g large onions, peeled, sliced and sautéed in 3 tbs olive oil over medium to low heat for 30–40 minutes until soft and turning golden. Season and stir in 1 tsp crumbled, mixed dried provençal herbs or 2 tsp chopped fresh thyme. Spread the onion over the dough, drizzle with oil, and leave to rise for 10–15 minutes. Bake, adding 100g stoned small black olives when you add the anchovies.

Savoury pancakes

Pancakes are very versatile; the batter can be made with a variety of flours, the pancakes flavoured with herbs or spices and filled with a variety of stuffings. You can serve them at once or make them in advance and fill them later.

Smoked fish and soured cream pancakes

Smoked fish is particularly good with herb pancakes, or pancakes made with buckwheat flour (p. 495).

For 6 pancakes	250g smoked trout, smoked salmon or smoked eel	120ml soured cream
6 pancakes (p. 494) made with half the quantity of batter		2 tbs chopped dill

Remove any bones from the fish and cut into small pieces. Spread the pancakes with the soured cream, top with the fish and dill. Roll up or fold and serve at room temperature.

Ham and mushroom pancakes

For 10–12 pancakes	250ml chicken or vegetable stock (p. 4) or milk	180g mushrooms, sliced
10–12 pancakes (p. 494)		200g cooked ham, diced
75g butter	salt and freshly ground pepper	2 tbs chopped parsley
25g flour		150ml single cream

Heat the oven to 180°C, 350°F, gas 4. Heat 25g butter, stir in the flour and then the heated stock or milk, a little at a time, whisking as you do so. Bring to the boil, season and simmer for 10 minutes. If it is at all lumpy, put the sauce through a sieve. Sauté the mushrooms in 25g of the remaining butter. Fold them into the sauce with the ham and parsley. Remove the pan from the heat. Put 2 tbs filling into the middle of each pancake, fold up the sides and then the ends to form oblong packages. Transfer them to a buttered shallow ovenproof dish. Spoon over the cream and dot with the remaining butter. Bake until lightly browned, about 20 minutes.

Variations
· Use cooked prawns or cold chicken to replace the ham.

Pumpkin pancakes

For 10–12 pancakes	10–12 pancakes (p. 494)	30g butter
		2 tbs grated Parmesan
	pumpkin purée	

Make a spicy pumpkin purée following the method for squash purée (p. 158), and fill the pancakes. Roll or fold them, brush with melted butter, sprinkle over grated Parmesan cheese and brown under the grill for 3–4 minutes.

Pancakes with spinach and ricotta

For 10–12 pancakes

10–12 pancakes
(p. 494)

2 tbs olive oil

1 shallot, peeled and
chopped

400g cooked spinach,
chopped

200g ricotta

salt and freshly ground
pepper

grated nutmeg

50g grated Parmesan

For the sauce

2 shallots, peeled and
chopped

1 tbs olive oil

350ml passata (p. 378
or bought)

salt and freshly ground
pepper

5 tbs single cream

handful of basil or
parsley leaves,
chopped

30g grated Parmesan

Heat the oven to 200°C, 400°F, gas 6. Heat the oil and fry the shallot until softened.
Stir in the spinach and ricotta. Season with salt, pepper and nutmeg and mix in the
Parmesan. Fill the pancakes and roll or fold them into parcels. Put them side by
side in a shallow baking dish.

To make the sauce, fry the shallots in the oil until soft, add the passata, season,
and simmer gently for 15 minutes so that it thickens somewhat. Stir in the cream
and the herb. Pour the sauce over the pancakes and sprinkle the Parmesan over the
top. Bake for 15 minutes, until the cheese has melted and the edges of the pancakes
are crisp.

German bacon pancakes

For 8 pancakes

4 eggs

200ml milk

150g plain flour

½ tsp salt

oil for frying

8 thin slices smoked
bacon, rind removed

Put the eggs, milk, flour and salt into a food processor and whiz to a smooth batter.
Leave to stand for 30 minutes. Cut each rasher of bacon into 2 or 3 pieces. Heat
½ tbs oil in a medium frying pan and fry 2 or 3 pieces of bacon on both sides. Swirl
the pan to coat the bottom with the oil and melted bacon fat. Pour over about one-
eighth of the batter, tilting the pan so that it coats the bottom, and cook until
golden brown underneath, about 1–2 minutes. Turn the pancake and cook the
other side. Fold in half and keep warm in a low oven, 150°C, 300°F, gas 2, while you
cook the rest of the pancakes, using 2 or 3 pieces of bacon and one-eighth of the
batter on each occasion.

Serve with a salad of rocket and corn salad or, as the Dutch do, with molasses or
maple syrup.

Potato and onion pancakes

For 4	½ tsp salt	oil for frying
750g potatoes, peeled	3 eggs	
2 onions, peeled	3 tbs plain flour	

Grate the potatoes and onions, draining off any liquid that accumulates. Add the salt, eggs and flour and stir to a batter. Heat a large frying pan, add 2 tbs oil and drop tablespoons of the batter into it, leaving space between them. Fry for 2 minutes each side and serve at once or keep warm in a low oven (150°C, 300°F, gas 2) while cooking the rest. It is best if you can work with two frying pans at once.

The pancakes can be flat and crisp all over or slightly thicker and soft inside, as you prefer.

Fruit and vegetable dishes

In addition to the few dishes given here, *see* the asparagus dishes, grilled aubergines, aubergine or spinach filo parcels, leeks vinaigrette, green beans with ham, courgettes baked with cheese and the gratin of pattypan squash in Vegetables.

Figs with mozzarella and mint

This simple salad depends completely on having very good ingredients – perfectly ripe figs and the best Italian buffalo mozzarella.

For 6	Maldon salt and freshly ground pepper	2–3 tbs extra virgin olive oil
8 large ripe figs	1 tbs balsamic vinegar	young leaves from 5–6 sprigs mint
300–350g buffalo mozzarella		

Slice the figs (from top to bottom quite thinly) and the mozzarella and arrange them on a serving platter. Season with Maldon salt and pepper. Drizzle over the vinegar and oil and scatter with the mint leaves.

Pear, raspberry and rocket salad

This intensely flavoured summer or autumn salad comes from Angelo Lancellotti of the renowned Da Lancellotti restaurant in Soliera, near Modena in Italy. Sadly, the restaurant has closed this year. The Lancellottis grew all their own salad greens and herbs, made their own traditional balsamic vinegar and served beautiful, inventive food firmly rooted in local tradition. Use the best balsamic vinegar you have for this salad.

For 4	2 sprigs tarragon, chopped finely	1 tbs balsamic vinegar
4 tbs raspberries		violet or borage flowers
3 perfect pears	2 tbs extra virgin olive oil	
100g rocket leaves, coarsely chopped		

Crush the raspberries to a purée with the back of a fork. Quarter, core and slice the pears. Mix together the fruit, rocket and tarragon, allowing the raspberries to coat the pears. Add the olive oil, then the vinegar, and toss. Scatter the flowers on top and serve at once.

Green beans with scallops

Thin beans are best for this dish.

For 4	a small piece of ginger, peeled and chopped finely	1 tbs wine vinegar
8 scallops		salt and freshly ground pepper
400g small green beans	6 tbs white wine	
2 shallots, peeled and chopped finely	3 tbs olive or walnut oil	

Slice the scallops in half and detach the corals. Cook the beans in water or steam until just tender, then drain them. While the beans are cooking, put the shallots and ginger into a pan with the wine. Bring to the boil, then lower the heat, add the scallops (including the corals) and simmer them for about 1 minute until they are opaque. Lift them out and arrange them with the beans on a serving dish. Add the oil and vinegar to the pan, season lightly, whisk together and reduce a little. Strain the sauce over the beans and scallops and serve.

Mushroom carpaccio

Use very fresh mushrooms for this simple Italian dish.

For 4	Maldon salt and freshly ground pepper	extra virgin olive oil
250g small mushrooms	lemon juice	60g Parmesan

Slice the mushrooms thinly and arrange on 4 plates. Season lightly with salt, more generously with pepper and sprinkle over a little lemon juice and olive oil. Shave the Parmesan thinly and scatter the shavings over the mushrooms. Grind over more pepper and drizzle with more olive oil.

Roasted peppers with olives

This dish can be eaten soon after it is made, or left for several hours (even overnight) for the peppers to marinate in the dressing.

For 4–6	2 garlic cloves, peeled	16–20 black olives
4 large red peppers	2 tsp chilli oil	6 anchovy fillets (optional)
salt and freshly ground pepper	100ml extra virgin olive oil	
handful parsley leaves		

Grill and peel the peppers (p. 151). Discard the seeds and white ribs and cut the peppers into strips. Put the strips in a shallow dish, season with salt and pepper. Chop the parsley and garlic together quite finely and scatter over the peppers. Mix the chilli oil into the olive oil and pour over the peppers. At this point the dish can wait for several hours, covered with clingfilm. Just before serving, arrange the olives over the peppers, and if you wish the anchovies, split down the middle.

Vegetable fritters

Vegetables to be coated in batter and fried should be dry and at room temperature; cut them into pieces of a uniform size. Make the fritter batter on p. 496 and *see* the instructions on frying (p. 99). Keep the cooked fritters in a dish lined with kitchen paper in a low oven while frying the remainder.

Raw sliced aubergines, courgettes and fennel hearts, whole small mushrooms, courgette flowers and sprigs of herbs can be coated with batter and fried.

Broccoli and cauliflower florets should be cooked until almost tender, drained well and dried before being dipped in batter and fried.

Whole beetroot, celeriac and parsnips should be boiled, drained and sliced before being battered and fried.

Serve vegetable fritters with tomato sauce (p. 366), skorthalia (p. 364), yogurt dip (p. 361) or a salsa or relish (pp. 380–4).

Vegetable kebabs with skorthalia

To grill or barbecue successfully the vegetables must all be of a similar size. If you wish, add a few pieces of streaky bacon or spicy sausage such as chorizo to the kebabs.

For 6	2 small courgettes, cut into thick slices	salt and freshly ground pepper
skorthalia (p. 364)	12 small onions or shallots, peeled	olive oil
12 firm cherry tomatoes	12 closed button mushrooms	
1 large red or yellow pepper, seeded and cut into small squares		

Prepare the skorthalia. Heat the grill or prepare the barbecue. Thread the vegetables in equal proportions onto 6 skewers, alternating them to create colour contrasts. Season well. Brush both the grill rack and the vegetables with oil. Grill the vegetables 6–8cm from the heat, turning them frequently until they are tender, about 12–15 minutes. Brush with more oil if necessary as they cook. Serve at once with the skorthalia.

Fish and seafood dishes

Many styles of fish and seafood dishes are suited to light dishes and first courses. Marinated raw fish, salads (pp. 83–6) and pâtés are easy to prepare and can often be made ahead of time. We have some of the best smoked fish in the world, so don't forget smoked salmon and smoked trout when you don't have time to cook.

Smoked mackerel pâté

For 4	juice of ½–1 lemon	To serve
250g smoked mackerel fillets, skinned	5 tbs thick yogurt	4 large ripe tomatoes, sliced
60g fresh mixed herbs (eg parsley, chives, marjoram, salad burnet, chervil), chopped	a few drops of Tabasco	1 small red onion, peeled and sliced in thin rings
	freshly ground pepper	4 tbs vinaigrette (p. 358)

Flake the mackerel with a fork and mix in the other ingredients, or for a smooth pâté whiz everything in a food processor. Serve as it is with toast, or for a more stylish first course arrange the tomatoes in a circle of overlapping slices on four plates with a few onion rings on top. Spoon over the vinaigrette. Using two tablespoons dipped in warm water, shape the pâté into ovals. Put one on top of each tomato salad and serve with toast.

Tuna rillettes

For 4	2 tbs double cream or crème fraîche	½ tsp paprika
200g canned tuna	1 tbs olive oil	salt and freshly ground pepper
juice of 1 lemon	1 tbs chopped dill	

Drain the tuna and crumble it with a fork or whiz it briefly in a food processor. Turn it into a bowl. Add the other ingredients and mix well with a fork. The rillettes should be quite rough in appearance, not a smooth paste. Taste and adjust the seasoning if necessary. Serve with toast, black olives and capers.

Ceviche

One of the very best marinated fish dishes, ceviche originates on the Pacific coast of Peru where it is served accompanied by slices of boiled corn and sweet potato. I prefer to serve it as a lighter dish with corn chips or good bread. Bass is usually used for this dish in Latin America, but I've made it successfully with monkfish, brill, lemon sole, salmon and, more expensively, with scallops. It is normally made with one type of fish only, but a combination can be used. Choose the freshest fish on the slab.

For 4	1 small mild onion, peeled and chopped	100ml olive oil
500g monkfish or other firm fish fillets	2 tomatoes, peeled, seeded and diced	salt and freshly ground pepper
juice of 3–4 limes		1 avocado
1–2 fresh chillies, seeded and sliced finely	3 tbs chopped coriander leaves	

Skin the fillets and remove all the bones, using tweezers if necessary. Cut the flesh into small cubes or thin slices. Put them in a dish with the lime juice, ensure all the fish is well coated, cover and leave to marinate in the refrigerator for 3–4 hours. The lime juice 'cooks' the fish; it loses its translucence and becomes white and opaque. Scallops will be ready in less time.

Drain most of the lime juice from the fish and combine the fish with the chillies, onion, tomatoes, coriander and olive oil. Season with a little salt and pepper. Arrange the ceviche on individual plates or a serving platter and surround with slices of avocado brushed with a little of the lime juice drained from the fish.

Salmon marinated with lemon and herbs

This is a dish I first ate in Italy some years ago, and found easy to reproduce. The salmon should be wild for maximum flavour and minimum fattiness, and very fresh, and the olive oil the best extra virgin. The salmon can be replaced successfully by swordfish or monkfish.

For 4	extra virgin olive oil	3–4 tbs fresh herbs (*see* below)
500g salmon fillet	freshly ground pepper	
40g sea salt	¼ tsp ground coriander seed (optional)	
juice of 2 lemons or 3 limes		

Skin the salmon and remove all pin bones with tweezers. Rub the flesh with the salt, cover and refrigerate for 2 hours, or longer if it is more convenient. Rinse quickly to remove the salt, transfer the salmon to a board and cut on the slant into thin slices, as if slicing smoked salmon. The salt will have made the flesh firm, so it is easier to slice. Spread the slices on a large platter, pour over the lemon or lime juice and return to the refrigerator for an hour or so. Drizzle over the olive oil, season with freshly ground black pepper and coriander. Choose one or two herbs – chives cut in 4cm lengths, chopped tarragon, shredded basil, marjoram or mint – and scatter over the salmon. Serve with good bread or warm toast.

Tuna tartare

If your fishmonger has extremely fresh tuna of the quality used for sashimi, that is the one to buy for this dish. Although the lime juice 'cooks' the fish, any fish to be eaten raw must be very fresh.

For 4	400g very fresh tuna loin	2 tbs capers, chopped finely
1 cucumber	juice of 1–2 limes	2 tbs chopped basil
salt	salt and freshly ground pepper	1 tbs extra virgin olive oil
2 tbs thick yogurt or soured cream	4 spring onions, sliced finely	mint or basil leaves to garnish
1 tsp Dijon mustard	1 small green chilli, seeded and sliced finely	
1 tbs shredded mint leaves		

Peel alternate strips from the cucumber, cut it in half, then in half lengthways and remove the seeds. Slice as thinly as possible (use a mandoline, *see* p. 528) and spread in a colander. Sprinkle the layers of cucumber generously with salt and leave to drain for 1 hour. Rinse them under cold water, then dry on a cloth. Whisk together the yogurt, mustard and mint leaves and stir the cucumber into the sauce. Set on one side.

Using a very sharp knife, dice the tuna finely. Put the fish into a bowl and pour over the lime juice. Lift the fish carefully with your fingers to mix it with the juice. Season with salt and pepper and add the sliced spring onion, chilli, capers, basil and olive oil. Combine well, then cover and marinate in the refrigerator for at least 1 hour.

Spoon a flattish circle of cucumber mixture onto each plate, put a mound of tuna tartare on top, garnish with mint or basil leaves.

Marinated herrings

This is a dish I discovered in Germany. The herrings are lightly fried and then marinated in vinegar and spices rather than cooked in the marinade as in the English dish of soused herrings. The principle is that used for the Spanish and Caribbean *escabeche*. It works well with small mackerel too.

Serve with a potato salad (p. 78, p. 347) to which you have added chopped celery or fennel, or with some good bread for a light meal, or as part of a buffet.

For 4	150ml water	1 tsp coriander seeds
4 herrings, weighing 200–230g each	1 small onion, peeled and chopped	1 tsp thyme leaves
seasoned flour	1 tsp black peppercorns	2 bay leaves
2 tbs olive oil	1 tsp mustard seeds (p. 76)	
250ml white wine vinegar or cider vinegar		

Have the herrings cleaned and the heads removed. Reserve the roes. Rinse and dry with kitchen paper. Roll the herrings in enough flour to coat them lightly. Fry them in 1½ tbs oil for 3–4 minutes on each side and drain them on kitchen paper. Fry the roes briefly in the remaining oil. Place the herrings in a dish with the roes on top.

Bring all the remaining ingredients to the boil then leave to cool. When the marinade is quite cold pour it over the fish. Cover with clingfilm and keep in the refrigerator for 12 hours before serving.

Serve the herrings whole or cut each one into 4 or 5 slices and pour over a little of the marinade.

Mussels in vinaigrette

For 2	4 tbs tarragon vinegar	1 ripe tomato, peeled, seeded and diced
1kg mussels	¼ tsp mustard	2 tsp capers
small bunch parsley	1 shallot, peeled and chopped finely	freshly ground pepper
2 bay leaves	¼ red pepper, diced	a little salt
150ml olive oil		

Scrub the mussels, remove the beards and discard any that float, are broken or remain open when tapped firmly. Put them in a pan with 100ml water, the stalks from the parsley and the bay leaves. Steam them open, remove from the pan and when cool enough to handle, take them from their shells which should be retained. Strain the cooking liquor through a fine sieve, lined with muslin (p. 528). Leave any obvious grit in the pan. Refrigerate or freeze the liquid to use as a soup base or to poach a fish – you don't need it for this dish but it is too good to waste.

Chop the parsley leaves and mix with the remaining ingredients to make a vinaigrette. Put the mussels in a bowl and pour over the vinaigrette. Cover and refrigerate for at least 12 hours before serving. Clean half of the retained shells and use them for serving the mussels. Put the mussels back in the shells, spoon over a little of the vinaigrette and serve with bread.

Roasted oysters

Oysters are now more plentiful and less expensive. Just opened, with a squirt of lemon juice and perhaps a little pepper or paprika, nestling on a bed of ice, they are excellent. The Americans and the French have long appreciated cooked oysters, using them for fritters, sautés and stews as well as inventing many ways of grilling or roasting them.

For 2	paprika	30g dried breadcrumbs
12 oysters	3 shallots, peeled and chopped finely	60g butter
coarse salt for baking		
2 tbs lemon juice	3 tbs chopped parsley	

Heat the oven to 180°C, 350°F, gas 4. Open the oysters, *see* p. 259. Put a layer of coarse salt on a small baking tray or two pie plates and bed the oysters firmly in the salt. Sprinkle over them the lemon juice and a little paprika. Combine the shallots, chopped parsley and breadcrumbs. Melt the butter and stir in the breadcrumbs. Spoon some of the mixture onto each oyster and bake for 4–5 minutes, until the oysters are just heated through. Serve at once with thin rye or wholemeal bread.

Oyster stew

For 4	2 shallots, chopped finely	dash of Tabasco
24 oysters	100ml vermouth	freshly ground pepper and a little salt
30g butter	200ml crème fraîche	2 tbs chopped chervil

Open the oysters, *see* p. 259. Remove them from their shells, reserving the liquor. Strain the liquor through a sieve lined with muslin (p. 528). Heat the butter and fry the shallot gently until softened. Add the vermouth, turn up the heat and let it reduce to 3 tbs. Stir in the cream and the oyster liquor. Season with Tabasco and pepper, and taste to see whether it needs salt – the oyster liquor is salty. When the cream is simmering, add the oysters and cook for 2–3 minutes until their edges curl. Remove the pan from the heat, scatter over the chervil and serve with bread.

Meat dishes

Some of the best meat for a first course is to be bought from a good delicatessen. Cured hams from Italy, Spain, Germany, Belgium; Italian and Hungarian salamis, and Spanish chorizo can be served alone or in a mixed meat platter. Ripe figs or melon partner Italian prosciutto; Serrano ham and Black Forest ham are best served on their own, while Ardennes ham from Belgium is sometimes served with asparagus. With the salamis and chorizo, olives and cornichons are good accompaniments. Decent bread, of course, is a must.

Chicken liver pâté

For 4	90g butter	salt and freshly ground pepper
250g chicken livers	3 tbs brandy or port	
1 shallot, chopped finely	pinch allspice	
	pinch crushed thyme	

Trim any green stringy bits from the livers. Sauté the shallot in 30g butter until soft, but not coloured. Add the whole livers and sauté until the outsides turn grey-brown. The livers should remain pink inside. Remove the livers and shallots to a food processor. Pour the brandy or port into the pan, stir and scrape up any bits stuck to the bottom and tip the contents into the food processor with the remaining butter. Add the seasonings. Process until smooth, adjust the seasoning if necessary and pulse briefly.

Turn the pâté into a bowl and chill for 1–2 hours before serving with toast or crusty bread.

To keep, melt more butter in a clean pan and pour it over the smoothed top of the pâté to cover it completely. There should be enough to form a layer about 2cm thick to seal the pâté completely. Cover the pot with foil. It will keep in the refrigerator for 2–3 weeks if completely airtight.

Carpaccio

For 4	2 tbs chopped flat-leaf parsley	freshly ground pepper
300g beef fillet		extra virgin olive oil
2 tbs chopped capers	3 anchovy fillets, cut in slivers	Parmesan
		lemon wedges

Trim all fat and connective tissue from the beef and put it in the freezer for about 45 minutes, until it is firm enough to be sliced thinly. Alternatively, slice the beef as thinly as you can, divide into four and put the slices for each helping between lightly oiled pieces of kitchen parchment. Pound with a mallet until they are very thin and rotate the parchment as you work so that all the slices are pounded evenly. Spread the flattened beef on four plates in overlapping slices. Handle it carefully or it may tear. Cover each plate and refrigerate.

When you are ready to serve the carpaccio, garnish each plate with capers, parsley and anchovy, grind over black pepper and drizzle with olive oil. Shave curls of Parmesan with a vegetable peeler and put them over the top. Serve with lemon wedges.

Moorish kebabs (Pinchitos morunos)

These spiced pork kebabs are found in tapas bars throughout southern Spain, and you can even buy ready-mixed spices for making them. They would normally be eaten with other tapas, but I find they make a good start to a meal on their own.

For 4–6	½ tsp dried thyme	3 garlic cloves, peeled and crushed
2 tsp ground cumin	salt	
1 tsp ground coriander	500g lean pork, cut into small cubes	2 tbs olive oil
1 tsp paprika		juice of 2 lemons
½ tsp turmeric	1 bay leaf, crumbled	lemon quarters

Combine all the spices and salt, and rub the mixture into the pork. Put it into a dish with the bay leaf and garlic distributed evenly. Stir through the oil and lemon juice. Cover the dish and refrigerate, leaving it to marinate for several hours, preferably as long as 12 hours. Thread the pork onto small skewers and grill on a barbecue, under an indoor grill or on a griddle plate until well browned. Serve with lemon quarters.

Grilled chicken wings

Very simple to prepare and very good finger food. Serve with Chinese or Thai dipping sauce (p. 369), a salsa (pp. 380–2) or coriander chutney (p. 383).

For 6	oriental marinade (p. 387)	4 tbs sunflower oil
1.5kg chicken wings		salt

Cut each wing in two and put them into a grill pan lined with foil and lightly oiled. Toss the wings in the marinade and leave for at least 2 hours, turning the pieces occasionally. Heat the grill to medium, drizzle oil over the wings and grill them about 8cm from the heat for 15–20 minutes, turning them once. Baste occasionally with the oil and marinade. Sprinkle with a little salt before serving.

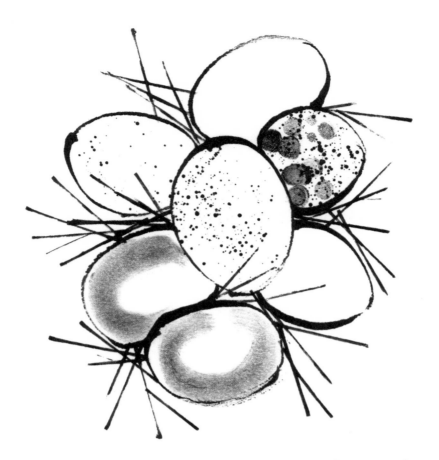

Eggs and cheese

Always in season, economical, handsome in form, eggs are one of
our most versatile and valuable foods. Used in a variety of ways in
all the world's cuisines, they can be quickly prepared as a snack or
more substantially as a main course, and have an important role in
desserts and baking. This chapter is essentially about hens' eggs. The much larger goose
and duck eggs are sometimes available and are best used in baking.
Quails' eggs are usually boiled and served in salads. Cheeses are
made to be eaten as they are, but that said, many dishes benefit in
flavour and texture from the addition of cheese, and cheese and eggs
are one of the best and most frequent combinations in both savoury
dishes and desserts.

Eggs

Choosing

Apart from size and colour, there is nothing to distinguish one egg from another in a shop. The colour of the shell has no relevance to quality; it is dictated by the breed of the laying hen. Labelling as organic or free-range is accurate, although many free-range birds are intensively farmed. Indications such as 'farm fresh' make no distinction between the traditional farmyard and the battery farm. Eggs produced by hens fed on a diet of grains and grass have a better flavour, and darker, richer yolks – but yolk-colourants can be fed to battery hens, so a deep yellow yolk does not always signify quality. Organic eggs usually have thicker shells because the hens have more calcium in their diet, and thicker shells are more impervious to bacteria and will protect the egg longer during storage. Only buy eggs with clean undamaged shells; cracked shells lead to rapid spoilage.

Eggs are graded very large, large, medium and small, but in practice only medium and large are widely available. The boxes, and often the eggs themselves, carry a 'best before' date corresponding to three weeks after laying.

Freshness

Eggs have a small air pocket in the rounded end which gets larger as the egg gets older and loses moisture through the pores in the shell. If you immerse an egg in cold water, a new-laid egg will lie flat, an older egg is more buoyant and will tilt and eventually stand upright in the water. If it floats to the surface it is too old and should be thrown away.

Another way to determine freshness is to crack the egg onto a small plate. A fresh egg will have a rounded well-centred yolk to which most of the viscous translucent white clings, and a narrow runny outer layer. In an older egg, the yolk moves out of the centre of the white and eventually flattens; the white becomes progressively thinner and finally quite watery.

For most purposes, the fresher the egg, the better, but there are some preparations for which a very fresh egg is not the best. To make mayonnaise use an egg that is at least 1 day old; for poaching use eggs that are at least 2 days old; and for meringues eggs that are at least 3 days old. Eggs that are less than 3 days old are difficult to peel when hardboiled. Most of us, of course, buy our eggs from a shop, and never experience eggs as fresh as this.

Storing

Eggs are best kept at a constant cool temperature, either in a larder or in the least cold part of the refrigerator. Let eggs come to room temperature before using. Store them pointed end down. The porous shells allow contamination by bacteria and smells, so keep the eggs away from strong-smelling foods.

Separated whites and yolks can be kept tightly covered in the refrigerator – whites for up to 1 week, yolks for 1–2 days only, after which they start to dry out.

Composition and the effects of cooking

Egg yolks are a source of protein, vitamins, minerals and fats. Whites contain some protein (albumen) but are mostly water. The yolks have a relatively high cholesterol content, the whites none. Current medical advice for people at risk from high cholesterol is that eggs can be eaten in moderation; cholesterol-lowering diets allow up to 2 whole eggs per week and, of course, as much white as is wished.

Salmonella bacteria, which can cause serious food poisoning, are very occasionally found in raw eggs. This is why it is not recommended to give raw or very lightly cooked egg to children, pregnant women, the elderly or anyone whose immune system may be at a low ebb.

When an egg is cooked the proteins thicken and solidify. The white cooks more quickly than the yolk. The effect is most clearly seen when cooking a whole egg; the white is set and firm, but the yolk remains soft and moist. Eggs need gentle heat; if cooked at too high a temperature or for too long, the whites become tough and rubbery and, when cooked whole, the yolks become dry and crumbly. Omelettes or batters turn leathery, and beaten egg used in custards or to thicken soups and sauces will curdle and become watery and grainy if overcooked.

Using whites and yolks

Separating eggs

Crack the shell in half over a bowl, tip the yolk carefully from one half shell to the other, letting the white fall into the bowl. Egg whites will not whisk to a snow if any of the yolk falls in, so separate them carefully to keep the yolks whole. If any bits of yolk fall into the bowl use one of the shell halves to scoop them out or a piece of kitchen paper to blot them up. Put the yolks into a shallow bowl.

If you are apprehensive about allowing the white to drain from the shell, crack the egg onto a saucer, place an egg cup over the yolk and drain off the white.

Beating eggs

Whole eggs and yolks For an omelette the eggs should be beaten lightly just before cooking. They can be beaten with a fork or a whisk in a small basin.

When eggs are used to aerate a mixture, the beating incorporates air, which expands when the mixture is heated. Whole eggs and yolks can be beaten to greater volume with an electric whisk or a balloon whisk. Sugar is often added if the mixture is for a cake; this helps the mixture to thicken.

Whites Egg whites must be completely free of yolk, and the bowl and balloon whisk should be scrupulously clean: a speck of grease may prevent the whites whisking to their maximum volume. The egg white whisking attachment on food processors does a reasonable job of whisking quickly, but the whites will attain greater volume if the job is finished by hand. A copper bowl is the professional choice for beating egg whites, but a stainless steel or glass bowl can also be used.

A pinch of salt added before beating will help the whites to stiffen. Lightly beaten egg whites look foamy and remain quite liquid. To whisk further, lift the whisk to beat in as much air as possible. Stiffly beaten whites are shiny and form peaks when the whisk is raised, and will cling to the whisk above the bowl. To make a meringue, sugar is added once the whites have begun to stiffen. Whites whisked for too long become grainy.

Folding in egg whites

If the beaten egg whites are to be added to a heavy mixture, first stir in a small amount of the egg white to lighten the consistency. To fold in the remainder, use a rubber spatula or a metal spoon, and cut down through the centre of the mixture, across the bottom and up the sides of the bowl, turning the mixture in a rolling motion. Turn the bowl and repeat the folding until the whites are evenly incorporated to give a light, airy mixture.

Eggs for thickening

Whole eggs, or more often yolks, are used to enrich and thicken sauces and soups. The success of the operation depends on cooking the mixture below boiling point otherwise the egg will curdle. For a sauce, use a heavy pan or a double boiler to heat the egg gently while whisking it to a mousse (p. 373). To thicken a soup, whisk the egg, then stir in a ladleful of the hot soup and return the mixture to the soup off the heat or over very low heat, and stir while gently heating through.

Boiled eggs

The first thing to be said is that boiled eggs should be simmered, not boiled. Boiling toughens the whites and rattling around in a pan of boiling water might crack the shell, allowing the egg to leak. Piercing the round end with a pin can prevent the shell cracking during cooking. If you salt the water it stops the white leaking out if the shell should crack.

The best way is to put eggs at room temperature into a pan of simmering water, bring the water to the boil, immediately lower the heat so that it returns to the simmer and cook for the required time. Start timing from the moment the eggs go into the water.

A soft-boiled egg (white set firm enough to hold the yolk, and soft yolk) will take 3–4 minutes, an *oeuf mollet* (white firm, yolk almost set, but runny in the middle) will take 5–6 minutes and a hardboiled egg (white and yolk set) 10–12 minutes. Eggs cooked longer than this will be rubbery, with a crumbly yolk which will probably have a green-black rim around it. A new-laid egg will take a minute longer for the white to set. Once cooked, plunge hardboiled eggs into cold water to stop them cooking further.

To shell an *oeuf mollet* or a hardboiled egg, it is best to crack it all over with a spoon and peel off the inner skin with the shell. Keep eggs in a bowl of water, once shelled, to prevent them drying out.

Hardboiled eggs can be served with a herb or plain mayonnaise (p. 362) on a bed of lettuce and rocket, in salads, in kedgeree or chopped as a garnish. Use *oeufs mollets* as you would poached eggs.

Quails' eggs should be added to simmering water and cooked for 5 minutes for hardboiled. Plunge them into cold water to arrest further cooking. For *oeufs mollets*, allow 1½ minutes' simmering time, then stand for another 30 seconds off the heat before draining.

Chinese tea eggs

These aromatic eggs with their marbled whites are often served for Chinese New Year celebrations, but they make a good supper, served hot with puréed spinach or quick tomato sauce (p. 378); the eggs cold are excellent for picnics or sandwich fillings. Choose a Chinese tea such as Keemun or Yunnan for preference.

For 6	600ml water	2 tbs dark soy sauce
6 hardboiled eggs	1 star anise*	1 tsp salt
1½ tbs black tea leaves	4cm piece cinnamon	

Craze the egg shells gently by tapping them or rolling them on a table so that they are cracked all over but do not come loose. Put the eggs into a pan with all the other ingredients. Bring slowly to the boil and simmer for 45 minutes. Allow the eggs to cool in the liquid to intensify the flavour if you intend to serve them cold. To serve hot, lift them out, remove the shells, showing the veined marble effect of thin brown lines, and serve.

Tea eggs will keep refrigerated and unshelled for 3–4 days.

Poached eggs

The eggs must be fresh, otherwise the whites will not cling to and coat the yolks when immersed in the water. Do not attempt to poach more than 4 eggs at a time because it is too difficult to regulate the temperature of the water. Break each egg into a cup or small bowl (if the whites look too runny and you have no fresher eggs available, change plans and make another dish). Bring 6–7cm water to the boil in a sauté pan or deep frying pan with a tablespoon of mild vinegar to help stop the white breaking up. Do not add salt. Slide in the eggs, cover the pan and turn off the heat. Leave undisturbed for 3 minutes. The whites should be set and the yolks soft and covered with a light coating of white. Lift them out with a slotted spoon and transfer to a bowl of cold water to arrest the cooking.

They can be stored in the refrigerator for 2–3 days in the bowl of water. To use, lift them out with a slotted spoon and drain on kitchen paper. Trim off any thin ragged edges of white if you wish.

Serve poached eggs on toast, alone or on top of a slice of smoked salmon or some sautéed mushrooms. They are also good added to a crisp salad of frisée, cos lettuce or rocket with lightly fried pancetta*, or with spinach leaves (p. 71).

Quails' eggs can be poached in 1–1½ minutes.

Poached eggs with fines herbes

This very good and very simple dish is Elizabeth David's, from *French Country Cooking.*

For 2	2 tbs chopped herbs (parsley, chives and tarragon)	squeeze of lemon juice
40g butter		
4 poached eggs or *oeufs mollets* (p. 50)		

Melt the butter in a small shallow pan, put in the eggs and sauté them without letting the butter burn. Sprinkle in the herbs and a squeeze of lemon juice and eat immediately. The process only takes about 2 minutes, provided that the eggs are prepared beforehand and the herbs ready chopped.

Eggs benedict

An American brunch favourite that is rich and satisfying. Serve it alone or with asparagus or green peas.

For 4	4 slices cooked ham	8 tbs hollandaise sauce (p. 373)
4 slices bread or 2 English muffins halved	4 poached eggs or *oeufs mollets* (p. 50)	
butter		

Toast the bread or muffins lightly and butter them. Warm the slices of ham and put them on the toast. Set the eggs on the ham and coat each one with 2 tbs hollandaise.

Poached eggs with spinach

For 2	salt, freshly ground pepper and nutmeg	8 tbs double cream
500g spinach		grated Parmesan (optional)
25g butter	4 poached eggs or *oeufs mollets* (p. 50)	

Remove any big stalks from the spinach, wash thoroughly and put it into a large pan with just the water that clings to the leaves from washing. Turn over heat until it is all softened, and simmer for 2–3 minutes. Drain and squeeze out all the moisture in your fist. Chop the spinach. Melt 20g butter and toss the spinach in it until any excess moisture has evaporated. Season.

Butter two ramekins or small ovenproof dishes, each large enough to hold 2 eggs and spread a layer of spinach in each one. Make 2 hollows in each bed of spinach and put in the eggs. Spoon over the cream, and sprinkle with Parmesan if you wish. Put the dishes under a preheated grill until the cream is bubbling and lightly browned.

Variation
· Use mornay sauce (p. 371) instead of the cream.

Poached eggs with lentils and lardons

For 4

250g lentils, preferably Puy or Castelluccio (p. 140)	3 tomatoes, peeled and chopped	salt and freshly ground pepper
2 bay leaves	2 garlic cloves, peeled and chopped	100g streaky bacon
100ml olive oil	1 tsp chopped fresh thyme leaves	4 poached eggs
		2 tsp wine vinegar

Wash the lentils and cook them in 450ml water with the bay leaves. Whilst they are cooking, heat 80ml oil in a wide pan and gently stew the tomatoes and garlic. Season with the thyme, salt and pepper, and cover. When the lentils are cooked through, season them, drain any water that has not been absorbed and remove the bay leaves. Add them to the tomato mixture. Cut the bacon into lardons* and fry in the remaining oil. Make 4 hollows in the lentils and put in the poached eggs. Cover and allow them to heat through, about 3–4 minutes. When the eggs are ready, scatter over the lardons, add the vinegar to the frying pan, swish it around, then pour over the eggs and lentils and serve from the pan.

Baked eggs

Eggs can be baked in lightly buttered individual ramekins or even in ovenproof cups standing in a bain-marie*. They can be baked as they are, but a little cream will stop them becoming dry. A tablespoon or two of another flavouring – finely diced cooked bacon, spinach purée, thinly sliced sautéed mushrooms, flaked smoked fish, peeled, seeded and chopped tomato, chopped fresh herbs – makes a pleasant variation. Put the flavouring in the bottom of each ramekin, season, then break the egg on top. Add a tablespoon of cream and put the ramekins into a bain-marie of hot water to come half to two-thirds of the way up the sides. If you don't use cream, cover the ramekins with foil to stop the eggs drying. Set the pan over low heat and maintain the water at a steady simmer. Alternatively, put the bain-marie in a preheated oven, 180°C, 350°F, gas 4. In either case it will take 6–8 minutes; the whites should be just set while the yolks remain soft. Don't overcook: the eggs will go on cooking for a minute or two after being removed from the heat.

Another method is to bake eggs *sur le plat* in shallow gratin dishes with a more substantial garnish. Butter each dish, add cooked and chopped or sliced vegetables, meat or fish, season and break the egg into a hollow in the centre of the other ingredients. Season, add cream, or a tiny knob of butter, and bake in a preheated oven, 180°C, 350°F, gas 4, for 6–8 minutes.

Eggs baked in tomatoes

For 6	2 tbs chopped tarragon	salt and freshly ground pepper
6 large ripe tomatoes	6 eggs	
50g butter		

Heat the oven to 200°C, 400°F, gas 6. Cut a slice from the top of each tomato and reserve these; scoop out the seeds and core. Turn the tomatoes upside down to drain for a few minutes if they appear watery. Using half the butter, put some into each of the tomatoes, and add the tarragon. Break an egg into each tomato, season with salt and pepper and replace the lid. Use the remaining butter to grease a baking dish just large enough to hold the tomatoes. Stand the tomatoes in the dish, cover with a lid or foil and bake in the oven for 15–20 minutes, until the eggs are cooked.

Chakchouka

This dish of baked eggs and vegetables comes from Tunisia. A good supper dish, it can be made more substantial with the addition of 4 sliced merguez sausages at the same time as the onions.

For 4	4 tomatoes, chopped	100ml water
4 tbs olive oil	2 small potatoes, peeled and diced	salt and freshly ground pepper
2 onions, peeled and finely sliced	1–2 fresh green chillies, seeded and chopped	4 eggs
2 red peppers, peeled (p. 157), seeded and chopped		

Heat the olive oil in a sauté pan or other shallow pan and fry the onion until it has softened. Add the remaining vegetables and 100ml water; season. Cover the pan. Simmer for about 25 minutes, until everything has softened. If the mixture is too liquid, simmer for a little longer without the lid.

Make 4 hollows in the vegetable mixture and break an egg into each one. Cover again and cook until the eggs are set, about 4 minutes.

Fried eggs

Fry eggs in butter, olive oil or bacon fat and be sure to keep the heat low or the white will be crisp and dry around the outside before the yolk has barely heated through. Break the eggs into the pan once the fat is hot and baste so that the eggs cook on top as well as underneath. Covering the pan with a lid for about 1 minute will set the white around the yolks. The eggs are ready when the underside of the whites is lightly browned, the top set and the yolks moist and shiny.

Scrambled eggs

Scrambled eggs need care and time to cook them slowly to an even creamy consistency. They should not be stringy and lumpy nor only partly set. Use a pan with a heavy base or, if you prefer, stand your pan in a bain-marie*. Butter the pan generously, beat the required number of eggs gently and season them. Put them into the pan with another 7g of diced butter for each egg and stir continuously over very low heat. Scrape the base and sides of the pan since this is where the eggs cook first. When the mixture begins to thicken and turn creamy, remove the pan from the heat and continue stirring. The residual heat will cook the eggs to a soft consistency. Serve at once on warm plates.

Scrambled eggs can be varied with the addition of small amounts of chopped herbs (chervil, tarragon, and parsley all go well with scrambled egg), cooked vegetables (asparagus tips, sliced mushrooms, small broccoli florets), crumbled crisp bacon, diced ham, slivers of smoked salmon or poached and flaked smoked haddock. The most delicious (and most expensive) flavouring is a sliced black truffle, which should be added to the beaten eggs an hour or so before cooking so that the flavour permeates the eggs thoroughly.

Scrambled eggs with chicken livers

For 4	splash of Worcestershire sauce	4 eggs
8 chicken livers		1 tbs chopped parsley
60g butter	salt and freshly ground pepper	

Trim any green or stringy bits from the livers, cut them into pieces and fry gently in half the butter, with a splash of Worcestershire sauce, for about 2 minutes. Season and keep them warm. Add the remaining butter to the pan and scramble the eggs, *see* p. 55. Put the livers in the centre of a serving dish and put the eggs around them and a little chopped parsley over the top.

Spiced scrambled eggs

In India this is served for breakfast with chapattis, puris or dosas, and very good it is too. But if you find it too daunting, even for brunch, try it for supper.

For 4	2 green chillies, seeded and chopped	salt
2 tbs sunflower oil or ghee*	2cm piece of ginger, peeled and grated	4 eggs
2 small onions, peeled and chopped finely	3 tomatoes, chopped	1 tbs chopped coriander leaves
	½ tsp ground cumin	½ tsp turmeric

Heat the oil or ghee in a deep frying pan or sauté pan and fry the onion, chillies and ginger for about 5 minutes, until the onion has softened and is turning golden. Add the chopped tomatoes and season with cumin and salt. Stir and cook until the juice from the tomatoes is absorbed. Break the eggs into a bowl and add the coriander and turmeric. Tip the eggs into the pan and stir constantly over moderate to low heat until the eggs are just set – it will take a minute or so, no more. If you haven't got Indian breads, serve with toast.

Pipérade

This is based on Boulestin's recipe from *What Shall We Have Today?* He observes that some people make it like scrambled egg, others like omelette, but that neither is correct. The dish should have the appearance of a frothy purée in which it is hard to determine which is vegetable and which is egg.

For 4	1 garlic clove, peeled and crushed	salt and freshly ground pepper
2 large red peppers	4 large tomatoes, peeled and chopped	4 eggs
2 large green peppers		
3 tbs olive oil		

Seed the peppers and slice them. Heat the oil and gently stew the peppers. When they have softened, add the garlic and tomatoes and season. Let the vegetables simmer until they become a purée, then break in the eggs, one by one, without beating them. Stir quickly over the heat until the eggs are cooked and serve at once.

Omelettes

Folded or rolled omelettes

A good folded omelette depends on having a heated and properly seasoned or non-stick pan, fresh eggs, butter and any flavouring you choose prepared and to hand, and it will be ready in less than 2 minutes.

An omelette pan must have a heavy base so that it will cook the egg evenly. If your pan is not non-stick, season it before using for the first time. Pour in 1½cm oil, heat the pan until the oil starts to smoke, then pour it away. Let the pan cool a little then wipe it dry with kitchen paper. Once seasoned, a pan should never be washed but wiped clean with kitchen paper while still warm. The pan must be scrupulously clean and dry before cooking begins.

The size of the pan is important in relation to the number of eggs: an 18–20cm pan will make a 2-egg omelette for 1 person, a 23cm pan a 4-egg omelette for 2. It is best to make small folded omelettes rather than attempt anything larger, because it is tricky to get the cooking right to achieve a lightly set edge and bottom, and a moist, creamy centre.

Beat the eggs lightly, just enough to combine yolks and whites, not to make them frothy. Season, and add any light flavouring such as chopped herbs or finely diced ham. Heat the omelette pan briefly over fairly high heat, add the butter and when it has melted, tilt the pan so all of the base is covered. When the butter stops foaming and starts to smell nutty, pour in the eggs. Stir the eggs with the flat back of a fork and shake the pan gently by the handle. As soon as the base begins to set – it takes about 30 seconds – lift the edges of the omelette with the fork and tilt the pan so that any runny egg goes underneath. Cook for a few seconds more; the top may be runny or lightly set, as you wish.

To fold the omelette, tilt the pan away from you and, with the fork, fold the edge nearest to you into the centre. Lift the further edge with the fork and flip it over the rest of the omelette, then slide it out onto a warm plate.

A filling that will complement the flavour of the eggs rather than override it can be added just before the omelette is folded. Put 2–3 tbs down the centre of the omelette so the filling will be enclosed when the omelette is folded. Grated cheese, peeled, seeded and chopped tomato, sautéed sliced mushrooms, shredded sorrel leaves softened in butter, cooked asparagus tips, cooked small peas, crumbled crisp bacon, diced smoked salmon all make suitable fillings.

Soufflé omelettes

Soufflé omelettes are usually served as desserts. Separate the yolks and whites, beat the yolks well with sugar or seasonings and whisk the whites to peaks. Stir a spoonful of the whites into the yolks and fold in the rest (p. 49). Make the omelette in the same way as a folded omelette, but cook over more gentle heat and spread the mixture evenly through the pan. Shake the pan from time to time. When the bottom is lightly browned, put the pan under the preheated grill for 1–2 minutes to brown the top, or into a preheated oven (190°C, 375°F, gas 5) for 4–5 minutes. You can of course continue cooking on the stove, but the top will not brown. Serve the omelette flat or folded once.

Fillings should be light. Cheese or herbs are suitable for savoury omelettes; for sweet omelettes use jam or fruit such as stoned cherries heated briefly in a little cream or a sliced apple sautéed in butter.

Flat omelettes

The frittate of Italy and the tortillas of Spain are less delicate fare in which the egg acts as a binding agent for the other ingredients. The eggahs of the Arab world and kookoos of Iran are more substantial still. Flat omelettes have a high proportion of filling to egg; vegetables are the most common filling, sometimes combined with cooked meats.

Flat omelettes are usually served in wedges like a cake and most are successful at room temperature as well as hot. Cook the ingredients for the filling and stir them into the beaten eggs and start cooking in a hot pan as for a folded omelette. Smooth the top of the mixture, cover with a lid, reduce the heat and cook for 3–4 minutes until the top is beginning to set. To set it further, the easiest method is to slide the pan under a hot grill for a minute. Alternatively, hold a plate upside down over the pan, tip the omelette onto it and return it to the pan upside down to finish cooking.

Omelette aux fines herbes

For 1 2 eggs	1 tbs finely chopped and very fresh herbs (parsley, chervil, chives and a little tarragon)	salt and freshly ground pepper 20g butter

Break the eggs into a shallow bowl, add the herbs and season. Heat a small frying pan, *see* opposite, add the butter and tilt the pan to coat the base and sides. Beat the eggs just enough to mix yolks and whites, pour them into the pan and cook and fold the omelette as described above. It will only take about 1 minute. Serve straight away on a warm plate.

Middle Eastern omelette with herbs

This dish is something between a tortilla and a gratin, and can be cooked on top of the stove or in the oven. It is called an eggah in Arab countries, a kookoo in Iran. Cooked vegetables, meat or fish all make suitable fillings.

For 4–6	3–4 lettuce leaves	2 tsp plain flour and
200g flat-leaf parsley	4 spring onions, chopped	1 tsp baking powder , or 2 tsp self-raising flour
200g dill	3 tbs chopped walnuts	salt and freshly ground pepper
100g coriander	6 eggs	3 tbs oil
small bunch chives		

If you intend to bake the omelette, heat the oven to 180°C, 350°F, gas 4. Remove and discard the big stalks from the parsley, dill and coriander and chop these herbs with the chives and lettuce. Add the spring onions and walnuts. Beat the eggs with the flour (and baking powder if using), and season well. Stir the herb mixture into the eggs. Heat the oil in a shallow ovenproof dish, making sure to coat it well, pour in the mixture and bake for 45–50 minutes, until the omelette is golden brown.

Alternatively, heat the oil in a frying pan, coating it well on the base and sides, pour in the mixture, cover and cook over low heat for about 25 minutes. Turn the omelette by reversing it onto a plate held over the pan, and cook the other side for 10–15 minutes, uncovered.

Serve hot or at room temperature, with bread and a bowl of yogurt.

Leek frittata

For 4–6	salt and freshly ground pepper	2 tbs chopped tarragon
4 medium leeks	6 eggs	2 tbs grated Parmesan (optional)
3 tbs olive oil		

Remove the outer layers of the leeks, and use only the white and pale green part, after washing them well. Cut them into thin slices and stew gently in the oil until soft. Season with salt and pepper. Beat the eggs lightly and add the tarragon and Parmesan if you are using it. Pour the eggs over the leeks and cook over moderate to low heat until the bottom and edges of the frittata are lightly browned. Put the pan under a hot grill to brown the top a little. Serve warm or at room temperature, cut in wedges.

Variations

Instead of the 4 leeks:

- Use 2 leeks and 250g chopped wilted spinach, and parsley instead of tarragon.
- Use 300g sliced mushrooms, 2 peeled and chopped shallots and 2 tbs chopped parsley.
- Use 250g thinly sliced courgettes, 2 peeled and chopped shallots and 2 tbs chopped mint.
- Use 1 small chopped onion, 1 shredded fennel bulb, and 60g diced ham.

Potato and onion tortilla

For 4	1 large onion, peeled	4 eggs
3 large potatoes, peeled	3 tbs olive oil	salt and freshly ground pepper

Cut the potatoes into small dice and chop the onion finely. Heat the oil in a frying pan, preferably non-stick, and gently sauté the potatoes. Shake and stir the pan regularly, turning the potatoes. They will take about 25 minutes to cook, and should turn golden, but not brown. Add the onion for the last 6–8 minutes, it may burn if put in earlier. Beat the eggs lightly and season with salt and pepper.

Remove the pan from the heat, lift the potatoes and onion out and stir them into the eggs. If there is not enough oil in the pan to fry the omelette add 1 tbs more. When it is hot, pour in the egg mixture, spreading it evenly with a spatula. Shake the pan to ensure the tortilla does not stick to it. When the bottom of the tortilla is golden, reverse it onto a plate held over the pan, and slide it back upside down to cook the other side. Again, if necessary, add a little more oil to the pan.

Serve hot or at room temperature, cut in wedges, with a plate of olives or a salad, or cut into smaller pieces to serve with drinks.

Variations

- Instead of the potatoes and onion, use 3 peeled, seeded and diced tomatoes, 3 red peppers, skinned (p. 151) and sliced, and 2 garlic cloves, peeled and chopped.
- Replace 2 of the potatoes and the onion with 100g sliced chorizo and a sliced chilli.

Soufflés

Soufflés are a blend of a well-flavoured sauce or purée to which first yolks are added then stiffly beaten egg whites. The air trapped in the whites expands during cooking to give the soufflé its light texture and to push the top of the soufflé above the dish. Soufflés use more egg whites than yolks to ensure the necessary expansion is achieved. However, don't overwhisk the whites or the soufflé won't rise. The base can be made in advance, but the whites should be whisked and folded in (p. 49) just before cooking.

Use a straight-sided dish, either a porcelain or glass soufflé dish or a casserole, and fill it three-quarters full with the soufflé mixture so that it will rise above the rim. A 1.4-litre soufflé dish will hold a mixture made with 4–5 whites, a 2-litre dish one made with 6–7 whites. Bake on the middle rack in a preheated oven to give the soufflé room to rise. Avoid opening the door during cooking, but if you need to, do it gently to avoid draughts.

Oven temperature affects the consistency of the soufflé. A large soufflé baked in a moderate (190°C, 375°F, gas 5) oven takes 30–40 minutes. For a firm consistency cook at a lower temperature and increase the time; for a soft centre increase the temperature and decrease the cooking time. Don't overcook the soufflé or it will shrink and the outside will become leathery.

It is ready when it is risen, browned lightly and slightly wobbly on top. If you are not sure, insert a thin flat skewer or knife in the centre; if it comes out clean, the soufflé is ready. Once baked, the soufflé ideally should be served at once, but it will not come to serious harm if it has to wait for up to 10 minutes, in which case, turn off the oven and leave it inside.

Cheese soufflé

Just about any cheese is suitable for making a soufflé, so choose your favourite.

For 4	salt and freshly ground pepper	125g grated cheese
50g butter		5 egg whites
50g plain flour	grated nutmeg	
300ml milk, heated	4 egg yolks	

Heat the oven to 190°C, 375°F, gas 5. Melt the butter in a heavy pan and stir in the flour, blending well. Pour in the hot milk, a little at a time and away from the heat, whisking continuously to achieve a smooth mixture. Return the pan to the heat and stir for a few minutes, until it thickens. Season and leave to cool a little. Beat in the yolks, one at a time, and then add all but 1 tbs of the cheese.

Butter a 1.4-litre soufflé dish. Whisk the whites with a pinch of salt until they form peaks, stir a large spoonful into the cheese mixture, then fold in the rest (p. 49). Pour the mixture into the dish – it should be about three-quarters full – and sprinkle the remaining cheese over the top. Bake for 35–40 minutes, until the soufflé is well risen and lightly browned.

Spinach soufflé

For 6	1 small onion, peeled and chopped finely	¼ tsp paprika
500g fresh spinach or 300g frozen	300ml milk	grated nutmeg
50g butter	50g plain flour	5 egg yolks
	salt	6 egg whites

Heat the oven to 190°C, 375°F, gas 5. Remove large stalks from fresh spinach, wash the leaves well and put them into a large pan with just the water that clings after washing. Turn over heat until it is all softened, and simmer for 2–3 minutes. Drain. Cook frozen spinach according to the instructions on the label and drain. Squeeze the spinach in your fist to remove excess water and chop.

Heat the butter and stew the onion slowly until softened. Heat the milk in a separate pan. Stir the flour into the butter and onion, and blend. Remove the pan from the heat and gradually whisk in the milk. When the mixture is smooth, return the pan to a low heat, add the spinach and stir for a few minutes until the mixture thickens. Season with salt, paprika and nutmeg. Remove the pan from the heat again and when the sauce has cooled somewhat, beat in the egg yolks one at a time. Butter a 2-litre soufflé dish. Whisk the egg whites with a pinch of salt until stiff, stir a large spoonful into the spinach mixture to loosen it, then fold in the rest (p. 49). Turn the mixture into the dish and bake for 40–45 minutes. The soufflé should be well risen and golden brown.

Variation
Mushroom soufflé Replace the spinach by 350g finely sliced mushrooms and sauté them with the onion before stirring in the flour.

Courgette soufflés with tomato sauce

For 6	50g butter	4 egg yolks
350g courgettes, grated	30g plain flour	5 egg whites
salt and freshly ground pepper	150ml milk	6 eggs
2 shallots, peeled and chopped finely	½ tsp crushed fennel seeds or aniseed	tomato sauce (pp. 378–9)

Arrange the grated courgettes in layers in a colander, sprinkling each layer with salt, and leave to stand for 30 minutes. Next squeeze them repeatedly with your hands to get rid of all excess moisture. Heat the oven to 180°C, 350°F, gas 4.

Sauté the shallots in the butter until pale golden, add the courgettes, tossing and stirring the mixture until it is well dried and lightly coloured. Sprinkle over the flour and stir it in. Remove the pan from the heat. Heat the milk in another pan and gradually pour it into the courgette mixture, whisking well. Season with pepper, crushed fennel or anise and a little salt. When the mixture is smooth return the pan to the heat and stir until it thickens. Remove the pan from the heat again, then beat in the egg yolks one by one. Butter 6 individual ramekins. Whisk the egg whites, with a pinch of salt, to peaks; stir a spoonful into the courgette mixture to loosen it, fold in the remainder (p. 49).

Spoon the mixture into the ramekins, filling them two-thirds full. Bake for 12–14 minutes, until risen, golden and firm. Run a knife around the soufflés to loosen them and turn them out onto warmed plates on which you have spooned some of the hot tomato sauce. Serve at once.

Twice-baked cheese soufflés

This recipe comes from Richard Olney's *French Menu Cookbook*.

For 6	grated nutmeg	3 egg yolks
250ml milk	30g butter, cut into small pieces	2 egg whites
40g plain flour	100g grated Parmesan	350ml double cream
salt and freshly ground pepper		

Heat the oven to 180°C, 350°F, gas 4. Bring the milk to the boil, leave until lukewarm then pour it over the flour, whisking to avoid lumps forming. Season with salt, pepper and a little nutmeg to taste. Whisking constantly, stir over moderate heat until the mixture thickens. Let it cool, then add the butter, two-thirds of the cheese and the egg yolks. Mix thoroughly. Butter 6 individual ramekins. Whisk the egg whites with a pinch of salt until stiff. Stir a large spoonful into the cheese mixture and gently fold in the rest (p. 49). Spoon the mixture into the ramekins, until two-thirds full, place them in a large ovenproof dish and pour enough hot, but not boiling, water into the dish to immerse the ramekins by two-thirds. Poach in the oven for about 20 minutes, until firm and spongy to the touch. Unmould the soufflés after running a knife around the edges to loosen them. If you wish, the dish can be prepared in advance to this point.

Butter a shallow baking dish that will hold the soufflés side by side, but not touching. Pour over enough cream to immerse them by half, sprinkle over the rest of the cheese and return to the oven for 15–20 minutes. Almost all the cream will have been absorbed and a light golden gratin formed. Serve at once.

Quiches

Open tarts with a variety of fillings are sold as quiches, but the real thing contains only eggs, cream and bacon and originates from the French province of Lorraine. In other parts of France, similar tarts are made with Parmesan or Gruyère cheese, with soft white cheese and spring onions, or with onions alone.

A tart is not a receptacle for all the leftovers in the refrigerator, but very good tarts can be made using one main ingredient with the eggs and cream. Vegetables such as asparagus, mushrooms, spinach and chicory work well; crab makes a superb tart and smoked salmon can be used as an alternative to the bacon in the original.

In Alsace and Lorraine egg and cream tarts are also made with fruit fillings.

Quiche lorraine

For 6	shortcrust pastry for a	2 eggs
250g smoked streaky bacon	28cm tin, baked blind (pp. 490–1)	2 egg yolks
	400ml double cream or crème fraîche	salt and freshly ground pepper

Heat the oven to 190°C, 375°F, gas 5. Cut the bacon into strips and fry them gently in their own fat in a small pan. Arrange the pieces in the pastry case. Beat the cream and whole eggs and yolks together and season, bearing in mind that the bacon will be salty. Pour the mixture into the tart and bake for 25–30 minutes until it is puffed and golden. Let it rest for a few minutes after taking it from the oven: it will be easier to cut.

Variation

Quiche with fromage frais This is Elizabeth David's version. Use a 22cm tart shell that has been baked blind, and for the filling 250g smoked streaky bacon, 125g fromage frais, young goat's cheese or cream cheese, with 150ml double cream, 3 egg yolks and 1 whole egg. Fry and arrange the bacon as above. Whiz the other ingredients in the food processor until smooth before pouring the mixture into the tart shell. Bake at 200°C, 400°F, gas 6, for 20 minutes, then reduce the temperature to 180°C, 350°F, gas 4, for another 10 minutes.

Cheese

There is scarcely a chapter where some form of cheese is not used: with salads, in sauces, with pasta and risotto, in gratins, in soufflés and quiches, sweet tarts and desserts. Of the hundreds of cheeses that are available, many can be cooked with good results, whether young curd and cream cheeses, soft and semi-soft cheeses like Brie and Taleggio, blue cheeses, semi-hard and hard English Lancashire, Cheddar, Double Gloucester, or really hard Parmesan, Pecorino, Gruyère or Manchego.

Young cheeses can be beaten into a mixture, whereas soft to semi-hard cheeses must be crumbled or cubed and hard cheeses grated before cooking. Most soft cheeses liquefy when heated, although curd cheeses tend to retain a grainy texture and mozzarella turns into gooey threads. English cheeses will melt in a sauce and when grilled or baked they melt to a soft paste that hardens on cooling. The Italian hard cheeses melt, but Gruyère and other Swiss cheeses become slightly stringy. Overcooking at too high a temperature or for too long can cause cheese to separate into its fat and protein elements, leaving you with an oily surface and rubbery texture.

There are a few dishes in which cheese is the principal ingredient, and some of those are given here.

Cervelle de canut

This spread of curd cheese mixed with fresh herbs and wine is a speciality of Lyons. It gets its strange name from the workers in the old silk factories who were called *canuts*, for whom it was a traditional, almost daily, dish.

For 6–8	1 small garlic clove, peeled and chopped finely	2 tbs white wine
500g curd cheese		½ tbs white-wine or tarragon vinegar
salt and freshly ground pepper	25g chives, chopped finely	3 tbs single cream (optional)
	25g tarragon leaves, chopped finely	

Beat the cheese, season it with salt and pepper and beat in the garlic and herbs. Add the wine, vinegar, and cream if you wish, and serve with bread or toast. The cheese will keep for a few days, covered, in the refrigerator and the flavours will develop.

Crème lorraine

This is another French regional dish, lighter and more delicate than a soufflé.

For 4	150g grated Gruyère or a mixture of Gruyère and Parmesan	1 egg
6 rashers streaky bacon		salt and freshly ground pepper
	250ml double cream	

Heat the oven to 180°C, 350°F, gas 4. Fry the bacon in its own fat until crisp and break it into small pieces. Mix together the cheese and cream, add the well-beaten egg, seasonings and bacon, stir well and fill buttered individual soufflé dishes. Bake for about 20 minutes; the mixture should be set, just coloured and very slightly risen. If you bake the cream in a large soufflé dish it will take about 35–40 minutes.

Cheese croquettes

For 4	50g butter, softened	salt and freshly ground pepper
6 large potatoes, boiled and mashed	250g grated Cheddar, Gruyère or Manchego	dried breadcrumbs
4 eggs		oil for frying

The croquettes should be made with newly mashed warm potatoes. Whisk the eggs and stir three-quarters of them into the potatoes with the butter and cheese. Season well with pepper and a little salt. Form the mixture into small balls or ovals. Spread the breadcrumbs on a plate. Dip the croquettes in the remaining beaten egg, then coat them well in breadcrumbs and fry until browned. If they are not well coated the cheese may ooze out.

Welsh rabbit

Whether you prefer rabbit or rarebit, here are the simple instructions for this snack.

For 4	250g grated Cheddar, Cheshire or Double Gloucester	150ml ale or milk
50g butter		4 slices wholemeal bread, toasted
	2 tsp made mustard	

Melt the butter and stir in the cheese, mustard and ale or milk. Cook gently and just long enough for the cheese to melt to a smooth, creamy texture. While the cheese is melting, toast the bread. Spread the mixture on the toast and serve at once or brown quickly under the grill if you prefer.

Variation

Buck rabbit Put a poached egg (p. 51) on top of the Welsh rabbit.

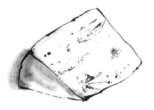

Cheese tart

There are many recipes for cheese tart, using a wide variety of cheeses. I have used Cheddar here, but use what you have to hand.

For 6	250g grated Cheddar	freshly ground pepper
shortcrust pastry for a 28cm tart, baked blind (pp. 490–1)	250ml single cream	grated nutmeg
	4 eggs	cayenne

Heat the oven to 190°C, 375°F, gas 5. Mix together the cheese and cream. Whisk the eggs and add them. Season well with pepper, a grating of nutmeg and a pinch of cayenne. Turn the mixture into the tart shell and bake for 30–40 minutes until golden brown and set. If the tart is browning too quickly cover the top with foil. Serve hot.

If you prefer to make small cheese tarts, this quantity will make about 16 and they will take about 20–25 minutes to bake.

Gorgonzola and walnut turnovers

Other blue cheeses can be used for these turnovers, but if you choose a dry rather than creamy cheese you may need to add a tablespoon or two more cream.

For about 18 turnovers	3 eggs	100g walnuts, chopped
1 pack ready-rolled puff pastry (425g)	180g Gorgonzola, cut into small cubes	60ml cream
		freshly ground pepper

Heat the oven to 220°C, 425°F, gas 7. Roll out the pastry a little more thinly and cut it into rounds of about 10cm diameter. Whisk 2 eggs and mix with the cheese, walnuts and cream. Season with pepper. Put 2 tsp of the mixture into the centre of each circle of pastry. Beat the remaining egg with a little water and brush the edges of the pastry lightly. Fold one side of the pastry over the filling and press it down on the opposite side so you have a semicircle. Press the edges well to seal in the filling. Brush the top of each turnover with the remaining egg wash and prick with a fork. Transfer them to a baking sheet and bake for 15 minutes, then turn down the heat to 200°C, 400°F, gas 6 and bake for a further 8–10 minutes, until golden.

Salads

Salad can be a stimulating start to a meal with bright flavours and
varied textures or a palate cleanser between the main course and dessert.
A substantial salad can also make a meal in itself. Lettuces, salad leaves,
vegetables, fruit, flowers, grains, eggs, meat, seafood, poultry, even bread
are all good in salads, and it goes without saying that the produce must
be very fresh. If you have even a small garden it is worth growing a few herbs and salad greens.
They don't need much space; many herbs and salad plants are attractive enough to be grown
amongst flowers, and cut-and-come-again lettuces will provide for the salad
bowl for several weeks. If it is not possible to grow anything outdoors, keep
pots of herbs in a light place indoors. Buy what is in season, looks fresh and
is appealing to the eye.

The possibilities for salads are unlimited and the recipes that follow should be seen as suggestions, ideas to build on. In composing salads it is important to be aware of different flavours, textures and colours, to use ingredients that complement or contrast with each other rather than make a jumble of tastes.

Dressings are as important as the contents of the salad: extra virgin olive or nut oil, a wine or herb-flavoured vinegar, a scrap of garlic, salt and freshly ground pepper – all will dress a green leaf salad beautifully. Tomatoes and other acidic fruits may not need vinegar at all; fresh lemon or lime juice complements fish and seafood, as does mayonnaise; soy-based oriental dressings are good with vegetable salads; robust salads of vegetables and grains need robust dressings. *See* the dressings and sauces on pp. 358–63.

Simple leaf salads

Green salad

The simplest salad, but it deserves careful treatment.

Lettuces like cos or romaine and the various chicories are fairly robust, but other lettuces and leaves are fragile and should be handled gently. Use small inner leaves of lettuces; outer leaves that are worth eating are best kept for shredding for a mixed salad or for cooking. Oak leaf, curly endive, chicory, cos or romaine, Little Gem, Webbs, corn salad, rocket, cress, baby spinach, purslane, chervil, chives all taste good in a green salad.

| For 4 | 250–300g young mixed salad leaves | vinaigrette (p. 358) |

Toss the salad leaves with just enough vinaigrette to coat them lightly and give the leaves a sheen. Serve at once.

Salad of bitter and peppery greens

In contrast to the green salad above, this salad offers a mixture of rough textures and pronounced flavours. Use a combination of radicchio, chicory, escarole, endive, rocket, young sorrel, watercress, nasturtium leaves, depending on what is available.

| For 4

about 300g salad leaves | a few chives, cut in short lengths | garlic or anchovy vinaigrette (pp. 358–9) |

Discard any tough outer leaves and tear the others into pieces, arrange them in a salad bowl, scatter with the chives and toss with the dressing. Serve at once.

Variation

Salad of sausage and bitter greens Grilled or fried sausages go very well with bitter and peppery greens. Choose 2 of your favourite sausages per person. While they are cooking, toss the salad in the soy, honey and garlic dressing on p. 360. Arrange the salad on individual plates, cut the cooked sausages into diagonal slices and put them on top of the salad.

Spinach salad with poached eggs

For 4	300g baby spinach	4 eggs
1 red pepper, peeled (p. 151)	garlic croûtons (p. 3)	tomato vinaigrette (p. 359)

Remove the seeds and inner ribs from the pepper and cut the flesh into small squares. Arrange the spinach on individual plates with the pieces of pepper and the croûtons. Poach the eggs (p. 51). Toss the salad lightly with the vinaigrette just before the eggs are ready and arrange the eggs on top of the salad.

Variations

Goat's cheese and mixed leaf salad Use a combination of leaves: escarole, curly endive, spinach, radicchio, corn salad or watercress. Omit the croûtons and replace the eggs by 2 small young goat's cheeses. Cut them in half horizontally and bake on a lightly greased tray in the oven (preheated to 200°C, 400°F, gas 6) for 5–6 minutes, until bubbling and golden. A walnut oil vinaigrette (p. 358) is good with this salad.

Wilted salad with bacon Replace the red pepper by 150g sliced small mushrooms, and the tomato vinaigrette by a bacon vinaigrette (p. 359). Keep or omit the croûtons and eggs as you wish. Use spinach, curly endive, radicchio or escarole, singly or two or three in combination.

Warm endive or spinach salad with chicken livers Omit the red pepper and poached eggs. Keep or omit the croûtons as you wish. Peel and finely chop 1 shallot and add to the greens. Toss them in a light mustardy vinaigrette (p. 359). Trim any discoloured or stringy bits from 150g chicken livers and sauté them gently in butter. Deglaze* the pan with 3–4 tbs single cream, scraping up any bits stuck to the bottom. Season lightly and distribute the livers and cream over the salad.

Salad leaves with smoked salmon and quails' eggs Use a mixture of salad leaves, including some spinach if you wish. Instead of red pepper, croûtons and poached eggs, use 125g smoked salmon cut in thin strips and 12 hardboiled quails' eggs (p. 50). Shell the eggs or not, as you wish; they look prettier in the shell. Dress with a lemon vinaigrette (p. 359).

Chicory, walnut and Roquefort salad

Walnuts have an affinity with Roquefort cheese and both combine well with the crisp flavours of the chicory and apple.

For 4	vinaigrette made with half walnut, half extra virgin olive oil (p. 358)	100g Roquefort
2–3 heads of chicory		60g walnuts, coarsely broken
1–2 crisp eating apples		

Separate the leaves of the chicory. Quarter and core the apple and slice finely; peel it or not, as you wish. Put the chicory and apple into a salad bowl and toss with the dressing. Cut the cheese into small pieces, or let it crumble, but not too finely. Scatter the cheese and walnut pieces over the salad and serve at once.

Variations

- Use another crumbly blue cheese such as Stilton, St-Agur or Bleu d'Auvergne if you can't get Roquefort.
- Replace the Roquefort by small cubes of Gruyère.
- If you have two perfect pears (*see* below), use them instead of the apples.

Chicory, apple and smoked fish salad Replace the Roquefort and walnuts by 200g smoked trout broken into large flakes or smoked eel cut in short lengths. Make a lemon juice or tarragon vinegar vinaigrette (p. 359). Add 2 tbs toasted flaked almonds if you like.

Corn salad, watercress and pear salad

Western pears have to be just yielding to the touch and at the point of juicy ripeness to be good, whether for salad or eating alone. Asian pears, which are apple-like in shape and range in colour from yellow to russet brown, always stay firm and have a refreshing crisp texture. Either can be used for this salad.

For 4	2 pears	2 tbs roasted and coarsely chopped hazelnuts (p. 488)
about 100g watercress	vinaigrette made with half extra virgin olive oil and half hazelnut oil (p. 358)	
about 100g corn salad		

Remove the big stalks from the watercress and put the small sprigs and corn salad in a salad bowl. Quarter and core the pears and slice finely, peel them or not as you wish, and add them to the salad leaves. Toss with the vinaigrette, scatter the hazelnuts over the salad and serve.

Variations

· Other nuts go well in this salad: dry-roasted* pine nuts, fresh walnuts, or try dry-roasted* pumpkin or sunflower seeds. You could also add shavings of Pecorino, Parmesan or Manchego cheese, or crumble over a little white Wensleydale or Caerphilly cheese.

Watercress and orange salad

This is a clean-tasting and refreshing salad which goes well after a roast or a rich meat casserole.

For 4	16 black olives	2 tbs rice vinegar
200g watercress	2 tbs orange juice	1 tbs sunflower oil
2 large oranges	2 tbs light soy sauce	

Remove the large stalks from the watercress. Peel the oranges and remove all the pith. Working over a bowl to catch the juice, separate the oranges into segments. Use a very sharp small knife to cut the flesh from between the membranes, and discard the pips. Put the watercress and orange pieces in a salad bowl. Add the olives. Whisk the soy sauce and vinegar into the orange juice collected in the bowl, stir in the oil and toss the salad in the dressing.

Composed salads

Salade composée

A salade composée does not have a formula, but represents an imaginative mixture of whatever salads and vegetables are in season. It is fairly substantial; it can be elaborate or constructed from just a few elements; served as a first course or comprise a meal in itself. Richard Olney was the master of the salade composée, making one virtually every day for his lunch and for any guests. Watching and helping Richard and eating his excellent salads led me to appreciate the diversity and richness of these salads and willingly to spend the time constructing my own.

Fennel, celery, cucumber, tomatoes, onions, mushrooms, radishes, courgettes, grilled and peeled red peppers (p. 151), cooked potatoes, green beans, asparagus, peas or broad beans marry well with all kinds of salad greens. I like to have about half salad greens to other ingredients, but you can vary the salad according to what you have and your own preference. Herbs and flowers – nasturtiums, violets, herb flowers – contribute extra flavours and colour. Leftover meat, poultry or fish cut in slivers or flaked, sautéed chicken livers, anchovy fillets, canned tuna or crab, hard-boiled or *oeufs mollets* (p. 50), thinly sliced omelette, cubes of cheese can all be used.

With such diverse choice it is important to make sure that the flavours of the ingredients selected are compatible and do not cancel each other out. It is best not to mix meat and fish, or either of these with cheese.

The salad needs a well-flavoured vinaigrette (p. 358) and should be tossed just before it is served otherwise leaves and other delicate vegetables become limp. Choose a large deep bowl, make the dressing in the bowl, and put into the dressing any ingredient – onion for example – that will benefit from macerating for a while. Cross the salad servers over the dressing to prevent other ingredients falling into it. Put vegetables and sturdy leaves at the bottom and build up with lighter ingredients arranging them attractively, with an eye to colour and contrast. Place flowers or asparagus tips, a few pieces of meat, poultry or fish, sliced radishes, red peppers or quarters of hardboiled egg on the top. The salad should look pretty and inviting. Admittedly the decorative effect will be spoiled when it is turned to dress it, but it should be composed to be admired first.

Caesar salad

For 6	1 egg yolk	150ml extra virgin olive oil
2 young heads cos or romaine lettuce	1 tsp Dijon mustard	
	2 tbs lemon juice	30g Parmesan cheese, shaved
2 garlic cloves, peeled	freshly ground pepper	
10 anchovy fillets		toasted garlic croûtons (p. 3)

Tear the lettuce leaves into pieces, discarding any tough central ribs. Pound the garlic and half the anchovy fillets to a paste with the egg yolk and mustard. Stir in the lemon juice, season with pepper, then whisk in the olive oil, a little at a time, to form an emulsion. Cut the remaining anchovy fillets into slivers. Dress the lettuce and toss with the anchovy slivers and Parmesan. Scatter over the croûtons and serve.

Greek salad

For 6	1 red onion, peeled and diced	150g feta cheese, cubed
2 heads firm lettuce such as cos	6 ripe tomatoes, cut into wedges	20g black olives
1 cucumber, cut into cubes		garlic vinaigrette (p. 359)

Tear the lettuce leaves into pieces or shred them in a chiffonade*. Combine the salad ingredients, toss with the dressing and serve at once.

Salade niçoise

There are many versions of salade niçoise. The basics are tomatoes, small black olives, green pepper, hardboiled eggs and basil. Other vegetables such as small broad beans, tiny artichokes, cucumber or onions are used according to the season or the inclination of the cook. *Fines herbes* (tarragon, chervil and chives) can replace the basil; tuna in oil, or grilled fresh tuna, can replace the anchovies. Some cooks, but not, as far as I can discover, those from the region, also add salad leaves. Occasionally one finds versions that have just about all of the above. The recipe I use follows but you can adapt it with these notes in mind; 300g tuna would be about the right amount to replace the anchovies.

For 6	12 anchovy fillets	vinaigrette made with white-wine or herb vinegar (p. 358)
8 large ripe tomatoes	3 hardboiled eggs	
salt	100g small black olives	10 basil leaves
1 green pepper	200g thin french beans, cooked	

Slice the tomatoes and salt them lightly. Leave them on the board while you prepare the remaining ingredients. Slice the pepper into thin rounds, discarding the seeds. Cut the anchovy fillets into two or three pieces. Cut the eggs in quarters or slice them.

Arrange the tomatoes in a shallow serving dish. Place the pepper, anchovies, olives and french beans over the tomatoes in an attractive way. Put the pieces of egg round the edge of the dish. Spoon over the vinaigrette and scatter the salad with torn basil leaves.

Vegetable salads

Carrot and apple salad

A crisp winter salad. Mint is the suggested herb because it is available all year, but if you grow lovage, try a little of it, chopped, instead when it is in season.

For 4	250g crisp eating apples, peeled and grated	salt and freshly ground pepper
250g carrots, peeled and grated		juice of 1 lemon
	1 tbs chopped mint	2–3 tbs sunflower or olive oil

Combine the carrot, apple and mint in a bowl. Make a lemony dressing with the remaining ingredients (p. 359) and toss the salad in it.

Spicy carrot salad

This is another of my favourite salads: lightly spiced carrots coated in yogurt are garnished with mint and cashew nuts. It is based on a recipe in Julie Sahni's *Classic Indian Vegetarian Cooking*.

The tiny dark brown mustard seeds are widely used in Indian cooking, and should be found in the spice rack in the supermarket or in Indian shops. When fried or dry-roasted*, they develop an earthy aroma, and the flavour is nutty, slightly bitter and hot. Mustard oil is a viscous pungent oil pressed from mustard seeds and is available from Indian shops. If you are unable to find the asafoetida, you can make the salad without it and it will still be good.

For 4–6	2 green chillies, seeded and chopped finely	pinch ground cloves
500g carrots	pinch asafoetida*	salt
1 tbs mustard oil or sunflower oil	2 tsp sugar	60ml plain yogurt
1 tsp mustard seeds	1 tsp curry powder	2 tbs cashew nuts, dry-roasted* and chopped
	squeeze of lemon juice	fresh mint leaves

Peel and slice the carrots very thinly or grate them. Heat the oil in a large frying pan and add the mustard seeds. Cover with a lid when they start to pop and jump about. As the spattering subsides add the chillies, asafoetida, sugar and curry powder. Shake the pan and stir for a few seconds.

When the sugar has dissolved add the carrots and toss well to separate the slices or shreds and to coat them with the oil and spices. Cook for 3–4 minutes, then transfer to a bowl and leave to cool. Stir the lemon juice, cloves, salt and yogurt into the carrots and toss. Sprinkle the nuts and mint leaves over the salad and serve at room temperature.

Cucumber salad with a cream dressing

This salad is particularly good with cold poached salmon or other fish, but if it is not to accompany fish, you could stir some prawns into it. Dill or chives can replace the chervil.

For 4–6	1 tbs lemon juice or mild vinegar	salt and freshly ground pepper
2 cucumbers	3 tbs chopped chervil	4 tbs soured cream

Peel the cucumbers or not as you wish, cut them in half lengthways, remove the seeds and slice the halves very thinly. Put the slices in a colander set over a deep plate, sprinkling each layer with salt as you put them in. Leave the cucumber to drain for at least 1 hour. Rinse well and press with your hands to extract as much water as possible, then dry the slices on a clean cloth or with kitchen paper.

Stir the lemon juice or vinegar, chervil and some pepper into the cream and mix in the cucumber. Taste for seasoning and serve chilled.

Fennel salad

Crisp slices of fennel make an excellent refreshing salad on their own (which is how I tend to serve them) or mixed with thin slices of apple or orange or red onion.

For 4	vinaigrette made with lemon juice and a dash of mustard (p. 359)	chopped chives
3–4 heads fennel		

Remove the tough outer layer from the fennel and slice the inner part thinly from top to bottom. Arrange the fennel on a plate, spoon over the dressing and sprinkle with chives.

Variation

Fennel and walnut salad Dress the salad not with a vinaigrette but with 3–4 tbs single cream into which you have stirred a little lemon juice, salt and pepper, then scatter over 30g chopped walnuts.

Salad of cooked peppers and tomatoes

This unusual and richly flavoured salad from Tunisia makes an excellent first course. It also goes well with grilled chicken or fish. It can be easily made in larger quantities and will keep for several days in the refrigerator.

For 4–6	salt and freshly ground pepper	4–6 garlic cloves, unpeeled
2kg ripe tomatoes	1 tsp paprika	1 preserved lemon (p. 513)
6 tbs olive oil	5–6 red peppers	4 tbs chopped parsley

Heat the grill. Peel, seed and chop the tomatoes and cook them gently in the olive oil, seasoned with salt, pepper and paprika. Keep the heat low, stir from time to time, and cook until all the water has evaporated and you have a thick sauce that begins to fry in the oil. This can take up to 30 minutes if the tomatoes are watery. Remove from the heat.

While the tomatoes are cooking, put the peppers and garlic under the grill, turning until the skins of the peppers are blackened on all sides and the garlic skins are crisp. The garlic will be ready before the peppers. Leave the garlic to cool, then squeeze it between your fingers and the cooked purée will pop out. Stir this into the tomatoes. Remove the peppers to a plastic bag and leave to cool.

Peel the peppers, remove the seeds and dice the flesh. Dice the skin of the preserved lemon, discarding the flesh. Add the peppers, lemon and parsley to the pan and put this back over a very low heat for about 15 minutes, stirring frequently to prevent sticking. Leave to cool before serving.

Potato salad

Only waxy, firm yellow-fleshed potatoes will produce a good salad. In recent years the variety on the market has increased and there are a number of varieties to choose from: Belle de Fontenay, Bintje, Charlotte, Pink Fir Apple, la Ratte, Rosa. For the best results, boil the potatoes in their skins and drain them well as soon as they are cooked. Avoid over-cooking.

For 6–8	1 glass white wine	150–180ml soured cream
1kg salad potatoes	1 medium red onion	
salt and freshly ground pepper	1 tbs lemon juice	2tbs small capers or 4 tbs chopped dill

Boil the potatoes in their skins in salted water until just tender. Drain and peel while still warm and slice into a large dish. Pour over the white wine, toss and stir to coat all the potatoes. Set aside to cool.

Peel and slice the onion finely. Stir the lemon juice into the cream and dress the potatoes. Season with pepper and a little salt. Stir in the onion and capers or dill, and serve at room temperature.

Spiced tofu salad

You can change the vegetables for this salad to suit your taste or what is available. Celery, cucumber, crisp apple, radishes, red or yellow peppers, water chestnuts are all suitable; what is important is to have crisp textured vegetables to contrast with the soft tofu.

For 4	1 bulb of fennel	2 tbs chopped raw peanuts
300g firm tofu	1 green pepper	
60g french beans	1 small red onion	oriental vinaigrette (p. 359)
1 carrot		

Drain the tofu and press it between sheets of kitchen paper with a plate on top for 30 minutes to make it more firm. Cut the beans into short lengths and parboil them until just tender. Drain and leave to cool. Peel the carrot and cut it in thin strips, remove the outer layer from the fennel and slice the bulb lengthways and then into strips, cut the pepper into thin strips, discarding the seeds and white membrane, peel and slice the onion finely. Cut the tofu into cubes. Combine all the ingredients in a salad bowl and toss with the dressing.

Variations

Spiced oriental salad Use a mixture of vegetables as described above, but instead of tofu – or in addition to make a more substantial salad – use some cooked prawns, shredded chicken, pork or crab meat.

Hearty salads

Haricot bean salad

There are all sorts of bean salads. This one from Turkey with onions, tomatoes, hard-boiled eggs and olives is one of my favourites.

For 4	1 small green pepper, sliced into thin rings	12 black olives
250g haricot beans, soaked overnight	2–3 tomatoes, cut in wedges	3 tbs chopped parsley
2 onions, peeled		lemon juice vinaigrette (p. 359)
salt	2 hard-boiled eggs, cut in wedges	

Cook the beans in unsalted boiling water with 1 whole onion until they are tender, about 1 hour. Let them cool in the liquid, then drain and discard the onion. Slice the other onion finely, sprinkle with salt and leave for 3–4 minutes. Rub the onion with your fingers to squeeze out the juice, then rinse.

Combine the beans and onion and arrange them in a serving dish. Taste and season with a little salt if necessary. Put the pepper rings over the beans and decorate further with the tomatoes, eggs, olives and parsley. Spoon over the dressing and serve.

Warm chick pea salad

This salad is served regularly in Provence in winter to accompany poultry and meat; it can also be served with two or three other salads to make a meal. In Syria, they make a similar warm salad with ground cumin in the seasonings.

For 5–6	salt and freshly ground pepper	100ml extra virgin olive oil
400g chick peas soaked overnight	2 garlic cloves, peeled and chopped finely	1 red onion, peeled and sliced in fine rings
1 onion, peeled	2 tbs red wine vinegar	4 tbs chopped parsley
1 bouquet garni*		

Drain and rinse the chick peas, bring them to the boil in unsalted water with the whole onion and bouquet garni. Reduce the heat to a fast simmer, partly cover the pan and cook until tender; they can take 1–2 hours, depending on their age and size. Top up with boiling water if necessary, and taste to see when the chick peas are ready: they should be quite firm and grainy but not hard. If they are cooked before you are ready to serve the salad, leave them in the pan off the heat, then reheat. Drain and discard the onion and bouquet garni. Combine the seasonings, garlic, vinegar and oil to make a dressing and toss the hot chick peas in it. Add the red onion and parsley, toss again and serve.

Couscous and vegetable salad

For 4–6	250g small mushrooms, quartered	4 tbs chopped coriander
300g couscous	6 spring onions, sliced	3 tbs lemon juice
100–120ml olive oil	4 tomatoes, peeled and diced	salt and freshly ground pepper
6 garlic cloves		
3 courgettes, halved lengthways and sliced	200g cooked chick peas (*see* above)	

Cook the couscous according to the instructions on the packet (or *see* p. 202). Fork 2 tbs olive oil into it and leave to cool. Heat 4 tbs oil in a pan and gently fry the whole peeled garlic cloves until coloured on all sides but not charred; it will take 5 minutes or so to do this. Lift out the garlic, crush and chop it and set aside. Add the courgettes to the pan and fry over medium-high heat until lightly browned. Remove them and fry the mushrooms until they are just cooked.

Combine the couscous with all the vegetables, most of the coriander and any oil left in the pan. Whisk the lemon juice with the seasonings and the remaining oil. Fork the dressing through the salad and scatter over the remaining coriander.

Variation
Chicken and couscous salad Grill, poach or steam a large chicken breast, cut the flesh into cubes and add them to the salad.

Lentil salad

Small slate-green lentils such as Puy from France or Castelluccio from Italy (p. 140) are best for this salad because they have a good flavour and retain their shape and texture. However, I recently tried similar small grey-green lentils from Canada with good results.

For 4	generous quantity of vinaigrette (p. 358)	3 spring onions, sliced
250g lentils		2 hardboiled eggs, cut into wedges
1 small onion, peeled	salt and freshly ground pepper	
1 garlic clove, peeled	3–4 tbs chopped herbs – chives, parsley, chervil, tarragon	1 lemon cut into wedges

Cook the lentils in unsalted boiling water with the onion and garlic until tender. Drain thoroughly, discarding the onion and garlic. Put into a dish, coat well with the vinaigrette and leave to cool. Taste and season with salt and pepper if necessary.

To serve, mix in the chopped herbs and spring onion, and top with the eggs and lemon.

Variation

Lentil and chorizo salad Spicy chorizo sausage and lentils make a good combination. Fry chorizo and cut it into slices. Stir these into the salad and omit the hardboiled eggs and lemon.

Herbed rice salad

If you wish, add diced tomato, roasted red pepper strips (p. 151) or olives to this salad.

For 4	2–3 tbs olive oil	3–4 tbs chopped fresh herbs
125g long grain rice	1 tbs tarragon vinegar	
salt and freshly ground pepper	1 small red onion, peeled and chopped finely	chive, hyssop or nasturtium flowers to garnish

Put the rice in a bowl, pour over boiling water, stir and leave for 5 minutes. Drain and rinse with cold water. Bring 150ml salted water to the boil, put in the rice, bring to the boil again, cover and turn down the heat so that the pan just simmers. Leave for 10 minutes or so to do this. By this time the water should be absorbed and small holes should have formed on the surface of the rice. Remove the pan from the heat. Pour over 2 tbs oil, cover with a tea towel and the lid and leave for 10 minutes. The rice should be tender but still have a light bite.

Turn it out into a large bowl, using a wooden fork in order not to break the grains. Allow it to cool, then, still using the fork, stir in a little more oil if needed and the vinegar. Stir in the chopped onion and herbs and season with pepper. Decorate the salad with a few flowers and serve.

Tabbouleh

This is a traditional Lebanese salad that is popular throughout the Middle East. Proportions of wheat to herbs and tomatoes vary, but the cracked wheat (bulgur) plays only a background role. The salad should be predominantly green and red, with specks of cream, and taste vibrantly of parsley and lemon.

For 6	6 spring onions	100ml extra virgin olive oil
90g fine cracked wheat (bulgur)	2 bunches flat-leaf parsley (350–400g total weight)	salt and freshly ground pepper
750g tomatoes, chopped, with the juice reserved	60g mint leaves	½ tsp allspice
	juice of 1 lemon or more to taste	small cos or Little Gem lettuce leaves

Soak the bulgur for 15–20 minutes in a large bowl of cold water until soft and swollen. Taste a grain or two to see if it is tender, then drain thoroughly, pressing out excess water.

Put the bulgur in a large bowl. Spread the tomatoes and their juices over the bulgur. While the tomato juices are soaking in, slice the spring onions thinly, and scatter them over the tomatoes. Chop the parsley, then the mint very finely, and spread the herbs over the onions. Mix together all these ingredients – I find it easiest to do this with my hands. Make a dressing with lemon juice, olive oil, salt, pepper and allspice and pour it over the salad. Stir it into the tabbouleh and let the salad stand for 30 minutes to give the flavours time to blend. Taste and add more lemon juice or other seasonings if necessary.

Serve with lettuce leaves for scooping up the tabbouleh out of the bowl.

Seafood salads

Spiced prawn and papaya salad

A refreshing light salad. The mint, lime juice and garam masala give a sharp clean taste to the creamy dressing. Alternatively, you can replace the papaya by mango or melon; avocado also goes well with this dressing.

For 4	½–1 tsp garam masala*	20–24 tiger prawns, cooked and peeled
2 ripe papayas	2–3 tbs lime juice	3–4 sprigs mint
90ml single cream	salt and freshly ground pepper	
90ml double cream		

Cut the papayas in half, scoop out the seeds, peel and slice the flesh. Reserve any juices. Blend together the creams, ½ tsp garam masala and 2 tbs lime juice. Add the papaya juices and season with a little salt and pepper. Taste and add more garam masala or lime juice if you wish. Run a knife down the centre back of the prawns and remove the black intestine thread.

Arrange the papaya and prawns on a serving plate or on individual plates, spoon the dressing over the salad. Shred the mint leaves and scatter them over the top.

Prawn, spinach and mushroom salad

For 4	4 tbs soy sauce	250g cooked medium prawns (shelled weight)
200g button mushrooms	½ tsp caster sugar	
	2 tbs sunflower oil	½ tsp paprika
4 tbs lemon juice	100g baby spinach	

Cut the mushrooms in halves or quarters depending on their size and the size of the prawns. Whisk the lemon juice, soy sauce and sugar together until the sugar has dissolved, whisk in the oil and toss the mushrooms in half of the dressing, coating them well to stop them discolouring.

Put the spinach leaves into a salad bowl, arrange the mushrooms and prawns over the leaves. Spoon the remaining dressing over the spinach and prawns. Dust with paprika. Toss well before serving.

Crab and avocado salad

This is a quickly made salad that can easily be made in larger quantities. The fresh mixed herbs in the vinaigrette enhance the flavours of both crab and avocado; choose from parsley, chervil, chives, tarragon.

For 2	salt and freshly ground pepper	handful of rocket or other salad leaves
125g white crab meat	2 tbs extra virgin olive oil	pinch cayenne
juice and grated rind of 1 unwaxed lime		4 cherry tomatoes
½ tsp Dijon mustard	1 small avocado, peeled	1 tbs dry-roasted* pine kernels
2 tbs chopped fresh herbs	¼ small melon, peeled	

Shred the crab meat and remove any bits of shell or cartilage. Whisk together the lime juice, rind, mustard, herbs and seasonings, then whisk in the oil. Cut the avocado flesh and the melon into cubes and toss in a little of the dressing. Toss the salad leaves also with a little of the dressing and arrange them on two plates. Spoon the avocado and melon into the centre of the leaves. Toss the crab with most of the remaining dressing and a good pinch of cayenne. Spoon the crab on top of the avocado and melon. Cut the tomatoes in half, spoon a little dressing onto them and arrange them on the plate. Scatter over the pine kernels and serve.

Crab and green bean salad with pickled ginger

The beans for this salad must be very thin. Beans and crab go well together and the ginger provides a light sharpness as well as a pretty pink colour to offset the green beans and creamy-white crab.

Finely sliced spring onion can replace the ginger.

For 4	salt and freshly ground pepper	2 tbs pickled ginger (p. 193), drained, or 3 spring onions, sliced finely
350g very thin french beans	250g crab meat, without shell or cartilage	
2 tbs sherry vinegar		
3 tbs sunflower oil		

Cook the beans in boiling water for 6–7 minutes. They should be firm but have no trace of rawness. Drain them and refresh in cold water. Drain again. In a shallow dish, whisk together the vinegar and oil and season well. Arrange the beans in the dish, place the crab in the centre and put the slivers of ginger or the spring onion over the top. Toss before serving.

Warm salad of scallops with Jerusalem artichokes

One of my favourite winter salads, this is a version of a recipe originally published by Jeremy Round in the *Independent*.

For 4	400g Jerusalem artichokes	2 tbs sherry vinegar
8 large scallops, cleaned (p. 260)	½ tsp grated unwaxed orange rind	1 shallot, finely chopped
3 tbs olive oil	½ tsp grated unwaxed lemon rind	150g small salad leaves (such as oak leaf, corn salad, watercress, Little Gem, radicchio)
3 tbs sunflower oil	salt and freshly ground pepper	
2 tbs lemon juice		

Detach the corals from the scallops and slice the white flesh horizontally into two or three pieces. Lay the scallops in a bowl. Whisk together the oils and mix 2 tbs of the oils with 1 tbs lemon juice. Spoon this mixture over the scallops, making sure all the pieces are coated on both sides, and marinate in the refrigerator for an hour or more.

Peel the artichokes, drop them into a pan of salted water acidulated with the remaining lemon juice. Bring to the boil and cook until tender, about 15 minutes. Drain and slice them into rounds. While they are cooking, blanch the orange and lemon rind for 1 minute, drain, refresh with cold water and drain again. Stir salt and pepper to taste into the vinegar, then whisk the vinegar into the remaining oil and stir in the shallot.

Put the warm artichokes on an ovenproof plate in a single layer and lightly coat on both sides with a little vinaigrette, including some of the shallot. Grind over more pepper.

When you are ready to serve the salad, heat the grill, toss the salad leaves in the remaining vinaigrette and arrange them on four plates. Heat a dry, heavy, non-stick frying pan until very hot. Put the plate of artichokes under the grill briefly to heat through. Sear the sliced scallops on both sides for 20–30 seconds, no more or they will become tough. Do not fill the pan too full, it is better to work in small batches. Arrange slices of artichoke and scallop on the salad leaves. Quickly sear the corals and arrange them on the top of the salad. Sprinkle over the citrus rind and serve.

Poultry and meat salads

Oriental chicken salad

This salad with flavours of south-east Asia is quickly assembled. The other ingredients can be prepared while the noodles are soaking. Cellophane noodles made from vegetable starch do not need cooking. If you are allergic to peanuts, the salad is still good without them.

For 4–6	2 spring onions, sliced finely	60g bean sprouts, tails trimmed
80g cellophane noodles	3 tbs chopped mint	2 tbs raw peanuts
250g cooked chicken	3 tbs chopped coriander	juice of 1 lime
1 stalk lemon grass*	½ cucumber	2 tbs fish sauce
1 small chilli, seeded and sliced finely	3 stalks celery	2 tsp sugar
		2 tbs water

Soak the noodles in hot water for 10 minutes, drain and rinse them in cold water and cut them into short lengths with scissors. Shred the chicken and put it in a bowl. Discard the outer layer of the lemon grass and, using the bottom third only, slice it finely. Combine the lemon grass, chilli, spring onions and herbs and add to the chicken. Cut the cucumber in half lengthways, discard the seeds and cut it into julienne* strips. Remove strings from the celery, and cut it into similar strips. Stir the noodles, cucumber, celery and bean sprouts into the chicken. Dry-roast* the peanuts and crush them coarsely. Combine the lime juice, fish sauce, sugar and water to make a dressing. Toss the salad in the dressing and scatter over the peanuts.

Turkey and avocado salad

A pretty red, cream and green salad, and a useful way of using up leftover turkey. It is also good with smoked chicken or turkey. Pomegranates are in season in autumn and the early winter months. Their bright, crisp seeds add an agreeable crunch and juiciness to the salad as well as being decorative.

For 4	1 large avocado, peeled and sliced	3 tbs hazelnut oil
1 large head radicchio	2 tbs pomegranate seeds	2 tbs olive oil
250g cooked turkey, sliced	2 tbs sherry vinegar	salt and freshly ground pepper

Tear 8–10 radicchio leaves into small pieces and arrange them in a shallow bowl. Arrange the turkey and avocado on the leaves and scatter over the pomegranate seeds. Whisk the vinegar, oils and seasonings together to make a dressing and spoon it over the salad. Make sure all the avocado slices are coated or they will discolour.

Thai beef salad

This salad, very popular in Thai restaurants, is made with barbecued or grilled steak, cooked rare. The citrus and chilli dressing gives it a pleasant piquancy.

For 4	1 stalk lemon grass*	freshly ground pepper
350g fillet or sirloin steak	2–3 shallots, peeled and sliced finely	2 tsp fish sauce (p. 520)
6 lettuce leaves, shredded	3 garlic cloves, peeled and crushed	juice of ½ small lime
leaves from 3–4 large coriander sprigs	3 chillies, seeded and chopped	2 tsp sugar
		mint sprigs

Grill or barbecue the steak until rare or medium-rare (*see* p. 314 for timing). Leave to cool, then cut the steak in thin strips. Put the lettuce in a bowl, tear the coriander leaves roughly and add them. Discard the outer layer of the lemon grass and, using the bottom third only, slice it finely. Put the steak over the lettuce and top it with the lemon grass and shallot. Pound the garlic, chillies and a generous amount of pepper, or blend to a paste in a food processor, adding the fish sauce, lime juice and sugar to achieve a smooth consistency. If necessary add a tablespoon of water. Pour the dressing over the salad and toss lightly. Top with the mint sprigs and serve.

Pork and crab salad

A fresh-tasting salad in which ingredients can be changed according to what is available: chicken and prawns may replace pork and crab. The inspiration for the salad is Vietnamese so bean sprouts or bamboo shoots in place of tomatoes and peppers would be quite authentic. It is important to have a large quantity and variety of herbs.

For 4	1 Little Gem or small cos lettuce	2 carrots, peeled and cut in long slivers
100g pork loin	2 plum tomatoes, seeded and sliced in strips	3 spring onions, sliced finely
100g cooked crab meat		
1 tbs sesame seeds		*for the dressing*
4 large sprigs basil	2 green peppers, preferably the thin-skinned, long pale green type, seeded and sliced in strips	1 tbs chilli oil
8 large sprigs coriander		2 tsp sugar
6 sprigs mint		3 tbs water
2–3 sprays fennel or dill	½ cucumber, sliced thinly	2 tbs fish sauce
		4–5 tbs lime juice

Put the pork in a small pan with just enough water to cover, bring to the boil, reduce the heat and simmer until tender, 15–20 minutes. Leave to cool in the water for 10 minutes, then strain and put aside until cold. Slice the meat into very thin rounds and shred the crab meat, removing any bits of shell or cartilage. Dry-roast* the sesame seeds. Pluck individual leaves or small sprigs from the basil, coriander and mint. Break the fennel or dill into small sprays.

Line a platter with the lettuce leaves. Arrange the vegetables and herb leaves on the lettuce. Top with the pork and crab meat, then scatter over the sesame seeds.

Mix together the ingredients for the dressing. Taste and adjust if necessary, then spoon the dressing over the salad and serve.

Vegetables

The choice of vegetables has never been greater: potatoes labelled by variety, three or four types of onion or tomato, several different squashes, a selection of fungi and mushrooms, a profusion of salad leaves – all are regularly to be found in greengrocers' and supermarkets. The growth of farmers' markets has also extended the choice of varieties and made local produce more accessible. Recent years have seen a huge increase in the availability of organically raised fruit and vegetables, thanks to consumer demand. Generally, they have more nutrients and more flavour, and there is the assurance that they have not been waxed or sprayed with pesticides. Vegetables play a greater and more central role in most people's cooking today than previously, and quality and flavour are of the utmost importance.

Choosing

Look for vegetables that are firm, bright in colour, unblemished and unwrinkled, and not frost-bitten. Leaf vegetables should not be limp or yellowing; cabbage stalks should not be dried out or slimy; root vegetables should be stiff, not rubbery, and potatoes should not be sprouting or have any green patches. Choose green beans or mange-tout that are crisp and bright; asparagus with firm tips and closed scales; corn-on-the-cob with green husks, golden brown tassels and plump unwrinkled kernels; cauliflowers with a tight, creamy white head; pale, crisp bean sprouts without brown ends; onions and garlic that are firm and dry, without green shoots. Ripe avocados yield to gentle pressure; courgettes should not, they should be firm. Mushrooms soon shrivel so buy only those that are very fresh and slightly moist and don't buy more than you will use quickly. Turnips, celeriac, aubergines and pumpkins should be firm and feel heavy, an indication that they will be more succulent. Tomatoes are best when ripened on the vine. Young and small vegetables are usually more tender and have more flavour than old and large, although the baby vegetables now widely available look pretty, but many have little taste. Baby fennel and carrots and young spinach are exceptions.

The only frozen vegetables worth buying are artichoke hearts and bottoms, small peas (petits pois), broad beans, sweetcorn and spinach.

Storing

Root vegetables, onions, garlic and pumpkins are best stored in a cool dark place, although once cut they should be refrigerated. Remove root vegetables from plastic bags because they will sweat and go mouldy. Unwashed root vegetables keep better than the washed ones sold in supermarkets. It is preferable not to store tomatoes, aubergines, peppers and courgettes in the refrigerator but keep them at room temperature. Pale tomatoes will turn red, especially if a deep red tomato is among them, exuding ethylene gas which is responsible for the colour change. Most other vegetables, but especially leaf vegetables and herbs, are best kept in perforated plastic bags in the salad drawer of the refrigerator. Leaves not kept in plastic bags quickly go limp. Wrapping in clingfilm is an alternative for beans, fennel, radishes and the like. Do not keep mushrooms in plastic; a paper bag is the best way of keeping them fresh.

Throw away any vegetable that shows signs of deterioration because it can affect others stored with it.

Quantities

Much depends on what else is to be served at the meal, whether the vegetable is an accompaniment to another dish or is the main dish itself. Some guidelines are given below to help when buying.

Vegetables with thick peel, such as pumpkin, squash, celeriac: allow 300g per serving.

Vegetables that cook down a lot, such as spinach and chard leaves: allow 300g per serving.

Vegetables to be shelled, such as peas and broad beans: allow 300–400g of the un-shelled vegetable per serving, and reckon roughly that 400g peas in the pod will yield 100–120g shelled. Broad beans are more difficult to assess, and may well yield a little less.

Artichoke (large), corn-on-the-cob: allow 1 per serving.

Asparagus (white has to be peeled, thin green does not, so you could allow less), fennel, leeks: allow 250–300g per serving.

Aubergines, broccoli, Brussels sprouts, cabbage, carrots, cauliflower, parsnips, peppers: allow 200g per serving.

Green beans, mushrooms, onions: allow 150g per serving.

Preparing vegetables

Washing

Don't wash, wipe or scrub vegetables until you are about to cook them, or they may become limp or their outer layers harden.

Wash leaf vegetables in plenty of water to which you have added a teaspoon of salt, which will flush out any bugs. They may need washing more than once; spinach can be particularly sandy. Dry salad leaves in a spinner or a clean tea towel.

Leeks also conceal more sand and grit than it first seems. Remove the outer leaves and the coarse green tops and split them in two or in four, depending on size, almost to the root and wash well. If you are going to chop or slice them, do that immediately after taking off the outer leaves and then wash them.

Peeling

Edible skins (e.g. of carrots) that have not been treated can be cleaned and eaten, but if you are not sure, it is better to peel them, since a high proportion of pesticides is retained in the skin. Vegetables that may have been waxed (e.g. cucumbers) should be peeled too.

Potatoes absorb less water if boiled in their skins, and can be peeled afterwards. So can Jerusalem artichokes which can be rather wasteful as well as tedious to peel raw if they are very knobbly. Scorzonera, a delicately flavoured long black root vegetable, and salsify, a similar long root with a creamy skin and succulent flesh, are easier to peel when cooked. Unfortunately neither is easy to find in Britain. Scrub beetroot, taking care not to damage the skin or it will bleed when cooked.

Stalk vegetables – celery, chard, fennel – should have the coarse stringy bits removed. A potato peeler does the job well; otherwise, break the stalk and pull away the threads. White asparagus and the fatter stalks of green need peeling. Large broccoli stalks are best peeled. Runner beans, large green beans, snow peas and mange-tout may need to have the strings peeled from either side.

Mushrooms may be peeled, especially the large portobellos which have a tougher skin, but they usually need only a wipe or to be brushed.

Remove the outer leaves of Brussels sprouts, chicory, cabbage, cauliflower and the base of the stalk of the latter; the husk and silk of corn-on-the-cob; the outer skin of onions and garlic cloves; the tails of bean sprouts.

Shallots and small onions can be peeled more easily after they have been blanched in boiling water for 10 seconds. Drain and rinse in cold water. Trim the root and the top, and the skin will come loose. They can also be blanched in the microwave (p. 146).

Some vegetables – globe artichokes, Jerusalem artichokes, celeriac, salsify, scorzonera – should only be cut with a stainless steel knife and, once peeled, should be dropped into water acidulated with lemon juice or vinegar or they will discolour. Avocados also discolour when cut and the cut sides should be rubbed with lemon juice.

Cutting and slicing

Vegetables to be cooked together should be of a similar size so that they cook evenly. A food processor will cut, chop and slice and is very convenient, even though you may have to pick out any rough bits that have escaped the blade. It is particularly useful for slicing onions (although they will release a great deal of juice) or hard vegetables such as potatoes, for shredding courgettes, carrots and other roots and for chopping vegetables to go into a stew, but don't chop for so long that you end up with pulp. Cutting by hand needs a very sharp knife, and is essential if you want uniform dice, neat chunks or julienne strips.

Stalks of celery and chard look better cut on the slant, as do thick slices of courgette. Runner beans are cut in fairly thin diagonal slices. Some Asian dishes call for roll-cutting, which is cutting on the slant, but rotating the vegetable a quarter-turn before each cut.

To cut julienne strips, slice the vegetables, stack the slices and cut through them lengthways to make thin strips. To dice vegetables, slice them, stack the slices and slice through them to make strips, and cut across the strips to make dice.

To make a chiffonade – of lettuce, spinach, cabbage – roll several leaves together and slice finely across into ribbons.

To slice a cabbage, cut it in half, or quarters if it is very big, and cut out the thick central stalk. Put the cabbage cut side down and slice through the leaves finely. Discard any thick ribs. You can also feed quartered cabbage onto the slicing plate of a food processor.

To cut very thin slices from cucumber, or from root vegetables for making crisps, you either need a large extra-sharp knife and a steady hand, or a mandoline (p. 528).

To slice ribbons from courgettes, carrots, parsnips and mooli use a potato peeler.

To slice an onion, cut the peeled onion in half through the root, put the cut side down on a board and cut it into vertical slices. Hold the onion half with your finger tips pulled back and knuckles forward so that the knife passes your knuckles and doesn't accidentally slice into your fingers.

To chop an onion, peel it, leave the root on to hold it together and cut it in half through the root. Make horizontal cuts from the top down to, but not through, the root. Make a similar series of vertical cuts. Holding the onion with your finger tips pulled back, slice through crosswise. To chop it more finely cut through the mound of pieces holding the point of the knife blade against the board with your non-cutting hand and chop briskly up and down. Discard the roots.

To chop herbs, remove large stalks and chop the herb coarsely with a large knife. Hold the point of the blade on the board with the finger tips of your non-cutting hand and chop briskly up and down, scooping the herb into a pile with the flat of the blade.

Stuffing

Almost any vegetable can be stuffed, although the most usual ones are peppers, aubergines, tomatoes, courgettes and onions. Stuffings vary greatly; the most familiar ones are those which originated in the Middle East. Be inventive, experiment with different textures and flavours, but always remember that the stuffing must complement the flavour of the vegetable it is used with.

Stuffed vegetables, served hot or cold, make excellent first or main courses. You can provide a very impressive meal by serving a variety of vegetables with different fillings. Many stuffings work equally well with several different vegetables: for instance, that given for aubergines (p. 106) is perfect for courgettes.

Cooking methods

Cooking in water

Boiling has a bad name when it comes to cooking vegetables yet if they are properly cooked in water the results can be very good. It is basically a question of timing. All overcooked vegetables lose their flavour and nutrients and have a poor texture; overcooked brassicas release sulphur compounds which produce that unmistakable cabbagey smell associated with institutional cooking (school dinners).

Vegetables are usually cooked in salted water (about ½ tbs to 1 litre water) and this reduces the need for seasoning later. Don't fill the pan too full.

Cooking in a covered pan preserves nutrients and reduces fuel costs, but it causes discolouration because enzymes released from the vegetables collect in the condensation on the lid and drop back into the water. Root vegetables do not discolour and are usually cooked in a covered pan. They need to be cooked through to the centre, but not left to go soggy. Put them in cold water, bring slowly to a simmer, and cook until a knife point or thin skewer pierces the centre. Start timing from the time the water is bubbling. Timing depends on the vegetable, the variety and the size of the pieces; start testing small pieces after 5 minutes; whole or halved potatoes will take 10–20 minutes.

There is little risk of overcooking green vegetables if you plunge them into boiling water, bring the water quickly back to a simmer and cook, uncovered, for 1–4 minutes. Again, start timing from the moment the water returns to the boil. The vegetables should still have a crisp bite, but not be half raw. Drain the vegetables quickly and toss in a little butter or olive oil or serve with a sauce. Young leeks can be tied in bundles before cooking to keep the leaves together. Asparagus can also be tied in the same way, but I prefer to cook it loose in a wide sauté pan and lift the stalks out with tongs when they are done.

Parboiling and *blanching* soften vegetables before they are cooked further. Put the vegetable into boiling water, bring the water quickly back to the boil and start timing. Small pieces or leaves take only a few seconds to blanch, large slices or dense whole vegetables can take 4–5 minutes.

Strongly flavoured vegetables such as onion, cabbage or Brussels sprouts are blanched to reduce their smell and flavour. Baby onions can be blanched in the microwave (p. 146).

Vine leaves, spinach or cabbage leaves which are to be used to wrap other food are blanched to soften them.

Cooking in minimal water is a method I like for spinach. Put the leaves into a large pan with only the water that clings to them from washing, set the pan over moderate heat and turn the leaves as the water evaporates so that they don't stick to the pan. Serve them as soon as they have wilted (1–2 minutes is all they need), tossed with olive oil or butter, and maybe a handful of toasted pine nuts.

Chard leaves can be cooked the same way, but they should be cut in a chiffonade* first.

Steaming

Steaming vegetables over simmering water helps retain minerals and vitamins that might be leached out by cooking in water. It seems to give a purer flavour too. Most vegetables can be steamed, but green vegetables tend to lose their colour quickly. I would avoid steaming the more pungent brassicas; they are better tempered by cooking in water. Cooking times are longer than for the same vegetable cooked in water: for example, steaming thin green beans will take 6–8 minutes, compared to 3–4 if simmered. A full steamer basket will also take longer than one that is only half full.

Don't salt vegetables before steaming: it draws out the moisture.

Chinese cabbage and mustard greens, chard, celery, fennel, green beans, leeks, mange-tout and snow peas, pattypan squash and purple sprouting broccoli are particularly successful steamed.

Purées and mashes Vegetables for mashing or puréeing are boiled, steamed, microwaved or occasionally baked first. To keep some texture in a mash, crush the vegetables by hand with a potato masher. A masher is the only way to prepare potatoes and other starchy vegetables because they turn gluey if put in a food processor. Mash small amounts at a time so that you don't leave lumps. Mashes are easier to make while the vegetables are hot.

A food processor will produce a purée very quickly; if you want a rough texture, stop the machine in time. A blender works well for very soft vegetables like aubergine or pumpkin, but you can also mash those with a fork. Stringy vegetables, or those with skins like peppers, need to be sieved after puréeing or the texture will be unpleasant.

Purées and mashes can be made of single vegetables or a mixture. The Dutch are the masters of mixed vegetable mashes, which they call *stamppot* (*stampen* being the verb for mashing). Potato is the dominant partner, mashed to a purée to which is added the same or a smaller amount of cooked shredded cabbage, kale or cos lettuce, finely sliced sautéed leek, apple purée, sauerkraut or fried onions. Sometimes chopped lightly fried bacon is added too. Irish colcannon is made with potatoes mashed with milk and cooked shredded cabbage beaten in; for champ, spring onions are cooked in milk and both are mixed into mashed potatoes. Celeriac, parsnip, swede and turnip used half and half with potatoes make good mashes.

Mashes and purées can be made with butter, cream, milk, yogurt, olive oil or any of the nut oils or with some of the cooking water. Really good potatoes make a well-flavoured mash just beaten with some of their cooking liquid. Seasonings are important too. Apart from salt and pepper, nutmeg, mace or turmeric are good with most winter roots, cinnamon with sweet potatoes, mint with peas, ginger with pumpkin and turnip, ground coriander with carrots and parsnips. I make my favourite mashed potato with saffron and olive oil. Potatoes with lots of chopped herbs and olive oil also make an excellent mash. Other good flavourings are Dijon mustard, pesto (p. 366), horseradish and grated cheese. Garlic – crushed, roasted, or puréed itself – goes with most things. A splash of whisky, Armagnac or rum is good with sweet potatoes, pumpkin or turnip; so is Pernod in a fennel and potato mash.

Vegetable cakes Stiff vegetable mashes can be made into cakes. Use only 3–4 tbs liquid to 500g vegetable, and flavourings as above. 500g vegetable will make 8 cakes, cylinders or balls. Shape the cakes, coat them in beaten egg and then dried breadcrumbs. Ideally, leave the cakes to stand for 30 minutes at this point; they will firm up and keep their shape better. Fry or grill for 4–5 minutes each side, or bake in a hot oven, 220°C, 425°F, gas 7, for 15–20 minutes.

Braising

Slow cooking is an ideal way to cook root vegetables, stringy vegetables like fennel, celery and chard stalks, whole heads of chicory, leeks, onions, artichokes and cabbage. Toss the vegetables in butter or oil first, add seasonings and a small amount of liquid – stock, wine, tomato juice, water – so that the vegetables are partly immersed. Use a heavy pan so that the vegetables cook slowly and don't burn, and cook in the oven or on the stove.

Grilling and barbecuing

Many vegetables can be grilled, char-grilled on a ridged griddle plate or barbecued successfully, as long as they are basted regularly with oil.

Slice aubergines into thick rounds, courgettes into thick strips, fennel from top to bottom. Cut radicchio in half or in quarters, keeping the leaves attached at the base. Cut peppers in quarters, onions in slices or in half. Toothpicks pushed through onions and fennel will hold the pieces together on the barbecue. Snap asparagus at its break point and thread a few spears onto a skewer to make it easier to turn them. Leave mushroom caps whole but discard the stalks. Leave tomatoes whole on the barbecue, but cut in half to put under the grill or on a ribbed griddle plate. Corn-on-the-cob barbecues beautifully in its husk, once the silk is removed. Potatoes can be grilled or barbecued but they must be parboiled first and then sliced. Pieces of vegetables cut to the same size can be made into kebabs for barbecuing, but inevitably some will cook more quickly than others. Slices or pieces of small vegetables are easier to handle on the griddle or under the grill.

Marinate vegetables, if you wish, in oil, lemon juice or white wine and herbs. Other flavourings can be added for cooking: ground cumin or coriander, fennel seeds, chilli flakes, coarsely ground pepper, chopped thyme, rosemary or savory can be stirred into the basting oil.

Brush the vegetables lightly with oil and grill or barbecue 8–10cm from the heat source. If you are using a griddle plate, heat it for 2–3 minutes before putting on the vegetables. Under a grill or on a griddle, most vegetables will be ready in 5–8 minutes, asparagus needs less time, 4–6 minutes. Turn the vegetables once when they become soft and have brown patches. On a barbecue the times are likely to be a bit longer. Corn-on-the-cob in its husk will take about 20 minutes.

Serve the vegetables with extra virgin olive oil and lemon juice, with young goat's cheese and chopped salad herbs, with pesto (p. 366), a fresh chutney or relish (pp. 382–3) or a salsa (pp. 380–2).

Baking and roasting

Cooking in the oven needs time, but it is a very good way to preserve flavour. Vegetables with a hard protective skin can be baked, provided the skin is pricked to let steam escape: aubergines, potatoes and small squashes come into this category. Beetroot is an exception; the skin should not be pierced or it will bleed. Baked potatoes or a small squash will take about 45 minutes at 200°C, 400°F, gas 6, aubergines 15–20 minutes. Beetroot wrapped in foil or in a covered pan will take 40 minutes to 1 hour, depending on size.

Root vegetables are best parboiled before roasting. Peeled vegetables and those with a soft skin are roasted with added fat. Cut them into chunks or leave whole, coat lightly with olive oil or butter, add sprigs of herbs or a sprinkling of ground spices and roast in a hot oven (200°C, 400°F, gas 6) for about 45 minutes. Turn them so that they become crisp on all sides and to prevent them sticking to the tin. You can bake vegetables in a pan with a lid if you prefer.

Onions, peppers, tomatoes, courgettes, okra, aubergines and garlic all roast well in a moderate oven (180°C, 350°F, gas 4).

Sautéing, frying and stir-frying

Sautéing in a little butter, olive oil or animal fat is a successful method of cooking for many vegetables. Duck or goose fat gives a rich flavour to sautéed potatoes but for other vegetables a mixture of butter and oil is best. Make sure the fat is hot before adding the vegetables so that they do not stick, and do not fill the pan too full. Keep the heat fairly low and turn the vegetables in the hot fat to brown evenly. Quickly cooked vegetables such as mushrooms will take only a few minutes; potatoes will need about 20.

Firm vegetables may be sautéed initially, then covered and left to simmer in their own juices or finished by adding a few tablespoons of liquid and, if you wish, a flavouring – herb or spice, diced shallot, grated citrus peel, a splash of balsamic vinegar, a teaspoon of sugar, chopped bacon or ham – to the pan. Put on the lid and cook until the vegetables are just soft but not mushy. They will take between 5 and 15 minutes.

Shallow frying needs more fat and the heat is kept higher than for sautéing. Aubergine slices, broccoli, okra, onions and par-boiled green beans can all be fried successfully, either alone or with the addition of chopped bacon or pancetta*, chopped garlic or shallot, grated cheese. Small vegetable fritters can be shallow-fried in a frying pan.

Stir-frying is an excellent way of keeping vegetables crunchy. The cooking is done fast over high heat, but more time is spent on preparation, cutting everything into bite-sized pieces. It is important to heat the wok or a large heavy frying pan without oil until you can feel the heat rising when you hold your hand above it, then put in the oil, swirl it around to coat the wok and start cooking. Stir-fried vegetables will be cooked in 2–3 minutes.

Deep-frying

Oil for deep-frying must be very hot (190°C, 375°F) before the vegetables are put in otherwise they will absorb it and become unpleasantly fatty. Test the temperature by frying a cube of bread; if it browns in about 40 seconds the oil is ready; if it takes longer, let the oil heat more; if it browns more quickly, reduce the heat. If the oil is smoking, it is too hot and will burn the outside of the food before the inside is cooked. Only deep fry a few pieces at a time since overcrowding the pan lowers the temperature too much. Chips and root vegetable crisps are fried without any coating, but most vegetables need a coating or batter to protect them from the hot oil. The coating also reduces spattering when the vegetables go into the oil. Vegetables are ready when the coating turns golden brown. They should be drained on kitchen paper and served quickly while still crisp.

Sweating

Chopped vegetables are sweated in a little butter or oil in a covered pan to release their juices and flavour. They should be tender but not browned. Aromatic vegetables – onions, shallots, carrots, celery, leek – are those most often sweated. They are used to form the basis of sauces, soups, poached and braised dishes such as chicken with tarragon (p. 289) and Tuscan braised beef (p. 321).

Microwaving

Their high water content makes virtually all vegetables suitable for microwaving. They cook quickly, retain their vibrant colours and a high proportion of their nutrients. Microwaving tends to emphasize the inherent flavours of foods, so the taste of microwaved vegetables is quite pure. They also require no or very little salt, and this is best added after cooking. Use pepper sparingly too; taste and add after cooking. Clean and prepare the vegetables as you would for cooking by other methods. The times are for a 600–700 watt oven with a carousel, at 100 per cent power. Err on the side of undercooking: the vegetables can always be put back if they are not quite ready.

Make sure you use a dish that is suitable for microwave cooking and cover it with a lid or microwave plastic film; in an uncovered dish, the moisture from the food evaporates too quickly. The steam held in by the cover ensures that the food cooks evenly. When the dish is ready, slit the plastic film to release steam and peel it off carefully. Alternatively, make a parcel of vegetables in a sheet of microwave cling film or put them in a microwave plastic bag.

Assorted vegetables to be microwaved together should be about the same size; pieces of 6–8cm are the optimum size. Arrange the vegetables with those that require longest cooking around the outside of the dish and those that cook quickly in the middle. The pieces should not be touching.

I have given cooking times for some common vegetables and for those where there is the greatest saving in time compared with other methods. Most of these timings are based on Barbara Kafka's excellent *Microwave Gourmet*, and they are given under the relevant vegetable.

Artichokes – globe

To prepare whole globe artichokes

Twist off the stalk, pulling with it any fibres from the centre. Pull off all the tough lower outer leaves and cut the base flat, exposing the white part. Rub it with a cut lemon. Slice the top third off the artichoke, and trim any sharp leaves with scissors. Drop the prepared artichokes into boiling water, put a plate or small lid on top to keep them submerged and simmer for 20–40 minutes, depending on size, until a leaf from the middle can be pulled out easily and the bottom is tender. Drain the artichokes upside down.

To microwave, put each artichoke in a microwave plastic bag or wrap in microwave plastic film. For artichokes weighing 250–350g, cook 1 for 7 minutes, 2 for 10 minutes, 4 for 15 minutes. The artichokes are ready when the bottom gives if pressed lightly. Stand for 5 minutes before pricking the plastic and unwrapping.

Serve hot with melted butter, warm or at room temperature with a vinaigrette (p. 358) or ravigote sauce (p. 359), plain or flavoured mayonnaise (p. 362), or a garlicky sauce such as skorthalia (p. 364). To eat, take off a leaf, dip the soft base in the butter or sauce and then pull it between the teeth. Discard the upper part of the leaf. When you get to the centre, lift out the cone of pale or pinkish leaves, use a spoon to dig out the fibrous choke and discard that. The cone of young leaves is edible. Next you have the best part, the firm bottom that was under the choke.

Eating an artichoke is a prolonged and messy business, but well worth it.

To prepare artichoke bottoms

Break off the stalk, pulling any tough fibres with it. Pull off the lower outer leaves and trim the base, cutting round it spirally, and removing the leaves so that only tender pale green ones remain. Rub exposed parts with a cut lemon as you work. Put the artichoke on its side and cut four-fifths of the top away, then remove the choke. This leaves the flat base which must then be put into acidulated water.

If you want cooked bottoms or hearts you can, of course, cook the whole artichokes and then finish the preparation as described above.

Artichoke and broad bean stew

Use young broad beans for this dish; the outer skins on old broad beans are likely to remain tough and spoil the dish.

For 4–6	500g broad beans, shelled weight	salt and freshly ground pepper
4 tbs olive oil	2 garlic cloves, peeled and chopped	200g merguez sausages (optional)
2 onions, peeled and chopped	¼ tsp ground cumin	150ml water
8 large artichoke bottoms, fresh or frozen ones, blanched	¼ tsp ground coriander	

Heat the oil and sauté the onion for a few minutes. When it has softened, put in the artichokes, cut in four, the broad beans and the garlic. Season with cumin, coriander, pepper and a little salt. If you wish, add the sausages, sliced 1cm thick. Sauté for 4–5 minutes, then pour over the water. Cover and simmer briskly for 10 minutes, lower the heat and simmer more slowly for a further 20 minutes, or until the vegetables are tender. Check that there is enough water, and if necessary add a little more.

Tian of artichokes and fennel

The inspiration for this dish is provençal, where tians or gratins of vegetables, topped with a sauce or a layer of breadcrumbs, are often served as a separate course.

For 8	3 bulbs of fennel	salt and freshly ground pepper
10 artichoke bottoms, fresh or frozen ones, blanched	3 tbs chopped herbs – parsley, basil, savory, thyme	5 large ripe tomatoes
5 tbs olive oil		2 tbs fresh breadcrumbs (p. 455)

Heat the oven to 170°C, 325°F, gas 3. Slice the artichoke bottoms and fry lightly in 2 tbs oil. Cut the fennel in half lengthways, discard the outer layers and parboil the pieces for 8 minutes. Drain and slice when cool enough to handle. Lightly oil a gratin dish and combine in it the artichokes, fennel and herbs. Season with pepper and salt. Slice the tomatoes and put them in overlapping layers over the other vegetables. Scatter over the breadcrumbs and drizzle over the remaining oil. Bake the tian for about 40 minutes, until the vegetables are tender. Serve hot or warm.

· If you prefer, use 300ml tomato coulis (p. 378), instead of sliced tomatoes.

Asparagus

Most asparagus grown and sold in Britain is green. To prepare it, bend each spear to find the breaking point and snap it there. This ensures that the tough part is discarded which is not always the case if the bottom of the stalk is trimmed and then peeled.

White asparagus has a thick skin which must be peeled from just below the tip. Break off the bottom of the stalk.

See notes on choosing vegetables (p. 91), cooking in water (p. 95) and grilling and barbecuing (p. 97).

Asparagus with ham

Asparagus with cooked ham and hard-boiled eggs and served with melted butter or mayonnaise is the classic way of serving it in Holland and Belgium, where they prefer white asparagus, but the dish is just as good with green. The ham should be well flavoured and preferably carved from the bone.

For 4	2 hard-boiled eggs, peeled and cut in half	100ml melted butter or 250ml mayonnaise (p. 362)
1kg asparagus	4 slices cooked ham	
salt and freshly ground pepper		

Break the bottoms from the asparagus; they can be used to flavour a soup. Bring a wide pan of salted water to the boil, put in the asparagus and simmer for 4–6 minutes, or steam for 8–10 minutes. Do not overcook, but timing varies greatly according to the thickness of the spears. Lift them out and drain well. Arrange the asparagus on a platter with the eggs and ham. Season lightly. Serve the melted butter or mayonnaise separately.

Variation

Asparagus with prosciutto Wrap small bundles of 4–5 stalks of cooked asparagus in slices of prosciutto. Serve with melted butter or extra virgin olive oil, or make a sauce by heating gently 200ml crème fraîche with 1 tbs finely chopped tarragon, 2 tbs chopped chives and a squeeze of lemon juice.

Oriental asparagus

For 4	2 tbs light soy sauce	1 tsp sugar
1kg asparagus	3 tbs rice or white wine vinegar	2 tbs sesame oil
1 tbs sesame seeds		

Break off the bases from the asparagus, cut off the tips and cut the stalks into 3cm pieces on the slant. Bring a wide pan of water to the boil, plunge in the asparagus tips and stalks, bring back to the simmer and cook for 1 minute. Drain well. While the water is heating, dry-roast* the sesame seeds in a heavy pan, shaking it so they don't burn. Remove the pan from the heat when the seeds start to pop. Whisk together the soy sauce, vinegar, sugar and sesame oil to make a dressing.

Arrange the asparagus on a serving dish, pour over the dressing and scatter over the sesame seeds or, if you prefer, grind the seeds while still warm with a pestle and mortar and then scatter them over the asparagus.

Grilled asparagus

Grilled asparagus makes a pleasant change from boiled or steamed, and cooks just as quickly. Use a griddle pan, or put the asparagus under a hot grill.

For 4	4 tbs extra virgin olive oil	salt and freshly ground pepper
1kg asparagus	a sprig of lemon thyme	

Break the bottoms from the asparagus spears; they can be used to flavour a soup. Thread the asparagus onto skewers and brush lightly with a little of the oil. Grill for 2–3 minutes on each side. Heat the remaining oil gently in a small pan with the lemon thyme, crushing the thyme so that it flavours the oil. Discard the thyme. When the asparagus is ready transfer it to a platter, remove the skewers, season with good sea salt (Maldon salt is very good) and black pepper and drizzle over the flavoured oil.

Variations
- Instead of the oil, drizzle 1 tbs of balsamic vinegar over the asparagus before serving.
- Omit the herb, whisk the unheated oil with 2 tbs lemon juice, spoon this dressing over the asparagus and top with fine shavings of Parmesan.

Asparagus risotto. See p. 193.

Aubergines

Aubergines come in a variety of sizes and colours. Tiny, bitter green ones, the size of peas, and creamy white egg-shaped and -sized ones are both much used in southeast Asian cooking. The ones most usually available in Britain are the fat oval purple ones and sometimes the long, thin ones or egg-sized purple ones. *See* notes on choosing (p. 91) and the various cooking methods (pp. 97–9).

Many cooks suggest slicing and salting aubergines (1 tbs salt per kg) an hour or so before cooking them to remove any bitter juices. I don't find that today's aubergines are bitter and so don't usually salt them. However, if they are salted, rinsed and dried they will absorb less oil if they are to be fried, an important consideration since otherwise aubergines tend to soak up oil like a sponge. Parboiling also helps reduce the amount of oil aubergines absorb.

Aubergines are very versatile vegetables, and one of the best ways to cook them is to grill or roast them whole (*see* below). To microwave, prick the skin of whole aubergines several times to allow steam to escape. Put them on 2 layers of kitchen paper, uncovered, and cook for 8 minutes for an aubergine weighing 250g, or 12 minutes for one of 500g.

Grilled whole aubergines

The skins of aubergines should be pricked a few times to prevent them bursting when being grilled or roasted. Grilled over an open fire aubergines acquire a smoky flavour; you can achieve a similar effect indoors by roasting whole aubergines over a gas ring. To roast in the oven, *see* p. 98. The purée from the cooked and peeled aubergines can be flavoured with herbs or spices, yogurt or tahini* and lemon juice (p. 25).

This version with an oriental sauce is best made with the long thin aubergines, allowing one per person.

For 4	3 tbs sunflower oil	2 spring onions, sliced finely
4 long aubergines or 2 larger ones	1 tbs fish sauce	
	1 tsp chilli flakes	1 tbs chopped coriander

Prick the aubergines and grill until the skin is blackened and they feel soft. When they are cool enough to handle, peel them and pull off the stalks. Cut the flesh into long strips and arrange on a serving dish. Heat the oil, stir in the fish sauce, chilli flakes and spring onion. As soon as it is sizzling, pour this sauce over the aubergines and garnish with the coriander.

Grilled sliced aubergines with cheese and pine nuts

Thanks to Simon Hopkinson I have come to realize that for grilling in slices, aubergines are better peeled first; the skin invariably gets drier than the flesh. Don't slice the aubergines too thinly; 1cm is about right.

For 3–4	2–3 tbs olive oil	3 tbs dry-roasted* pine nuts
2 large aubergines, peeled and sliced thickly	100g ricotta	salt and freshly ground pepper
	2 tbs chopped mint	

Brush the aubergine slices with oil and grill on a barbecue or on a griddle plate until they are soft and lightly browned, about 4–5 minutes each side.

Crumble the ricotta and mix it with the mint and pine nuts. Season well. Put a spoonful of the mixture on each grilled aubergine slice.

Serve as a first course, or with other grilled vegetables, or to accompany grilled lamb chops.

Variation

Grilled aubergines with salmoriglio or tomato salsa Serve the slices topped with salmoriglio sauce (p. 377) or with salsa cruda (p. 380).

Stuffed aubergines

Although Turkish *imam bayaldi* may be the most famous of the stuffed aubergine dishes, there are countless others just as rewarding. This recipe is also Middle Eastern in origin.

For 6	3 large garlic cloves, peeled and finely chopped	4 ripe tomatoes, peeled, seeded and cubed
3 medium aubergines	½ tsp ground allspice	2 tbs red wine vinegar
salt and freshly ground pepper	50g raisins, soaked in warm water for 10 minutes	1–2 tsp sugar
100ml olive oil		handful of chopped parsley
3 medium onions, peeled and finely chopped		about 150ml water

Cut the aubergines in half lengthways, scoop out and reserve most of the flesh, leaving a layer next to the skin. Sprinkle the shells with salt, turn them upside down and leave to drain for 20 minutes, then blanch in boiling water for 2–3 minutes. Heat the oven to 200°C, 400°F, gas 6.

Heat 3 tbs oil and gently cook the onions and garlic until soft, then add the aubergine flesh, chopped. If necessary, add a little more oil, season with salt, pepper and allspice and cook for 4–5 minutes, stirring frequently to prevent the mixture sticking to the pan. Add the raisins and tomatoes, the vinegar and sugar; taste for balance and sweetness before adding all the sugar. Simmer until you have a thick stew, about 5 minutes. Stir in the parsley.

Arrange the aubergine shells in a wide ovenproof casserole or baking tin in which they fit side by side, and fill them with the mixture. Mix the remaining oil with 150ml water and pour over the aubergines; it should come almost to their tops – add more water if necessary. Cover and bake for about 1 hour. These stuffed aubergines are best served cold.

Aubergine filo pie

Filo pastry is usually brushed with melted butter, but for savoury pies such as this, I prefer oil. You could use finely crumbled feta cheese or a well-flavoured Cheddar, grated, instead of the Parmesan.

For 4	2 garlic cloves, peeled and chopped finely	350ml passata (p. 378 or bought)
2 onions, peeled and chopped	2 tsp chopped or rubbed dried oregano or mixed Mediterranean herbs	1 packet (270g) filo pastry
4 tbs olive oil		olive oil for the pastry
400g aubergines, peeled and cubed	salt and freshly ground pepper	125g grated Parmesan

Sauté the onion in 2 tbs oil until it starts to colour, then add the remaining oil and the aubergines. Cook, stirring occasionally, until the aubergine is almost tender, then add the garlic, herbs and seasoning. Pour over the passata, and cook, covered, over low heat for 15 minutes. Heat the oven to 190°C, 375°F, gas 5.

When working with filo pastry it is important to keep all except the sheet you are using covered with clingfilm or a tea towel, otherwise the pastry will dry out. Each piece has to be brushed lightly with oil, so pour about 80ml olive oil into a small bowl and have ready a brush. Take a shallow baking tray or ovenproof dish (the one I use is 20 x 30 x 3cm) and line it with a sheet of filo. Brush the pastry with oil and repeat with 2 further sheets. If necessary cut the sheets and patch them in the dish. Spread the aubergine mixture over the pastry and cover it with 2 more sheets of oiled filo. Sprinkle half the cheese over this and cover again with 2 sheets of filo. Scatter the remaining cheese over this layer, cover with 2 more sheets of pastry. Score the top lightly into serving pieces, but do not cut through.

Bake until golden, about 30–35 minutes. Leave the pie for 10 minutes before serving.

Variations

Spinach filo pie (*Spanokopitta*) This Greek pie is made in the same way as the aubergine pie. Replace the aubergine by 1kg fresh spinach, blanched and chopped, or the equivalent amount of frozen spinach, thawed and chopped. Combine the spinach with the sautéed onion, the garlic and a large handful of chopped parsley instead of the oregano. Season with salt, pepper and a little nutmeg. Omit the passata and stir in the cheese. Line the dish with half of the pastry, make a layer of the spinach mixture and cover with the rest of the pastry. Bake as above.

Aubergine or spinach parcels or triangles Make small parcels or triangles of filo pastry (p. 493) filled with a spoonful of the aubergine or spinach mixture above, lay them on a baking sheet and bake for 15–20 minutes at 190°C, 375°F, gas 5. Serve warm.

Moussaka

This Middle Eastern dish has many variations, some with potato, some with fresh meat, some with no meat at all, some with a tomato sauce. It is a dish to experiment with, rather than a formula to follow. Moussaka can be prepared a day in advance as far as layering the vegetables and meat sauce and kept refrigerated. Let it come to room temperature and heat the oven while you make the sauce.

For 4–5	500g cooked or raw lamb or beef, cubed or minced	1 tbs plain flour
2 large potatoes, peeled		300ml hot milk or stock or half and half
2 medium aubergines	2 tbs tomato purée	
oil for frying	1 tsp cinnamon	grated nutmeg
2 onions, peeled and chopped	salt and freshly ground pepper	salt and freshly ground pepper
2–3 garlic cloves, peeled and chopped	**For the sauce**	150g grated Parmesan or Gruyère
	15g butter	

Parboil the potatoes for 10–12 minutes, drain and slice them. Slice the aubergines. To prevent them absorbing too much oil, parboil them or salt and leave to drain (pp. 95, 105) Fry the aubergine slices lightly in oil until they are golden on both sides. Drain them on kitchen paper, and fry the potatoes briefly in the same oil. Drain them too. Wipe the pan clean and put in 2 tbs new oil. Add the onion, cover the pan and sweat* gently over low heat until soft. Add the garlic, meat, tomato purée and seasonings. Stir well; if you are using cooked meat, heat through gently for about 10 minutes. If it is fresh meat, cook it until tender, about 20 minutes.

While the meat is cooking, melt the butter and whisk in the flour. Off the heat, add the heated liquid – a little at a time – to make the sauce. Whisk to avoid lumps and season with a little nutmeg, salt and pepper. Place the pan over low heat and cook, stirring from time to time, until the sauce thickens. Stir in half the cheese.

Heat the oven to 180°C, 350°F, gas 4. To assemble the moussaka, put a layer of potato in the bottom of a deep ovenproof dish, sprinkle with some of the remaining cheese, then a layer of aubergine followed by some of the meat mixture. Season each layer. Repeat until all the ingredients are used up, finishing with a layer of potato or aubergine. Pour over the sauce. Bake for about 40 minutes until golden.

Variations

Vegetarian moussaka To make a meatless moussaka, use 2 more aubergines and grill or bake them whole until tender. Peel them and mash the flesh to a purée. Chop 4 tomatoes. Mix the purée and tomatoes with the onion instead of the meat and make layers as above.

· Another possibility would be to sweat* 500g chopped courgettes with the onion, then add 4 chopped tomatoes and cook together for a few minutes.

Escalivada. *See* p. 152.

Indian braised potato and aubergine. *See* p. 157.

Broad beans

Tiny young broad beans are best; their flavour and texture are excellent and they need only simple treatment. Large old broad beans taste much nicer if you remove the outer skin of each bean after cooking. They come loose while being boiled, and it is easy to nick the skin at one end, press out the bean and discard the empty shell. It is a bit time consuming, but it will make a big difference to the taste of your dish.

Broad beans alla romana

The Italians have some of the best dishes for young broad beans, and this one has several interpretations: with tomatoes, with pancetta or with both; with sage, with basil, with neither. Experiment to see which version you prefer. If you leave out the tomatoes, use just enough water to cover the beans.

For 4–6	125g pancetta* or bacon, cut in strips	4 large tomatoes, peeled and chopped
2kg broad beans (will give about 500g shelled beans)	a handful of basil leaves, torn or chopped coarsely	salt and freshly ground pepper
2 tbs olive oil		
1 onion, peeled and chopped		

Pod the beans. Heat the oil and sauté the onion until golden. Add the pancetta or bacon, let it release its fat, then stir in the beans and basil. Stir and cook for a minute or two, then add the tomatoes and season. Cover the pan and simmer for 20–25 minutes, until the beans are tender. Add a little water if necessary from time to time to prevent the beans sticking to the pan. Serve hot.

Broad beans with coriander

The flavours of broad beans and coriander complement each other beautifully in this simple dish.

For 4–6	2 shallots, peeled and chopped	salt and freshly ground pepper
2kg broad beans (about 500g shelled)	1 tbs white wine vinegar	large handful of coriander leaves, chopped
3 tbs olive oil		

Pod the beans and boil until just tender, and drain. Heat the oil and sauté the shallots until they just start to colour. Stir in the vinegar and add the beans. Season and stir the pan to coat the beans in the sauce. Stir in the coriander and serve.

Broad bean purée

A very good way of serving large older beans. *See also* purées and mashes (p. 96).

For 4	1 bay leaf	salt and freshly ground
2kg broad beans	2 sprigs savory	pepper
(about 500g shelled)	100ml olive oil	lemon juice
2 spring onions		

Pod the beans and boil them with the spring onions and herbs until tender. Drain them, discard the onions and herbs, and remove the tough pale skins from the beans (p. 109). Purée the beans in a processor or through a sieve. If you are using a processor, put in some of the oil with the beans and season them. If you sieve the beans, add the olive oil a little at a time to create a smooth purée, and season well. You may not need all of the oil, or you may need a little more to obtain a smooth well-flavoured purée. Use a tablespoon or so of lemon juice to heighten the taste.

Dressed with a little garlic crushed with salt, more lemon juice and olive oil, and left to cool, this makes a good first course with pitta bread.

Dried beans

There are dozens of types of dried beans, usually associated with a particular part of the world and its style of cooking. We are fortunate that we can buy many of them easily, dried or canned. For many dishes, good canned beans can be used, but it is important to rinse them well to get rid of the canning liquid.

If your beans are supermarket-packaged, they should be free of bits of stone or wood or earth. If you bought them loose, check them over for foreign bits and then wash well to get rid of dust. Beans and whole peas require soaking for several hours or overnight before being cooked in water. If you forget to soak them in time, a quicker method is to put them in a pan with plenty of water, bring to the boil and boil fast for 2 minutes, then remove the pan from the heat and leave to stand for 1 hour. Drain and cook as indicated in the recipe. They may need to cook a bit longer than usual, but cooking times for pulses vary not only according to how long they are soaked but also according to how old they are. Chick peas take the longest time, lentils the shortest.

Salt pulses only at the end of cooking otherwise they will harden.

Although there are classic dishes which call for a particular bean, they can to some extent be used interchangeably between recipes, so experiment.

Mexican refried beans

Mexican food is invariably associated with refried beans. They are usually made with black or brown beans, but red kidney beans are good too. There are many styles of refried beans, some smooth from puréeing in a food processor, some rough, some with lots of onion and garlic, some spiced with chilli, so there is plenty of choice. Lard is the fat most used in Mexico, but oil is starting to replace it.

The beans are simmered, traditionally in an earthenware pot, until creamy when they make a good dish without further treatment, just served with a salsa (pp. 380–2). Refried beans go well with rice and a salad, with sausages or bacon; use them to stuff peppers or eat them on their own with tacos.

For 6	1 onion, peeled	1–2 chillies (optional)
250g beans, soaked overnight	1 litre water	salt
	1 tbs oil	

Put the beans in a deep pot with the onion cut in half, cover with the water and bring to the boil. Reduce to a simmer, add the oil and whole chillies (if using), and cook, half covered, until the beans are tender. They will take an hour or more, but much depends on the age of the beans and how fast they are cooking, so check after 45 minutes. Keep the water about 1cm above the beans, not more. Add hot water as needed. When the beans are almost tender, season with salt. The skins and inside of the beans should be tender but they shouldn't be broken and disintegrating. Most of the liquid should have been absorbed, what remains will be thick and creamy.

for refrying the beans

For 6	3 garlic cloves, peeled and chopped	60g grated cheese or crumbled feta (optional)
2–3 tbs oil	the cooked beans	
2 onions, peeled and chopped	salt	

Use a large non-stick frying pan to fry the onions until golden, but don't burn them. Add the garlic and cook a little longer. Scoop about a quarter of the beans out of their pan (it doesn't matter if there is a little of the cooking liquid with them) and mash with a potato masher or large fork. You could purée some of the beans in the food processor, but crush some by hand to give the dish a more interesting texture. Keep adding the beans to the frying pan and mashing them until all are used. Add a ladleful of the bean liquid, or water, and stir it in, then another, and a third if necessary. The beans can absorb quite a lot of liquid and will dry once they reach the table, so it is best to start with them slightly on the soupy side. Salt them and if you are using cheese, stir it in towards the end of the mashing time.

Tuscan beans

Cannellini or borlotti beans are the beans most suitable for this dish. The beans are usually served hot or warm, on their own, dressed with fruity olive oil, or to accompany a meat dish. Cold, they make a delicious salad with chopped parsley, finely sliced onion and chunks of tuna fish.

For 3–4	2 garlic cloves, peeled and crushed	2 tbs olive oil
250g cannellini beans, soaked overnight	3 sage leaves	1 litre water
1 small onion, peeled and cut in half	1 tsp chopped thyme leaves	salt
		12 slices pancetta*
		extra virgin olive oil

Put the beans in a deep pot (earthenware would be used in Tuscany) with the onion, garlic, herbs and 2 tbs olive oil and pour over about 1 litre of water. Bring the beans to the boil, reduce to a simmer and cook very slowly for 1–2 hours, until the beans are tender. Add salt to taste about 15 minutes before the beans are ready.

Just before the beans are done, grill the pancetta until crisp. Drain the beans and sprinkle them liberally with extra virgin olive oil. Serve with the pancetta crumbled over the top, and a bowl of roasted garlic (p. 136).

Green beans

There are many green beans on the market, from tiny French beans to the larger flat beans (sometimes green, sometimes almost white or yellow), round bobby beans and, of course, runner beans. Small French beans have the best flavour. The following recipes are based on small to medium-sized beans. If necessary, remove any strings, cut large beans on the slant in 2–3 pieces, and adapt the cooking time. *See* notes on choosing (p. 91), cooking in water and steaming (pp. 95, 96). To microwave, sprinkle beans with water and wrap in microwave plastic film, or put them in a microwave plastic bag or a covered dish. Cook 250g for 4½ minutes, 500g for 7–8 minutes.

Green beans with walnut sauce

For 4	a handful of parsley, chopped	¼ tsp ground coriander
500g beans, cut in short lengths if large	½ tsp chilli flakes or ¹/₄ tsp cayenne	salt and freshly ground pepper
120g walnuts	¼ tsp ground cinnamon	50g fresh breadcrumbs
1 garlic clove, peeled and crushed		100–150ml olive oil
		2–3 tbs lemon juice

Boil or steam the beans until just tender, then drain them. While they are cooking, whiz together in a processor the walnuts, garlic, parsley, spices, salt and pepper and breadcrumbs. Trickle in the olive oil as though making mayonnaise. Use enough to make a creamy but not stiff sauce. Add the lemon juice and taste for seasoning. Spoon the walnut sauce over the beans and turn them to coat them well. Serve the beans with poached or grilled fish, grilled or roast chicken or a steak.

Green beans with tomatoes

This is a combination of vegetables which is found in many countries. These two recipes are Italian and French in origin.

Italian version	2 tbs olive oil	small handful of basil leaves, chopped
For 4	handful of parsley leaves, chopped	1 glass of good red wine
500g small green beans	1 garlic clove, peeled and chopped finely	salt and freshly ground pepper
400g tomatoes		

Boil or steam the beans until just tender. Drain them. Peel, seed and chop the tomatoes. Heat the oil and sauté the parsley, garlic and basil. Add the tomatoes to the pan and stir well. Add the beans, pour over the wine and season. Simmer uncovered for about 30 minutes, until the wine has reduced to make a sauce.

French version	400g tomatoes	½ tsp chopped thyme leaves
For 4	2 tbs olive oil	salt and freshly ground pepper
500g small green beans	1 garlic clove, peeled and chopped finely	

Cook the beans in water or steam until just tender, and drain them. Peel, seed and dice the tomatoes. Heat the oil and lightly sauté the garlic. Add the tomatoes and thyme leaves when the garlic starts to colour; season well. Simmer for 2–3 minutes, then add the beans. Toss all together and serve.

Green beans with ham

This dish has been a firm favourite in our house since we discovered it many years ago in Menorca. It is nicest with Serrano ham, but works well with any other cured rather than cooked ham, or with smoked bacon.

For 4	125g Serrano ham or bacon, cut in strips	50g grated Manchego or Parmesan
500g green beans		
5–6 tbs olive oil	2 garlic cloves, peeled and chopped	freshly ground pepper

Cook the beans in water or steam until just tender, then drain them. Heat the oil in a heavy frying pan, add the ham or bacon and garlic and fry them gently, making sure the garlic doesn't burn. Add the beans, stir to combine, and cook for 10 minutes, stirring occasionally. Add the cheese and grind over plenty of black pepper. Continue to cook until the cheese melts, then serve.

Beetroot

Beetroot has had a revival, and it is now recognised that there are many more interesting things to do with this vegetable than pickle it in vinegar or tip it into a bowl with lettuce and tomato and call it salad. *See* notes on preparing vegetables (p. 92), cooking in water (p. 95) or baking and roasting (p. 98). To microwave, put baby beetroot in a microwave dish and cover. Allow 8 minutes for 250g, 12 minutes for 500g. Wrap large beetroots individually in microwave plastic wrap and arrange them in a circle on the carousel. Allow 20 minutes for one 300g beetroot, 25 minutes for 6 beetroots with a total weight of 1kg. For immediate use, cool slightly, unwrap and peel off the skin. To keep, leave the beetroot in their skins until needed.

Beetroot with orange

This is a version of a lovely recipe in John Tovey's *Feast of Vegetables*, sadly now out of print.

For 4	1 tbs walnut, hazelnut or sesame oil	30g walnuts or hazelnuts, dry-roasted* and chopped coarsely
300g raw beetroot	juice and grated rind of 1 unwaxed orange	

Peel and grate the beetroot quite finely. Heat the oil and add the orange juice and rind. Tip in the beetroot and fry, tossing and stirring for 5–6 minutes. Put the beetroot and pan juices in a warmed serving dish and scatter over the nuts. Serve with baked pork chops (p. 339), pot-roasted pork fillet (p. 341), a grilled steak or as a separate vegetable course. Cold, it also makes an excellent salad.

Variation
Beetroot with balsamic vinegar and dill Prepare the beetroot as above, then sauté it in 2 tbs olive oil for 4–5 minutes; stir in 1 tbs balsamic vinegar and 2 tbs chopped dill.

Beetroot with cream

This is a standard dish of central and east European cooking. It works well with soured cream, crème fraîche or, as here, with double cream laced with mustard.

For 4	50g butter	1 tbs Dijon mustard
500g cooked beetroot (*see* above)	2 tsp wine vinegar	100ml double cream
	salt	

Dice the beetroot. Heat the butter in a frying pan and stir in the beetroot. Add the vinegar and season with salt. The vinegar will turn the beetroot a vivid red. Stir the mustard into the cream, add to the pan, stir to coat all the beetroot with the sauce and allow to heat through. Serve with baked rabbit (p. 354), a plainly grilled venison steak or with game birds.

Broccoli

Large-headed calabrese is the broccoli most often on sale, but in spring purple sprouting broccoli, with small deep-coloured heads and dark green leaves, appears in the shops. Purple sprouting has an excellent flavour when young, but discard most of the stalks which are often stringy. The cauliflower recipes can also be used for broccoli, and broccoli can replace the spring greens in the stir-fry recipe on p. 119.

To microwave, put broccoli spears into a round dish with the heads in the centre and the stalks pointing outward. Add 1 tbs water to 250g, cover and cook for 4–6 minutes; add 1½ tbs water to 500g, cover and cook for 6–8 minutes. Put florets in a dish that holds them in a single layer, cover and cook for 2½ minutes for 250g, 4 minutes for 500g.

Broccoli stir-fried with garlic, chilli and ginger

For 4	a small piece of ginger, chopped finely	2 garlic cloves, peeled and chopped finely
500g broccoli		
2 tbs oil	1 small red chilli, seeded and sliced	3 tbs rice wine* or sherry
		salt

Cut the broccoli into small florets, peel the stalks and cut them into short lengths. Heat a wok and when it feels hot when you hold your hand above it, add the oil. Swirl it around, then add the ginger, followed by the chilli, garlic and broccoli. Stir-fry vigorously for 2 minutes, then add the wine and a little salt. Keep stirring so the broccoli is well tossed with the other ingredients. It will be ready after a further 2–3 minutes.

Broccoli with oil and lemon

This is a popular Italian way of serving vegetables. Green beans, chard, spinach all benefit from this treatment, but I find the lemon particularly good with broccoli.

For 4	80–100ml extra virgin olive oil	salt and freshly ground pepper
500g broccoli		
	juice of ½–1 lemon	

Cut the broccoli into florets, trim and peel the stalks and cut them into short lengths. Cook the broccoli for 3–4 minutes in boiling water or steam it for 5–6 minutes; it should still be crisp but not raw. Drain and put into a serving dish. Whisk together oil and lemon juice to your taste, making enough to dress the broccoli. Season with pepper and a little salt and pour over the broccoli. Serve hot or warm.

Brussels sprouts

I am not a fan of Brussels sprouts. Even the small, fresh bright green ones have a pronounced cabbagey flavour, quite out of proportion to their size. I find the other members of the brassica tribe more subdued and pleasing. Brussels sprouts are tempered by nuts, or breadcrumbs lightly fried in butter.

Brussels sprouts with breadcrumbs

For 4	6 tbs fresh	salt and freshly ground
500g small Brussels sprouts	breadcrumbs	pepper
	50g butter	

Boil the sprouts in water for 6–8 minutes, until just tender. Drain them. Fry the breadcrumbs in the butter until crisp and lightly browned. Add the sprouts, season and toss together. Serve at once.

Variations
· Replace the breadcrumbs with 6 tbs slivered almonds or chopped pecans.
· Use half the amount of braised chestnuts (p. 130) to cooked sprouts and toss them in 50g butter.

Brussels sprouts with olive oil and lemon

For 4	4 tbs olive oil	salt and freshly ground
500g small Brussels sprouts	2 garlic cloves, peeled and sliced	pepper
		2 tbs lemon juice

Boil the sprouts until almost tender, about 5–6 minutes. Heat the oil in a large pan and fry the garlic gently until it turns brown. Scoop it out and discard it. Put in the drained sprouts, season and cook for 2–3 minutes, stirring and shaking the pan. Add the lemon juice, stir it in and serve.

Cabbage

Cabbage is an under-appreciated vegetable. There are so many varieties to choose from: crinkly Savoy, firm heads of round and pointed white cabbage, spring greens, red cabbage and the currently fashionable Italian cavolo nero as well as the Chinese varieties. Cabbage should be cooked for a very short time to retain texture and flavour, or baked or braised for a long time. Anything in between produces a sulphurous-smelling unappetising mush. *See* notes on preparation (pp. 93–4) and the various cooking methods (pp. 95–6).

Savoy cabbage rolls

For 4–6	200ml soured cream	5–6 tbs chopped dill
1 Savoy cabbage (about 750g)	salt and freshly ground pepper	80g butter
300g thick fromage frais or curd cheese		2 tbs dried breadcrumbs

Heat the oven to 200°C, 400°F, gas 6. Separate the cabbage leaves and cook the large and medium sized ones in boiling water in an uncovered pan for about 5 minutes (keep the heart for another dish). Drain the leaves well and cut out the thick part of the central stalk. Blend the cheese, soured cream and seasonings together, then stir in the dill. Put some of the mixture on each of the leaves, and roll them up like pancakes. Lightly butter an ovenproof dish and coat it with breadcrumbs. Put in the cabbage rolls and dot generously with butter. Bake in the oven for 15–20 minutes until the top is lightly golden.

Spring greens with oyster sauce

You can, of course, stir-fry any of the Chinese cabbages or greens, and flavourings can be varied to include soy sauce or finely chopped ginger. A sprinkling of sesame oil at serving time is good with cabbage. I find oyster sauce has a particular affinity with spring greens.

For 2–3	2 tbs oil	3 tbs oyster sauce
300g spring greens	2 garlic cloves, peeled and crushed	

Shred the spring greens. Heat a wok over high heat until the heat rises, then add the oil and swirl it around the sides. Put in the garlic, then the cabbage. Toss it quickly – tongs are useful here unless you are skilled with chopsticks. The greens will spit, so be careful. Stir-fry for 3–4 minutes, then add the oyster sauce. Coat the greens with it and serve.

Spiced red cabbage

Most recipes for red cabbage suggest long braising; this one is cooked quickly so that the cabbage retains some bite. Good with roasted winter vegetables (p. 165), sausages and venison dishes.

For 6	2 tbs raisins	1 tsp ground coriander
1 red cabbage (600–700g)	1 tsp chopped thyme or rosemary	salt
1 red or white onion, peeled and sliced finely	4 tbs olive oil	1 large glass good red wine
1 large tart apple, grated	2 cardamom pods*, crushed	2–3 tbs balsamic or red wine vinegar

Cut the cabbage in four, remove the stalk then shred the leaves. Combine the cabbage with the onion, apple, raisins and thyme or rosemary; mix it all well together with your hands. Heat the oil slowly in a large pan, add the vegetable mixture, turning it over to coat everything in the oil. Stir in the spices and salt to taste. Turn up the heat, pour in the wine and cover the pan. Cook briskly for about 8 minutes, stirring and occasionally shaking the pan. Add a splash of water if it is getting too dry. Take the pan from the heat, add the vinegar which will provide a lively note, and serve.

Braised red cabbage

Finely sliced red cabbage can be braised for 30–45 minutes in butter with a splash of water or wine vinegar. Then give added flavour with chopped soaked prunes, a spoonful or two of a sweet chutney, a handful of cranberries, and cook for another 15 minutes or so for the flavours to blend.

Steamed bok choi

Use baby bok choi if you can get it and keep the heads whole. Cut large ones in half. They make an attractive accompaniment to steamed sea bass (p. 243).

For 4	salt	50g walnuts, broken or chopped coarsely
500g small heads of bok choi	3 tbs sesame oil	

Remove the outer stalks from the bok choi. Put the heads in a steamer and cook over simmering water for 7–10 minutes. The stalks should still retain some bite. Season with salt. Heat the sesame oil in a small pan and lightly fry the nuts for a minute or two. Put the bok choi on a dish, pour over the oil and nuts and serve.

Braised cavolo nero

This newcomer with its deep blue-black leaves is a type of kale. It provides an agreeable addition to the supermarket vegetable racks. Its texture remains firm when cooked. It is best sautéed with garlic in olive oil, or braised as here with onions, garlic and wine. A final sprinkling of Parmesan is beneficial whichever method you use.

For 4

400g cavolo nero

80ml olive oil

2 onions, peeled and sliced finely

4 garlic cloves, peeled and finely chopped

salt and freshly ground pepper

100ml white or red wine

80ml water

60g grated Parmesan

Discard the large central stalks and shred the leaves finely. Heat the oil in a large pan and sauté the onion until it is a light gold, then add the garlic. Sauté a minute or two longer, and stir in the cabbage. Keep stirring until it is all coated in the oil and starting to wilt. Season with salt and pepper and pour over the wine and water. Cover the pan, turn the heat very low and simmer for 50 minutes to 1 hour. Turn the cabbage from time to time. Check for seasoning. The cabbage should be tender but will still have a bite. Stir in the Parmesan and serve.

Carrots

Young tender carrots need only be rinsed and brushed; older ones need scraping and may benefit from a very small amount of sugar in the cooking. *See* notes on the various cooking methods (p. 95–8). To microwave, slice or julienne* the carrots, put them in a microwave plastic bag and cook for 6½ minutes for 250g, 8 minutes for 500g. Carrots make an excellent purée if simmered in orange juice and water and then whizzed with a little double cream.

Carrots glazed with lemon and coriander

For 4

500g carrots

30g butter

1 tsp brown sugar

salt and freshly ground pepper

½ tsp ground coriander

2 tbs lemon juice and grated rind of 1 small unwaxed lemon

3 tbs chopped coriander leaves

It is important to cut the carrots to the same size so that they cook evenly. I suggest strips about 3cm long and ½cm wide, otherwise slice the carrots finely. Melt the butter in a heavy pan, add the carrots, sugar, salt, pepper and ground coriander and just enough water to cover the carrots. Bring to the boil and simmer, uncovered, for 10–15 minutes. The carrots should be fairly tender and the liquid quite well reduced. Turn up the heat and watch the pan so that the vegetables do not stick as the last of the liquid evaporates, leaving the carrots coated in the butter and sugar glaze. Add the lemon juice and rind and the chopped coriander and serve.

Variation

Carrots in cream sauce Cook as above and add 2–3 tbs double cream after adding the lemon juice. The coriander leaves could be replaced by chives or mint.

Carrot and celeriac cake

Celeriac are large so you will certainly have some left if you cut one to make this cake. Cover the cut surface of the remaining piece tightly with clingfilm and refrigerate. It may discolour a little but you can cut off a slice before using the rest.

For 4

250g carrots, peeled

250g celeriac, peeled

50g butter

1 tsp sugar

salt and freshly ground pepper

150ml vegetable stock or water

1 tbs olive oil

3 shallots, peeled and chopped

2 eggs

50g grated Parmesan or Gruyère

50g ricotta

50ml double cream

2 tbs chopped parsley

Heat the oven to 220°C, 425°F, gas 7. Slice the carrots thinly and the celeriac into pieces of a similar size. The easiest way to do this is to slice both in a food processor, cutting the celeriac into chunks first. Heat the butter in a heavy pan and cook the vegetables until lightly coloured. Add the sugar and seasoning, and pour over the stock. Cover and simmer for 20 minutes, by which time the liquid should have almost evaporated. If it hasn't, turn up the heat and let it reduce further.

While the carrots and celeriac are cooking, heat the oil and sauté the shallots until softened. Remove the carrots and celeriac from the pan and chop them coarsely; again, a food processor will do it for you. Beat the eggs with the cheeses and cream and stir in all the chopped vegetables and the parsley.

Butter a 16cm soufflé dish or a ring mould and fill it with the mixture. Cover the dish with foil and bake in a bain-marie* for 30–40 minutes until set. Turn out carefully onto a serving plate and serve at once with broad bean purée (p. 110) or peas.

Cauliflower

Cauliflower is quickly cooked when broken into florets – *see* notes on the various cooking methods (pp. 95–6) – and it benefits from strong flavourings, whether western or oriental. To microwave, put florets in a dish that holds them in a single layer and cook for 4 minutes for 250g, 7 minutes for 500g. *See also* the broccoli recipes, which can be made equally well with cauliflower.

Cauliflower with anchovy dressing

This is a dish from southern Italy where different versions are found, sometimes adding strong local cheese to the sauce.

For 6	3 garlic cloves, peeled and sliced	12 black olives, stoned and sliced
1kg cauliflower, cut into florets	6 anchovy fillets, chopped	freshly ground pepper
60ml olive oil		

Boil the cauliflower for 4–5 minutes so that it still retains a bite, and drain. Heat the oil in a heavy pan and sauté the garlic. Let it turn golden, but be careful that it doesn't burn. Add the anchovy, the olives and the cauliflower. Season with a twist or two of pepper. I find the dish has enough salt from the anchovies and olives. Stir all together over low heat for 4–5 minutes and serve.

Cauliflower with almonds

This looks most attractive if the cauliflower is served whole, but it tastes just as good made with florets.

For 4–6	50g flaked almonds	salt and freshly ground pepper
1kg cauliflower	60g fresh white breadcrumbs	
80g butter		

To cook the cauliflower whole, turn it upside down and dig out most of the central stalk. Boil it for 10–12 minutes or steam for about 15. Lift it out carefully onto a warm dish, season and keep warm. (Cook florets for 4–5 minutes.) Melt the butter in a frying pan, and pour a little over the cauliflower.

Fry the almonds and breadcrumbs in the rest of the butter until golden. Scatter the breadcrumb and almond mixture over the cauliflower and serve.

Spiced braised cauliflower

For 4	1 tsp cumin seeds	½ tsp turmeric
1kg cauliflower	2 cm piece of ginger, chopped finely	salt
3 tbs oil		3 tbs water
½ tsp black mustard seeds (p. 76)	1 tsp ground coriander	½ tsp garam masala*
	¼ tsp chilli powder	1 tbs lemon juice

Cut the cauliflower into florets. Heat the oil in a large pan or wok and fry the mustard seeds, cumin seeds and ginger. When the mustard seeds start to pop and fly about, add the cauliflower. Stir well and add the coriander, chilli powder, turmeric and salt. Fry until the cauliflower is lightly browned. Add 3 tbs water, put on the lid, lower the heat and cook for 6–8 minutes. Shake the pan from time to time; if the cauliflower is sticking add another spoonful of water. When it is tender, transfer it to a serving dish, sprinkle over the garam masala and lemon juice and serve.

Celeriac

Although not a root vegetable (it is actually the swollen lower stem of celery), celeriac can be prepared in much the same way and can be stored through the winter months. Celeriac discolours once cut, so it is best put into acidulated water. *See* notes on the various cooking methods (pp. 95–6). To microwave, cut into 1cm dice, put in quantities up to 200g in microwave plastic bags and cook for 5 minutes for 250g, 8½ minutes for 500g.

Celeriac with olive oil

This is a Turkish way of cooking all kinds of vegetables – carrots, leeks, green beans, artichokes – to be eaten cold. The vegetables are stewed briefly in olive oil, then flavourings and a liquid, usually water, are added and they are cooked slowly to leave a rich sauce as the water is driven off. It is a particularly good way of preparing celeriac. The oil must be the best extra virgin olive oil. Choose small celeriac roots because the big ones are often woody.

For 6	10 baby onions or	1 tsp sugar
700–800g celeriac	1 onion, peeled and chopped	250ml water
lemon juice	80ml extra virgin olive oil	4 tbs chopped dill
1 carrot, peeled		50g young peas, fresh or frozen
1 potato, peeled	salt	1 lemon

Peel the celeriac, cut it in half and discard the woody centre if necessary. Parboil the two halves for 5 minutes in water acidulated with a squeeze of lemon juice. Drain and cut into cubes. Cut the carrot and potato into pieces the same size as the celeriac. Put the carrot, potato and onions into a large pan with the oil and fry for a few minutes over medium heat. Add the celeriac, salt to taste, the sugar and the water. Bring to the boil, then reduce the heat, cover the pan and cook for 20–30 minutes, adding the dill and peas for the last 5 minutes. All the vegetables should be tender and the liquid considerably reduced. Leave the vegetables to cool in the pan. Serve at room temperature with lemon wedges as a separate course.

Celeriac and potato cakes

This dish evolved from eating latkes, the celebrated potato cakes of Jewish cookery; I find this unorthodox version has more flavour.

For 4	3 tbs chopped parsley	salt and freshly ground pepper
2 eggs	250g potatoes	
3 tbs flour	300g celeriac	oil for frying

Beat the eggs lightly, mix in the flour and parsley. Peel the potatoes and the celeriac, discard any hard woody parts of the latter, grate both, and combine quickly with the egg to prevent discolouring. Season.

Heat 2–3 tbs oil in a frying pan and form the mixture into 8 cakes. Fry over moderate heat for 4–5 minutes on each side. Pressing the cakes flat with a spatula or fish slice helps them to brown evenly.

Celeriac crisps

Celeriac crisps make an attractive garnish, provided they don't get nibbled before they reach the table. Sweet potato and parsnip crisps can be made in the same way.

200g piece of celeriac, peeled	oil for deep-frying

Cut the celeriac into very thin slices on a mandoline (*see* p. 528) or with a potato peeler. Heat the oil in a deep-fryer to 180°C, 350°F. Drop in the pieces of celeriac a few at a time; they will turn crisp very quickly. Drain them on kitchen paper and season with salt.

Carrot and celeriac cake See p. 122.

Celery

Cooked celery is very different from the raw vegetable traditionally served with cheese. Easily overcooked, its most common use is as a flavouring for soups and stews, but it can be excellent braised. *See* notes on preparation (p. 93) and the various cooking methods (pp. 95–8).

Celery braised with ham

This quickly assembled dish can make a supper dish for 2 or a vegetable serving for a meal for 4.

For 2–4	150g Serrano or smoked ham, cut in strips	salt and freshly ground pepper
2 heads of celery		½ tsp cornflour mixed with 1 tsp water
50g butter	1 garlic clove, peeled and sliced	
1 onion, peeled and chopped		150ml yogurt
	2 tbs chopped parsley	2 tbs dried breadcrumbs

Heat the oven to 180°C, 350°F, gas 4. Remove any strings from the celery and cut into 5cm pieces. Blanch in boiling water for 2 minutes and drain thoroughly. Heat 10g butter and sauté the onion and ham for 2–3 minutes, add the garlic and sauté 1 minute more. Take a little of the remaining butter to grease a shallow ovenproof casserole. Put in the contents of the frying pan and spread the parsley and celery on top. Season well. Beat the cornflour and water into the yogurt to stabilize it during cooking and pour it over the vegetables. Scatter the breadcrumbs over the top and dot with the rest of the butter. Bake for 35–45 minutes until the top is browned.

Chard

Most of the chard in the shops looks tired, as if it has been there for days – and it probably has, since few people seem to know this lovely vegetable. Vegetable gardeners certainly know it and grow it for its beauty – large dark green leaves rising above white or (with rainbow chard) magenta, red or yellow stalks – as much as for its flavour. It is a vegetable which can be prepared in a variety of ways; the leaves and stalks are often cooked, and served, separately. Leaves can be cooked in the same way as are spinach leaves and used to make a stuffing for pasta or served as a cooked salad; the stalks can be sautéed, cooked as a gratin (*see* over) or braised with ham (*see* above); *see also* curried ham and leek gratin (p. 345).

While writing this I was brought armfuls of chard from a friend's allotment, and so had plenty of opportunity to try all sorts of recipes. *See also* the notes on preparation (pp. 92–3).

Chard with oil and lemon

For 6		
1kg chard	2 garlic cloves, peeled and chopped finely	juice of ½ lemon
6 tbs extra virgin olive oil	salt and freshly ground pepper	¼ tsp chilli flakes (optional)

Separate the leaves and stalks. Remove the stringy bits from the stalks with a potato peeler, and cut them in 2cm diagonal slices. Blanch the stalks for 2–3 minutes in boiling water and drain. If the leaves are very big, roll them and cut them in a chiffonade*, otherwise tear them into 2 or 3 pieces. Heat the oil in a large sauté pan and add the garlic. As soon as it starts to colour, put in the chard leaves and a little salt. Turn them in the oil and when they have wilted, if all the water that was clinging to them from washing has evaporated, add the stalks. If necessary, turn up the heat to get rid of the moisture before you put in the stalks. Sauté for 5–6 minutes, tossing the vegetables around in the oil. Both leaves and stalks should retain a bite. Season with pepper, lemon juice and chilli flakes if you like, and serve hot or at room temperature.

Gratin of chard stalks

This is a traditional dish from Provence, where chard is as popular as it is in Italy. It is simple to prepare, and the cream and cheese combine well with the fresh taste of the parsley to bring out the delicate sweetness of the chard. The overall quantity of chard needed for this and the next recipe depends on the size of the chard but as a guide you would need about 1–1.2kg.

For 4	salt and freshly ground pepper	200ml double cream
600g chard stalks		2 egg yolks
sunflower oil	3 tbs chopped parsley	2–3 tbs dried breadcrumbs
¼ tsp ground nutmeg or mace	150g grated Parmesan	

Heat the oven to 180°C, 350°F, gas 4. Remove the stringy bits from the stalks with a potato peeler, then cut the stalks into sticks 5–6cm long and 1cm wide. Blanch the stalks for 3–4 minutes in boiling water and drain. Lightly oil a shallow ovenproof casserole or gratin dish. Put in a layer of stalks, season with nutmeg or mace, salt and pepper and scatter over some of the parsley and cheese. Make further layers, finishing with a good layer of cheese, until everything is used. Heat the cream gently and whisk in the lightly beaten egg yolks. Pour the cream over the chard and sprinkle the breadcrumbs over the top. Bake for 15–20 minutes until the top is lightly browned.

Variation

For a less rich version, use thick yogurt stabilised with ½ tsp cornflour mixed with 1 tsp water (p. 127) instead of the cream and egg yolks. I find grated feta better than Parmesan with yogurt.

Sautéed chard leaves

For 4

600g chard leaves; *see* above

4 tbs olive oil

1 onion, peeled and chopped

3 garlic cloves, peeled and chopped

salt and freshly ground pepper

¼ tsp ground mace

1 large tomato, peeled, seeded and diced

Slice the leaves into a chiffonade*. You will need a very large pan or a wok to cook this much chard in one go. Heat the oil and sweat* the onion until it softens. Add the garlic to the pan, leave uncovered, but do not let it brown. Add the chard leaves, a handful or two at a time, turning them to coat in the oil. Cook for 8–12 minutes until they have softened; with a large quantity it is easiest to cover the pan for part of the time, but still turn the leaves as they cook. When they have softened, leave the pan open to drive off the moisture. Season with salt, pepper and mace. Add the diced tomato and cook for another 5 minutes.

Chestnuts

Not a vegetable, of course, but chestnuts are often used as a vegetable or with vegetables. They have a particular affinity for cabbage, celery, mushrooms, especially wild mushrooms, pumpkin and squash and Brussels sprouts. In the mountain regions of Italy, France and Spain, chestnuts are staple food. In addition to their role in vegetable cooking, stuffings and soups, chestnuts also make delectable desserts (p. 473).

To peel chestnuts, cut a cross on the flat side, bring them to the boil in a pan of water, simmer for 5 minutes, then take the pan from the heat. Take out the chestnuts, one at a time, and peel off the outer and inner skin. They need to be hot to get the peel off, so if necessary put on gloves. Reheat the water if the chestnuts are getting too cool.

A microwave offers a quick and efficient way of peeling and cooking chestnuts. Cut a cross on the flat side of each one, arrange them in one layer in a dish and cook uncovered for 6 minutes for 250g, 8 minutes for 500g. Peel as soon as they are cool enough to handle. To cook further, put the shelled nuts in a single layer in a dish and cook, again uncovered, for 4 minutes for 250g, 6 minutes for 500g.

Vacuum-packed cooked chestnuts save greatly on the slow task of peeling them. Dehydrated chestnuts must be soaked in water for several hours before cooking. Cans of chestnuts and chestnut purée may be plain or sweetened, so check the label when you buy.

Braised chestnuts

For 4–6	2 shallots, chopped	salt and freshly ground pepper
500g chestnuts, peeled	1 bay leaf	
150ml white wine	150–200ml vegetable or chicken stock (p. 4)	30g butter
1 stalk celery, sliced		

Put the chestnuts in a pan with the wine, celery, shallots and bay leaf. Add enough stock just to cover them, season and bring to a simmer. Cover and simmer over very low heat for about 20 minutes, until the chestnuts are tender. Take care that they don't disintegrate. If the liquid has not reduced enough, take out the chestnuts and boil it down in the uncovered pan. Whisk in the butter and serve. The chestnuts make a good accompaniment to venison stew with cherries (p. 352), lamb with pumpkin, prunes and apricots (p. 333), and roast goose (p. 298) unless you have used a chestnut stuffing.

Chestnut purée

For 4	125ml double cream	salt and freshly ground pepper
500g chestnuts, shelled	60g butter	
	pinch of ground mace	

Boil the chestnuts for about 30 minutes, then drain and purée them. If you do this in a food processor you may need to add a tablespoon or two of the cream because the chestnuts will be fairly dry. Return the purée to the pan. Heat the cream a little and add it to the purée with the butter, stirring all the time over low heat. Season with mace, salt and pepper and serve with Savoy cabbage rolls (p. 119), or partridge with red cabbage (p. 300).

Wild rice and chestnut casserole. *See* p. 196.

Chick peas

Also known as garbanzo beans and in India as Bengal gram. Chick peas resemble hazelnuts in shape. They require long soaking (for notes on preparation, *see* those under Dried beans, p. 111) and never lose their shape. Canned chick peas are a great time-saver. A 240g can is the equivalent of 125g raw chick peas.

Chick pea tagine

The Moroccans are very fond of chick peas and use them in all sorts of vegetable and meat stews. This dish concentrates on the chick peas. It makes an excellent accompaniment to meat and poultry dishes and vegetable stews.

For 4	3 garlic cloves, peeled	½ tsp saffron threads
250g chick peas, soaked overnight	1 red chilli	2 tbs chopped coriander
1 onion, peeled and chopped finely	1 tbs paprika	3 tbs olive oil
	1 tsp black pepper	salt

Drain the chick peas and remove any loose skins. Put them in a pan with the onion, whole garlic cloves, whole chilli, the spices, coriander and oil. Add 900ml water and bring to the boil. Reduce the heat and simmer, covered, for at least 1 hour. Season with salt, and taste to see whether the chick peas are ready; if they are still firm cook longer, but don't let them disintegrate. There should be only a little liquid left. Remove the chilli before serving.

Bulgur pilaf with chick peas. See p. 201.

Spinach with chick peas. See p. 160.

Hummus. See p. 26.

Chicory

Chicories form a rather large family, but the one I am dealing with here is the firm white Belgian variety known as *witloof* in Flemish (for radicchio, *see* p. 159). It makes an excellent salad vegetable, and is well worth serving cooked. Chicory goes well with steamed or baked fish, grilled or roasted birds and meat, with ham and gammon, and braised or baked in the oven it is a good separate vegetable course.

Heads of chicory vary greatly in size, so choose ones that are similar so they will cook in the same time. If they are huge, 3 or 4 may be enough for 6 depending on what else is to be served and the size of your appetites. If they are small, allow one per person.

Buttered chicory

For 6	1 tbs lemon juice	salt and freshly ground pepper
6 heads of chicory	80g butter	

Cut the heads of chicory in half lengthways and rub with a little lemon juice. Steam over bubbling water for about 8 minutes. The root ends should still be firm, but the leaves should have become translucent. Heat the butter slowly in a wide pan, put in the chicory and season with salt and pepper. Turn the pieces to let them absorb the butter and serve.

Braised chicory

For 4	50g butter	100ml chicken stock (p. 4) or water
4 heads of chicory	salt and freshly ground pepper	

Cut the chicory heads in half lengthways. Melt the butter in a casserole which will hold the chicory side by side. Put in the chicory and turn the pieces in the butter. Season and pour over the stock. Cover and braise for about 10 minutes. Remove the lid and simmer gently for another 5 minutes. The chicory should be tender and the liquid reduced to a few tablespoons. If you prefer, the chicory can be cooked in the oven at 200°C, 400°F, gas 6 for about 20 minutes.

Chillies

Preparing fresh chillies can be unpleasant, even painful, for the capsaicin in the fruit causes a burning sensation. Hands can remain contaminated by capsaicin long after you've finished preparing the chillies, and if you touch another part of your body the irritation will spread there. Above all, do not rub your eyes. Rinse them at once with plenty of cold water if you do inflame them accidentally. If you have a very sensitive skin wear rubber gloves; always wash your hands in soapy water after handling chillies. Wash the board and the knife too.

Chillies can be used whole or sliced, with or without their seeds. There is more capsaicin in the seeds and white membranes than in the skin, therefore more heat.

Fresh chillies freeze well; although they will be soft when thawed, they retain their bite.

Courgettes

Small courgettes are delicious and merit careful treatment; overcooked they are watery and lose all taste. They adapt well to most cooking methods (pp. 96–9) and combine well with other vegetables such as young carrots and peas for a summer stew or with aubergines, tomatoes and peppers for Mediterranean flavours. To use the beautiful flowers you will have to grow your own.

Courgettes a scapece

Courgettes in vinegar are a speciality of the region of Naples. Meant to be eaten at room temperature, they are very good with bread for a snack and great for picnics and outdoor eating. Do use good-quality vinegar.

For 4	salt	2 garlic cloves, peeled and chopped
6 courgettes	1 tbs chopped mint or tarragon leaves	
3–6 tbs olive oil		4 tbs red wine vinegar

Slice the courgettes lengthways, making slices about ½cm thick. Heat a little oil in a frying pan and put in a layer of courgette slices. Fry them gently, moving them around so they cook evenly and turn a couple of times. They should be golden brown. If necessary, turn up the heat to brown them. Fry the courgettes in batches, adding more oil to the pan if necessary. Put the fried courgettes into a flat dish, sprinkle with salt and scatter over the mint or tarragon leaves. Add the garlic to the oil when the last courgettes have been fried, and cook for a few seconds over low heat, then add the vinegar. Pour this dressing over the courgettes and leave to cool.

Sweet-sour courgettes

For 4	2 tbs raisins	salt and freshly ground pepper
500g courgettes	1 tsp cinnamon	
3 tbs olive oil	1 tbs sugar	1 tbs chopped parsley or coriander
3 tbs wine vinegar		

Cut the courgettes into 4–5cm slices. Heat the oil and fry them gently, turning so they cook evenly. Add all the other ingredients except the parsley or coriander, stir and shake the pan until the juices become syrupy. Transfer the courgettes to a dish, sprinkle over the parsley or coriander and serve hot, warm or cold, but not chilled.

Courgettes baked with cheese

For 4	salt and freshly ground pepper	150g grated Gruyère or Cheddar
500g courgettes		
	3 eggs	2 tbs flour
4 spring onions, chopped		30g butter

Heat the oven to 180°C, 350°F, gas 4. Slice the courgettes thinly and blanch them in boiling water for 2–3 minutes. Drain well and combine them with the onions. Season with salt and pepper. Beat the eggs and add the cheese and flour, then stir in the vegetables. Lightly grease an ovenproof dish and pour in the mixture. Dot the top with butter and bake for about 30 minutes. The top should be lightly coloured.

Courgette gratin

Follow the recipe for gratin of pattypan squash on p. 158, replacing the pattypans with courgettes.

Fennel

Florentine or bulb fennel can be eaten raw in a salad, with a dressing of extra virgin olive oil, lemon juice and good salt, or grilled, with shavings of Parmesan. *See* notes on preparation (p. 93). Fennel roasts and braises well; *see* roasted winter vegetables (p. 165), notes on braising (p. 97) and celery braised with ham (p. 126). To microwave, cut fennel bulbs into 3 or 4 wedges, wrap in microwave plastic wrap and for 1 bulb weighing 250–300g cook for 3½ minutes, allow 5 minutes for 2 bulbs.

Fennel braised in olive oil

For 6	6 tbs olive oil	salt and freshly ground pepper
6 bulbs of fennel (about 1.5kg total weight)	2 garlic cloves, peeled and crushed	4–5 tbs water or white wine
	1 tsp fennel seeds, crushed	chives to garnish

Cut the fennel bulbs in half lengthways and cut each half in two or three equal pieces. Put the pieces in a pan, pour over the olive oil, add the garlic and fennel seeds and season with salt and pepper. Cook for 5–6 minutes over moderate heat, turning the pieces carefully in the oil.

Add 4–5 tbs water or white wine, cover the pan and put on low heat for about 20 minutes. Shake the pan occasionally, and check to see if a little more water is needed. The fennel is ready when it can be pierced with a knife, but don't cook it until it gets too soft; fennel tastes better with a slight bite. There should be just a little liquid in the bottom of the pan, which can be poured over the fennel before serving. Garnish with the chives.

Fennel with preserved lemon

For this dish the fennel may be cooked in the microwave (p.134) or steamed (p. 96). To make preserved lemons, *see* p. 513.

For 2	2 tbs olive oil	¼ preserved lemon, skin sliced thinly (p. 513)
2 fennel bulbs (500–600g total weight)	salt and freshly ground pepper	

Cut the fennel bulbs in half down the middle and cut each piece in half again. Chop some of the green fronds. Wrap each bulb in a large piece of microwave plastic wrap. Close the parcels well and cook at 100% for 5 minutes. Leave to rest for 2 minutes, then unwrap the fennel. To steam it, allow 10–12 minutes. Put the pieces on a serving dish, pour over the oil, season with salt and pepper and scatter over the preserved lemon and the chopped fennel leaves.

Tian of artichokes and fennel. See p. 102.

Garlic

This pungent flavouring is one that few cooks will be without. Many dishes depend on it for their characteristic flavour, but it is not often used in large quantities in British cooking. When it is cooked, garlic becomes mellow-tasting and smells quite fragrant. The recipes given here make good accompaniments to roast or grilled meat, to game and poultry dishes or to root vegetables, and the purée can be stirred into dishes of beans or used to flavour soups or sauces. Use unblemished heads of firm garlic, avoiding any that have a green shoot because that is indigestible.

Chop garlic finely or crush it with the back of a heavy knife. The dry skin will come loose as you crush it. Another method is to crush the clove with a little salt in a mortar to produce a paste. I do not recommend using a garlic press; these gadgets tend to intensify the smell and taste of the sulphur compounds present in the plant oils. They are also more fiddly to clean than a knife or a pestle and mortar.

Garlic purée

| Enough for 1 small jar | salt | 2 tbs olive oil |
| 6 heads young garlic | | |

Put the whole garlic heads in a pan and cover with boiling water. Simmer for 15–20 minutes until the flesh is soft. Drain and leave to cool, then remove the skins and blend. Season the purée with salt and stir in the oil. The purée will keep for 1–2 weeks in the refrigerator, stored in a jar and covered with a layer of olive oil.

Variations
· Instead of blending the garlic with olive oil, add 150ml crème fraîche for a rich purée, or 150 ml stock and a tablespoon or two of cream to finish an almost cholesterol-free alternative.

Fried garlic

| 6–8 cloves per person | olive oil |

Simmer the peeled cloves of garlic in water to cover for 2–3 minutes, then drain well and dry with kitchen paper. Heat some oil in a frying pan and fry the garlic until golden, but don't let it turn brown or burn. Drain on more kitchen paper.

Roasted garlic

This can be made with the garlic available all year, but it is particularly good with the new (green) garlic that arrives in early summer. Roasted garlic is wonderful spread on good bread and drizzled with fruity olive oil.

| 4 heads garlic | 2 tbs olive oil | 2–3 tbs water |

Heat the oven to 180°C, 350°F, gas 4. Separate the heads into cloves, but don't peel them. Put them into an ovenproof dish, preferably earthenware, and pour over the oil. Make sure all the cloves are coated. Add 2–3 tbs water. Roast for about 30 minutes, basting from time to time. When the garlic is ready, the cloves slip out of their skins easily.

Variation

- Leave the heads whole, but slice the top off to show the cloves. Put the heads in a shallow ovenproof dish and brush with 4 tbs olive oil. Cover with foil and roast for 50–60 minutes, basting occasionally.

Jerusalem artichokes

Of North American origin, these tubers are not related to globe artichokes, but to sunflowers. Some people suffer severe wind problems from eating them, caused, according to Harold McGee in *The Curious Cook*, by a type of carbohydrate that is seldom encountered in our diet and so we have not evolved enzymes to digest it. He says that long cooking can help reduce the wind-provoking problem.

Jerusalem artichokes have a slightly sweet flavour; they make an excellent soup (p. 12) and benefit from braising or parboiling and roasting. The knobbly tubers can be wasteful as well as tedious to peel raw; where the recipe allows it is easier to peel them once they are cooked.

Daube of Jerusalem artichokes

The delicate nutty flavour of Jerusalem artichokes is enhanced in this slow-cooked dish and they retain their texture and shape.

For 4	1 tbs olive oil	bouquet garni*
750g Jerusalem artichokes, peeled	salt and freshly ground pepper	5 garlic cloves, peeled
1 small onion, peeled and chopped	grated nutmeg	1 glass dry white wine

Cut the artichokes into 3 or 4 pieces. Sauté the onion in the oil until lightly coloured, then put in the artichokes, season with salt, pepper and nutmeg, tuck in the bouquet garni and the whole garlic cloves. Cover and sweat* over very low heat for 15 minutes, turn the artichokes once and shake the pan so they don't stick. Add a glass of white wine, simmer for another 5–10 minutes, then uncover the pan, let the wine reduce by half, leaving a small amount of sauce in the pan. Discard the bouquet garni before serving. Serve the daube as a main course with rice or to accompany game or poultry.

Purée of Jerusalem artichokes

For 6	salt and freshly ground pepper	6 tbs crème fraîche or double cream
1kg Jerusalem artichokes	100g butter	

Boil or steam the artichokes until tender, then drain and peel them. Season, then put them in the food processor with the butter and cream and blend to a purée. If it is too thin, put the purée in a pan and stir over moderate heat to drive off the water. Serve it with beef or veal.

Kohlrabi

Our European neighbours are more enthusiastic about kohlrabi than we are. The green or purple globes – bulbous swellings in the stem of a type of cabbage – are readily available in their markets. You have to hunt for them here. They are worth finding because they add variety to winter vegetables, but do not buy any larger than a tennis ball because they are likely to be woolly. If they come with leaves, these can be cooked as spring greens or spinach. Kohlrabi can be simmered or steamed and served with a sauce or braised.

Kohlrabi braised with tarragon

For 4	60ml white wine	salt and freshly ground pepper
800g kohlrabi	4 sprigs tarragon, chopped	
2 tbs olive oil or 30g butter		

Peel the kohlrabi and cut a thick slice from the bottom. Cut the flesh into thickish strips. Fry them lightly in the oil or butter over low heat. Add the wine and tarragon, and season with salt and pepper. Cover the pan and simmer for 12–15 minutes, until the kohlrabi is tender. Serve with roast meats or stews; it goes particularly well with carbonnade of beef (p. 323).

Leeks

To the French, the leeks are 'poor man's asparagus' and they often prepare them in similar ways. We are fortunate that small leeks are now available in summer for dishes like leeks vinaigrette. Leeks combine well with other vegetables, make an excellent accompaniment to steamed fish (steamed brill with mushrooms and leeks, p. 251) and a very good tart.

For instructions on cleaning this often very soil-encrusted vegetable *see* p. 92, and *see also* the various cooking methods (pp. 95–7).

Leeks vinaigrette

This is a good way to serve leeks, particularly young leeks. The leeks seem to soak up a great deal of the mustardy sauce, so make a large amount – it will certainly get mopped up if you serve some good bread as well. Parma or Serrano ham goes well with the leeks.

For 4	1 shallot, peeled and	salt and freshly ground
12 medium leeks or 20 small ones	chopped finely	pepper
	1½ tbs Dijon mustard	120ml sunflower oil
	2 tbs red wine vinegar	chives to garnish

Clean the leeks and wash them thoroughly. Keep the pale green part. Leave small leeks whole and tie them together in a bundle, they will cook more slowly and be easier to remove from the pan. Cut large leeks into 5cm lengths. Simmer the leeks until tender, 5–10 minutes depending on size, lift them out carefully and drain well on a cloth. Whisk together the shallot, mustard, vinegar, salt and pepper and whisk in the oil, little by little, to form a creamy sauce. Arrange the hot leeks on a warm dish, spoon over the sauce and scatter over a few chopped chives. Serve lukewarm or cold, but not chilled.

Braised leeks with red pepper

The bright colour of the pepper contrasts well with the pale white and green of the leeks. I've put a star anise – a spice used in Chinese cookery and in Chinese five-spice powder – into this dish because I like the anise note which it gives to the leeks, but it is not essential to the dish.

For 6	1 small red pepper, diced	1 star anise* (optional)
8–10 leeks		2–3 tbs stock or water
30g butter	salt and freshly ground pepper	1 tbs parsley

Prepare the leeks, keeping some of the green part. Cut them into 2cm rounds. Heat the butter in a heavy pan and sauté the leeks gently, turning them in the butter. Add the diced pepper, season and put in the star anise if you wish. Add a little stock or water, cover the pan and simmer over low heat for about 20 minutes. Take out the star anise before serving. Put the leeks and pepper in a dish and scatter over the parsley.

Lentils

Lentils are available in several varieties. The small red ones disintegrate quickly and are best used for purées. Slate-coloured Puy lentils, small Italian Castelluccio lentils and the large brown ones need longer cooking but keep their shape and texture. I have recently tried some small grey-brown Canadian lentils which were similar to those from Puy and Castelluccio in taste and texture. Pick lentils over and wash them before cooking. They do not need to be soaked. Like other pulses, lentils should only be salted towards the end of the cooking time.

Lentils with herbs and cream

The best lentils for this dish are the small slate-coloured Puy lentils or the green-brown ones from Castelluccio; both have a fine flavour. Serve the lentils with poultry, grilled chops, other vegetable dishes. If there are any left, they make a good salad.

For 4	1 litre water	freshly ground pepper
300g lentils	salt	2 tbs chopped coriander
1 onion, peeled and cut in half	1 garlic clove, peeled and crushed	
2 bay leaves	80–100ml double cream	2 tbs chopped mint
2 tbs olive oil		2 tbs chopped chives

Put the lentils in a pan with the onion and bay leaves. Add the olive oil and about 1 litre of unsalted water. Bring the pan to the boil, reduce to a simmer and cook until the lentils are tender, about 20 minutes. Check that there is enough water during the cooking and, if necessary, top up with hot water. Add salt to taste in the last 5 minutes.

Drain the lentils and return them to the pan, discarding the bay leaves. Stir the garlic into the cream and pour over the lentils, turning to coat them well. Season with pepper, stir in the herbs and serve.

Lentils with apricots and walnuts

This lentil dish comes from the Caucasus.

For 4	1 onion, peeled and chopped finely	50g walnuts, chopped
250g Puy lentils	40g butter	2 tbs chopped parsley or coriander
50g dried apricots, soaked in warm water and chopped coarsely	salt and freshly ground pepper	

Bring the lentils to the boil in a large pan of unsalted water, then simmer until tender, about 20 minutes. Drain them, rinse out the pan and return the lentils to it.

While the lentils are simmering, sauté the drained apricots and the onion in the butter until they begin to soften. Season with salt and pepper. Add this mixture and the walnuts to the cooked lentils and place over very low heat for 5 minutes so that the lentils dry out. Stir in the chopped parsley or coriander and serve.

Lentil purée

Follow the spiced split pea purée (p. 151). Vary the spicing if you wish with a 3cm piece of cinnamon, 1 tsp cumin seeds and 2 crushed cardamom pods*, and omit the turmeric. Put the cinnamon into the pan with the lentils. Fry the cardamoms with the garlic and cumin.

Mange-tout

Mange-tout and snow peas are much alike, and can be used interchangeably. Mange-tout are flat whereas snow peas are tender pods with more noticeably developed peas. In both cases, the whole pod is eaten. *See* notes on de-stringing, p. 93. Stir-frying suits them well. To microwave, put the peas in a microwave plastic bag or a covered dish and cook for 3 minutes for 250g.

Stir-fried mange-tout with water chestnuts and pork

For 4	1 garlic clove, peeled and chopped finely	120g water chestnuts, sliced
120g lean pork, cut in strips	180g mange-tout	2 tbs soy sauce
3 tbs fish sauce	4 spring onions, cut in 4cm lengths	1 tsp sugar
2 tbs oil		80ml stock or water

Put the pork in a small bowl and marinate for 10 minutes with 1 tbs fish sauce. Heat a wok until very hot, add the oil and fry the garlic until golden brown. Put in the pork and stir-fry until it is brown. Add the mange-tout, spring onions and water chestnuts, toss for a minute, then add the remaining fish sauce, soy sauce, sugar and stock. Stir constantly and cook until the pork is firm and the vegetables still crisp, about 3–4 minutes.

Mushrooms and fungi

Finding wild mushrooms, or fungi, in our shops has become relatively easy, although 'wild' is perhaps a dubious adjective as many are now raised commercially (even though they don't conform to the controls applied to most vegetable and fruit production). Most fungi have more flavour than cultivated field mushrooms. Button mushrooms are good for salads and mushroom carpaccio (p. 36).

Probably the best of the wild mushrooms are ceps (porcini in Italian), large mushrooms with bulbous cream stems, rounded brown caps and a rich flavour. Girolles and chanterelles, closely related to each other, with golden or brown flattened caps and spindly stalks, have a delicate apricot flavour that is complemented by herbs and garlic. The brown-black horns of plenty, called trompettes des morts by the French, are also related to girolles; their undulating caps are indeed horn-like. More fragile, they are less easy to find. Creamy coloured hedgehog fungi are somewhat like firmer versions of girolles, but they have spines not gills beneath their caps. Most of these fungi are found in autumn, but morels are spring fungi. They have pitted tall caps and hollow stalks and are highly prized for their smoky flavour. They are also the most expensive. Other fungi occasionally found for sale are puffballs – creamy white spheres, sometimes as big as a football, with dense flesh – and parasol mushrooms with their long stalks and large caps.

I have never developed a great liking for shiitake, the cultivated oriental mushrooms with firm brown meaty caps and woody stalks, finding their flavour obtrusive, but some people love them. Oyster mushrooms I am seldom tempted by, finding the taste bland and the texture too watery.

Brush mushrooms or wipe with a damp cloth. After brushing fungi, cut off any dubious-looking or slimy bits and trim the ends of the stalks. Use whole or slice, depending on size.

Cooking mushrooms and fungi

Mushrooms and fungi are best quickly sautéed, grilled or baked to preserve their flavour and aroma. All mushrooms and fungi give off liquid when cooking, some in large amounts. Unless they are to be grilled, it is easiest to sauté them in hot oil or butter to sear them, otherwise they will go on exuding juices. If there is a lot of liquid in the pan, cook until it evaporates. To microwave, put 250g sliced mushrooms in a dish, add a sprinkling of water or lemon juice, a dab of butter if you wish, and cover tightly. Cook for 3 minutes.

Dried mushrooms

Ceps (usually sold as porcini since most of them come from Italy), morels and shiitake are all available dried. Their flavour is concentrated and you need use only a few, so although they are expensive to buy, they will last for some time. All dried mushrooms need to be soaked in hot water for about 20 minutes. They can then be chopped and added to the recipe. Strain the soaking liquor (there may be grit in it) and use it in the recipe as part of the liquid needed, or put it in a soup or stew. Don't waste it, the flavour is too good.

Sautéed ceps

This will make a main dish for 2 or part of a meal for 3 or 4	a small slice of raw ham	1 small glass white wine
	2–3 tbs olive oil	salt and freshly ground pepper
400g ceps	2 shallots, peeled and chopped finely	2 tbs chopped parsley

Remove the caps from the ceps and slice them. Cut the stalks into large dice. Cut the ham into thin slivers. Heat the oil and sauté the ham and shallot quickly. Pour over the wine. Let it simmer for 5 minutes, then put in the ceps. Season and cook for 10–15 minutes. The ceps will exude some juice, but there should not be too much liquid, so keep the heat fairly high and shake the pan regularly. Add the parsley, turn the ceps into a dish and serve.

Sauté of girolles and pumpkin

For 4–5	4–5 tbs walnut oil	2 tbs white wine vinegar
500g pumpkin flesh	salt and freshly ground pepper	2 tbs chopped chives
300g girolles		

Cut the pumpkin flesh into thin strips. If the girolles are large, cut them into 2 or 3 pieces. Heat 2 tbs walnut oil in a non-stick pan over moderate heat and gently sauté the pumpkin, turning the strips in the oil. Turn up the heat and add the girolles, sautéing them quickly to avoid them shedding their liquid. Season and remove the vegetables to a warm serving dish.

Add the remaining oil to the pan, let it heat through, add the vinegar and swirl it around, scraping up any bits in the pan. Pour over the vegetables and serve with the chives sprinkled over.

Mushrooms with cream

Chestnut mushrooms, whether buttons or caps, are good for this dish, but if you prefer an all-white dish, stick to the standard variety. Dill can replace parsley.

For 4–5	500g mushrooms, sliced	salt and freshly ground pepper
30g butter	150ml double cream	2 tbs chopped parsley

Heat the butter and sauté the mushrooms over medium heat, stirring briskly for 2–3 minutes. Heat the cream gently to thicken it and add it to the pan. Season with salt and pepper. Cook, stirring, for about 2–3 minutes. Sprinkle over the parsley and serve.

Mushroom ragoût

This dish is best made with an assortment of field or cultivated mushrooms and fungi. Serve as an accompaniment to veal, to rice or as a pasta sauce.

For 6	2 garlic cloves, peeled and chopped finely	salt and freshly ground pepper
1kg assorted mushrooms	1 tsp chopped thyme leaves	2 tomatoes, peeled, seeded and chopped
4 tbs olive oil	pinch ground cloves	6 tbs double cream
2 shallots, peeled and chopped		

Discard any dubious bits and slice the mushrooms including the stalks. Heat the oil in a large pan and sauté the shallots for 1 minute. Add the garlic, thyme and cloves, stir them in the oil, then put in the mushrooms, increase the heat and stir the mushrooms frequently until they become soft. Season with salt and pepper. Add the tomato and cream. Simmer, with the pan half covered, for 20–25 minutes until the juices thicken.

Mushroom risotto. *See* p. 192.

Okra

Okra is now on sale in many supermarkets, and is well worth trying. It has a place in the cooking of the West Indies, the southern USA, the Middle East and India, so several styles of cooking suit okra. Buy bright green young okra, large pods with a yellowing colour and brown marks tend to be tough. Okra is easy to prepare: the cap is cut off, and the pod may be cooked whole or sliced when it has an attractive pattern. Okra is a sweet-tasting vegetable, but it is slippery and sticky – slimy even, and some people do not like this texture. In Louisiana it is prized for its sticky juices which thicken soups and stews. Once fried or sautéed, the sticky quality tends to disappear and the okra is crisp. Okra goes well with lamb and chicken dishes.

Steamed okra with sesame dressing

For 4	400g okra	*dressing* as for oriental asparagus (p. 104)

Slice the stalks and caps from the okra without cutting into the pods. Steam over briskly simmering water for 4–6 minutes, until the okra is tender. Prepare the dressing while the okra is cooking. Pour it over the okra to serve.

Variation

· Serve the okra cool with a vinaigrette dressing,

Spiced sautéed okra

For 4	small piece ginger, chopped finely	1 garlic clove, peeled and chopped finely
400g okra	½ tsp ground cumin	salt
3–4 tbs sunflower oil	½ tsp ground coriander	2–3 tbs water
1 onion, peeled, cut in half and sliced thinly	½ tsp ground pepper	1 tbs lime or lemon juice

Slice the okra into thin rounds. Heat a heavy pan and when it feels hot to your hand held over it, add the oil. Put in the onion, reduce the heat somewhat and sauté for 3 minutes, until the onion starts to colour. Add the spices, garlic and salt. Put in the okra, toss it in the spices, then sprinkle over 2–3 tbs water. Cook, stirring from time to time, until the okra is tender but still crisp, about 6–8 minutes. Sprinkle over the lime or lemon juice and serve.

Onions

Chopped onions are a staple flavouring ingredient at the heart of so many dishes that it is easy to forget how delicious they can be in their own right. *See* notes on choosing (p. 91), storing (p. 91), preparation (p. 94) and all the cooking methods (pp. 95–100).

Onions do not brown well in a microwave, but if cooked with butter in an uncovered dish, sliced onions will caramelize: cook 500g onions with 60g butter for 30 minutes. Microwaving is also a useful way of cooking small whole onions without fat. Arrange them in one layer in a dish. Cook 250g onions with 100–125ml liquid in a covered dish for 8 minutes; for 500g use 250ml liquid and cook for 15 minutes.

Baby onions, their roots trimmed first, can also be blanched in a microwave before further cooking; this is also an easy way to avoid the fiddly business of peeling small raw onions. Put unpeeled onions in a dish, add 1 tbs water for 250g, cover and cook for 1 minute. For 500g, add 2 tbs water, cover and cook for 2 minutes. Slip off the skins when they are cool enough to handle.

Baked onions

This dish is capable of many variations, the recipe below using halved onions and taking nearly an hour to cook. It can also be made with small whole onions, which will cook in about half the time, or with sliced onions, tossed first in the oil and vinegar and spread in a dish with herbs scattered between them. These will take about 40 minutes to cook.

A couple of bay leaves can be added or used to replace the herbs given below. A wine or cider vinegar is fine, but gives less depth of flavour than sherry or balsamic vinegar.

For 4	1 tbs brown sugar	3 tbs olive oil
4 large onions, peeled	salt and freshly ground pepper	6 tbs water
1 tbs chopped rosemary or thyme or 8 fresh sage leaves	3 tbs sherry vinegar or balsamic vinegar	

Heat the oven to 200°C, 400°F, gas 6. Cut the onions in half, across, and put them cut side down in an ovenproof dish just big enough to hold them side by side. Sprinkle over the herbs and sugar and season with salt and pepper. Spoon over the vinegar, oil and water and bake, covered, for 20 minutes, then uncovered for a further 30–40 minutes. Baste the onions frequently. Add a little more water if the juices are reducing too quickly.

Roasted onions

A simple way of cooking onions in the oven is to roast them in their skins. They take a long time in a low oven, but can be cooked at the same time as a casserole. The onions are juicy and caramelize slightly in their skins.

For 4	salt and freshly ground pepper	chopped parsley or mint
4 large or 8 medium onions, unpeeled	olive oil or butter	

Heat the oven to 170°C, 325°F, gas 3. Put the whole onions in a baking tin and cook them, uncovered, for 2–2½ hours. Serve as they are (taking the skins off at the table) with salt and pepper, olive oil or butter and a small bowl of chopped herbs.

Roasted red onions

Red onions are best grilled or roasted; their flavour seems to dissipate with long slow cooking.

For 5–6	1kg red onions	6–8 tbs olive oil

Heat the oven to 200°C, 400°F, gas 6. Slice the onions thickly or cut them in wedges. Brush well with the oil, put them in a lightly oiled baking tin and roast for about 20 minutes, turning once. They should be crisp and slightly charred at the edges.

Onions in cream

For 6	¼ tsp ground mace	80ml double cream
1kg onions, peeled	salt and freshly ground pepper	30g butter

Heat the oven to 190°C, 375°F, gas 5. Blanch the onions, whole, in boiling water for 3–4 minutes. Drain thoroughly and chop them. Turn the onions into a buttered ovenproof dish, season with mace, salt and lots of black pepper. Stir in the cream and dot with the remaining butter. Bake for 25–30 minutes.

Onion tart

One of my favourite dishes is this simple onion tart from Alsace, taken several years ago from a local paper where it was called *Tarte paysanne*.

For 6	750g onions, sliced thinly	70g grated Gruyère
shortcrust pastry for a 28cm tart tin (p. 491)	2 eggs	salt and freshly ground pepper
100g butter	200ml double cream or crème fraîche	

Heat the oven to 190°C, 375°F, gas 5. Roll out the pastry thinly and line the tin. Prick it with a fork and follow the notes on blind baking on p. 490. Melt the butter in a heavy frying pan and cook the onions slowly, covered, for about 30 minutes. Stir from time to time to make sure they aren't sticking; the onions should be soft and pale gold. Beat the eggs with the cream, stir in the cheese and season. Put the onions into the tart, cover with the egg and cream mixture and bake for 30 minutes.

Parsnips

This most versatile of winter root vegetables can be fried, baked, boiled, steamed or braised. Its natural sweetness combines well with spices, chopped fennel leaves, mint, parsley or coriander and it benefits from being enriched with butter and cream. In *Acetaria*, John Evelyn recommends boiled parsnip with oil, vinegar and 'something of spicy' as a winter salad. *See* notes on choosing and storing (p. 91) and the various cooking methods (pp. 95–100). To microwave, cut parsnips into chunks, spread them in a dish, add 125ml liquid for 250g, cover and cook for 5 minutes; for 500g add 250ml liquid, cover and cook for 8 minutes.

Parsnips with ginger

The idea for this recipe also came from reading John Evelyn who uses this spicing in a root vegetable pudding.

For 4	100ml madeira or sherry	pinch nutmeg
500g parsnips, peeled		salt and freshly ground pepper
30g butter	3 pieces ginger in syrup, chopped finely	

Slice the parsnips thinly. Melt the butter and stew them gently for 10–15 minutes, turning them frequently. Do not let them brown or stick to the pan. Pour over the wine, stir in the ginger and season with nutmeg, salt and pepper. Cover the pan and simmer on very low heat for about 30 minutes. Check the liquid at intervals; the parsnips absorb quite a lot. Add a little more wine or water if necessary. Good with roast and casseroled meats.

Parsnip purée

Parsnips make an excellent purée, particularly if spiced with ground ginger, mace, coriander or cumin. Toasted pine nuts can be scattered over the purée. *See* the notes on purées and mashes, p. 96.

Parsnip crisps

These are made in the same way as celeriac crisps (p. 126).

Peas

Only if you grow your own are you likely to have fresher and better peas than small frozen peas (petits pois). What the greengrocers and supermarkets have for sale tends to be second best.

Petits pois à la polonaise

This is Edouard de Pomiane's name (in *Cooking with Pomiane*) for an early summertime dish of peas and carrots cooked together in butter. Use very fresh young peas and new carrots. The pale orange carrots contrast with the green of the peas and also give the dish their natural sweetness.

For 3–4	300g new carrots	100ml water
1.5kg young green peas (350–400g shelled)	90g butter	salt

Shell the peas. Remove the green tops off the carrots and rinse and brush them. Cut them in long strips and then crosswise into dice not much larger than the peas. Cook the peas and carrots together with half the butter, the water and salt to taste in a covered pan over low heat for 30 minutes. Taste to see if the vegetables are ready. To serve, add the remaining butter to the pan, let it melt and stir it into the vegetables.

Variation
- Add a bunch of small spring onions, cut off above the bulb.

Peas in saffron cream

For 6	1 tsp sugar	2 tsp water
60g butter	salt and freshly ground pepper	150ml double cream
4 tbs water		½ tsp flour
2.25kg peas (about 600g shelled)	10 saffron threads, crushed	1 tbs chopped dill or chives

Bring the butter and water to the boil. Put in the peas and sugar, and season with salt and pepper. Simmer, covered, over low heat for 8–10 minutes, until the peas are almost tender. If more than a few spoonfuls of liquid are left in the pan, leave it uncovered for the moisture to evaporate. Blend the saffron with 2 teaspoons of water and stir it into the cream with the flour. Pour the cream over the peas, as soon as it comes to the boil, stir in the dill or chives and serve the peas.

Spiced split pea purée

For 6	salt	1 tsp cumin seeds
300g yellow split peas	4 tbs oil	½ tsp chilli powder
¼ tsp turmeric	4 garlic cloves, peeled and chopped finely	3 tbs chopped coriander
about 1 litre water		

Rinse the split peas well and put them in a deep pan with the turmeric and 900ml unsalted water. Bring to the boil, reduce the heat and cook, covered, for about 1 hour. Check from time to time that there is enough water in the pan. If there is too much towards the end of cooking time, uncover the pan to allow it to evaporate. Salt the split peas and purée through a sieve or in a food processor. Heat the oil and fry, briefly, the garlic, cumin seeds and chilli powder. Add the garlic, spices, oil and coriander to the purée and stir.

Peppers

Thin-skinned tapering red peppers from Spain and Italy have much more flavour than the squat ones usually produced hydroponically in greenhouses. The same is true of the long pale green peppers imported from Turkey, and sometimes sold as white peppers. I seldom use dark green peppers because they can be indigestible.

The tapering red and green peppers do not need peeling, but the texture of the red, yellow and green peppers most usually available is improved by having the skin removed. Long slow cooking will loosen and remove them if you don't mind having little bits of skin in a dish.

The best way to remove the skin is to roast or grill the pepper until the outer skin is charred. Cut the pepper in half and put it, outer side up, in a hot oven or under the grill for 10–12 minutes. Alternatively put the whole pepper over a gas flame or barbecue, turning it until it is charred. Now put the charred and softened pepper in a covered pan or a plastic bag and leave it for 10 minutes or so, when the skin will peel away easily. Remove the core, seeds and ribs. Rinse the pepper under the cold tap to get rid of any black bits.

Baked peppers

The traditional Piedmontese recipe for these peppers fills them with garlic, a bit of anchovy and tomatoes. I have suggested an alternative here. I have at times also added pesto and tiny bits of sun-dried tomatoes to the original version, with success.

For 4–6	12 green olives, stoned and chopped	salt and freshly ground pepper
4 red or yellow peppers		
80–100g feta, crumbled	2 tbs finely chopped coriander	2–3 tomatoes, sliced
		2–3 tbs olive oil

Heat the oven to 180°C, 350°F, gas 4. Cut the peppers in half lengthways; remove the stalks, seeds and white pith. Put them on a baking tray and fill them with a mixture of the Feta, chopped olives and coriander. Season with pepper and a little salt if you wish (Feta is salty). Cover the filling with tomato slices. Drizzle over the olive oil and bake the peppers for 30 minutes; they should not be completely soft. Serve at room temperature.

Escalivada

This excellent Catalan dish of roast or grilled vegetables is now becoming popular outside Spain. If you can roast the aubergines and peppers on a barbecue or over a gas hob, the flavour will be improved.

For 6	2 tomatoes	4–5 tbs extra virgin olive oil
500g aubergines, not too big	salt and freshly ground pepper	
3 red peppers		

Prick the skins of the aubergines so the steam can escape during the cooking. Grill the aubergines and peppers, turning them regularly. The skins should get quite charred. After 10 minutes, put the tomatoes to grill until the skins split, then remove them. The aubergines and peppers are ready when they are soft. Put them into a covered pan until cool enough to handle. Remove all the skin, then cut or tear the aubergines and peppers into strips, making sure to discard the seeds from the peppers. Peel the tomatoes and cut into pieces. Arrange the aubergines and peppers on a serving dish, top with the pieces of tomato, season with salt and pepper and pour over the oil. Serve hot, warm or cold.

Variations

- In some versions of escalivada, onions and potatoes are added for which the cooking time will need to be much longer. Sometimes the vegetables are dressed with a vinaigrette with crushed garlic.
- You can also bake the vegetables in a moderate oven, 180°C, 350°F, gas 4.

Stuffed peppers

Dried porcini and morels combined with olives and sun-dried tomatoes give these peppers a rich flavour which complements the sweetness of ripe peppers. Choose peppers which can stand upright.

For 4	6–8 tbs fresh breadcrumbs	salt
5–6g dried porcini mushrooms	4 tbs coarsely chopped parsley or coriander	freshly ground pepper, or 1 tsp harissa*
4 dried morels	8–10 black olives, stoned and chopped	about 500ml tomato juice or passata (p. 378 or bought)
4 large red, orange or yellow peppers	4–6 pieces sun-dried tomato, chopped	

Cover the mushrooms with hot water and soak for 20 minutes. Heat the oven to 180°C, 350°F, gas 4. Turn the peppers over a gas flame until the skin has blackened. Leave them to cool, then peel off the skin. Slice the top off and reserve this to make a lid; remove seeds and white membranes. Stand the peppers upright in an earthenware dish which fits them as closely as possible.

Lift the mushrooms from the soaking liquid. Strain and reserve the liquid. Chop the porcini but leave the morels whole unless they are very large in which case cut them in half lengthways. Combine the porcini with the dry ingredients and add enough of the soaking liquid to make a moist mixture. Season with a little salt and rather more black pepper or harissa.

Fill the peppers with the mixture, putting the morels in the middle. Pour tomato juice or passata into the dish, to come to about three-quarters the way up the peppers. Pour a little juice over the tops of the peppers, then close them with their lids. Bake for 45 minutes.

Compote of tomatoes and peppers. *See* p. 168.

Potatoes

It is good to see so many varieties now on sale everywhere, but sad that information on how they will behave when cooked is still seldom provided. I remember many years ago looking with admiration at three potato stands next to each other in a Dutch market: each had half a dozen different varieties, each labelled with origin, soil-type and uses. *See* notes on preparing (p. 92) and all cooking methods (pp. 95–100).

In spite of all the claims that baked potatoes can be cooked in a microwave in a fraction of the time taken in the oven, the result is not the same. The texture of the potato is different and the skin is flabby. However, if you are going to use a microwave, prick the skin in several places and stand the potatoes on a layer of kitchen paper. One large potato will take 10 minutes, for 2 allow 13–15 minutes. New potatoes are more successful, cooked in one layer in a dish. For 500g add 2 tbs water, cover and cook for 10 minutes.

Mashed potatoes

The best varieties for boiling and mashing are Desirée, King Edward, Romano and Wilja. For suggestions about different types of mash, *see* p. 96.

Baked potatoes

Heat the oven to 220°C, 425°F, gas 7. Scrub the potatoes and bake for about 1¼ hours, or until soft. Cut the top of the potato open, or cut it in half, and add butter, soured cream, yogurt, olive oil or a dressing (pp. 360–1).

Roast potatoes

Firm-fleshed Cara, Maris Piper and Wilja are among the best potatoes for roasting. Take time to roast potatoes. To produce crisp potatoes, parboil them first for 10 minutes so that their surfaces are rough.

For 6	1 head of garlic	100ml olive oil
1kg potatoes	a few sprigs of thyme	

Heat the oven to 220°C, 425°F, gas 7. Peel the potatoes and parboil for 10 minutes. Drain thoroughly. Cut them in half or quarters, depending on size. Separate the cloves of garlic, but do not peel them. Put the potatoes in a roasting tin, distribute the garlic and thyme sprigs among the potatoes, pour over the oil and make sure all the potatoes are well coated. Put the tin into the oven and roast for about 40–45 minutes. Baste and turn the potatoes once or twice.

Variation

- To roast new potatoes, leave them unpeeled, parboil for 5 minutes and roast for 20–25 minutes.

New potatoes baked with garlic

Garlic and potatoes are an excellent combination, and if you can get new season's garlic to go with the potatoes, the dish will be even better. Any type of new potatoes can be used.

For 4	12 garlic cloves, unpeeled	thyme sprigs
500g small new potatoes, unpeeled	3 tbs olive oil or 50g butter, melted	3 tbs water

Heat the oven to 220°C, 425°F, gas 7. Put the potatoes and garlic in an earthenware casserole and pour over the oil or butter. Turn the vegetables around with your hands to coat them well. Tuck in a sprig or two of thyme. Add 3 tbs water. Cover the dish tightly and put it in the oven. After 20 minutes, turn the vegetables and check that nothing is sticking to the dish. Return the casserole to the oven and cook, uncovered, until the potatoes are ready, about 15–20 minutes more.

Variation

- Omit the oil or butter and bake the potatoes and garlic on a bed of coarse sea salt. Put 2 tbs of the salt in the bottom of the casserole and scatter another 2 tbs over the potatoes and garlic. Close tightly and bake. These potatoes will not need turning, and they will take about 50 minutes to 1 hour to cook.

Gratin dauphinois

This is perhaps the best-known French potato dish, and one of the best loved. It must be made with waxy potatoes such as Cara or Kipfler, and with double cream for the best results. It is a very rich dish, but everyone always eats more than you expect. Serve on its own or with roast meat.

For 4	1 garlic clove, peeled	50g butter
500g waxy potatoes	and crushed	salt and freshly ground
	300ml double cream	pepper

Heat the oven to 180°C, 350°F, gas 4. Slice the potatoes thinly. Put the garlic and cream into a small pan and heat slowly. Butter a gratin dish generously with half the butter and arrange the potatoes in layers, seasoning with salt and pepper. Pour over the cream, discarding the garlic. Dot the top with the remaining butter. Cover with foil and bake for 30 minutes. Remove the cover and return the dish to the oven for a further 20–30 minutes. Stick a flat skewer into the gratin to check that the potatoes are tender right through. If the top is not colouring, turn up the heat for the last 10 minutes to form a bubbling, golden crust. Let the gratin stand for a few minutes before serving because it will be very hot.

Variations

- A combination of celeriac and potatoes makes a delicious gratin.
- A few dried porcini (*see* p. 142), soaked for 20 minutes in warm water and then drained and chopped, can be put as a middle layer in the gratin.

Jansson's temptation

This was a dish I had read about but never eaten until it was served to me by a Swedish friend. It is quite wonderful, a simple peasant dish enriched with cream. Do not omit or reduce the amount of anchovies; they are essential to the dish and not overwhelming.

For 6–8	1kg waxy potatoes	14–16 anchovy fillets,
40g butter	(such as Cara or	rinsed (if very salty)
	Kipfler), peeled	and chopped
	1 large onion, sliced	250ml double cream

Heat the oven to 200°C, 400°F, gas 6 and butter a gratin dish with half the butter. Cut the potatoes into thin sticks. Arrange half of the potatoes in the dish then add the onion and anchovies as a second layer. Cover with the rest of the potatoes. Smooth the top and pour over the cream. Dot with the remaining butter. Bake in the oven for 50–60 minutes. If the top is browning too quickly, cover with foil. Leave the dish for a few minutes before serving because it will be very hot.

Swiss potato cake (Rösti)

For 4–6

1kg waxy potatoes (such as Cara or Kipfler), unpeeled

1 medium onion, peeled and chopped finely

salt and freshly ground pepper

50g butter

2 tbs vegetable oil

Parboil the potatoes in their skins for about 10–12 minutes. Drain, peel, and coarsely grate them. Mix thoroughly with the onion; season well. Heat half the butter and half the oil in a heavy frying pan. Put in the potato mixture and press it flat. Fry over medium heat until crisp and browned – about 10 minutes. Slide the cake out onto a plate. Heat the remaining butter and oil in the pan; fry the other side of the cake until crisp – somewhat less than 10 minutes. Serve at once.

Indian braised potato and aubergine

For 6

500g potatoes, peeled

500g aubergines

2 onions, peeled

6 tbs sunflower oil

¾ tsp fennel seeds

2 tsp garam masala*

¼ tsp chilli powder

2 tsp lemon juice

salt

150ml water

Cut the potatoes and aubergines into cubes and chop the onion coarsely. Heat the oil in a heavy pan and when it is hot, but not smoking, put in the fennel seeds and fry for a few seconds until they darken. Add the vegetables, lower the heat and fry, stirring and shaking the pan, for 10 minutes, then add the remaining spices, lemon juice and a little salt. Pour over 150ml water, cover the pan, lower the heat further and simmer for 15–20 minutes. Serve hot or at room temperature.

Pumpkin and squash

I have put pumpkins and squash together since they are of the same family and the recipes can be used interchangeably for pumpkins and the hard-skinned squash. Pretty pale green summer pattypans, better known to gardeners than to the supermarkets where they only make an occasional brief appearance, can be cooked in the same way as courgettes (pp. 133–4). *See also* notes on choosing and storing (p. 91) and cooking methods (pp. 95–100).

Thick-skinned acorn and butternut squash cook very well in a microwave. Cut in half and remove the seeds and fibre. Put a little ground ginger, mace or cinnamon in the cavity, and, if you wish, coat the flesh with 1 tbs honey or maple syrup mixed with 1 tsp lemon juice. Cover each piece tightly with microwave plastic film and put them in a dish. Cook 250g for 5 minutes, 500g for 8 minutes.

Gratin of pattypan squash

Use small pattypans since they lose their flavour by the time they get big.

For 4	60g day-old bread, crusts removed and soaked in water	a handful of chopped parsley
500g pattypans		100g grated Gruyère
salt and freshly ground pepper	2 garlic cloves, peeled and crushed in a mortar with a little salt	1 egg
		olive oil

Heat the oven to 220°C, 425°F, gas 7. Top and tail the pattypans and slice them thinly. Put them into a wide pan with a little salt and enough water to half cover them. Put the pan over medium heat and cook, shaking and stirring from time to time, until the water evaporates.

Squeeze the bread dry and mix it with the garlic, parsley and most of the cheese. Season with salt and pepper and mix in the egg. A fork is the best implement for mixing all this. Combine the pattypans with this mixture and pour it into an oiled gratin dish. Put the remaining cheese over the gratin, drizzle a bit more oil over the top, and bake for 30 minutes.

Squash purée

The hard-skinned squashes – acorn, butternut, kabocha – make wonderful light purées in varying shades of gold. They respond well to spicing – ginger, cardamom, cinnamon or cloves are all suitable – and to a dose of alcohol.

For 2	¼–½ tsp ground spice, see above	150–200ml double cream
1 medium squash		
salt and freshly ground pepper	60–80g butter	2 tbs rum or whisky

Cut the squash in half and remove the seeds, then bake in the oven at 190°C, 375°F, gas 5 for 30–45 minutes depending on the size and the variety. Alternatively, cook the squash in the microwave: see the instructions and timing above.

Scoop the flesh out of the skins and purée with salt and pepper, the spice of your choice and enough butter and cream to make a smooth purée. Stir in the rum or whisky. You can keep the purée hot in a low oven for 10–15 minutes.

Curried pumpkin in coconut milk

This is a south Indian dish which I learned from village women living in the beautiful backwaters of Kerala. The gourd they used was, of course, different, but our standard Hallowe'en pumpkin makes a good substitute. The Keralans use coconut oil for cooking, but a vegetable oil, such as sunflower, can be used, although it does not have the richness of coconut oil.

For 4	3 cardamom pods*, crushed	3 green chillies, seeded and sliced
1kg pumpkin, weight with skin	1 shallot, peeled and sliced finely	400ml can coconut milk (p.524)
2 tbs oil	2 garlic cloves, peeled and sliced finely	salt
½ tsp mustard seeds (p. 76)	a small piece of ginger, sliced finely	300g spinach, cut in a chiffonade*
a small piece of cinnamon		
2 cloves		

Cut the pumpkin flesh into cubes. Heat the oil in a large pan and fry the spices, shallot, garlic, ginger and chillies for a minute or two. Add the coconut milk and a little salt and bring to the boil. Put in the pieces of pumpkin and simmer for 10 minutes, then add the spinach, bring the coconut milk just to the boil, simmer for another 5 minutes or so, until the pumpkin is tender, and serve.

Barley and pumpkin casserole. See p. 204.

Sauté of girolles and pumpkin. See p. 144.

Radicchio

The red varieties of the chicory family may be tight and cabbage-shaped or have a looser form like a cos lettuce. They make good bitter salad leaves. They are best cooked only briefly. To grill, cut the heads in quarters or half, leaving them held together by the root, brush with olive oil and cook under a grill or on a griddle plate, turning occasionally until slightly browned and wilted.

Radicchio is also good in risotto: shred the leaves finely and add them to the pan after the onions have coloured; *see* p. 192 for the risotto recipe.

Wilted radicchio

For 4	3 tbs olive oil	salt and freshly ground pepper
2 heads radicchio	2 tbs wine vinegar or sherry vinegar	

Trim the radicchio and cut the leaves into strips. Heat the olive oil in a large pan and sauté them for 1 minute, then cover the pan and cook for 2–3 minutes more when the leaves will be wilted. Add the vinegar, season and serve at once with grilled or roast meats and game birds or as a separate vegetable course.

Spinach

Very young raw spinach with its crisp texture and bright colour is excellent for salads. Older leaves need to be cooked after thorough washing and discarding tough stalks. Spinach can be blanched and added to other dishes, or wilted in a little water or butter. It combines beautifully with eggs, cheese, nuts and pulses, makes a good filling for ravioli or pancakes and the perfect purée to serve with gammon or pork chops.

Spinach with chick peas

This combination of vegetables turns up in many cultures from Spain, across the Mediterranean and the Middle East to India.

For 6	1 tsp paprika	250g cooked chick peas (p. 80)
3 tbs olive oil	750g spinach, coarsely chopped	salt and freshly ground pepper
3 garlic cloves, peeled and chopped	2 tbs wine vinegar	150ml water
½ tsp ground coriander	2 tomatoes, peeled and chopped	
½ tsp ground cumin		

Heat the oil in a large pan and fry the garlic with the spices for 1 minute, then add the spinach. Stir to turn the spinach in the oil so that it wilts. Add the vinegar, tomatoes and chick peas. Season with salt and pepper and pour over the water. Stir to combine the contents of the pan and simmer for 20 minutes.

Spinach with raisins and pine nuts

Another dish found in many different food traditions. Some versions add garlic or leave out the raisins.

For 4	4 anchovy fillets, chopped	60g pine nuts
60g raisins		salt and freshly ground pepper
1kg spinach	4 tbs chopped parsley	
	100ml olive oil	large pinch nutmeg

Soak the raisins in hot water for 15 minutes. If the spinach leaves are very large cut them in half. Shake them well after washing, but leave some water clinging to them. Pound together the anchovies and parsley. Heat the oil in a large pan and cook the parsley and anchovy mixture over low heat. Add the spinach, drained raisins, pine nuts and seasonings. Mix well and cook for 10 minutes, stirring occasionally. Serve hot.

Spiced spinach in yogurt

Spinach and yogurt is another combination that occurs in many cuisines, from Greece and Turkey across to India. The spicing varies from country to country, rice is sometimes added to the dish and in India it is often made with paneer, the local soft white cheese. The quantity of yogurt used varies as well: in India it tends to be little, in the Middle East rather more, and in Turkey some versions use almost as much yogurt as spinach.

For 4	pinch of nutmeg	1 small onion, peeled and chopped finely
1½ tsp ground coriander	1 green chilli, seeded and sliced	250ml thick yogurt
½ tsp ground ginger	1kg spinach	2 garlic cloves, peeled and crushed to a paste with a little salt
¼ tsp chilli powder	salt	
	2 tbs sunflower oil	

Heat a small heavy frying pan and briefly dry-roast the coriander and ginger. Tip them into a bowl and combine them with the chilli powder, nutmeg and green chilli. Put the spinach into a large pan of boiling water and cook for 4–5 minutes. Drain, and squeeze out all the water. Chop it to a rough purée and season with salt. Heat the oil in a large pan and fry the onion. When the onion turns golden add the spices and stir to blend.

Put in the spinach, stir to mix thoroughly and cook over low heat for 5 minutes. Mix the yogurt and garlic. Remove the pan from the heat, stir in the yogurt and serve.

Spinach filo pie. *See* p. 108.

Sweetcorn (corn-on-the-cob)

Corn-on-the-cob is the only cereal crop native to the Americas (where it is known simply as 'corn'). From there come many good corn dishes, not surprisingly, since it is a basic food that nourished native Americans for thousands of years and still fills that role today for all Americans from Chile to Canada. It was adopted more slowly in Europe than most other New World food plants, probably because it had to compete with our wheat, barley, oats and rye. We are now all familiar with tortillas, the flat Mexican corn bread, and nacho chips, not to mention cornflakes. In South American dishes, corn is often cooked with tomatoes, chillies, potatoes, beans and pumpkins, all indigenous ingredients.

See notes on choosing (p. 91) and the various cooking methods (pp. 95–100) and the use of corn in baking (pp. 199–200). To remove the kernels from the cob, cut down from the tip to the stalk with a sharp knife, scraping well to get all the milky juice.

Corn and mushrooms with chillies

For 4		
3 tbs vegetable oil	500g tomatoes, peeled and chopped; or a 400g can chopped tomatoes	300g corn kernels, fresh, frozen or canned
2 onions, peeled and chopped		400g mushrooms, halved or quartered
3 green chillies, seeded and chopped	salt and freshly ground pepper	2 tbs chopped coriander
1 garlic clove, peeled and chopped		

Heat the oil in a large pan and sauté the onions until golden. Stir in the chillies and garlic and sauté for another minute, then add the tomatoes and season. Cook for 3–4 minutes until the tomato mixture starts to thicken, then add the corn and mushrooms. Stir to mix everything together, and simmer for about 5 minutes, until the corn and mushrooms are tender and most of the liquid has evaporated. Stir in the coriander and serve.

Corn and prawn fritters

I first ate these corn and prawn fritters in an Indonesian restaurant in Holland and eventually tracked down a recipe in an old Dutch Indonesian cookery book. They are quick and easy to make. Serve as a snack or with rice, stir-fried vegetables (p. 117, p. 119) or a sambal (p. 384).

For 4–6	3 spring onions, chopped	½ tsp ground cumin
350g corn kernels, fresh, frozen or canned	1 stick celery, chopped	½ tsp turmeric
250g large cooked prawns, shelled weight	1 red chilli, sliced	3 tbs plain flour
	1 tsp ground coriander	1 egg
2 garlic cloves, peeled		oil for frying

Very fresh corn scraped straight from the cob can be used as it is; thaw frozen corn or drain canned. If the fresh corn kernels look a little tired, cook them in boiling water for 3–4 minutes and drain well. Put the prawns (cut into pieces if they are very large), garlic, onions, celery, chilli and spices into a food processor and pulse 2 or 3 times. Add the corn and pulse 2 or 3 times until all is coarsely chopped. Sift the flour and make a batter with the beaten egg. Mix in the other ingredients. Add a little water if the mixture is too dry. Pour a little oil into a frying pan and when it is hot, but not smoking, drop in spoonfuls of the batter. Fry for 2–3 minutes on each side until brown and drain the fritters on kitchen paper. Serve hot or warm.

Pastel de choclo

Choclo is the Spanish American word for an ear of corn, and versions of this dish are found throughout the Andean countries. This one with chicken in the filling is from Bolivia.

For 6	60g raisins	1 tsp ground chilli
6–8 corn cobs (about 750g)	2 tbs sunflower oil	100g black olives
80–100ml milk	2 onions, peeled and chopped	1kg cooked and boned chicken, cut into small pieces
60g butter	2 tomatoes, peeled, seeded and chopped	
salt and freshly ground pepper	1 tsp oregano, chopped	2 hardboiled eggs, chopped (optional)
2 eggs	1 tsp ground cumin	1 egg white

Heat the oven to 200°C, 400°F, gas 6. Grate the corn from the cobs, or take off whole kernels and blitz them once or twice in the food processor with a little of the milk to keep a coarse texture. Melt the butter and heat the corn, seasoned with salt and pepper, then stir in 80ml milk. Beat in the eggs one at a time, over very low heat, making sure that the mixture does not boil. If it becomes too thick, add a little more milk. Set aside.

Soak the raisins in warm water for 10 minutes. Heat the oil and sauté the onion until golden, then add the tomato, oregano, cumin, chilli, salt and pepper. Drain the raisins and stir them in with the olives. Remove from the heat and mix thoroughly with the pieces of chicken and hardboiled egg, if using. Put a thin layer of the corn mixture in a greased soufflé dish, cover with the chicken mixture and top with the rest of the corn. Whisk the egg white lightly and brush the top with it. Bake in the oven for 50 minutes to 1 hour. The top should be lightly browned. Serve hot.

Sweet potatoes

The most common sweet potatoes available in Britain are pink-skinned with white flesh and brown-skinned with deep orange flesh. The texture of the white flesh is often dry whereas the orange flesh is moist and sweet. Although they are not related to potatoes, sweet potatoes can be cooked in the same ways. They boil, bake and roast well, make a good mash (p. 96) and terrific crisps.

Sweet potato casserole

For 6	salt and freshly ground pepper	4 tbs sweet wine or port
1.5kg sweet potatoes		
80g light brown sugar	grated rind of 1 unwaxed orange and juice of 2	60g butter
large pinch allspice		
¼ tsp cinnamon		

Heat the oven to 200°C, 400°F, gas 6, and bake the potatoes until soft, about 45–50 minutes. Lower the heat to 170°C, 325°F, gas 3. Peel and slice the potatoes and make layers in a shallow buttered ovenproof dish. Sprinkle with the sugar, spices, salt and pepper, and grated orange rind. Spoon over the wine and orange juice. Dot with butter and bake for about 25 minutes until the top is golden.

Sweet potato crisps

Follow the instructions for Celeriac Crisps, p 126.

Roasted winter vegetables

Use a mixture of winter vegetables depending on what you like and what is available. A suggested list follows. You will need about 2–2.5kg for 6 people if other dishes are being served, 3kg if this is the main course (weight before preparation in both cases).

For 6		
1–2 sweet potatoes	300–400g pumpkin or squash flesh	4 tbs olive oil
1–2 parsnips	300–400g celeriac flesh	salt and freshly ground pepper
2–3 small turnips	1–2 fennel bulbs	1 tbs chopped dried herbs – oregano, thyme, savory, rosemary
2–3 carrots	3–4 onions	
3–4 Jerusalem artichokes	6 garlic cloves	

Heat the oven to 200°C, 400°F, gas 6. Peel all the vegetables, then cut them all, except the garlic, into slices or wedges of similar size. Leave the garlic whole. Grease a baking dish into which the vegetables will fit without being crowded and heat the oil in it on the stove. Add the vegetables, turning them in the oil, season them and sprinkle over the herbs. Transfer the dish to the oven and roast the vegetables for 45 minutes to 1 hour, turning them occasionally. Serve with mustard fruits (mostarda di Cremona) or a tomato chutney (p. 511).

Tofu

Made from soy beans, tofu or bean curd is extremely high in protein, low in carbohydrates, calories and cholesterol. It has only a faint flavour of its own, which makes it a versatile ingredient since it readily absorbs the flavours of foods cooked with it. Tofu is important in the diet of Japan, China and parts of south-east Asia. It is eaten in soups, in one-pot dishes, grilled and fried. It can be bought from most supermarkets and oriental shops. Fresh tofu will keep for up to 5 days and must be refrigerated. It keeps best in water, which should be changed daily. Some brands can be kept in the cupboard and only need to be refrigerated after opening; dried tofu is also available.

Firm or 'cotton' tofu is most common. It can be grilled, fried, poached or braised.

When it is to be fried or added to salads, tofu needs to be pressed before using to remove excess water: wrap the block in kitchen paper, stand it on a plate, put another plate on top and leave for 30 minutes to 1 hour. Tofu is quite fragile and it needs to be cut and stirred with care or it will break.

'Silk' tofu, as the name suggests, is soft, fine textured and delicate; it should not be pressed. It is used for soup.

Tofu stir-fried with vegetables

The vegetables can be changed according to what looks best when you are shopping: shredded Chinese cabbage or mustard greens, sliced leeks, bamboo shoots, water chestnuts can all be used. If you don't want to use oyster sauce, use more soy sauce and rice wine.

For 2	80g mange-tout or snow peas	1 tbs rice wine* or dry sherry
250g firm tofu, pressed (*see* above)	80g oyster mushrooms, sliced	½ tsp sugar
4 tbs sunflower oil	1 tbs soy sauce	2 tbs oyster sauce
2 sticks celery, sliced		2 spring onions, sliced finely

Cut the tofu in 3cm cubes. Heat a wok and add 3 tbs oil. Fry the tofu in batches until the pieces are golden on all sides, about 3–4 minutes. Drain well on kitchen paper. Pour off the oil and wipe the wok clean. Heat the remaining oil and stir-fry the celery, mange-tout and mushrooms for 3–4 minutes until cooked. Combine the soy sauce, rice wine, sugar and oyster sauce and add to the wok with the fried tofu. Stir-fry carefully. As soon as the tofu is heated through and the ingredients are mixed, add the spring onions and serve.

Braised tofu

For 4	100g canned straw mushrooms or button mushrooms	1 tbs soy sauce
300g firm tofu		2 tsp sugar
4 tbs oil	300g leeks, cut in very thin slices	100ml stock or water
2 garlic cloves, peeled and chopped	1 tsp cornflour	1 tbs chopped coriander
2cm ginger, chopped		

Press the tofu (*see* above) to get rid of excess water, then cut it into 3cm cubes. Heat a wok, add 3 tbs oil and fry the tofu in batches until golden, 3–4 minutes. Drain thoroughly. Wipe the wok clean. Heat the last tbs oil and stir-fry the garlic and ginger. Add the mushrooms and leeks and toss for 2–3 minutes. Combine the cornflour, soy sauce, sugar and stock and pour over the vegetables. Let the liquid come to the boil, lower the heat, cover and simmer for 5 minutes. Return the tofu to the pan, simmer 5 minutes more, then scatter over the coriander and serve.

Tomatoes

Life without tomatoes may have become unthinkable, but life with only the tasteless tomatoes on most supermarket shelves does not bear thinking about either. In late summer, Greek and Turkish and sometimes small shops in the country have riper, well-flavoured tomatoes that may be misshapen but are likely to taste better than anything bought from the supermarket. Even the 'plum' and 'vine' tomatoes now in vogue are not as good as they should, and could, be – they are grown for long shelf-life, uniformity and colour with scant attention to flavour. We often rely on canned tomatoes, passata* and tubes of tomato purée to boost or replace our commercial watery tomatoes. Sun-dried tomatoes from southern Italy are intensely flavoured; make sure to chop them finely and use sparingly. If you buy them dry rather than in oil, soak them before using to get rid of some of the salt. Semi-dried (*mi-cuit*) tomatoes from France have a rich taste and softer texture.

See notes on storing (p. 91) and all cooking methods (pp. 95–100).

To peel tomatoes, pour boiling water over them, leave for 1 minute, drain and the skin will come off easily. If you leave the tomatoes longer in water the texture suffers.

To remove the seeds, cut the tomato in half around the middle and squeeze each half gently to get rid of the seeds. Do this over a bowl if you want to use the seeds and juice, over a bowl and a sieve if you only want the juice.

Slow-roasted plum tomatoes

Roasting concentrates the flavour of tomatoes, but do start off with the best flavoured ones you can find. Serve these tomatoes with cold meats or pâté, as part of a mixed hors-d'oeuvre, on bruschetta, in salad, or to accompany grilled meat, poultry or fish.

| For 4 | salt and freshly ground pepper | 4 tbs olive oil |
| 500g ripe plum tomatoes | | 2 tbs balsamic vinegar |

Heat the oven to 150°C, 300°F, gas 2. Cut the tomatoes in half lengthways and put them in an ovenproof dish face up. Season with salt and pepper and drizzle over two-thirds of the oil and vinegar. Put them in the oven and roast for 2 hours. When you take them out drizzle over the rest of the oil and vinegar and leave them to cool; they are best eaten lukewarm. They will also keep in the refrigerator for 1–2 days; bring them back to room temperature before serving.

Compote of tomatoes and peppers

For 6	8 large ripe tomatoes	2 tbs chopped parsley
2 slices day-old bread, crusts removed	2 red peppers, peeled (p. 151)	2 tbs chopped basil
olive oil	salt and freshly ground pepper	1 tsp capers

Heat the oven to 220°C, 425°F, gas 7. Brush the bread lightly on both sides with olive oil and put the slices on a baking tray. Bake for 4–5 minutes until lightly golden, then take the tray from the oven. When the bread has cooled down a little, crumble it coarsely with a rolling pin or in a food processor. Put the crumbs in a bowl and set aside.

Lightly oil a shallow ovenproof dish of 18–20cm diameter. Slice the tomatoes thickly and slice the peppers in strips, removing their seeds. Place a layer of tomatoes in the dish, season and add some of the herbs. Make a new layer of peppers, then another of tomatoes and herbs. Continue until all the vegetables are used, finishing with a tomato layer. Drizzle oil over the vegetables, scatter the capers over the top and then the breadcrumbs. Bake in the oven for 20–25 minutes. Serve cold.

Tomato, basil and olive tart

A good summer tart capable of variations. I have made it spreading tapenade (p. 28) on the base, interspersed slices of roasted, peeled red peppers with the tomatoes, added chopped anchovies to the shallots, replaced the shallots with garlic. Make sure the tomatoes are ripe.

For 3–4

1 sheet frozen puff pastry, thawed

3 tbs pesto (p. 346)

2 shallots, peeled and chopped finely

5–6 ripe tomatoes, sliced

16 small black olives

2 tsp caster sugar

salt and freshly ground pepper

2 tbs olive oil

1 tbs shredded basil leaves

Heat the oven to 220°C, 425°F, gas 7. Unroll the pastry onto a lightly floured baking sheet, prick with a fork and bake for 8 minutes. Remove it from the oven and let it cool slightly. Reduce the oven temperature to 200°C, 400°F, gas 6. Spread the pesto over the pastry, leaving a narrow clear rim. Scatter over the shallots. Arrange the tomato slices in overlapping circles. Scatter over the olives and season with sugar, salt and pepper. Drizzle over 1 tbs oil and bake for 35–40 minutes. Take the tart from the oven, scatter over the basil and sprinkle with the remaining oil.

Turnips and swedes

I confess I have little enthusiasm for these roots of the cabbage family, not even the tiny white and purple turnips. When I cook them I combine them with potatoes, either in a mash (p. 96), in a gratin of the type given below or in a mixed vegetable winter soup or dish of roasted vegetables. It is best to choose small to medium swedes: they have a better flavour and are not woody. To microwave, cut into 1cm dice or slice thinly, put in a dish with 4 tbs water for 500g, cover and cook for 12 minutes.

Turnip and potato gratin

For 4

300g potatoes, peeled

300g turnips, peeled

30g butter

½ tsp ground cardamom*

salt and freshly ground pepper

200ml double cream

1 garlic clove, peeled and crushed

60g grated Gruyère or Cheddar

Heat the oven to 180°C, 350°F, gas 4. Parboil the potatoes for 15 minutes and the turnips for 12. Drain them and rinse with cold water, then slice them. Using half the butter, grease a small gratin dish and put in a layer of turnips. Season with a little cardamom, salt and pepper, and follow with a layer of potatoes. Repeat the layers until all the vegetables are used. Heat the cream gently with the garlic, then strain it over the vegetables. Sprinkle over the cheese, dot the top with the rest of the butter and bake for 20–30 minutes until the vegetables are tender and the top crusty.

Vegetable stews

There are a number of vegetable stews which all make good main course dishes. They come from different parts of the world and would be served with rice, bread, couscous, bulgur, beans or potatoes, depending on their origin. Follow your own inclination when choosing your accompaniment.

Summer vegetable ragoût

For 8

8 shallots, peeled and sliced

4 whole cloves new garlic, peeled

50ml olive oil

hearts of 3 small fennel bulbs, quartered

6 small carrots, cut in half or in quarters, lengthways

4 small globe artichokes, cleaned, quartered and choke removed (p. 102)

400ml water

salt and freshly ground pepper

3 courgettes, cut in quarters lengthways

3 young leeks, sliced

100g shelled peas (approx. 400g original weight)

100g shelled broad beans (approx. 450g original weight)

200g asparagus, cut in short lengths

leaves from a sprig of tarragon

2 tbs chopped parsley

15 basil leaves, torn

1 tbs balsamic vinegar

Sauté the shallots and garlic in the oil over medium heat. When lightly coloured, add the fennel, carrots and artichokes. Cook gently for 3–4 minutes, then add the water and season. Bring the open pan to the boil, lower the heat and simmer for 10 minutes. Add all the remaining vegetables, the tarragon and parsley; simmer for another 10 minutes, then test the vegetables – they should remain firm but not half raw. When they are ready, stir in the basil and check the seasoning. The liquid should be reduced to a few spoonfuls. Turn all into a serving dish and sprinkle over the balsamic vinegar.

Turkish vegetable stew

Versions of this stew are also found throughout the Balkan countries, once part of the Ottoman empire.

For 6–8

2 onions, peeled and chopped

3 courgettes, sliced

1 medium aubergine, cubed

100g okra, stalked but pod intact

200g green beans, cut in 2 or 3 pieces

200g shelled peas (approx 750g original weight)

1 green pepper, cut in squares

500g tomatoes, peeled and chopped or a 400g can

a large bunch of parsley, chopped

2 tsp paprika

salt

6 tbs sunflower oil

Heat the oven to 190°C, 375°F, gas 5. Put all the vegetables and parsley into a wide, deep ovenproof casserole. Season with paprika and salt and pour over the oil. Mix all the ingredients thoroughly, cover and put the dish in the oven and bake for 1 hour. Remove the lid, check the progress of the vegetables and cook for a further 15–30 minutes. Serve hot.

Tunisian vegetable stew

North African markets have tempting, wonderful displays of vegetables and spices. Both are used extensively in different types of stew. This one is adapted from Edmond Zeitou's *250 recettes classiques de cuisine tunisienne*. Serve it with couscous (p. 202).

For 8

4 tbs sunflower oil

1 tsp black peppercorns, freshly ground

1 tbs paprika

½ tsp cinnamon

½ tsp ground coriander

1 tsp harissa*

2 onions, peeled and chopped coarsely

4 garlic cloves, peeled and crushed

4 tomatoes, peeled and chopped

2 tbs tomato purée

1 litre water

3 carrots, peeled and sliced thickly

3 small white turnips, peeled and quartered

4 courgettes, sliced thickly

2 red peppers, cut in squares

3 stalks celery, sliced thickly

4 potatoes, peeled and cut in chunks

120g chick peas, soaked overnight, or 1 can chick peas, rinsed

a large handful of coriander leaves, chopped

salt

Heat the oil in a large pan, put in the spices, harissa, onion and garlic and stir-fry over medium heat for 2–3 minutes, then add the tomatoes and tomato purée and fry for a few minutes more. Add 1 litre of unsalted water, all the vegetables and the coriander. Bring to the boil, then simmer, covered, until the vegetables are cooked, about 45 minutes. Add salt to taste.

172   *Couscous with grilled vegetables See* p. 202

Avial

I ate this dish several times on a visit to the Malabar coast of India and always found it delicious. You can use any mixture of root and green vegetables, but not leaves. Potatoes, pumpkin, gourd, okra, aubergine, beans – even bananas – were all used there; back in England I've used carrots, peas, courgettes and peppers as well. Onions are essential. In India the dish is finished with coconut oil but I've used sunflower oil here.

For 6	4 sprays of curry leaves (p. 257), preferably fresh	4–6 green chillies
1.5kg mixed vegetables		1 tsp cumin seeds
2 onions, peeled	120g fresh grated coconut or 60g unsweetened desiccated coconut (*see* below)	200ml thick yogurt
pinch turmeric		salt
		2 tbs sunflower oil

If you are using desiccated coconut soak it in 120ml water for 1 hour before cooking, then drain it.

Clean all the vegetables – peeling and shelling as required – and cut them, where necessary, into fairly small pieces. Put them in a pan with the turmeric and enough boiling water to half cover the vegetables. Put in the curry leaves, cover the pan tightly and simmer very gently so that the vegetables steam, until just cooked. Put the coconut, chillies and cumin into a food processor and whiz until finely ground, adding a little water if needed. Mix this paste into the yogurt and stir into the vegetables, taking care not to break them. Add salt to taste. Simmer over very low heat for 5 minutes for the flavours to blend. Pour over 2 tbs oil, stir it through and serve at once.

Malay vegetables in coconut milk

Three or four vegetables would normally be used for this type of stew; choose from aubergine, green beans, okra, Chinese cabbage, spring greens, courgettes, bamboo shoots, carrots, pumpkin, potatoes.

For 4	1 small onion, peeled and chopped	600ml coconut milk (p. 524)
500g mixed vegetables	1 garlic clove, peeled and chopped	2 lime leaves*
1 stalk lemon grass*		salt
2 red chillies, seeded and sliced	1 small piece ginger, peeled and chopped	

Cut the peeled vegetables into similar small-sized pieces. Discard the outer layer of the lemon grass and, using the bottom third only, slice it finely. Pound together, or whiz in the food processor, the chillies, onion, garlic, lemon grass and ginger to make a paste. Heat half the coconut milk until the oil starts to separate, then stir in the paste until the aromas rise from it. Add the vegetables and lime leaves, and season with salt. Cook for 10 minutes, then add the rest of the coconut milk and cook until the vegetables are tender.

Thai vegetable curry

The red curry paste used for this curry can be bought, but it is not difficult to make your own, and what is not used for this recipe will keep in a jar in the refrigerator for 2–3 weeks. Select the vegetables according to what looks best when you shop.

For 4–6	4 lime leaves*	2 tsp chopped galangal root* or ginger
1 tbs red curry paste (*see* below)	2 large red chillies, seeded and sliced finely	2tsp chopped lemon grass*, using bottom third only
1 tbs sunflower oil	1 tbs fish sauce (p. 520)	
600ml coconut milk	10 basil leaves	1 tsp chopped coriander
200g green beans, cut in short lengths	**For the curry paste**	2 tsp coriander seeds
3 courgettes, sliced	5–8 red chillies, fresh or dried, seeded	1 tsp kaffir (*see* below) or ordinary unwaxed lime peel
200g broccoli or cauliflower florets	2 shallots, peeled and chopped finely	
200g bamboo shoots, sliced	2 garlic cloves, peeled and chopped finely	1 tbs sunflower oil (optional)
1 small aubergine, cubed		

First blend together all the ingredients for the curry paste. The easiest way is to put everything in a blender or food processor, adding the oil if necessary to lubricate the spices. If you do not like very hot dishes, reduce the number of chillies. Kaffir limes are knobbly round fruits from the same tree as lime leaves; only the peel is used in cooking. Although the leaves are now in many supermarkets, the fruits are seldom found; you can use ordinary lime peel instead, but it won't taste quite as strong.

Fry a tablespoon of the curry paste in the oil for a minute or two until it is very aromatic and oil seeps around the edges. Add the coconut milk. Stir in the vegetables and flavourings and bring to the boil. Simmer until the vegetables are tender – this will take 15–20 minutes depending on how well cooked you like your vegetables.

Variation

Vegetable and tofu curry Add 350g pressed tofu (p. 166), cut into 2cm cubes. Before starting to fry the oil and curry paste, heat 100ml oil in the pan and fry the cubes of tofu in a single layer for 3–5 minutes, turning to brown them on all sides. Drain on kitchen paper and repeat with remaining pieces if necessary. Pour off all but 1 tbs oil from the pan and continue with the recipe. Keep the tofu aside and add 5 minutes before the curry is ready.

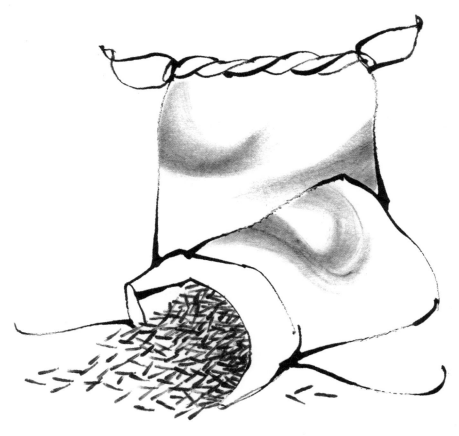

Rice and other grains

Grains provide the world's staple foods. Rice is the main food crop in the hot humid regions of Asia; wheat and barley prefer a temperate climate and do not flourish in very cold or dry, arid places. Rye, oats and buckwheat withstand the cold and are the staples of northern and east European cooking; millet withstands desert conditions and is cultivated in those regions of Africa and Asia. Maize or corn, native to the Americas, has now been adopted all over the world. The Americas have two other native grains that are less well known: the extremely nutritious quinoa that grows at high altitudes in the Andes, and 'wild rice', not a rice but another grain, still gathered by the North American Indians but now also grown commercially.

Rice

Choosing

It is important to understand the different types of rice so you can buy the right kind for the food you want to prepare. All good-quality rice looks vibrant and glistens slightly, so do not buy anything that looks dull. Avoid broken grains. Good-quality rice should have a pleasant aroma, be resistant to splitting during cooking and be agreeable to chew. It also needs little salt.

Brown rice

This may be short or long grain, and is rice which has undergone minimal milling and still retains the bran layer. It has a nutty flavour and retains more vitamins, minerals and fibre than white rice. It is always chewy.

White rice

This may be short or long grain, and is rice which has been milled to remove hull and bran, leaving a translucent polished grain. It is easier to digest than brown rice.

Long grain rice

Known as Indica, this is slender, and has a high percentage of amylose starch which keeps the grains separate after cooking. It is grown in China, Iran, India, Thailand and the USA. Most Chinese rice is long grain, but not as dry as basmati, which is difficult to eat with chopsticks. Chinese black rice, a recent arrival on the market, keeps its colour well and has a pleasant, light texture. Long grain rice is used for pilafs and salads, and for rice served on its own as an accompaniment.

Basmati has a fragrant flavour and when cooked is light and dry with separate grains.

Jasmine or *fragrant Thai* is also aromatic but has a softer texture than basmati.

Medium and short grain rice

Called Japonica, this rice is mostly grown in northern China, Japan, the USA, Italy and Spain. Medium grain rice has a short grain but is not round; short grain is almost round; both are slightly sticky and cling when cooked, because of the amount of amylopectin, another starch, in their composition. These rices absorb up to three times their weight in liquid and the starch which is released gives the dish a creamy texture. Short and medium grain rice are used for croquettes, timbales and puddings.

Bomba from Calasparra in Murcia is the best Spanish variety and is used for paella, baked rice dishes and stews.

Risotto rice The Italians use *arborio* widely; two other varieties to note are *carnaroli* which keeps its shape well and is hard to overcook, and *vialone nano*, with large grains which makes a very creamy risotto.

Red rice In recent years there has been a revival of rice growing in the Camargue in the Rhone delta and a medium grain red rice is now exported. Not as nutty as brown rice, it has a more pronounced flavour than white rice.

Glutinous or sticky rice

Grown in Japan and south-east Asia, this rice is very high in amylopectin. It is usually short grain, although a black long grain variety is now available from Thailand, which stays chewy when cooked and has separate grains. Japanese medium grain rice absorbs less water than some others and is slightly less sticky. In a few regions glutinous rice is eaten on a daily basis, but it is mainly used for snacks and sweets and most notably for sushi. It is also the rice from which rice-based alcohols and wines are made. Although called glutinous, sticky rice is gluten-free like all rices.

Parboiled rice

This is usually long grain rice that has been partly cooked and should be cooked further according to the instructions on the packet. The grains remain moist and separate after cooking.

Instant rice

This is rice that has been cooked and then dried, and need only be rehydrated to eat. Follow the instructions on the packet.

Storing

White rice will keep indefinitely. Brown rice can get infested if it is old or if stored in humid conditions for too long. It should keep for up to 1 year in a cool dry place, and you can freeze it. Cooked rice will keep for up to 3 days tightly covered in the refrigerator.

Quantities

Quantities are difficult to give because rice lovers eat large amounts compared to people who eat it seldom. 500g will soak up 650ml water or more and should feed 4–6 people.

Preparing rice

Long grain and glutinous rice should be washed before cooking, except par-boiled rice which is cooked straight from the packet. Many rices are soaked from 30 minutes to several hours, depending on the cooking method. Pre-soaked rice needs less water for cooking. Italian and Spanish rice are used dry. *See* information in the recipes.

Cooking methods

All rice is cooked in water, stock or milk to make it edible. It may also be lightly fried before being simmered or steamed. It is important not to overcook rice; rice cooked longer than necessary softens and splits open. The right amount of water to rice, the cooking time and the intensity of the heat are all important.

Simmering

The simplest way to cook long grain rice is to boil it in lots of water. Wash the rice, bring a large pan of water to the boil and tip in the rice. Stir well to stop the grains sticking to the pan, bring back to the boil and then simmer, uncovered, until the rice is ready. It should retain a slight bite and be tender, not split and mushy. Brown rice will take about 50 minutes to 1 hour, white rice 15–20 minutes. Taste to see if the rice is ready and drain it. Put it into a warm dish and toss with bits of butter or a little olive or sunflower oil. Use forks (wooden ones are best) to toss it, spoons tend to crush the grains.

Steaming

Sometimes called the absorption method of cooking rice, this depends on having the correct proportions of rice and water. The water is absorbed by the time the rice is cooked. Use a heavy-based pan to reduce the risk of the rice sticking to the bottom, and make sure it is big enough. Measure rice and cooking liquid by *volume*. It doesn't matter what sort of container you use to measure, but use the same one for rice and cooking liquid. The basic proportions are one measure of rice to two of water, but this may vary slightly according to the age and type of rice, the shape and size of the pan. Put the rice in the pan, cover with cold water, swish it around with your fingers, drain into a sieve and rinse until the water runs clear. Put the rice back in the pan with the correct measure of cold water, bring to the boil and stir once. Reduce the heat to a simmer, stir briefly and cover the pan. Leave for 15–20 minutes for white rice, 50 minutes to 1 hour for brown. Camargue red rice is also cooked by this method, and needs about 40 minutes. When the rice is cooked there will be small steam holes over the surface and all the water will be absorbed. Check the pan towards the end of cooking time. The rice should be tender but still have a slight bite. Because types of rice vary you may need to allow a bit longer, or use a little more or a little less water, as necessary. If you buy the same rice regularly you will soon know just how much liquid it needs. Fluff the rice with wooden forks before serving.

Note
An electric rice cooker cooks by this method, and will cook white, brown and glutinous rice. Follow the manufacturer's instructions about using it.

Soaked and steamed rice
This is my preferred way of cooking basmati and jasmine rice. Use 1 measure of rice to 1¼ measures of cooking water. Rinse the rice under running water, put it into a bowl, pour over hot water, stir so that the grains don't clump together and leave to soak for about 30 minutes. Drain it and rinse under the cold tap until the water runs clear. Bring the measured water to the boil, put in the soaked rice, bring the water to the boil again and immediately cover it and transfer to the lowest possible heat. Use a heat diffuser if necessary. White rice will be almost ready in 12–15 minutes; there will be steam holes in the surface. At this point you can drizzle melted butter or oil over the rice if you wish, or leave it plain. Take a clean folded tea towel and put it under the lid, folding up the corners so that it is not in contact with the heat source. Leave the pan on the very low heat for another 5 minutes, then turn off the heat and leave it undisturbed for at least 5 minutes. It can also be left for up to 15 minutes and will stay hot. Turn the rice out with a wooden fork. It will be light and very dry because the tea towel absorbs any excess moisture.

Japanese rice is always soaked for about 30 minutes, usually in cold water, and then cooked this way.

Microwaving long grain rice
Use 2 measures of water to 1 of rice. Rinse the rice in water until it runs clear. Put the rice in a suitable container and pour over twice the volume of hot water. Add salt. Microwave, uncovered, on full power for 10 minutes for 3 cups (about 500g) rice. Remove the dish from the oven – the contents will still be quite liquid – and add a little oil. Now cover the dish and cook for a further 2½–3 minutes. For a smaller amount of rice (1 cup, about 175g), allow about 4 minutes for the first cooking and 2–2½ for the second.

Fluff with a fork before serving.

Cooking glutinous rice

Glutinous rice is always soaked, often for several hours, and then steamed over boiling water. In south-east Asia it is put in a woven bamboo basket over the pan. It takes about 20 minutes. Let it rest for 5 minutes before serving. Serve it as an accompaniment as you would a non-sticky rice.

Fried rice

Most countries where rice is grown have a repertoire of fried rice dishes. Chicken, pork, ham, prawns, tofu, green beans, mushrooms, carrots, peas, tomatoes, spring onions and eggs are frequent additions. The flavourings vary according to the country: soy sauce in China, fish sauce and lime juice in Thailand, chilli and dried prawn paste in Malaysia and Indonesia, soy sauce and rice wine* in Vietnam. The choice is great, but if you experiment do not be tempted to put more than 3 or 4 ingredients into your rice, and select flavours that complement each other.

Use long grain rice and it must be cold; fried rice does not work successfully with hot rice. The other ingredients are stir-fried first and then the cold rice is added to them. The seasonings are added as you mix together the rice and other foods over low heat, giving time for the rice to warm up and for the flavours to blend.

Thai fried rice

For 3–4

2 tbs sunflower oil

6 garlic cloves, peeled and chopped finely

1 small onion, peeled and sliced finely

1 chicken breast, cut in thin strips

125 g small mushrooms, sliced

100g frozen young peas

½ tsp chilli powder

600–700g cooked long grain rice, cold

2 tbs fish sauce (p. 520)

1 tbs soy sauce

1 lime

accompaniments

½ cucumber, cut in half lengthways and sliced

3 tbs chopped coriander

6–8 spring onions

2 limes cut in wedges

Heat a wok and when it is hot add the oil and swirl it around. Stir-fry the garlic and onion for 1 minute. Put in the chicken strips and stir-fry for 2–3 minutes, then add the mushrooms, peas and chilli powder. Let them soften. Lower the heat, and add the rice. Mix it with the vegetables, letting it heat through. Season with the fish and soy sauces, taste and adjust amounts if necessary. Squeeze the juice of the lime over the rice and serve with its accompaniments.

Chinese fried rice

For 3–4

2 tbs sunflower oil

3 spring onions, chopped

200g cooked ham, diced

4 eggs, whisked lightly with 1 tbs water

600–700g cooked long grain rice, cold

2 tbs soy sauce

Heat a wok and add the oil when it is hot. Stir-fry the spring onions rapidly and add the ham. Turn it in the oil, then add the eggs, breaking them up as they cook so you have a scrambled effect. Put in the rice, lower the heat and mix it thoroughly with the other ingredients. Keep stirring the rice to make sure it heats through. Stir in the soy sauce, taste and serve.

Pilafs and polos

These are the rice dishes of the Middle East, central Asia and India. Basmati is the best rice to use. The way of cooking the rice varies from region to region, but it is usually soaked and then steamed (p. 179) or fried lightly before the liquid is added. Pilafs are sometimes plain, sometimes simply flavoured with herbs or spices and perhaps a few almonds or pistachios, or the rice may be cooked with vegetables, fish or meat. Some of the most delicious pilafs are made with dried fruits. Stock often replaces water as the cooking liquid.

Malabar spiced pilaf

Pilafs with whole spices are found in many parts of India; this one comes from the Malabar coast, home of cardamom and pepper. Except for the cumin seeds, the spices are not eaten, but if you accidentally chew any of the others, you won't come to any harm.

For 4–6

500g basmati rice

30ml sunflower oil or clarified butter*

1 large onion, peeled and chopped

8 cardamom pods*

1 stick cinnamon

8 cloves

1 tsp cumin seeds

12 black peppercorns

1 tsp salt

15–30g butter or 1–2 tbs sunflower oil (optional)

Measure the rice, wash it in cold water, drain and rinse until the water runs clear, then soak for 30 minutes or longer. Heat the oil in a heavy pan and fry the onion until golden. Bruise the cardamom pods, break the cinnamon in three and add all the spices to the onion. Fry gently for about 30 seconds until the spices are slightly puffed.

Drain the rice and add it to the pan. Fry for about 3 minutes, stirring occasionally, until the rice becomes translucent, then add 1¼ measures of boiling water for every 1 measure of rice. Season with salt. Stir frequently and bring back to the boil.

Reduce the heat to very low, cover the pan and simmer for 15 minutes. The water will have been absorbed and the surface of the rice will be covered with tiny steam holes. If you wish, add melted butter or oil to the rice now. Fold a tea towel, put it over the pan, replace the lid and fold up the corners of the tea towel over the top. Leave the pan over low heat for 5 minutes, then turn off the heat and leave to steam undisturbed for a further 5–10 minutes. Turn the rice out onto a warmed serving dish with a wooden fork, fluffing it as you do so.

Saffron pilaf with lamb and almonds

Pilafs with lamb and spices are found throughout the Middle East and central Asia. They are usually made with a small amount of fresh meat, as here, but you can make a successful pilaf with diced cooked lamb; simply omit the meat from the frying process. The spicing in this pilaf is mild; you could increase the amounts of cinnamon and nutmeg if you wish, but more clove might make it taste harsh.

For 4–6	50g slivered almonds	large pinch nutmeg
500g basmati rice	1 onion, peeled and chopped	large pinch ground cloves
½ tsp saffron threads		
2 tbs rose-water (p. 139) or plain water	200g lamb, diced	salt
	¼ tsp ground pepper	1 tbs sunflower oil
15g butter	¼ tsp ground cinnamon	about 650ml chicken stock (p. 4)

Measure the rice. For every measure of rice you will need 1¼ measures of chicken stock, in all about 650ml. Wash the rice well in cold water, drain and rinse under running water until the water is clear, then soak in warm water for 1 hour. Crush the saffron and blend it with the rose-water or plain water. Heat the butter in a frying pan and gently fry the almonds until golden.

Put them aside and fry the onion, then add the lamb and spices and fry, stirring from time to time. Add salt to taste.

Drain the rice well. Heat the oil in a large pan, put in half the rice, then the meat and onion on top and cover with another layer of rice. Add the stock and the saffron mixture. Cover the pan with a tea towel and lid, tucking up the ends of the tea towel over the lid. Cook on medium heat until it starts to boil, then turn the heat very low and simmer for 25–30 minutes until all the liquid is absorbed. Scoop the rice onto a warm serving dish and scatter over the almonds.

Lime and cashew nut pilaf

This pilaf from Mysore in southern India is made with cold cooked rice. It works well with lemon juice, too.

For 4–6	8–10 curry leaves (p. 257), preferably fresh	2–3 tbs water, if necessary
3 tbs sunflower oil		salt
½ tsp mustard seeds (p. 76)	pinch of asafoetida*	4 tbs chopped coriander
2 red chillies	2 cups cooked basmati or other long grain rice	60g dry-roasted* cashew nuts, coarsely chopped
½ tsp turmeric	100ml lime juice	

Heat the oil in a large pan and fry the mustard seeds and whole chillies. The mustard seeds will pop and the chillies will darken. Stir constantly for 2–3 minutes. Stir in the other spices, then add the rice, coating it well with the spiced oil. Pour in the lime juice and if necessary the water or a little more lime juice. How much liquid you need varies with the rice. Season with salt. Cover the pan and steam over low heat (use a heat diffuser if possible) for 5–10 minutes, until the rice is heated through. Leave to rest for 5 minutes, then use a wooden fork to stir through half the coriander and cashews. Put the rice on a warm serving dish and sprinkle over the rest of the nuts and coriander.

Variation

· Use 1 more tbs sunflower oil and add 2 peeled and finely sliced onions to the pan with the turmeric and other spices and fry until the onions are golden before adding the rice.

Iranian polo with herbs

This is a beautiful dish with layers of rice interspersed with layers of herbs and a crust on the bottom of the pan. In Iran, it is the traditional dish to eat at the new year, or Noo Rooz festival in March which marks the beginning of spring. Fresh herbs are best, but Iranian shops sell bags of exceptionally fragrant dried herbs for cooking rice. You will only need 25–30g of dried herbs to flavour 500g rice. Fresh herbs must be dry when they are added to the rice. A salad spinner will drain them well before they are chopped, or wrap them in kitchen paper or a tea towel.

For 4–6	3 tbs water	100g coriander, finely chopped
500g basmati rice	100g dill, finely chopped	100g chives or spring onions, finely chopped
salt	100g parsley, finely chopped	
100g butter or sunflower oil		

Put the rice into the pan, pour over cold water, swish around and then drain and rinse until the water runs clear. Return it to the pan and soak it for several hours in salted water. Drain it. Add 1 tbs salt to 2½ litres water, bring to the boil and put in the rice, stirring to make sure it does not stick. Boil, uncovered, for 2–3 minutes and test to see whether the rice is almost tender. It should be soft on the outside but still have a firm core in the centre. Drain and rinse the rice in lukewarm water. Put half the butter or oil and 3 tbs water in a non-stick pan if you have one large enough for the rice; otherwise rinse the pan you boiled the rice in and use that. When the butter has melted or the oil is hot, put in a layer of rice, then a third of the mixed herbs. Repeat this layering, making each layer a bit narrower than the one before so that you have a cone-shaped mound in the pan. Finish with a layer of rice. With the handle of a wooden spoon, poke 2 or 3 holes through the cone down to the bottom of the pan to allow the steam to escape. Pour over the rest of the butter or oil.

Cover the pan with a folded tea towel and then the lid, flip the ends of the tea towel up over the lid to keep them away from the heat. Cook on high heat for 3–4 minutes until the rice is steaming, then turn down the heat and steam for 30 minutes. The rice will keep warm for another 20–30 minutes once the heat has been turned off, as long as the cloth and lid are left in place.

To serve, turn the rice gently onto a warm serving dish. Lift out the crust from the bottom of the pan and put it around the rice.

Rice with pulses

Rice and lentils, rice and chick peas, rice and beans, such dishes are found all over the world. They provide simple, cheap and sustaining food.

Mujadara

All the countries of the Middle East have versions of this dish of rice and lentils with onions. The lentils, onions and rice are usually cooked together, but the rice can be cooked separately and stirred into the lentil and onion mixture before serving.

For 6–8	150ml olive oil	salt
400g brown lentils	3 large onions, peeled, cut in half and sliced finely	
200g basmati rice		
1 litre water		

Wash the lentils and rice separately in cold water and rinse them well under running water. Put the lentils in a large pan and cover them with l litre boiling water. Simmer for 12–15 minutes until they are almost cooked. Heat the oil and fry the onions. Take out half of them when they are just lightly browned and continue to fry the others until dark brown, but not burned. Add the lightly browned onions and the rice to the lentils and add salt. Stir to mix the ingredients, cover the pan and simmer over low heat for about 20 minutes. The rice should be cooked and the liquid absorbed. If necessary add a little more boiling water; both lentils and rice vary greatly in their capacity to absorb water. Turn the rice and lentils out onto a serving dish and garnish with the darker onions and pour over their oil. Serve hot, warm or cold. A bowl of yogurt is a good accompaniment.

Arroz al horno

This Spanish dish of rice and chick peas is baked in the oven. Spanish rice is medium grain, but if you cannot get Spanish, use an Italian rice rather than a long grain rice. The chick peas are cooked in advance (or you could use canned ones) and then the dish takes only 30 minutes or so to prepare and cook. It is cooked with a whole head of garlic in the centre which flavours the dish beautifully and is mellow to eat.

For 4–6	1 tsp paprika	750ml vegetable or chicken stock (p. 4)
1 head garlic	salt	400g rice
80ml olive oil	120g cooked or canned chick peas (p. 80)	
3 tomatoes, peeled and chopped		
2 potatoes, peeled and sliced thinly		

Heat the oven to 200°C, 400°F, gas 6. Remove any loose outer skin from the garlic but keep the head intact. Wipe it clean, parboil for 5 minutes and drain. Heat the oil in an ovenproof casserole – in Spain it would be an earthenware casserole – and sauté the tomatoes and potatoes for a few minutes. Season with paprika and salt, then add the chick peas. Heat the stock. Tip the rice into the dish and stir well to mix, then pour over the stock. Push the garlic into the rice and vegetables in the centre of the dish. Bring to the boil and simmer for 2–3 minutes, then transfer the dish to the oven and cook for about 20 minutes. Check that the rice is done and remove the dish from the oven. Separate the cloves of garlic to serve them with the rice and take the dish to the table.

Variations

· In some places, bits of blood sausage or chorizo are added, sometimes raisins plumped in water, elsewhere haricot beans replace the chick peas. Arroz al horno can be interpreted in different ways, but keep, roughly, the same proportions of rice and chick peas or beans and keep the head of garlic.

Rice with vegetables

In those parts of the world where rice is the staple food, it is most frequently accompanied by or cooked with vegetables; meat and fish are reserved for special occasions or just included in tiny quantities as a flavouring. In Europe, vegetable paella from Spain, vegetable risottos from Italy and stuffed vegetables from Greece are among the most imaginative ways of combining rice and vegetables.

Rice baked with herbs and chilli

For 4	2 garlic cloves, peeled and chopped	large handful of coriander, chopped
1 tbs sunflower oil	3–4 green chillies, seeded and chopped	200ml soured cream
4 spring onions, chopped	2 cups cooked long grain rice, cold	180g grated Cheddar

Heat the oven to 180°C, 350°F, gas 4. Lightly grease a shallow ovenproof casserole of 1-litre capacity. Heat the oil in a small frying pan and fry the onions, garlic and chillies for 2–3 minutes. Stir the contents of the pan into the rice. Stir the coriander into the soured cream. Put a layer of rice in the dish, smooth it down and cover with a layer of cream and coriander, then sprinkle over some of the cheese. Repeat the layers, finishing with rice, but keeping some of the cheese back to sprinkle over the top. Bake for 25–30 minutes.

Vegetable paella

The vegetables for this paella can be varied: green beans, broad beans, cauliflower, small artichokes, peas and peppers are those most commonly used. The dish is best made in a *paella*, the thin two-handled metal pan used for many Spanish rice dishes cooked on the stove. If you don't have one, use a big frying pan.

For 6

80ml olive oil

200g cauliflower florets

4 small artichokes, cleaned and cut up (p. 102) or 6 artichoke hearts, halved

1 red pepper, cut in squares

100g green beans, cut in 5–6cm lengths

100g broad beans or peas (400g in the shell or use frozen)

3 large ripe tomatoes, peeled and chopped

300g Spanish or other short or medium grain rice

4 garlic cloves, peeled and chopped

about 800ml vegetable stock (p. 4)

½ tsp ground saffron

1 tsp paprika

salt and freshly ground pepper

Heat the oil in a 30–40cm *paella* (*see* above) or a large frying or sauté pan and fry the cauliflower, artichokes, red pepper, green and broad beans, turning them frequently for 5 minutes. Add the tomatoes and garlic and cook over moderate heat for a further 5 minutes and bring the stock to the boil in a separate pan. Stir the rice into the vegetables, coating it well with the oil and juices. Pour over the hot stock, season with saffron, paprika, salt and pepper and simmer gently for 15–20 minutes until the rice is done. Leave to stand for 5 minutes before serving.

Baked rice with spinach and prunes

This Iranian dish looks beautiful and tastes marvellous, the flavours of spinach, prunes and saffron-yogurt rice complementing each other so well. Allow time to soak the rice for 2 hours or longer.

For 4–6

250g basmati rice

125g prunes

30ml sunflower oil

1 onion, peeled and chopped

350g spinach

salt and freshly ground pepper

50g butter

2 egg yolks

4 tbs thick yogurt

½ tsp ground saffron

Soak the rice in cold water for at least 2 hours; you can leave it for much longer without it coming to any harm. If the prunes need soaking, do so for the length of time indicated on the packet, then cook them in the soaking water for about 20 minutes, or until soft. Drain them and remove the stones. Ready-to-eat prunes can be used instead.

Heat the oil in a large pan and fry the onion until golden. Set aside 10–12 large spinach leaves and add the remainder to the onion. Season and cook for 5 minutes, until the spinach has wilted. Remove the pan from the heat. While the vegetables are cooking, bring a pan of water to the boil and blanch the large spinach leaves for 1 minute. Lift them out of the water carefully and spread on kitchen paper.

Melt the butter and use some to brush generously a 1-litre ring mould or a 20–22cm shallow baking dish or cake tin. Line it with the blanched spinach leaves.

Heat the oven to 180°C, 350°F, gas 4. Drain the rice, bring 1 litre of salted water to the boil in a large pan. Stir in the rice, bring back to the boil and simmer, uncovered, for 3–4 minutes. Drain and rinse the rice with cold water. Beat the egg yolks with the yogurt and saffron and stir in half the rice. Arrange half of this rice in the mould, smooth it down and lay the prunes over it. Cover them with the remaining yogurt rice. Now make a layer with the spinach and onion mixture and fill the mould with the plain rice. Flatten the surface and pour over the remaining butter. Cover tightly with foil. Bake the rice for 1½ hours. Turn out onto a warmed serving dish.

Rice with seafood

This is a popular combination in many countries, made with short or long grain rice and the locally available seafood. Sometimes seafood and meats such as chicken or ham are used together, as in the internationally renowned Spanish paella, a flamboyant interpretation of the traditional Valencian dish which uses chicken or rabbit, snails and green beans as its principal ingredients, and of course saffron-scented rice. Just as popular within the south-eastern states of America is Louisiana jambalaya.

Jambalaya

Louisiana is renowned for its seafood and rice dishes: oysters, crab, crawfish, shrimps are served up as gumbos and étouffées on top of a dish of rice or as an integral part of a rice dish, as in a jambalaya. The basis of the dish, as with so many Creole and Cajun dishes, is onion, celery and green peppers stewed together. Jambalaya varies according to the cook and what is available, but a mixture of seafood and meat is common.

For 4

2 tbs sunflower oil

200g spicy or smoked sausage, sliced

200g ham, preferably smoked, diced

1 onion, peeled and chopped

2 stalks celery, sliced

1 green pepper, seeded and diced

2 bay leaves, crushed

1 tsp dried thyme

1 tsp dried oregano

3 spring onions, chopped

2 garlic cloves, peeled and chopped

3 large tomatoes, peeled and chopped

4 tbs parsley, chopped

600ml fish or chicken stock (p. 6, p. 4)

salt and freshly ground pepper

½ tsp cayenne

200g long grain rice

20 tiger or other large prawns, cooked and peeled

Heat the oil and gently sauté the sausage and ham for 4–5 minutes, then remove the meats and sauté the onion, celery and green pepper. Let them start to brown, then add the dried herbs, spring onion and garlic. Cook for 5 minutes, stirring occasionally, then return the meats to the pan and add the tomatoes, half the parsley and the stock. Season with salt if necessary and with black pepper and cayenne.

When the stock comes to the boil stir in the rice. Let it come back to the boil, cover and reduce the heat. Simmer for about 20 minutes, stirring occasionally with a wooden fork, until the rice is done, but still has a slight bite. Add the prawns, stirring them carefully into the mixture, and simmer, uncovered, for 5 minutes or so until they are heated through. Stir with a wooden fork to fluff the rice and keep the grains separate. Check the seasoning and stir in the rest of the parsley. Serve hot.

Rice with monkfish and prawns

Instead of monkfish you could use another firm fish such as halibut. Use short or medium grain rice, and cook the rice in a *paella* (p. 187), or in a large frying or sauté pan.

For 4	3 tomatoes, peeled and chopped	400g short or medium grain rice
1 monkfish tail, weighing about 400g	2 garlic cloves, peeled	250g medium uncooked prawns, with or without shells
lemon juice	1 tsp paprika	
80ml olive oil	salt	
1 onion, peeled and chopped	about 1 litre fish stock (p. 6)	

Remove the bone and filmy skin from the monkfish and cut it into slices 2–3cm thick. Sprinkle it with lemon juice. Heat the oil in a *paella* or a wide frying pan and fry the pieces of monkfish for 2–3 minutes, turning once to sear the sides. Put the fish aside, add the onion to the pan and fry for 1–2 minutes, then add the tomato and garlic. Season with paprika and salt. Cook for a few minutes and bring the stock to the boil in a separate pan.

Add the rice to the tomato mixture, stir it well and pour over the hot stock. Cook over medium heat for 10 minutes, then reduce the heat, put the slices of monkfish and the prawns on top of the rice and simmer for 10–12 minutes. Turn the fish and the prawns after 6–8 minutes; the prawns should have turned pink on the underside. The rice should still have a slight bite. Remove the pan from the heat and leave to stand for 5 minutes before serving.

Kedgeree

This English dish evolved from *khichri*, a moghul dish of rice and lentils cooked with spices. It became popular as a breakfast dish in late Victorian times and then turned into a lunch or supper dish. Smoked haddock is my favourite fish for kedgeree, but salmon is good too (it is a useful way of finishing the remains of a large fish) and so are prawns and mussels. Mussel liquor can be used to cook the rice. Do not stint on the proportion of fish to rice.

For 4	2 tbs olive oil	2 hardboiled eggs, chopped
500g smoked haddock fillet	1 tsp curry powder	1 tbs chopped parsley
1 medium onion, peeled and sliced	180g long grain rice	grated rind of 1 unwaxed lemon
	60g butter	
	salt	

Pour boiling water over the haddock fillet and set aside for 5 minutes, then drain, discard the skin and bones, and flake the fish. Lightly brown the onion in a heavy pan. Stir in the curry powder and then the unwashed rice. Pour over 600ml water and cook steadily, uncovered, for about 15 minutes until the liquid is absorbed and the rice tender. If necessary, add a little more hot water to the pan. Add the fish and butter to the pan, mixing them in carefully with a wooden fork in order not to break the rice. Taste and season with salt if necessary. Turn the kedgeree out onto a warm serving dish, arrange the chopped egg over the top and sprinkle over the parsley and lemon rind. Serve with lemon quarters and mango chutney.

Risotto

Risotto is one of the triumphs of Italian cooking, a creamy dish of rice with each grain whole and separate, *al dente*. The creaminess comes from the starch released by the rice during cooking, so rice with a high starch content is essential to the success of a risotto. The three short grain Italian rices to choose from are arborio, carnaroli and vialone nano (p. 177).

Risotto has the reputation of being hard to make, but it isn't – provided some quite simple procedures are followed. Rice is stirred to release its starch. Arborio, which has less starch than the other two, needs constant stirring for the dish to reach the right consistency, whereas carnaroli and vialone nano will become creamy if left to absorb the stock and stirred only right at the beginning and again at the end. If you stir a risotto after the initial stirring, you will have to continue throughout the cooking time. The other important points are to use a heavy-based pan, only a little butter or olive oil, to cook the shallot or onion gently so that it barely colours, and to have the stock hot. You will need roughly twice the volume of stock to rice.

Saffron risotto

This saffron-flavoured risotto is prepared with minimum stirring, *see* above. Make sure you have twice the volume of liquid to rice; measure both carefully.

For 4		
about 800ml vegetable or chicken stock (p. 4)	2 shallots, peeled and chopped finely	1 glass white wine (optional)
100g butter	400g carnaroli or vialone nano rice	salt and freshly ground pepper
	¼–½ tsp saffron threads, ground to a powder	2 tbs freshly grated Parmesan

Heat the stock and keep it simmering. Heat half the butter in a heavy pan and gently fry the shallot until golden. Add the rice and stir for 2–3 minutes until it is coated with butter. Steep the powdered saffron in 3 tbs hot stock for 5 minutes. If you are using the wine remember to include it as part of the volume when determining how much liquid to add. Pour the wine and stock over the rice, add the saffron liquid and season with salt and pepper. Stir once gently, cover the pan and simmer for 16–18 minutes. Stir in the rest of the butter and 2 tbs Parmesan cheese. Check the seasoning, stir gently and serve with more Parmesan.

Mushroom risotto

Use some dried porcini and/or morels (p. 143) for this risotto to give it a lovely depth of flavour and use the soaking liquid as part of the stock. This quantity will serve 2 as a main dish or 4 as a first course. The mushroom recipe is made following the method which adds small amounts of water at a time and requires continuous stirring; see above for more information.

For 2–4		
10g dried porcini and/or morels	2 tbs olive oil or 30g butter	1 glass white wine
about 500ml chicken or vegetable stock (p. 4)	2 shallots, peeled and chopped finely	salt and freshly ground pepper
	200g fresh mushrooms	50g butter
	250g risotto rice	freshly grated Parmesan

Soak the dried fungi in 200ml hot water for 20 minutes, then drain them, reserving the liquid. Chop the fungi and strain the liquid through a muslin-lined sieve (p. 528) to remove any grit. Measure the liquid and use it to replace part of the stock. Heat the stock and the soaking liquid and keep it at a gentle simmer. Heat the oil or butter in a heavy pan and gently sauté the shallots until they soften. Cut the fresh mushrooms into pieces and add them to the pan. Cook until they are soft, then add the rehydrated fungi and the rice. Stir for about 2 minutes to coat the rice in the oil and when the grains are glistening and hot, pour over the wine, stir gently and wait until the wine is absorbed. Season and add a little hot stock, stirring as you do so. When it is absorbed add more, still stirring as you do so. Continue to do this until the rice is tender and creamy but still with a slight bite at the centre; it will take about 18–20 minutes.

Remove the pan from the heat, stir in the butter and 2 tbs grated Parmesan. Cover the pan and let it stand for 3–4 minutes, then serve. Offer more Parmesan with the risotto.

Variation

Asparagus risotto Replace the mushrooms by 400g asparagus. Find the break point of the asparagus (p. 103) and discard the bottoms. Keep the tips intact and cut the stalks into small pieces. Sauté the stalks with the shallots. Stir in the tips during the last 5 minutes of cooking.

Sushi

Sushi is not that difficult to make, with a bit of attention and practice, and it is fun and will impress your friends. It is important to have Japanese sushi rice and rice vinegar. The other thing you need is a pack of dried nori (laver – a type of seaweed) sheets. Some supermarkets and food shops sell the whole kit together. The simplest sushi for a beginner are nori rolls, or *nori-maki,* in which the rice is wrapped around pieces of very fresh raw or smoked fish or around vegetables such as cucumber, spring onion or avocado and then rolled in a sheet of nori seaweed which holds it all together. To roll the sushi you will need a bamboo sushi mat from a Chinese shop.

Wasabi, which accompanies raw fish dishes, is sometimes known as Japanese horseradish because it is an edible root with a fierce aroma and biting, cleansing taste. Outside Japan it is not found fresh, but can be bought as a powder and as a paste packed in tubes from Japanese shops, delicatessens and some supermarkets.

Thinly sliced, pale pink pickled ginger (*gari*) is served with sushi as a digestive condiment; it is available from oriental shops, delicatessens and some supermarkets which stock Japanese foods.

Nori rolls (Nori-maki)

For 8–10	600ml water	1½ tbs sugar
For the rice	5 tbs rice vinegar	1 tsp salt
500g sushi rice		

Wash the rice well in a sieve, running your fingers through it until the water runs clear; this will take a few minutes. Drain it and put it into a pan with the water, cover and bring to the boil. Lower the heat and simmer for 10 minutes, then remove the pan from the heat and leave undisturbed for another 10 minutes. Check the rice; it should be a little harder than normal boiled rice.

While the rice is cooking stir the vinegar, sugar and salt together until dissolved. Once the rice is ready it must be cooled quickly. Spread it in a large shallow bowl using a wooden spatula. Dribble over the vinegar mixture, and with one hand turn the rice with the spatula to blend it in, with the other, fan it with a piece of card or a newspaper to speed up the cooling process. Two people working together can achieve this more easily. Add the vinegar gradually, you may not need it all. When the rice has cooled to room temperature it should have a sheen and the grains should remain separate.

For the nori rolls	½ cucumber	1 pack (10 sheets)
1 medium avocado	180g smoked salmon	sushi nori (*see* above)
		wasabi paste

Peel the avocado and cut the flesh into thin strips. Squeeze a little lemon juice over it to prevent it discolouring. Split the half cucumber lengthways, remove the seeds and cut the flesh into thin strips. Cut the salmon into thin strips, too.

If you can buy toasted nori, that is the most convenient. Plain, black nori should be toasted by passing it quickly over a gas flame until it turns bright green and is crisp. Place the nori, toasted side down, on the sushi mat. Use the spatula to spread a layer of rice over the nori, leaving a 3cm border at the end furthest from you. Make an indentation across the rice, about 10cm from the edge nearest to you, with the edge of the spatula. Put a very light coating of wasabi along this hollow, then fill it with the strips of avocado, cucumber and salmon. They should reach the width of the rice and the nori. To roll up the nori, lift the edge of the mat so that the nearest edge of the nori rolls up to meet the top of the rice. Press the mat to shape the roll. Taking care not to let the edge of the mat catch in the roll, roll the nori into a tight cylinder. The edge of the nori should seal with the moisture from the rice, but if it doesn't, wet your finger, rub the nori and press it to seal. Put the roll seam side down on a platter. Repeat with the other sheets and filling until all is used up.

If the sushi are not to be served straight away cover the rolls with clingfilm. Cut them just before serving. With a very sharp dampened knife, cut each roll in half and then each half in four. Wipe and wet the knife between cuts.

Serve with more wasabi, pickled ginger or a dipping sauce made with 3 tbs rice vinegar and 4 tbs soy sauce.

Variations
- For alternative fillings use tomato (seeded and cut in strips), carrot (blanched and cut in thin strips), blanched spring onion, other smoked fish or very fresh top-quality raw fish such as salmon or tuna, cut in strips.

Wild rice

Wild rice is not related to rice, but is a grass that grows wild in marshlands in North America, and these days is also grown commercially in paddy fields. It has a nutty, slightly spicy flavour and is always sold as dark brown-black whole grains. Wild rice is high in proteins, minerals and fibre, low in fat and extremely nutritious. It is expensive but it goes a long way because it triples in volume when cooked, and you need add only a small amount to a salad, a soup or a rice pilaf to appreciate its distinctive taste. The real 'wild' rice still harvested each autumn from small lakes and marshes between the Great Lakes and the Midwest has a superior, slightly smoky flavour compared with the commercially grown types. Wild rice can be stored for up to one year.

Plain wild rice

The amount of liquid and the length of time needed to cook wild rice vary greatly from one brand to another, so read the instructions on the packet. The following are just general guidelines. Take 1 measure of wild rice, put it into a large bowl, cover with hot water and soak for 1 hour. Drain the rice and measure out a volume of water 2½ times that of the dry rice. Bring it to the boil, add stir in the rice, turn down the heat and simmer gently for 40 minutes. Bite on a grain to see if it is done; if not, cook longer: wild rice can take up to an hour. When it is ready the water should have been absorbed. Stir in a little butter or olive oil.

Wild rice with chicken livers

For 4–6	250g chicken livers	250g mushrooms, sliced
2 tbs olive oil	flour	250g cooked wild rice
30g butter	salt and freshly ground pepper	100ml chicken stock (p. 4)
2 medium onions, peeled and sliced	1 small glass brandy or madeira	

Heat the oven to 180°C, 350°F, gas 4. Heat 1 tbs oil and the butter and sauté the onion lightly. Clean the livers, discarding any stringy or greenish bits, and cut each in two. Dust them with seasoned flour and add them to the pan. Cook gently for about 3 minutes, then pour over the brandy or madeira and let it bubble and reduce. Heat the remaining oil in another pan and sauté the mushrooms. Stir the chicken livers and mushrooms into the wild rice and moisten with the stock. Put the mixture into a lightly greased ovenproof casserole, cover and bake for about 15 minutes to allow the rice to heat through and the flavours to mingle.

Wild rice and chestnut casserole

For 6

30g butter

1 onion, peeled and chopped

2 stalks celery, sliced

1 measure wild rice (about 250g)

3 measures vegetable or chicken stock (p. 4)

salt and freshly ground pepper

150g cooked chestnuts (p. 129), broken into pieces

80g dried apricots, soaked and chopped

60g raisins, soaked

juice of 1 orange

2 tbs chopped tarragon

Melt the butter in an ovenproof casserole and sauté the onion and celery until lightly golden. Add the rice, stir well to coat the grains with butter, then add 2½ measures of stock. Season with salt and pepper, bring to the boil, then turn down the heat and simmer for about 45 minutes. Taste to see if the rice is cooked.

Heat the oven to 180°C, 350°F, gas 4. Stir the chestnuts and drained fruits into the rice with the orange juice and some or all of the remaining stock. Add the tarragon, taste for seasoning and bake, covered, for 15 minutes.

Corn

This section covers cornmeal and other corn products made from the varieties that are allowed to dry on the stalk in the field, converting sugar to starch. The juicy immature corn sold as corn-on-the-cob is dealt with in the vegetable chapter.

Cornmeal and polenta are available in coarse or fine grades, yellow or white. The yellow has a clear corn flavour, the white is more delicate. Choose the coarse meal if you want to make a robust dish in which you can still feel the grains with your teeth; for a softer, smoother dish take a fine meal. Cornmeal and polenta will keep for several years in tightly closed containers.

Polenta

Polenta is the staple food of northern Italy, made by stirring polenta flour into water until it becomes dense and thick. It can be used when just made, warm and soft, to accompany meat stews or dishes of poultry or game birds with a lot of sauce that the polenta will soak up. It can be left to cool, when it becomes firm enough to slice, and then fry, grill or bake it. Polenta is bland and readily absorbs the flavours of foods served with it.

Soft polenta

Polenta demands time and attention if you make the real thing, but it is far superior to pre-cooked polenta. I prefer to use coarse flour because the finished polenta has a more interesting texture.

For 4–6	1 tsp salt	1 tbs olive oil or 15g butter
1.5 litres water	300g coarse polenta	

Bring the water to the boil with the salt. As soon as it boils, trickle in the polenta flour slowly, whisking hard. Don't stop whisking or the grains may stick together, and keep the water at a steady boil until all the polenta is in the pan. It will bubble violently. Reduce the heat to very low and simmer for about 30 minutes, stirring frequently with a wooden spoon, always in the same direction, to prevent a skin forming on top. The polenta is ready when it comes away from the sides of the pan. Stir in the olive oil or butter.

Leave the polenta to rest for 5 minutes, then put it into a bowl and serve with more olive oil or butter, grated Parmesan or a sauce, or as an accompaniment to a stew.

Firm polenta

Cook the polenta as described above and have ready a lightly greased shallow baking tin. As soon as you have stirred in the olive oil or butter, spread the polenta in the tin, smoothing the top to make a layer about 1.5cm thick. Cover the top with a sheet of greaseproof paper and leave to cool. When it is cool and firm, cut it into slices or squares. They can be brushed with olive oil, toasted under a pre-heated grill or fried, or used as layers in a composite dish.

Pre-cooked polenta

Pre-cooked polenta lacks the taste and texture of the real thing, but it is passable if you are in a hurry. It is cooked in the same way, using the prescribed amount of water and will be ready in 5 minutes.

Sage-flavoured polenta with mushrooms and anchovies

For 3–4	1 garlic clove, peeled and crushed	3 tbs chopped parsley
150g coarse polenta		½ tbs chopped sage leaves
salt and freshly ground pepper	100g mushrooms, sliced finely	
	50g anchovy fillets, chopped	flour
600ml water		8 whole sage leaves
olive oil		

Make the polenta following the method described above, and as soon as it is simmering heat 3 tbs oil in a frying pan and lightly sauté the garlic and mushrooms for 3–4 minutes, then add the anchovies and chopped herbs, season and cook for 1–2 minutes more. When the polenta is three-quarters ready, stir in this mixture and leave to finish cooking. Turn the polenta out into a shallow greased tin, smooth the top and allow to get cold. Then slice the polenta, coat the slices lightly in flour. Heat about 2cm oil in a frying pan, put in the whole sage leaves to flavour it and fry the polenta on both sides until crisp and golden. Serve very hot.

Polenta crostini with Gorgonzola

This recipe comes from *Il libro della polenta* by Luigi Carnacina and Vincenzo Buonassisi.

For 8	100g butter	¼ tsp paprika
8 slices of cold polenta (*see* above)	200g Gorgonzola	2 tbs brandy

Toast the polenta lightly on a griddle plate or under a grill. Whiz or mash together the butter, Gorgonzola, paprika and brandy. Spread the paste onto the warm slices and serve at once.

Cornmeal

We do not have the American tradition of cooking extensively with corn in its various dried forms – meal, grits, hominy – nor have we widely adopted the practice of using Mexican *masa harina* to make tortillas, but here are two simple recipes for corn bread and corn cakes which are well worth knowing about.

Corn cakes

For 16–18 cakes	½ tsp salt	30g butter, melted
60g plain flour	1 tsp sugar	1 egg, beaten
100g coarse cornmeal	180g fresh corn kernels	½ red pepper, diced
1 tsp baking powder	300ml buttermilk	oil for frying

Mix together the dry ingredients. Put half of the corn into a food processor and purée, then remove it to a large bowl. Put the buttermilk, butter and egg into the processor and whiz. With the motor running slowly, add the dry ingredients a little at a time through the feeder tube. Turn the batter into the bowl with the puréed corn. Fold them together and add the remaining corn and the red pepper. If the mixture is very thick, thin it with a little more buttermilk.

Heat a non-stick frying pan, coat it with a film of oil and spoon in the batter to make cakes 7–8 cm in diameter. Fry until golden brown, 2–3 minutes each side.

Serve the cakes instead of rice or couscous with a stew, or with avocado and orange salsa (p. 381) and grilled prawns for a light meal or first course.

New Mexican chilli corn bread

In New Mexico, almost everything comes with chillies, and I like the mild kick they give to this bread, but you can leave them out if you prefer. Jalapeño chillies are available canned, and occasionally fresh, from some supermarkets and specialist grocers, but you can use any fresh green chilli. Corn bread is the staple bread of the southern states of the US and appears for nearly every meal.

For 1 loaf	1 tsp salt	250ml milk and 50ml single cream – or 300ml milk
60g plain flour	1 tsp sugar	
180g cornmeal	1 tsp ground cinnamon	
1½ tsp baking powder	3 eggs	2–3 jalapeño chillies, seeded and chopped finely
	60g butter, melted	

Heat the oven to 190°C, 375°F, gas 5. Mix together the dry ingredients. In another bowl, whisk the eggs well, then whisk in the butter, milk, cream and chillies. Beat this mixture into the dry ingredients until they are well mixed and the batter is smooth. Grease thoroughly a 25cm cast-iron skillet, cake tin or other baking tin, pour in the batter and bake for about 20 minutes, until the bread has risen and is golden brown. Test with a flat skewer in the centre; it will come out clean when the bread is ready. Serve warm, cut in wedges. This is great with bacon, sausages or eggs for brunch, with barbecued foods or with vegetable stews. Any leftover bread can be sliced and toasted or fried.

Wheat

Recipes for bread, cakes and pastry are in Bread (pp. 439–58) and Cakes, Pastry and Batters (pp. 459–76). This section is concerned with cracked wheat, called bulgur or burghul, and with couscous.

Bulgur

Bulgur is made from wheat berries that have been parboiled and hulled, then dried and cracked. It is available in grades from fine to coarse. It is steamed in the same way as rice (p. 178) and served as a pilaf; use coarse or medium bulgur for pilafs. It is the everyday staple in countries such as Turkey and the Balkans where no rice is grown.

The nutty flavour of bulgur makes a pleasant change from rice as an accompaniment to meat and poultry or vegetable stews. Bulgur is also used to make a dessert with spices, walnuts and grape juice, a spiced winter drink, savoury patties, and one of the triumphs of Middle Eastern cooking, kibbeh. Kibbeh are small balls or ovals with a crisp outer shell, made of fine bulgur moistened and mixed with minced lamb, and a filling of meat, spices, nuts or vegetables. Fine bulgur soaked in water, but not cooked, is the basis of the popular salad, tabbouleh (p. 83).

Bulgur can turn rancid, but it can be kept (airtight) for up to 6 months.

Plain bulgur pilaf

For 4–6

4 tbs olive oil

1 medium onion, peeled and chopped

300g medium or coarse bulgur

2 tomatoes, peeled and chopped

600ml vegetable or chicken stock (p. 4)

salt and freshly ground pepper

2–3 tbs chopped mint

Heat the oil in a large pan and gently sauté the onion for 3–4 minutes, then stir in the bulgur, coating it well with the oil. Fry for 4–5 minutes, add the tomatoes and continue to cook for a further 3–4 minutes. Meanwhile bring the stock to the boil. Pour the stock over the bulgur, adding salt if you wish. Cover the pan and cook for 3 minutes over medium heat, then 10–15 minutes on low heat. The bulgur will absorb the stock and holes appear on the surface. Put a folded tea towel over the pan and put back the lid, tucking up the ends of the cloth over the lid. Leave on the lowest possible heat, with a heat diffuser, for 10 minutes, then turn off the heat and leave to stand for another 5–10 minutes. Lift the grains with a slotted spoon or a wooden fork to fluff them, season well with pepper and add the mint.

Variations

- Add 1 small thin-skinned pale green pepper, chopped, at the same time as the bulgur.
- Add a few sultanas at the same time as the stock, and/or 60g chopped blanched almonds or pine nuts just before serving.

Bulgur pilaf with chick peas

For 4–6

80g olive oil or butter

1 medium onion, peeled and chopped

300g bulgur

600ml vegetable or chicken stock (p. 4)

150g cooked chick peas (p. 80)

salt and freshly ground pepper

½ tsp red pepper flakes

2–3 tbs chopped coriander

Heat the oil or butter in a large pan and sauté the onion gently for 5–6 minutes. Stir in the bulgur and turn well to coat the grains in the fat. Cook for 4–5 minutes, and meanwhile heat the stock. Add the chick peas and hot stock to the pan, add salt if you wish. Cover the pan and simmer over medium heat for 5 minutes. Lower the heat and continue to cook for a further 10–15 minutes until the stock is absorbed and steam holes appear in the top of the bulgur. Put the pan on a heat diffuser, put a folded tea towel under the lid, tucking up the ends of the cloth over the lid, and cook very gently for 10 minutes, then remove the pan from the heat and leave for 5–10 minutes. Lift the pilaf with a wooden fork or slotted spoon, stirring in black pepper and red pepper flakes as you do so. Sprinkle over the coriander and serve.

Couscous

Native to the Berbers of North Africa, couscous is a mixture of fine and coarse grain semolina rolled together and sieved to achieve a uniform size. The grain is traditionally steamed over the stew, also called couscous, with which it is served. This type of couscous, which needs soaking and then steaming, is more difficult to find now, as supermarkets and Middle Eastern shops stock instant or quick-cooking couscous, which is ready in 10–15 minutes or less and needs no actual cooking. It means that preparing couscous is now easy and the only time-consuming part is making the stew.

Quick-cooking couscous is covered with boiling water with some olive oil and salt if you wish. It is left, covered, to swell, then fluffed with a wooden fork and usually a little more oil is stirred through. Follow the instructions on the packet for the proportions of couscous and water. Couscous stored in an airtight container will keep for up to two years.

The stews for serving with the grain are usually made with lamb or chicken, sometimes beef, merguez sausages or fish. Combinations of root vegetables, cabbage, courgettes, onions, aubergines and pumpkin are used in all the stews, and to make the classic vegetable couscous *au sept légumes* (with seven vegetables). Plenty of herbs are used, principally dill, coriander and parsley, and the spicing is combinations of cumin, saffron, turmeric, paprika, chilli, coriander, cinnamon and black pepper.

The Tunisian vegetable stew (p. 171) goes well with couscous. An early summer vegetable stew of broad beans, artichokes, courgettes, fennel, peppers and celery seasoned with paprika, coriander, chilli and plenty of dill is good, too.

Couscous with grilled vegetables

Couscous is a good accompaniment to grilled vegetables. Vary the vegetables according to your taste and what is available; cook them under a grill or on a ribbed griddle plate.

For 4

3 courgettes, sliced thickly

2 red peppers, seeded and quartered

2 yellow peppers, seeded and quartered

2 red onions, peeled and quartered (if necessary, hold the pieces together with a toothpick)

4 large mushrooms, quartered

100ml olive oil

3 tbs lemon juice

½ tsp paprika

½ tsp ground cumin

salt and freshly ground pepper

300g quick-cooking couscous (*see* note on preparation, above)

150g cooked chick peas (p. 80)

3 tomatoes, peeled and diced

4 spring onions, sliced

4 tbs chopped parsley

4 tbs chopped dill

Put the courgettes, peppers, onions and mushrooms in a large bowl; mix together half the oil, the lemon juice, spices, salt and pepper, and pour over the vegetables. Toss to coat them with the marinade and leave to stand for 20 minutes. Heat the grill or griddle plate. Cook the couscous, stir in the remaining olive oil and fork it through. Put in the chick peas, tomatoes, spring onions and half the herbs, and keep warm.

Take the vegetables from the marinade and put them under the grill, 8–10cm from the heat source, or on the griddle plate. Turn occasionally and baste them as necessary with the remaining marinade. They will take 6–10 minutes.

Turn the couscous into a warmed serving dish, arrange the grilled vegetables over and around it and scatter over the remaining herbs.

Chicken couscous

For 6–8

4 tbs sunflower or olive oil

1.5kg chicken, cut into serving pieces

2 onions, peeled and chopped

1 tbs tomato paste

1 tsp paprika

½ tsp ground black pepper

½ tsp turmeric

½ tsp ground cumin

1 litre water

salt

3 carrots, peeled and cut in chunks

3 small white turnips, peeled and quartered

2 tomatoes, peeled and chopped

100g cooked chick peas (p. 80)

2 green peppers, seeded and cut in squares

2 courgettes, cut in chunks

4 tbs chopped coriander

500g quick-cooking couscous (*see* note on preparation, above)

harissa* or other chilli sauce

Heat the oil in a large pan and fry the chicken pieces until turning golden, 3–4 minutes. Lift them out, add the onion and when it starts to brown add the tomato paste and spices. Stir well, put back the chicken and pour over the water. Season with salt, bring to the boil and simmer, covered, for 20 minutes. Add all the vegetables and continue to simmer until the chicken and vegetables are ready, 25–30 minutes. Stir in the coriander.

Prepare the couscous when the stew is almost ready. To serve, mound the couscous in a bowl, make a slight hollow in the centre and spoon some of the vegetables into the hollow and around the sides of the pyramid. Spoon over a little of the cooking liquid. Take a spoonful or two of the liquid and thin the harissa. Put the chicken and remaining vegetables and sauce in another bowl. Serve hot with the harissa on the side.

Barley

Most barley available in our shops is highly polished pearl barley that has shed most of its nutrients. Pot barley is whole barley with its bran retained. It takes longer to cook than pearl barley. Wash barley thoroughly and cook in water or stock. It needs 2 or 2½ times its volume of liquid. The water will be absorbed, leaving the barley dry and ready to serve.

Cooked barley is good in salads, as a base for grilled or roasted vegetables (*see* couscous with grilled vegetables, p. 202), as an alternative to rice for a vegetable stuffing, and in soups.

Barley and pumpkin casserole

For 4–6	500ml vegetable or chicken stock (p. 4)	500g pumpkin, peeled weight, cubed
50g butter	1 tsp fresh thyme leaves or ½ tsp dried	2 tbs sunflower or olive oil
2 onions, peeled and chopped	salt and freshly ground pepper	120g cashew nuts
200g pearl barley		2 tbs chopped chives or parsley

Heat the oven to 180°C, 350°F, gas 4. Melt the butter in an ovenproof casserole and sauté the onion gently for 5 minutes, then measure the barley and stir it in. Coat the grain with the butter, then add the same volume of stock as barley; add the thyme, season with salt and pepper. Bring to the boil, cover and transfer the casserole to the oven.

Rub the pumpkin with the oil, put it into a lightly oiled roasting tin and roast while the barley is cooking. Turn the pieces once or twice. It will take about 20 minutes.

After 30 minutes, add more stock to the barley and carefully stir in the pumpkin and cashews. Return the casserole to the oven for another 30 minutes, taste to see if the barley is ready. It should be turning creamy rather than chewy. If necessary, add more stock and cook a little longer. Garnish with chives or parsley.

Variations

- Replace the pumpkin by sautéed mushrooms or leeks, cooked chestnuts or Brussels sprouts. If you use chestnuts, omit the cashews.
- Replace the cashew nuts by 100g toasted, slivered almonds, but only add them for the last 10 minutes of cooking time.
- Sautéed chicken livers, or sliced cooked firm sausages such as merguez or chorizo, can also be added for the last 15 minutes' cooking time.

Buckwheat

Buckwheat is not a grain, although it is used in similar ways and is nutritionally akin to wheat and other grains. It has a slightly nutty flavour, and is easy to digest. It is a three-sided seed that originated in central Asia and grows well in cold climates and poor soils. Unroasted buckwheat is pale green in colour; roasted it is chestnut brown. Buckwheat flour is used to make Russian blinis and Breton crêpes; in America it is also used for pancakes and muffins. Japanese soba noodles are made from buckwheat. Buckwheat is easier to find in health food shops than in the supermarket and is also sold under its Russian name *kasha*.

Buckwheat pilaf

Essentially buckwheat is steamed in the same way as rice (p. 178), and served as an accompanying dish for meat and poultry. It needs about twice as much water by volume as grain, so measure the buckwheat and liquid in the same container.

For 4–5	2 measures water or chicken stock (p. 4), about 400ml	1 tbs sunflower oil
1 measure buckwheat (200g)		salt and freshly ground pepper

Toast the buckwheat in a dry pan for 2–3 minutes, until it is fragrant, then add the water or stock and the oil. Season with salt. Bring to the boil, cover tightly, lower the heat and simmer gently for about 20 minutes, until the water is absorbed. Take the pan from the heat and leave, covered, for 10 minutes, then fluff the buckwheat with a wooden fork and season with pepper and more salt if you wish.

Variations
· Add a sautéed chopped onion with the water or stock.
· Add 100g sautéed slivered almonds just before serving.

Pasta and noodles

Pasta and noodles – the name changes with the country of origin – are made from flour mixed with a liquid, usually egg or water. The dough is kneaded, rolled, cut, maybe stuffed, then boiled, steamed, baked or fried, and served with a sauce or broth. Asian noodles have become increasingly popular in recent years, but to judge by the number of pasta shops and restaurants, pasta now almost seems to be our national dish. The noodle dishes of central and eastern Europe and the Middle East are less well known, but perhaps our enthusiasm for pasta will eventually extend to some of these excellent dishes. In Asian cities you never have to go far to find a vendor offering steaming appetising bowls of noodles served in broth or with a sauce.

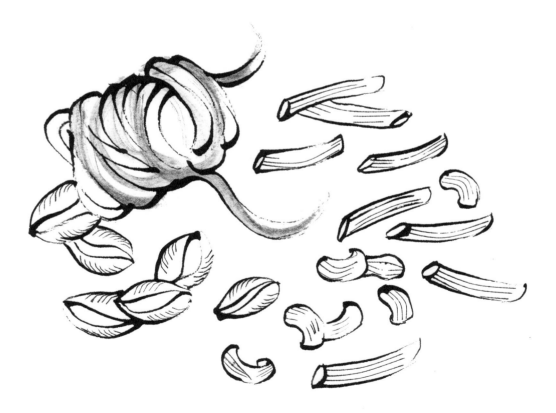

European pasta

Types of pasta and cooking methods

Italian pasta

Ribbons, sticks, tubes, shells, twists, small shapes for soup and other more fanciful forms of pasta can be bought fresh or dried.

Ravioli, capelletti, agnolotti and all the other regional Italian-named shapes for stuffed pasta can be bought fresh, but it is easy to make your own fillings, and you can buy sheets of fresh pasta if you don't want to make the dough yourself.

Pasta should be cooked in a large pan with plenty of boiling water. For up to 500g of pasta, 4 litres of salted water is the right amount; there should be plenty of room for the pasta to move around in the pan. For larger quantities use two pans. The pan should be no more than three-quarters full to ensure it doesn't spill over when you add the pasta. Put in the pasta all at once, stir with a wooden fork, bring the pan back to the boil and stir occasionally to make sure the pasta doesn't stick to the pan.

Italians cook pasta *al dente*; that means it should still be slightly chewy, with a bite. It should not be soggy and limp, nor tough and hard when it will have a raw taste. Cooking times vary with the freshness and thickness of the pasta. Homemade pasta cooks in a couple of minutes, bought fresh pasta takes a little longer; dried pasta takes 5–15 minutes, depending on the type. Use the instructions on the packet as a guideline only; they tend to produce overcooked pasta. Taste a piece or two before the recommended cooking time is up.

As soon as the pasta is ready, drain it in a colander and immediately turn it into a sauce, if using one, or coat it with olive oil or butter and Parmesan cheese. Stuffed pasta rises to the surface and balloons slightly when ready. It is better to scoop the shapes out with a large slotted spoon than to tip them into a colander. Do not rinse pasta under cold water.

Central European pasta

Noodle dishes can be made with flat ribbons or vermicelli, and stuffed shapes such as Jewish kreplach or Polish pierogi can be made using a flour and egg pasta dough or sheets of bought pasta. The cooking methods and times are the same as for Italian pasta. Noodles are often served to accompany meat or poultry.

Quantities

Appetites for pasta vary greatly but, as a guideline, allow 80g of fresh or 50g of dried pasta per person for a first course and 1½ or 2 times as much for a main course. If the sauce is substantial you may need less pasta.

In the recipes which follow, the servings given are for a main course, since that is how we tend to serve pasta.

Making pasta

Basic proportions for making pasta are 100g flour to 1 egg, but the exact amount will vary according to the flour and the size and freshness of the eggs. Italian 00 flour, a soft wheat flour, is recommended by many cooks, but I find a mixture of soft flour with durum, hard wheat flour, more successful; the texture and taste of the pasta are improved. Strong white bread flour combined with unbleached plain flour can also be used.

Basic pasta recipe

This recipe will make 475–500g pasta dough.

Enough for a main course for 4	150g 00 or unbleached plain flour	3 medium eggs
150g durum or white bread flour	1 tsp salt	

Sift the flours and salt together in a bowl. Make a well in the centre and break in the eggs. Mix with a fork or your fingers, drawing the flour into the egg a little at a time to produce a thick mass. If it feels very sticky add a little more flour, if it is dry add a little water. Draw the dough together and knead on a lightly floured surface for 8–10 minutes until the dough is silky and elastic (*see* p. 443 for notes on kneading). Form it into a ball, cover with clingfilm or a cloth and leave to rest for an hour. If you want to leave it longer, put the covered dough in the refrigerator, but allow it to come back to room temperature before working with it.

If you prefer to make the pasta in a food processor, put the flour and salt in the machine and process briefly to blend. Lightly beat the eggs in a jug and pour in the egg, a little at a time, through the feeder tube. Process until the mixture forms a compact ball. Knead briefly by hand, then cover and leave the dough to rest.

Flavoured pasta

Mix the flavouring with the eggs before drawing in the flour.

Green pasta: for each egg add 100g spinach, cooked, squeezed dry and chopped.

Red pasta: for each egg add 1 tbs tomato purée.

Herb pasta: for each egg add 50g blanched chopped herbs: basil, lovage, marjoram, parsley and rocket are all suitable.

Rolling and cutting pasta with a machine

Cut the dough into 6 pieces, keep all but the one you are working with covered. Flatten the piece a little, flour it lightly, set the space between the machine's rollers as wide as possible and pass the dough through. Do not stretch or pull it. Fold the strip in three, turn it through 90 degrees and roll it again. Repeat this 4 or 5 times. Reduce the space by one notch and roll the dough again. Do not fold this time. Repeat this pattern, each time reducing the width of the rollers by one notch until you have a long thin sheet of pasta. Flour it lightly and hang it over the back of a chair or a clean garden cane supported at either end. Repeat with the other pieces of dough.

Leave the pasta to dry for about 10 minutes. It should still be supple but not sticky, and should not be allowed to dry so much that it starts to crack. Pass the pasta sheets through the machine on the thinnest setting of the rollers, to cut broad or narrow ribbons as you need.

Rolling and cutting pasta by hand

Divide the dough in three, keep two pieces covered and lightly knead the third into a disc. Roll the dough on a lightly floured surface, turning it at intervals to produce a round sheet. Do not push down on the rolling pin, but press the dough away from you, always rolling in one direction. When you can see the surface through the dough, it is ready. Put it over the back of a chair or on a dry tea towel to dry for about 20 minutes, until it looks dull and leathery. Repeat with the other pieces. Rolling pasta is more tricky than rolling pastry, but with practice you will get the hang of it.

To cut the pasta into ribbons, roll up the sheet of dough loosely and cut across with a sharp knife to the width you want.

Keeping pasta

Fresh pasta can be cooked straight away. To use later in the day, spread out the ribbons on a tea towel. Pasta can also be left to dry in small nests on a lightly floured tea towel. After 24 hours, store it in an airtight container.

Sauces for pasta

The proportion of sauce to pasta must be judged carefully. Non-Italians tend to serve too much; the sauce is intended to coat the pasta, not to turn it into soup. Less is more, in the case of pasta sauces. In Italy you are served a helping of spaghetti with a small ladleful of sauce in the centre, in which you then toss your pasta.

There are some basic rules about the type of sauce to serve with different types of pasta. Long thin pasta is suited to oil-based and light purées and seafood sauces because the strands hold the sauce well when twirled around a fork. Flat ribbons are well paired with sauces based on cream, butter or cheese which coat them well. Tubular pasta, coils and rounded shapes are best dressed with a chunkier meat or vegetable-based sauce. With this in mind, use the pasta you prefer in the recipes.

Several sauces in Sauces, Salsas and Marinades can be used with pasta: pesto and its variations (p. 366), uncooked passata (tomato coulis) (p. 366), and other tomato sauces (pp. 377–80) and Bolognese sauce (p. 379).

Spaghetti aglio e olio

This is one of the simplest pasta dishes: spaghetti with olive oil, garlic and chillies. Use dried pasta.

For 5–6	4 garlic cloves, peeled and chopped finely	2 tbs chopped parsley
500g dried spaghetti	½ tsp chilli flakes	salt and freshly ground pepper
120ml extra virgin olive oil		

Cook the spaghetti al dente and drain thoroughly. While it is cooking, heat the oil gently and add the garlic. When it starts to colour, add the chilli flakes and parsley, and season. Cook a minute or two longer and remove the pan from the heat. Turn the spaghetti into a warm serving bowl and toss with the sauce. Serve at once.

Spaghetti alla carbonara

This is a Roman dish that has become popular worldwide.

For 5–6	150g streaky bacon or pancetta*, chopped	100g grated Parmesan, or half Parmesan and half Pecorino
500g dried spaghetti	4 eggs	
30g butter		salt and freshly ground pepper

Cook the spaghetti al dente and drain well. While it is cooking, heat the butter and fry the bacon until lightly coloured. Take the pan from the heat and keep warm. Whisk the eggs in a bowl and stir in three-quarters of the cheese. Season well with pepper and a little salt. Return the spaghetti to the pan (off the heat), add the egg and cheese mixture and toss to coat the spaghetti with the sauce. Add the bacon and the remaining cheese, toss once more and serve at once.

Spaghetti alla puttanesca

Whether this dish is named for the whores of Naples or Rome seems to be in dispute, but either way it is well-flavoured and easy.

For 5–6	500g ripe tomatoes, peeled and chopped, or 1 x 400g can chopped tomatoes	120g black olives, stoned and sliced
6 tbs olive oil		1 tbs capers
3 garlic cloves, peeled and chopped finely		salt and freshly ground pepper
¼ tsp chilli flakes	2 tsp chopped fresh oregano or ½ tsp dried	500g dried spaghetti
6 anchovy fillets, chopped		

Put the oil in a pan with the garlic, chilli flakes and anchovies, and fry gently, stirring and mashing the anchovies to a paste. Add the tomatoes, oregano, olives and capers, season with pepper and taste to see whether salt is needed. Simmer gently for 15 minutes, partially covered, and meanwhile cook the spaghetti al dente. Drain thoroughly, turn into a warmed bowl and toss with the sauce.

Linguine with herbs

Only make this if you have good fresh herbs and extra virgin olive oil. The texture of the herbs will be much better if you chop them by hand rather than in a food processor.

For 4–5	1 sprig rosemary	1 shallot, peeled and chopped finely
4 sprigs basil	1 sprig sage	3–4 tbs fresh breadcrumbs
6 sprigs flat-leaf parsley	100ml extra virgin olive oil	600g fresh or 400g dried linguine
3 sprigs marjoram	salt and freshly ground pepper	

Discard the large stalks from the herbs and chop the leaves and small stalks. Infuse them with all but 30ml of the oil in a large serving bowl and season with salt and pepper. Heat the remaining oil and sauté the shallot and the breadcrumbs over moderately high heat until the breadcrumbs are crisp. Cook the linguine al dente and drain thoroughly. Toss the pasta in the oil and herb mixture, scatter over the shallot and breadcrumbs and serve.

Linguine with mussels

This is a Neapolitan dish which can also be made with clams.

For 5–6	2 garlic cloves, peeled and chopped	3 tbs chopped parsley
1kg mussels		salt and freshly ground pepper
4 tbs white wine or water	350ml passata (p. 378, or bought)	
3 tbs olive oil	1 bay leaf	750g fresh or 500g dried linguine
	1 sprig thyme	

Clean the mussels and remove the beards (p. 259), discarding any that are open or broken. Put them in a heavy pan with the wine or water, cover and steam over high heat, until the mussels open (discard any that don't). Shake the pan occasionally. Scoop the mussels from the pan with a slotted spoon and remove the shells. Strain the cooking liquor through a fine sieve lined with muslin (p. 528) into a clean pan, then reduce by a third over high heat. Heat the oil in a heavy pan, lightly fry the garlic, stir in the passata, bay leaf, thyme, half the parsley and the mussel liquor, and season with salt and pepper. Partially cover the pan and simmer gently for 15 minutes.

Cook the linguine al dente and drain thoroughly. Just before the pasta is ready, add the mussels to the sauce and keep it over very low heat so they just warm through. Remove the thyme and bay leaf.

To serve, put the linguine into a warmed serving bowl, toss with the sauce and scatter over the remaining parsley.

Fettuccine with mushroom ragoût

For 5–6	750g fresh fettuccine	mushroom ragoût (p. 144)

Have the mushroom ragoût ready; if it seems a little dry, add 1–2 more tbs cream. Cook the fettuccine al dente, toss with the ragoût and serve.

Tagliatelle with leek

For 5–6

1kg leeks (to give about 600g cleaned)

3 tbs olive oil

1 red pep
small squ

salt and f
pepper

Remove the outer layers, clean and slice
the oil in a covered pan for about 15 mi
stick add a little water. Add the red pep
Season well. There should be only a few
too much, leave off the lid and turn up t
cream. Simmer until the cream has heat
the cooker or over a heat diffuser while o
pasta well, turn into a warmed bowl and
Parmesan.

Tagliatelle with ch

I have tried several chicken liver sauces for pasta, but the one I always come back to
is this simple one with tomato and red pepper. Duck livers can also be used.

For 2

150g chicken livers

1 tbs olive oil

50g pancetta*, diced

1 large garlic clove, peeled and chopped finely

1 small red pepper, cut in small squares

salt and freshly ground pepper

¼ tsp chilli flakes

2 ripe tomatoes, peeled, seeded and chopped

250g fresh tagliatelle

Clean the livers, removing any green or stringy bits, and cut them in pieces. Heat
the oil and lightly fry the pancetta until it starts to colour, then add the garlic and
red pepper and cook over low heat for 6–8 minutes. Add the chicken livers, season
with salt, pepper and chilli flakes and cook over medium heat for 3 minutes. Add
the tomatoes, cook for a further 2–3 minutes. Remove the sauce from the heat.
Cook the tagliatelle al dente and drain thoroughly. Turn the pasta into a warm
dish, toss with the sauce and serve at once.

Riccioli with peas, watercress and prosciutto

This is a lovely dish to make in the summer with young fresh peas; at other times, frozen petits pois would be better than big peas. Use small pasta shapes or twirls; ribbons will not hold the sauce. The sauce is also good without the prosciutto if you prefer.

For 2	2 spring onions, sliced finely	125ml crème fraîche
bunch watercress		salt and freshly ground pepper
1 tbs olive oil or 15g butter	125g shelled peas (about 400g in the pod)	200g fresh pasta
2 slices prosciutto, cut in thin strips		

Remove tough stalks, ageing leaves and whiskers from the watercress and chop the rest coarsely. Heat the oil or butter and lightly fry the prosciutto and spring onions for 2–3 minutes. Add the peas and 2 tbs water. Lower the heat, cover and cook for 5 minutes. Add the watercress and cook 3–4 minutes longer. Stir in the crème fraîche, season and simmer very gently a few minutes more.

Cook the pasta al dente and drain well. Turn into a warm bowl and toss with the sauce. Serve at once. The dish will keep its fresh taste better without added Parmesan.

Farfalle with broad beans and asparagus

For 5–6	90ml olive oil	salt and freshly ground pepper
400g shelled small broad beans (about 1.8kg in the pod)	1 onion, peeled and chopped	basil leaves
600g asparagus	150g pancetta*, chopped	3–4 tbs grated Pecorino
500g farfalle	400g tomatoes, peeled, seeded and diced	

Boil the beans for 6–8 minutes, depending on their size, and drain. Trim the asparagus and parboil them in salted water for 2–5 minutes (depending on thickness). They should remain crisp. Drain, and cut into 2cm lengths. Put on the farfalle to cook al dente and drain thoroughly.

While the pasta is cooking, heat the oil and lightly fry the onion and pancetta.

Add the asparagus, beans and tomatoes. Taste for seasoning and simmer for 3–4 minutes until the tomatoes are lightly cooked. Turn the pasta into a warm bowl, toss with the sauce and top with torn basil leaves and Pecorino cheese.

Fusilli with ragù

For 4–5 | 400g fusilli | ragù (p. 379)

The quantity of ragù in the recipe is sufficient for this quantity of pasta. Cook the pasta al dente and serve tossed with the sauce.

Penne with courgettes and pesto

| For 4–5 | 400g courgettes, cut in batons | salt and freshly ground pepper |
| 400g penne | | pesto (p. 366) |

Cook the penne al dente and drain thoroughly. While they are cooking, cook the courgettes in boiling salted water for 2 minutes, then drain them. They should remain crisp. Toss the pasta with the courgettes and pesto, season and serve with grated Parmesan.

Penne with four cheeses

This is a classic well-flavoured dish best made with a firm pasta such as penne, macaroni or rigatoni. Other cheeses can be used, but try to maintain a balance of sharp and mild flavours.

For 5–6	100g Fontina, cut in small cubes	100g Gorgonzola, cut in small cubes
500g penne		
80ml single cream	100g mozzarella, cut in small cubes	100g grated Parmesan
		freshly ground pepper

Cook the penne al dente. While they are cooking, heat the cream gently in a large heavy pan, add the Fontina, mozzarella and Gorgonzola, stirring constantly so that the cheeses melt. Stir in half of the Parmesan. Season with pepper and keep the sauce over very low heat. When the penne are ready, drain them and tip them into the cheese sauce and mix quickly. Serve straight from the pan and top with the remaining Parmesan.

Ravioli filled with ricotta and walnuts

For 5–6

250g ricotta

100g grated Parmesan

1 egg yolk

100g walnuts, chopped fairly finely

salt and freshly ground pepper

¼ tsp cinnamon

fresh pasta, made with 200g flour and 2 eggs (p. 209) or an equivalent amount of bought fresh pasta

100ml extra virgin olive oil or quick Italian tomato sauce (p. 378)

handful of basil leaves

Soften the ricotta with a wooden spoon and add the Parmesan, egg yolk and walnuts. Season with salt, pepper and cinnamon.

Make the pasta, keep most of it wrapped in clingfilm while rolling one piece. When it has been through the machine on the thinnest setting, put it on a lightly floured surface and cut it into rounds of about 6–7cm diameter (around the rim of a small cup, or with a pastry cutter) – it will make 60 rounds. Place a teaspoon of the filling in the middle of one piece. With your finger or a pastry brush moisten the edges of the pasta and put another round over the top. Press the edges together to make sure they are sealed. Repeat with the remaining pasta and filling. Put the ravioli on a tray lined with silicone paper so they are not touching each other. They can be made up to 6 hours in advance of being cooked and kept in a cool, dry place.

If you are using olive oil, heat it; otherwise, have the tomato sauce ready and keep it warm.

To cook the ravioli, bring 4 litres of water to the boil, add salt and cook the ravioli. They will be ready when they rise to the surface and puff up a little, 5–8 minutes. Test the sealed edge of one to see that it is al dente. Drain carefully with a slotted spoon and transfer the ravioli to a warm serving platter. Spoon over the oil or tomato sauce, top with the basil leaves and serve hot.

Spinach and mushroom lasagne

For 6–8

25g dried porcini (p. 143)

4 tbs olive oil

500g fresh mushrooms, sliced

1kg spinach

2 shallots, peeled and chopped

2 garlic cloves, peeled and chopped

400ml passata (p. 378, or bought)

1 bay leaf

2 tsp chopped fresh thyme or 1 tsp rubbed dry thyme (p. 517)

salt and freshly ground pepper

fresh pasta made with 400g flour and 4 eggs (p. 209), or an equivalent amount of bought fresh pasta

150ml double cream

30g grated Parmesan

Soak the dried porcini in 250ml warm water for 20 minutes. Heat 2 tbs oil and sauté the fresh mushrooms for 4–5 minutes and set them aside. Wash the spinach, removing any large stalks and blanch it for 1 minute in plenty of boiling water, refresh in cold water and squeeze dry. When ready, remove the porcini from the soaking liquid, which should be retained, and slice or chop them. Strain the liquid through a muslin-lined (p. 528) sieve.

To make the sauce, fry the shallots and garlic in the remaining oil. When they are lightly coloured, add the passata, the porcini and most of their reserved soaking liquid, and the herbs; season with salt and pepper. Simmer for 15 minutes, partly covered. The sauce should be of a thick pouring consistency, so if necessary add more mushroom liquid. Remove the bay leaf before using the sauce.

Roll out the pasta as thinly as possible and cut into strips 12–15cm wide. Cook the strips, two or three at a time, in at least 4 litres of boiling salted water. They will only take 2–3 minutes and should be quite firmly al dente. Drop the sheets into a bowl of cold water, then drain on tea towels.

Heat the oven to 190°C, 375°F, gas 5. Lightly oil a rectangular ovenproof dish and smear a little of the tomato sauce over the bottom. Cover with a layer of pasta followed by a layer of mushrooms, another layer of pasta and a layer of sauce. Make another layer of pasta, spread the spinach over it and top with the remaining sauce. Make the top layer of pasta and cover this with the cream. Scatter over the Parmesan.

Bake the lasagne for about 30 minutes until the top is browned. Remove it from the oven and leave for 5 minutes before serving.

Fettuccine baked with crab and fennel

The flavours of fennel and crab complement each other well in this rich dish. Add a few fennel seeds if you like, to emphasize the clear fennel taste. Have the velouté sauce ready before you start on the dish.

For 4–5
2 shallots
2 fennel bulbs
2 tbs olive oil
juice of ½ lemon
½ tsp fennel seeds (optional)

salt and freshly ground pepper
300g crab meat, flaked
a few drops of Tabasco sauce
2 tbs chopped parsley

½ quantity of velouté sauce (p. 372), made with fish or vegetable stock (p. 6, p. 4)
100ml crème fraîche or double cream
500g fresh fettuccine

Heat the oven to 200°C, 400°F, gas 6. Peel and chop the shallots; strip the outer layers from the fennel, cut the remainder in vertical slices and then in strips. Fry the shallots in the oil until just coloured. Add the fennel and fry for 2–3 minutes more, then pour over the lemon juice, season with fennel seeds, salt and pepper, cover and simmer over low heat for 5 minutes. Remove the pan from the heat, stir in the crab meat, Tabasco and parsley.

Combine the velouté sauce and cream and simmer for 2–3 minutes, then add to the fennel and crab. Cook the fettuccine until just al dente, drain thoroughly and add to the sauce. Butter a large gratin dish, turn the pasta mixture into it and bake for 15–20 minutes until the top is golden brown.

Baked shells with chard and ricotta

For 4
400g pasta shells
200g chard leaves

300g ricotta
125ml crème fraîche
½ tsp ground cinnamon

salt and freshly ground pepper
20g butter
3 tbs grated Parmesan

Heat the oven to 190°C, 375°F, gas 5. Cook the pasta shells almost al dente and drain well. While they are cooking, blanch the chard in boiling water for 1 minute, refresh in cold water and squeeze dry. Put the chard in a food processor with the ricotta, crème fraîche and seasonings and purée. Mix the cooked shells with the chard purée and turn into a buttered gratin dish. Dot with the butter and sprinkle over the Parmesan. Cover the dish with foil and bake for 15 minutes, then remove the foil and return to the oven to brown for 5 minutes.

Goat's cheese macaroni

A new version of an old dish.

For 4	250g goat's cheese	3 tbs chopped parsley
1 garlic clove, peeled	350g macaroni	1 tbs olive oil
80ml single cream	freshly ground pepper	

Pound the garlic to a paste in a mortar, if necessary with a little salt, and stir it into the cream. Cut half the cheese into small cubes and add them to the cream. Cook the macaroni al dente and drain well. Toss it with the garlic and cheese cream, a good grinding of pepper and 2 tbs parsley. Heat the grill. Turn the macaroni into a shallow ovenproof dish, slice the remaining goat's cheese and arrange it over the pasta. Grind over a little more pepper, sprinkle over the olive oil and grill, not too near to the heat source, for about 5 minutes, until the cheese is bubbling and turning golden here and there. Scatter over the remaining parsley and serve at once.

Pastitsio

This Greek pasta dish is usually made with a meat sauce and a white sauce, rather like lasagne alla Bolognese. I find both of those dishes rather heavy and prefer this vegetable pastitsio based on a recipe in Anna Thomas's *Vegetarian Epicure*.

For 8	½ tsp cinnamon	100g cooked chick peas (p. 80)
3 tbs olive oil	½ tsp chopped rosemary	500g penne
50g butter	½ tsp rubbed dried oregano (p. 517)	100g grated Parmesan
2 onions, peeled and chopped finely	salt and freshly ground pepper	*béchamel sauce made with:*
2 garlic cloves, peeled and chopped	1kg tomatoes, peeled and chopped or 2x400g cans	40g butter
1 large aubergine, cut into small cubes	2 tbs sun-dried tomato paste	3 tbs flour
3 courgettes, cut into small cubes		600ml milk
		3 eggs

Heat the olive oil and butter in a large heavy pan and fry the onions until soft and translucent. Add the garlic, aubergine and courgettes, the cinnamon and herbs, salt and pepper and stir to mix. Cover and simmer for 10 minutes, stirring once or twice. Add the tomatoes, tomato paste and chick peas and simmer for another 15 minutes. Stir occasionally. The sauce should be thick, but if it is too thick or is sticking to the pan, add a little water.

Heat the oven to 200°C, 400°F, gas 6 and butter an ovenproof casserole or rectangular dish. Cook the penne until just al dente and drain well. Make a layer with half the penne in the dish, sprinkle with a third of the Parmesan and cover with half the vegetable sauce. Repeat the layers. You can make the dish to this point if you wish and refrigerate it until later.

Make the béchamel as on p. 370. Whisk the eggs in a large bowl and pour the béchamel over them, whisking all the time. Pour this sauce over the pastitsio. It should drain all the way through to the bottom; if necessary, make a few slits with a knife to allow it to dribble through. Sprinkle with the rest of the cheese. Cover the dish and bake for 50 minutes to 1 hour. Remove the cover for the last 10 minutes to brown the top. Serve hot.

Asian noodles

Types of noodles and cooking methods

Asian rice noodles

Rice noodles, rice sticks and rice vermicelli are used in southern China and throughout south-east Asia; most are available dried, and a few fresh, from oriental shops. They can be boiled in unsalted water or deep-fried.

Fresh rice noodles are briefly soaked in hot water and then boiled in a large quantity of unsalted water for 1–2 minutes. Dried rice noodles are soaked in warm or hot water for up to 15 minutes so that they soften, and then rinsed in cold water. Vermicelli can then be deep-fried, stir-fried or added to soups straightaway. Thicker noodles are cooked for 2–6 minutes and thoroughly rinsed in cold water. They should remain al dente.

Chinese wheat noodles

Noodles from the north of China are usually made with wheat flour and egg, and can be bought fresh or dried from oriental shops. Fresh noodles are rinsed in warm water for 3–4 minutes and then boiled as Italian pasta in 4 litres of boiling water – do not add salt. Fresh noodles cook quickly, and can be ready in 1–4 minutes, depending on their thickness; dried noodles take a little longer, about 4 minutes for thin noodles to 10 minutes for thick ones. Taste before the recommended cooking time is reached and do not overcook. Drain, rinse in cold water, and drain again thoroughly to get rid of starch. They can now either be used immediately or left to be eaten cold. If they are to be kept for some time, put the well-drained noodles into a bowl and toss with 1 tbs oriental sesame oil to coat the strands and keep them separate. To reheat noodles, dip them briefly into a pan of boiling water or pour boiling water over them in a colander.

Japanese noodles

Noodles are Japanese fast food. Every village has its noodle shops and their dishes have been introduced to Britain in recent years by chains of noodle restaurants, providing nourishing, quick and inexpensive food. In the south of Japan, wheat flour noodles, called udon, are most widely used; they are either ribbon-like or round. Somen are fine wheat noodles used in soups. Ramen are similar to Chinese wheat noodles. Soba noodles, made with buckwheat flour, are popular in Tokyo and the northern part of the country; Korea, too, has buckwheat noodles. Buckwheat noodles are brown-grey in colour and firm textured.

The Japanese have a different method for cooking their noodles: they keep adding cold water to the pan and bringing it back to the boil. Add noodles gradually to 4 litres of boiling water so that the water stays at the boil and stir to prevent them sticking to the pan. When the water returns to a rolling boil add a little cold water and bring back to the boil again. Repeat this process a few times, depending on the type of noodle being cooked. Dried soba (buckwheat) noodles usually need 3 additions of water and can be left to soak for 8–10 minutes after the last boiling. Udon (wheat) noodles need 3–4 additions and are then left to soak for about 15 minutes. Somen (wheat) noodles cook very quickly; after one addition of water they are likely to be ready when the water returns to the boil. Taste the noodles frequently to check progress.

If you find this process too much hassle, Japanese noodles can be cooked in the way described above for Chinese wheat noodles.

Whichever cooking method you use, once the noodles are al dente, drain them and rinse well to rid them of starch. They can be reheated by dipping in boiling water.

Cellophane or beanthread noodles

Noodles made from vegetable starch, usually mung bean starch, are soaked in boiling water for 15 minutes to soften them. Drained and added to other dishes, they soak up flavours and can be braised for up to 20 minutes without losing their texture.

Alternatively, they can be quickly deep-fried so that they puff up and become crunchy. Noodles to be served separately may need cooking for 1–5 minutes. Cellophane noodles turn transparent when they are ready.

Quantities

120–150g fresh or 80–100g dried wheat, buckwheat or rice noodles would serve as individual helpings. For cellophane (beanthread) noodles, allow 50–70g per serving for a main course. If the noodles are to be added to a soup or another dish, 20–30g per person should be enough.

Singapore noodles

Singapore has a great variety of noodle dishes that draw on the food traditions of the Chinese, Malay and Indonesian inhabitants. This is a Malay dish of fried rice vermicelli, prawns and pork or chicken.

For 4		
300g dried rice vermicelli	4 shallots, peeled and chopped	200g small cooked prawns, shelled weight
4 red chillies, seeded	4 tbs sunflower oil	200g bean sprouts, tails trimmed off
3 garlic cloves, peeled and sliced	200g pork fillet, cut in very thin strips	150ml water
	3 tbs light soy sauce	salt to taste

Soak the rice vermicelli in warm water until soft, about 15–20 minutes, then drain them and set aside. Pound the chillies, garlic and shallots to a paste in a food processor, or by using a pestle and mortar. Heat a wok or frying pan and when it is hot, add the oil and swirl it around to coat the bottom and sides. Cook the chilli paste until lightly coloured; do not let it get too dark or it will taste burnt. Add the pork and stir-fry for 1–2 minutes. Add the soy sauce and toss for 1 minute, then put in the prawns and the bean sprouts, toss briefly and add the noodles. Toss to coat them with the oil and paste, then add the water and salt. Toss until everything is well mixed. Serve at once.

Thai crisp noodles (Mee krob)

This is a spectacular dish of rice vermicelli puffed up by deep-frying and then stir-fried with pork, chicken, prawns and egg.

For 5–6

200g dried rice
vermicelli

oil for deep-frying

2 tbs lime juice

2 tbs rice vinegar

2 tbs soy sauce

2 tbs fish sauce
(p. 520)

2 tsp grated unwaxed
lime rind

2 tbs dark brown sugar

1 large onion, peeled
and chopped

4 garlic cloves, peeled
and chopped

2–4 red chillies,
seeded and sliced
finely

200g pork fillet, cut
into thin strips

1 large chicken breast,
skinned, boned and cut
into thin strips

100g small prawns,
cooked or raw

4 eggs, beaten

100g bean sprouts,
tails trimmed

2 spring onions, sliced
finely

3 tbs chopped
coriander leaves

The vermicelli need to be separated into handfuls before frying. The easiest way to do this is in a large plastic bag, otherwise they fly all over the kitchen. In a wide heavy pan or wok heat 5–6cm oil. The oil must be very hot, or the noodles will be tough. When a strand of vermicelli puffs up instantly when dropped into the oil, it is hot enough. Fry the noodles a handful at a time. As they puff up, turn them over, pushing the noodle 'cake' into the oil. It will take only 30–40 seconds for the noodles to become crisp and pale golden. Drain on paper towels and repeat the frying with the remaining batches. Pour off all but about 3 tbs oil from the pan.

Combine the lime juice, vinegar, soy and fish sauces, grated rind and sugar, then set aside.

In the oil remaining in the pan, stir-fry the onion, garlic and chilli until softened, then add the pork and brown it lightly. Add the chicken and continue to stir-fry for 3–4 minutes. Lower the heat, add the prawns and the lime juice mixture. Toss and stir for another minute or until the prawns, if raw, turn pink.

Make a hole in the middle of the ingredients and pour in the eggs. Turn up the heat a little to set them lightly, then stir to distribute them. Add the bean sprouts and fried noodles, a batch at a time, tossing to coat them lightly with the sauce. The noodles are very brittle, take care they don't break up too much. Transfer to a warm serving dish and garnish with the spring onion and coriander.

Variation

· For a vegetarian version, replace the pork, chicken and prawns by 200g tofu cut in cubes and deep-fried and 150g sliced fresh shiitake or oyster mushrooms. You can omit the fish sauce too.

Laksa

This is another Malay dish that has started to appear on menus in Britain in recent years. Laksa has wonderfully clean fresh flavours backed up by a spicy bite. It is always served very hot. Thick rice noodles, spices, coconut milk, chicken or seafood are the main ingredients, and there are dozens of regional variations of this popular dish throughout Malaysia and Singapore. Seafood versions invariably use prawns and often ready-prepared fish balls or fish cakes. They can be bought from Chinese shops (use 2 fish cakes, sliced, or 16–20 fish balls), or you can use fish fillet as I have done here.

Candlenuts are hard, oily nuts that taste slightly bitter. They are used as a thickening agent in Indonesian and Malay cooking; macadamia nuts can be substituted.

For 6–8

3 stalks lemon grass*

2 garlic cloves, peeled and crushed

4cm ginger, peeled, or galangal*, chopped coarsely

2–3 red chillies, seeded

½ tsp turmeric

8 shallots, peeled and sliced

2cm slice dried shrimp paste (p. 513)

5 candlenuts or macadamia nuts

500g dried thick rice noodles

300g bean sprouts, tails trimmed

3 tbs sunflower oil

800ml fish or vegetable stock (p. 6, p. 4)

800ml coconut milk

500g white fish fillet cut into 3cm pieces

400g cooked small prawns

salt

juice of 1 lime

3 spring onions, sliced finely

½ cucumber, seeded and cut in strips

mint leaves

Discard the outer layer of the lemon grass and, using the bottom third only, slice it finely. Purée the first 8 ingredients to a coarse paste in a food processor or using a pestle and mortar. Bring a large pan of water to the boil, put in the noodles, bring it back to the boil and cook for about 6 minutes until they are tender. Drain, rinse thoroughly in cold water. Blanch the bean sprouts for 1 minute, drain and rinse – it helps keep them crisp.

Heat a large pan or wok, add oil, swirling it to coat the base and sides. Add the spice paste and fry, stirring briskly, until the paste is fragrant and the oil separates from the solids. Add the stock and bring to the boil, stirring to blend it with the paste. Lower the heat, add the coconut milk and simmer for 2–3 minutes, then add the fish and simmer until the fish is almost done. Add the prawns. Stir in salt to taste and the lime juice.

Serve laksa in deep bowls. Put a helping of noodles in the bottom, topped with bean sprouts and pour over some of the broth and seafood. Garnish with spring onion, cucumber and mint.

Noodles with broccoli and beef

This Thai dish is quick and easy. Pork or chicken can replace the beef.

For 4		
300g egg noodles	200ml meat or vegetable stock (p. 5, p. 4)	250g broccoli cut into small pieces
250g lean beef, cut in thin strips	2 tbs sunflower oil	2 tbs fish sauce
	3 garlic cloves, peeled and chopped finely	2 tbs oyster sauce
		salt and freshly ground pepper

Cook the noodles until just tender in plenty of boiling water. Drain and rinse them under cold water. Simmer the beef in the stock until lightly cooked. Heat a wok and when it is hot, put in the oil and swirl to coat the bottom and sides. Fry the garlic until golden, add the broccoli and stir-fry for 2 minutes. Add the noodles and toss for 2 minutes, then add the beef and its stock. Let it come to the boil, put in the fish sauce and oyster sauce, season and serve with rice.

Vegetable chow mein

Chow mein means stir-fried noodles, and the dish can be made with meat or seafood, or with vegetables as here. Dried Chinese shiitake mushrooms, sometimes sold as black mushrooms, are available from oriental shops and some supermarkets.

For 4		
6 dried Chinese shiitake mushrooms	3cm ginger, peeled and chopped finely	60g carrots, peeled and cut in thin strips
250g dried egg noodles	4 spring onions, sliced finely, diagonally	6 water chestnuts, sliced thinly
2 tbs sunflower oil	60g bamboo shoots, cut in thin strips	2 tbs light soy sauce
3 garlic cloves, peeled and chopped	60g celery, sliced finely, diagonally	2 tbs mirin* or sherry
		80g bean sprouts, tails trimmed

Soak the mushrooms in hot water for 30 minutes, drain them, discard the stalks and cut the caps in thin slices. Cook the noodles in plenty of boiling water until tender, then drain and rinse them with cold water.

Heat a wok and add the oil, swirling it to coat the bottom and sides. Fry the garlic and ginger for 20 seconds, add all the vegetables and stir-fry for 3–4 minutes. Add the well-drained noodles, soy sauce and mirin, toss and stir for 2 minutes until they are heated through and the vegetables and noodles are well mixed. Stir in the bean sprouts, toss once more and turn into a warm serving dish.

Noodles with chicken

This is a simple Japanese dish which can be made with soba (buckwheat) or udon (wheat) noodles. Japanese noodle broth is based on dashi, a stock made with dried bonito flakes and kelp (*konbu*). You can buy dashi powder or granules in oriental shops which will give a reasonable stock, although not as good as the real thing. Alternatively use a well-flavoured chicken stock. Seven spice powder (*shichimi togarashi*) is a popular Japanese spice mixture used both in cooking and as a table condiment to flavour soups, noodles and grilled meats. It is available from Japanese shops and some supermarkets.

For 4	1 litre dashi or chicken stock (p. 4)	2 tbs mirin* or sherry
350g dried soba or udon noodles	2 tbs light soy sauce	6 spring onions
350g chicken breast, skinned and boned	2 tbs dark soy sauce	seven spice powder

Cook the noodles in plenty of boiling water until tender, drain and rinse in cold water. Fill the pan with water again and put it to boil. Cut the chicken into small pieces. Put the dashi or chicken stock, soy sauces and mirin into the pan and bring to the boil. Add the chicken pieces and simmer gently until cooked, about 8 minutes. Split the spring onions lengthways and cut across into 4cm lengths. Add the onions to the pan and simmer 1 minute more. Remove from the heat.

Reheat the noodles by immersing them in boiling water until just hot. Drain, and divide them among 4 large warmed bowls. Ladle over the stock and arrange the chicken and onions on top. Sprinkle over seven spice powder and serve.

Ramen noodles with vegetables

Ramen are the Japanese equivalent of Chinese egg noodles (which can be used as a substitute). The vegetables can be varied according to what is in season.

For 4

300g dried ramen noodles

1 litre vegetable stock (p. 4)

2 small leeks, quartered lengthways and cut into short lengths

2 courgettes, cut in thin strips

250g mange-tout, trimmed

4 oyster mushrooms, sliced thinly

200g baby spinach

3 spring onions, sliced finely diagonally

Cook the noodles in plenty of boiling water until tender, drain and rinse in cold water. Heat the stock and simmer the vegetables until softened: start with the leeks, courgettes and mange-tout, add the mushrooms after 3–4 minutes and the spinach 2–3 minutes later. They will then need only 1 minute more. Scoop out the vegetables, bring the stock back to the boil and add the noodles. Let them heat through for 1 minute, then put the noodles into 4 deep warmed bowls, ladle over the broth, arrange the vegetables on top and scatter over the spring onion.

Variation

· Instead of cooking the vegetables in stock, stir-fry them in 2 tbs oil, adding them to the wok or pan in the order given, and finish with 1 tbs light soy sauce. Serve as in the main recipe.

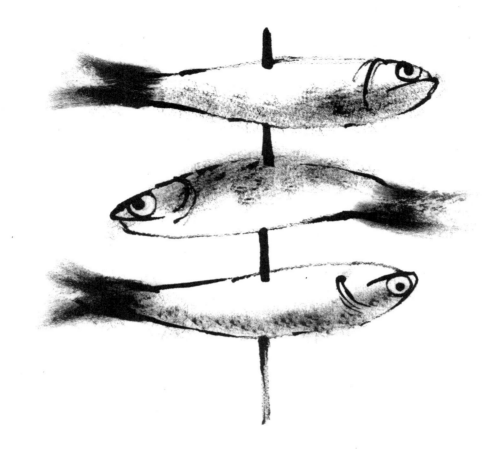

Fish and seafood

There are more than sixty varieties of fish available in the UK. Sea bass, halibut, red and grey mullet, monkfish and turbot are usually available at good fish counters alongside the familiar cod, haddock, sole and plaice. Fish from warm waters – pomfret, swordfish, parrot fish, snappers and breams – are increasingly common. Although small native brown shrimps are now hard to find, except as potted shrimps, the variety of seafood has widened with the arrival in our shops of spiny Mediterranean lobsters, tiger prawns from Thailand and huge shrimps from the west coast of Africa. The best suppliers identify the source – region, country or ocean – of their fish, although distance is not always a criterion in determining what is freshest.

Fish

Choosing

Buy your fish from a fishmonger or supermarket counter with a fast turnover; check how many customers there are and how appetising the fish looks on the slab. A good fishmonger will give advice about what's on sale and the best methods for cooking each one. He will also scale, gut and fillet fish, so unless you are a keen fisherman, there is no need to know how to do these jobs yourself. Don't forget to ask for the bones if you want to make stock.

Nothing beats *really* fresh fish just out of the water, but for most of us that is seldom attainable. However, icing or freezing top-quality fish on the fishing vessel immediately after it is caught does preserve flavour and freshness. The fish is cleaned and kept chilled in ice at 0°C until (ideally) it reaches the customer in a few days' time. Alternatively it is flash-frozen to very low temperatures, and when thawed may have better flavour and texture than a 'fresh' fish that has spent too long in transit from the docks. Freshness is the key to successful fish cookery, so it is a good idea to go shopping with an open mind rather than a planned menu, and buy what is best.

Fish and health

The connection between eating unsaturated fats and the low incidence of heart disease was recognised some years ago and fish is an excellent source of unsaturated fats; white fish have less than 1% fat.

Oil-rich fish such as herring, mackerel, salmon, sardine and tuna are even more beneficial. They supply omega-3 fatty acids which have been shown to help reduce fats in the blood and lessen the risk of a heart attack.

Whole fish

The best whole fish look as though they are alive, with an overall bright appearance, undamaged shiny scales, red gills and full rather than sunken eyes. The flesh should feel elastic and firm when pressed and the smell be clean and sweet – the smell of the sea, in fact.

Fillets and steaks

If possible, have fillets and steaks cut to order because whole fish keep better than pieces. If not, look for cuts that are translucent and bright, with no blemishes or bruises. The flesh should be resilient when touched; ask the sales person to press a finger into it, and if it leaves an indentation, buy something else. Avoid fillets and steaks that are dry or show yellowing edges or are standing in too much water – they will have no taste and a soggy texture. As with whole fish the smell must be sweet and clean. If you buy pre-packed fish, inspect it as much as you can; bad fish and shellfish can be smelled through the packaging, but if it is just about to go off, the odour may not yet penetrate.

Fishermen should take time to gut their catch to eliminate as quickly as possible the main source of bacterial infection, and then keep it properly iced.

Farmed fish

The quality of farmed fish varies greatly depending on the conditions in which they are raised. Farmed fish are fattier because they have less exercise. Farmed salmon often have a fatty deposit along the belly and may have white streaks of fat in the flesh which are almost certainly a sign that they have been farmed in sheltered waters. Salmon farmed offshore in water with strong currents where they swim a lot will, however, be more like wild salmon. Density makes a difference: 14–18kg per cubic metre allows the fish room to swim; if they are packed in at 25–30kg per cubic metre they obviously have less space. Feed is important, too; a high percentage of fat will make the fish grow quickly but will not improve texture.

Apart from looking for excessive fat when buying fish, it is almost impossible to tell a well-farmed fish from a poor one. If you have a good fishmonger it is reasonable to suppose that he buys from a reliable source, and he should be able to tell you about it. Most salmon on sale these days is farmed, as is rainbow trout and the rather tasteless so-called sea trout which is nothing more than a rainbow trout grown to a larger size in sea cages – a far cry from a wild sea or salmon trout. Farmed bass, gilt head and other breams, cod, halibut and turbot are also on sale, often through supermarkets. My fishmonger reckons bream and bass are acceptable, although the flavour of the bass is diminished because of its limited diet, but he finds the texture and flavour of turbot and halibut poor and will not stock them. However, given the severe problem of over-fishing in some waters, it is likely that we shall see more and more farmed fish in our shops. But on the farming front there are problems other than the quality of the fish. There is evidence that intensive salmon farming is depleting stocks of wild salmon as the fish become infested with sea lice from the farms and die. Poor farming practices are also causing marine pollution, which governments have to address.

Cured fish

Before refrigeration, preserving fish to last through the winter was a necessity for survival. Drying, salting and smoking are now practised because we like the taste, whether of kippers or caviare. Smoked salmon and trout, Finnan haddock and Arbroath smokies are the specialities of our islands. With the exception of smoked salmon and trout which are eaten raw, cold-smoked fish such as kippers and haddock are best gently poached. Hot-smoked fish like eel, mackerel, Arbroath smokies and cod roe do not need cooking, although they can be lightly grilled. Salt herring is popular in northern France and Belgium. The Dutch consume huge quantities of lightly salted maatjes and green herring as soon as the season starts at the end of May; their other delicacy, smoked eel, is available all year. In Germany and Scandinavia they prefer soused herrings and rollmops, and the Swedes have their renowned gravadlax.

The peoples of the Mediterranean basin salt anchovies and have a passion for salt cod imported from Norway and Iceland. Whole books of recipes are devoted to it in Portugal and in Venice, the salt cod capital of Italy. New England and the eastern seaboard of Canada also have a tradition of salt cod stews, chowders and boiled fish dinners. Although not much appreciated in Britain, where it is hard to buy good quality salt cod, it is well worth trying; buy the best you can find from a Spanish, Portuguese or Italian shop and soak it for 12–24 hours to get rid of the salt.

Storing

Fish is best eaten as soon as possible after purchase. If it is properly iced when bought, fish can keep for a day or two, perhaps longer; much depends on when it was caught. Ideally, fish should be kept at 0°C, which is lower than the temperature of a domestic refrigerator (usually around 4°C). Put steaks and fillets in a covered dish and stand it on an ice pack. Gutted and wrapped whole fish keep well between ice packs.

Quantities *(for a main course serving)*

In general, you need less of a rich meaty fish than of a light lean fish. Quantities also depend on how the fish is to be cooked, what other ingredients will be used and whether you plan to make a rich sauce. When buying steaks or fillets of a dense-fleshed fish such as tuna, swordfish or salmon, allow 150–180g per person; for round fish and larger flatfish such as halibut or turbot allow 200–250g; of the more delicate flatfish such as flounder or plaice you may need to allow 300g. For fish on the bone allow about 450g per person, but if the fish has a large head and heavy bones (e.g. John Dory, snapper) you will need more. If you are cooking a large whole fish, about 350g per person should be enough. Buy one small fish (about 250g), such as red mullet or trout, per person.

Cleaning and preparing

Normally the fishmonger will do the work for you, but if you need to do it yourself – for instance, if you are lucky enough to be given a fish freshly caught from river or sea – here are the essentials you need to know.

Trimming

Use scissors to cut away the fins on either side, along the belly and the back, and to cut the tail into a 'V' shape.

Removing the head

If the head is to be removed – and some fish are cooked with their heads intact – insert a heavy knife behind the gills, cut firmly and deeply, cutting through the bone.

Scaling

Scaly fish are almost always scaled before cooking. It is a messy job because scales tend to fly about, but it is quite easy – simply scrape the scales with the back of a knife or a fish-scaler, working from the tail to the head. I prefer to work on a large board, holding the fish by the tail, but some people find it easier to work under running water.

Gutting

Using a small knife make a slit along the belly from the anal vent to the gills. If there is roe, detach the sacs carefully and put them aside for cooking. Loosen the innards with your fingers and pull them out, then scrape out the kidneys that remain attached to the backbone. If the fish is to be cooked with the head on, the gills must be removed because they taste bitter. Either pull them out through the stomach cavity or lift the gill flaps, cut the gills loose with scissors and then remove them. Discard the guts and gills and wash the fish thoroughly, getting rid of all blood.

Cutting steaks from round fish

Start behind the head and with a heavy knife cut thick even slices. If necessary, hit the back of the knife with a wooden mallet to cut through the spine. Make sure to keep the knife vertical.

Boning a round fish

Continue the cut made to gut the fish down to the tail. Hold the upper fillet back and run a knife blade between the transverse bones and the flesh of the side that is lying on the work surface. For a small delicate fish this is better done with the fingers.

When the bones are loose along one side, turn the fish over and perform the same operation on the other side.

Taking care not to tear the flesh, open the fish as wide as possible and run the knife down both sides of the spine. Again, for a delicate fish, do this with your fingers. Use scissors to cut through the spine at either end and lift it out.

To bone small oily fish (herring, mackerel) remove the head, open the fish as wide as possible and place it, skin side up, on a board. Press firmly with the fingers along the bone. Turn the fish over and lift out the bone; cut it loose at the tail and remove any small bones left behind.

Filleting round fish

You need a long-bladed filleting knife for this job. Lay the cleaned fish on a board with the backbone towards you. Insert the knife horizontally and cut through the skin from head to tail along one side of the backbone with a long continuous stroke. Now cut down to the backbone just behind the gills. Hold the fish steady and, with the knife still horizontal, slice into the fish behind the head, feeling for the backbone with the blade. Keep the knife in contact with the bone as you cut down the length of the fish, slicing the fillet away from the bones. Turn the fish over and repeat with the other fillet. Tidy up any ragged edges. Use tweezers to remove any pin bones.

Filleting flat fish

Use a knife with a long pliable blade. Put the fish, dark skin side up and tail towards you, on a board. Cut round the edge of the fish with the point of a knife to outline the fillets. You will feel the little bones that support the fins. Next, cut the fish to the bone around the head. Cut through to the backbone from head to tail. Insert the knife, almost flat, between the head end of one fillet and the ribs and cut with long strokes to free the flesh. Keep the blade in contact with the bones. When the upper part of the fillet is freed, lift it and continue cutting along the length. Turn the fish round and repeat to remove the second upper fillet. Turn the fish over and follow the same procedure for the lower fillets. Trim any ragged edges.

Skinning fillets

The skin is easier to remove after cooking and most fish are roasted or grilled with the skin on. If the skin has to be removed before cooking, put the fillet, skin side down, on a board. Make a small cut at the tail end with a sharp heavy knife to separate skin and flesh. Hold the skin firmly and slip the knife between the skin and the flesh. With the knife almost parallel to the skin, use short strokes to separate them, keeping the skin taut and lifting and pushing the fillet in front of the knife.

Use the bones and skin to make stock (p. 6).

Skinning whole flat fish

The dark skin (and sometimes the light one) of flat fish is removed before frying and grilling. Remove the upper dark skin by cutting it across where the tail joins the body. Loosen the skin with the tip of the knife until you can grasp it firmly. Salt your fingers to give them a better grip, or use a cloth to hold down the tail with one hand and pull the skin decisively towards the head with the other.

To remove the white skin, turn the fish over when you reach the head, hold the fish by the head and keep pulling the skin down the white side until you reach the tail. Alternatively, repeat the process described for the dark skin, cutting it loose at the tail.

Remember to remove the gills and gut before cooking.

Cooking methods

With the exception of large whole fish, fish cooks very quickly and you can prepare a meal in minutes. The flesh needs only to become opaque – remove it from the heat as the last translucence disappears; if cooked at too high a temperature or for too long, fish becomes dry and loses its flavour and may disintegrate. It is best to err slightly on the side of undercooking, and take into account that the fish continues to cook while being served.

Whatever the cooking method, the cooking time for whole fish, steaks or fillets (but not seafood) is calculated by the thickness of the fish at its thickest part, not by its weight or length. After a long period of extensive tests, the Canadian Department of Fisheries published the rule that fish should be cooked for 10 minutes per 2.5cm of thickness. This is a reliable method to follow, but it is not quite foolproof because, for example, if the sides of a whole fish are slashed at intervals the heat will reach the centre more quickly than with an uncut fish. Also, for a very large whole fish the overall size should be taken into account.

To see if fish is done, press the thickest part with your finger; it should feel firm and slightly resistant. Another method is to insert a fork or the tip of a knife into the thickest part and gently flake a little of the fish to see if it is opaque. With a whole round fish, the spines of the dorsal fin will pull loose when it is ready.

Poaching

Poaching is a simple way of cooking fish as long as some basic rules are observed. The fish is immersed in simmering liquid, which must barely move, and certainly never bubble for that will overcook the fish and make the flesh fall apart. It is most suitable for large fish to be cooked whole – salmon is the classic example – but works well too for sea bass, carp, a small cod, and for flatfish like brill and turbot. Smoked haddock fillets are extremely good poached in milk and water.

Fish is poached in a court-bouillon (p. 5) flavoured with herbs and vegetables or in a fish stock (p. 6) made with fish bones and trimmings as well as vegetables. The fish remains quite plain when poached, so it is a good idea to reduce some of the cooking liquid to make a sauce.

In any event, don't throw out the court-bouillon after poaching your fish; use it for a soup or stew or boil it down and freeze it for later use.

Steaming

Steaming is cooking over rather than in liquid, which may be water or a court-bouillon (p. 5). Fish needs gentle even steam produced by simmering water; the blasts of steam produced by water at a rolling boil will overcook it. Steaming is a plain method, but the fish can be enhanced with herbs, spices or vegetables, or placed on a bed of seaweed. The Chinese, who are masters of fish steaming, use black beans (p. 242), spring onions and ginger as flavourings. Put a piece of foil or a plate with a rim under the fish in the steamer basket so that the juices from the fish are not lost.

Steaming is best suited to small to medium-sized whole fish such as sea bass, grey mullet or bream or to fillets and steaks.

Stewing and braising

Stewing is similar to poaching, but the liquid in which the fish is cooked is served as part of the dish. The fish or seafood may be sautéed first and the stew will include vegetables and flavourings. A stew should only simmer, not boil, or the fish will break up. Cut the fish to pieces of similar size to ensure even cooking; more delicate fish and shellfish may be added towards the end of the cooking time.

Firm-fleshed fish such as sea bass, monkfish and conger eel work well in stews; flaky fish such as cod and hake are good too, but must be timed carefully so they do not fall apart. Stewed octopus is terrific.

To braise fish, sauté it and combine with vegetables and flavourings as above, but add only a little liquid. A whole fish, such as red snapper, bream, salmon, turbot or carp is excellent braised on a bed of vegetables. Shark, monkfish and other firm fillets or steaks, cut into evenly sized pieces, are also good for braising.

Grilling and barbecuing

These are two of the most successful ways of cooking fish and seafood. Both are suitable for small to medium-sized whole fish, for meaty steaks or kebabs of tuna or swordfish, salmon or monkfish. Oily fish such as sardines, herring and mackerel will baste themselves from within. Thin flatfish fillets – sole, plaice, dabs – are not suited to barbecuing, but will grill well. Flaky white fish – cod, haddock, hake – are also best grilled because they start to collapse almost as soon as they are done.

For the barbecue it is worth buying a fish basket which can be adjusted to hold the fish tightly; its long handles make it easy to turn. Whether grilling or barbecuing, the heat should not be too high when cooking fish. Slash the sides of whole fish and rub with oil and chopped herbs. Alternatively marinate fish and use the marinade to baste the fish while cooking.

Baking and roasting

Baking or roasting, whichever name you choose, is a good method for cooking a whole fish. Slash the sides at intervals, put flavourings in the cavity and cook at medium or high heat. The skin protects the flesh and the spine conducts heat evenly. Use only thick steaks or fillets for roasting. Fish is usually roasted with vegetables with which it is served. Baste it from time to time with oil, stock or wine.

Whole fish can be wrapped in foil, or fillets enclosed in a *papillote*, a parcel made with foil or parchment paper, and then baked. Preparation is quick and none of the juices or flavour is lost.

Sautéing, frying and stir-frying

A non-stick frying pan is a great help; the fish will not stick and you need less fat. Before sautéing heat the pan. When it is really hot, add the fat – clarified butter* which can be heated to higher temperatures than ordinary butter without burning, or a mixture of clarified butter and oil. The fat must be hot enough or it will be absorbed by the fish, but if it gets too hot the fish will burn on the outside before it is cooked through. Add the fish to the pan over medium to high heat, sear the outside, then lower the heat and turn the fish to finish cooking. Avoid overcrowding. The fish should be crisp on the outside and moist inside. Drain it on kitchen paper and do not cover it or it will lose its crispness.

Fish to be sautéed can be dusted with flour or breadcrumbs, either plain or flavoured with dried herbs or spices. You can make a quick sauce by adding liquid – fumet or stock (p. 6), wine, lemon juice, water – to the pan after the fish has been taken out, boiling it down to thicken a little, flavouring it, and finishing it with a spoonful or two of oil or butter or cream. Alternatively a salsa (pp. 380–2) makes a good accompaniment to sautéed or fried fish.

Sautéing works well for small and medium-sized flatfish – sole, flounder, plaice – and for small round fish such as trout, red mullet, mackerel; also for most fillets and steaks.

Many oriental dishes of fish and vegetables are stir-fried. As with sautéing, it is important to heat the pan or wok before the oil is added, and to maintain a high temperature, otherwise as liquid is given off by the vegetables the food will start to steam. Only fish with a firm texture are suited to stir-frying; delicate flaky fish will disintegrate. Foods for stir-frying are cut to a fairly small size to ensure even cooking in a very short time.

Deep-frying

For deep-frying, small whole fish (for example, whitebait) or small fillets are best; thick pieces of a bigger fish are likely to frizzle on the outside, leaving the inside raw. Protect the flesh with a coating of flour, egg and breadcrumbs or batter (*see* fritto misto of scallops and vegetables, p. 266, and tempura batter, p. 497) and dry the surface of the fish as much as possible before coating so that there is less spattering when it goes into the hot oil. The oil must be very hot so that the coating crisps and seals the flesh; if it is not hot enough the fish will absorb it and become 'fatty'; too hot and the fish will burn. *See* p. 99 for more details on deep-frying temperatures. Only cook small quantities at a time because the temperature of the oil will drop when the fish is put in. The fish is ready when the coating is golden brown – a matter of minutes – and should be drained on kitchen paper and eaten straight away before it loses its crispness. Do not cover it. Japanese tempura uses a light batter to coat fish and vegetables which are deep-fried and served with a dipping sauce.

Microwaving

The microwave comes into its own for fish cooking, especially if you are cooking small quantities. The precise timing of the microwave helps ensure perfectly cooked fish but, as with other methods, err on the side of undercooking initially and if necessary reset the oven for short intervals until it is cooked through. Microwaving is best for simple dishes in which the fish would otherwise be poached, steamed or braised, but in the microwave the amount of liquid used is tiny. For more complicated dishes, I find it more trouble than it is worth. Whole fish should be slashed on each side so the skin doesn't burst. Position fillets or steaks with the thicker parts to the outside of the dish. Make sure to use a dish that is suitable for the microwave and cover with the lid or microwave plastic film. If it is not covered the moisture in the fish evaporates too quickly.

Remove the skin from fillets; gut and remove heads, tails and fins from whole fish. No liquid is necessary since the fish will cook in its own juices, but if you wish to add stock, wine or lemon juice for flavouring do not put in more than 4 tbs per 150g of fish. Marinating fish before microwaving works well.

By far the best book on everything to do with the microwave is Barbara Kafka's *Microwave Gourmet*; I have followed her advice for the cooking times given here. The times given are for a 600–700 watt oven with a carousel at 100 per cent power.

To steam		*To steam*	
1cm-thick fillets of 180–200g		*2cm-thick fillets or steaks of 200–250g*	
1 fillet	2 min	1 fillet/steak	3 min
2 fillets	2½ min	2 fillets/steaks	4½ min
4 fillets	5 min	4 fillets/steaks	6 min

Arrange fillets side by side; steaks should be placed with the thin belly flaps to the centre. Cover tightly.

To steam	
whole fish of 250–300g	
1 fish	2 min
2 fish	3–3½ min
4 fish	5–6 min

Arrange very small fish with their tails to the centre; bigger fish can be placed head to tail. Cover tightly, or wrap in microwave film before putting on a plate. Leave whole fish to rest, covered, after cooking.

Marinades

Marinades are important in preparing fish to be grilled, roasted or fried; they tenderize the flesh and enhance flavour. In most cases, fish needs only 1–2 hours marinating before cooking, and it is best done in the refrigerator, but bring to room temperature before cooking. The marinade can be used to baste the fish during cooking. Some recipes here have a marinade included; for more choice, *see* pp. 386–8.

Round large-flaked fish

Essentially members of the cod family – cod, coley, haddock, hake, whiting – these fish have white flesh that breaks into large thick flakes when cooked. The taste is mild. They are very adaptable; apart from being the usual fish for fish and chips, members of the cod family can be poached, steamed, braised, pan-fried, grilled or baked (*see* cooking methods pp. 235–9). Well-flavoured sauces – mustard (*see* below), tartare, horseradish (p. 365), salse verde (p. 367) – make good accompaniments.

See also bourride (p. 255) and fish curry (p. 257).

Poached cod with mustard sauce

This is a quick and easy recipe: even if you have to make the court-bouillon, it won't add more than 20 minutes to the preparation time. Hake or haddock could replace the cod.

For 4		
½ quantity of court-bouillon (p. 5)	200ml white wine	salt and freshly ground pepper
2 shallots, peeled and chopped	200ml water	4 pieces of cod fillet, with skin, weighing 170g each
	100ml crème fraîche	
	100g butter	
	1 tbs Dijon mustard	

Heat the court-bouillon gently, and meanwhile prepare the sauce. Put the shallots, wine and water in a pan, bring to the boil and cook until only a small amount of liquid remains. Stir in the crème fraîche and reduce by half. Now add the butter, a little at a time, using a whisk to blend it in. Do not have the heat too high for this operation. When all the butter is incorporated, stir in the mustard, taste and season with salt and pepper. Remove the pan from the heat and keep warm.

Bring the court-bouillon to the boil if it is not yet there, slip in the cod fillets, bring back to the boil and simmer for 10 minutes. Lift out the fish, draining it thoroughly, and remove the skin. Strain the court-bouillon and use as the base for soup or a sauce.

Serve the cod with the sauce and new or mashed potatoes.

Roast cod with couscous and pomegranate and avocado salsa

Other firm fish fillets such as haddock or monkfish or tuna steaks could be used instead of cod.

For 4		
pomegranate and avocado salsa (p. 382)	5–7 tbs olive oil	1 red or yellow pepper
250g couscous	3 shallots, peeled	1 tbs chopped mint
	2 courgettes	4 cod fillets, about 170g each

Start by preparing the salsa and leave it at room temperature for an hour or two for the flavours to mingle.

Heat the oven to 200°C, 400°F, gas 6. Next prepare the couscous according to the instructions on the packet; or *see* p. 202. Dress with a little of the olive oil. Chop the shallots finely, dice the courgettes and pepper. Heat 1–2 tbs oil and sauté the shallots for 2 minutes, add the courgettes and cook for 2 minutes more. In a separate pan, sauté the pepper in 1 tbs oil for 2 minutes. Use a fork to combine the vegetables with the couscous, add the mint and keep warm.

Lightly oil a baking dish which will hold the cod in one layer. Heat 2 tbs oil in a frying pan and quickly sauté the fillets, 1 minute on each side. Transfer them to the baking dish and roast for 5 minutes.

To serve, spoon couscous into the centre of each warmed plate and place a piece of cod on top. Spoon some of the salsa to one side.

Roast hake on a bed of vegetables

Hake is often underrated in Britain, and much of the catch finds its way to Spain where it is prized. If you can buy a good-sized hake, this is an excellent way to cook it; bream, grey mullet, salmon or bass can also be cooked in the same way. In the south of France, a monkfish tail on the bone (called a *gigot de mer*) is often roasted on a bed of vegetables after being spiked with slivers of garlic, as would be a leg of lamb. The vegetables can be varied, according to what is available – aubergines, green or red peppers, fennel bulbs are all suitable.

For 4–6	3 courgettes, cut in 1½cm slices	salt and freshly ground pepper
a small bunch of mixed herbs – thyme, rosemary, oregano, savory	4 garlic cloves, peeled and crushed	1 hake weighing 1.5–2kg
5 tbs olive oil	6 tomatoes, peeled, seeded and coarsely chopped	juice of 1 lemon
2 onions, peeled and finely sliced		200ml white wine

Heat the oven to 190°C, 375°F, gas 5. Chop the herbs finely. Heat 3 tbs olive oil in a pan and sauté the onions for 3–4 minutes until soft, then add the courgettes and crushed garlic. When the courgettes are lightly coloured, stir in the tomatoes and most of the herbs, season with salt and pepper. Cover and simmer for 10 minutes.

Lightly oil a gratin or other oven dish big enough to hold the fish and vegetables. Slash the sides of the fish in 2 or 3 places, rub it with salt and pepper, press some of the remaining herbs into the cuts and put the rest into the cavity. Spread the vegetables over the dish, lay the fish on top, pour over the lemon juice and wine and drizzle 2 tbs of oil over the top. Roast for 30–40 minutes; test with the point of a knife near the backbone – the flesh will flake easily when it is ready. Serve straight from the dish.

Fish steaks with black bean sauce

The Chinese often cook a whole fish in black bean sauce for a special celebration. The same sauce can be used for steaks with great success. Cod, haddock, hake and salmon are all suitable. In Singapore they add chopped chillies; if you like hot food add 2–3 chillies to the garlic and ginger paste.

Black bean sauce is a thick Chinese sauce based on fermented soy beans and is particularly good as a base for cooking fish and vegetables. It is available in jars from supermarkets and oriental shops.

For 4	3 tbs sunflower oil	1 tbs light soy sauce
2 garlic cloves, peeled and crushed	4 fish steaks, weighing about 180g each	4 spring onions cut in 3cm pieces
1 tsp peeled and chopped ginger	3 tbs black bean sauce	lemon or lime juice
	120ml water	1 tbs sesame oil

Pound the garlic and ginger to a paste with a pestle and mortar. Heat a frying pan or wok, add the oil and fry the fish for 1 minute on each side. Remove from the pan and set aside. Add the ginger and garlic to the oil and stir-fry for 1 minute, then put in the black bean sauce and stir-fry for 1 minute. Return the fish to the pan, pour over the water and soy sauce, bring to the boil and simmer, uncovered, for 4–5 minutes, depending on the thickness of the steaks. Put in the spring onions for the last 2 minutes.

The sauce should have reduced to a few tablespoons, but if necessary, put the fish on a serving dish, keep warm and boil the sauce down a bit more. Taste – it probably won't need more salt, because the beans and soy sauce are salty – and add lemon or lime juice.

Pour the sauce over the fish, sprinkle with the sesame oil and serve with rice.

Round firm fish

These fish vary greatly in size from the small red mullet to huge swordfish and tuna. In between come sea bass, a number of breams, grey mullet, gurnard, monkfish, salmon and snapper. Small fish are sold whole or filleted for poaching, grilling and baking; larger fish are usually sold only as steaks or fillets. The flesh varies in texture from neat, small flakes with a delicate flavour (bass, bream) to firm medallions (monkfish) or meaty steaks (swordfish or tuna); these are best braised, grilled or baked and served with a well-flavoured sauce.

Steamed sea bass

Steaming is the best way to cook a really fresh fish. This recipe uses Chinese flavourings which also work well with bream, snapper or carp. Sichuan pepper (*fagara*) is a small red-brown berry, the fruit of a prickly ash tree. It is used extensively in Chinese cooking and has a spicy-woody fragrance and a numbing effect in the mouth rather than a pungent peppery taste. Discard any loose black seeds since they are bitter. It is available from oriental shops and some supermarkets.

For 2–3	2 tsp sesame oil	*garnish*
1 bass weighing 750–900g	¼ tsp crushed Sichuan pepper or white peppercorns	3 spring onions, chopped finely
50g finely chopped smoked ham	3cm piece fresh ginger, peeled and chopped finely	1 tbs sunflower oil
1 tbs light soy sauce		1 tbs sesame oil
1 tbs rice wine* or dry sherry	1 tsp salt	

Clean the fish thoroughly and make 3 slashes in each side. Combine the ham, soy sauce, wine, oil, pepper and ginger and mix well together. Rub the fish all over and in the cavity with salt. Push some of the flavourings into the slashes, rub them over the skin and put the remainder into the cavity.

Place the fish on a plate with a rim, curving it if necessary, and put the plate in the steamer or on a rack in a wok. Pour 6–8cm hot water into the steamer or wok, cover and steam over simmering water for 12–15 minutes. Make a small cut near the backbone to see if the flesh flakes easily, but don't let out too much steam while doing so.

Lift out the fish, keeping all the juices on the plate with it. Scatter the spring onions over the top. Heat the two oils slowly in a small pan and when very hot pour the liquid over the fish and serve at once. If you wish, offer the dipping sauce below.

Soy and ginger dipping sauce Combine 4 tbs light soy sauce with 2 tsp shredded fresh ginger.

Bream baked in a salt crust

No dish could be simpler than this: all you need is a handsome fish and a lot of coarse sea salt. A bream would be my first choice, but bass and snapper can also be used.

For 4	1 bream weighing 1–1.5kg	about 1.5kg coarse sea salt

Heat the oven to 220°C, 425°F, gas 7. Have the fish gutted and trimmed but not scaled. Put an even layer of salt, about 1cm thick, in a baking dish just big enough to hold the fish and lay the fish on it. Cover the fish entirely with salt until you have a mound of salt and no sign of the fish. Bake for 25 minutes for a fish weighing 1kg, 35 minutes for one weighing 1.5kg. For a fish weighing less than 1kg, cook for 20 minutes. Remove from the oven, break and carefully lift off the salt crust, and then remove the skin. Lift off the top fillets, take out the backbone and remove the lower fillets.

Serve with extra virgin olive oil, lemon quarters and a mill of black pepper or with salsa verde (p. 367) or sauce vierge (p. 360).

Red mullet with sauce vierge

This is a quick dish to make during the summer when the garlic is young and tomatoes are ripe.

For 4	2 tbs olive oil	salt and freshly ground pepper
sauce vierge (p. 360)	8 red mullet fillets	

Have the sauce ready before cooking the fish. Heat the oil in a frying pan and fry the mullet fillets, skin side down, for 2 minutes, then turn and fry the flesh side for 30 seconds. Lift the fillets onto a warm serving dish, season lightly, spoon over the sauce and serve.

Poached salmon

I learned to poach salmon from Jane Grigson's *Fish Cookery*, and I give her instructions here. You will need a fish kettle; if you don't own one, your fishmonger may have one for hire. Alternatively, an approximation to poaching can be achieved by baking in the oven (p. 237, p. 246).

Tear off a piece of foil large enough to wrap the salmon. If the fish is very large make two straps out of more foil to help lift it when it is cooked. Lay them across the big piece to either side of the centre, then brush the foil with oil. Put the cleaned salmon in the middle of the foil and fold up the sides and ends to make a loose parcel. Twist the edges to close tightly.

For salmon to be served cold: Put it on the tray in the fish kettle; if necessary turn the tail up the side of the pan. Add cold water to fill the pan almost to the top. Bring slowly to the boil, allow the water to bubble a few times, then remove the kettle from the heat and put it in a cool place. Leave undisturbed for several hours, until the water is quite cold. Lift out and unwrap the parcel and you will have a perfectly cooked salmon.

For salmon to be served hot: Fill the fish kettle half full with water and bring to the boil. Put in the wrapped salmon on the strainer tray. Bring back to a steady simmer, then start the timing. For fish weighing up to 2kg allow 5 minutes per 500g; up to 3kg 6 minutes. Let stand for 10 minutes before unwrapping the parcel.

Don't forget when cooking a large fish that thickness should be more of a guide to cooking time than weight alone. If you have a very large fish, cut it in two or three pieces, wrap and cook each one separately, then mask the joins with a garnish when it comes to serving.

To serve, lift the salmon on its straps onto a long dish or oiled piece of wood. Remove the skin from the top fillet, leaving head and tail intact. Garnish simply with a bunch of watercress and, if you wish, very thin rounds of lemon or cucumber along the fish. Serve cold with mayonnaise (p. 362) or salsa verde (p. 367) or hot with béarnaise (p. 374) or sorrel sauce (p. 377).

Microwaved salmon with ginger and lime

For 4		
2 tsp sesame oil	1 tbs dry sherry	salt
2 tsp soy sauce	1 unwaxed lime	2 spring onions
1 tbs peeled and finely chopped ginger	4 pieces of skinned salmon fillet, 1cm thick, each weighing 180g	

Combine sesame oil, soy sauce, ginger and sherry and rub the mixture into the salmon. Marinate for 30 minutes. Grate the rind from the lime and squeeze out 4 tsp juice. Arrange the fish in a microwave dish, season lightly with salt and pour 1 tsp lime juice over each fillet. Cover tightly and steam at full power for 5 minutes. Serve the salmon with its juices, sprinkled with lime zest and chopped spring onion with wedges of lime on the side.

Salmon trout baked in foil

Baking in foil is a simple and quick method of preparing a fish weighing 1–2kg. Bass, bream, grey mullet can all be cooked in this way. I have used flavourings of shallot, tarragon sprigs and lemon for the salmon trout because it has a delicate flavour; a more robust fish would benefit from crushed garlic and coriander leaves. When baking the fish, reckon 10 minutes per 2.5cm thickness at its thickest part, but also bear in mind the overall size of the fish. A 1.5kg fish will take about 40–45 minutes.

For 4–6	2 lemons, peeled and sliced thinly	2 tbs white wine or vermouth
1–2 tbs olive oil		
3 shallots, peeled and chopped	1 salmon trout weighing 1–1.5kg	2 tbs fish fumet (p. 6), optional
4–5 sprigs tarragon	salt and freshly ground pepper	

Heat the oven to 220°C, 425°F, gas 7. Tear off a piece of foil large enough to make a baggy wrapping for the fish, making sure there is enough foil at each end of the fish to close the parcel tightly. Place the foil on a baking sheet and oil the central part lightly. Scatter shallots, tarragon and lemon on it, lay the fish on top, put more flavourings inside and on top of the fish. Season with salt and pepper. Lift up the long sides of the foil, then the short sides so that the fish lies in a sort of box. Pour in 1 tbs oil, the wine or vermouth and the fumet if you have some. If not, depending on the size of the fish, you may wish to add a little more wine. Bring the long sides of the foil together, close the top seam of the parcel, folding it at least double and pinching it closed. Make similar seams at the head and tail ends. The parcel should be loose, but airtight.

Bake the fish, following the guidelines on cooking time above. Open the parcel carefully from the top and insert the point of a knife near the backbone. If the fish flakes easily it is ready. Transfer the fish to a warmed serving dish, remove the upper skin and spoon over the juices, or if you are not confident about lifting it out, transfer the whole parcel and serve it from that.

Baked snapper with chermoula

Chermoula is an excellent Moroccan seasoning mix for fish. Garlic, onion, parsley, coriander, chilli powder and paprika form the basis, together with one or more of the other staple spices of Moroccan cooking – saffron, cumin or cinnamon. Sometimes the peel of a preserved lemon is added to the mixture. Chermoula can be used for a whole fish as here, or with steaks that are pan-fried. Grey mullet, bass, bream or hake are all suitable.

The list of ingredients may look forbiddingly long, but the marinade is quickly prepared, and the rest is done in the oven.

For 4–6	For the chermoula	
1 large or 2 medium snappers weighing 1.5–2kg, scaled and gutted	3 garlic cloves, peeled	1 tsp paprika
	1 tsp salt	¼ tsp chilli powder
800g–1kg ripe tomatoes	I onion, peeled and chopped finely	½ tsp cumin
salt to taste	small bunch flat-leaf parsley, chopped	peel from 1 preserved lemon (p. 513), chopped finely (optional)
150g cracked green or purple olives	small bunch coriander, chopped	6 tbs olive oil
		juice of 1 lemon

Wash the fish and pat dry. Make sure all the scales are removed because you can't see them once the fish is covered with the chermoula, and it is unpleasant to get one in your mouth. Slash the sides in two or three places.

Crush the garlic with the salt and combine with the other chermoula ingredients to make a thick paste. Rub well all over the fish, making sure some goes into the slashes and into the cavity. Put the fish in a dish and leave in the refrigerator for at least 2 hours, or even overnight, to allow the flavours to develop.

Take the fish from the refrigerator at least 30 minutes before it is to be cooked and place it in an ovenproof dish. Heat the oven to 190°C, 375°F, gas 5. Slice the tomatoes and put them over the fish. Season lightly with salt and scatter around the olives. Spoon over any remaining chermoula. Drizzle a little oil over the top if there is not much chermoula left.

Cover with foil and bake for 35–45 minutes, depending on the size and number of fish. Serve from the dish.

Variations

· Replace the tomato slices with thin slices of lemon from which you have removed the pith and rind.

- If you wish, slice thinly and parboil 1kg potatoes and put them in layers under the fish before baking.
- If you have used the chermoula to marinate fish steaks, pat the fish dry with paper towels, dust with flour and fry until golden brown on both sides. Serve with lemon wedges.

Swordfish kebabs

I've chosen swordfish here, but kebabs can be made with any firm textured fish; tuna and monkfish are other excellent choices. Other marinades for fish are given on p. 386.

For 4		
700g swordfish steaks	1 garlic clove, peeled and chopped finely	1 tsp paprika
½ small red onion, peeled and chopped finely	2 bay leaves, torn	salt to taste
	handful flat-leaf parsley, chopped	3 tbs white wine or vermouth
		4 tbs olive oil

Cut the fish into 3cm cubes. Combine all the other ingredients except for 2 tbs oil and rub over the fish. Leave to marinate for at least 2 hours. Thread the swordfish cubes onto skewers (if you use wooden ones, soak them in water for 10 minutes first) and brush the fish with the remaining oil. Grill over charcoal or under a very hot indoor grill, turning once.

Allow about 3 minutes per side. Serve with quartered lemons and salmoriglio (p. 377). Other good accompaniments would be coriander chutney (p. 383), tarator sauce (p. 364) or tomato vinaigrette (p. 359).

Microwaved trout with gremolata

For 2		
1 unwaxed lemon	salt and freshly ground pepper	1 large garlic clove, peeled and chopped finely
1 trout, weighing 400–500g	3 tbs chopped parsley	

Grate the rind from the lemon and squeeze out 2 tsp juice. Sprinkle a little of the juice inside the fish and season well. Mix the parsley, garlic and lemon rind. Stuff the cavity with half of this gremolata mixture. Season the outside of the fish, splash over the remaining lemon juice and wrap the fish tightly in microwave plastic film. Put it on a plate and steam at full power for 1½ minutes. Turn the fish and steam for another 1½ minutes. Leave to stand for 1–2 minutes before unwrapping. Lift the top fillet, remove the bone, then the lower fillet. Scatter over with the remaining gremolata.

Tuna steaks with Seville orange marinade, olives and pine nuts

This dish has Sicilian influences in the flavourings: pine nuts or almonds, green olives, capers, parsley or mint, sometimes raisins or currants and, of course, garlic occur in many dishes from that beautiful island. If it is not the season for Seville oranges, use the juice of 1 sweet orange and 1 lemon.

For 4	2 bay leaves	2 tbs pine nuts
small bunch of parsley	salt and freshly ground pepper	20 green olives, stoned and cut in half
4 tuna steaks, weighing 150–180g	2 tbs olive oil	1 tbs capers
juice of 2 Seville oranges and grated rind of 1		

Strip the parsley leaves off their stalks. Marinate the tuna steaks in half the orange juice with the parsley stalks and bay leaves for up to 1 hour. Lift out the steaks, season with salt and pepper on both sides and brush lightly with oil. Grill, or fry in a hot non-stick pan, for 2–3 minutes on each side, depending on thickness.

Meanwhile heat the remaining juice in a small pan with the grated orange rind, pine nuts, olives and capers and cook gently for 2–3 minutes. Spoon the sauce over the steaks and garnish with the chopped parsley leaves.

Oil-rich fish

This group, also round in form, includes anchovies, herring, mackerel and sardines. They are small, sleek fish with fairly soft flesh. In varying degrees, they are rich in fats, including omega–3 fatty acids. Salmon and tuna are also oil-rich but are included in Round firm fish on p. 243 because they are firm and can be cooked in a greater variety of ways than the small, soft-fleshed oily fish.

Poach, grill, bake or fry these with herbs and spices and serve with sharply flavoured sauces (mustard, p. 359 and horseradish, p. 365) and salsas to counteract the oiliness. *See also* marinated herring (p. 40).

Barbecued sardines

Fresh sardines straight from the grill are perfect garden and beach food. Serve them with parsley, salsa cruda (p. 380), or tomato sambal (p. 384).

For 4	juice and grated rind of 1 large or 2 small unwaxed lemons	2–3 sprigs of thyme
12–16 sardines, scaled and gutted		½ tsp crushed black peppercorns
	2 tbs sunflower oil	salt

Put the sardines in a shallow dish, mix together all the other ingredients and pour over the fish, making sure they are all coated. Leave to marinate for 20–30 minutes. Grill, turning once, and allow 3–4 minutes on each side. Brush with the marinade after turning. Serve with the salsa or sambal and crusty bread.

Baked mackerel with orange and coriander

For 4	1 tsp finely crushed coriander seeds	2 tbs chopped coriander leaves
4 small mackerel, filleted	salt and freshly ground pepper	
juice of 1½–2 oranges		

Heat the oven to 190°C, 375°F, gas 5. Arrange the mackerel fillets in a shallow ovenproof dish and pour over the orange juice. Season with coriander seed, salt and pepper. Cover the dish and bake for about 15 minutes. Serve from the dish with the fresh coriander leaves scattered over the top.

Variation
Baked stuffed mackerel Stuff 4 medium mackerel with a mixture of 50g fresh breadcrumbs, 1 finely chopped shallot, 1 tbs chopped tarragon, 1 tbs chopped parsley, 2–3 tomatoes, seeded and diced, the juice and grated rind of 1 unwaxed lemon, salt and freshly ground pepper. If you remove the backbone first (p. 234), they will be easier to stuff. Bake, covered, in a well-buttered dish for 25–30 minutes at 190°C, 375°F, gas 5.

Flat fish

This is another group that varies greatly in size, from the large halibut and turbot to brill, John Dory, skate, the various soles, plaice and dabs. Turbot and dover sole have succulent firm flesh and are rightly prized. Brill is somewhat softer, while halibut tends to be drier. John Dory is firm fleshed and well flavoured, though often neglected because of its ugly appearance and fierce spines. The small fish – lemon sole, plaice, dabs – have soft flesh that is easy to overcook. Halibut and turbot are usually sold as steaks; the smaller fish are sold whole and may be cooked whole or filleted. Skate is different from the others in that it has a cartilaginous rather than a bony structure; it is sold as wings which have a fine-textured flesh. Flat fish can be poached, steamed, fried, grilled or baked.

Béarnaise (p. 374), sauce vierge (p. 360) and sorrel sauce (p. 377) make fine accompaniments.

See also fish and shellfish ragoût (p. 255).

Steamed brill with mushrooms and leeks

Brill is a rather neglected flatfish, somewhat smaller than a turbot with a similar texture and fine flavour, and it is much cheaper. I've used small cap mushrooms in the recipe, but wild mushrooms such as pieds de mouton or chanterelles, even for part of the quantity, would enhance the flavour. I don't recommend large field or portobello mushrooms because they darken the sauce.

For 4	2 tbs olive oil	90g butter
400g mushrooms	100ml fish stock or use the brill bones and head to make stock (p. 6)	1 brill, weighing about 1.5kg, filleted
400g leeks, white part only		
1 shallot, peeled and chopped finely	salt and freshly ground pepper	

Slice the mushrooms. Slice 300g of the leeks into rounds; cut the remainder in half lengthways, then into 10cm lengths and cut each piece into julienne* strips. Put the shallot to soften in the olive oil and add the mushrooms when it has taken colour. Sauté, stirring, until the mushrooms have given up their liquid and absorbed it again. Stir in the sliced leeks, pour over the stock and season with pepper and salt. Cover and simmer.

Heat 20g of the butter in a small pan and sauté the julienned leeks, shaking and stirring the pan, until it is just cooked, but retains a bite. Set aside.

Season the brill, place the two fillets on plates with rims that will fit inside the steamer, and steam over simmering water for about 5 minutes. If the fillets are thick they may take a little longer.

While the fish is steaming, stir small pieces of the remaining butter into the vegetables. To serve, spoon the mushroom and leek onto a warm serving dish or individual plates; divide each brill fillet in two, remove the skin, and place the fish on top and garnish with the sautéed leek.

Poached skate with vinaigrette

For 4	½ tbs chopped parsley	½ fennel bulb, chopped finely
1 recipe for court-bouillon (p. 5)	½ tbs chopped tarragon	2 small tomatoes, peeled, seeded and diced
1kg skate wings	½ tbs chopped chervil	
1 tbs lemon juice	1 tbs capers	salt and freshly ground pepper
1 tbs olive oil		

Heat the court-bouillon gently in a wide pan until it boils. Cut the skate wings into sections if they are very large. Add the fish to the pan, bring back to the boil and simmer for 8–10 minutes. Lift out the skate, draining it well. Strain the court-bouillon and pour 100ml into a bowl. Add the lemon juice, olive oil, herbs, capers, fennel and tomato, and season to taste.

Remove the skin from the skate, pour over the vinaigrette while the skate is warm and leave to marinate for 15 minutes. Serve at room temperature.

Grilled sole

The sole is the finest of the small flat fish and it responds well to simple treatment. Plaice, flounder and lemon sole may all be grilled too, but will cook in about half the time.

For 2	2 tbs lemon juice	salt and freshly ground pepper
2 Dover sole, each weighing 300g	30g butter, preferably clarified butter*	

Remove the skin from both sides of the fish (p. 235) or ask the fishmonger to do this. Sprinkle with lemon juice and brush with melted butter. Under a pre-heated grill, cook for 4–5 minutes a side, turning the fish once. Season lightly and serve with pats of savoury butter (p. 385) on top.

Steamed turbot with sorrel sauce

Turbot is a beautiful firm-fleshed fish with an excellent flavour and a price to match; halibut or if you can find it, John Dory, make good and more affordable substitutes.

For 2	2 pieces of turbot fillet, each weighing 170g	salt and freshly ground pepper
sorrel sauce (p. 377)		

Make the sauce. Season the turbot fillets, put them on a plate with a rim that fits inside the steamer and steam over simmering water for 6–8 minutes, depending on the thickness of the fish. Test with the point of a knife; the flesh should flake easily.

Arrange the turbot on warm individual plates, spoon a little of the sauce over each piece and serve the rest separately.

Fishcakes

Good fishcakes are delicious; they need a high proportion of fish to potato and lively flavourings. The English version is flavoured with tarragon and shallot, the second uses classic Indian spicing. Almost any fish can be used for this recipe, but salmon is the only oily fish I find successful.

English fishcakes

For 4	2 shallots, peeled and chopped finely	salt and freshly ground pepper
500g potatoes, peeled		flour
30g butter or 2 tbs olive oil	2 tbs tarragon leaves, chopped	1 egg and dried breadcumbs (optional)
500g fish fillet, skinned	2 tsp anchovy essence (optional)	oil for frying

Boil the potatoes in salted water, drain and mash them with the butter or olive oil. Poach the fish for 8–10 minutes until it becomes opaque or steam it in the microwave, which will take 3–3½ minutes depending on the thickness of the fillets (p. 239). When it is cool enough to handle, remove all bones and flake the fish. Mix it carefully with the potato, adding the shallots, tarragon and, if using, anchovy essence. Season with pepper and a little salt; the anchovy essence will provide more salt. Shape the mixture into 8 flat cakes in your hands and coat them in seasoned flour – using a plain pastry cutter you can shape the outside more evenly – then pat the cake flat with a knife. Do not make the cakes too big, they are fragile. I prefer to cook my fishcakes like this, but if you wish for a firmer, crunchy coating, lightly whisk the egg, then pass the floured fishcakes through the egg and coat them in breadcrumbs.

Heat a little oil in a frying pan and fry the fishcakes over moderate heat for 2–3 minutes each side. Turn them carefully with a spatula. Drain on kitchen paper. Serve with lemon quarters.

Indian spiced fishcakes

Mashed sweet potato makes a pleasant change from ordinary mash in spiced fishcakes.

For 4		
500g sweet potatoes, peeled	seeds of 3 cardamom pods*	1 small onion, peeled and chopped finely
30g butter or 2 tbs sunflower oil	2 tsp coriander seed	salt
500g fish fillet, skinned	1 tsp anise or fennel seed	flour
	½ tsp chilli powder	1 egg and dried breadcrumbs (optional)
		oil for frying

Boil the potatoes in salted water, drain and mash them with the butter or oil. Cook and flake the fish as described above. Grind together the cardamom, coriander and anise or fennel seed, and combine with the chilli powder. Mix the fish, potato and onion; season with the spices and with salt. Form the mixture into 8 flattened cakes with your hands and coat in flour. For more crunchy fishcakes, lightly whisk the egg, pass the floured fishcakes through it and then coat in breadcrumbs. Fry in a little hot oil over moderate heat for 2–3 minutes on each side, turning once. Drain on kitchen paper and serve with coriander chutney (p. 383) or raita (p. 384).

Fish stews

Why, I wonder, do the English have no native fish soup or stew? The Scots have Cullen Skink, but further south nothing. For islanders, we are certainly rather conservative, basic even, in our fish tastes, and yet nothing could be simpler than a fish stew. Just about every country in the world that has a coastline has recipes for fish stews.

Bourride

This is a classic provençal dish which is less well known than bouillabaisse, but infinitely easier to make outside the region because it does not rely on such a wide variety of local fish. Use whatever white fish looks good when you go shopping: choose 2 or 3 different types – cod, bass, whiting, monkfish, gurnard are all suitable. Oily fish are best avoided. What is important is to take the time to make an aïoli and to take care that it does not curdle when adding it to the broth.

For 4	1.5–1.8kg fish fillets including heads and bones	8 slices of french bread, slightly dried out in the oven
aïoli (p. 363)		
700ml fish stock made from the trimmings (p. 6)		

Make the aïoli and set aside. Strain the stock into a wide shallow pan and bring to a simmer. Poach the fish fillets or steaks over very low heat for 10 minutes. If the stock starts to boil, remove the pan from the heat. Lift out the fish, cover and keep warm. Set aside 1 tbs of aïoli per person. Put the rest into a pan and add a ladleful of broth off the heat. Stir well with a wooden spoon. Add the rest of the broth, a little at a time, making sure it blends in. Put the pan on a very low heat and stir constantly until the broth thickens enough to coat the spoon. The texture should be smooth and velvety. Pay close attention because if it curdles, it cannot be retrieved.

To serve, put the slices of bread in a deep dish or soup tureen and pour over the broth. Serve the fish and the reserved aïoli to accompany the soup.

Fish and shellfish ragoût

For 6	150ml vermouth	150ml single cream
300g red mullet fillet	300ml fish stock (p. 6)	a little lemon juice
250g firm white fish fillets (sole, brill, monkfish, or a mixture)	2 leeks, white part only, sliced finely	salt and freshly ground pepper
500g mussels	500g medium or large cooked prawns, peeled	50g butter
150ml white wine		

Cut the fish fillets into equal-sized pieces, about 50g each. Scrape the mussel shells clean and pull out the beard protruding from between the shells. Discard any that are broken or that won't close when tapped. Put them in a heavy pan with the white wine, cover and cook over high heat for 3–4 minutes until they have opened: discard any that don't. Tip them into a colander placed over a bowl to collect the cooking liquor. Remove the mussels from the shells, keeping 8 or 12 of the best-looking mussels for the garnish.

Pour the vermouth into a heavy pan and reduce to 3 tablespoons. Add the stock and the strained mussel liquor, and reduce by half. Add the leek and simmer for 1–2 minutes, then carefully put in the pieces of fish. Simmer for another 1–2 minutes, then add the prawns and mussels and let them heat through. Lift out all the fish and shellfish and arrange them in 4 warmed bowls.

Add the cream to the pan and simmer for 2 minutes. Do not let it boil. Taste and season with a squeeze of lemon juice, salt and pepper. Finally, whisk in the butter in small pieces. Spoon the sauce over the fish, garnish with the reserved mussels and serve.

Waterzooi

This Flemish stew is usually made with freshwater fish (perch is good) or chicken, but in Antwerp and other coastal towns it is often made with monkfish.

For 4	30g butter	juice of 1 lemon
1kg monkfish	4–5 saffron threads	4 tbs finely chopped parsley
2 shallots, peeled	200ml dry white wine	
2 leeks, white part only	300ml fish stock (p. 6)	150ml single cream
2 carrots, peeled	salt and freshly ground pepper	2 egg yolks
2 inner stalks celery		

Bone the monkfish, remove all the filmy grey skin and cut into slices about 3cm thick. Chop the shallots finely, cut the leeks, carrots and celery into julienne* strips. Heat the butter in a large heavy pan and gently sweat* the vegetables until soft, but make sure they do not brown. Crush the saffron and soak in a little hot water for a few minutes. Lay the pieces of fish on top of the vegetables and pour over the wine, stock and saffron. Season with salt and pepper. Bring to the boil, then simmer over moderate heat for 10 minutes.

Remove the fish and keep warm, bring the liquid back to the boil, add the lemon juice and parsley, taste for seasoning. Beat together the cream and egg yolks, stir in a ladleful of the cooking liquor, then pour this mixture back into the pan and stir for a moment or two over very low heat. Do not let it boil or the egg will curdle.

Distribute the fish among 4 warm soup plates, pour over the broth and vegetables. Serve with bread or boiled potatoes.

Fish curry

This is a richly flavoured curry which is not too hot – if you would like it hotter, add more chillies. It is easy to make in larger quantities for a party. When it is available, pomfret is a good choice, but I've used cod, hake and monkfish successfully too. Fresh curry leaves can be bought from Indian shops; if you can't find them you can try dried leaves, but often they don't have much flavour. Even without curry leaves the dish will still have a good taste. If you take the trouble to heat the whole cumin and coriander seeds in a dry frying pan for a few minutes or two before grinding them, the flavour will be improved.

For 4		
1 tbs tamarind* paste (or 2–3 tbs lime juice)	2 onions, peeled and chopped	6 green chillies, split in 2 and seeds removed
2 tbs sunflower oil or ghee*	2 garlic cloves, peeled and chopped	2 tomatoes, quartered
½ tsp mustard seeds (p. 76)	1 tbs peeled and chopped fresh ginger	salt to taste
2 sprays curry leaves (optional)	½ tsp turmeric	200g coconut cream blended with 350ml hot water
	1 tsp ground cumin	750g fish steaks
	1 tsp ground coriander	

Soak the tamarind paste in 2–3 tbs water. Heat the oil and put in the mustard seeds and curry leaves. Cover with a lid because the seeds will pop and fly about. When this has happened, add the onions and fry gently until they soften and turn a light gold, about 5–8 minutes. Now put in the garlic and ginger and fry for 2–3 minutes, stirring frequently. Stir in the spices, chillies and tomatoes. Add salt if you wish.

Pour in the tamarind liquid and half the coconut milk. Stir well to mix all the ingredients together. Bring to a simmer. Put in the fish steaks and the remaining coconut milk. Cover and simmer until the fish is cooked – about 5–10 minutes, depending on how thick it is. Serve with plain rice, or rice garnished with chopped dill.

Seafood

Choosing

Freshness is especially important for shellfish, and this is helped by much of it being still alive when sold. Whole clams, mussels and oysters must be alive with their shells closed; do not buy them if many have gaping shells. If a shell is slightly open, it will respond to a light tap and close up if the mollusc is alive; if it doesn't, discard it. Opened oysters are best avoided; they have often been rinsed in water before being put on ice. This ruins the flavour and starts deterioration. Scallops are still occasionally found live in their shells; the fishmonger will open and clean them. If they are ready cleaned, look for firm glistening flesh; avoid any that are withered or flabby, or scallops lying in water because they absorb it.

In contrast to the indifferent quality of much farmed fish, shellfish such as mussels, oysters and queen scallops are raised very successfully with no loss of flavour.

Live crabs and lobsters should move quite energetically when you buy them; if they have spent too long in a tank or a box of seaweed they may be sluggish. Small lobsters tend to have a better flavour than the very large ones. Crabs and lobsters should feel heavy for their size. To buy a cooked crab or lobster, go to a reputable fishmonger who boils them himself. Do not buy a crab with a crack or hole in its shell because the meat will be watery and overcooked. Spiny or rock lobsters which have no claws are usually sold as tails, either frozen or precooked.

Prawns and shrimps are sold cooked or raw, but most have been frozen straight after the catch. Avoid dry-looking cooked shrimps and prawns since they will be overcooked.

The flesh of squid and cuttlefish should be creamy beneath the outer membrane; octopus has white flesh beneath a grey skin. Squid and cuttlefish are often frozen immediately after the catch and are still frozen on the fishmonger's slab. If you buy them frozen, thaw in the refrigerator. Avoid any that are lying in water because they, too, absorb it. Medium- and smaller-sized creatures tend to have more tender flesh than the huge ones sometimes on offer.

As with fish, all shellfish should smell sweet with no hint of ammonia.

Storing

Molluscs need to breathe, so keep them in a bowl or open bag in the refrigerator. They will keep for 1–2 days if necessary at the normal refrigerator temperature. Lobster and crab should be cooked the day they are bought; put them in a box of seaweed or on wads of damp kitchen paper in the refrigerator until you are ready to cook.

Thawed prawns and shrimps will only be good for a day or two at most; but frozen will retain flavour and texture for up to 3 months if stored in the freezer. Defrost them in the refrigerator.

Remove the innards from squid and its relations when you get them home (if bought frozen, wait until thawed) and store in the refrigerator for no longer than a couple of days.

Quantities

For 1 person, allow 350–500g mussels in the shell, or about 150g shelled. Allow 6–12 oysters or clams and 4–6 scallops or large prawns per person, depending on how they are to be served. A 1.25–1.5kg lobster will satisfy 2 people; a crab weighing 750g–1kg will yield about 350g meat, enough for 3. For squid, cuttlefish and octopus, allow about 180–200g per serving before cleaning.

Cleaning and preparing

Mussels

Put them in a large bowl or sink full of cold water. Discard any that have broken or gaping open shells. Scrape any barnacles from the shells and remove the beard by tugging it firmly. As each one is cleaned, place it in a bowl of clean water. Cook the mussels immediately after cleaning. Never leave them standing in fresh water.

Oysters

There are many different types of oyster, but all are opened in the same way, and you will need a proper oyster knife: this has a short strong blade and guard between the blade and the handle. Scrub the shells briefly under running water. Hold the oyster in a cloth in the palm of your hand, flat shell uppermost, or hold it firmly on a cloth on a flat surface. Insert the blade between the shells near the hinge – this may take a bit of force. Lever and twist the blade and run it around until you sever the muscle that holds the shells together. Lift off the top shell and run the knife around the oyster to loosen it from the bottom shell. Wipe away the inevitable bits of broken shell; if they are too fine, strain the liquid through muslin (p. 528); the strained liquid may either be returned to the shell or added to a sauce. If the oyster is gritty, rinse it in its own liquid but do not add water since that will ruin the flavour.

If you intend to cook the oysters, opening them is made easier by steaming briefly or cooking for a minimum time (about 2 minutes for 6, 3½ minutes for 12 in a covered dish) in a microwave oven until the shells open slightly. Don't leave them for too long or they will start to cook.

Clams

Open clams in the same way as oysters.

Scallops

Cut off the dark intestinal thread along the side, and any traces of the brownish skirt and the tough white muscle on the side. The red or orange coral is edible. If the scallops are of very different sizes, slice the large ones horizontally to achieve the same thickness.

Prawns and shrimps

To shell prawns and shrimps, twist the head to detach it from the body. Peel back the 'legs' and pull them and the shell away from the flesh. Hold the tail shell and gently pull the flesh loose.

Crab and Lobster

See pp. 261–2 and p. 263.

Squid

Squid may appear daunting and strange, but they are very easy and quick to clean. Pull and twist the head to separate it from the body, removing the innards with it. Cut the tentacles from the head just above the eyes; they will remain joined together by a thin circle of flesh. Within the circle of flesh is the hard 'beak' which you squeeze out with your fingers and discard. Discard too the head and innards, keeping the ink sac if you want to use it in the sauce. The transparent pen, as the rudimentary bone is called, can be hooked out of the body with your finger and discarded. Wash the tentacles and body, removing any mucus from inside the pouch. Peel off the reddish-purple skin with your fingers; it comes away easily. Pull off the edible fins on either side of the body and skin them too. The squid (body, fins and tentacles) is now ready for use.

If you are making an oriental dish or intend to grill it, you may need to score the squid. Cut the body open and put it onto a board, inside uppermost. With a sharp knife, cut lightly into the flesh in parallel lines, then turn the squid and make another set of cuts at right angles, to create a diamond pattern. The cuts help to tenderize the squid.

Cuttlefish

Cuttlefish can be prepared in the same way as squid, but it is easier to cut the body open, and lift out the oval bone. Discard the membrane that covers the innards. If you want to use the ink, remove the sac carefully, otherwise discard it with the rest of the guts. Cut the tentacles from the head and press out the beak, as with squid. Wash thoroughly and strip away the outer skin; having a much thicker membrane than the squid, it needs to be pulled firmly.

Octopus

Sever the ring of tentacles. Turn the body inside out and discard the guts and the beak (*see* above), also the ink sac unless you wish to use it. The skin is quite tough; rubbing it with salt may help to remove it, but it is more easily peeled off after cooking. Baby octopus are tender enough, but larger ones would benefit from beating with a mallet. At the Sydney fish market, you can see them being thrown around in cement mixers. At home, a good way to tenderize octopus is to plunge it into a large pot of boiling water for a few seconds, lift it out to cool slightly, then repeat the process twice more. Then add flavourings, bring the water back to the boil, put in the octopus and simmer until tender.

Cooking methods

For more detailed information on cooking methods, *see* pp. 236–9. Take care not to overcook seafood; it quickly becomes tough and rubbery.

Boiling

Prawns, raw in the shell, are plunged into well-salted boiling water and cooked until they turn pink. They will take 2–5 minutes, depending on size. Taste one to see if they are ready; undercooked prawns have a mushy texture, overcooked they are tough.

Boiling is too vigorous a method, in fact, for cooking most seafood, but crab and lobster are brought to the boil and simmered.

Crab Many people feel squeamish about cooking crabs and lobsters, but they do taste so much better than most that can be bought ready-prepared unless you have a source which you know prepares dressed crabs daily. Crabs become less active if put in the refrigerator for a few hours or in the freezer for an hour before cooking. Put the crab into very well-salted water (use 100g salt per litre of water), bring to the boil and simmer for 10 minutes per 500g. Remove to cool in a colander.

When it is cool enough to handle, lay the crab on its back and twist off the claws and legs. Crack them with a mallet or nutcracker and, using a flat metal skewer where necessary, scrape out all the flesh. To remove the flesh from the shell, twist back the tail flap and lift out the body section. Discard the grey-white gills and the small stomach sac just behind the mouth. Pick the flesh into two bowls, one for white meat, the other for brown. Take your skewer again and a teaspoon and poke out the flesh from all the crevices of the body. Make sure you do not put bits of thin shell or cartilage in with the meat. This is a long and fiddly, but rewarding, job.

If you want to serve the meat in the shell, break off the jagged edge, scrub out the shell and arrange brown meat down the side and white on either side. For purists, freshly dressed crab needs only a little freshly ground black pepper and lemon juice, but mayonnaise or remoulade sauce (p. 363) go well with it too.

Soft-shell crabs, which are crabs that have moulted and not yet grown into a new hard shell, are in season in late spring. Except for the gills they can be eaten whole and are excellent sautéed or stir-fried.

Lobster The easiest way to cook a lobster is by boiling. Use plenty of well-salted water – 100g salt to 1 litre of water – or a court-bouillon (p. 5) and, after weighing the lobster, plunge it in head-first when the water is at a rolling boil. When the water returns to the boil, lower the heat so it simmers and start to time the cooking, allowing 10 minutes for the first 500g and 4 minutes for each additional 500g. Remove the lobster from the pot and wait until it is cool enough to handle.

To serve in the shell, insert the tip of a large heavy knife in the cross mark behind the head and cut down to the tail. Return to your starting point and cut through the head. Discard the gravel sac just behind the eyes, the feathery gills and the grey-black intestinal thread that runs down the tail. Remove the creamy light green tomalley and, from a female lobster, the roe (both can be used for sauces).

To remove the flesh from the shell, put the lobster on its back, twist off the legs close to the body and extract the meat with a skewer. Detach the claws and crack them with a mallet or sturdy knife and remove the meat neatly, discarding the cartilage. Cut along each side of the body. Remove the stomach sac, the tomalley and any roe. Lift the flesh from the tail end, loosening it if necessary with a small knife, and detach it from the shell.

Lobster can be served hot with hollandaise sauce (p. 373) or cold with mayonnaise, gribiche sauce (p. 362) or a light aïoli (p. 363).

Poaching

This is a particularly good method for cooking scallops; they will take about 1 minute to become opaque. Cook shelled prawns in the same way; they will take 1–3 minutes to turn pink, depending on size.

Steaming

This is a successful method for prawns and scallops; allow a little longer than you would for poaching. Mussels and clams steam in their own juices in a closed pan.

Stewing and braising

Uncooked lobster, octopus and squid, cut into even-sized pieces, can benefit from long cooking in a sauce.

Grilling or barbecuing

Prawns and scallops can all be grilled or barbecued. Mussels and clams can be put on the grill over a barbecue; when their shells open, they are ready. Squid can be cooked very fast on a barbecue or griddle plate if it has been opened and scored (*see* 260); otherwise, it needs long slow cooking. Anything in between turns the texture rubbery.

Baking and roasting

This is good for prawns and scallops, especially in a *papillote*, a parcel made with foil or parchment paper.

Sautéing and stir-frying

Sautéing works well for soft-shell crabs, lobsters, prawns, scallops and squid. Lobsters, prawns and scallops all stir-fry beautifully. Seafood must be raw: if it has been cooked in advance, it will get tough, although you can stir a few cooked prawns into a sautéed dish at the last moment.

If you want to prepare a sautéed lobster dish, you need first to kill the lobster by driving a knife through the spinal cord. Put the lobster in the refrigerator for a few hours or freeze for 1 hour to reduce activity. Drive the tip of a very sharp knife through the centre of the cross behind the head. Cut decisively and firmly. Death is instantaneous. Follow the instructions above for splitting a lobster in two or, if you want to keep the tail in whole slices, chop across the join between the head and tail with a heavy cleaver. Now cut off the claws and legs and crack them. Cut the tail in slices following the joints in the shell. Split the head lengthwise and remove stomach sac and gills, tomalley and roe. Keep the latter two for the sauce.

Deep-frying

This is successful with squid rings and small shellfish – such as prawns, scallops, oysters. They are usually coated in a batter (p. 266, p. 247). *See* p. 99 for more details on deep-frying temperatures.

Microwaving

It is advisable to keep microwaving for small quantities and simple dishes. The cooking times given below are again from Barbara Kafka's *Microwave Gourmet*.

To steam

medium and large prawns

in shell, 250g	2–3 min
in shell, 500g	3–4 min
shelled, 250g	2–3 min

Cover the plate or dish tightly.

To steam

scallops

250g	2 min
500g	3 min

Cover the plate or dish tightly.

Marinades

The marinades given on pp. 387–8 are used mostly for prawns, which only need to be marinated briefly.

Mussel and potato stew

A simple cold weather supper dish.

For 4		
small bunch of parsley or coriander with long stalks	4 stalks celery	2 garlic cloves, peeled and chopped
	4 medium potatoes	
2kg mussels	2 tbs olive oil or 30g butter	freshly ground black pepper
75ml water	1 onion, peeled and chopped	4 tbs chopped parsley or coriander leaves
1 glass dry white wine		

Strip and reserve the leaves off the parsley or coriander. Clean the mussels (p. 259). Put them in a large pan with the water, wine and herb stalks over high heat. Cover and shake the pan from time to time. When the mussels are open (discard any that don't), scoop them into a colander standing in a bowl, and remove them from their shells to a small bowl. Spoon over a little of the cooking liquid and cover so they don't dry out; if you are going to wait some time to finish the dish, put them in the refrigerator. Strain all the mussel liquor through a fine sieve lined with muslin (p. 528), leaving any large bits of grit in the pan.

Peel the strings from the celery (use a potato peeler) and cut the stalks into 2cm pieces; peel and cut the potatoes to chunks of a similar size. Heat the oil or butter in a heavy pan and lightly sauté the onion until it is transparent. Add the garlic, celery and potatoes, season well with black pepper. The mussels usually provide enough salt. Stir all the vegetables in the fat for a moment or two, then pour over the mussel liquor. Cover the pan and bring to the boil, then simmer for 15–20 minutes until the potatoes are almost ready. If there is too much liquid, remove the lid for the last 5 minutes so that it reduces somewhat. Add the mussels to the pan and allow them to heat through for 2–3 minutes. Taste for seasoning, add the chopped parsley or coriander leaves and serve with crusty bread.

Variation
- For a richer dish, whisk together 2 egg yolks and 100ml thick cream, pour in a ladleful of the cooking juices, then pour the whole back into the pan. Do not let the stew boil or it will curdle. Let it thicken and serve at once.

Seared scallops with tomato and basil butter

For 2	15g basil leaves	60g butter
8 large scallops	salt and freshly ground pepper	2 tbs lemon juice
6 ripe plum tomatoes		2 tbs olive oil

Detach the roes (coral) from the scallops and save for another dish such as a fish stew or soup. Cut the scallops into 2 or 3 discs. Peel and seed the tomatoes and cut them into dice. Tear the basil leaves into small pieces; combine with the tomatoes and season. Melt the butter, stir in the lemon juice, then the tomato and basil mixture. Taste and season lightly. When the tomato has warmed through, put the pan to one side. Heat a non-stick frying pan, add the oil and sear the scallops for 1 minute until browned. Turn and sear the other side for 30 seconds, no more. It is very easy to overcook scallops, so only put a few in the pan at a time. Arrange the scallops on warmed plates and spoon the sauce around them.

Fritto misto of scallops and vegetables

Scallops take well to deep-frying in a light coating batter which seals in their flavour. I do not much like the roe (coral) deep-fried and prefer to keep that for a fish soup or other dish. Sliced young artichokes or pieces of red pepper could be used instead of the vegetables given here.

For 4	8 large scallops	pinch of salt
2 fennel bulbs	oil for deep-frying	2 eggs
3 small courgettes	**For the batter**	2 tbs olive oil
8 medium mushrooms	4 heaped tbs flour	6 tbs water

Remove the outer layers from the fennel bulbs and cut each one into 8 pieces. Trim the courgettes and cut lengthways into 4 or 6 pieces, and then into 5cm strips. Cut the mushrooms in half and cut the scallops into two rounds.

To prepare the batter, sift the flour and salt into a bowl, make a well in the centre and add the eggs and oil. Mix in the flour and gradually stir in the water until you have a smooth thick cream. Make sure the oil is hot before starting to fry. If you have a deep-fat frying thermometer, 190°C, 375°F is the correct temperature; if not, test with a bread cube (p. 99). Above all, do not let the oil reach smoking point. Fry the foods in the order listed. Dip each piece into the batter and lower into the oil on a wire scoop or slotted spoon. Do not fry more than a few pieces at a time. They will be done after 3–4 minutes. Lift them out, drain on kitchen paper to remove excess oil, and keep warm in a low oven until the scallops are ready. Pile up on a warm dish and serve with lemon quarters immediately, while the batter is crisp.

Barbecued prawns with sweet chilli sauce

Choose large tiger or king prawns for this dish. Grilling over charcoal gives the prawns a better flavour than putting them under an indoor grill.

For 4	½ small chilli, sliced finely	pinch salt
16 large uncooked prawns	1 small garlic clove, peeled and sliced finely	3 tbs sunflower oil
1 stalk lemon grass*	½ tsp sugar	sweet chilli sauce (p. 370)

Shell the prawns and remove the black vein. Discard the outer layer of the lemon grass and, using the bottom third only, slice it finely. Put 8 short wooden skewersin water to soak so that they will not burn. Put the prepared chilli, garlic and lemon grass in a bowl with the sugar, salt and oil and marinate the prawns for 30 minutes, during which time the sauce can be prepared.

Take 4 prawns, push 1 skewer through the tail end of each, leaving space between them, and push a second skewer through the 'head' end (so that you have a small ladder). Nick the flesh of each prawn on the underside. Repeat with the rest of the prawns. Brush with a little of the oil from the marinade and barbecue or grill over medium heat for about 2 minutes each side.

Serve with the chilli sauce and, if you wish, a salad of cucumber and mint, dressed with 3 tbs rice vinegar, 3 tbs water, 2 tbs sugar and a pinch of salt.

Microwaved spiced prawns

For 2	¼ tsp freshly ground pepper	good pinch salt
250g medium uncooked prawns	¼ tsp garam masala*	1 tsp lemon juice
¼ tsp turmeric	2 tsp chilli sauce (p. 518)	salad leaves lightly tossed in a vinaigrette

Shell the prawns and remove the black vein. Put them into a dish, combine all the other ingredients except the salad leaves and toss with the prawns to coat them. Cover and marinate for 10 minutes. Arrange the prawns with their tails to the centre on a plate suitable for the microwave, cover and cook at 100% heat for 2–2½ minutes. To serve, arrange the prawns on a bed of salad leaves.

Crab tart

For 6	2–3 tbs dry sherry	2 tbs chopped parsley
shortcrust pastry for a 26cm tin, baked blind (pp. 490–1)	salt and freshly ground pepper	400g white crabmeat
	good pinch cayenne	2 eggs
200g ricotta or curd cheese	2 tbs chopped chives	about 60ml single cream or milk

Heat the oven to 190°C, 375°F, gas 5. Mix the ricotta with the sherry, seasonings and herbs. Pick over the crabmeat to remove any bits of shell or cartilage and stir into the ricotta. Whisk the eggs lightly and stir them in with enough milk or cream to make a smooth mixture. Turn the filling into the pastry shell and bake for 30–40 minutes until it is set and lightly browned. Cool on a rack for a few minutes before removing from the tin.

Lobster Courchamps

I find lobster best boiled and served cold with a sauce. Mayonnaise and its related sauces – gribiche, remoulade (pp. 362–3) – are good but to my taste rather too rich. I prefer the Courchamps sauce given by Elizabeth David in *An Omelette and a Glass of Wine*. She named it after the Comte de Courchamps, author of one of the books in which she found the recipe. He called it Sauce for Boiled Lobster.

For 2		
1 lobster, boiled (p. 262)	leaves from 2 sprigs tarragon, chopped	24–30 drops soy sauce
2 shallots, peeled and chopped finely	2 tbs chopped parsley	6 tbs fruity olive oil
	salt and freshly ground pepper	juice of ½ small lemon
	1 tsp Dijon mustard	1 tsp anisette or Pernod

Once your cooked lobster has cooled, cut it in half. Extract the red and creamy parts from the split lobster and pound them in a mortar. Mix with the shallots, tarragon and parsley. Add the seasonings, and gradually stir in the olive oil, then the lemon juice. Finally add the anisette or Pernod. Put the sauce into two small bowls next to each plate so that the lobster can be dipped into it. The lobster can be cut into thick slices and replaced neatly in the shells.

Squid with peas

For 6		
1kg small squid	2 garlic cloves, peeled and chopped finely	salt and freshly ground pepper
3 tbs olive oil	100ml white wine	300g small fresh or frozen peas
1 small onion, peeled and chopped finely	100ml water	
	2 tbs chopped parsley	

Clean the squid as described on p. 260. Slice it into 1cm rings and divide the rings of tentacles in two. Heat the oil in a heavy pan and sauté the onion until it turns a golden colour. Add the garlic and continue to sauté, but do not let it brown. Pour in the wine and water, and add the squid and parsley. Season with salt and pepper. Cover the pan and simmer over low heat for 30 minutes. Add fresh peas to the pan now and continue to cook for a further 15–20 minutes. Cooking time for squid varies greatly, so check to see if it is cooked – when it is ready it can be pierced easily with the point of a knife. Frozen peas should be added when the squid is almost tender since they take only a few minutes to cook. Taste for seasoning before serving.

Poultry and game birds

Poultry includes domesticated birds bred for the table:
chicken, turkey, goose, duck and guinea fowl. These days
most of our chickens and poussins (baby chickens),
turkeys and some ducks are intensively reared. Geese and guinea fowl have largely
escaped intensive rearing, hence their higher price. Some
game birds – pheasant, partridge, pigeon, quail – are now
farmed and can be bought all year round. They tend to have
a bland flavour, probably because they are not hung as long
as wild game. The season for wild game birds is quite short
and varies according to the bird.

Choosing

Poultry

Most of our chickens are raised in highly commercial large-scale operations in artificial conditions in order to meet consumer demand. Intensively reared in artificially lit and heated sheds and fed a controlled diet, these chickens reach 1.5kg or more in weight at 6–7 weeks, when they are killed. They do not develop any flavour, the meat is uniformly pale and has little texture.

Most birds labelled 'free-range' are reared in conditions little better than broiler birds, although they can get into outdoor runs. Unless you know the producer to be one who rears high-quality birds, it is realistic to assume that a free-range bird is semi-intensively produced. Genuinely free-range and organic chickens have a better-developed bone structure, thicker skin, firm breast meat, plump darker-coloured thighs and a much richer flavour. The price is considerably higher, too.

The colour of the skin depends on the breed and the diet. A young chicken should have a smooth, slightly moist skin. A boiling fowl has a rigid breastbone, a mottled skin and darker flesh.

Most turkeys are also intensively reared, with unnaturally large breasts to suit the market. Their flesh tends to be bland and dry compared to that of traditionally raised birds, which are hung for about a week to increase flavour. It is best to avoid turkeys that are 'self-basting' because of the substances in the basting liquid injected into them.

Geese and domesticated ducks have larger, heavier skeletons and more fat in proportion to meat than do chickens and turkeys. Their appearance is slightly waxy, the flesh is darker and has a rich and succulent flavour as long as it is not overcooked. A goose more than a year old can be tough and is better braised than roasted.

Choose a bird with an unblemished, unbruised skin. Do not buy a packaged bird if it is sticky or contains a lot of liquid or has even the faintest smell.

Game

Our most common game birds are now farmed, often quite intensively and, when buying, particularly in a supermarket, it is very hard to know what you are getting. If the bird is farmed, it is likely to be young and has probably been hung for the minimum time, so it will not have acquired a very gamey flavour. A game dealer should be able to tell you the sex (hen birds are smaller and usually considered to have a finer flavour) and perhaps the age of the bird, and his stock should have been hung for longer.

Game is hung before cleaning. Hanging permits bacteria and enzymes in the flesh to break down the tissues, rendering it more tender and giving it a richer flavour.

Game that has been properly hung should not smell unpleasant, any more than should properly hung beef.

Game is likely to have shot marks and tears in the skin, and occasionally shot in the flesh. When you get it home, check for shot and remove it if possible; the presence of shot is often indicated by bloody patches on the skin. If you buy oven-ready game, as with chicken, make sure that the package looks and smells wholesome. Avoid birds with badly crushed limbs, they have been badly shot.

The season for wild birds is:
- *Grouse* 12 August – 10 December
- *Partridge* 1 September – 1 February
- *Pheasant* 1 October – 1 February
- *Pigeon* all year
- *Quail* all year
- *Wild duck* 1 September – 31 January

Storing

Poultry and game should be stored for a short time only: 2–3 days in the refrigerator for small birds, up to 4 days for goose and turkey. Remove the packaging and wrap loosely. Remove giblets from the cavity and cook straight away because they deteriorate faster.

Thaw frozen birds in the refrigerator, allowing plenty of time; a turkey can take up to 2 days to thaw completely. If you are really in a hurry, thaw pieces of chicken in cold water. Once thawed, cook promptly.

Poultry, in particular chicken, may carry a form of salmonella which causes food poisoning. However, it is very rare to get food poisoning from properly cooked poultry because salmonella is destroyed by high heat. Contamination is more likely to come from raw or lightly cooked foods that have been in contact with infected poultry. The way poultry is stored and prepared is of great importance. Keep poultry chilled, out of contact with other foods, and make sure the juices can't drip onto anything else. As soon as you have finished handling and preparing raw poultry, wash the knife, the board and your hands thoroughly in soapy water.

Quantities

The amount needed per serving depends on how the bird is cooked and what else is included in the dish. As a guideline, allow 250–300g meat on the bone per person from the larger lean birds. A guinea fowl, depending on its size, will serve 3–4. A pheasant can serve 4, but the legs are quite tough, so it may be better to count it as 2 generous servings only. A grouse, a partridge or a pigeon will serve 1, a poussin 1–2, and allow 1 quail per serving for a first course and 2 as a main dish. Ducks and geese have a lower proportion of meat to bone, so allow 400–450g on the bone per person.

Preparing poultry and game

Bring all birds to room temperature before cooking. Rinse the cavity and the skin and dry with kitchen paper, or wipe it with damp paper.

Most of the fat in a bird is in and immediately under the skin, so if you wish to avoid excessive fat, remove the skin and use other means to prevent the flesh drying out – a marinade, or cook in a sauce or liquid. Of course a bird to be roasted cannot be skinned, but it is best to remove excess fat from the opening of the cavity.

Preparing a whole bird

If the wishbone is cut out, the breast is easier to carve. Fold back the skin of the neck cavity and cut around the wishbone with a small knife.

I seldom truss a bird, but use small skewers to secure the cavity if it is stuffed. The shape may not be so neat, but for carving and serving it makes little difference. To roast a goose or a turkey, tying the legs together helps keep the cavity closed. A ball of crumpled foil will fill the cavity opening of a large bird.

If you want to truss a bird, here are the instructions. Cut a piece of string about 1 metre long. Put the bird, breast side up, with the legs towards you, and the neck flap tucked under at the back. Put the centre of the string under the parson's nose and cross the two ends over the top of the parson's nose. Pull the string tightly, then pass it under the ends of the drumsticks. Cross the string over again, and hold it tight, then pass it under the tip of the breastbone. Now take the string backwards over the part where the thighs join the body. Turn the bird over, bring the ends of the string together on the back, pinning the wings to the body as you do so. Tie in a knot and cut off the ends of the string.

Jointing a bird

Poultry and game can be jointed into 4, 6 or 8 pieces, depending on size and how it is to be cooked.

Put the bird, breast side up, and cut around the leg with a sharp knife. As you cut pull the leg away from the body until the thigh bone comes out of the socket. Cut down between the ball and the socket to remove the leg. Repeat on the other side.

To separate the thighs from the drumsticks, hold the leg in both hands and bend it to crack the joint. Put it skin side down and cut through the joint.

With the breast uppermost, hold one of the wings and use a pair of poultry shears or a heavy knife to cut along the breastbone, splitting it in half. Turn over and cut out the backbone and ribs, so you now have two breast pieces with wings attached. Cut through the breasts diagonally, so one piece has the wing attached.

Don't discard the bones; use them for stock (p. 4)

Spatchcocking a bird

Cut through the ribs on either side of the backbone and take out the bone. Turn the bird breast uppermost and press hard on the breastbone to flatten it. This requires a certain amount of force, since you need to break the bones. Make two slits in the skin either side of the end of the breast and push the ends of the drumsticks through them. This keeps them in place for cooking.

Boning a breast

Work the ribs free from the flesh with a sharp knife, cutting close to the bones. Ease the meat back in one piece as you cut. Discard the bones and the white tendon.

Cutting a duck in four

Ducks are more awkward to joint, so it is easier instead to cut them in quarters with a pair of poultry shears or a heavy knife. Cut along the breast bone, then cut along either side of the backbone and remove it. Now cut each half duck diagonally and you have 4 pieces ready to cook.

Cooking methods

Roasting

All young birds can be roasted, which means almost all poultry wherever you buy it, and certainly if it is described as 'oven ready'. However, there is little point in roasting an intensively reared broiler because it does not have sufficient flavour to withstand this simple treatment. Intensively reared chickens need the aromatics of a marinade or to be cooked with other ingredients which will impart their flavour. Older birds benefit from braising or poaching. If you buy game birds and are not sure of their age, it is better to braise rather than roast them.

Ducks and geese, which have a high amount of fat in and under the skin, are best started at a high temperature to allow the fat to run, and the temperature is reduced to moderate for the rest of the cooking time. Most other birds roast well at 200°C,

400°F, gas 6 for the whole cooking period, although some game birds roast better at a higher temperature.

Allow the bird to rest for 5–20 minutes according to size, loosely covered with foil, in a warm place – at the back of the cooker or in the turned off oven with the door open – before carving. This allows the juices to be reabsorbed into the flesh.

Roasting lean poultry One of the problems with roasting is that the breast meat of lean birds tends to dry out before the legs are ready. Except with very large birds which are too heavy to turn, start roasting the bird on one side, turn it to the other side a third of the way through the cooking time, and put it breast up to finish. This helps protect the breast meat and allows juices to run into it and, at the same time, exposes the legs so that they cook more thoroughly.

The simplest way to protect the breast is to rub butter or olive oil over it and cover it with foil. You can also cover it with streaky bacon or pork fat, or best of all, mash together some butter and a flavouring such as chopped herbs and spread it under the skin (p. 281). If you use some kind of covering, remove it for the last 15 minutes so that the skin can brown. Baste every 15–20 minutes. If you are preparing a chicken for two, you can remove the legs and keep them for another dish, and just roast the breast. Small birds can be cooked in a *papillotte*, a parcel made with foil or parchment paper. The bird cooks in the steam created in the parcel and is well flavoured by the ingredients put with it.

Roasting duck and goose Prick the skin of ducks or geese all over to help the fat escape whilst retaining the juices. Baste the bird with its fat every 20 minutes which helps to melt more fat, and pour or spoon the fat out of the tin if necessary during cooking. Stand the bird on a rack so it is not sitting in the fat it has released.

Roasting game With the exception of quail, game birds are usually served with the breast pink, but not bloody. The times given below should produce faintly pink breast meat; increase the cooking time a little for meat that needs to be more well done. All game birds are lean, and the breast needs protecting by barding with a piece of pork back fat (p. 326) or by rubbing well with butter. As with lean poultry, if you roast the bird breast side down except for the last few minutes, it will dry out less. The legs are invariably tough, and can be kept and cooked longer in a stew.

Stuffing poultry and game Do not let a stuffed bird wait around so stuff a bird just before cooking. Allow about 150g stuffing per 500g weight of bird. Pack it loosely into the body cavity so that it will heat through properly in the oven. Close the cavity with skewers or by trussing (p. 272). A large bird can also be stuffed at the neck end.

Stuffing can soak up the bird's juices but not the fat in or under the skin which escapes down the outside of the flesh, not into the cavity.

Stuffing can also be cooked separately and served with the bird, and this method should be adopted if you prefer to roast a large turkey at a low temperature since the inside of the bird may not reach a sufficiently high temperature to cook the stuffing.

Roasting times Remember to include the weight of the stuffing in the total weight for cooking. For duck and goose, calculate the total cooking time from when the bird goes into the oven.

Poultry	Oven temperature	Cooking time	Resting time
chicken	200°C, 400°F, gas 6	20–25 min per 500g	+ 15 min
spatchcocked	200°C, 400°F, gas 6	18–22 min per 500g	+ 15 min
poussin	200°C, 400°F, gas 6	25–35 min	+ 8 min
spatchcocked	200°C, 400°F, gas 6	20–25 min	+ 8 min
guinea fowl	200°C, 400°F, gas 6	20 min per 500g	+ 10–15 min
capon	190°C, 375°F, gas 5	25 min per 500g	+ 15–20 min
turkey			
up to 5kg	180°C, 350°F, gas 4	20 min per 500g	+ 20 min
from 5–7kg	180°C, 350°F, gas 4	18 min per 500g	
above 7kg	180°C, 350°F, gas 4	16 min per 500g	
duck	220°C, 425°F, gas 7	first 20 min	
	180°C, 350°F, gas 4	rest of cooking time	
		20 min per 500g*	+ 15–20 min
goose	220°C, 425°F, gas 7	first 30 min	
	170°C, 325°F, gas 3	rest of cooking time	
		20 min per 500g*	+ 20 min

*total cooking time

Game	Oven temperature	Cooking time	Resting time
quail	220°C, 425°F, gas 7	20–25 min	+ 5 min
partridge	220°C, 425°F, gas 7	30–35 min	+ 5 min
pigeon	200°C, 400°F, gas 6	25–30 min	+ 5 min
grouse	200°C, 400°F, gas 6	35 min	+ 10 min
wild duck	220°C, 425°F, gas 7	30–40 min	+ 10 min
pheasant	200°C, 400°F, gas 6	20 min per 500g	+ 10 min

To test if the bird is done Pierce the thickest part of the thigh with a small flat skewer; the juices will run clear if the bird is cooked. If a bird is not sufficiently cooked, return it to the oven for another 10–15 minutes and then test it again. If you have a meat thermometer, it can be useful for testing a large bird. Put it into the flesh between the thigh and the breast, avoiding the bone, before roasting. It should read 75°C/170°F when the bird is ready. When you lift out the bird, tip the juices from the cavity into the pan. Put the bird onto a serving dish, cover and leave to rest.

Making simple gravy While the bird is resting, pour or skim off the fat in the pan, leaving the juices behind. There will be copious amounts of fat from duck and goose, less from chicken and turkey. Heat the pan and add a glass of wine, sherry or madeira. If you have no wine available, use chicken stock or water (from cooking the vegetables). Stir well, scraping loose any bits stuck to the bottom. Tip in the juices that have collected under the bird while it is resting. Taste, season, and add a squeeze or two of lemon juice. This will make a little thin gravy to serve with a small bird.

If you wish you can add chopped herbs or chopped tomatoes, sautéed mushrooms or other vegetables for a more substantial sauce, or enrich it with cream.

For a larger bird, or just for more gravy, follow the method above, then add 100ml chicken stock to make gravy for a chicken or up to 700ml chicken stock for a large turkey or goose. A tablespoon or two of red currant jelly provides sharpness for the richer meat of duck and goose. Simmer for 2–3 minutes. To thicken gravy, mix 2 tsp plain flour into 2 tsp softened butter and add it, little by little, to the pan, stirring as you do so. Add as much as is needed to thicken the gravy to the consistency you want. Alternatively, if you are making a large quantity of gravy, whisk 1 tbs cornflour dissolved in 2 tbs water into the pan and simmer until it thickens. Gravy should not get lumpy, but if it does, put it through a sieve. Taste and season if necessary.

Making giblet gravy Pre-packed chickens are seldom sold with giblets, but butcher's chickens still are. Cut the neck into pieces, the heart in two lengthways and open up the gizzard at the lobes. Put them in a pan with a small peeled and chopped onion, a peeled and chopped carrot, a sliced stick of celery, a sprig of thyme and a bay leaf. Season and cover with 1 litre of water. Bring to the boil, then simmer for about an hour and strain. Discard the solids. Add the giblet stock to the roasting pan after deglazing* it, simmer and thicken as necessary. If you wish, sauté the liver in a little butter until just cooked, then dice it. Add the liver and let it heat through for 1–2 minutes before serving.

Carving a chicken or turkey Put the bird, breast side up, on a board or large platter. Use a carving fork and a knife with a long flexible blade. Hold the bird steady with the fork, and cut down between the thigh and the body. Prise the thigh outwards to expose the joint and cut through it, removing the whole leg.

For a turkey, separate the thigh and drumstick by cutting between the bones. The meat can be sliced from both thigh and drumstick, cutting parallel to the bone and turning the drumstick to cut slices from all sides. Leave chicken legs whole unless very large.

After removing the leg on one side, remove the wing. Push the wing outwards to reveal the joint and cut down through the lower corner of the breast and the joint to sever it.

Slice the breast parallel to the bone, holding the top of the bird steady with the fork. Remove each slice. Repeat on the other side. Serve quickly once the bird is carved, on hot plates.

Carving duck or goose Use a heavy firm knife to cut through the skin around the leg, then push the leg away from the body to expose the joint and cut through it. Separate the thigh and drumstick on a goose. Cut the wing away from the body at the shoulder, it has virtually no meat. Take a flexible long-bladed knife and carve the breast into slices, or take the breast meat off each side as one piece and cut it into slices across the grain.

Repeat on the other side and serve quickly on hot plates.

Carving small birds Small birds can be cut in half along the breastbone and the backbone. Pheasants and guinea fowl are carved as chicken and turkey.

Grilling and barbecuing

Poultry is best marinated for 1–2 hours before grilling or barbecuing so that the tender meat does not dry too quickly when exposed to the heat. Use a marinade based on oil (p. 386) or simply whisk together oil and lemon juice and add sprigs of fresh herbs. Leave the skin on jointed birds for greater protection. Whole small birds, such as poussin, quail or guinea fowl, will cook more evenly if spatchcocked (p. 273). Baste frequently with the marinade or oil or a barbecue sauce (p. 376). Turn the pieces with a spatula or tongs; if they are pierced by a fork, the juices are lost. Breast meat is very difficult to keep moist and is easiest to grill when cubed and cooked as kebabs after prolonged marinating.

Make sure the grill or barbecue is hot before starting, and whether cooking under or over the heat source, keep the heat moderate and position the poultry 10–15cm away from it. Drumsticks will take about 20 minutes, wings and kebabs 10–15 minutes, large pieces up to 30 minutes.

Grill spatchcocked birds skin side to the heat for 5 minutes, then turn and complete the cooking cut side to the heat. Quail will need a further 10–12 minutes; a poussin weighing up to 500g, 15–20 minutes; a guinea fowl or other bird weighing up to 1kg, 25–35 minutes.

To test whether the poultry is ready, pinch the meat or press with the tongs; if it is firm it is ready, if it is soft it needs further cooking. Alternatively, pierce with a flat skewer and if the juices run clear it is cooked.

Frying, sautéing and stir-frying

Chicken pieces, quail, duck breasts (magrets) and turkey breast escalopes are all suited to frying. A coating of flour or breadcrumbs helps keep the juices in the meat. Chicken pieces will take 30–40 minutes, but boneless breasts require only 12–15 minutes. Quail take about 15 minutes. Duck breasts to be served pink need 10–12 minutes, turkey escalopes 5–6 minutes. Make sure the pan is hot and the oil or butter hot but not burning before adding the poultry. Poultry cooked with its skin will need less fat than skinned pieces.

Herbs and vegetables added to a bird after browning, together with stock, water or wine and left to simmer, will produce a sauté. Do not attempt to make one with duck breast fried with its skin because it releases too much fat.

Small pieces of chicken, turkey or duck cut to the same size can be used for stir-frying. As with frying and sautéing, it is important to heat the wok or pan before the oil is added and to maintain a high temperature. If the temperature is too low the food starts to steam in the liquid given off by the vegetables.

Pot-roasting and braising

Chicken, guinea fowl, and game birds that may be dry, such as grouse and pheasant, are eminently suited to pot-roasting with a few flavourings and a little liquid. Game birds benefit from marinating first. The flesh of a pot-roasted bird remains moist, the bird carves easily and the liquid supplies the gravy.

Older birds for braising are usually jointed, although small game birds such as partridge or pigeon can be braised whole. A braised dish incorporates more flavouring ingredients and more liquid than a pot-roast, and the cooking time is longer.

You can vary the bird in many recipes for slow-cooked poultry, and even use domesticated and game birds interchangeably.

Stewing

Stews are intended for mature birds and have more liquid than braised dishes. The joints or whole birds are immersed in liquid, vegetables and flavourings are added and the pot is left to simmer for a long time.

Poaching

Poaching is a beautifully simple method: the bird is cooked in barely simmering water, and the poaching water can be reduced and used as stock. Essentially, this is a method for cooking whole mature birds, usually chicken, with vegetables for added flavour.

Steaming

Small pieces of poultry – breasts, thighs, quarters – steam better than whole birds, and I find it a method more suited to birds with lean flesh like chicken, guinea fowl and pheasant. The water or stock over which the bird cooks should simmer gently to produce even steam.

Boned breasts and thighs take 12–15 minutes, on the bone a minute or two longer, chicken quarters 20–25 minutes.

Leftovers

Cold chicken and turkey are good in salads, whether in small amounts, as in Thailand and Vietnam, or to make more substantial dishes accompanied by a chutney or a salsa. They combine well with cooked green beans, skinned peppers, raw mushrooms, potatoes dressed with mayonnaise or a vinaigrette.

For further cooking, these dry meats need a sauce or other liquid. Mushroom sauce, cheese sauce and lightly curried sauce are good for heating chicken or turkey to serve as a separate dish, to fill pancakes, make a pasta sauce or provide the basis for a casserole or pie.

Small pieces of chicken or turkey can be added to soups (p. 7 and p. 111) or to a pilaf (p. 182), or used to stuff vegetables.

Chicken

Roast chicken

This is roast chicken at its simplest, and to me its best. In essence it is Simon Hopkinson's recipe from *Roast chicken and other stories*.

For 4		
1.5–1.8kg chicken	salt and freshly ground pepper	3–4 garlic cloves, peeled and crushed
100g softened butter or 80ml extra virgin olive oil	2 lemons	
	a few sprigs of thyme	

Heat the oven to 200°C, 400°F, gas 6. Have the chicken at room temperature and rub the butter or olive oil all over it. Season well with salt and pepper. Prick one lemon all over with a fork and put it into the cavity with the thyme and garlic. Put the chicken in the roasting pan on its side and roast for 20 minutes, basting it a couple of times. Turn the bird to the other side and again baste from time to time. After 20 minutes, put it breast up and pour over the juice of the second lemon. Continue basting occasionally until the chicken is ready. The juices should flow clear when the thickest part of the thigh is pierced with a skewer, and the bird is golden brown all over. Tip the chicken up over the pan to add the juices from the cavity to the tin, then let the chicken rest in a warm place, covered loosely with foil for 15 minutes to allow the flesh to relax before carving (p. 274).

Whisk the liquids in the pan together, strain if necessary and serve with the chicken.

Roast stuffed chicken

Fill the cavity loosely with one of the stuffings below or that on p. 294 and rub the chicken with butter as above. Roast the bird on one side, then turn, and finally put it breast uppermost. Remember to add the weight of the stuffing when reckoning total cooking time (*see* chart on p. 275).

Spiced fruit stuffing

A good stuffing for all types of poultry.

Makes enough to stuff a 1.5–1.8kg bird	1 tsp cinnamon	80g raisins, soaked briefly and drained
60g butter	½ tsp ground ginger	50g walnuts, chopped coarsely
1 onion, peeled and chopped	large pinch cloves	
	salt	50g almonds, chopped coarsely
2 garlic cloves, peeled and crushed	80g dried apricots, soaked, drained and chopped	1 under-ripe pear, cored and chopped

Heat the butter and soften the onion, then add the garlic, spices and salt. Stir for a minute or two, then add the fruit and nuts. Mix all well together to form rather a loose stuffing.

If you wish, you can add ½–¾ cup of cooked rice or couscous to the stuffing, to extend it or to replace some of the fruit and nuts. You may also need to add a little liquid: 1–2 tbs of wine or sherry or chicken stock.

Herb and apple stuffing

Good for chicken and turkey.

Makes enough to stuff a 1.5–1.8kg bird	2 large apples, peeled, cored and chopped	3 tbs chopped fresh herbs (parsley, thyme, marjoram, savory, tarragon)
30g butter	grated rind and juice of ½ unwaxed lemon	salt and freshly ground pepper
1 large onion, peeled and chopped finely	8 tbs fresh white or brown breadcrumbs	1 egg
2 stalks celery, sliced		

Soften the onion in the butter until lightly coloured, then stir in the celery and apples, lemon rind and juice, breadcrumbs and herbs. Mix well and season with salt and pepper. Beat the egg lightly and bind the mixture.

Richard Olney's stuffed baked chicken

This stuffing is placed under the skin of a spatchcocked bird, giving it a rounded plump appearance. Richard used to grill it over the open fire in his kitchen, but it bakes beautifully in the oven. It isn't as difficult to prepare as the lengthy instructions suggest. Once the skin is loosened from the flesh, introducing the stuffing is quite easy. The courgettes and onions can be prepared while the chicken is marinating.

For 4	100g butter	salt and freshly ground pepper
1.5–1.8kg chicken	500g courgettes, cut into julienne* strips and salted for 15 minutes	1 tbs finely chopped marjoram leaves and flowers, or fines herbes
1 tsp crumbled mixed dried herbs (thyme, oregano, savory)		
3 tbs olive oil	90g ricotta or cream cheese	1 large egg
For the stuffing	60g fresh white breadcrumbs	2–4 tbs grated Parmesan
1 medium onion, peeled and chopped finely		

Split and flatten the chicken as described (p. 273). Loosen the skin. Starting at the neck, work your fingers between the skin and the flesh, moving towards the tail, to loosen the skin over one side of the breast. Free the skin gradually from the leg, leaving it attached only at the end of the drumstick. Do the same on the other side of the bird. Take care not to tear the skin.

Sprinkle the chicken on both sides with the dried herbs and rub generously with olive oil. Leave to marinate for an hour or two.

Stew the onion gently in 15g butter without letting it colour and leave to cool. Squeeze the salted courgettes to remove all excess liquid and sauté them in 30g butter, then leave to cool.

Mash the ricotta, breadcrumbs and remaining butter together with the salt and pepper and herbs, using a fork. Add the egg, mashing; then mix in the onion and the courgettes, and, finally, the Parmesan, adding enough to bring the stuffing to a firm, stiff consistency.

To stuff the chicken, push the filling under the skin from the neck with one hand, using the other to mould and settle it in place from the outside. Stuff the drumsticks and thighs first, then put a layer over the breast. Finally tuck the neck flap over the opening and under the bird. If there is no neck flap, put less stuffing towards the neck.

Tuck in the drumsticks next to the breast. Place the bird in a roasting tin and shape it, smoothing the skin so that it looks like a rounded version of the bird's natural shape. Roast the bird in a preheated oven, starting at 230°C, 450°F, gas 8, and turning the oven down to 190°C, 375°F, gas 5, some 10 minutes later. Start basting regularly after 30 minutes. Allow 50 minutes to 1 hour roasting time, depending on the size of the chicken and weight of stuffing, and if, after about 40 minutes, it seems to be colouring too rapidly, turn the oven down further, placing a sheet of foil loosely over the bird.

Transfer the bird to a round, heated serving platter. Don't serve the juices, they are too fat, and the dish needs no sauce. To carve, split the bird in two through the breast. Use a very sharp knife, cutting through the skin and stuffing. To remove the legs, cut along the curved creases between the thighs and the body.

Grilled chicken with honey and spices

This is quick to prepare and to cook, but do allow time for the chicken to marinate for up to 1 hour. Grill under an indoor grill, on a ribbed griddle pan or on a barbecue.

For 4	½ tsp curry powder	2 tbs sunflower oil
2 tbs honey	¼ tsp paprika	4 drumsticks
1 tbs Dijon mustard	salt and freshly ground pepper	4 thighs
½ tsp turmeric		oil

Heat the honey, spices, salt and pepper and oil in a small pan, whisk them together and use to coat the chicken pieces on all sides. Leave to marinate for up to 1 hour.

Brush the grill bars or the griddle pan lightly with oil because the honey may stick, and grill 10–15cm from the heat source for 15–18 minutes, turning the chicken and basting occasionally. Serve the chicken with raita (p. 384) or mango and red pepper salsa (p. 381).

Chicken yakitori

This method of preparing skewers of chicken and vegetables comes from Japan. They are very good served with drinks or as a snack.

For 4	4 small leeks, cleaned	75ml mirin*
500g boned and skinned chicken breast or thigh	250g small mushrooms, preferably fresh shiitake	150ml soy sauce
		1 tbs sugar
6 chicken livers	75ml saké	

If you are using wooden skewers, put them in water to soak. Cut the chicken into bite-sized cubes. Trim the livers, removing any discoloured bits, and cut them in half. Discard the green part of the leeks and cut the white into 2cm lengths. Discard the mushroom stalks. Thread pieces of chicken onto the skewers alternating with the livers and vegetables.

Combine all the other ingredients to make a marinade. Put them into a small pan, bring to the boil and pour over the skewers. Let them marinate for 30 minutes. Grill on a barbecue or under an indoor grill for 5–6 minutes, turning once, then dip the kebabs in the marinade again and grill again until the chicken is done.

Country captain

This is a dish I ate while staying at the Koorghully Estate in Coorg in the south-west of India. My host there, Ted White, who grows coffee and pepper, served this simple but excellent chicken dish for lunch. It is a dish from the days of the Raj. How it got its name I do not know.

For 4	½ tsp turmeric	4 chicken legs, separated into thighs and drumsticks and skinned
100ml sunflower oil	2 tsp ground cumin	
500g onions, peeled and sliced	2 tsp ground coriander	
½ tsp chilli flakes	1 tsp freshly ground pepper	salt

Heat the oven to 150°C, 300°F, gas 2. Heat the oil in one large or two smaller frying pans and fry the onions until golden brown; don't crowd them too much. Transfer them to a baking tray, leaving behind most of the oil, and put them low down in the oven to become more crisp and darken in colour.

Divide the chilli flakes and spices evenly between the pans and let them fry over low heat, while stirring, for 2 minutes. Add the chicken, and turn the pieces to coat them in the spiced oil. Raise the heat to medium, and fry the chicken until it is browned, then reduce the heat and fry, turning from time to time until it is cooked through. It will take 30–40 minutes. Pierce the thickest parts with a skewer and if the juices run clear the chicken is ready. Season with salt. While the chicken is cooking, check the onions from time to time. If they are browning too much, turn off the oven and leave them there. If they have not darkened and crisped, increase the heat slightly. Serve the chicken surrounded by the onion. Rice and peas are the traditional accompaniments.

Chicken and cashew nut stir-fry

This dish can be made with Chinese or Thai flavourings. I have given both, so you can choose the one you prefer. The vegetables can be varied too : thin green beans, mange-tout, small peas, bamboo shoots would all be suitable. ι can also experiment with and vary the flavourings. Duck breasts with the fat removed could be used instead of chicken. Rice or noodles are the standard accompaniment.

Chinese stir-fry

For 3–4		
300g chicken breast, skinned and boned	75g cashew nuts	small piece of ginger, chopped finely
	2 tbs hoisin sauce	
1 egg white	1 tbs soy sauce	1 red pepper, seeded and cut in thin strips
2 tsp cornflour	2 tsp sesame oil	80g mushrooms, sliced
large pinch salt	1 garlic clove, peeled and chopped finely	2 spring onions, chopped finely
3 tbs sunflower oil		

Thinly slice the chicken. Combine the egg white, cornflour and salt, toss the chicken in the mixture and put in the refrigerator for 20 minutes. Heat 1 tbs oil in a wok or large frying pan and stir-fry the cashews until lightly browned. Remove them and reserve. Combine the hoisin sauce, soy sauce and sesame oil and set aside. Add the rest of the oil to the wok and when it is hot, add the garlic and ginger and stir-fry for 30 seconds. Put in the chicken and toss for 1 minute, then add the red pepper and mushrooms. Stir-fry until the chicken turns white, which will take 1–2 minutes. Pour over the sauce and stir-fry for another 2 minutes, coating all the ingredients with the sauce. Add the cashew nuts and spring onions for the last 30 seconds. Serve at once.

Thai stir-fry

For 3–4	1 tsp sugar	80g small fresh or frozen peas
300g chicken breast, boned and skinned	1 tbs lime juice	
	2 tbs soy sauce	80g bamboo shoots, sliced
3 tbs sunflower oil	2 garlic cloves, peeled and chopped finely	1 tbs chopped coriander
75g cashew nuts		
2 tbs fish sauce	1 chilli, seeded and sliced finely	1 tbs chopped basil

Slice the chicken thinly. Heat 1 tbs oil in a wok or frying pan and toss the cashews in it until lightly browned. Set them aside. Combine the fish sauce, sugar, lime juice and soy sauce and set aside. Add the rest of the oil to the pan and stir-fry the garlic and chilli for a few seconds, then add the chicken. After 1 minute, add the vegetables and continue to toss and fry. When the chicken has turned white, which takes 1–2 minutes, add the sauce. Coat all the ingredients well with the sauce and fry for 1–2 minutes more. Add the chopped herbs and cashews for the last 30 seconds.

Chicken with mushrooms

Chicken and mushrooms are a happy combination, whether you use wild or cultivated mushrooms. If you use cultivated fresh mushrooms, add a few dried mushrooms, soaked for 20 minutes in warm water; this will make a huge difference in taste. Strain the soaking liquid and use it instead of part of the stock.

For 6	1 tbs olive oil	4 shallots, peeled and chopped finely
6 chicken breasts, skinned and boned	60g butter	
	400g mushrooms, preferably wild	400ml chicken stock (p. 4)
2 tbs flour		
salt and freshly ground pepper		250ml crème fraîche

Toss the chicken breasts in seasoned flour. Heat the oil and half the butter in a wide pan that will comfortably hold the breasts in one layer. Sauté the chicken until golden, about 4 minutes on each side. Take out the chicken and keep warm.

While the chicken is cooking, trim the mushrooms, removing any big stalks, and cut in half or in quarters. Add the remaining butter to the pan and lightly fry the shallot until it softens, then add the mushrooms and cook for 3–4 minutes. Lift out the mushroom and shallot mixture and add to the chicken.

Scrape loose any bits stuck to the bottom of the pan and pour in the stock. Increase the heat so that the stock boils, and let it reduce by half. Lower the heat again and stir in the crème fraîche. Return the chicken mixture to the pan and simmer gently, covered, for 10–12 minutes until the chicken is cooked. Remove the pan from the heat, and serve. Rice makes a good accompaniment, so do sautéed potatoes.

Chicken with orange and saffron sauce

For 4–6	salt	2 tsp flour or cornflour
1.5–1.8kg chicken pieces	½ tsp paprika	juice of ½ lemon (optional)
2 tbs sunflower oil	150ml water	flaked toasted almonds to garnish
2 onions, peeled and sliced	3 unwaxed oranges	
	15 saffron threads	

Sauté the chicken pieces in the oil until golden brown on all sides. Lift out the chicken and sauté the onion until golden. Return the chicken to the pan and season with salt and paprika. Pour over the water, bring to the boil, cover the pan and simmer very gently for 20 minutes, turning the chicken once.

Remove the peel only (not the pith) from 2 of the oranges and cut it into fine strips – a potato peeler does the job well. Put the strips into a small pan, cover with water and bring to the boil and simmer for 3 minutes to remove any trace of bitterness. Drain and rinse. Squeeze the juice from all the oranges. Crush the saffron threads and blend them with 1 tbs orange juice.

Mix the remaining orange juice with the flour or cornflour and the saffron liquid. Stir this mixture into the chicken pan together with the orange peel, and simmer for 20–30 minutes more, until the chicken is tender and the sauce thick. Taste and add a little lemon juice if you would like a sharper sauce. Garnish with the almonds and serve with rice.

Garlic chicken

People who don't like garlic have been converted by this simple French dish in which a few whole heads of garlic are cooked to a mellow purée.

For 4	salt and freshly ground pepper	bouquet garni* of thyme, parsley, rosemary, bay leaf and sage
3 or 4 heads of garlic		
50g butter	4 chicken legs, separated into thighs and drumsticks	
80ml olive oil		

Heat the oven to 180°C, 350°F, gas 4. Separate the garlic cloves, discarding the head's outer skin, but don't peel the cloves. Heat the butter and oil in a heavy casserole, season the chicken and brown it on all sides. Fill the gaps between the chicken pieces with the cloves of garlic, turning to coat them in the fat. Tuck the bouquet garni into the centre. Put a double layer of foil over the dish and then the lid so that it is tightly closed. Put it low down in the oven and cook for 1½ hours. The aromas when you open the pot are wonderful, the chicken will be very tender and the garlic squeezes easily from its skin. Serve straight from the casserole with potatoes baked in the oven at the same time, or do as they sometimes do in Provence and serve slices of toasted country bread on which to spread the garlic purée.

Pot-roasted chicken with provençal vegetables

Once the vegetables are prepared, this dish needs little attention; all you have to do is turn the chicken. If you make the dish early in summer, use fresh wet garlic. It has a milder flavour than dried garlic and long cooking makes it particularly delicate.

For 4–6	250g aubergine, diced	250g tomatoes, chopped
1.5–1.8kg chicken	250g small courgettes, halved lengthwise and sliced	½ tsp thyme
12 garlic cloves, unpeeled if new, and cut in half across the middle		½ tsp summer savory
	2 red peppers, seeded and cut in pieces	½ tsp oregano or marjoram
salt and freshly ground pepper	1 onion, peeled and chopped very finely	1 glass white wine
3 tbs olive oil		

Heat the oven to 190°C, 375°F, gas 5. Put half of the garlic into the cavity of the chicken, season it well and rub the bird all over with 1 tbs olive oil. In a dish, combine the remaining garlic and all the vegetables and herbs, season well and toss in the remainder of the oil. Make a bed of the vegetables in a heavy casserole just large enough to hold them and the chicken, put the chicken on its side on top. Pour over the wine. Cover tightly, using foil under the lid if necessary, and cook for 30 minutes. Turn the chicken over and carefully turn the vegetables in the juices. Cover the pot again and return to the oven for a further 30 minutes. Finally, put the chicken breast uppermost and return the open pot to the oven for 10 minutes or so, to brown the breast a little. Lift out the chicken, straining the juices into the vegetables. Keep the vegetables warm whilst you carve the chicken.

Coq au vin

There are many recipes for this well-known dish; I find this one works admirably.

For 4–6	1.5–1.8kg chicken pieces	1 bottle red wine (use something you wouldn't mind drinking)
60g butter	salt and freshly ground pepper	
2 tbs olive oil		250g small mushrooms
100g salt pork or bacon, cubed	1 bouquet garni*	
250g button onions, peeled	1 small glass brandy	1 tbs flour
		croûtons (p. 3)

Heat all but 15g butter and 1 tbs oil in a heavy casserole and brown the salt pork or bacon cubes and onions lightly. Lift them out, season the chicken pieces and fry them in the fat, turning to brown them on all sides. Add the bouquet garni, return the salt pork and onions to the pan, then pour over the brandy and the wine. The chicken should be just covered. If necessary, add a little more wine or stock or even water. Cover and simmer very gently for about 40 minutes. The chicken should be tender but not falling from the bone.

Heat the remaining oil and lightly fry the mushrooms. Add them to the chicken and cook for another 5 minutes. Work the remaining butter and the flour together with a fork to make beurre manié (p. 358) and cut it into small pieces. Lift out the chicken and vegetables onto a serving dish and keep warm. Discard the bouquet garni. Boil the cooking liquid to reduce it to about 500ml. Skim off any fat. Add the bits of beurre manié to the pan over low heat, stirring until they have melted into the sauce. It will thicken in less than a minute. Let it come just to the boil and immediately remove the pan from the heat. It must not continue to boil. The sauce will now be smooth and shiny. Pour it over and around the chicken and serve with croûtons.

Chicken with tarragon

This is a standard dish of French bourgeois cooking and simple to prepare. It has a clear yet unobtrusive flavour of tarragon which complements the chicken well. Poaching is usually thought of as a good method for cooking tough older birds, but a poached chicken makes a very succulent dish. Some of the poaching liquid is used for the sauce; the rest will make a good soup.

For 6	2 onions, peeled and sliced finely	salt and freshly ground pepper
30g butter	1¾ litres chicken stock (p. 4)	1 egg yolk
3 carrots, peeled and sliced finely	1.5kg chicken	100ml crème fraîche
2 sticks celery, sliced finely	200ml dry white wine	1 tsp flour
	small bunch tarragon	

Heat the butter in a large pan and stew the carrots, celery and onion gently, with the lid on. Do not let them brown. Heat the stock in a separate pan. Put the chicken on top of the vegetables and pour over the stock and wine. There should be enough liquid to cover the chicken, if necessary add a little water. Bring to the boil over moderate heat and skim off any scum that rises to the surface. Lower the heat. Put aside 3 tbs of the tarragon leaves for the sauce and add the rest of the bunch to the pan. Season with salt and pepper. Cover tightly and let the chicken poach for 50 minutes to 1 hour. The stock should just shudder, not bubble. Check to see if the bird is ready by inserting the point of a knife where the thigh joins the body – there should be no trace of blood.

When it is ready, lift out the chicken, draining it well over the pan, carve it and keep it warm while you make the sauce. Chop the reserved tarragon leaves. Strain the stock, pour 400ml into a pan and boil to reduce it by half. Beat the egg yolk with the crème fraîche and the flour. Remove the stock from the heat, let it cool a little, then whisk in the egg mixture to make a smooth creamy sauce. Add the chopped tarragon. Serve the sauce separately. New potatoes, glazed carrots, young broad beans or peas make good accompaniments.

Steamed chicken breasts with a ricotta stuffing

For 6

6 chicken breasts, skinned and boned

125g ricotta or curd cheese

2 tbs pine nuts, toasted and coarsely chopped

12 green olives, pitted and chopped

a handful of basil leaves, shredded

salt and freshly ground pepper

With a long knife make a slit down the plump side of each breast for a pocket. Drain the cheese if necessary and mix with the pine nuts, olives and basil. Season well. Use a teaspoon and your fingers to stuff the mixture into the pockets and close them with toothpicks. Steam over simmering water for 15–18 minutes. Pierce with a skewer in the thickest part; if the juices run clear the chicken is ready. Serve with a tomato sauce (pp. 378–9): put a spoonful of sauce on each warmed plate and put the chicken breast on top. Serve the rest of the sauce separately.

Poussin

A poussin will serve 1 or 2, depending on appetite. The roast and baked chicken recipes on p. 279 and p. 281 are good for poussins; *see* the chart on p. 275 for roasting times. Halved poussins are excellent pot-roasted with garlic (p. 287); whole ones with provençal vegetables (p. 287). For more variety, use the guinea fowl and pigeon recipes on pp. 292–3 and p. 302.

Baked poussins with lavender

Lavender is not usually thought of as a kitchen flavouring, yet it is very good provided it is used in small quantities. Other herbs can replace it: thyme, rosemary, marjoram and tarragon all suit poultry. For an oriental flavour, use 2 tsp chopped lemon grass*, garlic and ginger for each poussin, or stir 1 tsp turmeric or a few saffron threads into the butter.

For 4

4 poussins

salt and freshly ground pepper

2 tbs fresh lavender flowers (about 6 heads) or 2 tsp dried

80g butter

Heat the oven to 200°C, 400°F, gas 6. Season the cavities of the birds and put in the lavender flowers. Close the cavities with a toothpick and tie the legs together so that they stay in place during cooking. Melt half the butter in a frying pan and brown the poussins all over. Cut 4 pieces of foil big enough to make a loose parcel around each poussin. Melt the remaining butter and brush the centre of each piece of foil. Place the poussins on the buttered part and pour the remaining butter over them. If there is butter left in the pan, use that too. Fold up the sides and close tightly on top, making sure there are no gaps where the juices can leak or the steam escape. Put the parcels on a baking sheet and bake for 30–35 minutes. Test one of the parcels to see that the poussin is ready, close it up again and let them all be opened at the table.

Roast poussins with kumquat sauce

The amount of cardamom in this recipe may seem excessive but the taste does not dominate the dish. Remove the seeds from the cardamom pods and crush them with a pestle and mortar or give them a quick whirl in a coffee grinder (cardamom gives a wonderful flavour to coffee, too).

For 4	50g melted butter	seeds from 8 cardamom pods*
4 poussins	**For the sauce**	250ml chicken stock (p. 4)
2 tbs sunflower oil	6 kumquats	
½ tsp turmeric	juice of 3 oranges	1 tbs cornflour
4 tbs fresh white or brown breadcrumbs	2 tbs orange liqueur (eg Grand Marnier, Cointreau)	2 tbs water
seeds from 15 cardamom pods*		

Heat the oven to 200°C, 400°F, gas 6. Cut the poussins in half and remove the backbones (p. 273). Put the birds in a lightly oiled roasting tin, skin side up, and brush them with the oil into which you have stirred the turmeric. Roast for 10 minutes. Mix the breadcrumbs and coarsely crushed cardamom seeds with a little melted butter. Remove the poussins from the oven, let them cool a little, then press the breadcrumb coating over them. Return the poussins to the oven to finish cooking, and baste once or twice with the butter and the pan juices. They will take another 12–15 minutes.

To make the sauce, slice the kumquats thinly and take out the seeds. Blanch them for 1 minute in boiling water, drain and rinse under cold water. Put the orange juice, liqueur, cardamom and stock into a small pan, bring to the boil, then simmer briskly to reduce by half. Add the kumquats.

Blend the cornflour with the water and whisk the mixture into the sauce off the heat. Return the pan to the heat and stir until the sauce thickens. To serve, spoon some of the sauce onto warm plates and place the poussins on top.

Guinea fowl

Smaller than a chicken, a bit larger than a pheasant, guinea fowl has a flavour somewhere between the two. Recipes for either bird can be used for guinea fowl, but the flesh is quite dry, so it is better to pot-roast, braise or casserole than to roast or grill. If you have a young bird to roast, bard it with fat or streaky bacon (p. 326), or rub it well with butter or olive oil and cover with foil.

Pot-roasted guinea fowl with chestnuts

I use vacuum-packed prepared chestnuts because they are so convenient. To prepare fresh chestnuts, *see* p. 129.

For 3–4		
1 tbs sunflower oil	1 small glass brandy or whisky	60ml madeira or port
60g butter	salt and freshly ground pepper	60ml water
1 guinea fowl		100ml white wine
80g streaky bacon or pancetta*, cut into lardons*	250g peeled chestnuts	2–3 tbs double cream
	2 sticks celery, chopped	

Heat the oil and 20g butter in a heavy casserole in which the bird fits snugly and brown it on all sides. Add 50g of the lardons and let them brown. Put the guinea fowl on its side. Pour over the brandy or whisky and let it bubble briefly. Season the bird, then cover the casserole tightly and put it over a very low heat to simmer for about 50 minutes. Turn the guinea fowl over at half time.

Once the guinea fowl is in the pot, chop the chestnuts roughly. Heat the remaining butter and sauté the celery and remaining lardons for a minute or two. Put in the chestnuts, the madeira or port and the water. Season. Cover the pan and cook gently for about 20 minutes.

When the bird is ready, lift it out, carve it and keep warm on a serving dish. Add the wine to the pan and let it boil briskly to reduce and thicken slightly. To finish the chestnuts, stir in the cream and put them around the guinea fowl. Spoon over the sauce.

Guinea fowl braised with lemon and herbs

In this dish of Iranian origin, split peas are used to thicken the sauce. If you don't have any, use small red lentils which also disintegrate as they cook. The quantities of herbs may seem large, but together with the lemon juice they give the dish a wonderfully fresh flavour.

For 3–4	¼ tsp turmeric	3 garlic cloves, peeled and crushed
3 tbs sunflower oil	¼ tsp ground cinnamon	70g chopped parsley
1 guinea fowl, cut into pieces	80g split peas	70g chopped coriander
2 leeks, sliced finely	salt	30g chopped mint
¼ tsp ground ginger	250ml water	juice of 2 lemons

Heat 2 tbs oil and sauté the guinea fowl, browning it lightly on all sides. Remove it from the pan and sauté the leeks for 3–4 minutes to soften them. Return the guinea fowl to the pan, add the spices and stir for another minute, then add the split peas and season with salt. Pour over the water, bring to the boil, then cover the pan and simmer very gently for 30 minutes. Check occasionally that there is enough water as it is absorbed by the split peas.

Lightly fry the crushed garlic with the herbs in the remaining oil. Stir this mixture into the guinea fowl and simmer for 15 minutes. Add the lemon juice and simmer for another 10–15 minutes. Serve with rice.

Turkey

By far the most popular choice for the Christmas celebration, turkey is now available all year, both whole and jointed. It can be sautéed, poached, stir-fried, grilled or braised – *see* the chicken recipes for suggestions.

Roast turkey

Roasting a turkey can be a daunting prospect the first time, particularly if it is for a large Christmas celebration. Make sure the bird is at room temperature, that you have weighed both it and its stuffing in order to calculate the roasting time correctly, and remember it will need regular basting.

For 12–14	2 tbs chopped tarragon	4–5kg turkey
125g butter, softened	2 garlic cloves, peeled and chopped finely	1 onion, peeled (optional)
2 tbs chopped thyme leaves	salt and freshly ground pepper	100ml chicken stock (p. 4)
2 tbs chopped parsley		

Heat the oven to 180°C, 325°F, gas 4. Mash the butter with a fork and work into it the herbs and garlic. Season with salt and pepper. Work your fingers in between the skin and the flesh of the turkey, carefully easing the skin loose from the breast. Spread the herbed butter over the flesh of the breast, letting the skin fall back to hold it in place. If you wish, stuff the turkey with the mixture below or with one of the stuffings on pp. 280–1. Otherwise, season the cavity and put in a quartered onion and some sprigs of herbs. Crumple a ball of foil to close the cavity or fasten it with skewers. Tie the legs together.

Put the bird, breast down, on a buttered V-shaped roasting rack that will hold it in place over a shallow roasting tin. Baste the turkey regularly with warmed stock and the pan juices. Roast for 20 minutes per 500g. An hour before the turkey is ready, remove it from the oven and turn it breast uppermost. This is quite tricky to do, and almost impossible with a bird larger than this. It is important not to break the skin. I have found the best way is to take a clean pair of oven gloves and lift it, but you can also manoeuvre it round with heavy wooden spoons. It helps to have someone else holding the pan and rack steady. Return the turkey to the oven. When it is ready the juices will run clear if you prick the thickest part of the thigh.

Let the turkey rest in a warm place for at least 20 minutes under a loose covering of foil before carving (p. 274). To make gravy, *see* p. 276.

Chestnut, celery and apple stuffing

Good for all types of poultry. Pack it loosely into the turkey's cavity. If there is any left over, put it in a buttered oven dish and bake it in the oven for the last hour of the turkey's cooking time, basting occasionally with the pan juices. I find the vacuum-packed cooked chestnuts very good and suggest using them for the stuffing. If you prefer to cook your own, *see* p. 129.

For enough to stuff a 4–5kg turkey	1 onion, peeled and chopped	4 tart apples
60g butter	8 sticks celery and young leaves, chopped	salt and freshly ground pepper
the turkey liver	750g chestnuts, peeled	3 tbs brandy, whisky or rum

Melt the butter in a frying pan and brown the trimmed liver. Remove it from the pan. Add the onion and celery and cook gently for 4–5 minutes. Meanwhile dice the liver. Chop the chestnuts roughly. Core the apples and chop the flesh. Mix the liver, onion and celery and any juices from the pan with the chestnuts and apples. Season well and stir in the brandy, whisky or rum. Stuff the turkey with the mixture.

Turkey saltimbocca alla romana

For 6	6 thin slices buffalo mozzarella	60g butter
6 thin escalopes of turkey breast	salt and freshly ground pepper	2 tbs olive oil
6 thin slices of Parma ham	6 basil leaves	½ glass dry white wine

Put the escalopes between two pieces of clingfilm and flatten them gently with the heel of your hand or a rolling pin. Place a slice of Parma ham on each escalope, then a slice of mozzarella, trimming them if necessary to fit just inside the escalope. Season. Place a basil leaf in the centre of each one and roll up, securing the rolls with toothpicks. Heat the butter and oil in a frying pan and sauté the rolls for about 6 minutes, turning them to colour all sides golden brown. Pour over the wine. When it bubbles, lift out the rolls and remove the toothpicks. Scrape any bits from the bottom of the pan, pour the juices over the meat and serve.

Duck

Duck is often avoided because it is thought of as being excessively fat. It does indeed have a thick layer under the skin, but below that the flesh is rich and well flavoured. The fat melts into the pan during cooking leaving succulent meat and a crisp skin. Duck responds well to flavouring with fruits and spices, particularly oriental spices.

Roast duck with figs

The idea for this dish comes from Spain where it is made with large dried figs. The small semi-dried Middle Eastern figs can be used too; they do not need to soak for more than 3–4 hours, and you will need to increase the quantity. The sweet wine for soaking the figs can be a Spanish moscatel, a French muscat such as Beaumes de Venise or Frontignac, or a white port.

For 4–5	2.5–3kg duck	salt and freshly ground pepper
24 dried figs	1 unwaxed lemon	
½ bottle sweet wine		300ml chicken (p. 4) or duck stock

Soak the figs in the wine overnight. Heat the oven to 220°C, 425°F, gas 7. Remove excess fat from the edge of the cavity, rub the duck all over with the juice of half the lemon and some salt. Season the cavity with salt and pepper and put in the half lemon shell and the other half, cut into four. Prick the skin all over, so that the fat will be released as the duck cooks, and put the bird, upside down, on a rack over a baking tin. After 20 minutes reduce the temperature to 180°C, 350°F, gas 4 and remove all the fat from the pan with a ladle or baster. Turn the duck so its breast is uppermost. Drain the figs and use the wine to baste the duck. During the next 30–40 minutes baste it frequently until the wine is used up. If the duck is browning too fast, lower the heat to 150°C, 300°F, gas 2.

After 1 hour add the figs and the stock to the pan. Continue basting the duck with the pan juices; it will take a further 30–45 minutes to cook. Test to see if it is ready by piercing the thickest part of the thigh with the point of a sharp knife; if the juices run clear it is ready. Let the duck rest for 15–20 minutes, loosely covered (p. 274), in a warm place before carving. Lift the figs out of the pan and keep them warm whilst you siphon off or blot up the remaining fat. I find the most effective way is to lay a sheet of kitchen paper over the liquid in the pan to absorb the fat. Repeat until all the fat is removed. Whisk the pan juices and scrape up any bits sticking to the bottom of the pan to make a sauce to serve with the duck and figs.

Duck breasts with green peppercorns

I have been making this dish for several years, since I published Prue Leith's *Dinner Parties* in 1984. Prue's recipe calls for a whole duck from which you cut the breasts and use the carcass (having removed the legs for another dish) to make the stock needed. Since duck breasts are now readily available I take the quick way: buy breasts and use chicken stock.

| For 6 | salt | 4 tbs green peppercorns |
| 3 large or 6 small boned duck breasts | 400ml chicken (p. 4) or duck stock | 100g butter |

Heat a non-stick dry pan and put the duck breasts in, skin side down, and fry for 10 minutes over moderate heat. The fat will run copiously from the skin. Turn them the other way up and cook for 3 minutes. Remove the breasts to a board, lift off the skins and put to one side. Transfer the breasts to a plate, cover with another plate and keep hot in a low oven; this allows the flesh to relax a little. Cut the skin into matchsticks, and put back in the pan for 1–2 minutes, until it is brown and crisp all over. Drain on kitchen paper and salt lightly. Pour the fat from the pan, put in the stock and boil to reduce by half. Add the peppercorns and then whisk in the butter, a little at a time, to make a rich, velvety sauce. Slice the breasts and arrange on a serving platter, pour round the sauce and scatter the skin on top.

Duck breasts with glazed apples

For 6		
3 tart eating apples	3 large or 6 small boned duck breasts	400ml chicken (p. 4) or duck stock
50g butter	20g caster sugar	100g butter
3 tbs brown sugar	200ml sherry vinegar	salt and freshly ground pepper

Peel, core and slice the apples thickly. Heat the butter and brown sugar and fry the apples until softened and glazed. Keep the slices whole. Set aside and keep warm. Heat a non-stick dry frying pan and put in the breasts, skin side down. Fry over medium heat for 10 minutes – the fat will run freely – then turn them and fry for a further 3 minutes. Transfer the breasts to a plate, cover with another plate and keep hot in a low oven; this allows the flesh to relax a little. Pour the fat from the pan and reduce the heat to low. Sprinkle on the caster sugar and let it caramelize gently. Deglaze* the pan with the vinegar and when it has reduced by half, add the stock. Bring to the boil, let the stock reduce by half too, then whisk in the butter, a bit at a time, to make a smooth sauce. Season if necessary. Slice the duck breasts, arrange them on a platter, pour the sauce around and garnish with the apple slices.

Goose

Goose is my favourite festive meat, the bird I would always choose for large celebrations. Undeniably rich, the layer of fat between the skin and the breast keeps the meat succulent and well-flavoured as it melts. Like duck, goose benefits from fruit flavours in a stuffing or as an accompaniment.

Roast goose with a fruit stuffing

It is important to roast goose on a rack so that it doesn't sit in its own fat, to keep basting it regularly so that more fat melts, and to remove as much fat as possible from the tin 3 or 4 times during the roasting period.

Goose and duck fat is delicious for frying potatoes but better not indulged in if you have a cholesterol problem. Carefully roasted goose flesh is not fatty or greasy but has a rich flavour and firm texture. In spite of the large amount of fat, it is possible to overcook goose which will make the flesh dry and stringy, so be attentive to the cooking time.

I find this fruit stuffing goes well with goose, but the stuffings on pp. 280–1 could be used instead.

For 8–10	½ tsp marjoram	600g tart eating or cooking apples
4.5–5kg goose	400g prunes, soaked overnight	100g raisins
salt and freshly ground pepper		

Rub salt into the goose an hour or two before you are ready to roast it. Heat the oven to 220°C, 425°F, gas 7. Season the cavity with salt and pepper and the marjoram. Drain and stone the prunes and cut in half, peel and core the apples and cut into cubes. Mix together the prunes, apples and raisins and use to stuff the cavity loosely. Close it with a ball of foil or skewers. Prick the skin of the goose all over to help release the fat.

Tuck the wings under the body, tie the legs together and put the goose on a rack over the largest baking tin that will fit into the oven. You need a big tin to catch the copious amount of fat that runs out. Roast the bird for 30 minutes, then turn the oven down to 170°C, 325°F, gas 3. Baste it with the fat in the pan, and remove the fat from the pan with a ladle or baster at regular intervals. Calculate the cooking time at 20 minutes per 500g, including the weight of the stuffing in the total weight. If the breast is darkening too quickly, cover it with a butter paper or foil. If it is too pale, turn up the heat for the last 15 minutes to brown the skin. The goose is ready when the juices run clear if you insert the point of a knife in the thickest part of the thigh.

Let the goose rest for 20 minutes in a warm place, loosely covered (p. 274). This allows the flesh to relax and makes carving easier. To make the gravy pour off all the fat remaining in the tin and follow the instructions on p. 276.

Game birds

Many game birds are now on sale in supermarkets, although you may have to go to a game dealer for grouse or wild duck. If you are not sure you like a gamey flavour, try farmed game such as quail or pheasant first since it will have the mildest flavour. The recipes for braised and pot-roasted chicken and those for guinea fowl can be used with pheasant.

Barbecued quail

This is one of the best ways to cook these small birds, but do marinate them for several hours or overnight first. You could use a simple marinade of white wine, vinegar and a herb or the oriental one given here.

For 8	2 shallots, peeled and sliced	8 quail
4 tbs soy sauce	4 garlic cloves, peeled and chopped	4–6 tbs sunflower oil
6 tbs sherry or saké		2 tbs chopped coriander
2 tbs sugar	a small piece of ginger, peeled and sliced	2 spring onions, sliced finely
juice and rind of 1 unwaxed lime	freshly ground pepper	

Combine the first 8 ingredients for the marinade. Split the quail from top to bottom and put them in a shallow dish. Spoon over the marinade, cover and leave for several hours in the refrigerator. Turn the pieces from time to time.

Take the birds from the marinade, wiping them clean of any bits that are sticking to them. Thread the quail onto skewers to hold them flat, pushing the skewers through the leg and the wing. Brush them with oil and put them on an oiled rack, 12–15cm from the heat, starting with the cut side down. Turn from time to time and baste with the oil. They will take 12–15 minutes. Scatter over the coriander and spring onions and serve.

Braised quail with grapes

For 4	sprigs of rosemary or 8 sage leaves	small glass brandy
8 quail	60g butter	150ml white wine
salt and freshly ground pepper	3 shallots, peeled and chopped finely	150g seedless green grapes

Season the quail with salt and pepper and put a little rosemary or a sage leaf in the cavity of each one. Heat 40g butter in a heavy pan and brown the quail on all sides for 5 minutes. Add the shallots and let them soften in the butter. Heat the brandy over moderate heat in a ladle, ignite it and pour it over the quail. Shake the pan. When the flames have died down, pour over the wine. Cover the pan, bring slowly to the boil, then simmer for 5 minutes. Add the grapes and cook for a further 10–12 minutes. Lift out the quail, stir the remaining butter into the pan and pour the sauce over the birds.

A sweet potato purée (p. 96) flavoured with Armagnac or brandy goes well with these quail.

Partridges with red cabbage

Partridge and cabbage seem to have a natural affinity. Most recipes call for white or green cabbage but I like this version with red cabbage which I first discovered in Germany.

For 4	2 bay leaves	4 partridges
red cabbage weighing about 500g	salt and freshly ground pepper	4 sage leaves
60g butter	¼ tsp ground cloves	4 rashers fat bacon
1 onion, peeled and sliced	2 tbs wine vinegar	2 slices day-old bread
1 tart eating apple	125ml red wine	60g streaky bacon, cut into lardons*

Remove the outer leaves of the cabbage, cut it in four, remove the stalk and shred the leaves finely. Melt half the butter in a pan and soften the onion without letting it brown. Peel, core and slice the apple, then add the cabbage, apple and bay leaves to the onion. Season well with salt, pepper and cloves and stir to mix all together. Add the vinegar and wine, cover the pan and simmer over low heat for about 30 minutes. Check occasionally that the mixture is not sticking to the pan; if necessary add a little water.

While the cabbage is cooking, heat the oven to 220°C, 425°F, gas 7. Season the partridges inside and out and put a sage leaf in the cavity of each one. Cover the breasts with the fat bacon, and hold it in place with string. Melt the remaining butter in a small roasting dish with a lid and brown the partridges on all sides. Transfer them to the oven and roast for 20 minutes, basting occasionally with the pan juices. Reduce the heat to 180°C, 350°F, gas 4. Put the cabbage mixture around the partridges, put on the lid and return the pan to the oven for another

30 minutes. Check to see if the partridges are ready. If necessary, cook them a bit longer, adding a little water to the pan.

When the partridges are cooked, take the dish from the oven. Remove the crusts from the bread and cut it into cubes. Heat the oil in a small frying pan and fry the bacon lardons until crisp, then add the bread and fry the croûtons until crisp. Season with pepper.

Remove the bacon from the partridge breasts and cut the birds in half, removing the backbone (p. 273). Put the cabbage mixture in a serving dish with the partridges on top and scatter over the croûtons and lardons.

Braised partridges with fennel and walnuts

For 2		
2 partridges	60g butter	1 large or 2 small bulbs of fennel, sliced
salt and freshly ground pepper	4 shallots, peeled and chopped	60g walnuts, halved
	200ml chicken stock (p. 4) or water	100ml single cream

Split the partridges in two and remove the backbone (p. 273); season with salt and pepper. Heat half the butter in a heavy pan and sauté the partridges gently, browning them on all sides. Lift them out and sauté the shallots for 2–3 minutes. Return the partridges to the pan, pour over the stock or water, cover the pan and simmer for about 1 hour, until the birds are tender.

Towards the end of the cooking time blanch the fennel in salted water for 1–2 minutes. Drain and rinse it under the cold tap, then sauté it in the rest of the butter until tender. Stir in the walnut halves. When the partridges are ready, remove them to a serving dish and keep warm in a low oven.

Add the cream to the pan and whisk to make a sauce. If it is too thin, let it bubble to reduce. Pour the sauce over the partridges and surround with the fennel and walnuts.

Pigeons with raisins and pine nuts

For 4	8 small onions, peeled	60g raisins
65g butter	350ml chicken stock (p. 4)	3 tbs pine nuts
4 pigeons		2 tsp flour
80g pancetta* or salt pork, diced	salt and freshly ground pepper	

Heat the oven to 170°C, 325°F, gas 3. Heat 50g butter in a casserole and brown the pigeons slowly on all sides. Lift them out and lightly fry the pancetta or salt pork and onions. Return the pigeons to the pan, pour over the stock, season, cover and transfer the pan to the oven. After 30 minutes, check the pigeons; they should be almost ready. Add the raisins and pine nuts to the pan and cook for a further 10–15 minutes. Lift out the pigeons, detach the legs and cut the breast meat from the bone. Put the meat on a serving dish and keep warm while you thicken the cooking liquid. Work the remaining butter into the flour with a fork to make beurre manié (p. 358) and cut it into small pieces. Add the bits of beurre manié to the pan over low heat, stirring until they have melted into the sauce which will thicken very quickly. Let it come just to the boil and immediately remove the pan from the heat. It must not continue to boil. The sauce will now be smooth and shiny. Check the seasoning, pour the sauce over the pigeon and serve.

Pot-roasted grouse

For 2	salt and freshly ground pepper	4–5 tbs stock
20g butter		1 small glass red wine
1 grouse	2 tbs brandy or whisky	

Melt the butter in a heavy pan just large enough to hold the grouse and brown it lightly on all sides for 6–8 minutes. Season the grouse and put it on its side. Pour over the brandy or whisky and stock, let it bubble briefly, then cover tightly, lower the heat and simmer for about 40 minutes. Turn the bird halfway through the cooking. Forty minutes should be long enough, although an old bird may need longer. Take out the grouse and keep warm; add the red wine to the pan, turn up the heat to let it reduce and thicken a little and serve it as the sauce.

Casserole of wild duck with olives

The sun-dried tomatoes and olives make a rich sauce for a gamey wild duck. Large juicy olives such as kalamatas are best.

For 4	1 tbs sun-dried or plain tomato paste	salt and freshly ground pepper
2 wild duck, each cut into four (p. 273)	2 garlic cloves, peeled and crushed	200ml red wine
2 tbs sunflower oil	8 sun-dried tomatoes, chopped	500ml chicken stock (p. 4) or water
2 onions, peeled and sliced	2 bay leaves	30 black olives, pitted
1 tbs flour		3 tbs chopped parsley

Heat the oven to 180°C, 350°F, gas 4. Brown the pieces of duck in the oil in a large casserole. Lift them out and add the onions. When they have coloured lightly sprinkle over the flour. Stir well to blend it with the fat and the onions, then stir in the tomato paste. Add the garlic, tomatoes and bay leaves and season well with salt and pepper. Return the duck to the pan, pour over the wine and enough stock or water just to cover the duck. Cover tightly and transfer the pan to the oven. Cook until the duck is tender, about 1–1¼ hours. Add the olives and parsley 5 minutes before serving.

Sautéed pheasant with herbs

A young pheasant is quickly sautéed and has a delicate flavour.

For 2	salt and freshly ground pepper	2 sprigs thyme or marjoram
2 tbs olive oil	2 garlic cloves, peeled and crushed	150ml white wine
1 pheasant, cut into 4 (p. 272)	2 shallots, peeled and quartered	30g butter

Heat the oil. Season the pheasant and sauté it over moderate heat, turning to brown it on all sides. Allow it to cook gently for 5–6 minutes. Add the garlic, shallots, thyme or marjoram and wine to the pan. Cover and simmer over low heat, turning the pheasant occasionally until it is tender. This will take 20–30 minutes, depending on size. Put the pheasant on a serving dish and keep warm. Whisk the butter, little by little, into the pan juices to make a sauce. Remove the herb and pour the sauce over the pheasant. Serve with a vegetable purée (p. 96).

Pheasant chilindron

This is a dish from Navarra in northern Spain, where it is made with lamb, chicken or rabbit. I tried the method with guinea fowl and pheasant some years ago and enjoyed both, so here is the recipe. Chilindron refers to the use of red peppers which are one of the main crops of Navarra. For a more refined version of the dish, roast and peel the peppers first (p. 151).

For 4

2 pheasants, each cut into 4 (p. 272)

salt

3 tbs olive oil

150g Serrano ham (or bacon), cut in thin strips

3 garlic cloves, peeled and chopped

1 onion, peeled and chopped

3 red peppers, seeded and cut in strips

500g tomatoes, peeled, seeded and chopped, or a 400g can

Season the pheasant pieces with salt, heat the oil and sauté them until browned on all sides. Lift them out and cook the ham lightly in the same oil. Scoop out the ham and put aside while you cook the garlic and onion over gentle heat until the onion has softened. Return the ham to the pan with the red peppers and tomatoes. Cover and simmer for 10 minutes then return the pheasant pieces to the pan. Taste and add a little more salt if necessary. Simmer, covered, for 1 hour or so, until the pheasant is tender. If the sauce becomes too thick, add a little water. Serve with boiled or roast potatoes.

Meat

Only animals raised humanely and non-intensively on natural
feeds yield well-flavoured meat. What happens to them afterwards
– slaughtering, butchering, hanging – also contributes greatly to
quality. This means that it takes times and money to produce good meat, and that it is
expensive to buy. But attempts at cooking poor meat soon convince
that quality and flavour are worth paying for, even if it means
eating less meat and less often. Buy the right cut for the way you
intend to cook it; a well-prepared stew will always taste better than
a lesser cut grilled or roasted.

Choosing

'A skilful, experienced butcher treats his meat almost as a tailor does his cloth. If it is stretched out of shape, if there are seams in the wrong places, if he has to make up a respectable looking joint by adding a piece here, skewering in some fat there, he knows that as soon as the meat is exposed to violent heat it will contract: unnaturally stretched muscles will spring back into place; it will cook unevenly; it will end up looking like a parcel damaged in the Christmas mails. No wonder people say that the cheaper cuts are a false economy. But if that same piece of meat had been stripped of membrane, sinew and gristle before it was rolled and tied, it would be a compact little joint which would keep its shape during cooking and which could be quite successfully roasted.' Elizabeth David in *House and Garden*, February 1958.

A good butcher will always give you better service, and almost always better meat, than you can get in a supermarket. Unhappily, their numbers are dwindling. A butcher should not only be able to prepare the cut you want, but also tell you where the meat came from, probably the breed, how it was reared and for how long it was hung. When checking out a butcher, see if the meat on display is well cut and that the shop smells fresh. Shops with slabs full of plastic bags of meat that is hard to identify are best avoided. Large joints like a loin of pork or a rib roast of beef are difficult to find in a supermarket, but a good butcher will be able to supply them, and bone out the pork or chine the beef as a matter of course. For cheap cuts like shin of beef or belly of pork, not to mention tripe, seldom stocked in supermarkets, you will also need a butcher.

Supermarkets certainly offer more choice than they did a few years ago, and have extended their range to include cuts that were not common in Britain until recently. In the last few years they have also responded to demand by stocking organic meat, yet there is still some ambiguous labelling such as 'farm-assured' or 'traditional' – how are we to know what these mean? Similarly, they woo the consumer who is concerned about fat in the diet with clearly labelled leaner meats, but the leaner meat is frequently obtained by intensive breeding and feeding programmes – a point which is not mentioned.

Scares related to agriculture, especially the rearing of animals, and the quality of food occur with alarming regularity, BSE being the most serious. Consumers have moved in large numbers to buying humanely reared or organic meat. Farmers who persisted in or have returned to the methods of the pre-intensive farming days, producing top-quality meat from animals raised by methods which promote their welfare, are selling all they can produce, as are organic farmers. They raise their animals non-intensively, feed them a natural diet and only use minimal antibiotics when it is essential. Herds tend to be small, and animals are not stressed or forced beyond their natural growth limits. The 'organic' label ensures these and other criteria of sustainable farming have been met; labels such as those of The Real Meat Company or Freedom Foods have similar strict standards of husbandry.

Good-quality meat has always been expensive: the cheapest way to buy is from the farm shop, or by mail but then it can be difficult to buy small quantities. A small amount of good meat is always better than a large slab of something indifferent. As a nation, it seems we are consuming less meat, particularly red meat. The roast meat and two veg stereotype of an English meal is being challenged as we turn to small, trimmed French or Italian cuts, or use a little meat with plenty of vegetables in the Asian manner. There is also more awareness that fish, pulses and grains are all excellent sources of protein.

Appearance

Unfortunately the appearance of a piece of meat does not necessarily give an indication of quality, nor whether it comes from a naturally or intensively raised animal, but here are some basic guidelines.

The surface should look moist but not sticky or slimy. The fat should be firm, white on lamb and pork, cream-coloured on beef. Marbling of fat through the muscle is a good sign; the meat should be tender and have a good flavour. Avoid bright red beef because it will not have been hung for long; beef should have a deep rich colour, with a tawny tinge if very mature. Veal from naturally reared calves, fed (after weaning) on grass and hay, is pink; it cannot be mistaken for the pallid white meat that comes from calves reared in crates and fed on a milk diet. Very young lamb has rosy-pink flesh; later in the season it is darker, tending to purple, but still pink, not red. Pork is sold as young meat and should have glistening pink flesh (beige-pink rather than rosy pink) and white fat. The muscle looks softer and smoother than that of other animals.

Basic mince is best avoided; it is usually made from the poorest cuts that have a high proportion of fat and connective tissue. It tends to look grey. Better-quality minced beef is dark red and has less obvious blobs of fat. Other minced meats are sometimes available. In the supermarket read the label to see what percentage fat they contain. Sinew and connective tissue are never mentioned. The best way to get good mince is to select a piece of meat and ask the butcher to mince it.

Offal spoils quickly. Liver and kidneys should look moist and have a glossy sheen; sweetbreads should be pale in colour. Avoid any offal that looks sweaty or slimy or has a strong smell.

Dry-cured bacon is the best for flavour and value. It doesn't shrink in the pan and ooze white goo as the wet-cured injected bacon does. Some bacon is smoked after salting; this enhances the flavour but also hardens the bacon a little.

Ham and gammon should be firm with not too much fat and not too dry. However, if the flesh is very moist it is likely that it was injected with water.

Ageing meat

All meat needs to be aged to allow enzymes to break down the tissue and tenderize it and to allow the flavour to develop. One of the difficulties today is that most meat is not hung for long enough. A good butcher who hangs meat will tell you how long it has hung and may be willing to hang it longer if you wish.

Storing

Meat from the butcher should be taken out of its packaging, loosely wrapped in plastic and put on a plate in the coldest part of the refrigerator. Meat in airtight plastic packs can be kept as is. Large joints will keep for 4–5 days, chops and cubed meat for up to 3 days, mince and offal are best eaten within a day. Lamb and beef will keep longer than veal or pork.

Quantities

Quantities needed vary according to how the meat is to be cooked and what other ingredients will be used in the dish. As a guideline, allow 120–150g trimmed, fairly lean meat off the bone or 250–300g on the bone per person.

Preparation

See notes under individual animals.

Cooking methods

Tender cuts of meat can be roasted, baked, grilled or fried, whereas tougher cuts should be pot-roasted, braised or stewed. Poaching is as successful with a prime fillet of beef as with shin. The tender cuts come from the parts of the animal that do least work whilst it is on the hoof – the centre back of the animal; tougher cuts come from the shoulders and legs.

Cooking times for tender cuts are relatively short, and vary according to how well done you want the meat to be; but beware, tender cuts become tough if overcooked. Guidelines for roasting and grilling times are given on pp. 310–12 and 314; don't follow them slavishly, use your nose and eyes too. If there is an appetising smell of roast meat and if the juices are seeping to the surface of the meat, it is almost ready.

All the tougher cuts need long slow cooking to break down tissue. You can't really overcook a braised or stewed dish, although you can let it dry out if you don't check the amount of liquid and adjust the cooking temperature if necessary. Slow-cooked dishes can always be reheated. The recipes for slow-cooking different meats and poultry are often interchangeable: for example, you can make an excellent beef stew following the recipe for coq au vin (p. 288), a lamb stew with artichokes instead of veal (p. 328) or pork instead of beef in the carbonnade (p. 323).

Cook the meat you buy by an appropriate method. Do not be tempted to buy an inexpensive cut and then roast rather than braise it. Remember too that expensive cuts often have less waste than cheaper ones.

Roasting

Roasting is most suited to large joints of meat; cuts weighing less than 1.5kg are better braised or pot-roasted. Meat for roasting should be at room temperature before cooking starts. Include any stuffing in the total weight when calculating cooking time. The shape and thickness of a joint also affect cooking time: a compact shape requires longer than an elongated joint of the same weight; a joint on the bone will take longer than the same cut boned. The bigger the roast, the shorter the cooking time per unit of weight and, after searing, the lower the temperature. A boned roast may be placed on its bones to prevent it stewing in the juices in the bottom of the pan; alternatively, use a rack. A layer of fat around a joint bastes it whilst it cooks, keeping the flesh moist, but for lamb I prefer to remove most of the fat and rub it with olive oil. Most lean cuts (veal, pork fillet, venison) should be barded with a sheet of fat (p. 326) but fillet of beef needs only to be rubbed with butter. Roasts need regular basting with the fat that falls into the pan; or, towards the end of cooking, stock, wine or a reserved marinade may be used instead.

Always rest a roast before serving: if it is carved immediately, the juices will all pour out and the texture will be on the rubbery side. Cover the meat loosely with foil and keep in a warm place – the turned-off oven, with the door open, or on the back of the cooker. After 15–20 minutes, depending on size, the juices will be reabsorbed into the flesh and the meat tender. Serve the meat on hot plates as soon as it is carved.

Your oven and your own experience ultimately determine how you use the timings in the charts below. The timings are intended as guidelines to be used in conjunction with the notes on roasting.

Beef

Beef is best roasted rare or medium to produce a supple texture and bring out maximum flavour; well-cooked roast beef can be dry and is rather a waste of top quality meat.

On the bone

Cuts to choose: rib roast, sirloin on the bone

Doneness	Time per weight	Oven temperature	Cooking time
rare	15 min per 500g	230°C, 450°F, gas 8 reduce to 180°C, 350°F, gas 4	first 15 min rest of time + 15–20 min rest
medium	20 min per 500g	as above	as above
well done	25 min per 500g	as above	as above

Off the bone

Cuts to choose: rolled sirloin, rump and topside

Doneness	Time per weight	Oven temperature	Cooking time
rare	10–12 min per 500g	230°C, 450°F, gas 8 reduce to 180°C, 350°F, gas 4	first 15 min rest of time + 15–20 min rest
medium	15–18 min per 500g	as above	as above
well done	20–22 min per 500g	as above	as above

Fillet of beef

A long thin piece like a fillet will cook more quickly than the same weight of a rolled roast, so follow the times and oven temperatures below.

Doneness	Time per weight	Oven temperature	Cooking time
rare	7 min per 500g	230°C, 450°F, gas 8	total cooking time + 10 min rest
medium	10 min per 500g	as above	total cooking time + 10 min rest

Veal

Veal dries out if it is roasted at too high a temperature so it is always cooked in a medium oven and for a longer time per 500g. Like pork, it is always eaten well done.

On or off the bone
Cuts to choose: loin, rump, shoulder, topside

Doneness	Time per weight	Oven temperature	Cooking time
well done	25–30 min per 500g	190°C, 375°F, gas 5	total cooking time + 15–20 min rest

Lamb

Lamb cooked pink tends to keep its flavour better than well-cooked meat. A thin joint like a rack, or a double rack as a guard of honour, will roast more quickly than a large joint, and so adjusted times are given below.

On or off the bone
Cuts to choose: leg, saddle, breast, shoulder, crown roast

Doneness	Time per weight	Oven temperature	Cooking time
rare	10–12 min per 500g	230°C, 450°F, gas 8 reduce to 180°C, 350°F, gas 4	first 15 min rest of time + 15–20 min rest
medium	15 min per 500g	as above	as above
well done	20 min per 500g	as above	as above

Rack of lamb, guard of honour

Doneness	Time	Oven temperature	Cooking time
rare	15 min	230°C, 450°F, gas 8	15–20 min
medium	20 min	as above	as above

Pork

Pork, like veal, is always well done. It is started at a high temperature to release the fat, then at a lower temperature to cook through.

On or off the bone

Cuts to choose: leg (knuckle or fillet), loin, shoulder, ribs

Doneness	Time per weight	Oven temperature	Cooking time
well done	25–30 min per 500g	220°C, 425°F, gas 7 reduce to 180C, 350°F, gas 4	first 15 min rest of time + 15–20 min rest

Venison

Venison is usually eaten pink or rare, occasionally medium cooked, but it becomes very dry if roasted for too long.

Cuts to choose: haunch, saddle

Doneness	Time per weight	Oven temperature	Cooking time
rare	15 min per 500g	220°C, 425°F, gas 7 reduce to 180°C, 350°F, gas 4	first 15 minutes rest of time + 15–20 min rest
medium	25 min per 500g	170°C, 325°F, gas 3	total cooking time + 15–20 min rest

Hare

The saddle is the prime cut from a hare, and it is always cooked rare.

Doneness	Time	Oven temperature	Resting time
rare	15 min	230°C, 450°F, gas 8	5 min

Testing for doneness A meat thermometer will give a reading of the internal temperature of the joint. Before putting the joint into the oven, push the thermometer into the thickest part of the meat, avoiding contact with bone. For rare beef, lamb or venison, the temperature should reach 60°C, 140°F; for medium beef or lamb

70°C, 160°F; and for all well-done meat 75°C, 170°F. However, since meat goes on cooking whilst it is resting, take the roast out of the oven when the temperature is a degree or two lower than those given above.

Another reliable method is to push a flat metal skewer into the thickest part of the meat, leave it for 30 seconds, then pull it out and test it against your wrist. If the skewer is cold the meat is not yet ready, if warm the meat is rare, if quite hot the meat is medium and if it is very hot the meat is well done.

Simple gravy Whilst the roast is resting, pour or skim off the fat from the pan and deglaze* with a little stock, water or white wine, scraping up any meat bits stuck to the bottom. Reduce a little and pour into a warmed jug to serve with the meat.

Carving It is easier to carve on a board than on a platter. Use a carving fork to hold the roast steady and, with a well-sharpened carving knife, slice through the meat across the grain.

Transfer the meat to a warm platter or individual plates; do not keep it waiting at this stage.

To carve a rib roast of beef The butcher will normally cut through the chine bone where it joins the ribs, so that when the meat is ready to be carved it can be removed. Now insert the knife horizontally between the bones and the meat to detach it, and slice down onto the ribs.

To carve a leg of lamb or pork A leg is more easily carved if the pelvic bone is removed before it is roasted (*see* p. 330). With the plumpest side uppermost, hold the leg steady with a carving fork near the shank and cut slices. Turn the carved side down and slice the other side, then cut small slices from the shank.

If a leg of pork has scored crackling, lift off the crackling 'shell', and cut out a wedge of meat near the end of the bone. Slip the knife in horizontally along the bone and release the meat from it. Now cut down in slices to the bone. Slice the crackling and serve with the meat.

To carve a shoulder of lamb or pork Do this in the same way as a leg, but since the bone is more awkward to carve around, the slices will be smaller.

Grilling and barbecuing

These are two excellent ways of cooking small tender cuts. Steaks, chops, cutlets, kebabs as well as sausages and burgers of beef, lamb or venison all respond well to searing followed by less fierce cooking. Meat should be at room temperature before grilling or barbecuing, and marinating is beneficial (*see* individual recipes and pp. 386).

Remove excess fat, leaving a narrow border only, and brush the meat with olive or sunflower oil before cooking. Do not salt, because salt draws out the juices and prevents proper sealing. Do not pierce the meat whilst it is cooking. Turn it once during cooking with a spatula or tongs.

Red meats should be seared quickly with high heat and then cooked more slowly so that the heat can diffuse inside the meat. Cooking time varies according to taste – *see* the table below.

White meats should be seared, but with medium heat, and then cooked gently until cooked through. Veal and pork should not be served underdone, but take care not to overcook and dry out the meat.

Beef
- *fillet steak, 5cm thick* 7–8 min for rare, 10–12 min for medium
- *entrecote, rump, sirloin, 3cm thick* 6–7 min for rare, 10–12 min for medium, 12–14 min for well done
- *porterhouse or T-bone, 3cm thick* 7–8 min for rare, 12–15 min for medium, 18–22 min for well done

A rare steak contracts slightly when touched, a medium steak is resistant when touched and juices seep on the sealed surface, a well done steak feels firm. Steak benefits from resting for a few minutes before being cut.

Veal
- *chops, cutlets* 6–8 min per side depending on thickness, turn once, baste regularly

Lamb
- *chops, cutlets* 3–7 min per side depending on thickness and how well you want them cooked

Pork
- *chops* 12–18 min per side depending on thickness
- *spare ribs* It is advisable to marinate these first. A whole rack takes 30–40 min to grill; it should be basted frequently and turned infrequently

Venison
- *cutlets* 3–4 min per side, turn once

Frying and stir-frying

The small cuts suitable for grilling and barbecuing can also be fried. Bring the meat to room temperature for an hour before cooking. For red meats have the pan very hot, add a little oil or oil and butter, and quickly sear the meat before reducing the heat. Cooking times are as above. Pork and veal should be sealed at a moderate temperature and then cooked until well done; for chops, follow the time guidelines above. Veal escalopes fried gently in butter and oil will be ready after cooking for 3–4 minutes on each side.

Good-quality steak or loin of pork, thinly sliced, is the best choice for stir-frying for oriental dishes.

Sautéing

A sauté is quickly made with small pieces of tender meat, sometimes dusted first in flour and fried. Vegetables and herbs are added after the meat has browned, and the pan is deglazed* with water, white wine or stock so that the meaty bits stuck to the bottom can be scraped loose. A spoonful or two of cream may be stirred in before serving.

Pot-roasting and braising

Slow cooking with a little liquid and flavourings is ideal for lean but less tender cuts such as topside, silverside or brisket of beef, chuck or blade steak. Veal is particularly suited to this treatment: all the leg cuts, the sliced shank (usually called osso buco), stuffed breast and joints from the shoulder. Braised lamb shanks make a rich satisfying dish and shoulder pot-roasts well. Pork fillet pot-roasts beautifully as do large less tender cuts such as rolled shoulder and the upper neck end. Ham and gammon will also braise well. Venison, like veal, is a dry meat which benefits from moist cooking; a boned shoulder or even a haunch are both suited to pot-roasting. Hare and rabbit joints also benefit from slow cooking.

Stewing

The extremities – neck, shin – make excellent stews and casseroles, as will cubed chuck or blade steak, veal flank or ribs, shoulder of lamb and shoulder of pork or hand and spring. Trotters and hock enrich stews as the gelatinous tissues break down.

Poaching

If meat is not to become tough, it must be poached in barely simmering water, never coming near the boil. One of the grandest poached dishes is a fillet of beef. Brisket, particularly if brined, poaches well. Otherwise the cuts which are suited to stewing are also good for poaching. Stuffed breast of veal makes a handsome dish. Fresh, salted and cured pork all respond well to poaching. A bonus of poaching is the stock created during the cooking.

Leftovers

Roast or braised beef, veal and pork are delicious cold; beef turns up as a salad all over the world, in a mustardy vinaigrette with gherkins and capers, with a dressing of orange juice, onion and herbs, with lemon grass*, fish sauce and a mild vinegar. Lamb is often considered to be too fatty to enjoy cold. The salad repertoire can be extended by following the Thais and Vietnamese and using small amounts of cooked meat in herb and vegetable salads (pp. 88–9).

There are many cooked dishes to be made with leftover meat, and there is one important principle to understand before making any of them. If the meat has been cooked by dry heat – roasting or grilling – it can be heated very gently for 5–10 minutes in a liquid and will remain tender. Longer cooking and higher temperatures will initially toughen it, and then it passes the tough stage and becomes tender again. If you decide to opt for longer cooking, slices of meat will need 1–1½ hours further cooking; diced or finely chopped pieces 30 minutes. Pot-roasted or braised meat is already past the tough stage and can be reheated for a shorter time.

The classic French ways to use leftover beef are to heat slices in white wine and add a mushroom or tomato sauce, to cook it further in a rich onion sauce, or to make a hash with potatoes, tomatoes and onions. In Alsace, they make a well-flavoured rather dense plate pie, or tourte, with finely chopped cooked pork. Many Middle Eastern dishes are based on vegetables to which a small amount of meat is added, usually minced or finely diced lamb. Leftover meat can be used in the same way, cut up small in fillings for vegetables, to stuff vine or cabbage leaves, in pilafs (p. 181) and grain-based casseroles (p. 204). Moussaka (p. 108) and shepherd's pie (chopped cooked lamb with cooked onions and carrots and a little stock or gravy, topped with mashed potato and baked for about 40 minutes at 180°C, 350°F, gas 4) are both dishes that are almost invariably made with cooked meat. If you use beef for the pie, it becomes cottage pie.

Beef

Cuts to choose

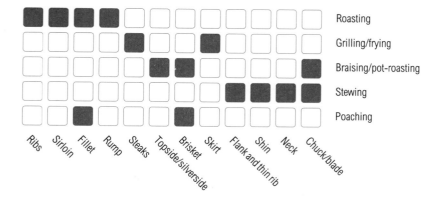

	Ribs	Sirloin	Fillet	Rump	Steaks	Topside/silverside	Brisket	Skirt	Flank and thin rib	Shin	Neck	Chuck/blade	
Roasting	■	■	■	■									
Grilling/frying					■			■					
Braising/pot-roasting						■	■					■	
Stewing									■	■	■	■	
Poaching			■					■					

Ribs. Forerib and back rib are prime cuts for rib roasts; the lean meat is marbled with fat and has an outer layer of fat which will baste the meat as it roasts. Best roasted on the bone for greater flavour, but a rib roast can also be boned and rolled. Rib steaks are sold as entrecôtes.

Sirloin. Extends from the ends of the ribs to the rump, providing tender, lightly marbled top-quality meat for roasting on or off the bone, or for cutting into steaks – T-bone, porterhouse and sirloin.

Fillet. Fillet lies below the backbone and offers the tenderest cut of beef. Sometimes sold as part of the sirloin, it is more generally removed and sold as a whole boneless piece for roasting or poaching, or cut into steaks – filets mignons, tournedos, châteaubriand and fillet steaks.

Rump. This has an outer layer of fat and is lightly marbled; sold as rump steaks or as joints for roasting.

Topside and silverside. These are lean joints from the upper leg, often sold with a separate piece of fat tied around. Best for pot-roasting or braising, although topside can be roasted. Salted silverside makes corned beef.

Brisket. The front of the breast, usually rolled and tied. A fatty meat which benefits from braising, pot-roasting or poaching. Brisket is also available salted.

Skirt. A small lean muscle within the flank. If marinated, it can be grilled as a (cheaper) steak and has a fine flavour.

Flank and thin rib. Fibrous meat running down from the loin. After trimming, it can be used for stewing or may be minced.

Shin. Sinewy but well flavoured; the connective tissue gives a rich gelatinous quality to slow-cooked stews. It is also good for making stock.

Neck. Inexpensive cuts with a high proportion of fat and connective tissue; usually sold cubed for slow cooking or as mince.

Chuck and blade. From the shoulder. Fairly lean joints or steaks are marbled and have a layer of outer fat. Best for braising or cubed for stewing.

Preparing a fillet of beef

Cut away the chain muscle from the side of the fillet; it is a tough sinewy piece but can be used for stewing or mincing. Lift and cut away any silvery-white membrane (it shrinks during cooking), leaving the meat free of all fat and sinew. Fold under and tie the tapered end if the fillet is to be roasted.

Preparing a steak

Trim excess fat, leaving an even layer. Snip through the fat into the edge of the meat at intervals so that the thin membrane lying between the fat and the meat does not curl as it cooks.

Roast fillet of beef

This may be horrendously expensive, but it is a prime cut with no waste. Treat it carefully and don't overcook it.

For 8	3 tbs olive oil	watercress
1 fillet of beef weighing 1.75–2kg	freshly ground pepper	béarnaise sauce (p. 374)

Remove the beef from the refrigerator an hour before it is to be cooked. Prepare it, if necessary, as described above. Tie it around with string in 4 or 5 places to keep it in shape, tucking under the tapering end. Heat the oven to 230°C, 450°F, gas 8. Brush the meat all over with 2 tbs olive oil and season it with pepper. Do not add salt. Use the remaining oil to grease the bottom of the roasting pan.

Roast the fillet 25–30 minutes for rare meat, 35–40 minutes for medium. Take it from the oven, wrap in foil and keep warm for 10 minutes. Garnish with watercress and serve with its own juices and béarnaise sauce. Serve quickly on hot plates.

New potatoes and a pea purée or wilted spinach make simple, clean tasting accompaniments.

Roast sirloin with mushroom sauce

For 6

1.5kg rolled sirloin

3 tbs olive oil

For the sauce

60g butter

1 onion, peeled and sliced finely

2 carrots, peeled and diced

3 tomatoes, skinned and chopped

bouquet garni* of bay leaf and thyme sprigs

600ml meat stock (p. 5)

salt and freshly ground pepper

1 rounded tbs flour or rice flour

2 tbs water

250g button mushrooms

4 tbs madeira

Bring the beef to room temperature for an hour before cooking. To make the sauce, melt half the butter in a heavy pan, add the onion and let it colour lightly. Add the carrots, cook gently for 10 minutes, then stir in the tomatoes and herbs. Increase the heat slightly so that the liquid from the tomatoes evaporates and the mixture thickens. Pour in the stock, season and simmer gently for 20 minutes.

Remove the pan from the heat. Mix together the flour and water and stir it, a little at a time, into the sauce. Return the pan to low heat and cook, stirring continuously, until the sauce thickens. Strain the sauce through a fine sieve, do not press too heavily on the vegetables. Return it to the rinsed-out pan and reheat gently. It should have the consistency of a thin cream soup.

Wipe the mushrooms and leave whole, unless they are larger than button mushrooms in which case cut them in four. Add them to the sauce and simmer for 10 minutes. Check the seasoning.

Up to this point the sauce can be made ahead of time and be kept warm or reheated.

To cook the beef, heat the oven to 230°C, 450°F, gas 8. Coat the meat with the oil (leaving a little to grease the bottom of the roasting tin) and season it with pepper. After searing the meat for 15 minutes, reduce the temperature to 180°C, 350°F, gas 4. Roast for 10–12 minutes per 500g for rare meat, 15–18 minutes for medium and 20–22 minutes for well-done meat. (To use a meat thermometer, *see* p. 312.) Wrap the joint in foil and keep in a warm place for at least 15 minutes before carving.

While the beef is resting, finish the sauce. Add the madeira and whisk in the remaining butter cut into small pieces. Carve the beef, spoon over a little of the sauce and serve the rest separately. Have hot plates ready.

Steak au poivre

This is one of those dishes by which you can judge the standard of cooking in a restaurant – well worth trying at home, and giving great satisfaction when you get it just right.

For 4	2 tbs black or green peppercorns	2 tbs sunflower oil
		4 fillet or sirloin steaks

Crush the peppercorns coarsely. Rub the steaks on both sides with a little of the oil and press peppercorns into both sides with the palm of your hand. Heat a heavy frying pan or ribbed griddle pan, coat it with the remaining oil and when it is very hot, sear the steaks for about 1 minute on each side. Wait for a crust to form before turning them. Reduce the heat and continue to cook for about 3 minutes on each side for rare fillet steaks or 4 minutes for medium rare. Sirloin steaks will take a minute or two longer on each side. Adjust times according to the thickness of the steaks. Serve at once.

Steak with mushroom sauce

Use 4 fillet or sirloin steaks and follow the recipe for Venison steaks with mushroom sauce on p. 351, omitting the juniper.

Beef teriyaki

This is a Japanese way of frying or grilling steaks. Teriyaki is a sauce based on saké (rice wine) and mirin (a syrupy rice wine used only in cooking) and soy sauce. It is used to baste or glaze grilled or fried fish and meat in the last stages of cooking. You can buy bottles of teriyaki sauce, but it is quite easy to make and keeps well in the refrigerator if you want to make a larger quantity. Saké and mirin can be bought from oriental shops and some supermarkets.

For 4	4 tbs dark soy sauce	4 sirloin or rump steaks
4 tbs saké	2 tsp sugar	
4 tbs mirin* ·	1 tbs sunflower oil	

First prepare the sauce: combine the saké, mirin, soy sauce and sugar in a small pan, bring to the boil and simmer until the sugar has dissolved.

Put a heavy frying pan over high heat and add the oil. When it is very hot, fry the steaks on each side for 3 minutes, turning once. Now spoon the teriyaki sauce over the steaks. It will sizzle fiercely and reduce. Coat the steaks with the glaze on both sides, turning them once, and serve.

If you prefer your steak medium rather than rare, fry each side for a minute or two longer.

To barbecue It is best to marinate the steaks in the sauce for up to 30 minutes, then transfer the meat to the grill and baste with the sauce as it cooks.

Sichuan stir-fried beef with leeks

This is a winter dish in Sichuan and it makes a good winter dish here, too, served with noodles or rice. You could use other vegetables – shredded Chinese cabbage or mustard greens, sliced celery or broccoli florets. The Sichuanese like chilli-hot food, but if you do not, reduce or leave out the chillies.

For 6		
800g lean beef, rump or sirloin	1 garlic clove, peeled and chopped finely	4 spring onions, white and lower green part, sliced finely
90ml soy sauce	4 slices ginger, peeled and chopped finely	2 tsp sugar
60ml rice or wine vinegar	2–3 chillies, seeded and sliced finely	4 tbs sunflower oil
		750g young leeks, sliced finely

Cut the beef across the grain into thin ribbons, discarding any fat. Combine the soy sauce, vinegar, garlic, ginger, chillies, spring onions and sugar and marinate the beef for 30 minutes. Heat a wok or heavy frying pan, add half the oil and when it is very hot stir-fry the leeks for 3 minutes. Remove them from the wok and add the remaining oil. Drain the beef, reserving the marinade. When the oil is very hot, add the beef. Toss and stir it rapidly for 1 minute. Return the leeks to the pan, mix well with the meat and pour over the marinade. Cook for a further minute and serve at once.

Tuscan braised beef

A satisfying and simple slow-cooked dish that can easily be extended for more people. In other parts of Italy, braised beef is cooked by the same method but the flavourings change: white wine is used instead of red; diced salt pork or bacon may be added with the vegetables; chopped anchovies and parsley may replace the cloves and nutmeg. Thyme, sage or rosemary also occur as alternative flavourings, but use sage and rosemary very sparingly.

For 6–8	2 large onions, peeled and chopped finely	a glass of red wine
2 tbs olive oil		2 cloves
30g butter	2 carrots, peeled and chopped finely	nutmeg
1.75kg topside or other braising cut	1 stalk celery, chopped finely	2 tomatoes, peeled, seeded and chopped, or 3 tbs passata (p. 378 or bought)
salt and freshly ground pepper	2 garlic cloves, peeled and chopped finely	80ml stock or water

Use a heavy pan with a well-fitting lid in which the meat fits snugly. Heat the oil and butter in the pan and put in the beef, well rubbed with salt and pepper, and brown it on all sides. Lift it out and sauté the onion, carrots, celery and garlic and continue cooking until they begin to take colour. Put the meat on top of the vegetables, pour over the wine and let it bubble for a minute or two, then add the cloves, a grating of nutmeg, the tomato and the stock. Cover tightly; if necessary put a piece of foil under the lid. Cook on a very low heat or, alternatively, in a low oven (150°C, 300°F, gas 2) for 3 hours. Turn the meat occasionally and baste with a spoonful of the liquid.

When it is ready, carve the beef into thick slices. Strain the sauce though a sieve, rubbing through as much of the vegetables as possible, and pour over the meat to serve. A dish of lentils makes a good accompaniment: if you prefer, add the vegetables from the sauce to the lentils, and serve the meat with a thinner gravy. Another possibility would be boiled potatoes.

In Tuscany it is usual to make the dish the day before it is eaten and leave it to mellow. Any fat can be lifted off before it is gently reheated.

Daube of beef

This is the classic beef stew of Provence. It can be made without marinating the meat, but a few hours in a marinade will give the daube more flavour. Like all stews, it benefits from reheating.

For 4	2 garlic cloves, peeled and crushed	100g salt pork or bacon, diced
1kg topside of beef	2 bouquets garnis*	strip of orange peel
2 onions, peeled and sliced	400ml red wine	3 cloves
2 carrots, peeled and sliced	2 tbs wine vinegar	salt and freshly ground pepper
	2 tbs olive oil	

Cut the beef into 8–10 pieces, put these in a bowl with the onion, carrot, garlic, one bouquet garni, the wine and vinegar and marinate for 4–5 hours, or longer. Turn the meat occasionally.

Heat the oven to 150°C, 300°F, gas 2. Drain the meat and vegetables, reserving the marinade liquor. Heat the oil in a heavy pan and sauté the salt pork, then brown the meat. Add the vegetables from the marinade, but discard the bouquet garni, and put in a new one. Put in the strip of orange peel and the cloves and season well with salt and pepper. Pour over the marinade. Slowly bring to the boil on the stove, and let the liquid reduce a little. Cover tightly, with a piece of foil under the lid if necessary, and transfer the pan to the oven for about 3 hours. Remove the bouquet garni before serving.

The dish is usually served with rice – traditionally the red rice from the Camargue – or a dish of macaroni moistened with some of the cooking juices.

Carbonnade of beef

This is a richly flavoured stew from the Flemish part of Belgium, made with a dark beer. It is best made in advance and reheated.

For 6	1 tsp mustard powder	2 tbs wine vinegar
2 tbs beef dripping or oil	1kg stewing steak, cut in large cubes	1 bouquet garni*
4 onions, peeled and sliced finely	300ml dark Belgian beer or stout	salt and freshly ground pepper
30g plain flour	100ml meat stock (p. 5) or water	a grating of nutmeg
		1 tbs brown sugar

Heat the oven to 150°C, 300°F, gas 2. Fry the onion in half the dripping or oil, allowing it to colour, but don't let it burn. Lift it out with a slotted spoon and put it into a shallow casserole. Combine the flour and mustard powder and coat the meat. Brown it quickly in the remaining dripping or oil and transfer to the casserole. Add the stout, stock and vinegar to the frying pan together with the seasonings and sugar and bring to a simmer. Pour over the meat and onions, cover tightly and cook for about 3 hours. Remove the bouquet garni before serving.

Serve with mash or lightly toasted slices of french bread to soak up the gravy.

Oxtail stew

An easy dish, perfect for cold winter days and quite inexpensive. It needs little preparation but several hours' cooking, and it is better if it is made a day in advance. The fat can then be removed from the top before the stew is reheated.

For 4	2 onions, peeled	4 cloves
2kg oxtail, in 5cm pieces	2 carrots, peeled	200ml red wine
2 tbs flour	2 stalks celery	800ml meat stock (p. 5) or water
salt and freshly ground pepper	2 tbs tomato purée	1 glass port (optional)
2 tbs sunflower oil	3 sprigs thyme	3 tbs chopped parsley
	2 bay leaves	

Heat the oven to 150°C, 300°F, gas 2. Trim excess fat from the oxtail and toss the meat in seasoned flour. Heat the oil in a large pan and brown the oxtail in batches. Chop the vegetables coarsely, by hand or in a food processor, and put them into the pan with the tomato purée, herbs and cloves. Replace the meat. Add the wine and stock or water, season with salt and pepper and bring to the boil. Skim off the scum that rises to the surface, cover the pan and transfer to the oven. Cook for 3 hours.

At this point the stew can be removed from the oven and left to cool. The next day, remove the fat from the surface before returning the uncovered pan to the preheated oven (150°C, 300°F, gas 2). If you continue cooking on the same day, remove the lid at this stage. Simmer for a further 1–2 hours; the meat should be loose from the bone and the sauce reduced and thickened. A glass of port stirred in 30 minutes before the end of cooking adds depth to the sauce.

Skim any fat from the surface, scatter over the chopped parsley and serve with noodles or potatoes.

Veal

Cuts to choose

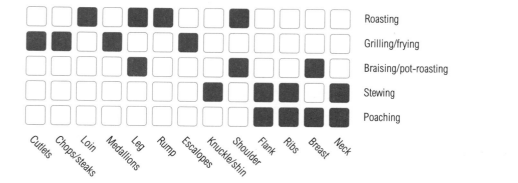

Roasting

Grilling/frying

Braising/pot-roasting

Stewing

Poaching

Cutlets Chops/steaks Loin Medallions Leg Rump Escalopes Knuckle/shin Shoulder Flank Ribs Breast Neck

Best end of neck. **Prime meat sold as cutlets. Because the meat is very tender it is best grilled or fried gently and basted.**

Middle neck. **Part of the shoulder; usually sold as cutlets or shoulder chops.**

Loin. **A choice cut of very lean meat with a thin layer of outer fat. Usually sold boned and rolled for roasting, or as cutlets. The fillet is frequently removed and sold sliced as medallions for frying.**

Leg fillet end (or cushion) and rump. **Good-quality cuts, sold as boned and rolled joints for roasting and pot-roasting. The meat is very lean and benefits from larding. Escalopes are cut from the fillet end of the leg.**

Knuckle and shin. **Cuts with marrow bones that make well-flavoured gelatinous stews such as ossi buchi. Also very good for making stock.**

Shoulder. **Usually sold boned and may be braised or roasted. Another good joint for stuffing. Also available cubed.**

Flank. **A thin cut with lots of connective tissue from the abdominal wall. It needs long moist cooking – stewing or poaching – to make it tender. Also sold as mince.**

Ribs. **Sold boned, ribs are for stewing or poaching, since the connective tissue needs to be broken down.**

Breast. **Once boned, this is an excellent cut for stuffing, rolling up and poaching or braising. Also sold cubed.**

Neck. **Sold cubed for stewing or poaching.**

Larding and barding

Very lean meats benefit from having fat added before roasting or pot-roasting, otherwise they become too dry. Larding is done internally, strips of pork fat in a larding needle are pulled through the meat. If you don't have a needle, make holes in the meat with a skewer and insert small pieces of fat: it is not as effective, but better than nothing. To bard a joint, wrap wider strips of fat around the meat and tie securely. If you can't get pork back fat, a lightly cured streaky bacon could be used.

Stuffing a breast of veal or lamb

Having got the butcher to bone the breast, lay it out flat, skin side down, spread it with the prepared stuffing and roll up, tucking one edge under the other. Tie into a neat shape, starting from the thick end.

Preparing veal escalopes

Escalopes do not need enthusiastic pounding, unless they are of very uneven thickness (which indicates poor butchering) or unless you want to stretch the meat to roll it around a filling. Cut away any connective tissue that will make the meat curl during cooking. Lay the escalopes between two sheets of plastic film or greaseproof paper and gently flatten them with the heel of your hand or a rolling pin. Escalopes are usually about 1cm thick when bought and are best flattened to half that thickness.

Veal escalopes with asparagus and balsamic vinegar

For 4	2 tbs olive oil	salt and freshly ground pepper
400g veal escalopes	40g butter	
300g green asparagus	150ml white wine	4 tsp balsamic vinegar

Flatten the escalopes gently (*see* above). Break the asparagus to give pieces 8–10cm long and use the rest of the stalks for soup. Thread the spears carefully onto thin wooden skewers. Heat the grill or a ribbed griddle plate.

Put 1 tbs oil and 30g butter into a frying pan and set the pan over medium heat. When the fat is hot, fry the escalopes in batches. Do not crowd the pan. Fry the escalopes for about 3 minutes on each side, turning once. They should only be lightly browned. When they are ready remove them to a plate and keep warm.

Meanwhile brush the asparagus spears with the remaining oil and put them under the grill or on the griddle plate. Grill for 5–6 minutes, depending on thickness, turning them once.

When all the escalopes are cooked, add the wine to the pan and scrape up any bits stuck to the bottom. Let the wine bubble until it is reduced to only a couple of tablespoons, then add the remaining butter and any juices from the escalopes. Season the meat with salt and pepper and return to the pan. Turn the pieces a few times in the pan juices, then add 3 tsp balsamic vinegar and turn the meat once more. Transfer the escalopes and any juices to a serving dish, remove the asparagus from the skewers and lay across the meat. Drizzle the last tsp of balsamic vinegar over the asparagus and serve at once.

Veal escalopes with onion and cider sauce

For 2	2 medium onions, peeled and sliced finely	salt and freshly ground pepper
200g veal escalopes		
60g butter	200ml dry cider	80ml crème fraîche or double cream

Flatten the escalopes lightly (*see* above). Heat half the butter in a frying pan and sauté the onions for 5 minutes. Pour over the cider, bring to the boil and reduce to 4 tbs. While the cider is reducing, heat the remaining butter in another pan and cook the escalopes for 3–4 minutes on each side. Remove them to a warm dish, season and keep warm. Scrape any bits from the bottom of the pan and add them to the onions. Stir the cream into the onions and season. Add the escalopes to the onions and reheat briefly in the sauce.

Veal with garlic (Aïllade de veau)

An easy supper dish, from an old provençal recipe.

For 2	4 garlic cloves, peeled and crushed	1 tbs dried breadcrumbs
1 tbs sunflower oil		
2 veal chops or steaks	3 large tomatoes, peeled, seeded and chopped	salt and pepper
		a glass of white wine

Heat a heavy frying pan, coat it with the oil and brown the meat on both sides. Take out the chops and keep to one side. Put all the other ingredients into the pan and simmer to make a sauce. After 20 minutes, put back the chops and continue to cook over low heat for a further 45 minutes. The sauce should be thickish; cover the pan if it is reducing too much, or add a little more wine or water.

Veal stew with artichoke bottoms

The veal should be marinated for some hours, even overnight, but the cooking time is quicker than for many stews. I have used frozen artichoke bottoms; to prepare fresh ones, *see* p. 101.

For 4	3–4 sprigs of thyme	6 sun-dried tomatoes, sliced
800g pie or stewing veal, cubed	4 tbs olive oil	2 tbs flour
300ml white wine	salt and freshly ground pepper	2 bay leaves
2 garlic cloves, peeled and crushed	2 large onions, peeled and sliced	400g frozen artichoke bottoms

Put the meat in a bowl, add the wine, garlic and thyme, stir, cover and leave for 3–4 hours. When you are ready to cook, lift out the veal and dry with kitchen paper. Strain and reserve the marinade. Heat half the oil in a heavy pan and seal the veal in batches. Transfer the meat to a casserole and season with salt and pepper. Add the remaining oil to the pan and lightly sauté the onions until they are transparent. Add them to the veal with the sun-dried tomatoes. Sprinkle the flour into the oil left in the pan and stir briskly as it slightly darkens in colour. Remove the pan from the heat and pour over the strained marinade, whisking steadily. Put the pan back on the heat, and bring to the boil, still whisking. Pour the sauce over the meat and vegetables, tuck in the bay leaves. The sauce should just cover the meat so it will probably be necessary to add a little hot water. Simmer over low heat for 1¼–1½ hours.

Blanch the frozen artichoke hearts for 2 minutes. Drain, cut them in half and add them to the veal. Simmer for a further 12–15 minutes to allow them to heat through, then remove the bay leaves and serve.

Lamb

Cuts to choose

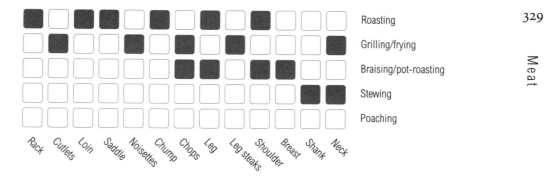

	Rack	Cutlets	Loin	Saddle	Noisettes	Chump	Chops	Leg	Leg steaks	Shoulder	Breast	Shank	Neck	
Roasting	■	□	■	■	□	■	□	■	□	■	□	□	□	
Grilling/frying	□	■	□	□	■	□	■	□	■	□	□	□	■	
Braising/pot-roasting	□	□	□	□	□	■	■	□	■	■	□	□	□	
Stewing	□	□	□	□	□	□	□	□	□	□	□	■	■	
Poaching	□	□	□	□	□	□	□	□	□	□	□	□	□	

Best end of neck. This has an even layer of outer fat and a little marbling in the flesh. Sold as a rack of lamb, it makes a perfect roast for two. Two racks with bones intertwined and fat side out form a guard-of-honour roast; two racks joined in a circle make a crown roast. Both may be stuffed in the middle. Best end is also sold as cutlets for grilling.

Loin. Usually sold as chops for grilling or frying. The meat is lightly marbled and there is a layer of fat on the outer edge of the chops. Loins left joined by the backbone can be sliced to form butterfly chops, or kept whole to roast as a saddle. A single loin can also be roasted, on or off the bone. Noisettes are cut from a boned, rolled loin.

Chump. A cut from between the loin and the leg; sometimes sold as a prime joint for roasting, but more frequently as chops.

Leg. The leg provides a succulent joint for roasting, either whole or divided into two small joints, the fillet end and the shank or knuckle. Steaks cut across the fillet end can be grilled or braised. A braised leg of lamb also makes a very good dish.

Shoulder. Has more fat and is more gelatinous than the leg. For roasting it is best boned and rolled, with or without a stuffing. Left on the bone it is difficult to carve. Shoulder can also be braised as a whole or half joint (blade or knuckle end). Boned and trimmed of fat and membrane, it can be cubed or minced.

Breast. A thin, fatty, well-flavoured cut, often sold boned when it can be stuffed and braised.

Shank. This gelatinous cut from the lower leg makes well-flavoured stews. Fore shanks are the meatiest, rear shanks are usually sold with the leg.

Neck. The middle neck is fatty and tough, best suited to stewing. The scrag is more bony; it is sometimes sold in slices and is also best stewed.

Preparing lamb loin chops

Cut off excess fat, especially from the long flap of skin, keeping the skin intact. Wrap the skin around the meat and secure with a toothpick. This makes a neater and easier shape to grill or fry, and the skin protects the meat.

Stuffing a breast of lamb. *See* p. 326.

Removing the pelvic bone from a leg of lamb

With the cut surface of the meat towards you, cut round the exposed surface of the pelvic bone with a small sharp knife, separating the flesh from the bone. Follow the shape of the bone, cutting deeper into the flesh until you expose the ball-and-socket joint that connects it to the thigh. Cut through the tendons joining the bones and the pelvic bone will become free.

Crown roast of lamb

For 6		
1 crown roast	1 tsp finely chopped rosemary leaves	salt and freshly ground pepper
1–2 tbs olive oil	1 tsp chopped thyme leaves	

Have the lamb at room temperature for an hour before you intend to roast it. Heat the oven to 230°C, 450°F, gas 8. Rub the meat with olive oil, sprinkle with the herbs and season with salt and pepper. Wrap the tops of the bones with foil to prevent them from burning. Roast for 15 minutes, then reduce the temperature to 180°C, 350°F, gas 4, and cook for a further 25–35 minutes, depending on how well cooked you want your lamb. Baste the meat from time to time as it roasts. Let it stand for 10–15 minutes in a warm place, covered with a piece of foil, before serving.

Just before serving, fill the centre with cooked vegetables tossed in a little butter or olive oil: new potatoes, peas, french beans, asparagus tips, small carrots in summer; Jerusalem artichokes, little onions, cubes of pumpkin in winter. Remove the foil from the tops of the ribs and carve down between the bones. Serve on hot plates.

Roast leg of lamb

For 8

1 leg of lamb weighing about 3kg

1–2 tbs olive oil

For the marinade

2 tbs finely chopped mixed herbs – thyme, marjoram, savory, parsley

1 garlic clove, peeled and crushed

freshly ground pepper

1 tbs olive oil

60ml white wine

For the gravy

400ml vegetable or chicken stock (p. 4)

3 garlic cloves, peeled and crushed

2 sprigs thyme

100ml white wine (or more stock)

Remove all excess fat from the lamb, and ideally remove the pelvic bone (*see* opposite). Combine the chopped herbs with the garlic, season with pepper and moisten with the oil to make a paste. Make slits in all sides of the meat and push in some of the paste. Rub the meat all over with any remaining paste and with the wine and marinate in the refrigerator for up to 5 hours. Take it out about an hour before cooking, so that the meat comes to room temperature.

Heat the oven to 230°C, 450°F, gas 8. Rub the lamb with olive oil. If you use a meat thermometer, insert it in the thickest part of the leg, but avoid contact with the bone. Roast for 10–12 minutes per 500g for rare lamb or 15 minutes per 500g for medium lamb, but after the first 15 minutes reduce the heat to 180°C, 350F, gas 4. (To use a meat thermometer, *see* p. 312.) Baste the meat from time to time with its juices. Allow the meat to rest, covered with foil, in a warm place for 15–20 minutes before carving.

Whilst the meat is resting, prepare the gravy. If there is excess fat in the pan blot it up with kitchen paper. Deglaze* the pan with the stock, scraping up any bits stuck to the bottom. Strain into a small pan. Add the garlic, the thyme and the wine, and reduce to about 200ml. Strain before serving. Serve the meat on hot plates.

Baked lamb chops with potatoes and tomatoes

For 4

8 loin chops or 4 chump chops

3 tbs olive oil

salt and freshly ground pepper

100ml red wine

500g potatoes, peeled and sliced thinly

8 garlic cloves, peeled and crushed

4 tomatoes, quartered

2 tsp finely chopped rosemary leaves

½ tsp paprika

100ml water

Heat the oven to 190°C, 375°F, gas 5. Remove excess fat from the chops. Heat the oil in a frying pan and brown the chops for 2–3 minutes on each side. Remove the chops, season with salt and pepper and set aside. Add the wine to the pan, scrape up any bits stuck to the bottom, and let the wine reduce by about half. Mix together the potatoes, garlic, tomatoes and rosemary. Put half of the mixture into a fairly shallow ovenproof dish, season with salt, pepper and paprika and place the chops on top. Spoon over the juices from the frying pan. Put the rest of the vegetables over the top, season and pour over water to cover. Cover and bring to the boil. Transfer the dish to the oven and bake for 45 minutes, then remove the lid and bake for another 30–40 minutes. Add a little boiling water if the dish seems to be drying out.

Grilled lamb noisettes

For 4	8 noisettes	½ tbs crushed black peppercorns
1 large onion, peeled	1½ tbs mixed chopped herbs – thyme, savory, marjoram, rosemary or herbes de Provence	
1 tsp salt		
3 tbs olive oil		

Chop the onion very finely and put in a small bowl. Sprinkle the salt over it and leave for 5–10 minutes. Now squeeze the onion in your fist to extract the juice, combine this with the oil and rub the mixture into the noisettes on both sides. Scatter half the herbs and peppercorns in a shallow dish, put in the noisettes in a single layer and scatter the rest of the herbs and pepper on top. Cover and marinate for 2–3 hours, or longer if you prefer.

Heat the grill or a ribbed griddle pan and grill the noisettes until brown outside but still pink inside – they will take 6–9 minutes, turned once, depending on their thickness and how pink you like your lamb. Serve at once with lemon quarters.

Note
Chops can be prepared in the same way, but take longer to cook. Thick loin chops will need about 12 minutes, chump chops up to 20 minutes. If you have more meat increase the other ingredients accordingly.

Lamb fillet with aubergine purée and yogurt dressing

The lamb and aubergine can be baked in the oven, or grilled on a barbecue. A thick yogurt is best for the dressing; if you prefer to use a low-fat yogurt, strain it first.

For 4	2–3 tbs lemon juice	2 aubergines, about
2 garlic cloves	200ml yogurt	350g each
salt and freshly ground pepper	4 tbs chopped mint	3 tbs olive oil
		2 lamb fillets

First prepare the yogurt dressing. Crush the garlic with a little salt. Whisk half of it into the yogurt with 1 tbs lemon juice. Season with pepper and stir in the mint. Set aside until needed.

Prick the aubergine skin in 2 or 3 places and bake in the oven preheated to 230°C, 450°F, gas 8, for 20–30 minutes, until the aubergines are soft. Then put them in a pan or bowl and cover with a lid and leave until they are cool enough to handle. Turn down the oven to 200°C, 400°F, gas 6.

Heat 2 tbs oil in a small roasting tin, and seal the lamb fillets quickly over high heat. Transfer the tin to the oven and roast for 10–12 minutes for lamb that will be still pink in the centre or 14–16 minutes for medium lamb.

While the lamb is cooking, peel off the aubergine skin, put the flesh into a bowl, add lemon juice to taste, the remaining garlic and oil; season. Blend to a purée with a fork. Keep the purée warm.

Slice the lamb fillets, arrange them on a bed of aubergine purée and serve the yogurt dressing separately.

To barbecue Grill the pricked aubergines for about 20 minutes and the lamb for 8–10 minutes to serve pink or 12–14 minutes for medium, turning once.

Lamb with pumpkin, prunes and apricots

The peoples of the Caucasus have a rich tradition of lamb stews with fruit and vegetables. Herbs play a more important part in the flavouring than spices.

For 4–6	2 onions, peeled and chopped	750g pumpkin (first weight), peeled, seeded and cubed
150g dried apricots	1 tsp allspice	4 tbs chopped dill
150g prunes	salt and freshly ground pepper	4 tbs chopped mint
50ml sunflower oil		
800g leg or shoulder of lamb, cubed		

Soak the apricots and prunes for 3–4 hours unless you are using ready-to-eat fruit. Stone the prunes. Heat the oil in a large pan and sauté the lamb and onion until the lamb is browned on all sides. Sprinkle over the allspice, salt and pepper. Pour in enough water just to cover the lamb, cover the pan and simmer over low heat for 45 minutes. Taste to see if the lamb is getting tender. If it isn't, let it simmer longer. Add the pumpkin and the fruit. Cover the pan and simmer for a further 30–40 minutes. Check the seasoning, stir in the herbs and serve.

Lamb tagine

The Moroccans have some of the best slow-cooked dishes in the world, usually based on lamb or chicken, with the addition of vegetables (artichokes, peas, broad beans, carrots) or fruits (apricots, dates, prunes, quinces), each with subtly different seasoning. This version is flavoured with olives and preserved lemons and is based on a recipe from a little book of the 1950s, *Fes vue par sa cuisine,* by Z. Guinaudeau. A tagine is a handsome earthenware dish with a tall conical lid; as in many cultures, the pot has given its name to the food cooked in it.

For 4–5	salt	150g green or violet olives
1kg lamb, shoulder or leg	100ml water	2 preserved lemons (p. 513)
½ tsp saffron threads	2 garlic cloves, peeled and crushed	juice of ½ lemon
100ml olive oil	1 large onion, peeled and chopped finely	
1 tsp ground ginger		
½ tsp ground chilli or red pepper flakes	a small bunch each of parsley and coriander	

Trim any excess fat from the lamb and cube the flesh. Soak the crushed saffron in a little hot water. Put the oil, spices and salt to taste in a heavy pan, stir thoroughly whilst pouring in, a little at a time, 100ml water, as if making mayonnaise.

Turn the meat in this emulsion over moderate heat until it colours, then add just enough more water to cover it. Bring to the boil, cover the pan and simmer over very low heat for 1 hour. Add the garlic, onion and bunches of herbs to the pot, cover again and simmer for a further 45–50 minutes, until the meat is very tender. Whilst it is cooking, stone the olives, remove the pulp from the lemons and cut the peel into strips. Add the olives, peel and lemon juice 10–15 minutes before the end of cooking.

Remove the meat and keep it warm in a tagine or other earthenware dish, boil down the sauce rapidly to about 350ml. Discard the herbs, check the seasoning. Spoon the sauce over the lamb, arranging the olives and lemon peel on top.

Lamb shanks with garlic

This dish is simple, quick to prepare and can be simmered for up to 3 hours without coming to harm – the meat just gets more tender. It is unwieldy to make in large quantities though and having a couple of large pans on the cooker can be a nuisance. The shanks could be braised in a low oven, at 170°C, 325°F, gas 3.

For 4

4 lamb shanks, weighing 300–500g each

3 tbs olive oil

1 large onion, peeled and chopped

8 or more garlic cloves, peeled

bouquet garni* of thyme and bay leaves

2 tomatoes, peeled, seeded and quartered

2 sun-dried tomatoes, chopped

salt and freshly ground pepper

200ml white wine

300ml vegetable or chicken stock (p. 4) or water

Trim excess fat from the shanks. Heat the oil in a large pan which will hold the shanks side by side and brown them on all sides. Add the onion and stir occasionally until it starts to colour, then put in the garlic, herbs and both lots of tomato; season with salt and pepper. Pour over the wine and stock. Bring slowly to the boil, cover tightly and simmer over very low heat for 1½ hours or until the meat is starting to come loose from the bone. Check the pot from time to time to see that it is simmering gently, and that it is not necessary to add a little more stock or water.

Remove the lid and simmer for another 30 minutes or so. The meat should be very tender and the sauce reduced. Skim off excess fat before serving. If there is still too much liquid, remove the shanks to a bowl and keep warm whilst you skim the cooking liquid and boil it down further over high heat.

A potato or celeriac mash (p. 154) would go well with this.

Variation
· Add 100g small black olives for the last 30 minutes of cooking.

Saffron pilaf with lamb and almonds. See p. 182.

Rogan josh

This mildly spiced dish thickened with yogurt or curds comes from northern India. Rogan josh reheats well, and is even better the second day.

For 4

1kg lamb, leg or shoulder

60ml oil or 60g ghee*

pinch asafoetida* (optional)

1 tsp ground ginger

4 cloves

250ml thick yogurt

1 tbs coriander seed, dry-roasted* and ground

1–2 tsp chilli powder

seeds from 4 cardamom pods*, crushed

½ tsp ground mace

salt to taste

1–2 tsp garam masala*

4cm piece fresh ginger, peeled and shredded

Cut the lamb into pieces about half the size of a postcard. Heat the ghee or oil in a heavy pan and stir in the asafoetida, ground ginger and cloves. Add the meat and about a third of the yogurt. Cover the pan and simmer until the liquid dries up. Stir in another third of the yogurt, scraping up any bits sticking to the pan. Cover and simmer again until the liquids dry up. The meat should be golden brown. Remove the pan from the heat and again scrape up any bits that are sticking.

Return the pan to the heat, add the coriander, chilli, cardamom and mace with the rest of the yogurt. Stir thoroughly. Add just enough water to cover the meat, put on the lid and simmer until the lamb is tender, about 1 hour.

Taste and add salt if necessary. Sprinkle over the garam masala and shredded ginger, cover again and simmer for 15–20 minutes until the flavours are well blended. Serve with rice.

Pork

Cuts to choose

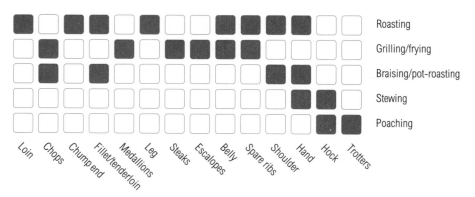

Loin. A prime tender cut with a thin outer layer of fat. It makes a very good roasting joint, especially if boned and stuffed. It is otherwise sold as chops for grilling, barbecuing or frying. Back bacon is cured loin.

Chump end. This is the back part of the loin, usually sold as chops which are much meatier than the loin chops. It can also be roasted whole.

Fillet or tenderloin. Lies beneath the middle loin and the chump end. From a small animal, it is sold as part of the loin, but may be separated out as a lean tender cut. Fillet is a good cut to pot-roast; for roasting it should be wrapped in fat or bacon so that the meat doesn't dry out. It can also be sliced into medallions. The meat has a delicate flavour and benefits from added liquid and flavourings.

Leg. Often sold as two joints – fillet end and knuckle or shank end. The fillet end is very good roasted on the bone, or it may be sold sliced like a steak or in smaller escalopes. The knuckle end is more bony but still a good roasting cut. It is also salted and sold as ham or gammon, depending on the cure.

Belly. A fatty cut from the abdominal wall that can be roasted or grilled. It is excellent salted as streaky bacon or as salt pork.

Spare ribs. These are cut from the thick end of the belly and may be barbecued, grilled or roasted, as a piece or separately, often glazed with a sauce.

Shoulder. Usually cut as two pieces: the upper neck end, mostly sold as chops, and the lower blade with the shoulder bone. The fatty tissue in the meat makes it suitable for braising and roasting. Collar bacon is cured neck end.

Hand. This cut from the foreleg is coarser than the meat from the hind leg and best suited to stewing, although the hand is also sold boned and rolled for roasting and braising.

Hock. The lowest part of the leg which is often cured in brine. Best for stewing and poaching.

Trotters. The feet need long slow poaching in court-bouillon, then they are rolled in breadcrumbs and grilled. In France, you can buy them ready-prepared for grilling. Their high gelatine content makes them useful for enriching stews and stocks.

Back fat is cut in thin sheets used for larding and barding, p. 326.

Salting pork

Pork is more intensively reared than other domesticated animals, has less fat than it used to have and less flavour. It benefits from a light salting; even rubbing sea salt over a piece of pork a few hours before cooking will improve the taste.

Removing the pelvic bone from a leg of pork or ham

Follow the instructions for a leg of lamb on p. 330.

Scoring pork for crackling

If you like crackling, with a very sharp knife cut parallel lines 1cm apart across the skin. Rub well with oil and salt to crisp the fat. Do not baste during roasting, or it will go limp.

Roast loin of pork stuffed with apricots

A roast loin of pork is a handsome and easy dish to prepare for several people. This version includes a stuffing, but if you don't want to go to that trouble, some crushed garlic and a few chopped herbs – rosemary, sage, thyme or fennel – spread over the meat before rolling and tying will flavour it well. Any leftover roast is excellent cold.

For 8

1 loin of pork, weighing about 2.5kg, boned and skin removed

For the stuffing

150g ready-to-eat dried apricots, chopped

1 small onion, peeled and finely chopped

100g unsalted pistachios, chopped

100g fresh white breadcrumbs

1 tsp thyme leaves, chopped

½ tsp ground coriander or anise seeds

salt and freshly ground pepper

juice and grated zest of 1 unwaxed orange

1 egg

Trim the pork fat to obtain an even layer. Combine apricots, onion, pistachios, breadcrumbs and seasonings, including the orange zest. Moisten with the orange juice and bind with the lightly beaten egg. If the result is too dry, add a little more orange juice. Spread the stuffing over the meat, roll up and tie. Weigh the stuffed joint to calculate the cooking time (*see* p. 312).

Heat the oven to 220°C, 425°F, gas 7. Roast the pork for 15 minutes, then reduce the temperature to 180°C, 350°F, gas 4. It will take about 2½ hours. Baste every 20 minutes with the pan juices. Pork must be well cooked and it is properly cooked through when a meat thermometer, if being used, shows 75°C, 170°F or when the juices run clear if the thickest part of the meat is pierced with a skewer. Leave to rest, covered, in a warm place for 15 minutes before carving. Serve on hot plates.

Baked pork chops

These baked chops make a quickly prepared supper dish and the flavourings can be changed to suit your taste. Replace the sage with ¼ tsp chilli flakes or paprika, or crush the garlic with ½ tsp fennel or coriander seeds.

For 4	8 sage leaves	1 tbs olive oil
4 pork chops	sprig of rosemary	a glass of white wine
salt and freshly ground pepper	2 garlic cloves, peeled	

Heat the oven to 190°C, 375°F, gas 5. Trim excess fat from the chops and season with salt and pepper. Chop the sage leaves together with the leaves from the rosemary, and the garlic. Rub the mixture into the chops on both sides. Lightly oil an ovenproof dish and put in the chops. Pour over the wine and add enough water just to cover the meat. Cover the dish and put it into the oven for 30 minutes, then remove the lid and continue to bake for a further 20–25 minutes or until the chops are well cooked and the sauce reduced. Test the chops; when they offer no resistance to a skewer they are ready. The cooking time depends on thickness as much as weight.

The chops are very good with a dish of quinces or apples stewed with onions.

Pork medallions with lime

For 4	2 small garlic cloves, peeled	2 tbs chopped parsley
2 unwaxed limes		salt and freshly ground pepper
5 tbs olive oil	8 medallions cut from the fillet, about 700g	

Prepare a marinade with the juice of ½ lime, 3 tbs oil and 1 crushed clove of garlic. Pour it over the meat and leave for an hour. Grate the zest of the whole lime and combine it with the remaining clove of garlic, finely chopped, and the parsley. Set aside to garnish the pork.

Heat the oven to 180°C, 350°F, gas 4. When you are ready to cook, pat dry the medallions with kitchen paper and heat the remaining oil in a frying pan. Season the meat with salt and pepper and brown it on both sides. Transfer to an oven dish and bake for 8–10 minutes, depending on the thickness of the medallions. Just before the meat is ready add the juice of the remaining limes to the frying pan and stir well, scraping up any bits stuck to the bottom. Put the pork onto a serving dish, spoon over the sauce, sprinkle over the garnish and serve.

Pork satay with peanut sauce

I first discovered satay in one of the many Indonesian restaurants in Holland and fell for the lightly spicy taste of the meat and decidedly moreish peanut sauce. For those who can't eat peanuts, try another relish, tomato sambal (p. 384), to accompany the satay. You can make satay also with chicken, beef or lamb, and adjust the flavours of the marinade to suit your taste.

Kecap manis is a thick, sweetish soy sauce from Indonesia and Malaysia. It is not interchangeable with Chinese or Japanese soy sauces, although one of those with a little sugar can at a pinch be used instead. It is available from oriental shops.

For 4	750g leg or fillet of pork, cut into small cubes	4 tbs smooth peanut butter (150g)
3 garlic cloves, peeled and crushed		2 tbs very thick coconut cream
1 tsp ground cumin	1 tbs sunflower oil	
1 tsp ground coriander	**For the peanut sauce**	3 tsp sambal* or similar chilli condiment
2 tbs soy sauce	4 medium onions (500g), peeled and chopped finely	2 tsp kecap manis or other dark soy sauce (optional)
1 tsp sugar	2 tbs sunflower oil	
1 red chilli, sliced	1 tsp ground cumin	

Combine the first six ingredients, and marinate the meat, turning it to coat it well as you put it into the dish. Cover and leave in the refrigerator for several hours.

The sauce needs time to cook and time to mellow, so make it well ahead of barbecuing the satay. Put the onion in a heavy pan with the oil and the cumin, stir to coat, cover and leave on a diffuser mat on medium heat for 20 minutes. Turn the heat to low and leave for another 30–40 minutes by which time the onions will be very soft and have made a fair amount of liquid.

Stir in the peanut butter and the coconut cream, and leave for another 30 minutes. Take the pan off the heat and stir in the sambal and, if you prefer a somewhat deeper flavour, the kecap manis. Leave to stand for several hours. When needed, heat through gently.

Remove the pork from the marinade and thread the cubes onto skewers. If you use wooden skewers, soak them in water first for 15 minutes so that they don't burn. Grill on the barbecue for 10–12 minutes, basting with oil and turning frequently, or cook under an indoor grill. Serve accompanied by rice and the sauce.

Stir-fried pork with cashew nuts

Follow the recipe for Chinese stir-fried chicken on p. 284, replacing the chicken by shredded pork. If you wish, use a mixture of vegetables instead of the mushrooms.

Pot-roasted pork fillet

For 2–3	salt and freshly ground pepper	2 garlic cloves, peeled and crushed
1 pork fillet (tenderloin), weighing 450–500g	30g butter	½ tsp ground coriander
	juice of 1 orange	

Trim the pork of any excess fat and sinew. Rub with salt and pepper.

Heat the butter in a heavy pan into which the pork just fits and brown it gently. Pour over the orange juice and stir in the garlic and coriander. Cover tightly, and cook over the lowest possible heat, using a heat diffuser if necessary, for 30–40 minutes. Turn and baste the meat once or twice while cooking. Pierce the meat with a skewer towards the end of cooking time; if the juices run clear, the pork is cooked through. It should be tender and moist.

Strain the juices (there won't be many), slice the pork and spoon the sauce over.

Chinese braised pork and vegetables

We tend to be more familiar with Chinese stir-fried and steamed dishes because these are the ones most commonly served in Chinese restaurants, but there are excellent braised and simmered dishes that are worth knowing about. This recipe can be made with beef if you prefer.

I have used bamboo shoots and snow peas, but mange-tout, Chinese cabbage or mustard greens cut in 1cm slices, sliced leeks or mushrooms or peppers cut in squares are all suitable substitutes.

For 2	1 tbs sugar	100g snow peas, topped and tailed
250g pork, fillet or leg	salt to taste	1 tsp cornflour or potato flour
2 tbs sunflower oil	100ml vegetable or chicken stock (p. 4)	
1 tbs rice wine* or sherry	100g bamboo shoots, sliced	1 tbs water
2 tbs soy sauce		

Trim the meat and cut into 2cm cubes. Heat a wok or pan over high heat until you can feel the heat rising from it when you hold your hand above it. Add 1 tbs oil, swirl it around and put in the pork. Stir-fry briskly until it is browned all over. Add the rice wine or sherry and toss for 30 seconds, then the soy sauce, sugar and salt (remember that soy sauce is salty). Toss again and add the stock. Bring to the boil, then immediately cover the pan, lower the heat and simmer gently for 45 minutes. Stir occasionally to make sure the meat has not stuck to the bottom, and check the stock level, replenishing if necessary.

Stir the bamboo shoots and snow peas into the pan and braise for a further 15 minutes. Just before the end of cooking time, check the quantity of sauce. If it is reduced to a few spoonfuls and just coats the food, serve as it is. If it is more liquid, mix the cornflour into the water, then stir into the sauce to thicken it slightly. Serve with rice.

Pork vindaloo

Indian restaurant vindaloos are all too often exercises in providing 'heat' from chillies rather than the robust but well-balanced flavours of the authentic stew evolved in Goa by the Portuguese who settled there. The name comes from the Portuguese for wine (*vinho*) and garlic (*alho*), and wine vinegar, garlic and chillies are the essential flavourings. The vinegar preserves the meat, and thus allowed it to be kept from one day to the next before the advent of refrigeration. A pickled version is also made, using more vinegar and mustard oil (p. 76). Vindaloo is often served with bread – usually chapatti – but rice also goes well with it.

For 4	4 cardamom pods*, crushed	3–6 dried chillies, seeded
500g lean pork, leg or shoulder, cubed	1 tsp salt	2cm cinnamon stick
2 tbs sunflower oil	1 tsp sugar	4 cloves
3 onions, peeled and sliced finely	2 green chillies, sliced	½ tsp turmeric
	4 tbs wine vinegar	6 garlic cloves, peeled and crushed
4 garlic cloves, peeled and sliced finely	200ml water	
	For the spice mix	2cm ginger, sliced
6 black peppercorns	½ tsp cumin	3 tbs wine vinegar

First prepare the spice mix. Grind together the cumin, chillies, cinnamon and cloves – an electric coffee grinder makes an excellent spice grinder. Put the mixture into a blender or mortar with the turmeric, garlic, ginger and vinegar and blend to a paste. Rub this mixture into the meat and marinate for at least 6 hours, turning occasionally. Twelve hours or more would be even better.

Heat a wide heavy pan, pour in the oil and fry the onion until browned. Add the garlic and spices and fry until the garlic starts to colour. Now put in the meat with its marinade, and a sprinkling of water and fry, turning the meat until it is browned all over.

Add the salt, sugar, green chillies, vinegar and water. Lower the heat, cover the pan and simmer for 40–50 minutes or until the pork is tender. If the meat is getting too dry add a little more water. The sauce should reduce and thicken; if it is too liquid, remove the lid and increase the heat for a few minutes at the end of cooking time.

Ham and gammon

Cured pork

Ham and gammon are prepared from the hind legs of the pig. Dry-salting produces the finest flavour and the most tender meat. Some hams are then air-dried, others smoked, depending on the climate and tradition. Both the feed given to the pigs and the wood used for smoking affect the flavour.

It is usually the less expensive hams that are cured in brine, and many are injected with the brine to produce faster – and inferior – results. Hams are sold whole or divided into knuckle and fillet pieces. Some hams – Ardennes, Bayonne, Black Forest, jamón serrano, prosciutto di Parma, prosciutto di San Daniele – are intended to be sliced thinly and eaten raw.

Boiled or cooked hams can be eaten cold or can be cooked further. They have a milder flavour than the raw hams.

To cook ham or gammon

Whole ham

If you buy a ham to cook, soak it in cold water for several hours to get rid of some of the salt. Follow the instructions from the producer, or the advice of your supplier. Change the water 2 or 3 times. A ham should be brought to a bare simmer, and poached in water that just shudders. Allow 20 minutes per 500g once simmering point is reached. Taste the water after half an hour; if it is very salty, throw it away and start again (remember to continue calculating the cooking time from simmering). Now is the time to add aromatic vegetables (carrot, onion, celery) and flavourings (bay leaf, thyme, peppercorns, allspice) if you wish. When it is ready, leave the ham to cool in the water until you can handle it comfortably. Lift it out, remove the skin and excess fat while the ham is still warm. The ham can be coated with breadcrumbs and served as it is, or baked.

A boiled ham to be baked can be covered with a herb and mustard coating or brushed with a glaze. Maple syrup, soy sauce mixed with honey and sherry, or brown sugar and apple juice all work well. Bake in the oven preheated to 170°C, 325°F, gas 3, basting frequently. Make sure the glaze doesn't scorch. About 35–40 minutes is long enough to set the coating for an attractive glaze, but should not dry out the meat. Serve hot or cold.

Gammon

Small pieces of gammon do not usually need soaking; bring the meat slowly to the boil in a large pot of water, drain and rinse in cold water. Remove the skin and excess fat. It can now be braised or baked. To bake, coat the fat side of the gammon with dried breadcrumbs or a herb and lemon zest mixture if you wish. Wrap the joint loosely in foil and put into the oven preheated to 170°C, 325°F, gas 3, for 35 minutes per 500g. Leave to stand for 40 minutes before unwrapping.

Carve ham and gammon into thin slices with a long flexible knife.

Gammon braised with honey and cider

For 4		For the sauce
1kg boneless gammon, after skin and excess fat removed	rind of 1 unwaxed orange without pith	3 Cox's orange pippins or similar apples
4 tbs honey	freshly ground black pepper	30g butter
2 tbs Dijon mustard	¼ tsp ground cardamom* (optional)	100ml dry cider
rind of 1 unwaxed lemon without pith	250ml dry cider	80ml double cream or crème fraîche
		lemon juice

Heat the oven to 170°C, 325°F, gas 3. Put the piece of gammon into a large pot and cover with cold water. Bring to the boil and drain at once. Rinse the gammon with cold water.

Mix together the honey and mustard. Put the gammon in an ovenproof casserole into which it just fits and spoon over the honey and mustard to coat the gammon on all sides. Add the citrus peel, pepper and cardamom. Heat the cider almost to boiling point and pour it over the gammon. Cover the casserole tightly and transfer the gammon to the oven. Cook for 1¼–1½ hours, then lift out the gammon and carve. The liquid is likely to be too salty for stock and is best thrown away.

Towards the end of the cooking time for the gammon, make the sauce. Peel, core and dice the apples, melt the butter in a pan and fry them gently until soft and lightly golden. Transfer the apple to a dish and keep warm. Deglaze* the pan with the cider, scraping up any bits stuck to the bottom and mixing in the buttery apple juices. Boil down the cider by two-thirds, stir in the cream, taste and add a squeeze of lemon juice if necessary, and stir the liquid into the apples. Serve with the gammon.

Grilled glazed gammon

For 2	For the glaze	2 tsp sherry vinegar
2 thick gammon steaks, about 200g each	4 tbs apricot jam 1 tbs preserved ginger, chopped finely	1 tbs finely chopped mint (optional)

Put the jam, ginger and vinegar in a small saucepan and bring gently to the boil; simmer for about 3 minutes, until smooth. For a somewhat fresher taste, if you like, stir in the mint. The glaze can be used hot; it will spread more easily.

Spread about half the glaze over one side of the gammon and grill, glazed side up, for 5–6 minutes. Turn the steaks, spread the other side with the rest of the glaze, return to the grill for another 5–6 minutes or until the glaze has browned well. Serve at once.

Variations

Cajun blackening spice. Combine 1 tsp each of paprika, dried thyme and dried oregano; ½ tsp each of freshly ground black pepper, ground cumin, mustard powder and cayenne pepper (a little less of the latter if the paprika is hot) and a pinch of salt. Mix well and rub the gammon with the mixture. Drizzle over a little oil before grilling.

Garlic and herb paste. In a mortar, crush 4 cloves of garlic to a paste with a little salt. Add 2 tsp of coarsely ground black peppercorns, 4 tbs finely chopped mixed fresh herbs (basil, oregano, parsley, rosemary, sage, tarragon, thyme) and 1–2 tbs olive oil. Mix well; use in the same way as the glaze.

Curried ham and leek gratin

This is a very adaptable dish: chicory, chard stalks or celery hearts (1 per slice of ham) can be used instead of leeks, a cheese sauce (80g grated cheese) or a spinach sauce (150g cooked, very well drained and chopped spinach) can replace the curry sauce. A tomato sauce (p. 378) is another possibility. You can prepare the sauce and blanch the vegetables ahead of time and finish the dish later.

Meat

For 4	1 small onion, peeled and chopped	1 tbs flour
8 thin leeks	½ tsp garam masala* or curry powder	400ml chicken stock or half stock, half milk
4 large thin slices cooked ham	¼ tsp ground coriander	salt
For the sauce	½ tsp freshly ground black pepper	80ml double cream
60g butter		

Parboil the leeks in salted water for 5 minutes and drain thoroughly. Cut them to the same length as the ham. Chop any leftover pieces finely.

Heat half the butter and soften the onion in it, then add any leftover leek. Cover and simmer for about 10 minutes, until the vegetables are just cooked. Stir in the spices and flour and add the heated stock a little at a time, whisking to thicken the sauce. Add salt to taste, and simmer for 10 minutes. Stir regularly to make sure it is not sticking to the pan. Transfer the mixture to a food processor or blender, purée, then stir in the cream. Taste for seasoning.

Heat the oven to 190°C, 375°F, gas 5. Wrap 2 leeks in each piece of ham and place them, with the join underneath, in a buttered gratin dish. Spoon over the sauce, dot with the remaining butter and bake for 15–20 minutes. The surface should be golden and bubbling. If it is not well browned, put the dish under a hot grill for a few minutes.

Sausages

Bangers and mash has taken on a new dimension with the wide variety of sausages now on sale. Most are still made from pork, but veal, beef, lamb (merguez), chicken, venison and wild boar are all available, as are a wide variety of blood sausages and black puddings. The range of flavourings – herbs, spices, vegetables, smoking – has increased, too. Our tradition is based on sausages that are best grilled, fried or baked, whereas many European sausages are intended for poaching.

Standard English sausages, long regarded as a cheap form of meat, are stodgy with a high percentage of bread to meat, and much of the meat is fat. Labelling is now better and indicates the amount of meat in the sausages, though it doesn't yet say how much of that meat is lean tissue rather than fat.

Garlic sausages with french potato salad

This is standard French bistro fare, and the success of this dish depends on the salad being warm. You can use other types of sausages equally well.

For 6

1kg salad potatoes (p. 78)

1kg garlic sausages

2 shallots, peeled and chopped finely

salt and freshly ground pepper

1–2 tsp Dijon mustard

3 tbs wine vinegar

100ml olive oil or a mixture of olive and walnut oil

1 glass white wine

Boil the potatoes until just done. While they are cooking, prick each sausage in 2 or 3 places and put them in a frying pan, add 3–4 tbs water, and cook over medium heat. The sausages will release their fat, and the water will eventually evaporate. Fry the sausages slowly, turning them to brown on all sides.

Combine the shallot, seasonings, mustard and vinegar and whisk in the oil to make a vinaigrette. Drain the potatoes, peel or not as you wish, but if you do peel them, work quickly and keep the potatoes warm. Slice them quite thickly, transfer them to a dish and pour over some of the white wine. Repeat until all the potatoes are ready and the wine used up. Pour over the vinaigrette, lifting the potatoes to coat them all. Be careful not to break them.

Drain the sausages on kitchen paper and serve with the salad.

Cotechino with lentils

Cotechino is a large pork sausage, subtly spiced, from the region of Emilia-Romagna in central Italy. It is poached and served with lentils, either whole or puréed, and often accompanied by an Italian speciality, mostarda di Cremona, fruits preserved in a mustardy syrup. You can buy the cotechino and mostarda in Italian delicatessens. If you fancy the idea of sausage and mash with a difference, the cotechino is excellent with mash too.

For 4–6

1 cotechino

350g lentils

3 tbs olive oil

1 small onion, peeled and chopped finely

2 stalks celery, sliced finely

salt and freshly ground pepper

Put the cotechino in a large pan and cover it with water. Bring to the boil, cover and simmer for 2 hours. Do not puncture the skin while it is cooking.

The lentils (use Castelluccio or Puy lentils, p. 140) will take 50 minutes to 1 hour to prepare, so start them about half way through the cooking time for the sausage. Heat the oil in a pan large enough for cooking the lentils and sauté the onion until lightly golden, put in the celery and sauté 1–2 minutes more. Add the lentils, stir them into the oil, then add water just to cover them. Bring to the boil, then simmer, covered, for 20–25 minutes, depending on the age and type of lentils, until they are tender. If the pan is getting dry, add a little more water. If there is too much water, uncover the pan towards the end of cooking time and turn up the heat, so that it evaporates. Season well.

Drain and slice the sausage and serve on top of the lentils.

Offal

France, Spain, Italy, the Middle East and China all have thriving traditions of offal cookery; we Anglo-Saxons are more squeamish about what, if any, offal we will eat, except for a few enthusiasts who adore it all.

Offal includes all the edible organs of the animal: brain, heart, kidneys, liver, sweetbreads (the thymus glands), testicles, tripe (the stomach) and the extremities (head, feet, and tail). Offal deteriorates quickly and is best cooked the day it is bought. Veal offal is prized above others for its delicate flavour and is correspondingly highly priced. Lamb's offal is tender and quickly cooked. Most beef offal and some pork is coarsely textured and very strongly flavoured.

Liver, kidneys and heart can be sautéed, grilled or braised. Calf's brains are no longer available in Britain, but lamb's are. Tongue is much underrated and very easy to poach at home, whether fresh or salted. Tripe is now sold parboiled, ready for poaching or braising.

With the exception of oxtail which makes a fine winter stew (p. 324), the extremities are more difficult to buy than the innards – even pig's trotters which have become fashionable in restaurants.

Preparing liver
Peel away the thin membrane with your fingers. Cut off any gristle, then slice thinly, and remove any internal ducts from the slices.

Liver with paprika

For 4

500g calf's or lamb's liver	salt and freshly ground pepper	small glass of white wine
flour	50g butter	handful of chopped parsley
2 tsp paprika	2 garlic cloves, peeled and crushed	150ml soured cream

Clean the liver (*see* above) and cut it into thin strips. Coat these with flour seasoned with paprika, salt and pepper. Melt the butter in a heavy pan and add the liver and garlic; sauté for 2–3 minutes over high heat, turning the liver until it is evenly browned. Take out the liver and keep it warm while you make the sauce.

Add the wine and parsley to the pan, scrape loose any bits that are sticking, and boil briefly. Reduce the heat; stir in the cream and heat through but do not boil. Put the liver into the sauce and serve.

Portuguese liver and bacon

For 4

500g calf's or lamb's liver	2 tbs white wine vinegar	salt and freshly ground pepper
100ml white wine	1 bay leaf	3 tbs olive oil
	2 garlic cloves, peeled and chopped	80g bacon, cut in thin strips

Clean the liver (*see* above) and slice into thin strips. Prepare a marinade with the wine, vinegar, bay leaf, garlic, salt and pepper. Pour it over the liver, cover and leave for 2–3 hours.

Take out the liver and pat it dry; reserve the marinade. Heat the oil in a frying pan and sauté the liver and bacon over moderate heat until the liver is tender. Take liver and bacon from the pan and keep warm.

Remove the bay leaf, then pour the marinade into the pan. Increase the heat a little and stir, scraping loose any bits from the bottom of the pan, until the marinade is reduced by a third. Pour it over the liver and bacon, and serve. Boiled potatoes are the usual accompaniment to this dish.

Preparing kidneys

Pull away the fat surrounding the kidneys and then peel off the membrane. Cut the kidneys in half lengthways and remove the fatty central core with scissors. Slice calf's kidneys into pieces; lamb's kidneys are left in half.

Kidneys with tomato

For 4		
500g lamb's or calf's kidneys	1 large onion, peeled and chopped finely	2 tbs chopped parsley
lemon juice	2 garlic cloves, peeled and chopped finely	salt and freshly ground pepper
2 tbs olive oil	3 large tomatoes, peeled, seeded and chopped	a small glass white wine

Prepare the kidneys (*see* above). Leave lamb's kidneys in halves, slice calf's kidneys. Soak them in a little lemon juice for 10 minutes, then pat dry. Heat the oil and sauté the kidneys quickly. Add the onion, garlic, tomato and parsley and season with salt and pepper. Stir to combine. Cook over gentle heat for 10 minutes, then add the wine. As soon as it starts to bubble remove the pan from the heat and serve.

Variation
Kidneys with sherry Omit the tomato, garlic and wine. Sauté the onion with the kidneys, add the parsley and seasonings. Pour over 150ml dry sherry and 50ml water, lower the heat and simmer for 12–15 minutes.

Game
Venison

The most common species of deer in Britain are red deer, roe deer and fallow deer, and the venison we buy may come from animals from the wild or from those raised in deer parks. The red deer is larger than the roe and fallow, so the size of the cuts is larger. Venison has less fat than farm-raised meats, the flesh is dark red, dense and fine-grained; a young animal has whiter fat than a mature one. It can have a gamey flavour or it can be almost insipid and lacking flavour, depending on its age and how long it has been hung. Unfortunately, unless you know the source of your venison, you will not know what you are getting. Venison is available from some supermarkets, from game dealers and by mail order.

A haunch (leg) or saddle of a young animal can be roasted; chops and medallions grilled or fried. The tougher meat from older animals needs slow cooking in liquid, as does that from the shoulder, neck and flank of a young deer. All venison benefits from marinating, and roasting joints may also be barded or larded (p. 326). Venison can be slow-roasted for several hours in a low oven or seared and quickly roasted at a high temperature if it is to be served rare. Farmed venison is available year round; summer is closed season for wild.

Venison steaks with mushroom sauce

Use wild mushrooms such as chanterelles, pieds de mouton or ceps if you can get them.

For 4	salt and freshly ground pepper	8 coarsely crushed black peppercorns
For the sauce		
2 shallots, peeled and chopped finely	150ml soured cream or crème fraîche	8 coarsely crushed juniper berries
30g butter	3 tbs finely chopped parsley	4 venison steaks
400g mushrooms, sliced		3 tbs olive oil or 45g butter

First make the sauce. Sauté the shallot in butter until it turns golden. Add the mushrooms, season them and cook until their juices evaporate. Stir in the cream and parsley and keep warm.

Press the peppercorns and juniper berries into both sides of the steaks. Heat the oil or butter over high heat and fry the steaks for 2–3 minutes on each side, so that they colour evenly. Turn once. They should still be pink inside. Serve at once with the sauce.

Braised venison

The recipe for Tuscan braised beef on p. 321 could be used for shoulder or haunch of venison. Marinate the joint for up to 24 hours (*see* pp. 386–8 for marinades) and wipe it dry before browning. Adjust the quantities of the other ingredients according to the size of the joint.

Venison stews

Venison makes an excellent carbonnade (*see* carbonnade of beef, p. 323) and the daube of beef on p. 322 also works well with venison. More surprising, perhaps, rogan josh (p. 335) is a good dish to make with mild-flavoured venison; the yogurt and spices complement the meat well.

Venison stew with cherries

Venison combines well with fruits and preserved cherries are particularly successful. I prefer the sourish morello cherries, but sweet cherries can be used. The dried cherries found in Middle Eastern shops are also good, but have to be soaked first.

For 6	1 bay leaf	salt and freshly ground pepper
80ml olive oil	1.5kg boned venison, cubed	1 glass port
juice of 2 lemons	1 tbs flour	300ml chicken stock (p. 4)
1 tsp crushed coriander seeds	1 large onion, peeled and chopped	300g cherries
6 crushed black peppercorns		

Combine half the oil, the lemon juice, coriander, peppercorns and bay leaf in a bowl and marinate the venison for 4–6 hours. Remove the meat from the marinade, dry it and coat lightly with flour. Brown the meat in the remaining oil, add the onion, season and pour over the strained marinade. Add the port and enough stock just to cover the meat. Bring slowly to the boil, then simmer over very low heat for about 2 hours or until the venison is tender. Shortly before the end of cooking, stir in the cherries and allow them to warm through for a few minutes, then serve with rice or triangles of bread, lightly fried in butter, and braised chestnuts (p. 130).

Wild boar

The wild boar available in Britain is not wild, but farmed; for the real thing, you have to go to southern Europe. The breed was reintroduced here some years ago; the animals are reared in spacious penned enclosures, and the meat is now available from some butchers and by mail order. The flavour is good, but more like lean top-quality pork from a traditional breed than the rich gamey flavour of European wild boar. Cook the meat as you would pork: roast or grill tender cuts, braise tougher joints. Use the baked chops recipe on p. 339 for wild boar steaks.

Hare

Hare and rabbit belong to the same family, but hares are bigger and longer-legged. Hare can sometimes be bought jointed and prepacked, but the butcher will joint a whole animal for you (it is a messier business than cutting up a rabbit). The meat is lean and dark in colour, the flavour pronounced and savoury. The saddle can be roasted (it will benefit from larding and barding – *see* p. 326), but other joints are best braised or casseroled. Several hours in a marinade of wine, vinegar, oil and flavourings will greatly enhance the flavour and tenderness of hare. Hare is at its best from October to March, the right time for making richly flavoured warming dishes.

Saddle of hare with soured cream sauce

This recipe comes from southern Germany, but similar dishes are found throughout the alpine region. Sometimes fresh cream and lemon juice are used instead of soured cream, and herbs or other spices replace the juniper.

For 2	salt and freshly ground pepper	1 stalk celery, chopped finely
1 saddle of hare	1 carrot, peeled and chopped finely	5 juniper berries, crushed
600ml water		
150ml vinegar	1 onion, peeled and chopped finely	100ml stock or white wine
60g butter		150ml soured cream

Remove as much thin membrane as possible from the hare and marinate the saddle in the water and vinegar for 2–3 hours. Pat it dry and discard the marinade. Heat the oven to 220°C, 425°F, gas 7. Melt the butter in a small roasting pan and brown the hare. Season with salt and pepper and add the vegetables and the juniper berries. Stir to coat the vegetables with the butter and transfer the pan to the oven. Baste frequently with the pan juices and a little of the stock or wine. Calculate 40 minutes per kg for the cooking time. When the hare is three-quarters cooked, remove the pan from the oven, discard the vegetables and keep the hare warm. Drain off the cooking liquid into a small pan to which add the remaining stock or wine and boil to reduce by half. Stir in the cream and pour the sauce over the hare. Return the pan to the oven to finish cooking, basting the hare regularly, then transfer the hare to a serving dish and strain over the sauce. Serve with noodles and an unsweetened apple purée.

Hare braised with onions

Follow the recipe for rabbit braised with onions (p. 355), without the sausage. Hare is likely to take a bit longer to cook than rabbit.

Rabbit

Both domesticated and wild rabbit can be bought all year round, the former sometimes sold jointed, the latter almost always whole. It is quite simple to cut up a rabbit: first, cut off the forelegs, then cut across the body where the hind legs join the saddle. Separate the hind legs. The saddle can be left whole or cut across into 2 or 3 pieces, depending on the size of the animal. Cut between the saddle and the ribcage. Remove kidneys, heart and liver (this can be cooked as chicken liver). If you don't want to do it yourself, ask the butcher to joint the rabbit for you.

Hutch rabbit has pale flesh and the flavour and texture are similar to chicken, whereas wild rabbit, not surprisingly, has a darker colour, a stronger, gamey flavour and the meat is tougher. Rabbit flesh is dry and needs moist treatment; the hind legs and saddle of a hutch rabbit can be roasted, sautéed or grilled, but need frequent basting; wild rabbit is best braised or stewed. Both kinds benefit from marinating.

Baked rabbit

An old English recipe, which produces succulent rabbit with a well-flavoured 'stuffing' spread over it.

For 3–4		
4 large onions, peeled and chopped coarsely	leaves from 2 sage sprigs, finely chopped	1 egg
	grated rind of 1 unwaxed lemon	1–2 tbs milk
250g fresh white breadcrumbs		1 tbs sunflower oil
	salt and freshly ground pepper	1 rabbit, jointed
		4 rashers streaky green bacon, rind removed

Heat the oven to 190°C, 375°F, gas 5. Put the onions in a pan, cover with cold water and bring to the boil. Strain and put them into a large bowl. Combine with the breadcrumbs, sage and lemon rind, and season with salt and pepper. Bind the mixture with the egg and a little milk. Oil a straight-sided casserole or a loaf or cake tin just big enough to hold the rabbit pieces in one layer. Season the meat and put it in. Cover with the bacon and lay the breadcrumb mixture as a crust over the top. Bake the dish for 2 hours; if the top is browning too quickly cover it with a piece of foil. Serve with a green salad.

Rabbit braised with onions

This dish is based on one I ate many years ago in Menorca. Now it is easy to buy chorizo, the spicy Spanish sausage, or you can substitute a firm Italian or French sausage, or even leave out the sausage altogether, although of course it does contribute to the texture and taste of the dish.

For 3–4	150g chorizo or other sausage, cut in chunks	paprika
4 tbs olive oil	500g onions, peeled and finely sliced	125ml vegetable or chicken stock (p. 4) or water
100g salt pork or streaky bacon, cubed	1 tbs wine vinegar	ground cinnamon
1 rabbit, jointed	salt and freshly ground pepper	

Heat 2 tbs oil in a heavy casserole and brown the salt pork or bacon, then the rabbit and finally the sausage. Remove the meats as they are ready. Add the remaining oil and fry the onion until golden. Stir in the vinegar, then put the meats back in the pot. Season with salt, pepper and paprika and pour over the stock or water. Cover and simmer over low heat until the rabbit is tender, about 1 hour. There should be a small amount of rich onion sauce. Check the seasoning and stir in ¼ tsp cinnamon. Serve with boiled potatoes.

Sauces, salsas and marinades

The extent to which our cooking has changed in the last decades
is most immediately reflected in the variety of sauces we use.
Traditional English and classic French sauces are still an important part of
the repertoire, but they are now joined by Italian sauces for pasta and other
dishes, salsas from central and south America, dips and
dressings from Asia, marinades and seasonings from
Australia, America and the Caribbean.

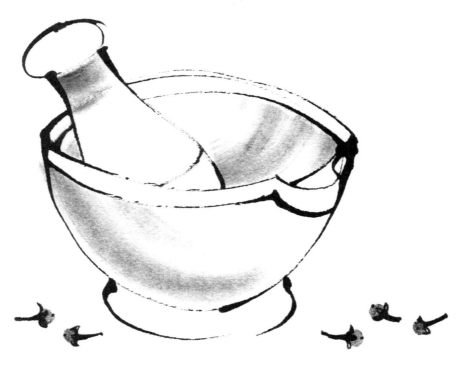

Sauces

Sauces are intended to enhance the flavours of the food they accompany, not to overwhelm or distort them. The concentrated flavours of a sauce add a dimension to a simply grilled steak, a steamed fish, a bowl of pasta or a salad. A sauce need not be complicated or difficult to make; the trickiest ones are the classic emulsion-based hollandaise and béarnaise family, but even these can be managed with a little care and confidence on the part of the cook. Other sauces are based on a flour and butter roux, on oil and vinegar, on cream or on vegetables or fruit. Many sauces, salsas and dips do not require cooking, some that were once made slowly by pounding or stirring can be made quickly with a food processor or blender.

The consistency of a sauce is important: it should not be so runny that the food is floating in it, nor so thick, especially when based on flour, that it is a solid, gluey blob on the plate and the tongue. A couple of spoonfuls, drizzled around, over, or on the side of the food is what you are aiming for to accompany a steak or a piece of fish; a coating consistency for a pasta dish; and a lightly whisked emulsion of oil and vinegar to dress a salad.

Most hot sauces are best eaten as soon as they are made or within an hour if they are kept warm in a bain-marie*. Stand the pan in a larger pan or deep baking dish of warm or hot water, depending on the sauce. Some cold sauces, such as mayonnaise, will keep for a couple of days; others can be refrigerated for a week or two. Vinaigrette can be kept in a jar; shake well before use.

Reducing a sauce

To reduce is to boil a liquid so that it evaporates and flavours are concentrated. Sauces based on stock are reduced by simmering, so that impurities rise to the surface and can be skimmed off with a spoon or ladle, leaving a clear, shiny sauce.

Alcohols and vinegars to be used in sauces are reduced to a small amount of concentrated flavouring, a few spoonfuls of a syrupy liquid.

Mounting a sauce with butter

Small pieces of unsalted butter may be whisked into a sauce at the last minute to give it a glossy appearance and to add richness. The butter is added off the heat so that it doesn't turn oily.

A small amount of arrowroot or potato flour mixed with a little cold water can be added to a boiling sauce and it will thicken immediately. Do not overdo the thickening agent, and do not simmer the sauce for more than 4–5 minutes after it has thickened.

Another way to thicken a sauce is with kneaded butter (beurre manié). Mash 15g unsalted butter with 1 tbs flour, using a fork. Whisk small bits of the butter into a hot sauce at the end of cooking to improve the texture and enrich the flavour. This amount will thicken 500ml of sauce.

Cold sauces
Vinaigrettes and dressings

Vinaigrettes are often the instant answer for a salad dressing, and indeed the choice of oils and vinegars now available offers much variety. Dressings made with cream or yogurt are just as quick to prepare and deserve to be better known.

Vinaigrette

This simple sauce is made in a few minutes and can be endlessly varied using different vinegars or oils, adding garlic, shallots, herbs or spices. Walnut and hazelnut oil make good dressings for green salads; herb and spice vinegars add aromatic flavours (p. 515); oriental rice vinegar is light and fresh tasting; sherry vinegar and balsamic vinegar give depth of flavour, but use the latter very sparingly. Vinaigrette keeps well for several days in a screw-top jar; just shake it thoroughly before using.

| For about 120ml | salt and freshly ground | 6 tbs extra virgin olive |
| 2 tbs vinegar of choice | pepper | oil |

Put the vinegar, salt and pepper in a small bowl and whisk until the salt has dissolved. Whisk in the oil until the sauce thickens a little and an emulsion forms. Use with salads and vegetables.

Variations
Anchovy vinaigrette Pound 4 anchovy fillets to a paste, whisk the paste into the vinegar before adding the oil. Add 2 tbs chopped parsley and 1 tbs chopped chives. Use with robust lettuces and chicory.

Garlic vinaigrette Add 1 small garlic clove, peeled and chopped finely, to the vinegar before whisking in the oil.

Lemon vinaigrette Replace the vinegar by lemon juice and, if you wish, add a little grated rind from an unwaxed lemon. Good for grated carrot, mushroom salad, crab and fish salads.

Mustard vinaigrette Add 1 tsp or more Dijon mustard to the vinegar and blend it in before adding the oil. It is particularly good with salads made of bitter leaves, meat salads and with lightly cooked vegetables such as young leeks.

Tomato vinaigrette Peel and remove the core and seeds from 1 large tomato. Cut the flesh into tiny dice and stir into the vinaigrette. Good with fish and meat salads.

Vinaigrette with bacon Fry 6 tbs diced streaky bacon until it is crisp and has rendered its fat. Drain the bacon on kitchen paper, then add it to a salad of spinach, corn salad or radicchio. Add the vinegar (one of the cheaper balsamic vinegars is particularly good for this) to the still-warm pan, scrape up the bits stuck to the bottom of the pan, stir briskly and pour the dressing over the salad. Toss well.

Ravigote sauce Add 1 tbs chopped capers, 1 tbs peeled and chopped shallot and 2–3 tbs chopped herbs (parsley, tarragon, chives and chervil) to the vinaigrette. Good with potato salad and grilled or poached fish.

Oriental 'vinaigrette'

Makes about 120ml	1 tbs fish sauce (optional)	2 tbs sunflower oil
2 tbs rice vinegar	½ tsp chilli oil or chilli flakes	salt
1 tbs light soy sauce		1 tbs chopped coriander (optional)
¼ tsp sugar	1 tbs sesame oil	

Whisk together the vinegar, soy sauce and sugar until the sugar dissolves. Add the fish sauce if you are using it, chilli oil or flakes, the sesame and sunflower oil and whisk to an emulsion. Taste and add salt if necessary; I find it seldom is, because the soy and fish sauce are salty. Stir in the coriander if you wish. Use to dress vegetable, fish and seafood salads.

Soy, honey and garlic dressing

Makes about 120ml

1 tbs light soy sauce

1 garlic clove, peeled and crushed

½ tbs honey

1 tbs sherry or mirin*

1 tbs sherry vinegar or red wine vinegar

4 tbs sunflower oil

Whisk all the ingredients together.

Sauce vierge

This is a good sauce to make in summer when there are really ripe tomatoes. It goes well with grilled and sautéed fish and vegetables, and with Bream baked in a salt crust (p. 244).

For 4

4 ripe tomatoes, peeled, seeded and diced

2 garlic cloves, peeled and chopped finely

2 tbs chopped parsley

2 tbs chopped tarragon

2 tbs chopped chives

1 tbs red wine vinegar

170ml extra virgin olive oil

salt and freshly ground pepper

Combine the tomatoes, garlic and herbs with the vinegar and then with the oil. Season well with salt and pepper and leave to stand.

Fromage blanc dressing

Use with green salads and crisp vegetable salads such as carrot and apple (p. 76) or fennel (p. 77).

Makes about 120ml

2 tsp Dijon mustard

½ small garlic clove, peeled and crushed

100ml low-fat fromage blanc

salt and freshly ground pepper

2 tsp sherry vinegar or wine vinegar

Whisk the mustard and garlic into the fromage blanc. Season with salt and pepper and whisk in the vinegar.

Soured cream dressing

This dressing is good with all green salads.

For about 150ml	salt and freshly ground pepper	2–3 tbs chopped fresh herbs – chervil, chives, marjoram, parsley, tarragon
1 tbs lemon juice or white wine vinegar		
8 tbs soured cream		

Stir the lemon juice or vinegar into the cream a little at a time. Season and stir in the herbs.

Yogurt and herb dressing

This quickly made sauce can be used for salads, baked potatoes and other vegetables, and as a dip. Use one or two herbs: coriander, dill, marjoram, mint, parsley and tarragon all combine well with yogurt. Fennel seeds can also be used.

Makes about 300ml	1–2 tbs lemon juice	salt and freshly ground pepper
4–5 tbs chopped herbs	250ml Greek yogurt	paprika
1 garlic clove, peeled and crushed		

Stir the herbs, garlic and lemon juice into the yogurt and season with salt, pepper and paprika.

Mayonnaise

This classic sauce is based on an emulsion of egg and oil. Make sure both are at room temperature before making the sauce or it will not thicken. Proportions are 1 egg yolk to 150ml oil. As you become more confident about making mayonnaise, you will find that for making larger quantities, you can increase the amount of oil per egg yolk. Serve mayonnaise with cold poached fish and seafood, cold roast chicken, eggs and vegetables.

Basic mayonnaise

For 5–6

2 egg yolks

salt and freshly ground pepper

1–2 tbs white wine vinegar or lemon juice

300ml olive oil

Whisk or beat the egg yolks with a wooden spoon. Add a little salt and pepper and 1 tbs vinegar or lemon juice. Whisk thoroughly. Now add the oil, drop by drop at first, whisking or stirring all the time. Increase the drops to a slow trickle. Do not try to hurry the process. When the sauce begins to thicken and emulsify, pour in the oil in a thin stream, whisking continuously. When you have a thick, jelly-like consistency, the mayonnaise is ready. Taste and add a little more vinegar or lemon juice if necessary. You can also thin the sauce with a tablespoon or two of warm water.

If the sauce separates because too much oil has been added at once, whisk another egg yolk in a clean bowl and slowly add the separated mayonnaise.

You can make mayonnaise more quickly in a food processor. Put the egg yolks and 1 tbs oil in the bowl and process for 4–5 seconds. Trickle the remaining oil through the feed tube with the motor running slowly. When all the oil has been absorbed, turn off the machine. Add salt and pepper, vinegar or lemon juice to taste and pulse briefly to combine. If the mayonnaise separates, take the mixture from the bowl, wash the bowl, put in another egg yolk and slowly add the curdled sauce.

Mayonnaise made in a food processor can be made with a whole egg instead of egg yolks, but it will not have the same texture as one made with yolks only.

To keep mayonnaise, cover with clingfilm and refrigerate for 2–3 days.

Variations

Green mayonnaise Blanch 100g watercress, spinach, parsley, or a combination of these, in boiling water for 2 minutes. Drain and refresh under cold running water. Squeeze out excess water, chop finely and add to the mayonnaise.

Gribiche sauce Use 2 hard-boiled egg yolks (instead of raw ones) mixed with 1 tsp Dijon mustard. Add salt, pepper, vinegar or lemon juice and oil as for mayonnaise. Stir in 1 tsp each of chopped parsley, chervil, chives, capers and gherkins.

Light mayonnaise Stir 60ml plain yogurt, lightly whipped cream or crème fraîche into the mayonnaise.

Remoulade sauce Add 1 tsp Dijon mustard and 1 pounded anchovy fillet to the egg yolks. To the finished mayonnaise, add 2 tsp each of chopped chervil, parsley, tarragon, capers and gherkins.

Saffron mayonnaise Grind 8–10 saffron threads and soak in 2 tbs warm water. Stir and add the liquid to the mayonnaise.

Tartare sauce Stir in 1 tsp each of chopped parsley, shallot, capers, gherkins and green olives to the mayonnaise.

Vegetable and fruit sauces

These sauces have a wide range of traditional uses. The garlic-based ones are excellent with fish and vegetables, horseradish accompanies both meat and fish, pesto is a classic pasta sauce and the fruit sauces are served with meats, both hot and cold.

Aïoli

This Provençal sauce is traditionally served with salt cod and is very good with poached fresh cod, baked fish, grilled rabbit or chicken and as a dip for raw and cooked vegetables. It is also stirred into bourride (p. 255), one of the fish stews of the region. A true Provençal would use more garlic than is given here.

For 3–4	salt	juice of 1 lemon
2–3 garlic cloves, peeled	2 egg yolks	
	150–180ml olive oil	

Put the peeled garlic in a mortar with a pinch of salt and crush to a paste. Add the egg yolks and bind with the garlic, then start to add the olive oil a drop at a time. Keep working the mixture with the pestle, always in the same direction. It takes longer than making mayonnaise because the garlic thins the egg yolks. When half the oil has been used, the colour will be paler and the sauce quite thick. Work in the lemon juice. Now add the oil in a steady trickle. When all the oil is amalgamated, add a few drops of water if it seems too thick. Aïoli can be made in a food processor, which makes a lighter sauce; *see* the notes on mayonnaise opposite for this and also for what to do should the aïoli separate.

Aïoli can be made with potato instead of egg yolk – good news for cholesterol watchers. Richard Olney notes in *Simple French Food* that about 100g boiled potato, cooled until tepid, can be pounded with the crushed garlic and salt before the oil is added. The resulting aïoli is less silken but more digestible.

Using cooked garlic also makes aïoli more digestible. Increase the amount of garlic and boil in salted water to cover for 10 minutes. Drain and when the garlic is tepid crush it and make the aïoli. Cover aïoli and refrigerate until it is to be served.

Skorthalia

Another garlic sauce, skorthalia comes from Greece where it is served with fried fish and vegetables. It is particularly good with fried aubergines and also makes a good dip for raw or lightly cooked vegetables. Skorthalia should be served at room temperature.

For 6	3 garlic cloves, peeled and crushed	3 tbs wine vinegar
6–8 thick slices white bread		200ml olive oil

Cut the crusts from the bread and soak it in cold water to cover for a few minutes. Squeeze out surplus water and put the bread in a food processor with the garlic and vinegar. Blend to a smooth mixture, then add the oil slowly through the feed tube to make a thick creamy sauce. If it is too thick, add a little water at the end. The sauce can also be made in a large mortar: crush the garlic and pound it with the bread and vinegar, gradually adding the oil.

Tarator sauce

This walnut and garlic sauce is Turkish. It is often eaten as a dip, or served with poached, steamed or fried fish or with vegetables and vegetable salads.

For 6	100g shelled walnuts	100–120ml olive oil
2 slices white bread, crusts removed	2 garlic cloves, peeled	salt
	3–4 tbs wine vinegar	

Soak the bread in water briefly, then squeeze out surplus water. Process or pound the bread, walnuts and garlic to a paste. Add the vinegar gradually and then the oil to achieve the consistency of thick yogurt. Taste and add a little salt if necessary. If the tarator is too dense, thin it with a few drops of water.

Horseradish cream

We tend to think of horseradish as an accompaniment to beef, but elsewhere in Europe it is just as likely to be paired with fish; it is indeed an excellent accompaniment to white fish and salmon as well as roast or boiled beef. Fresh horseradish is now available more frequently and is infinitely better than the bottled variety. I prefer soured cream for this sauce, but double or whipping cream could be used instead.

For 6–8	50g ground almonds	1 tsp sugar
80g grated horseradish	1 tbs lemon juice	1 tbs chopped chives (optional)
300ml soured cream		

Pour boiling water over the horseradish and leave for a few minutes. Drain it well and mix it into the cream with the almonds. Stir in the lemon juice and sugar, taste and add a little more if necessary. Put the cream into a dish and scatter over the chives.

Horseradish and apple sauce

This sauce is eaten in southern Germany and Austria with boiled beef, smoked meat and sausages as well as with fish. For a milder sauce, use more cream or add a few fresh breadcrumbs to the mixture.

For 4	2 tbs lemon juice	salt and sugar to taste
30–40g grated horseradish	1 medium cooking apple	80ml soured cream

Stir 1 tbs lemon juice into the horseradish so that it does not turn brown. Peel, core and grate the apple, mix it with the horseradish together with the remaining lemon juice. Season with a little salt and sugar, and leave for 10–15 minutes before stirring in the cream.

Red pepper coulis

This sauce dates, I believe, from the days of nouvelle cuisine. It is colourful and can be sharpened in flavour by the addition of a red chilli. Serve it with vegetables, fried polenta or couscous.

For 4–6	60–70ml olive oil	salt and freshly ground pepper
3 large red peppers		

Roast the peppers and remove their skins (p. 151). Remove the core, white membranes and seeds. Leave aside a little of the pepper and purée the remainder in a food processor with the oil and seasonings. Chop the pepper kept aside into small dice and add to the coulis.

Uncooked tomato coulis or passata

A coulis or passata is a smooth-textured purée which can be used on its own or to flavour other sauces. An uncooked tomato coulis is only worth making if your tomatoes are ripe, thin-skinned and bursting with flavour. If they aren't, a cooked sauce (pp. 377–8) will taste better.

Makes about 400ml	750g tomatoes, peeled	salt and freshly ground pepper

Cut the tomatoes in half around the circumference and squeeze out all the seeds. Chop the flesh coarsely and season with salt and pepper. Raw tomatoes contain a lot of water which will separate out. The best way to eliminate it is to strain the chopped and seasoned tomatoes for 30 minutes in a sieve over a bowl and then push the remaining flesh through a sieve or purée in a food processor. Taste for seasoning. Serve with cold fish or chicken, a fish or vegetable terrine, or as a sauce for pasta.

Variations
- You can stir in a tablespoon of thick cream, or add a squeeze of lemon juice to sharpen the flavour, or whisk in a tablespoon of vinegar and 2–3 of olive oil. Chopped herbs can be added too.

Pesto

Originally a Genoese sauce for pasta, pesto is now used with vegetables, on pizzas, in breads (p. 452), and as a dip or spread for crostini and bruschetta. It is still one of the best sauces for pasta and gnocchi

For 4 6 large handfuls basil 3 garlic cloves, peeled and crushed	3 tbs pine nuts 80g Parmesan or Pecorino, grated	150–200ml extra virgin olive oil

Put all the ingredients except the oil into a food processor and blend. Scrape down the sides and add the oil slowly through the feed tube until you have a thick green sauce. To make a thinner sauce, add more olive oil. If you don't have a food processor, start with the basil and garlic in a large mortar and pound with a pestle. Add the pine nuts a few at a time, then add cheese and olive oil alternately, pounding each addition thoroughly before adding more. When you have a thick paste add more oil to obtain the consistency you want.

Variations

Coriander pesto Use coriander instead of basil.

Parsley pesto Replace the basil with flat-leaved parsley and if you wish use walnuts instead of pine nuts.

Rocket pesto Use rocket with walnuts.

Watercress pesto Use watercress with walnuts.

Salsa verde

This versatile Italian sauce is made with a large quantity of flat-leaved parsley, a smaller amount of basil or mint, anchovies, capers and garlic. It sometimes includes hard-boiled egg yolks, or breadcrumbs soaked in vinegar. Serve with poached fish (it is particularly good with cod) or fish baked in salt (p. 244), grilled meats or sausages, or with vegetables such as artichokes, cauliflower or broccoli.

For 4		
about 200g parsley, leaves only, chopped	small bunch basil or mint, leaves only, chopped	6–8 anchovy fillets
	2 garlic cloves, peeled and crushed	150–200ml extra virgin olive oil
	2 tbs capers, chopped	salt and freshly ground pepper

Blend the herbs, garlic, capers and anchovy fillets in a food processor, scrape down the sides of the bowl and trickle in the oil through the feed tube to make a smooth sauce. Use enough oil for the consistency you want. Season to taste.

If you don't have a food processor, pound together the garlic, capers and anchovy, mix with the herbs, whisk in the oil and season to taste.

Mint sauce

Makes about 125ml

3 tbs chopped mint leaves

1 tbs light muscovado sugar

3 tbs boiling water

4 tbs wine vinegar

Pound the mint and sugar together. Add the boiling water and leave to infuse. When it is almost cold stir in the vinegar. Ideally the sauce should stand for an hour or two before serving with roast lamb.

Parsley and lemon sauce

For 4–5

80g parsley, chopped finely

2 shallots, peeled and chopped

1 tbs Dijon mustard

juice of 1 lemon

150ml extra virgin olive oil

salt and freshly ground pepper

Whisk all the ingredients together and serve with grilled fish or chicken.

Cranberry sauce

For 8–10

180g sugar

150ml water

100ml orange juice

grated rind of 1 unwaxed orange

350g fresh or frozen cranberries

Bring the sugar, water and orange juice to the boil over moderate heat, stirring to dissolve the sugar. Add the orange rind and cranberries, bring to the boil again and simmer until the cranberries begin to pop. Skim off any froth, cool and then refrigerate. Serve with roast turkey.

Cumberland sauce

One of the best sauces to accompany cold meats.

Makes about 150ml

1 unwaxed orange

4 tbs red currant jelly

1 tbs Dijon mustard

juice of 1 lemon

salt and freshly ground pepper

60ml port

Pare the rind from the orange, leaving behind the pith. Cut the peel into matchstick pieces and blanch them in boiling water for 3–4 minutes. Drain them. Put the red currant jelly, mustard, lemon juice and a light seasoning of salt and pepper in a bowl, put the bowl over a pan of simmering water and stir to melt the jelly. Add the orange peel and the port and stir for another 3–4 minutes. Leave to cool.

Dipping sauces

Dipping sauces are the oriental answer to dressing plainly cooked foods. Refreshing and aromatic, they are good with fried or grilled fish, prawns, grilled squid, spring rolls or chicken satay.

Thai dipping sauce (Nuoc cham)

This light dipping sauce is based on fish sauce diluted with water and flavoured with chillies, garlic, lime juice and sugar. Sometimes other flavourings, such as grated ginger, crushed dry-roasted* peanuts, chopped coriander or mint, are added.

Fish sauce has a pronounced flavour and is salty, so you may want to use less than is suggested here. Proportions of fish sauce, lime juice, chilli and sugar can be varied to taste.

Makes about 125ml	2 tbs lime juice	2 small chillies, seeded and chopped finely
3 tbs fish sauce (p. 520)	1 garlic clove, peeled and crushed thoroughly	1 tbs sugar
3 tbs water		

Combine all the ingredients and stir until the sugar has dissolved.

Note
If you don't want to use fish sauce, make the dressing with light soy sauce. It will, of course, taste quite different, but it can serve the same purpose.

Chinese dipping sauce

Makes about 100ml	1–2 tsp sugar	1 tbs finely chopped ginger
3 tbs light soy sauce	1 tbs finely chopped spring onion	
3 tbs rice vinegar		

Combine the soy sauce, vinegar and sugar and stir until the sugar has dissolved. Stir in the spring onions and ginger.

Sweet chilli sauce

This sauce is quick and easy to make, and if you make a larger quantity it will keep for 2 weeks in the refrigerator. Serve with barbecued prawns (p. 266).

Makes about 150 ml	3 garlic cloves, peeled and crushed	80ml rice wine or cider vinegar
125ml water	2cm piece of fresh ginger, peeled and sliced finely	1 tbs fish sauce (p. 520)
6 tbs sugar		small bunch coriander, chopped
4 medium red chillies, seeded and sliced finely		

Heat the water and sugar together to make a syrup, let it thicken a little, then stir in the chillies, garlic, ginger, vinegar and fish sauce. Bring to the boil and simmer for 3 minutes. Remove from the heat and pour into a bowl. When it has cooled, stir in the coriander. Taste for seasoning. I do not add salt because the fish sauce is salty, but you may wish to.

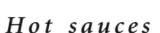

Hot sauces

Roux-based sauces

These sauces are based on a thickening of flour and butter combined with milk or stock. By adding flavours to the basic sauces, you can develop a varied repertoire. If you add a tiny amount of diced butter at the end, the sauce will have an attractive gloss.

Béchamel sauce

This is the French version of white sauce, which I prefer because, despite taking a little more trouble, it has more flavour from infused herbs and spices.

For 280–300ml	6 black peppercorns	salt and freshly ground pepper
300ml milk	30g butter	nutmeg
1 bay leaf	2 level tbs plain flour, sieved	

Heat the milk with the bay leaf and peppercorns until it almost reaches boiling point. Remove the pan from the heat, cover and infuse for 10 minutes. Heat the butter in a thick pan; as soon as it starts to foam, whisk in the flour. Keep whisking over low heat for 1–2 minutes, then remove the pan from the heat. Strain in a little of the milk, whisking until a smooth paste is formed. If you have a smooth base at this stage, the sauce is less likely to turn lumpy. Return the pan to the heat, strain in the rest of the milk, whisking all the time until the sauce boils. Season with a little salt, pepper and grated nutmeg. Put the pan on a heat diffuser and simmer very gently for 10 minutes, stirring or whisking frequently.

If the sauce does turn lumpy, put it through a fine sieve or blend it.

Keep it warm in a bain-marie* if it is not to be used at once, and put shavings of butter over the top while it is still hot to prevent a skin forming. Béchamel will also keep for 2–3 days covered with clingfilm in the refrigerator.

Variations

Thin béchamel sauce Use only 20g butter and 1½ tbs flour. This is a useful base to which other ingredients can be added.

Cheese sauce (Sauce mornay) This is a béchamel to which grated hard cheese is added. Parmesan, Gruyère and Cheddar are all suitable. Use a thin béchamel and stir 30g grated cheese into the finished sauce off the heat.

Cheese sauce is used with vegetables and fish, often for reheating them gently or as the base for a gratin; if it were made with a standard béchamel, it would become too thick.

Mushroom sauce Purée 60g small white mushrooms, raw, in a food processor and stir the purée into the thin or thick finished béchamel. Use with vegetables or as the base for a gratin.

Onion sauce (Sauce soubise) Cook 2 large onions in 60g butter in a covered pan until very soft. When they have softened to a pale mass, whiz them in a blender and incorporate the purée into the thick or thin béchamel. Add 60ml single cream. Onion sauce is an excellent accompaniment to roast or grilled lamb.

Parsley sauce Blanch 50g parsley leaves in boiling water for 1 minute. Drain and refresh under cold running water. Squeeze out excess water in your fist and dry the parsley on kitchen paper. Chop it finely and stir it into the sauce with 20g butter cut into small pieces. A squeeze of lemon juice is good if the sauce is to go with fish. Serve with poached fish, chicken, boiled or steamed vegetables.

Velouté sauce

Velouté sauce is made with chicken, fish or vegetable stock (pp. 4–6), depending on what it is to accompany.

Makes about 300ml	1½ level tbs plain flour, sieved	about 50ml crème fraîche or double cream
400ml stock		
20g butter	salt and freshly ground pepper	

Heat the stock. Melt the butter in a heavy pan and when it foams whisk in the flour. Cook for 1–2 minutes, then take the pan from the heat. Whisk in a little of the stock and keep whisking until you have a smooth paste. Return the pan to the heat, whisk in the rest of the stock and keep whisking until it comes to the boil. Lower the heat and simmer for 20–30 minutes to reduce the sauce. Stir from time to time. If any impurities rise to the surface, skim them off. Season with salt and pepper and add enough cream to give a consistency that coats the back of a spoon. Serve with fish or chicken.

You can keep the sauce warm in a bain-marie* for an hour. Once cooled, the sauce can be covered with clingfilm and refrigerated for 1–2 days.

Variations

Sauce Bercy Chop 2 peeled shallots finely and cook them in 100ml white wine, boiling to reduce the liquid by two-thirds. Add the shallots and their liquid to the velouté sauce before it is reduced and simmer for 20–30 minutes until it reaches a consistency which coats the back of a spoon. Take the pan from the heat and instead of cream, stir in a squeeze of lemon juice, 30g butter and a little chopped parsley. Serve with fish, chicken, steamed or boiled vegetables.

Tomato velouté sauce Stir 2–3 tbs tomato purée into the reduced velouté and serve with chicken, eggs or vegetables.

Bread sauce

Thickened with bread rather than flour, this mixture makes a moderately thick sauce. For a thinner sauce, add more cream; for a thicker one more breadcrumbs. The easiest way to make breadcrumbs is in a food processor or blender, and you can make the crumbs as coarse or as fine as you want. Serve with roast turkey, chicken, game or pork.

For 5–6	6 black peppercorns	60g day-old breadcrumbs
300ml milk	1 blade of mace	60ml double cream
1 onion, peeled and stuck with 2 cloves	1 bay leaf	30g unsalted butter, cut into pieces
	salt	

Bring the milk slowly to the boil with the onion, peppercorns, mace, bay leaf and a pinch of salt. Take the pan from the heat, cover and infuse for 30 minutes. Strain and bring the milk to the boil again. Stir in the breadcrumbs and simmer gently for 5–10 minutes, stirring occasionally, until the sauce thickens. Whisk in the cream. Take the pan from the heat and whisk in the butter.

Butter sauces

These sauces are mixtures of butter suspended in egg yolk. Mayonnaise, which uses oil not butter, is on p. 361. The recipes here are for hollandaise, béarnaise and similar sauces.

Hollandaise sauce

Hollandaise is excellent with poached fish, freshly boiled prawns, asparagus, artichokes and eggs (*see* eggs benedict, p. 50).

For 5–6	2 egg yolks	salt and freshly ground pepper
3 tbs wine vinegar or white wine	180g unsalted butter, chilled and cut into 8–10 small pieces	1–2 tbs lemon juice
1 tbs water		

Heat the vinegar or wine in a small heavy pan and reduce to about 1 tbs. Let the pan cool. Add 1 tbs water and whisk in the egg yolks and keep whisking over low heat until the eggs are thick and mousse-like. Make sure the pan does not overheat or the eggs will separate; a heat diffuser is useful here. If you prefer, make the sauce in a bowl set over simmering water or in a double boiler. Add a piece of butter and whisk it in thoroughly before adding the next. When all the butter is incorporated, the sauce should have the texture of thick cream. Season it with salt, pepper and a little lemon juice.

If the sauce should separate, try beating in 1 tbs of cold water. If that doesn't work, stir a new egg yolk in a clean pan or bowl and add the failed sauce a little at a time off the heat. As it thickens, continue with the recipe.

Hollandaise is best eaten as soon as it is made, but you can keep it for about an hour in a bain-marie*.

Variations

Maltaise sauce Whisk in the juice of a blood orange instead of lemon juice when the sauce is finished. This sauce is particularly good with asparagus.

Mousseline sauce Stir 60ml whipped cream into the finished sauce. Serve with crab, fish or chicken.

Béarnaise sauce

This is the perfect sauce for grilled steak or a fillet of beef.

For 5–6	3 shallots, peeled and finely chopped	180g unsalted butter, cut into pieces
100ml white wine		2 egg yolks
3 tbs tarragon or wine vinegar	3 tbs finely chopped fresh tarragon	salt and freshly ground pepper

Heat the wine and vinegar in a small pan with the shallot and 2 tbs tarragon; reduce to 2 tbs of syrupy liquid. Let it cool, then strain through a fine sieve, pressing the shallots and tarragon to extract all the flavour. Return the liquid to the pan. Melt the butter gently in a separate small pan and set aside to cool. Whisk the egg yolks into the wine and vinegar infusion over very low heat. Make sure the pan does not overheat or the eggs will separate; use a heat diffuser. You could make the sauce in a bowl set over simmering water or in a double boiler. Pour in a tablespoon or so of butter and whisk it in thoroughly before adding the next. Continue until all the clear butter is used, and leave the white residue in the pan. Stir in the remaining tarragon and season. Keep warm in a bain-marie* if necessary, and eat as soon as possible.

Should the sauce curdle, *see* the notes at the end of Hollandaise sauce, p. 374.

Variations

Sauce paloise This is made in the same way as béarnaise, using mint instead of tarragon. Paloise goes well with poached salmon, grilled chicken or lamb.

Green peppercorn sauce Make a béarnaise sauce without the tarragon and add 1 tbs crushed green peppercorns. Serve with steak.

White butter sauce (*Beurre blanc*)

This sauce is less tricky to make than hollandaise and its variations because it does not use egg yolks. It is an emulsion of butter and reduced wine and vinegar.

For about 5–6	2 shallots, peeled and finely chopped	salt and freshly ground pepper
80ml white wine		
80ml wine vinegar	250g unsalted butter, chilled and cut into small pieces	

Boil the wine, vinegar and shallots until reduced to 2 tbs. Turn the heat very low – a heat diffuser is useful here – and gradually add the butter, whisking in a few pieces at a time, and waiting until each lot is absorbed before adding more. Do not let the butter become oily. If the pan is too hot, remove it from the heat and whisk in more butter. When all the butter is absorbed, the sauce has a creamy consistency. Taste and season if necessary. Beurre blanc is best served at once. If you need to keep it for a few minutes, set the pan in a bain-marie*.

This sauce has a delicate flavour and is served with grilled or poached white fish; it is less successful with oily fish such as salmon. Beurre blanc is also good with boiled or steamed vegetables.

Variation
· Add 1–2 tbs finely chopped fresh herbs to the sauce with the shallots.

Vegetable and herb sauces

Vegetable purées are sometimes used as sauces on their own or to thicken and flavour more complex sauces. Sauces that rely only on a purée for thickening do not have the smooth glossy appearance of roux-based or butter sauces, but they have the concentrated flavour of the vegetable, and can be virtually fat-free. Purées can also be used in conjunction with roux-based sauces – *see* mushroom sauce and sauce soubise (p. 371). Hot herb sauces, like their cold counterparts, have very clear distinctive flavours.

Barbecue sauce

This is a version of the all-American barbecue sauce, originally derived from Helen Brown's *West Coast Cook Book*. Barbecue sauce is essentially for spare ribs, but can be served with grilled steaks, hamburgers or chicken.

For 6	1 medium onion, peeled and chopped	1 tsp dried oregano
6 garlic cloves, unpeeled	1 small green pepper, chopped	1 tbs chilli powder
100ml olive oil	300g tomatoes, peeled, seeded and chopped	salt
		50ml wine vinegar

Pour boiling water over the garlic and simmer for 10 minutes. Drain, rinse under cold water, peel and crush the garlic. Heat the oil and soften the onion and pepper. Add the tomatoes, oregano, chilli powder, garlic and a little salt. Simmer for 10 minutes, then stir in the vinegar. Cook slowly for a further 10 minutes, then sieve. Reheat before serving.

Courgette coulis

Makes about 300ml	2 tbs olive oil	salt and freshly ground pepper
300g courgettes, sliced	80–100ml vegetable stock (p. 4)	
½ tsp finely chopped rosemary leaves		

Lightly fry the courgettes and rosemary in the oil. Add 80ml stock and the seasonings, cover and simmer until the courgettes are soft. Purée in a food processor, and if the purée is too thick add a little more stock. Serve warm or cold with vegetables – it is very good with new potatoes and with early peas and carrots.

Salmoriglio

This potent oregano sauce comes from Sicily, where it is spooned over grilled fish, scallops or prawns, roast meat or green vegetables. Use it sparingly.

For 6–8	juice of 2 lemons	2 tbs finely chopped parsley
150ml olive oil	1 tbs finely chopped fresh oregano	salt and freshly ground pepper
3 tbs hot water		

Beat the oil and water together in a bowl over hot water or in the top of a double boiler until they form an emulsion. Gradually beat in the lemon juice and herbs. Season. Beat for 4–5 minutes over simmering water until a smooth sauce is obtained. Serve at once.

Sorrel sauce

Sorrel is one of the few herbs not readily found in the shops, which is a pity, but if you have a bit of spare space in the garden, do consider planting it since it grows in profusion. The leaves are soon cooked to a sauce for fish, eggs or other vegetables. I also like a thick sorrel sauce to accompany a rack of lamb or grilled lamb chops.

For 4	180–200ml double cream, or crème fraîche	salt and freshly ground pepper
300g sorrel leaves		lemon juice (optional)
30g butter		

Remove thick stalks and cook the sorrel gently in the butter. It will melt and turn a dull, khaki colour quite quickly. In a few minutes, you will have a sorrel purée. Stir in the cream gradually; sorrel is quite acidic and it is important to balance the sorrel and cream, so taste as you stir to find the balance that suits you. Season with salt and pepper and a dash of lemon juice if you wish. Serve hot.

Variation
Watercress sauce Replace the sorrel with watercress.

Tomato sauces
There are many different tomato sauces, from the simple uncooked tomato coulis or passata (p. 366) to complex long-simmered sauces with meat, vegetables and herbs. Plum tomatoes are probably the best tomatoes for sauce making, but more important

than the type is ripeness. An uncooked or lightly cooked sauce depends on perfectly ripe tomatoes. A cooked sauce made with pale, firm tomatoes picked before ripening can be given a boost with tomato purée or sun-dried tomatoes, herbs and spices. Canned tomatoes also need some help, but they tend to have more flavour than many watery supermarket tomatoes.

Tomato coulis or passata

Makes about 350ml	4 tbs olive oil	1–2 tsp sugar
1 small onion, peeled and chopped finely	750g ripe tomatoes	salt and freshly ground pepper
2 garlic cloves, peeled and chopped	3–4 sprigs fresh thyme or 1 tsp dried thyme	

Sauté the onion and garlic gently in the oil until soft, but don't let them turn brown. Cut the tomatoes in half around the circumference and squeeze out the seeds. Chop them and add to the pan with the thyme, sugar, salt and pepper. Simmer gently, uncovered, for about 30 minutes until nearly all the liquid has evaporated. Press the mixture through a sieve and taste for seasoning.

The coulis will keep for a few days refrigerated or you can freeze it. Serve hot or cold, either on its own or to flavour other sauces.

Quick Italian tomato sauce

This sauce comes from my friend Francesco Radaeli, an antiquarian bookseller who is an excellent cook. The quantity can easily be increased (this amount is enough for 2–3 people) and it makes a good rapid pasta sauce.

Makes about 250ml	2–3 garlic cloves, peeled and chopped finely	½ tsp chilli flakes
4 tbs olive oil		salt and freshly ground pepper
1 x 400g can chopped tomatoes, drained	½ tsp sugar	a few basil leaves, torn

Heat half the olive oil, add the tomatoes and garlic and bring to the boil. Season with sugar, chilli flakes, salt and pepper, and simmer for 15 minutes, until all excess liquid has evaporated. To serve, stir in the remaining olive oil and a few basil leaves.

Variations
· Diced pancetta* can be lightly fried in the oil before the tomatoes are added.

- Other herbs can be added to the sauce with the seasonings: oregano, marjoram and thyme are all good with tomatoes.

Rich tomato sauce

Makes about 500ml	2 tbs olive oil or 30g butter	1kg tomatoes, seeded and chopped
1 small onion, peeled and chopped finely	1 tbs flour	2 tbs tomato purée or sun-dried tomato paste
1 carrot, peeled and chopped finely	150ml vegetable or chicken stock (p. 4) or white wine	1 bouquet garni*
1 stick celery, chopped finely	2 garlic cloves, peeled and crushed	1 tsp sugar
		salt and freshly ground pepper

Sauté the onion, carrot and celery in the oil or butter until lightly coloured. Stir in the flour, and when the mixture bubbles and foams, turn down the heat and add the stock or wine. Stirring continuously, increase the heat somewhat and bring to the boil. Add the garlic, tomatoes, tomato purée or paste, bouquet garni and seasonings. Cover and simmer gently for about 1 hour, stirring occasionally.

Remove the bouquet garni, rub the sauce through a sieve, taste and adjust the seasonings if necessary. If it is too liquid, return the sauce to the pan, bring to the boil and reduce to the consistency of double cream. Serve hot.

The sauce will keep for a few days refrigerated and freezes well.

Bolognese sauce (Ragù)

There are many versions of this famous sauce, and too many of those served in restaurants are indifferent or even downright bad. It is not difficult to make, and a properly made, rich Bolognese sauce is one of the best sauces for pasta.

Makes about 500ml	100g pancetta*, diced	200ml meat stock (p. 5)
30g butter	100g lean beef, minced	200ml tomato coulis (cooked version, see opposite)
1 small onion, peeled and chopped finely	100g lean pork, minced	
1 carrot, peeled and chopped finely	1 tbs chopped fresh thyme and marjoram, or ½ tbs dried	salt and freshly ground pepper
1 stick celery, chopped finely	80ml red wine	

Heat the butter in a heavy pan and gently cook the onion, carrot, celery and pancetta until soft. Add the minced beef and pork and fry over medium heat, stirring constantly until the meat is browned. Sprinkle over the herbs, pour over the wine and half of the stock. Simmer until the liquid is absorbed. Add the remainder of the stock and simmer again until most of it is absorbed. Now pour in the tomato coulis, season and simmer for 15–20 minutes, to allow the flavours to combine and the sauce to come to a thick, rich consistency.

Serve hot with pasta – this quantity of sauce is enough for fresh tagliatelle made with 300g flour and 3 eggs (p. 209) or with polenta.

Salsas

Salsa is the Spanish word for sauce, but in English salsa is more specifically used to mean an uncooked sauce from Latin America or the Caribbean. Mexican salsas are the best known and often the simplest in terms of ingredients. In any restaurant in Mexico there will be a bowl of the salsa cruda on the table. All salsas have some heat from chillies, but you can add or subtract chillies according to your taste. The point of a salsa is to be piquant but not explosive, adding zip to the food it accompanies, not overwhelming it. Originally the food was most likely to be a corn-based dish of enchiladas or tamales or a dish of beans; try any of the salsas with the corn cakes (p. 199). Salsas are also perfect accompaniments to meat, fish and vegetables, especially when these are grilled or fried.

Make sure the ingredients are fresh and well flavoured; salsas made with pale unripe tomatoes or tired herbs don't work. Salsas are to be eaten fresh: don't make them too long in advance – an hour or two to allow the flavours to blend is about right.

Salsa cruda

This is the recipe for the everyday salsa which is often made with the juice of a bitter orange instead of vinegar. Seville orange juice can be used in season, otherwise use a mixture of orange and lime or lemon juice.

For 4	5 tbs finely chopped coriander	80ml sherry vinegar or a mixture of orange and lime juice
4 tomatoes, seeded and chopped		
3–4 jalapeño or other chillies, seeded and chopped	1 red onion, peeled and chopped finely	salt

Combine all the ingredients and serve at room temperature.

Avocado and orange salsa

For 5–6	4 spring onions, chopped	seeds of 2 cardamom pods*, crushed
2 oranges		
2 avocados	3 tbs chopped coriander	salt and freshly ground pepper
1 green chilli, seeded and diced	3–4 tbs lime juice	
1 red pepper, diced	3 tbs olive oil	

Peel the oranges, removing any pith, and cut the flesh into segments (p. 73). Work over a bowl to catch any juices. Cut the flesh into pieces and drop them into the bowl, discarding any pips. Peel, stone and dice the avocado and combine it at once with the orange to prevent it discolouring. Add the chilli, pepper, spring onions and coriander. Whisk together the lime juice, olive oil and seasonings and stir into the salsa. Taste and sharpen with a little more lime juice if necessary. This salsa goes well with ham, cold chicken or turkey.

Variation
• Replace the oranges with the flesh of half a small ripe pineapple.

Mango and red pepper salsa

For 5–6	1 red chilli, seeded and diced	4 tbs lime juice
1 large ripe mango		salt and freshly ground pepper
1 red pepper, seeded and diced	½ small red onion, peeled and chopped	
½ cucumber, seeded and diced	3 tbs chopped mint	

Peel the mango, cut the flesh away from the stone and dice it. Combine all the ingredients, taste and add more seasoning or lime juice if necessary. Cover and leave for an hour or two before serving to allow the flavours to blend. Serve with seafood (it is particularly good with crab), with grilled pork or chicken.

Variation

Papaya and melon salsa Replace the mango by a papaya, the cucumber by half a small melon and the mint by coriander. This salsa may also need a little more lime juice.

Pomegranate and avocado salsa

For 4	1 large avocado	salt and freshly ground pepper
1 small red onion, peeled	3 tbs olive oil	2–3 tbs lime or lemon juice
1 red chilli	2 tbs red wine vinegar	
1 large pomegranate	3 tbs chopped coriander	

Chop the onion finely, slice the chilli finely, extract the seeds from half the pomegranate and squeeze the other half for the juice, cut the peeled and stoned avocado into small cubes. Combine these with the oil, vinegar and coriander, taste and season with salt and pepper. Add enough lime or lemon juice to give a slight sharpness (pomegranates vary in sweetness). Leave at room temperature for an hour or two for flavours to mingle.

Relishes

Salsas are specific to Latin American cooking, even if we have adapted them and invented new versions. Other parts of the world have similar freshly-made sauces – chutneys, acars, sambals, raitas – depending on their origin. They are served with rice or flat breads, grilled or barbecued meat or fish, curries and vegetable dishes. Some add piquancy with spices and chillies, others have a cooling effect. Although best eaten soon after they are made, most of these sauces will keep for a few days if refrigerated.

Coriander chutney

This is a lively fresh-tasting chutney from India. Serve with kebabs, samosas, pakoras and fried or grilled vegetables.

For 4–5	1 tbs peeled and chopped ginger	salt to taste
250g coriander leaves and young stalks	50g sesame seeds, dry-roasted*	juice of 1–2 limes or 1 lemon
2 green chillies, seeded and chopped		

Put all the ingredients except the salt and lime juice into a food processor and blend to a paste. Scrape down the sides of the bowl a couple of times. Alternatively pound everything in a mortar. Add salt to taste and enough lime or lemon juice to loosen the paste a little; it should still be quite thick.

The chutney will keep refrigerated for up to a week.

Green mango chutney

For 8	small handful of mint or coriander leaves	small piece of ginger, peeled and chopped finely
1 tsp cumin seeds	2 green chillies, seeded and chopped	salt to taste
2 tsp coriander seeds		1–2 tbs sugar
1–2 green mangoes, about 600g		

Dry-roast* the cumin and coriander seeds. Peel the mango and cuts its flesh into cubes and blend it to a paste with the dry spices, mint, chillies, ginger, salt and 1 tbs sugar. For a sweeter chutney stir in more sugar.

Mint chutney

This is a cooling chutney to serve with spiced dishes. It is excellent with fried foods.

For 3–4	1–2 green chillies, seeded and chopped finely	½ tsp sugar
1 handful of mint leaves		salt to taste
		5 tbs plain yogurt

Blend the mint, chillies, sugar and salt to a paste in a food processor or pound them in a mortar. Blend in the yogurt.

Raita

A cooling Indian sauce to accompany curries; it can also be served as a dip.

For 4–5	½ tsp cumin	250ml yogurt
½ cucumber, peeled, seeded, and chopped or grated	2 tbs chopped coriander	

Whisk the yogurt and stir in the other ingredients.

Cucumber and pineapple sambal

Sambals combining fruit and vegetables with hot and sweet-sour flavours are popular in Singapore and Indonesia. This one goes well with satay, grilled fish or vegetables.

For 6	1–2 red chillies, seeded and chopped finely	2 tbs kecap manis (p. 340) or dark soy sauce
1 small pineapple		
1 cucumber	2 tbs sugar	1 tbs fish sauce

Peel the pineapple and remove the 'eyes'. Discard the central core and cut the flesh into small cubes. Peel the cucumber, remove the seeds and cut it into pieces the same size as the pineapple. Mix together the pineapple, cucumber and chillies. Dissolve the sugar in the kecap manis and fish sauces and stir into the pineapple and cucumber.

Tomato sambal

This sambal makes an excellent accompaniment to pork satay (p. 340) if you don't like or can't eat peanut sauce.

For 4	3 tomatoes, chopped	juice of 1 lime or lemon
4 shallots, peeled and sliced	3 tbs coarsely chopped basil or mint	salt to taste
4 chillies, seeded and sliced		

Combine all the ingredients and serve at room temperature.

Flavoured butters

Butters flavoured with herbs, spices and other flavourings such as anchovies make very good toppings for plainly cooked meat, poultry, fish and vegetables. They can be added to soups and sauces, or used as a basting liquid; they are good in sandwiches, too. Use unsalted butter at room temperature, and pulse butter and flavourings together in a food processor. Don't let the butter turn to oil. Alternatively, work the flavourings in with a wooden spoon.

Form the butter into a sausage and wrap in foil or clingfilm. Butters wrapped in this way can be stored in the refrigerator for 2 weeks (1 week if the butter contains a lot of garlic) or frozen.

Make flavoured butters an hour or more before you want to use them to allow the flavours to develop.

Anchovy butter

Makes about 180g

6 anchovy fillets

1 garlic clove, peeled and crushed (optional)

150g unsalted butter

2 tbs lemon juice

freshly ground pepper

Blend all the ingredients in a food processor. Serve with grilled fish or steak.

Variations

Garlic butter Combine 150g unsalted butter with 3 crushed garlic cloves, and season with a little salt and freshly ground pepper. Essential for making garlic bread, and good with grilled meat, boiled or steamed vegetables.

Herb butter Combine 150g unsalted butter with 4 tbs of a particular chopped herb and 1–2 tbs lemon juice. Serve basil butter with baked or grilled tomatoes or mushrooms; chive butter with peas or mange-tout; dill or fennel butter with fish or a dish of beans; mint butter with carrots, peas and grilled lamb. Parsley butter is traditionally served with grilled sole and grilled steak and it is perfect with courgettes; tarragon butter goes well with fish, poultry and pumpkin.

Snail butter Combine 150g unsalted butter with 1 peeled and finely chopped shallot, 2 crushed garlic cloves, 2 tbs chopped parsley, 2 tbs lemon juice, salt and freshly ground pepper. Good for heating through shelled mussels, snails of course, and lightly cooked mushrooms.

Marinades

Marinades are an important element in preparing meat or fish to be barbecued, grilled, roasted or stir-fried; they tenderize and enhance flavour and also help to preserve the food. Marinades are usually liquid, but in the Caribbean, Mexico and further south, cooks rub pastes onto the food.

Mix the marinade ingredients together in a container (glass, ceramic) that will not react with acid, immerse the food in the marinade and turn it occasionally. Cover and refrigerate. Meat should be marinated for 3–4 hours and can be left overnight; chicken can be marinated for 1–3 hours; fish and shellfish need only 1–2 hours. Take the food from the refrigerator 30 minutes to 1 hour before it is to be cooked to bring it to room temperature. The marinade can be used to baste the food while cooking. To use it in a sauce, bring it to the boil first to kill off any bacteria there may be from raw meat or fish.

Do not re-use a marinade.

Red wine marinade

For beef, hare and venison	2 garlic cloves, peeled and crushed	2 bay leaves
1 onion, peeled and sliced	4 allspice berries, crushed	sprig of rosemary
1 stalk celery, sliced	a few black peppercorns, crushed	4 tbs olive oil
		½ bottle red wine

French marinade

For poultry, game birds, rabbit or meaty fish such as swordfish and tuna	1 bay leaf	pinch salt
	2 sprigs thyme	4 tbs wine vinegar
1 small onion, peeled and sliced	a few parsley sprigs	4 tbs olive oil
1 garlic clove, peeled and crushed	a few crushed black peppercorns	200ml red or white wine

Mediterranean marinade

For pork, lamb or chicken.

1 garlic clove, peeled and chopped

1 tsp thyme leaves

1 tsp chopped oregano or rosemary leaves

juice of 2 oranges

juice of 1 lemon

1 glass white wine

Oriental marinade

For fish or poultry

2 garlic cloves, peeled and chopped

3cm fresh ginger, peeled and chopped

2 tsp sugar

1 chilli, sliced

4 tbs chopped coriander – root, leaf and stalk

juice of 2 limes

2 tbs fish sauce

5 tbs rice vinegar

Pernod marinade

For fish and seafood

3 tbs lemon juice

1 tbs fennel seeds or a handful of fresh fennel leaves and stalks

4 tsp olive oil

150ml white wine

3 tbs Pernod or other anise-based drink

Yogurt marinade

For roast and grilled lamb, and for fish

250ml plain yogurt

1 garlic clove, peeled and crushed

1 tsp ground cumin

1 tsp ground coriander

4cm ginger, peeled and chopped

¼ tsp chilli flakes

2 tbs chopped mint

Barbecue marinade

For steaks, pork chops or spare ribs

2 shallots, peeled and chopped finely

1 tbs chopped coriander

1 tsp freshly ground pepper

3 tbs light soy sauce

2 tbs sunflower oil

Jamaican jerk seasoning

For fish, chicken or pork to be barbecued

2–4 chillies, seeded and sliced

3 shallots, peeled and chopped

3 spring onions, chopped

3 garlic cloves, peeled and chopped

3cm fresh ginger, peeled and chopped

1 tbs fresh thyme leaves

1 tsp ground allspice

2 tsp ground black pepper

1½ tsp cinnamon

¼ tsp ground cloves

4 tbs sunflower oil

Put the chillies, shallots, spring onions, garlic, ginger and thyme into a food processor with a tablespoon of water and mix to a firm paste, scraping down the sides of the bowl. Add the spices and oil and blend to a thick paste. If necessary add a little more oil or water. Rub the seasoning onto the meat or fish.

This seasoning will keep for up to 6 weeks in the refrigerator.

Desserts

Desserts give pleasure and are often the best-remembered
part of dinner. Although a ripe peach or a slice of melon
may provide the perfect ending to a balanced meal, most people enjoy the aromas, sweet
flavours and attractive appearance of a well-prepared
dessert – be it a palate-cleansing fruit dish, a gap-filling
pudding or a moment of sheer indulgence.

Cold fruit desserts

Most of us at some time must have stopped to admire and then, unable to resist the temptation, to buy from a display of perfect fruit – a small box of pink and white wild strawberries with their haunting perfume perhaps, or downy yellow peaches patched with red, or tawny-gold Williams pears at that point of ripeness when you long to get your teeth into the white juicy flesh.

Apart from being good for us, fruits in season offer some of the easiest and best desserts; out of season they generally lack flavour and real ripeness, especially the fragile summer fruits flown over in winter. The same is true of some tropical fruits that are picked unripe in order to arrive in the shops in what is hoped to be pristine condition. The best guide to telling whether many fruits are ripe is your nose: smell before you buy. If the fruit has no aroma, it will almost certainly have no flavour either. Texture is important, too; most fruits should be firm but that is not the same as hard, which usually indicates a lack of ripeness.

In some of the recipes, one fruit can be substituted for another – berry fruits are very adaptable in this respect even though their flavours are very different; peaches, nectarines and sometimes apricots can be prepared in the same way; lychees and rambutans are interchangeable.

Dried fruit

Dried fruit may be naturally sun-dried or sulphur dioxide may have been used in the process. This information should be on the packet. Many dried fruits are now 'ready-to-eat' and need no soaking. Those that do require soaking may need as little as 1 hour or as much as 12; there should be instructions on the packet. When in doubt, soak the fruit for several hours; long soaking reduces the cooking time.

Citrus fruits

If you require grated citrus rind, buy organic or unwaxed fruit if possible; if not, wash and scrub the rind thoroughly before grating it.

Caramel apples

For 4–6	3 tbs raisins	30g muscovado sugar
6 tart eating apples	grated rind and juice of 1 unwaxed lemon	250g granulated sugar
60g butter		60ml water

Heat the oven to 220°C, 425°F, gas 7. Peel, core and slice the apples. Use a little butter to grease an ovenproof dish. Arrange the apples in layers, sprinkling each one with raisins, lemon rind and juice, muscovado sugar and a few dabs of butter. Cover the dish with foil, make a few slits in it, and bake the apples for 40 minutes. Remove the foil and cook for a further 10–15 minutes, until the apples are tender. They should be moist, so don't let them dry out; if there is too much liquid spoon some of it off. Let the apples cool to lukewarm.

Put the granulated sugar in a small heavy pan with the water, heat gently until the sugar melts, then turn up the heat so that the sugar starts to colour. Shake the pan if one part is turning dark before the rest. As soon as the sugar is a deep amber colour, pour it over the apples to coat them. A brush is useful for spreading the caramel. If it starts to harden in the pan, return the pan to the heat briefly and then work quickly to finish the job. Leave to cool for at least 30 minutes before serving the apples, either on their own or with thick cream.

Quick apple charlotte

For 4	grated rind of $\frac{1}{2}$ unwaxed lemon	100g fresh white breadcrumbs
500g eating apples		
30g granulated sugar, or to taste	1 tbs water	50g demerara sugar
	80g butter	

Peel, core and slice the apples. Put them in a pan with the granulated sugar, lemon rind and water. Cover and cook gently to a purée, stirring occasionally. If you prefer a smooth purée, sieve or blend the apples; I like a rougher texture for this charlotte and just crush the apples lightly with a large fork or a potato masher. Leave the purée to cool.

Heat the butter in a large frying pan and fry the breadcrumbs until golden. If necessary, do them in two batches to make sure they are all nicely coloured. Mix the crumbs and demerara sugar together. Spread half the mixture in the bottom of a small straight-sided dish, such as a soufflé dish, pour in the apple purée and top with the remaining crumbs.

You can make this dessert in advance, but serve it at room temperature, not straight from the refrigerator, with cream, thick yogurt or vanilla ice cream (p. 414).

Rose, date and banana salad

This exquisitely flavoured dish is one of my favourite summer desserts. It comes from *Rose Recipes* by Eleanour Sinclair Rohde. The more scented the roses, the better; it is not worth making with unscented flowers. You can buy rose petal jam from Middle Eastern and some Indian shops.

For 6	200g dates, chopped finely	200ml double cream, whipped, or clotted cream
2–3 very fragrant red or pink roses	6–8 tbs rose petal jam	
4 very ripe bananas	juice of 1 orange	

Cut the white heels from the base of the rose petals and cover the bottom of a serving dish with the petals, ensuring they come a little up the side to make an attractive border. Mash the bananas and mix them with the dates. Spread the mixture over the rose petals, making certain that the petals show well around the fruit. Cover the bananas and dates thickly with rose petal jam. Just before serving pour the orange juice over the fruit and cover with a thick layer of cream. Serve cool, not chilled.

Baked figs with orange and cardamom

This is a good way of preparing figs that are not quite ripe.

For 4	2 tbs caster sugar	100ml port, sweet sherry or other sweet wine
30g butter	thinly pared peel of 1 and juice of 2 unwaxed oranges	
8 firm figs		
4–5 cardamom pods*		

Heat the oven to 200°C, 400°F, gas 6. Butter a baking dish in which the figs will fit snugly. Remove their stalks and put the figs into the dish. Take the cardamom seeds from their pods and grind them with a pestle and mortar, or in a coffee grinder. Add ground seeds to the dish with the sugar. Tuck the pieces of orange peel among the figs. Pour over the orange juice and the wine. Dot with the remaining butter and bake for 20–30 minutes, depending on the ripeness of the figs. Lift out the figs and put them on a serving dish. Transfer the liquid to a pan, reduce a little then strain the sauce over the figs. Either serve at once or leave until cold – I prefer the figs cold.

Melon, lychee and passion fruit salad

This fragrant, light salad comes from Simon Hopkinson who suggests making the syrup a few days in advance so that the flavours mingle. He also points out that if you don't want to bother with the syrup, a few spoonfuls of elderflower cordial will flavour the fruit well. Rambutans could be used instead of lychees.

For 4	a large knob of ginger, unpeeled and sliced	1 melon, preferably charentais
200g sugar		
125ml water	4 pieces of thinly pared unwaxed lemon peel	300g lychees, peeled
100ml white wine		5 passion fruit
		mint (optional)

Put the sugar, water, wine, ginger and lemon peel into a pan. Bring to the boil and simmer for 5 minutes. Cool, and pour into a screw-top jar. Store in the refrigerator where it will keep for several weeks.

Cut the melon flesh into cubes or scoop it out with a melon-baller. Cut the lychees in half and remove the stones. Cut the passion fruit in half and scoop out the pulp. Mix all the fruits together gently (it is best to do this with your hands) and add several spoonfuls of strained syrup, to taste. Cover and macerate in the refrigerator for at least 1 hour. As Simon observes, a little chopped mint adds a summery note.

Melon with raspberries

For 4–5	250g raspberries	4 tbs kirsch
2 medium canteloupe or charentais melons	100g caster sugar	

Remove the melon flesh with a melon-baller or cut it into cubes. Mix it with the raspberries in a serving dish. Sprinkle with the sugar and kirsch. Cover and macerate in the refrigerator for at least 1 hour before serving. Melon sorbet (p. 418) or raspberry ice cream (p. 416) go well with this simple fruit salad.

Nectarines with strawberry purée

For 6	6 ripe nectarines	2 tbs light rum
200g sugar	500g strawberries	125ml whipping cream
200 ml water	50g icing sugar	

Heat the sugar and water to make a syrup. Immerse the nectarines in boiling water for 30 seconds, then drain and peel them. Put them into the syrup, cover the pan and simmer for 4–5 minutes. Turn them if they are not fully covered by the syrup. Lift out the fruit and drain. Cut them in half and remove the stones. Arrange them on a serving dish. Raise the heat and cook the syrup for 3–4 minutes more until it has thickened. Spoon 1–2 tbs over each nectarine, making sure to coat them well. When they are cold put them in the refrigerator for at least 1 hour.

Put the strawberries, cut in half if large, into a food processor with the icing sugar, and purée. If you mind the small seeds, pass the purée through a sieve. Stir in the rum, whip the cream and fold it into the strawberry mixture. Put this to chill for 1 hour, too.

To serve, pour the purée over the nectarines.

Iced peaches

This recipe comes from *Aromas and flavours of past and present* by Alice B. Toklas, who describes it as 'pure essence of Arabian nights'. Buy the most fragrant peaches you can find: English, French or Italian white peaches often have more flavour than the yellow fruits.

For 6	12 ripe figs	80g small strawberries
6 peaches	4 tbs kirsch	50g pistachio nuts, chopped
250g sugar	300ml double cream, whipped	
250ml water		

Immerse the peaches in boiling water for 30 seconds, then drain and peel them. Heat the sugar gently in the water, bring to the boil, then simmer for 5 minutes. Poach the peaches in the syrup for 8–10 minutes. Take them out and put them into a shallow serving dish. Cut the figs into quarters and blend them in a food processor with 4–5 tbs of the syrup. Turn the purée into a pan, add another 150–180ml of the syrup, depending on how thick your purée is, and simmer for 10 minutes to make a kind of fig marmalade. Let it cool, flavour it with the kirsch and stir in the whipped cream. Cover the peaches with the mixture and decorate with a few small strawberries and finely chopped pistachios. Chill for 1 hour before serving.

Peach and raspberry dessert

A quickly prepared dessert if you buy the sorbet or have it already made. *See* note on peaches above.

For 6	2 glasses white wine (choose something not too acidic, such as Pinot blanc or a light Chardonnay)	1 tsp orange flower water (p. 398)
4 peaches		½ litre raspberry sorbet
300g raspberries		10 mint leaves, chopped finely
	100g caster sugar	

Immerse the peaches in boiling water for 30 seconds, drain and peel them, cut them in half, and slice. Squash the raspberries gently with a fork. Stir together the wine, sugar, orange flower water and any peach juice until the sugar has dissolved. Arrange the raspberries in 6 bowls and put the sliced peaches on top. Spoon over the wine. Add 2 spoons of sorbet to each bowl, scatter over a little mint and serve.

Pears poached in spiced red wine

The spices can be varied according to what you have or prefer. I sometimes use bay leaves, cloves and thinly pared orange rind, or star anise*, rosemary and cinnamon.

For 6	¾ bottle decent red wine	½ vanilla pod
200g sugar	1 cinnamon stick	6 Conference or Comice pears
200ml water	3 cloves	

Heat the sugar and water in a pan just large enough to hold the pears. Bring to the boil and boil for 1 minute. Add the wine and spices, bring gently back to the boil and simmer for 5 minutes. Peel the pears, but leave on the stalks. Stand the pears upright in the wine. If necessary add a little more water or wine so that they are covered. Put a circle of baking paper on top of the liquid so that the pears stay immersed (the stalks can poke through). Bring back to the boil, lower the heat and simmer for about 25 minutes. The time will depend on the size and ripeness of the pears; the centre should still feel just firm when pierced with a thin skewer.

Lift out the pears with a slotted spoon and put them into a serving dish. Reduce the liquid by half, then strain it over the pears. Serve warm or cold, with a dollop of mascarpone or strained yogurt.

Pineapple, nectarine and grape salad

Prepare this salad in advance so the flavours have time to blend. For the wine, I suggest a perfumed Gewürztraminer or dry Muscat from Alsace, or a New World unwooded Chardonnay with aromas of melon and tropical fruit.

For 6	6 nectarines	100g seedless grapes
150g sugar	6 slices fresh pineapple, peeled	1 glass white wine
150ml water		

Make a syrup with the sugar and water (p. 399) and leave to cool. Pour boiling water over the nectarines, leave for 30 seconds, then drain and peel. Pour the syrup over the nectarines and leave to macerate for 1 hour. Lift out the nectarines and slice, retaining the syrup. Remove the core from the pineapple slices and cut into pieces. Combine all the fruits gently in a serving dish. Add the wine to the syrup, pour over the fruit, cover and chill for at least 1 hour.

Spiced rhubarb and apple purée

For 4–6	60g sultanas	grated rind of 1/2 unwaxed orange
1.5kg rhubarb	½ tsp ground cinnamon	
3 eating apples, peeled, cored and sliced		6 tbs light brown sugar or honey

Heat the oven to 170°C, 325°F, gas 3. Pull any stringy bits from the rhubarb and cut it into 2cm lengths. Mix together the rhubarb, fruits, cinnamon and orange rind in an ovenproof dish. Spoon over the sugar or honey. Cover and leave in the oven for about 4 hours. Take the dish out, stir through with a fork to mix the ingredients, then put into individual pots and chill. Serve on its own or with whipped cream or crème fraîche.

Strawberry and orange soup

For 4	500g strawberries, sliced or halved	150ml light red wine, such as Beaujolais
4 oranges	125g caster sugar	

Squeeze two of the oranges for their juice, peel the others, removing all pith, and cut out the segments carefully (p. 73). Do this over a bowl to catch the juices. Mix the strawberries and orange segments in a bowl. Heat the orange juice with the sugar until the sugar dissolves, then leave to cool. Add the wine to the syrup and pour over the fruit. Cover and macerate for at least 1 hour before serving.

Strawberries with balsamic vinegar

My first taste of strawberries with balsamic vinegar at the restaurant of the Lancellotti family, not far from Modena, was particularly special because the vinegar was their own traditional 15-year-old balsamic, dense and syrup-like with rich, complex flavours. It was equally spectacular with home-made vanilla ice cream (p. 414).

Use the oldest balsamic vinegar you can afford. Taste a drop on the tip of a spoon to determine its sweetness or acidity in order to judge how much to use. A teaspoon per serving, drizzled over ripe strawberries, is usually about right. Alternatively, slice the strawberries into a large bowl, drizzle over the balsamic vinegar and stir carefully. Leave for 10 minutes, then sprinkle with sugar and serve.

Summer pudding

For 4–6	300g black currants	200g sugar
500g raspberries	300g red or red and white currants	1 loaf of good quality, day-old white bread
500g strawberries		

Put the fruit into a pan with the sugar. Do not add any water. Cook for 3–4 minutes, until the juice runs. Slice the bread as if for sandwiches and remove the crusts. Line the bottom and sides of an 800ml–1 litre basin or soufflé dish with the slices, making sure they fit well together so that the juice will be contained. Fill the dish with the fruit and some of the juice. Cover with a lid of bread, then a small plate which just fits inside the dish. Put a weight on top and leave for several hours or overnight in the refrigerator. Put the reserved juice into a jug. Top up with a little more juice if the bread has absorbed the first lot unevenly. Turn the pudding out onto a dish and pour over the reserved juice. Serve with crème fraîche.

Variation

Autumn pudding Thanks to Franco Taruschio who often had this on his menu at the Walnut Tree.

Make the pudding in the same way as summer pudding, using autumn fruits such as plums, damsons, blackberries and autumn raspberries. Remove the stones from plums and damsons and adjust the amount of sugar according to the fruit you use.

Tropical fruit salad

For 6–8	1 small pineapple	juice of 1 lime
2 mangoes	3 oranges	30g caster sugar
400g lychees	3 kiwi fruits	6 tbs dark rum

Peel all the fruits, making sure no pith remains on the oranges. Remove the stones from the mangoes and lychees and the core from the pineapple. Leave the lychees cut in half, cut the oranges into segments (p. 73), the mango and pineapple into cubes; slice the kiwi fruits. Put all the fruit and their juice into a large bowl. Pour over the lime juice. Dissolve the sugar in the rum and pour over the fruit. Stir gently, cover and chill for at least 1 hour.

Dried fruit compote (Khosaf)

This is a Middle Eastern dessert, a fragrant compote of dried fruits, sometimes spiced with cinnamon or cardamom* or cloves, but most often the fruits are simply macerated with rose-water or orange flower water. These, produced from the respective blossoms, are light yet intensely fragrant waters used in many Middle Eastern dishes, both sweet and savoury. They are sold in Middle Eastern grocery shops and some supermarkets.

The dish must be macerated for 48 hours, and will keep longer. Apricots and sultanas are essential, prunes can be added or dried figs – the small semi-dried figs are delicious in khosaf. For the apricots, I suggest a combination of small whole Hunza apricots and larger halved fruits (preferably Turkish because they have a slight sharpness not found in Californian apricots). Blanched almonds, pistachios and sometimes pomegranate seeds are added before the compote is served, or I sometimes put the nuts in halfway through the macerating time.

If there is any of this compote left, it is great for breakfast.

For 6–8	200g semi-dried figs	100g blanched, slivered almonds, or pistachio nuts
400g dried apricots	125g sugar	
150g sultanas	2 tbs rose-water or orange flower water	seeds of 1 pomegranate (optional)

Put all the dried fruit into a large bowl and cover with water. Add sugar to taste; you may need none, but if you like very sweet things, add more. Add the rose- or orange flower water, cover and put the bowl in the refrigerator for at least 48 hours. Before serving, stir in the nuts and, if you wish, the pomegranate seeds – their deep red colour sets off the amber of the fruits and syrup very well.

Fruit purées and sauces

Fruit purées are quick to make and form the basis of fruit fools and mousses, ice creams and sorbets, sauces and some tarts and cakes.

Raspberries, strawberries, very ripe peaches and nectarines, tropical fruits such as mango, papaya and pineapple, can be puréed raw. Whiz the fruit in a blender or food processor with caster or icing sugar. Sieve raspberry and strawberry purée to get rid of the seeds. Bananas and melons can be crushed with a fork. Add sugar in the proportion of 50–100g per 500ml purée or 500g fruit, depending on how sweet the fruit is and your own taste.

Most firm fruits should be cooked in a syrup (*see* below). For 500g fruit, use 100ml water and 3 tbs sugar or to taste. A purée should have the consistency of a thick cream, so in most cases you will need to drain off the syrup before blending or sieving, depending on whether there are pips to be removed. Apples need very little water (p. 391); gooseberries and currants can be steamed in the water from washing them, just with the addition of sugar – about 125g sugar to 500g fruit.

Fruit sauces are usually based on a fruit purée combined with a sugar syrup. They are good to serve with sorbets and ice creams, soufflés and pancakes.

Fruit fool

Simplicity itself to make, a fool is a mixture of lightly sweetened fruit purée and thick cream, thick yogurt or fromage frais, or a combination of these with cream. The purée should be thick so cook the fruit with little or no syrup and drain it well. Tart fruits such as gooseberries and rhubarb are well set off by the cream.

Fool can also be made with custard (p. 402) but that is more time-consuming and I find the flavour of the fruit somewhat masked. Coconut cream (p. 401) makes a good fool with tropical fruits. Cream can be used straight or lightly whipped, as you prefer. The amount of cream, yogurt or fromage frais you use depends on whether you like a very creamy fool or one in which the flavour of the fruit dominates. For 500ml purée or 500g fruit, I find the minimum needed is 200ml, but you can use up to as much cream as fruit. Taste as you blend the fruit and the cream; you may need a little more sugar or a tablespoon of honey if the fruit is tart, a squeeze of lemon juice if the flavour needs heightening. Chill the fool before serving.

Sugar syrup

This is a general all-purpose syrup recipe suitable for poaching fruit and for use in sauces. Syrups with different ratios of sugar to water are used for caramel and for syrup for sorbets (p. 417).

250g sugar	500ml water

Bring the sugar and water gently to the boil. Simmer for 3–4 minutes until the sugar has dissolved. The syrup can be flavoured with spices and herbs – cinnamon, cloves, crushed cardamom pods*, star anise*, whole mace, vanilla bean, lemon grass*, lime leaves*, bay leaves, rosemary, lemon verbena, lavender – or with finely pared lemon, lime, orange or grapefruit peel, depending on the fruit to be poached and your taste.

Sugar syrup will keep for 4–5 days at room temperature and for several weeks in a screw-top jar in the refrigerator.

Fruit coulis

Ripe summer fruits such as peaches and nectarines, tropical fruits such as mango, and soft fruits and berries make the best uncooked purée or coulis. Add more sugar if you like a sweeter sauce, or if the fruit has a tart flavour. In winter, use fruits in syrup, drained, but do not add any further sweetening. Frozen fruit can also be used, but do not refreeze.

For 4	juice of ½–1 lemon	50ml sugar syrup (see above) or 3 tbs caster sugar
300g fresh fruit		

Purée the fruit in a food processor with lemon juice and syrup or sugar for 1–2 minutes. Sieve if you want to eliminate seeds. The coulis will keep in the refrigerator for 1 week in a screw-top jar; it can also be frozen for up to 6 months. If you freeze it, allow it to thaw overnight in the refrigerator before using and whisk it to restore the smooth texture.

Apricot sauce

For 4–6	400g apricots, halved and stoned	1 vanilla pod
300ml sugar syrup (see above)		

Put the syrup, apricots and vanilla pod into a pan and bring to the boil. Reduce the heat and simmer, uncovered, for 20–25 minutes until the apricots are reduced to a syrupy purée. Stir frequently to prevent the fruit from sticking. Remove the vanilla pod and purée the fruit in a food processor until smooth. Serve hot or cold. Keep for up to a week in a screw-top jar in the refrigerator or up to 6 months in the freezer.

Cassis sauce

Not strictly a fruit sauce, this is made with crème de cassis, the black currant liqueur used to make Kir.

For 4–6	2 tbs sugar	3 tbs crème de cassis
500ml white wine		

Bring the wine and sugar to the boil and cook over medium heat until reduced by two-thirds. Pour the wine into a jug and leave until cold. Stir in the liqueur and refrigerate until needed.

It goes particularly well with figs, a salad of summer fruits or of melon and grapes, and with ice cream.

Variation
Framboise sauce Replace the crème de cassis by the raspberry liqueur, framboise.

Coconut cream sauce

For 4	50g caster sugar, or to taste	150–160ml water or water and single cream
100g solid coconut cream (p. 524)		

Chop the coconut block into small pieces, put it into a food processor with the sugar and half the water. Whiz, adding the rest of the water through the feed tube until you have a creamy consistency.

Quick orange sauce

For 4–6	grated rind of 1 unwaxed orange	60g sugar
200ml fresh orange juice		2–3 tbs Grand Marnier or other orange liqueur

Put the juice, rind and sugar into a small pan and bring to the boil, stirring occasionally. Lower the heat and simmer for 3–4 minutes so that the sauce reduces a little. Add the liqueur. Strain if you want to eliminate the grated rind and leave to cool.

Pomegranate sauce

For 4	1 tbs sugar	2 tbs water
3–4 pomegranates	1 tsp potato flour or cornflour	

Break the pomegranates in half and then into pieces. Use your fingers to separate the seeds from the membrane and put the seeds into a food processor or blender and purée. Put the purée through a sieve and let the juice stand for at least 2 hours. A sediment will settle to the bottom of the bowl. Strain through a sieve lined with muslin (p. 528). Don't be tempted to squeeze the pomegranates on a lemon squeezer because the juice will have a bitter flavour from the membrane.

Heat the juice (there should be about 300ml) with the sugar until the sugar has dissolved. Stir the potato flour into the water and add to the juice. Stir well and cook for 15–20 seconds, until the sauce thickens somewhat. Chill before serving. A good accompaniment to cream desserts.

Custards and creams

Custard, made with eggs, sugar and milk or cream, is usually thought of as a sauce for hot puddings, but it is also the basis of many cold desserts. Chilled, it forms the basis of numerous ice creams; with the addition of gelatine, it becomes a bavarois (p. 404). Also included here are easy cream desserts and more elaborate confections for special occasions.

Custard (Crème anglaise)

For about 500ml	1 vanilla pod, split lengthways or ½ tsp vanilla extract	5 egg yolks
500ml milk		90g sugar

Heat the milk with the vanilla pod in a heavy pan and bring almost to the boil. Whisk the egg yolks and sugar together until the mixture is thick and pale.

Gradually pour the hot milk onto the yolks, stirring steadily. Remove the vanilla pod. Return the mixture to the pan and cook over low heat, stirring constantly, scraping the bottom of the pan, for about 5 minutes until the custard coats the back of a spoon. Do not let it boil. Strain the custard into a bowl and leave to cool. Stir every 3–4 minutes as it cools to prevent a skin forming. If you are using vanilla extract, add it now.

Custard can also be flavoured with a tablespoon of rum, cognac or a liqueur while it is cooling.

Note
If you are apprehensive about making a custard without letting it curdle, add ½ tsp arrowroot or potato flour for each 500ml milk when you beat the eggs and sugar. This tip I learned from La Cuisine de Madame St-Ange *when I first started cooking. She remarks that it prevents surprises and disasters should the milk boil, and recommends its use to beginners and for occasions when you have to keep your eye on a number of things all at the same time.*

Sabayon

A similar sauce to custard, this is made with wine instead of milk or cream, and is also a dessert in its own right – think of zabaglione. For a light sabayon, I use a white wine, but a sweet wine or a fortified wine such as Marsala or sherry can be used instead. A hand-held electric whisk is the best tool to use.

For about 250ml	120g caster sugar	200ml white wine
4 egg yolks		

Whisk the egg yolks and sugar together in a large bowl until thick and pale. Put the bowl over a pan of hot but not boiling water, so that the bottom of the bowl is immersed in the water. Keep whisking and add the wine. After a few more minutes' whisking, the mixture will be warm, frothy and mousse-like. Remove the bowl from the heat.

To eat the sabayon as a dessert, pour it into individual glasses and serve at once. For a cold sauce, set the bowl over ice cubes and whisk until cold.

Variation
Zabaglione To make zabaglione, add the grated rind of ½ unwaxed lemon to the egg yolks and use Marsala instead of white wine.

Coffee bavarois

For 6	3 egg yolks	15g powdered gelatine
100ml very strong coffee	80g caster sugar	3 tbs water
300ml milk	½ tsp arrowroot or potato flour (optional, *see* note p. 403)	150ml double cream

Use a flavourless oil and lightly oil a 1-litre mould or 6 individual moulds. Turn upside down on a plate to allow excess oil to drain off. If you don't have a mould, use a glass or other dish from which you can serve the bavarois.

Put the coffee and milk into a heavy pan, and bring almost to the boil. Cover and set aside. Whisk the egg yolks and sugar until thick and pale. If you are using arrowroot, add it to the yolks. Gradually pour the milk onto the eggs, stirring as you do so. Return the mixture to the pan and cook over gentle heat, stirring constantly and scraping the spoon over the bottom of the pan. Don't let the mixture boil as it will curdle. It is ready when the custard coats the back of a spoon, about 5 minutes. Remove from the heat and strain.

Sprinkle the gelatine over 3 tbs hot water in a small pan and stir briskly. The gelatine will start to swell. Heat very gently until it dissolves. Gelatine must not boil. When it is clear and warm, stir it into the custard. Lightly whip the cream and fold it into the cooled custard. Pour into the mould and refrigerate until set.

To turn out, run a knife round the edge of the bavarois or dip the mould very quickly in hot water.

Passion fruit bavarois

For 6	4 egg yolks	15g powdered gelatine
6 passion fruit	80g caster sugar	3 tbs water
500ml milk	½ tsp arrowroot or potato flour (optional, *see* note p. 403)	200ml double cream
1 vanilla pod, split lengthways		

Use an unflavoured oil and lightly oil a 1 litre mould or 6 small moulds. Turn upside down on a plate to allow excess oil to drain. Alternatively make the bavarois in a dish from which it can be served. Cut the passion fruit in half and scoop out the pulp. Heat the milk with the vanilla pod in a heavy pan until it almost comes to the boil. Remove the pan from the heat, cover and set aside. Whisk the egg yolks, sugar and arrowroot, if you are using it, until thick and pale. Remove the vanilla pod, whisk the milk into the egg yolks gradually, then return the mixture to the pan. Heat, stirring steadily and scraping the bottom of the pan until the mixture is thick enough to coat the back of the spoon. It will curdle if it boils. Remove from the heat and strain into a bowl.

Sprinkle the gelatine over the water in a small pan and stir as it starts to swell and dissolve. Heat it very gently and when it is clear and warm pour into the bavarois mixture. Gelatine must not boil. Stir occasionally until on the point of setting. Stir in two-thirds of the passion fruit pulp, whip the cream lightly and fold it in. Tip into the mould and refrigerate until set.

To turn out, run a knife round the edge or dip the mould briefly into hot water. Serve with the remaining passion fruit.

Crème caramel

Crème caramel remains ever popular. Properly made, it is delicious, whereas the packet variety tastes floury and has a dense texture.

For 6	100g sugar	For the caramel
500ml full milk	2 eggs	100g sugar
half a vanilla bean or a strip of unwaxed lemon peel, or a few drops vanilla extract	3 egg yolks	5 tbs water

First make the caramel. Put the sugar and water into a heavy pan over medium heat. It doesn't need to be stirred, but watch it because the sugar will caramelise quickly. The sugar dissolves, starts to bubble and turns golden, then deepens to amber after a minute or two. Remove the pan from the heat at once and add a few drops of cold water to stop the cooking. If it cooks further, the caramel will be bitter. Take a soufflé dish or other straight-sided dish of 800ml–1 litre capacity, and pour in the caramel, turning and tilting the dish to coat the sides and bottom with the caramel. Work fast because the caramel sets quickly.

Heat the oven to 170°C, 325°F, gas 3. Put the milk into a pan with the vanilla bean or lemon peel and the sugar and bring slowly to simmering point. Cover and leave to infuse off the heat. Whisk in a food processor or by hand the eggs and egg yolks with the sugar until thick. Remove the vanilla bean or lemon peel from the milk and pour the slightly cooled liquid onto the eggs. Whisk until the mixture is well blended. If you are using vanilla extract, add it now. Strain the custard into the dish and cover. Stand it in a bain-marie*. Bake for about 1 hour or a bit longer.

The custard should be firm, but slightly trembly and a thin skewer inserted in the centre should come out clean. Leave to cool, then chill for several hours. Only turn out the pudding shortly before serving.

Lemon posset

A simple, clean-flavoured cream which goes well at the end of a rich meal.

For 6–8	4 tbs dry sherry	sprigs of lemon verbena or twists of fresh lemon peel to decorate
600ml double cream	2 egg whites	
grated rind and juice of 2 unwaxed lemons	125g caster sugar	

Put the cream, lemon rind and juice and sherry into a large bowl and whisk until thick; it will take 5 minutes or more, but take care not to beat too much or the mixture will become grainy. Whisk the egg whites and sugar until stiff and fold lightly into the cream (p. 49). Spoon into glasses and chill lightly. Stick a small sprig of lemon verbena or a twist of lemon peel into each posset and serve with thin biscuits.

Raspberry and chocolate cream

A delicious, indulgent dessert; the raspberries and chocolate complement each other beautifully.

For 2	2 tbs kirsch	200g raspberries
150ml double cream	100g plain chocolate, grated	
2 tbs caster sugar		

Whip the cream until thick, stir in the sugar and kirsch and whip until it holds soft peaks. Stir in three-quarters of the grated chocolate. Put the raspberries into a serving dish, spoon over the cream and sprinkle the rest of the chocolate over the top. Chill for at least 1 hour before serving.

Strawberry cream

A wonderfully simple dessert to make with ripe strawberries.

For 4	60g caster sugar	1 egg white
400g strawberries	300ml double cream	

Set aside a few small strawberries and purée the rest with the sugar. Whip the cream until thick and whisk the egg white until stiff. Fold the cream and then the egg white into the strawberry purée. Turn the cream into a serving dish and chill for at least 1 hour. Stir in the reserved whole strawberries and serve.

Rêve au chocolat

For 4	2 tbs water	4 tbs sugar
250g plain chocolate	350g butter	4 eggs
2 tbs brandy		

Melt the chocolate with the brandy and water in a bowl over hot water. Cream the butter and sugar, then beat in the egg yolks. Pour in the chocolate and beat vigorously. It will take about 10 minutes by hand, but less than half that time with an electric beater. Whip the egg whites until stiff and fold them into the mixture (p. 49). Turn it into a serving dish and chill for 3–4 hours. Serve with single cream.

Mocha diplomate

This recipe from Claudia Roden's *Coffee* has been a family favourite for many years. It is foolproof to make and can be eaten after being chilled in the refrigerator, or after freezing for a few hours when it has a pleasant semi-freddo texture.

For 6	300ml double cream	3 packets lady finger biscuits
125g hazelnuts	150ml single cream	300ml milky coffee
5 tbs caster sugar	1 heaped tbs instant coffee	

Make a praline with the hazelnuts and 3 tbs caster sugar after removing the skins from the nuts (p. 487). Keep a few nuts whole for decoration.

Beat the two creams together, add 2 tbs sugar and the coffee powder dissolved in a tablespoon of warm water. Moisten the biscuits by dipping them briefly in the milky coffee. Don't let them soak up too much liquid or they will become soggy. Put a layer of biscuits in a 20cm square or round tin, with a loose base or detachable sides. Spread with a thin layer of the coffee cream and sprinkle with a little praline. Repeat the layers until all the biscuits are used, ending with a good layer of cream. Lift the diplomate out, on the base of the tin, or remove the sides. Spread a little cream around the sides and sprinkle all over with praline. Place the whole caramelised nuts on the top and refrigerate or freeze.

Tiramisu

This recipe comes from my friend Tiziana Zeri who has it from her grandmother. I first ate tiramisu in her house and became addicted, at least to this version.

For 8–10	4 tbs grappa	2 tbs sugar
4 egg yolks	2 egg whites	24–30 lady finger biscuits
100g caster sugar	1 glass water	
400g mascarpone	1 glass Marsala or sherry	plain chocolate for the decoration

Whisk the egg yolks with the caster sugar until pale and thick. Mix in the mascarpone, a tablespoon or two at a time to obtain a smooth cream. Stir in the grappa, cover and refrigerate for 1–2 hours. Whisk the egg whites to peaks and fold them carefully into the cream (p. 49).

Pour the water and Marsala into a wide shallow dish, add the sugar and stir to dissolve. Have ready a glass or china rectangular dish, about 20x30cm. Dip the biscuits into the water and wine bath and place a layer of tightly packed biscuits in the serving dish. Judging the dipping process is a bit tricky: too long and the biscuits start to disintegrate, too brief and the tiramisu will have dry spots. If it is to be kept for some hours before serving that is not a problem, because the mascarpone layers will provide additional liquid, but if it is to be eaten soon after making, the biscuits must be soaked enough. Over the layer of biscuits, put a layer of mascarpone cream. Repeat the layers with two more layers of soaked biscuits and two more layers of mascarpone cream. Refrigerate for at least 2 hours and up to 1 day.

Just before serving, grate a good covering of chocolate over the top of the tiramisu; if it stands for any length of time, the chocolate will start to melt.

Anselmo, Tiziana's husband, adds that tiramisu is best accompanied by a sparkling Moscato d'Asti, but if you prefer a dry wine, a Prosecco would be fine.

Variations

Tiramisu al caffè Use espresso coffee and grappa or another spirit such as rum or cognac for soaking the biscuits, and use that same spirit in the mascarpone cream.

Tiramisu all'amaretto This is a modern version. Soak amaretti biscuits in half water and half Amaretto di Saronno, and use Amaretto in the mascarpone. Do not use chocolate with this version, leave the top plain.

Black currant cheesecake

For 1 cake using a 20cm spring-form cake tin	120g caster sugar	**For the base**
	3 eggs	120g digestive biscuits
250g black currants	500g mascarpone	50g butter, melted
	100ml double cream	3 tbs light brown sugar

Put the black currants in a pan with half the caster sugar and 1 tbs water. Bring slowly to the boil and simmer until the fruit softens, about 5 minutes. Sieve, pressing out as much thick purée as possible. Leave to cool.

Heat the oven to 180°C, 350°F, gas 4, and grease the tin. To prepare the base, crumble the biscuits and the brown sugar in a food processor, and pour the melted butter in through the feed tube. Alternatively, put the biscuits in a plastic bag and crush them with a rolling pin, then mix the crumbs with the melted butter and sugar. Cover the base of the tin with the mixture. Press the crumbs evenly onto the base.

Beat the eggs until thick, add the rest of the caster sugar and beat until the mixture is light and fluffy. Lightly beat the mascarpone and add it to the eggs. Whip the cream lightly and fold it into the cheese mixture. Cover the base with the black currant purée and pour the cheese mixture on top. Bake for 1 hour and 10 minutes. Cover the top with foil if it is browning too much. When the cake is ready, turn off the oven but leave the cake inside until cold.

Variation

Apricot cheesecake Instead of the black currants, chop 150g ready-to-eat dried apricots and spread them in a layer over the biscuit base or mix them into the mascarpone and cream.

American cheesecake

For 1 cake using a 20cm cake tin	3 tbs lemon juice	450ml soured cream
	1 tsp vanilla extract	**For the base**
400g curd cheese	2 tbs cornflour	150g digestive biscuits or plain rusks
350g cream cheese	2 tbs plain flour	
3 eggs	1 tsp salt	60g soft brown sugar
80g caster sugar	125g butter	60g butter, melted

Grease either a spring-form tin or a square tin with a loose base. Heat the oven to 170°C, 325°F, gas 3. To prepare the base, crumble the biscuits or rusks in a food processor with the sugar and pour the melted butter in through the feed tube. Alternatively, put the biscuits or rusks in a plastic bag and crush them with a rolling pin; combine the crumbs with the brown sugar and butter. Press the mixture firmly into the base of the tin to form an even layer.

Mix together the curd and cream cheeses. Beat the eggs until thick, then beat in the caster sugar until the mixture is light and fluffy. Stir in the lemon juice and vanilla. Add the egg mixture to the cheeses. Sift the cornflour, flour and salt two or three times, then fold into the mixture. Melt the butter and stir it in. Fold in the cream. Turn the mixture into the tin and smooth the top. Bake for 15 minutes, then increase the temperature to 190°C, 375°F, gas 5, and bake for another 40 minutes. If necessary, cover the top with foil to prevent it browning too much. Turn off the oven and leave the cake for another hour. Refrigerate before serving.

Mousses and cold soufflés

Mousses and soufflés are made with similar ingredients – whole or separated eggs – but for a mousse the eggs are usually beaten whole, and the flavouring and cream folded in, whereas for a soufflé the egg yolks are beaten with sugar, flavouring and cream, and whipped egg whites are folded in. Both are lightly set with gelatine.

A soufflé is made in a soufflé dish heightened by a collar of double-thickness greaseproof paper tied around the top to stand 5–6 cm above the rim. The mixture is poured in so it rises above the rim of the dish, the mixture being supported by the paper collar. When it has set, the paper is removed and the soufflé has the appearance of a mixture that has risen. Mousses can be made in a large bowl or individual dishes.

It is important that the mixture for both should be quite thick and creamy before it is poured into the dish and refrigerated, otherwise it is likely to separate, with a jelly at the bottom and a light creamy top.

Blackberry yogurt mousse

For 6	180g caster sugar	150ml thick yogurt
500g blackberries	2 tsp powdered gelatine	2 egg whites

Reserve a few blackberries for decoration, purée the remainder in a food processor. Sieve if you want to remove the pips. Transfer the purée to a pan and add 150g sugar. Heat gently until the sugar dissolves. Dissolve the gelatine in 2 tbs of the purée over low heat, then mix it with the rest of the purée. Whisk in the yogurt. Whip the egg whites to soft peaks with the rest of the sugar and fold into the blackberry mixture (p. 49). Turn into a large bowl or individual dishes. Refrigerate and leave to set for at least 2 hours. Decorate with the reserved blackberries and serve with pomegranate sauce (p. 402).

Variation
Raspberry yogurt mousse Replace the blackberries by raspberries.

Chocolate and orange mousse

In this version of Elizabeth David's, the orange juice tempers the richness of the chocolate and adds an aromatic flavour. Try a Seville orange instead of a sweet one when they are in season.

For 6	4 eggs, separated	1 tbs Grand Marnier or other orange liqueur (optional)
125g plain chocolate	30g softened butter	
	juice of 1 orange	

Put the chocolate to melt in a bowl over hot water. Beat the egg yolks until thick with an electric whisk and stir them into the melted chocolate. Add the butter followed by the orange juice and the liqueur if you are using it. Whisk the egg whites to peaks and fold them into the mixture (p. 49). Spoon it into little dishes, glasses or coffee cups and chill.

Mango mousse

For 6–8	50g caster sugar	3 tbs water
500–600g ripe mangoes (whole fruit)	4 tbs white wine	250ml double cream
	15g powdered gelatine	chopped pistachio nuts to garnish
2 eggs		

Prepare a purée with the mangoes, as described on p. 398; you should obtain about 400g. Whisk the eggs, sugar and wine over gentle heat or in a bowl set over hot water until thick, or whisk on high speed in a bowl with an electric whisk. Sprinkle the gelatine over the water in a small pan, stir it in and as it starts to swell, heat gently until it dissolves and the liquid is clear. Do not let gelatine boil. Stir the gelatine into the egg mixture and add this to the mango purée. Lightly whip the cream and fold it into the mango mixture.

Spoon into a large glass dish or individual dishes and chill for at least 2 hours. Decorate with chopped pistachio nuts.

Chocolate chinchilla

Chinchilla is a kind of soufflé without egg yolks. It is well worth making on any account, but has the added virtue of being a handy way to use up a lot of egg whites. The flavour of cinnamon is particularly good with chocolate. The recipe comes from *Summer Cooking* by Elizabeth David.

For 4–5	90g caster sugar	5–7 egg whites
60g unsweetened cocoa	1 heaped tsp ground cinnamon	

Heat the oven to 170°C, 325°F, gas 3. Grease a ring mould or kugelhopf mould of 1 litre capacity. The central funnel in these moulds helps in the even distribution of heat throughout the mixture. If you have to use a soufflé dish, the chinchilla will stay moist in the centre after the rest is cooked.

Mix the cocoa with the sugar and cinnamon. Whisk the egg whites until firm, tip the cocoa mixture onto them and fold the two together, gently but thoroughly, with a large metal spoon or a spatula.

Turn the mixture into the mould, stand it in a baking tin with hot water to reach halfway up the sides. Bake for 45–50 minutes. It rises dramatically, but sinks when taken from the oven. Put it in a warm place, out of draughts, and leave to cool. It should turn out easily when cold.

Serve with single cream to which has been added a little sherry, rum or brandy.

Lemon soufflé

For 6	grated rind and juice of 2 large or 3 small unwaxed lemons	250ml double cream, whipped
4 eggs, separated		extra whipped cream to decorate
150g caster sugar	15g powdered gelatine	

Prepare a 14–15cm soufflé dish with a paper collar as described on p. 410.

Put the egg yolks, sugar, lemon rind and juice into a bowl and whisk with an electric whisk until thick and foamy and a trail is left across the surface when you raise the whisk. If you don't have an electric whisk, put the bowl over a pan of simmering water and whisk for 10–15 minutes until the mixture reaches the same point, and continue to whisk away from the heat until it is cool. Sprinkle the gelatine on 3 tbs water in a small pan; when it starts to swell, heat gently and stir to dissolve the gelatine completely. Do not let it boil. When the liquid is clear, stir it into the egg and lemon mixture and chill for about 30 minutes until it begins to thicken and set. Fold in the cream. Whisk the egg whites until stiff and fold them into the mixture (p. 49). Pour the mixture into the soufflé dish and refrigerate for at least 4–5 hours.

To serve, remove the paper collar and decorate the top with whipped cream.

Ice creams and sorbets

The quickest way to make an ice is to mix a flavouring – fruit, alcohol, coffee, tea, spice – with a syrup to make a water ice, or with cream and syrup to make an ice cream, and to freeze it. The simplest water ice, a granita, is a thick, grainy slush. A sorbet is frozen to a firmer texture and may have beaten egg whites, and occasionally cream, added. It should have the consistency of firm snow. An ice cream of cream, syrup and flavouring is light and delicate, most suited to summer fruits; ices with a richer texture are made with a custard of egg yolks and milk or cream. Ice creams made with custard tend to freeze to a better consistency.

Storage

Many ice creams and sorbets, especially those that are fruit-based, taste best when eaten the day they are made. Ice creams containing alcohol are best kept for at least one day for the flavours to develop. Ice creams keep well in the freezer for 1 month, sorbets are best eaten within 2–3 weeks. Ices need to be softened before serving to bring out the flavour and improve the consistency; from the freezer, put the ice in the refrigerator for 15–30 minutes, depending on the type of ice, before serving.

Freezing methods

The most satisfactory method is to use one of the small domestic ice cream machines which freeze and churn simultaneously. Follow the manufacturer's instructions for use.

Ices can also be frozen in shallow plastic containers in a freezer. Chill the mixture before putting it into the freezer and cover with the lid or a piece of foil. When the mixture freezes, ice crystals form, trapping air and fat in the structure. The consistency of an ice cream or sorbet is improved if you stir it every hour or so to break up the ice crystals. A mixture based on egg yolks and cream needs less beating than one that is less rich, but the more any ice is beaten the more air is incorporated and the smoother the texture.

When the mixture has set around the sides and on the bottom of the container, either beat it with an electric hand beater for a few seconds, or whiz it quickly in a food processor, or tip it out into a chilled bowl and beat vigorously. Then return it to the container and to the freezer. An ice cream frozen in this way will take about 6 hours to freeze and should be beaten at least 2 or 3 times. Ices containing alcohol take longer to freeze, but also need less time to soften before serving.

For a granita, spread the mixture or liquid no more than 2cm deep. It does not need beating; it is enough to stir the frozen edges into the middle with a fork because part of the appeal of a granita is the crunchy shards of ice. A granita will take about 3 hours to freeze.

Making ice cream

It is important not to let an egg-based mixture boil or it will curdle. After making an ice cream once or twice, it becomes easy to see when the mixture is thickening. Lift out the spoon you are stirring with, hold it flat and run your finger along it; if it leaves a clear mark through the mixture, the cream is ready. Take the pan from the heat while you test. If the mixture does boil, remove the pan from the heat, beat furiously and add a spoonful of cold milk or cream; this usually works.

All food has less taste when very cold, so slightly over-sweeten and over-flavour ice cream and sorbet mixtures.

Vanilla ice cream

| For 6 | 1 vanilla pod, split in half lengthways | 150g caster sugar |
| 450ml full milk or single cream | 4 egg yolks | 150ml double cream |

Put the milk or single cream and the vanilla pod into a heavy pan and bring slowly to the boil. Remove from the heat and leave to infuse for 20 minutes. Take out the vanilla pod and scrape the seeds into the liquid. Beat the egg yolks and sugar until thick and pale; an electric whisk is useful here. Gently reheat the milk or cream and beat a little of it into the egg yolks. Then pour the egg mixture into the pan and put the pan over low heat. Stir for several minutes until the custard is thick enough to coat the spoon, or when your finger leaves a clear mark on the spoon. Do not boil.

Strain through a fine sieve and continue to stir until almost cooled. You can speed up the cooling by standing the bowl in a sink of cold water. Whip the double cream lightly and fold it into the custard. Freeze (p. 413).

Variations

Cardamom ice cream Replace the vanilla pod by 8 lightly crushed cardamom pods*. Infuse for 30 minutes, then strain and follow the instructions above.

Cinnamon ice cream Replace the vanilla pod by 1 tbs finely ground cinnamon. There is no need to infuse; just follow the instructions above.

Cointreau ice cream Make the vanilla ice cream as above, and stir in 125g diced crystallised orange peel and 50ml Cointreau just before adding the double cream.

Lavender ice cream Replace the vanilla pod by 3 tbs lavender flowers. Infuse for 1 hour, then strain. Add 1 tsp finely chopped lavender flowers just before adding the double cream.

Lemon ice cream Replace the vanilla pod by the grated rind of 1 unwaxed lemon, 2 tbs lemon juice and a small handful of lemon verbena leaves. Infuse for 1 hour, then remove the verbena leaves.

Praline ice cream Make the vanilla ice cream as above, and stir in 100g hazelnut praline (p. 487) just before adding the double cream.

Chocolate ice cream

For 5–6	1 tsp vanilla extract or ½ tsp ground cinnamon	150g caster sugar
180g plain chocolate		6 tbs water
3 tbs water	3 eggs	200ml double cream

Melt the chocolate in 3 tbs water in a bowl set over a pan of hot water. Stir until smooth, then stir in the vanilla extract or the cinnamon. Whisk the eggs until frothy and pale, preferably in an electric mixer or with an electric hand whisk. Heat the sugar and 6 tbs water, boil for 2–3 minutes, then pour the syrup onto the eggs, whisking all the time. Keep whisking until the mixture thickens. Whisk in the chocolate and leave the mixture to cool. Whip the cream, fold it into the mixture and freeze (p. 413).

Cappuccino ice cream

For 5–6	3 egg yolks	1 tsp unsweetened cocoa
300ml full milk or single cream	170g caster sugar	1 tsp ground cinnamon
	2 tbs strong coffee powder	200ml double cream

Heat the milk or single cream slowly to boiling point in a heavy pan. Beat the egg yolks and sugar until pale and thick, then stir in the coffee, cocoa and cinnamon. Pour on a little of the hot milk or cream, whisking briskly, then pour the mixture into the pan and follow the instructions for vanilla ice cream (p. 414).

Strawberry ice cream

For 6–8	200g caster sugar	300ml double cream
500g strawberries	2 tbs lemon juice	

Purée the strawberries with the sugar (p. 398). Add the lemon juice, lightly whip the cream and fold it into the mixture. Freeze (p. 413).

Variations

Mango ice cream Replace the strawberries by chopped mango flesh, reduce the sugar to 100g and use lime juice instead of lemon.

Raspberry ice cream Use raspberries instead of strawberries and reduce the lemon juice to 1 tablespoon.

Frozen peach yogurt

For 6	2 tbs lemon juice	4–5 tbs honey
500g ripe peaches, stoned	2 tbs light rum or brandy (optional)	300ml plain yogurt
		2 egg whites

If the peaches are very ripe they can be puréed raw, otherwise they should be cooked in a syrup first. *See* the notes on fruit purées on p. 398. Whiz the lemon juice and rum or brandy if you are using it into the purée. Add the honey and yogurt and blend. Whisk the egg whites until they hold peaks and fold them in (p. 49). Freeze (p. 413).

Variations

Frozen strawberry yogurt Replace peaches with strawberries, rum with kirsch; omit the lemon juice.

Frozen raspberry yogurt Replace the peaches with raspberries, the rum with eau de vie de framboise or cassis; omit the lemon juice.

Syrup for sorbets

1kg sugar	1 litre water

Put the sugar and water into a heavy pan and bring slowly to the boil, stirring until the sugar has dissolved. Simmer for 5 minutes, and cool.

The syrup can be kept in a bottle in the refrigerator for up to 1 month.

Black currant and red wine sorbet

For 6	50ml water	100ml double cream
500g black currants	1 stick cinnamon	2 egg whites
150ml red wine	250g sugar	

Purée the black currants (p. 398) then pass through a sieve. Put the debris, wine, water and cinnamon into a pan, bring slowly to the boil, then simmer for 2–3 minutes. Strain and discard the solids. Add the sugar to the liquid and let it dissolve over low heat. Mix the wine syrup into the black currant purée and leave to cool. Whip the cream and stir it into the purée. If you are using an ice cream machine, whisk the egg whites until stiff, fold them in (p. 49) and freeze. To freeze in the freezer, freeze the mixture to a slush, then whisk the egg whites and fold them in. Return the container to the freezer and continue the freezing process (p. 413).

Lemon sorbet

For 5–6	400ml syrup (*see above*)	2 egg whites
250ml lemon juice		

Strain the lemon juice and combine with the syrup. Freeze in a plastic container in a freezer until it has turned into a slush and then add the whisked egg whites; continue to freeze as p. 413. If you have an ice cream machine, whisk the whites until stiff and fold them into the lemon syrup (p. 49) before freezing.

Mango sorbet

For 6	2–3 ripe mangoes (about 800g)	300ml syrup (p. 417)
		juice of 1 lime

Peel and slice the mangoes, scraping as much fruit as you can from the stone. Purée it (p. 398) and add the syrup and lime juice. Freeze (p. 413).

Melon sorbet

A refreshing, delicately flavoured sorbet. Choose a ripe, perfumed melon.

For 5–6	2 tbs lemon juice	100ml whipping cream
500g melon flesh	100g caster sugar	2 egg whites

Blend the melon, lemon juice and sugar in a food processor. Whisk the cream until stiff and fold into the purée. To freeze in the freezer, freeze the melon and cream mixture to a slush, then fold in the whisked egg whites; continue to freeze as p. 413. If you use an ice cream machine, whisk the egg whites until stiff and fold them in (p. 49) before freezing.

Eliza Acton's red currant and raspberry ice

This sorbet, from *Modern Cookery*, 1845, captures the very essence of summer flavours.

For 6–8	400g sugar	juice of 1 large or 2 small lemons (optional)
1kg red currants	300ml water	
250g raspberries		

Purée the fruit (p. 398) and rub through a sieve. To make the syrup, let the sugar dissolve slowly in the water, bring to the boil and simmer for 3–4 minutes. Leave to cool. Stir the syrup into the fruit purée, add lemon juice if you wish and freeze (p. 413).

Raspberry, wine and mint granita

This granita is good made with a dry rosé or light red wine.

For 6–8	150g sugar	300g raspberries
500ml rosé or red wine	10 mint leaves, lightly crushed	

Bring the wine slowly to the boil with the sugar and mint leaves, stirring to dissolve the sugar. Remove the pan from the heat and pour the wine into a large bowl. Purée and sieve the raspberries and add them to the wine. Stir well and leave to macerate for 1 hour, then remove the mint leaves. Stir again thoroughly and pour into a shallow container. Cover and chill, then transfer to the freezer for 2½–3 hours. From time to time scrape the frozen mixture from the sides of the container and bottom into the soft centre. To serve, scrape the granita into chilled individual glasses or a large glass bowl.

Coffee granita

Coffee granita is the most refreshing ice on a hot day.

For 6–8	80g ground espresso coffee	80g sugar
1 litre water		strip of lemon peel

Boil the water and pour it over the coffee and sugar. Stir and leave to brew for 10 minutes. Strain through a coffee filter then add lemon peel and infuse for 5 minutes. Discard the lemon peel, pour the coffee into a shallow plastic container, cover and refrigerate until very cold. Freeze, stir after an hour and then every half hour. Scrape the frozen mixture from the sides and bottom of the container with a fork and mix it with the more liquid part in the centre. It will take 2½–3 hours to freeze and should ideally be eaten straight away, but it will keep for a few hours if you stir it from time to time.

Serve with whipped cream.

Note
If you stir 150ml single cream into the frozen granita, it becomes the perfect iced coffee.

Tarts, pies and pastries

For simplicity I have divided these recipes according to the type of pastry used. Recipes for shortcrust and choux pastry and notes on lining tins, covering pies and baking blind can be found on p. 490. For notes on using filo pastry, *see* p. 493. For puff pastry follow the manufacturer's instructions for the preparation.

Shortcrust tarts

Alsatian apple tart

Alsace is a province with a long tradition of making excellent tarts. The best known is Flammekueche which is rather like a pizza topped with white cheese and sometimes onions or bacon. The onion tart on p. 148 is another speciality of the region. When it comes to desserts, all the fruits from the local orchards find their way into tarts, either fresh or dried. Most Alsatian fruit tarts are topped with a light custard, as is this one.

For one 30cm tart, for 8–10	1kg eating apples	125ml single cream
shortcrust pastry made with 250g flour (p. 491)	100g caster sugar	½ tsp ground cinnamon or caster sugar
	2 eggs	
	80ml milk	

Heat the oven to 200°C, 400°F, gas 6. Roll out the pastry and line the tin, preferably one with a removable base. Prick the pastry in several places to prevent it bubbling up while baking. Peel the apples, cut them in quarters and remove the core. If they are large cut each quarter again in half lengthways. Distribute the fruit over the pastry, sprinkle with 30g sugar and bake for 25–30 minutes. Make the topping while the tart is in the oven. Beat the eggs with the remaining sugar, making sure the sugar has dissolved. Whisk in the milk and cream gradually. When the apples are cooked through, pour over the cream and return the tart to the oven for another 10–12 minutes, or until the custard is set. Sprinkle with cinnamon or a little more caster sugar and serve warm.

Variations
Plum tart Make a plum tart in the same way. Cut the plums in half and remove the stones. Serve warm.

Blueberry tart Replace the apples by 500g blueberries. Before putting them into the tart scatter 3–4 tbs fine fresh white breadcrumbs or crushed biscuit crumbs over the pastry to absorb excess juice. For the custard, omit the milk and use 100ml single cream or crème fraîche. Bake for 18–20 minutes to cook the fruit, then pour over the cream and return the tart to the oven for another 10 minutes to cook the custard. Omit the cinnamon, sprinkle with caster sugar and leave to get cold before serving, but it should not be chilled.

Red currant tart This is a variant on the blueberry tart. Use 500g red currants. Scatter the tart base with crumbs as in the blueberry recipe. The red currants are too fragile to cook alone, so spread them over the crumbs, make the custard and pour it over the fruit straightaway. Bake at 200°C, 400°F, gas 6, for about 35 minutes.

Frangipane tart

This tart filled with almond cream can be topped with fresh apricots, peaches, plums or pears.

For one 24cm tart, for 6–8	shortcrust pastry made with 200g flour (p. 491)	1kg fresh fruit
frangipane cream (p. 487)		1–2 tbs caster sugar

Chill the frangipane cream for an hour or so, it will cook better. Heat the oven to 200°C, 400°F, gas 6. Roll out the pastry, line the tin, prick the base with a fork, and follow the instructions on baking blind on p. 490.

Cut the fruit in half, remove stones (or the core and peel from pears), then slice them. Spread the frangipane cream over the base of the tart and arrange the fruit slices on top of it. Sprinkle with caster sugar and bake for 30–35 minutes. The frangipane should be set and golden brown. Set the tin on a wire rack for a few minutes before turning out. Serve hot or cold.

Variation
Prune and dried apricot frangipane tart Soak 300g prunes and 300g dried apricots in sherry or brandy for several hours. Add 30g sugar and sufficient water to cover them and bake, uncovered, in a low oven, 170°C, 325°F, gas 3, for 30–40 minutes, until the fruit is just soft. Drain and let the fruit cool, cut in half and remove the stones.

Bake the pastry case as above, fill it with half the frangipane cream, arrange the fruit so that the flavours will marry and cover with the rest of the frangipane. Bake the tart for 10 minutes, then reduce the heat to 150°C, 300°F, gas 2, and bake for a further 20 minutes. Serve warm or cold.

Black currant meringue tart

Easy and absolutely delicious. Red currants are also good with the meringue.

For one 20–22cm tart, for 4–6	750g black currants	190g caster sugar
	3 tbs caster sugar	grated rind of 1/2 unwaxed lemon
shortcrust pastry made with 150g flour (p. 491)	**For the meringue**	
	6 egg whites	150g ground almonds

Heat the oven to 200°C, 400°F, gas 6. Roll out the pastry and line a tart tin, preferably one with a removable base. Stir the black currants and sugar together.

Make the meringue: whisk the egg whites until almost stiff, fold in the sugar and continue to whisk until they stand in creamy peaks. Fold in the lemon rind and the almonds. Place a layer of meringue on the pastry, using about a third of the mixture. Mix the black currants into the rest of the meringue and spread over the tart. Bake for 20 minutes, then lower the heat to 180°C, 350°F, gas 4, and bake for another 15–20 minutes until the tart is lightly golden. Serve warm or cold.

Fresh fruit tarts

These pretty tarts are easy to make. The baked tart shell is filled with pastry cream – the richness of the cream sets off the fresh fruit nicely – and topped with fruit. If you prefer not to use pastry cream, brush the tart shell with a glaze to stop the fruit juices making it soggy. The fruits can be whatever is in season: summer red fruits, quartered figs and blueberries and blackberries, cubes of mango and pineapple with green grapes or sliced banana. Individual tartlets can be made in the same way; the number of tartlets you can make depends on the size of your tins.

For one 24cm tart, for 6–8	pastry cream (p. 486)	**For the glaze**
	about 1kg fresh fruit	4 tbs apricot jam
shortcrust pastry made with 200g flour (p. 491)		1 tbs lemon juice
		2 tbs water

Heat the oven to 190°C, 375°F, gas 5. Roll out the pastry thinly and line the tin. Prick the pastry with a fork and follow the notes on baking blind on p. 490. Allow the tart shell to cool, then spread it with a layer of pastry cream, or brush with hot glaze. Arrange the fruits on the tart.

To make the glaze, heat the jam, lemon juice and water until syrupy. Strain and keep warm in a bain-marie* otherwise it will become too stiff to apply. Use the apricot glaze for yellow fruits, or make a red currant glaze in the same way but omit the lemon juice. If you want to glaze both fruit and pastry, make a double quantity of the glaze. Brush the hot glaze over and leave to set.

Lemon tart

This is a tart with very pure lemon flavours, and easy to make.

For one 24cm tart, for 6–8	shortcrust pastry made with 200g flour (p. 491)	150g sugar
		juice of 3–4 lemons, about 120ml
	3 eggs	4 tbs double cream.

Heat the oven to 200°C, 400°F, gas 6. Roll out the pastry and line the tin, preferably one with a removable base. Prick the pastry with a fork in several places and follow the notes on baking blind on p. 490. Lower the heat further to 150°C, 300°F, gas 2.

Just before the shell is fully baked, prepare the filling. Beat the eggs and sugar until thick and pale – an electric mixer or an electric hand whisk does the job well – and keep whisking as you slowly add the lemon juice and then the cream. Pour the mixture into the tart shell and bake for about 40 minutes until set. Leave to cool.

Pecan pie

A traditional pie from the southern states of America for which there are dozens of recipes. I use dark muscovado sugar, but corn syrup or molasses or even non-traditional maple syrup from New England can be used to replace part of the sugar.

For one 24cm tart, for 6–8	200g dark muscovado sugar	200g pecan nuts, coarsely broken
	1 tbs flour	150ml double cream
shortcrust pastry made with 200g flour (p. 491)	4 tbs milk	1 tbs icing sugar
2 eggs	4 tbs melted butter	1 tbs bourbon or Scotch whisky

Heat the oven to 200°C, 400°F, gas 6. Line a 24cm tart tin, preferably one with a removable base, with the pastry. Beat the eggs lightly, add the sugar, flour, milk and butter and stir until smooth. Stir in the pecans then pour the filling into the pastry shell. Bake for 10 minutes, then reduce the heat to 180°C, 350°F, gas 4, and bake for a further 35–40 minutes, or until set. Leave to cool. Serve with whipped cream flavoured with icing sugar and bourbon or Scotch whisky.

Tarte Tatin

This upside-down tart is usually made with apples, but pears, plums and figs are good too (although plums and figs release more juice which can make it tricky to turn the tart out). If you have a sturdy metal pie dish, 24–26cm in diameter, with sides 5–6cm high, use that. A paella or similar pan with metal handles would also do. Otherwise, caramelise the fruit in a frying pan and transfer it to another fixed-base tin or dish for baking.

For one 24–26cm tart, for 6–8	shortcrust pastry made with 200g flour (p. 491)	1kg medium eating apples
		75g butter
		75g sugar

Heat the oven to 190°C, 375°F, gas 5. Peel, quarter and core the apples. Heat the butter and sugar in the tin over low heat and cook until you have a dark golden caramel. Don't let it burn or it will be bitter. Remove the tin from the heat and put in the apples, rounded side down. Roll out the pastry and fit it over the fruit, letting the edges fall against the inside edge of the tin. Tuck it in between the tin and the fruit. Make a couple of slits in the pastry to allow steam to escape and bake for 45–50 minutes. The pastry should be golden brown, and the liquid bubbling up around the sides should be a rich brown syrup. If the pastry is getting too dark, cover it with a piece of foil.

To turn out the tart, wait for 10 minutes or so and then place a large plate over the tart and turn it over. The juices will be hot, so take care. If the apples are not nicely caramelised, sprinkle caster sugar over them and put the tart under a hot grill for a few minutes before serving. Serve the tart warm with crème fraîche.

Puff pastry tarts

Crisp apple tarts

For 6	5–6 crisp eating apples	3 tbs caster sugar
340g frozen puff pastry, defrosted	60g butter, melted	

Heat the oven to 220°C, 425°F, gas 7. Lightly grease two baking sheets. Cut the pastry into 6 equal pieces and roll out each piece thinly. Take a small plate or bowl with a diameter of about 15cm, place it on each piece of pastry and cut round it so that you have 6 discs. Place them on the baking sheets and prick with a fork in several places, but not around the outer edge. This is to stop the pastry rising too much or unevenly while baking.

Peel, quarter and core the apples and slice them thinly. Lay them in neat overlapping circles on the pastry, leaving a rim of about 1 cm round the edge. Brush the tarts, both fruit and pastry rim, with melted butter and sprinkle over the sugar. Bake the tarts for 12–15 minutes, swapping the trays over halfway through if you have one low down in the oven and the other near the top. The pastry should be crisp and puffed round the edges of the tarts. Serve hot.

Raspberry and cream tart

For 4	250g raspberries	1 egg, lightly beaten
1 sheet ready-rolled frozen puff pastry, defrosted	100g thick yogurt	50ml double cream
	100g ricotta	75g caster sugar

Heat the oven to 220°C, 425°F, gas 7. Unroll the pastry to fit onto a lightly floured baking tray (I use a 20 x 30cm tin with a shallow rim). Prick all over with a fork. Arrange the raspberries on the pastry. Whisk together the yogurt, ricotta, egg, cream and sugar and pour over the raspberries. Bake for 20–25 minutes, until the cream is just set. Serve warm or cold.

Variations

- Use shortcrust pastry made with 150g flour (p. 491) and line a 20cm tin.
- Combine red currants and raspberries.
- Replace raspberries by cherries or blueberries.

Filo pastries

For general notes on using filo pastry, *see* p. 493.

Baklava

This many-layered pastry with nuts and honey syrup is popular throughout the Middle East. The pastry shops are laden with all sorts of sumptuous cakes, but they are always rated by the quality of their baklava. This recipe uses walnuts, but baklava is also made with almonds or pistachios.

For 16–20 pastries	250g walnuts, chopped coarsely	150ml water
500g filo pastry		150g sugar
200g unsalted butter, melted	3 tbs caster sugar	4 tbs honey
	2 tsp ground cardamom seeds* or cinnamon	1 tbs lemon juice

Heat the oven to 170°C, 325°F, gas 3. While working with filo, keep the waiting sheets covered with a tea towel so that they do not dry out. Brush the sides and bottom of a Swiss roll or similar baking tin with butter. Lay half the sheets of filo in the tin, brushing each one with butter, and folding or cutting the sheets as necessary to fit.

Mix together the nuts, caster sugar and spice and spread the mixture over the pastry. Cover with the remaining sheets of buttered pastry. With a very sharp knife cut the pastry into lozenges or squares. Bake for about 1 hour, or until the pastry is crisp, puffed and golden.

While it is baking, prepare the syrup. Heat the water with the 150g sugar, honey and lemon juice, bring to the boil and simmer for about 5 minutes, until it thickens enough to coat the back of a spoon. Let it cool.

As soon as the baklava comes from the oven spoon the cool syrup over it evenly and leave to cool before lifting the pieces out onto a serving plate.

Cherry strudel

For 4–6	90g walnuts, chopped finely, or 50g fresh white breadcrumbs	1 jar or can (about 450g) morello cherries, drained well
6 sheets filo pastry		
50g butter, melted	90g sugar	

Heat the oven to 190°C, 375°F, gas 5. Spread a clean tea towel on the work surface. Put one sheet of filo on it, with the long side towards you. Keep the other sheets wrapped in another towel. Brush the filo lightly with butter. Take a second sheet and place it half over the first sheet, increasing the depth. Butter it lightly. Do the same with the third sheet. Place the fourth sheet on top of the first and repeat the sequence, buttering each sheet as you go.

Spread the walnuts or breadcrumbs and sugar along the front edge, leaving a border of 5–6 cm at either end. Pile the cherries on top of the nuts and sugar. With the help of the tea towel, start to roll the strudel into a sausage shape. Tuck in the sides to prevent the fruit falling out. Just before you get to the end, lightly butter the last strip of pastry so that it sticks firmly to the strudel. Use the tea towel to lift the strudel onto a baking sheet with the seam underneath. Bake for about 30 minutes until golden brown. Serve hot or cold.

Variations

Apple strudel Replace the cherries by 600g peeled, cored and very thinly sliced eating apples, 60g raisins, the grated rind of 1 unwaxed lemon, ½ tsp cinnamon, ¼ tsp ground cloves. In a bowl mix all these ingredients thoroughly with your hands and spread them on top of the nuts or breadcrumbs and sugar.

Mincemeat and apple strudel Replace the cherries by 350g mincemeat (p. 507) and 2 eating apples, peeled, cored and grated.

Choux pastries

Chocolate profiteroles

For 18–20 buns	250ml double cream	80ml water
choux pastry made with 3 eggs (p. 492)	30g caster sugar	30g butter
	For the chocolate sauce	80ml double cream
1 egg	150g plain chocolate	

Heat the oven to 200°C, 400°F, gas 6. Grease two baking trays. Drop large teaspoonfuls of choux paste onto the trays, leaving plenty of space between them, or pipe the mixture into small rounds. Beat the egg lightly and brush the buns with it to glaze them. Bake the buns for 20–25 minutes until brown and crisp.

Remove them to a rack to cool and make a slit in the side of each one to release steam. Whip the cream lightly with the caster sugar and spoon or pipe some into each bun when cool. Set them on a serving dish.

Melt the chocolate with the water in a bowl over hot water. Stir, and when it is smooth add the butter and cream. Keep the sauce warm over hot water. Pour it over the profiteroles just before serving.

Variations

- Replace the chocolate sauce by a fruit coulis (p. 400)
- Replace the whipped cream by ice cream. Keep in the refrigerator until ready to serve.

Hot fruit desserts

In addition to the desserts below, *see* the tarts in the preceding section.

Fruit fritters

Fruit can be sprinkled with sugar and spices, macerated in rum or kirsch or brandy for 30 minutes before being cooked. Dry the pieces well otherwise the batter won't coat them properly.

Prepare the fritter batter as described on p. 496. Peel and core apples and cut into rings; choose firm apricots, cut them in half and remove the stone; cut bananas into 3 or 4 pieces; choose firm peaches, peel, halve or quarter and remove the stone; choose firm pears, peel, core and quarter them; peel and slice pineapple, cut the slices in half and remove the hard centre; choose firm plums, cut them in half and remove the stone.

Dip the fruit pieces in batter and fry. Sprinkle them with sugar and serve at once.

Apple pancakes

For 10–12 pancakes	3 firm eating apples	2 tbs sugar
10–12 pancakes (p. 494)	30g butter	¼ tsp cinnamon

Heat the oven to 150°C, 300°F, gas 2. Peel, core and slice the apples and fry them gently in the butter. After 4–5 minutes they will soften and release their juices. Sprinkle over the sugar and cinnamon; turn the apples so that they caramelise lightly. Fill the pancakes with the apples, roll them up and put them in a shallow buttered baking dish. Cover with foil and heat through for 10 minutes. Serve with whipped cream.

Variations

Apricot and almond Mix 200g apricot jam with 2 tbs rum and 80g chopped blanched almonds, spread over the pancakes, roll, sprinkle with icing sugar and serve.

Fruit purée Make a thick fruit purée (p. 398), spread it over the pancakes, roll, sprinkle with icing sugar and serve.

Maple pecans Spread the pancakes with maple syrup, scatter over chopped pecans, roll up and serve.

Cream cheese and raisins Stir raisins and chopped nuts into well-drained cream cheese or mascarpone, spoon into the centre of the pancakes, fold in four and heat through for 10 minutes at 150C, 300F, gas 2. Top with soured cream or crème fraîche if you wish.

Baked apples

These apples are filled with soft muscovado sugar, but you could also stuff them with crushed stem ginger, raisins, mincemeat, chopped dates or prunes.

For 4	50g butter	125ml apple juice, cider or water
4 cooking apples	150–180g muscovado sugar	

Heat the oven to 200°C, 400°F, gas 6. Core the apples and make a shallow cut in the skin around the circumference of each one; this is to prevent the skins bursting. Butter an ovenproof dish just big enough to hold them without touching. Put in the apples, fill the cavities with sugar and pour the liquid around the apples. Dot each one with butter and bake for 40–50 minutes, until they can easily be pierced with a skewer.

Variation

· Baked apples can be cooked quickly in a microwave. Core them and remove a round of peel from the top. Fill the cavity, add 2 tsp apple juice to each apple and wrap tightly in microwave plastic. Put the apples into a dish and for apples weighing about 150g, microwave on full power for 2½ minutes. Leave to rest for 2 minutes before opening.

Apricot hazelnut crumble

For 6–8	60g caster sugar	100g plain flour
1kg apricots, halved and stoned	grated rind of 1 unwaxed orange	100g dark muscovado sugar
3 tbs port	100g hazelnuts	100g butter

Heat the oven to 200°C, 400°F, gas 6. Put the apricots in a shallow ovenproof dish with the port, caster sugar and orange rind. Roast and peel the hazelnuts (p. 488). Grind them fairly finely in a food processor. Add the flour and muscovado sugar to the nuts and whiz to combine them. Chop the butter into small pieces, add them and process until the mixture resembles breadcrumbs. Scatter the mixture evenly over the apricots and bake for 45–50 minutes. Serve hot or warm.

Variations
· Instead of apricots, use rhubarb, cut in short lengths, with 3 tbs orange juice instead of port.

Bananas with cinnamon and rum

A very quick winter pudding, or in summer you could grill the bananas on a barbecue.

For 4	½ tsp ground cinnamon	2 tbs light muscovado sugar
4 firm bananas	75ml dark rum	50g walnuts, chopped coarsely
50g butter		

Peel and cut the bananas in half lengthwise (for barbecuing leave them whole and cut them after grilling). Heat half the butter in a frying pan and stir in the cinnamon. Fry the bananas until soft, then lift them out onto a serving dish. Add the remaining butter to the pan, stir in the rum, sugar and walnuts. Cook for 3–4 minutes, then pour the sauce over the bananas and serve at once.

Blackberry and apple brown betty

For 6–8	½ tsp ground cinnamon	150g sugar
125g butter		125ml apple juice
150g day-old breadcrumbs	¼ tsp ground cloves	200g blackberries
750g tart eating apples	grated rind of ½ unwaxed lemon	

Heat the oven to 190°C, 375°F, gas 5. Melt the butter and fry the breadcrumbs lightly. Peel, core and slice the apples. Mix them thoroughly with the cinnamon, cloves, lemon rind, sugar and apple juice. Stir in the blackberries. Spread half the fruit in a pie dish or soufflé dish, cover with half the breadcrumbs. Repeat the layers. Cover the dish with foil and bake for 25 minutes, then remove the foil and bake for another 20 minutes until the crumbs are crisp. Serve with whipped cream or ice cream.

Clafoutis

This fruit and batter pudding comes from the Limousin region of France. It is traditionally made with cherries, but other fruits such as halved and stoned apricots or plums cooked in a little butter can be used instead.

For 6–8	3 eggs	pinch of salt
400g cherries, stoned	60g sugar	2 tsp vanilla extract (or use vanilla sugar*)
250ml milk or single cream	60g plain flour, sifted	icing sugar

Heat the oven to 200°C, 400°F, gas 6. Put the cherries in a shallow lightly buttered 1–1.5 litre ovenproof dish. Put the milk or cream, eggs, sugar, flour, salt and vanilla extract into a food processor or blender and whiz for 1 minute at high speed. Pour the batter over the fruit and bake for 30–35 minutes, until the clafoutis is puffed up and lightly browned. Serve warm, rather than hot, sprinkled with icing sugar.

Grilled nectarines with orange and ginger syrup

For 4–6	4 tbs clear honey	8 nectarines
400ml water	5cm unpeeled piece of ginger, sliced thinly	2 tbs icing sugar
juice of 2 oranges		30g butter

Put the water, orange juice, honey and ginger into a pan over medium heat. Stir until the honey dissolves, bring to the boil and simmer for 12–15 minutes, until the mixture is somewhat reduced and syrupy. Pour the syrup into a jug, cool and refrigerate. Leave it for at least 1 hour to get cold, or put it into the freezer for 10 minutes.

Cut the nectarines in half and remove the stones. Heat the grill. Put the fruit, open side up, on a grill tray lined with foil, sprinkle with icing sugar and dot with butter. Grill 5–6 cm from the heat source for 8–10 minutes until the nectarines are golden. Transfer them to a serving dish or individual bowls and pour over the strained syrup. Serve with shortbread fingers (p. 481).

Variations

Grilled nectarines with mascarpone and preserved ginger Fill the hollows in the nectarines with 125g mascarpone or fromage blanc mixed with 3–4 pieces of chopped preserved ginger. Grill, without added sugar or butter, and serve with a fruit coulis made with raspberries (p. 400).

Grilled peaches with coconut cream Prepare as above, allowing 1 large peach per person, and serve with coconut cream (p. 401).

Peach and raspberry brûlée

This is not the chef's way to make a brûlée with a carefully judged caramel poured over chilled cream, and a blow torch or hot iron to achieve a perfect finish – but it is very fast and easy, and tastes delicious.

For 4	125g raspberries	6 tbs light muscovado sugar
2 large or 4 small peaches	125ml soured cream or crème fraîche	

Heat the grill. Stone and slice the peaches and put them with the raspberries in a shallow ovenproof dish or in individual ramekins that can go to the table. Spoon the cream evenly over the fruit and rub the sugar through a sieve over the top. Put the dish under the hot grill for 3–4 minutes (put ramekins on a baking tray first) until the sugar melts and the cream is bubbling. Serve at once, or chill for 3–4 hours.

Variations
· Most soft fruits respond well to the brûlée treatment: bananas, blackberries, figs, mangoes, nectarines, passion fruit, pineapple, red currants, strawberries – choose a combination you like. And for a richer dish, use double cream.

Spiced pineapple

This recipe comes from Christine Manfield's excellent book *Spice*.

For 4–6	1 vanilla pod, split	2 tbs brown sugar
50g clarified butter*	2 star anise*	2 tbs honey
600g ripe pineapple	40ml dark rum	

Peel the pineapple, remove the hard core and dice the flesh. Melt the clarified butter in a frying pan and cook the pineapple with the vanilla pod and star anise over moderate heat until caramelised slightly. Stir in the rum, sugar and honey and cook for another 5 minutes. Remove the pan from the heat and discard the spices. Strain the pineapple and serve warm.

I serve this with ice cream, or with a chilled coconut cream (p. 401). Cooled, it can also be used to fill tarts.

Pancakes filled with walnuts

For 6 pancakes	1 tbs grated unwaxed orange rind	60ml milk
6 pancakes (p. 494)		2 egg yolks, beaten
100ml single cream	100g raisins	1 tsp cornflour
100g sugar	2 tbs brandy or rum	1 tbs unsweetened cocoa
250g walnuts, coarsely ground	**For the chocolate sauce**	
	125g plain chocolate	2 tbs caster sugar
	3 tbs water	2 tbs brandy or rum

Heat the oven to 150°C, 300°F, gas 2. Heat the cream and when it is simmering add the sugar, walnuts, orange rind and raisins. Simmer over very low heat for 1–2 minutes. Take the pan from the heat and stir in the alcohol. Spread a tablespoon of filling over the middle of each pancake and fold in four, to make a fan. Put the filled pancakes into a lightly buttered dish, cover with foil and put in the oven while you make the sauce.

Melt the chocolate with the water in a bowl over simmering water. Stir as it melts so that it remains smooth. Stir in the milk and egg yolks, then the dry ingredients and finally the brandy or rum. Keep stirring so that the sauce is smooth. If it is too thick, add a little more milk. Spoon a little of the sauce over each pancake to serve.

Favourite hot desserts

Hot chocolate soufflé

For notes on making soufflés, *see* p. 61.

For 4	30ml water or black coffee	50g vanilla sugar* or caster sugar
125g plain chocolate	4 egg yolks	6 egg whites

Heat the oven to 200°C, 400°F, gas 6, and butter a 1.2-litre soufflé dish. Put in a tablespoon of caster sugar, turn the dish around to coat the bottom and sides and tip out any excess.

Melt the chocolate with the water or coffee in a bowl over hot water. Remove from the heat and stir until the chocolate is smooth. Beat the egg yolks and sugar for 1–2 minutes until pale and add them to the chocolate. Whisk the egg whites until they hold stiff peaks and fold them into the chocolate mixture. Turn the mixture into the soufflé dish and bake for 20–25 minutes. Serve cold single cream with the soufflé.

Bread and butter pudding

For 4–6	5 eggs	300ml double cream
60g currants	2 egg yolks	1 vanilla pod or 1 tsp vanilla extract
60g butter	125g sugar	
12 thin slices of french bread	600ml full milk	icing sugar

Heat the oven to 180°C, 350°F, gas 4. Soak the currants in a little warm water for 10 minutes, then drain thoroughly. Butter the slices of bread, keeping a scrap of butter to grease a large shallow ovenproof dish. Scatter half the currants in the bottom of the dish, arrange the bread on top, buttered side up. Scatter the rest of the currants over the bread. Whisk the eggs, egg yolks and sugar until thick and pale.

Heat the milk and cream with the vanilla pod, but do not boil. Pour the milk and cream gradually into the eggs, stirring as you do so. Remove the vanilla pod; if you are using vanilla extract, add it now. Strain the custard over the bread.

Set the dish in a large roasting tin and pour in hot water to come about halfway up the sides of the dish. Bake for 45–50 minutes, at which point it will still be slightly wobbly in the middle. Remove from the oven, sprinkle generously with icing sugar and glaze quickly under a hot grill.

Louisiana bread pudding with cognac sauce

Bread pudding, usually served with a bourbon whisky or cognac sauce, is an established classic in the restaurants of New Orleans, and there are recipes for it in local cookery books from the late 19th century onwards. This version is based on the recipe in *The Plantation Cookbook*, compiled by the Junior League of New Orleans. I have added pecans, which are not in their recipe, but which were in some of the puddings I ate in New Orleans.

For 6	80g raisins	1 tsp vanilla extract
500ml full milk	80g pecan nuts, chopped	**For the cognac sauce**
50g butter	2 eggs	50g butter
125g sugar	pinch of salt	120g icing sugar
½ day-old french loaf, cubed	½ tsp grated nutmeg	30ml cognac

Heat the milk, add the butter off the heat and let it melt. Stir in the sugar. Put the bread, raisins and pecans in a large bowl and pour over the milk mixture. Leave to stand for 15 minutes. Heat the oven to 180°C, 350°F, gas 4. Whisk the eggs, add the salt, nutmeg and vanilla and pour into the bread and milk. Mix thoroughly. Grease a medium baking dish, tip in the pudding mixture and bake for 35–45 minutes.

To make the sauce, cream the butter and sugar and gradually add the cognac. Serve the pudding warm, topped with the sauce.

Indian rice pudding (Kheer)

Do not think of this as a relation of English rice pudding – it is utterly different, is cooked for several hours so that the rice breaks down and the pudding has the consistency of a very thick cream.

For 6–8

1 litre milk

75g long grain rice

about 125g caster sugar

75g raisins or mixed dried fruit

40g dried apricots, cut small

seeds of 6 cardamoms*, bruised

2–3cm cinnamon stick

rose-water (p. 398)

slivered almonds or pistachios (optional)

Bring the milk to the boil. Add the rice, stir and boil for a minute or two, then put the pan on a pre-heated diffuser on the lowest heat (to make the change-over less brutal) and cook, covered, for 1½–2 hours, stirring occasionally during the first 15 minutes.

Add the sugar (the amount depends on how sweet you like your pudding), the fruit and the spices; stir them through, then cook for another hour or longer – the pudding should be of a thick just-pouring consistency. It can then be eaten hot, but is much better chilled in individual pots and if possible left for the next day.

Before serving, sprinkle a little rose-water and/or slivered almonds or pistachios on top. In India, kheer is often decorated with edible gold or silver leaf (which can be bought from Indian grocers).

Rice pudding with meringue

I am not aware of contemporary English recipes for this rather elegant version of rice pudding, but it occurs in Eliza Acton's *Modern Cookery* of 1845, and in present-day Spanish cookery books.

For 4–6

800ml full milk

100g sugar

peel of 1 unwaxed lemon

125g short-grain rice

3 eggs, separated

3 tbs caster sugar

Bring the milk to the boil with the 100g sugar and lemon peel, add the rice and simmer very gently over a heat diffuser for 30–40 minutes, stirring frequently until the rice becomes creamy but not dry (the timing depends on the rice and its absorption capacity). Remove the pan from the heat, discard the lemon peel and stir in the egg yolks.

Heat the oven to 180°C, 350°F, gas 4. Butter a pudding dish and pour the rice mixture into it. Whisk the egg whites to soft peaks, sprinkle over them the caster sugar and whisk again until they are firm. Spread the meringue evenly over the pudding and bake for about 20–25 minutes until the meringue is golden; do not let it get too dark. Serve straight from the oven.

Budino di ricotta

In old English recipes for curd cheese desserts, the curd is often bound with ground almonds or fresh breadcrumbs, and baked in a tart crust. Spicing of cinnamon or cloves with nutmeg or mace was common.

For the Italian version, the ricotta must be dry, so if the one you buy is soft and moist, leave it to drain for an hour or two in a fine sieve.

For 4–6	¼ tsp grated nutmeg	40g raisins
500g ricotta	40g candied orange peel, diced	grated rind of 1 unwaxed lemon
5 eggs		
90g sugar	40g candied citron peel, diced	4 tbs rum
40g flour		icing sugar

Put the drained ricotta into a large bowl. Separate 4 of the eggs, and beat the yolks and the whole egg into the ricotta, one at a time. Beat in all the other ingredients in the order listed, except for the egg whites and icing sugar. The mixture should be very smooth. Whisk the egg whites until stiff, stir a large spoonful into the ricotta mixture to loosen it, then fold in the remainder (p. 49). Generously butter a 22cm cake tin. Spoon in the mixture; the tin should be about half to two-thirds full. Bake for 30–35 minutes until the budino is puffed and golden.

Sprinkle with icing sugar and serve. I find the pudding best hot, but leftovers are good cold.

Christmas pudding

My Christmas pudding recipe is from Eliza Acton's *Modern Cookery*. She includes several plum pudding recipes – this one is Ingoldsby Christmas pudding with proportions reduced to make one pudding rather than the three of Miss Acton's recipe.

I have always made what she describes as the very rich version, by cutting the amount of breadcrumbs and flour still further. As we have a vegetarian in the family, the pudding is always made with vegetarian suet.

For 8	120g currants	pinch of salt
60g fresh white breadcrumbs	120g sugar	½ tsp grated nutmeg
	120g candied peel, chopped	½ tsp mixed spice
60g flour		3 eggs
120g suet or vegetarian suet	grated rind of ½ unwaxed lemon	1 small glass of brandy
120g raisins		2 tbs apricot jam

Mix thoroughly the breadcrumbs and flour. Stir in the suet, raisins, currants, sugar, candied peel, lemon rind, salt and spices. Beat the eggs well, strain them into the mixture, add the brandy and the apricot jam. Turn the mixture into one large or two small pudding basins. The basin should be quite full, but not to the brim.

Cut circles of foil and greaseproof paper a few centimetres larger than the top of the basin. Cover first with greaseproof, then with foil, tying the covers firmly beneath the rim of the basin. Stand the basin on a rack or an inverted old saucer in a large pan, pour in boiling water to come two-thirds of the way up the basin, cover the pan and steam for 4 hours. Check from time to time to see if more water is needed and add more boiling water as necessary. Lift out the pudding when it is done, cool, replace the paper cover with a clean one and store in a cool place.

To serve, steam the pudding for a further 2 hours, and accompany with brandy or rum butter, *see* below, or sabayon sauce (p. 403).

Brandy butter

For 8–10	250g icing sugar	1 tsp lemon juice
450g unsalted butter	4 tbs brandy	a little grated nutmeg

Cut the butter into pieces, put it into a food processor with all the other ingredients and whiz for 2–3 minutes.

Variation
Rum butter As above except replacing the icing sugar by light muscovado sugar and the brandy by rum.

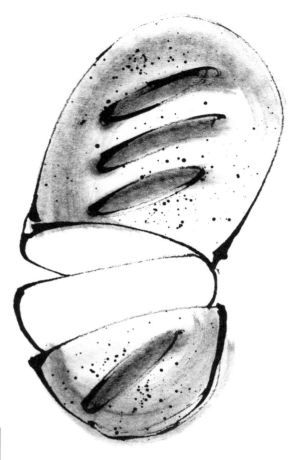

Bread

Good bread is the most satisfying of all foods and the smell
of freshly baked bread whets the appetite more than any
other. Bread making is not difficult, nor as time-consuming
as many people suppose. The bread needs time and warmth
for the yeast to do its work, but that does not require your time. Many non-yeast
breads and quick breads are mixed and baked within an hour. The basic ingredients for
bread are flour, water, salt and yeast or another leavening agent – a
sourdough starter or baking soda, baking powder or cream of tartar.
Bread can be enriched with milk, buttermilk or yogurt, oil or melted
butter, eggs, sugar or molasses, dried fruit or nuts, herbs or spices.

Flours

Flours are ground from seeds, principally from cereals. Wheat flour is the most adaptable and most widely used for baking. A wheat kernel consists of three parts: the bran or outer husk, the germ or embryo of the future plant, and the inner part of the kernel or endosperm that is full of starch and proteins. Flours milled from different types of wheat have different uses.

Wholemeal flour contains all of the grain. It tastes slightly nutty and has a high fibre content from the husk, and vitamins and oils from the germ. Wholemeal flour is primarily used for bread making. The particles of bran inhibit aeration, so wholemeal breads are heavier than white. Stoneground wholemeal is ground in the old way between circular stones and generally has a better flavour than roller-milled flour. Roller-milling produces a wholemeal that is finer in texture; the bran and germ are extracted during processing and then returned to the flour.

Any flour containing the wheat germ and its oil will not keep for more than 3–4 months without turning rancid.

White flours are milled from the inner part of the grain only. Stored in a cool dry place, white flours will keep for at least a year.

Strong plain white flour, also called bread flour, is mostly milled from hard wheat that has a high gluten potential. The proteins in wheat flour form gluten when liquid is added. Gluten expands during kneading, trapping the air, to produce an elastic dough that gives a lighter loaf that holds its shape well. Strong plain flour may be bleached or unbleached. It is usually roller-milled, but some stoneground flour is available.

Durum flour, or fine semolina, is a high-gluten flour from durum (the hardest) wheat, ground twice to produce a silky flour used primarily for making pasta. It also makes good bread if combined with unbleached plain flour.

OO and O flours. Italian hard wheat flours are classified by how much bran and grain have been removed in the milling process. OO is the most refined, a white, silky flour. O is less fine and contains more of the grain. Both are finer than English plain flour.

Plain flour is multi-purpose flour. Usually made with a high proportion of soft low-gluten wheat, it is frequently bleached. It absorbs less water than strong flour. Plain flour is good for pastry, cakes and batters, but bread made with plain flour goes stale quickly.

Self-raising flour is plain flour to which baking powder has been added. If the flour is old or has been badly stored, the aerating properties will be affected. It is generally better to use plain flour and add the necessary amount of baking powder according to the recipe.

Granary flour is a blend of wholemeal, white and rye flours with the addition of malted grains which give bread made with it a sweetish flavour.

Rye flour, which may be dark or light, inhibits gluten development. It is widely used for bread making in Scandinavia and northern Europe. Rye breads are very dense unless a blend of rye and wheat flours is used.

Barley flour lacks gluten and is best mixed with wheat flour. It adds an interesting earthy tang to bread.

Oatmeal also lacks gluten and is mostly used with wheat flour to give bread a more crunchy texture.

Cornmeal or maize meal is another gluten-free meal. It is used primarily in Italy and parts of the Balkans to make polenta (p. 197) and in the Americas to make non-yeast breads (p. 199). It has a gritty texture and sweetish taste.

Corn flour is milled from the endosperm of the maize kernels and is almost pure starch. Sometimes used with plain flour for baking, it is principally used for thickening sauces.

Buckwheat flour is speckled greyish brown and has a slightly bitter flavour. Gluten-free, it can be combined with wheat flour to make bread; it is also used for pancakes and noodles. Buckwheat flour will keep for 6 months.

Gram flour, also called besan, is made from a small variety of chick pea. Beige in colour, with an earthy note, the taste is pleasantly nutty. It gives a good flavour to flat breads. In India, it is used for the batter for fritters and vegetable bhajias, and is mixed with wheat flour for breads. Gram flour will keep for 6–9 months.

Rice flour is gluten-free but has more starch than wheat flour. It is easy to digest.

Potato flour is often used with other flours or alone to make sponge cakes. It has a light, creamy taste and is gluten-free. It is also used as a thickening agent.

Gluten-free flour is a blend of flours – usually rice, potato, buckwheat and cornmeal. It absorbs more water than wheat flours and can be used for all types of baking except yeast baking.

Tins and trays for baking

Non-stick are best but even non-stick tins sometimes stick, so it is best to grease them. For bread, use 500g or 1kg loaf tins or bake free-form loaves on trays dusted with flour or cornmeal. A re-usable cooking liner can be useful too. Muffins can be made in shaped trays or in paper cases.

Yeasts

Working with yeast is the aspect of bread making that many people find daunting, and I would recommend first time bread makers to use easy-blend yeast. These are tiny granules that are stirred into the flour with the salt. Fresh and dried yeasts must first be dissolved in water.

Fresh yeast is the yeast I prefer to work with. A few supermarkets and some bakers sell it. If you buy a quantity, cut it into 30g pieces and freeze them. The yeast remains in good condition for at least 6 months. Fresh yeast is dissolved in water heated to blood temperature (38°C, 100°F) before being added to the flour. If you can put your finger into the water and it feels to be the same temperature, you can add the yeast. Water that is too hot kills off the yeast.

Dried yeast is also reactivated by soaking in warm water. It needs 15–20 minutes for the granules to absorb enough water and make a frothy cream.

Easy-blend yeast is sprinkled over the flour and well mixed in. The addition of liquid activates it. As easy to use as the name indicates, it is a better choice than ordinary dried yeast.

Time and temperature are as important as the amount of yeast when it comes to how much yeast to use. For plain bread, 30g of fresh yeast will leaven 1.5kg flour in

2–3 hours. A yeast dough rises fastest in a warm room, but too much heat slows it down. The ideal rising time is 4–5 hours in a cool place; you can also leave the dough all day or overnight. In very cold weather, stand the bowl on a thick wodge of newspaper or tea towels on the central heating boiler.

For a long slow fermentation, 15g yeast will be enough for 1.5kg flour. Bread that has a long fermentation period has a better texture, more complex flavours and stays moist longer. To slow down the fermentation, put the dough in the refrigerator, but let it come back to room temperature before attempting to knead it. A larger amount of yeast does not make for a better loaf, it simply enables the dough to rise more quickly but, without the maturing provided by time, moisture and warmth, flavour does not develop in the bread. Too much yeast also makes the bread go dry and stale quickly.

Dried yeast is much more potent than fresh, and only one-third to half the amount (10–15g) is required for 1.5kg flour. For a small amount of dough for a pizza or small loaf, ¼ tsp granules is enough.

Easy-blend yeast is twice as potent as dried yeast, so you only need a quarter (7g or 1 sachet) or less of the amount of fresh yeast to 1.5kg flour.

Enriched doughs made with eggs, butter and fruit need more yeast than plain breads, but the proportions of 30g fresh yeast: 15g dried yeast: 7g easy-blend yeast still apply.

Chemical leavens

Breads raised with chemical leavens are easy and quick to make, require no or little kneading, but do not keep as well as yeasted breads.

Bicarbonate of soda, also known as baking soda, is the most widely used non-yeast leaven. In combination with an acidic liquid such as sour milk or buttermilk, it gives off carbon dioxide which expands the dough during baking and makes the bread rise.

Baking powder is bicarbonate of soda mixed with cream of tartar, an acid which causes the same reaction as the sour milk.

Making the bread

Mixing and kneading

Mix the basic ingredients in a large bowl. Flour varies in its ability to absorb water, so add the water a little at a time, especially towards the end. If the dough is too wet, add a little more flour; if too dry, add a little more water. The dough should be sticky, not runny or stiff. It is then ready to be kneaded.

Kneading develops the gluten, allowing the dough to trap the gas given off by the yeast and so to stretch and expand. Put the dough mixture on a floured surface. Hold it with one hand and with the heel of the other push the dough gently away from you until it starts to break. Fold it back and give the dough a quarter turn. Work lightly, but firmly. Set up a rhythm of pushing, folding and turning for 8–10 minutes until the dough feels firm, supple and smooth. If necessary, flour your hands lightly as you work, but do not incorporate more flour into the dough.

You can mix and knead dough in a food processor or electric mixer. Check how much your machine will hold and divide the ingredients into batches. It is important not to overheat and stress the dough, so run the machine at low speed and use the pulse function on a food processor.

If using a mixer, put in the flour and the yeast with its liquid and use the paddle to mix the dough. Add the water gradually. Replace the paddle with the dough hook and knead until the dough comes away from the sides of the bowl and collects around the hook.

If using a food processor, use the dough blade. Put in the flour and yeast and feed the liquid in through the tube and run the machine until the dough forms a ball. Leave to rest for a few minutes, then process again for 30 seconds to 1 minute.

In both cases, transfer the dough to a work surface and knead by hand for 2–3 minutes to improve its elasticity.

Proving and knocking back

After kneading the dough until it is smooth and elastic, put it into a bowl, cover with clingfilm or a cloth and leave to prove. *See* the notes on p. 442 about temperatures and rising times. Most breads need more than one rising to achieve an even crumb. The dough will double in size; do not let it rise too much. Press the dough with your finger: when it is ready it should feel spongy and the finger indentation should not spring back too quickly. When the dough has risen, knock it back by punching it in the middle to release the gases, divide it if necessary and knead each piece into a ball and then into the appropriate shape, with the folds underneath. To form a round, cup your hands around the piece of dough and apply light pressure downwards while rotating the dough. For a long loaf, make a ball then flatten it with your hand and fold it in three. Seal the folds together with lightly floured hands and put the seam underneath. For a tin loaf, shape as a long loaf and fold under the ends to fit the tin.

Put free-form loaves on a lightly warmed and floured baking tray; dough for a tin loaf into a pre-greased tin. Cover with a cloth and leave to prove again for about 50 minutes. Dough that half filled a bread tin should have almost reached the top.

Slashing the loaf

Cuts made in the surface allow the dough to expand as it bakes without cracking along the sides. Use a very sharp knife or scalpel. Cut decisively, making slashes of equal length and of about 1cm depth. Let the cut dough rest for 5 minutes before baking.

Glazing

A loaf can be glazed just before baking; this gives the crust a finished appearance and prevents it becoming tough or dry. Use a brush to spread the glaze over the top of the dough. The simplest glazes are olive oil, milk, salted water or an egg wash made by lightly whisking an egg with a teaspoon of water. Bread can also be glazed after baking while it is warm. Just brush the crust with water or olive oil. If you glaze the dough before baking, you can sprinkle it with nuts or seeds.

Baking the loaf

Heat the oven while the dough is proving for the second time. Bake for the time given in the recipe. To test whether the bread is done, turn the loaf upside down and rap the bottom with your knuckles. If it sounds hollow the bread is ready; if it doesn't, put it back and bake for a little longer. Cool the bread on a wire rack.

A steamy oven helps delay the formation of the crust, allowing the maximum expansion of the dough which improves the texture of the bread and eventually produces a crisp crust. Put a wide dish in the bottom of the oven and fill it with hot water. Using a plant sprayer, spray the inside of the oven before putting in the dough. Although not essential to producing good bread, this little extra trouble is worthwhile.

Problems that can occur when making bread

- *Dough doesn't rise:* stale yeast, not enough yeast, or water for creaming too hot.
- *Sour-smelling dough:* too much yeast or over-proved.
- *Bread doesn't rise:* the water for creaming the yeast may have been too hot, or the mixture was not kneaded enough. Using plain rather than strong flour can also give a poor rise. Doughs rich in fruit, butter and eggs may not rise if they have insufficient yeast.
- *Cracked crust:* not proved enough or not well shaped; oven too hot (crust sets while inner dough is still expanding).
- *Heavy bread:* too much liquid in the dough, or the dough did not rise enough before baking.

Storing and freezing bread

Store bread in a bin or tin with air holes; if kept in a sealed polythene bag or box it gives out moisture causing mould to form within a day or two.

The freezer is an excellent place to keep bread. It remains moist and fresh, although some of the crust may come loose. Thaw bread slowly at room temperature unless you have a microwave; in the microwave, bread thaws fast and the crust stays intact. Follow the manufacturer's instructions. Wrap the bread in a clean cloth for 10–15 minutes when it comes out of the microwave.

Basic bread

This bread is made with a mixture of wholemeal flour, preferably stoneground, and strong white flour. You can, however, vary the proportions or use all wholemeal or all white flour. The olive oil suggested for inclusion makes a slightly richer loaf.

To make the bread in a mixer or food processor, *see* p. 444.

For 2 loaves	20g fresh, 10g dried or 5g easy-blend yeast	approximately 700ml warm water
750g wholemeal flour		
250g strong plain white flour	1–2 tsp salt	2 tbs olive oil (optional)

Mix together the flours. Prove fresh or dried yeast in a little of the water (p. 442). Stir the salt and easy-blend yeast into the flour. Fresh yeast will prove in 5–10 minutes, dried will need 15 minutes or more. Make a well in the centre of the flour, stir the yeast to a cream and pour it into the well. Add a little more water, the olive oil if you are using it, and stir the liquid into the flour. Now add most of the remaining water and mix together to a firm, sticky dough. If it is too dry add the remaining water; too sticky, a little more flour. You can do this mixing with a spoon or by hand. The dough should come away from the sides of the bowl after a minute or two.

Turn it out onto a lightly floured surface and knead (p. 444) until it is smooth and elastic. Rinse and lightly oil the bowl, shape the dough into a ball, put it back in the bowl, cover with clingfilm or a cloth and leave to rise for about 1½ -2 hours. It will double in volume and look spongy, and if you press your finger into the surface the dent will disappear only slowly. Punch the dough down, remove it to a lightly floured surface and slap it down hard 3 or 4 times. The more the dough is knocked back now, the better the bread will be. Cut the dough in half and knead each piece into a ball. Cup your hands around the piece of dough, press lightly downwards on the sides, and turn the dough as you do so. Tuck the edges underneath. Continue until you have an even round ball. Put each one onto a warmed baking sheet sprinkled with wholemeal flour or fine cornmeal. Cover and leave to prove again until they have doubled in bulk, about 45 minutes to 1 hour.

Towards the end of the proving time, heat the oven to 230°C, 450°F, gas 8. Put a shallow dish on the bottom of the oven and fill it with hot water to create a steamy atmosphere in the oven. Cut a cross about 1cm deep in the centre of each loaf. Leave to stand for 5 minutes for the cuts to develop. Just before putting the dough into the oven spray the inside of the oven with water, using a plant sprayer.

Bake the loaves for 15 minutes, then lower the temperature to 200°C, 400°F, gas 6 and remove the dish of water from the oven. Bake for another 30–40 minutes. When it is baked the bread sounds hollow when you tap the bottom with your knuckles. Leave the bread to cool completely on a rack before putting in the bread bin or cutting.

Note

The bread can be baked in two 1kg tins. Grease and warm the tins, shape the dough to fit the tins, with the folds underneath. The dough will look inadequate for the size of the tins when you put it in, but it will rise to the top while proving the second time.

Variations

White bread Use all strong flour, preferably unbleached. You will need less water.

Herb or spice bread Herbs and spices can be added to the flour. Use 4–5 tbs finely chopped fresh herbs or 2 tbs dried for this quantity of flour. Aniseed, dill, poppy and fennel seed are also good in bread; use 2 tbs seeds.

Rolls Cut pieces weighing 30–50g from the dough after proving. Form round rolls by holding the ball of dough in one hand and folding the fingers of the other hand around it to shape it. Press and rotate the dough to form a compact ball.

To form long rolls, shape each piece into a fat baton by rolling it back and forth with your fingers. Leave rolls to prove for 20 minutes before baking at 220°C, 425°F, gas 7, for 12–15 minutes.

Rye bread

Rye flour (p. 441) is mixed with wheat flour for most breads because it lacks the capacity for gluten development. Rye breads slice thinly and keep well. A loaf made with white flour and a small amount of rye produces a delicately flavoured bread. This one uses wholemeal and is made with a starter dough which gives the bread a slightly sour taste.

For 3 loaves	200ml warm water	650g wholemeal flour
For the starter	For the dough	250g rye flour
125g wholemeal flour	20g fresh yeast or 10g dried yeast or 5g easy-blend yeast	1 tsp salt
30g rye flour		the starter dough
½ tsp fresh yeast or ¼ tsp dried yeast granules or ⅛ tsp easy-blend yeast	approximately 500ml warm water	

Make the starter 18–24 hours before you intend to bake the bread. Put fresh or dried yeast to prove in the water for 10–15 minutes, then stir in the flours and mix to a dough. Add easy-blend yeast directly to the flours and mix all at once with the water to a dough. Cover with clingfilm and leave for 18–24 hours in a warm place.

To make the bread, mix fresh or dried yeast in a little of the water and leave to prove for 10–15 minutes. Mix easy-blend yeast into the flours. Mix together the flours and salt, add the starter dough, the yeast and remaining water and mix to form a dough. Knead the dough with a dough hook in a food mixer on the lowest speed. Alternatively, knead by hand on a lightly floured surface for about 10 minutes until it is smooth and elastic (p. 443). Rinse and lightly oil the bowl, return the dough to it and cover with clingfilm or a cloth. Leave to rise until doubled in size, about 1½–2 hours. Punch down the dough, knead lightly, cut into 3 equal pieces and mould to fit 3 greased and warmed 500g tins. Make sure the folds are underneath.

Cover the tins and leave the dough to prove for a further 45 minutes. After 30 minutes heat the oven to 200°C, 400°F, gas 6. Lightly dust the loaves with flour. Bake for 55 minutes to 1 hour. Turn one loaf out of the tin, rap the bottom with your knuckles; if it sounds hollow the bread is ready. Leave the loaves to cool on a wire rack.

Elizabeth David's rice bread

This bread is very easy to mix and bake. It keeps well since the rice remains moist, and the texture is beautifully light. We often made it for taking on picnics when she was researching *English Bread and Yeast Cookery*.

For 1 large loaf	500g strong plain white flour	15–20g salt
85g uncooked rice (round or long grain)		about 250ml water
twice its volume of water	15g fresh or 7g dried or 1 tsp easy-blend yeast	

Put the rice into a 1-litre pan, cover with the measured water and bring to the boil. Cover the pan and cook steadily until the water is absorbed and little holes have formed over the surface of the rice. While the rice is cooking, prepare the other ingredients. Cream the yeast with a little warm water (if using easy-blend yeast this is added straight into the flour). Put the salt in a measuring jug and dissolve it in 150ml very hot water, then add cold water to make up 250ml.

When the rice is cooked and while it is still very warm, amalgamate it, very thoroughly, with the flour. Now add the yeast, then the salted water, and mix the dough. It will be rather soft. Cover it and leave it to rise for 1–1½ hours, until it is at least double in volume, and bubbly.

Probably the dough will be too soft to handle very much, so it may be necessary to dry it out a little by adding more flour before breaking it down and transferring it – very little kneading is necessary – to a warmed and well-greased tin or tins. For the quantity given, I use a 1kg loaf tin. The dough should fill the tin by two-thirds. Cover it with a cloth or piece of clingfilm, and leave it until has risen above the top of the tin.

Bake the bread at 230°C, 450°F, gas 8 for 15 minutes, then at 200°C, 400°F, gas 6 for another 15 minutes, before turning the loaf out of its tin and returning it to the oven, on its side, for a final 15–20 minutes at the same temperature. If the crust shows signs of baking too hard and taking too much colour, cover the loaf with a large bowl or an inverted oval casserole.

Walnut bread

This is Sally Clarke's recipe from *Sally Clarke's Book, Recipes from a restaurant, shop and bakery*.

For 2 loaves	15g fresh or 7g dried yeast or 1 tsp easy-blend yeast	50ml walnut oil
240g wholemeal flour		125g walnut halves, very roughly chopped
260g strong plain white flour	250ml warm water	
5g salt		a little extra walnut oil

In a mixer bowl, mix the flours with the salt and easy-blend yeast if you are using it. If you use fresh or dried yeast, prove it in half the warm water, then using the dough-hook attachment on your mixer at the slowest speed pour this into the bowl. Add the walnut oil and then most of the remaining warm water to produce a soft dough. Continue to knead until the dough becomes smooth, approximately 5–8 minutes, adding the remaining water if necessary. Alternatively, the mixing can be done by hand and the dough turned out and kneaded for 5–10 minutes until smooth. Place the dough in a bowl which has a light coating of walnut oil. Cover and leave in a warm place to rise to double its size. This may take up to 1 hour depending on the temperature of the kitchen and the weather.

Heat the oven to 180°C, 350°F, gas 4. Sprinkle a baking sheet with a little wholemeal flour. Remove the dough from the bowl and place it on a lightly floured surface. Sprinkle the walnuts on top and gently knead them in until they are evenly distributed, expelling the air in the dough at the same time. Cut in two and shape the loaves into balls or long sausage shapes and place on the baking sheet. Brush with a little walnut oil, cover with clingfilm or a cloth and allow to rise in a warm place to half the size again. Place on the middle shelf of the oven and immediately turn up the temperature to 200°C, 400°F, gas 6. Bake until crisp and dark golden brown. This may take up to 40–45 minutes, by which time the bread will sound hollow when the base is knocked. Cool, and use within 2 days.

Spiced flat bread

Throughout the Middle East there are flat breads topped with seeds or with zahtar, a blend of sesame seeds, thyme and sumac. The dried and ground berries of a sumac bush have a fruity sour flavour; sumac is available from Middle Eastern shops.

For 2 loaves	500g strong plain white flour	For the zahtar
15g fresh or 7g dried or 1 tsp easy-blend yeast	1 tsp salt	2 tbs sesame seeds
about 400ml warm water	olive oil	2 tbs fresh or 1 tbs dried thyme
		1 tbs sumac

First make the zahtar. Toast the sesame seeds in a dry frying pan, stirring and shaking the pan, until they darken; they will give out a little oil and a nutty aroma. Put them in a small bowl and leave to cool. Grind the thyme to a coarse powder in a coffee grinder or with a pestle and mortar. Add the sesame when it has cooled and grind it too. Transfer the mixture to a bowl and stir in the sumac. Zahtar will keep for some weeks in an airtight jar.

Prove fresh or dried yeast in a little of the warm water (p. 442), or add easy-blend yeast to the flour with the salt. Stir the yeast when it becomes creamy, make a well in the centre of the flour and add the yeast with enough of the remaining water to make a dough. Knead the dough on a floured surface until supple and elastic. If you prefer to work with the dough hook of a mixer or in the food processor, *see* p. 444.

Put the dough into a lightly oiled bowl, cover with clingfilm or a cloth and leave to rise until it has doubled in bulk, about 1½ hours.

Punch the dough down and divide in two. Roll the pieces out to rounds about 1cm thick and put them onto oiled baking sheets. Cover and leave to rise again for 30 minutes.

Heat the oven to 200°C, 400°F, gas 6. Brush the loaves with olive oil and sprinkle over each one a teaspoon of zahtar. Bake them for 10 minutes, then lower the heat to 170°C, 325°F, gas 3 and bake for a further 20–25 minutes. Cool on a rack and serve warm or at room temperature.

Variations
- Use 1 tsp aniseed, fennel seed, nigella, plain sesame seed or a mixture of sesame seeds and red pepper flakes instead of zahtar.
- Add seeds to the dough instead of scattering them on the top, and leave the top with just an oil glaze.

Herb batter bread

This is a quickly-made bread with a fast rising time that I have been making for years. The original recipe was, I think, American. I now make it in a food processor, which takes no time at all, but it can be mixed by hand, beating vigorously with a wooden spoon, or in a mixer. The dough is not kneaded. I have tried a variety of herbs and find fresh rosemary, fresh or dried thyme, dried mixed provençal herbs or the dried mixed Iranian herbs mentioned on p. 183 the best.

For 1 loaf		
150ml milk	7g fresh yeast or 3g dried yeast or ½ tsp easy-blend yeast	1 tsp rubbed and crushed dried herbs or 2 tsp finely chopped fresh herbs
½ tsp sugar	200ml warm water	
1 tsp salt	350g strong plain white flour	coarse salt
45g butter		

Heat the milk to simmering point, remove it from the heat and stir in the sugar, salt and 30g butter. Leave until lukewarm. Prove fresh or dried yeast in half of the water. Put the flour, herbs and easy-blend yeast, if you are using it, into a food processor and process for 10 seconds to sift. With the machine running on low speed, add the yeast and milk through the feed tube. When they are absorbed, add the remaining water, a little at a time as the flour absorbs it – the mixture should be quite slack and sticky. Either scrape down the sides, put the stopper in the feed tube and leave to prove for 45 minutes to 1 hour, or transfer the dough to a bowl, cover with clingfilm or a cloth and leave to rise. In a processor, pulse twice to knock it back, otherwise beat by hand for 30 seconds.

Towards the end of the proving time, heat the oven to 180°C, 350°F, gas 4. Grease thoroughly a shallow 18–20cm tin (I use a square 18cm tin with 3cm sides or a small loaf tin). Tip the dough into the tin, shake and tap it to fill evenly. Bake at once for about 45 minutes. Melt the remaining butter, brush it over the crust and sprinkle with coarse salt. Cool on a wire rack.

Pesto bread

This recipe is adapted from Carol Field's excellent book *The Italian Baker*, unfortunately not available in Britain as far as I have been able to discover.

For 2 loaves	500g strong plain white flour	2 tbs olive oil
20g fresh yeast, 10g dried yeast or 5g easy-blend yeast	1–2 tsp salt	100g pesto (p. 366)
	250ml warm water	

If you use fresh or dried yeast stir it into the water and leave until creamy, about 10 minutes. Mix flour and salt, and easy-blend yeast if you are using that, and with the water, oil and pesto stir to a soft dough. Knead on a lightly floured surface for 8–10 minutes (p. 444) until the dough is velvety and elastic. If you use a mixer follow the same procedure, using the basic paddle until the flour is well moistened, then change to the dough hook and knead until the dough is velvety and medium-soft, 3–4 minutes. Finish kneading briefly by hand.

With a food processor, sift the salt and flour (and easy-blend yeast if you are using it) together for 10 seconds, using the dough blade while (if you are not using easy-blend) the fresh or dried yeast is proving in 50ml water. With the machine running pour the oil, pesto and dissolved yeast through the feed tube, followed by 200ml cold water, as quickly as the flour can absorb it. Process 1 minute longer to knead, then knead for another minute by hand.

Put the dough in an oiled bowl, cover with clingfilm or a cloth and let it rise until doubled in size, about 1¼ hours. Cut the dough in half, punch each piece down and knead briefly to expel air. Shape each piece into a rounded loaf. Place the loaves on an oiled baking sheet, seam side down. Cover again, let the loaves rise until doubled in size, about 45 minutes to 1 hour. The dough must be very relaxed and fully risen before it is baked, so don't rush it.

Heat the oven to 230°C, 450°F, gas 8. Place the loaves in the oven, immediately turn down the heat to 200°C, 400°F, gas 6; the initial heat helps expand the dough quickly. Bake for 30–40 minutes. The loaves will sound hollow when tapped on the bottom if they are ready. Cool completely on a wire rack.

Variation
Tomato bread Replace the pesto by 100g sun-dried tomatoes puréed in oil.

'Ciabatta'

This recipe for a ciabatta-like loaf baked in a flat tin was developed by the food writer Lynda Brown and Italian restaurateur Giorgio Rocca of da Felicini restaurant in Monforte d'Alba. The dough is made in a food processor fitted with a dough blade, requires no kneading and produces a flattish loaf with large holes, a somewhat crumpet-like texture and a crisp crust. It keeps for 4–5 days.

The real thing is much more difficult to make; the dough is wet and sticky and requires energetic mixing and kneading, so I have settled for buying my ciabatta, and making 'Rocca's *pane*', as Lynda calls it, at home.

For 1 loaf	3.5g fresh yeast or 1/4 tsp easy-blend yeast	4–6 tbs extra virgin olive oil
360g unbleached strong white flour	½ tsp salt	320–350ml lukewarm water

Put the flour, yeast, salt and olive oil into a food processor. With the motor running, pour the water through the feed tube and process for 1–2 minutes. Add just enough water to make a thick batter. Scrape down the lid and the sides of the processor, put the stopper in the feed tube and leave to prove for 3–6 hours. The dough will be puffy and sticky. Scrape it gently into a shallow non-stick tin (I use an 18cm square tin). The dough should just fill it. Leave to rest for 30–40 minutes.

Meanwhile heat the oven to 220°C, 425°F, gas 7, with a flat baking sheet on the middle rack. Put the bread tin onto the baking sheet and bake for 35–40 minutes. The crust will be golden brown, and the hot baking sheet under the tin ensures a crisp bottom crust too. Cool the loaf on a wire rack.

In her experiments Lynda discovered that the proving time for the dough could be extended to as much as 24 hours to give the bread deeper, more complex flavours.

Focaccia with olives

Focaccia has been almost as widely adopted in Britain as its cousin the pizza. It is an easy bread to make and can be flavoured with aromatic herbs – thyme, oregano, rosemary or sage – with sautéed onions or with a topping of coarse sea salt. Use small olives, either all black or a combination of black and green.

For 1 focaccia	375g strong plain white flour	4–5 tbs olive oil
15g fresh or 7g dried or 1 tsp easy-blend yeast	250ml warm water	180g small olives, stoned
	1 tsp salt	

Put fresh or dried yeast to prove in half of the water for 10–15 minutes, or sprinkle the easy-blend yeast over the flour with the salt. Stir the yeast mixture until creamy and add it to the flour with 3 tbs olive oil. Stir in the remaining water a little at a time to make a soft dough. Knead on a lightly floured surface until elastic and springy (p. 444). You can prepare the dough by hand or with the dough hook of a mixer on the lowest speed. In a food processor, pulse for 1 minute, adding the water through the feed tube. Once the dough has gathered together, pulse 15 seconds longer to knead it to a sticky ball, then finish the kneading by hand.

Put the dough in a lightly oiled bowl, cover with clingfilm or a cloth and leave to rise for about 1 hour, until it has doubled in volume. Heat the oven to 190°C, 375°F, gas 5. Oil a baking sheet.

Punch the dough down and knead it again on a lightly floured surface. Form it into a ball and roll it into a disc or square about 1cm thick. Place it on the baking sheet, cover and leave to rise again for 20–30 minutes.

Make dimple marks in the top with your fingertips, then push the small olives into the dough. Brush with olive oil and bake for 20–25 minutes until risen and golden.

Cool on a wire rack. Eat focaccia, cut into wedges or squares, warm or at room temperature the day you make it.

Soda bread

Every time I go to Ireland I eat huge amounts of soda bread – white, brown, scones, fruit bread. It almost becomes an addiction, and I get into the habit of making soda bread again when I get home.

Stoneground wholemeal flour is unsurpassed for flavour for brown soda bread, used alone or with a small proportion of strong plain white flour. White soda bread is always rather cake-like, and I prefer it with added dried fruit or made into scones. The dough should be supple; if it is too stiff the bread is likely to be leaden. Soda bread is made with sour milk or buttermilk, the acidity of the sour liquid being necessary to the action of the soda. Soda bread needs little or no kneading.

For 1 large or 2 small loaves	125g strong plain white flour	350–380ml sour milk or buttermilk
400g stoneground wholemeal flour	1 tsp baking soda	
	scant tsp salt	

Heat the oven to 220°C, 425°F, gas 7. Mix together all the dry ingredients and moisten with the sour milk to make a supple but not soft dough. Flour a baking sheet, form the dough into one large round or cut it in half and make two taller small rounds. Cut a deep cross in the top of a large loaf so that when it is baked it can be divided into four. Bake at once for 30–35 minutes and cool on a rack.

Variation
White soda bread Make white soda bread in the same way, and if you wish add 2 tbs sugar, 3–4 tbs raisins and a little chopped mixed peel to the dry ingredients.

Breadcrumbs

Brown or white bread can be used to make crumbs and the better quality the bread, the better the crumbs, in texture as well as taste.

Fresh breadcrumbs Use bread that is 1 or 2 days old. Discard the crust. Put pieces of bread into a blender or food processor and reduce them to crumbs. Make the crumbs as coarse or as fine as you wish. Store in the refrigerator for 2–3 days or freeze for a year or more.

Dried breadcrumbs Dry bread by putting slices in a very low oven (150°C, 300°F, gas 2) for 30–40 minutes. When dry, reduce to crumbs in a blender or food processor, or crush with a rolling pin. Store in an airtight container for 6–8 months.

Croûtons and croûtes. See p. 3.

Fruit breads and muffins

These recipes use baking soda or baking powder as raising agents. Once mixed, the doughs must be baked quickly or the raising agents will not do their work effectively. Make sure to heat the oven before you start preparing the dough.

Barmbrack

A traditional Irish fruit bread that is good on its own or with butter.

For 1 loaf	100g chopped candied peel	1 tsp baking powder
200g raisins	200g soft brown sugar	½ tsp cinnamon
200g sultanas	200ml strong black tea	1 tsp mixed spice
	250g plain white flour	3 eggs

Put the fruit, peel and sugar in a bowl and pour over the tea. Cover and leave to soak for several hours or overnight. Heat the oven to 170°C, 325°F, gas 3. Grease a 1kg loaf or cake tin. Sift together the flour and baking powder, add the spices. Beat the eggs. Add the flour and eggs alternately to the fruit and beat well. Pour the mixture into the tin. Bake for 1½ hours or until a skewer comes out clean. Leave to cool in the tin for 10 minutes on a wire rack before turning the bread onto the rack to cool completely.

Prune and pecan loaf

For 1 loaf	125g pecan nuts, chopped	1 egg
150g prunes, stoned and chopped	1 tsp baking soda	1 tsp vanilla extract
	150ml water	250g plain white flour
125g raisins or sultanas		60g soft brown sugar

Heat the oven to 180°C, 350°F, gas 4. Grease a 500g loaf tin. Put the prunes, raisins and nuts in a bowl with the baking soda and pour over 150ml boiling water. Leave to cool. Beat the egg lightly and stir in the vanilla extract. Stir the egg into the cooled fruit mixture with the flour and sugar. Add more water as necessary to make a dough of a soft consistency. Turn the mixture into the tin and bake in the middle of the oven for 1 hour. Stand the tin on a wire rack for 10 minutes before turning out the loaf to cool completely. This tea bread is best kept for a day before being cut.

Variations

• The fruit and nuts for this bread can be varied; try dates with walnuts or semi-dried apricots with pistachios or almonds.

Banana bread

For 1 loaf	250g plain white flour	pinch salt
90g butter	2 tsp baking powder	2 large ripe bananas, mashed
125g caster sugar	1 tsp cinnamon	
1 egg, beaten	grating of nutmeg	60g pecans, coarsely chopped or 60g raisins

Heat the oven to 180°C, 350°F, gas 4 and grease a 1kg loaf tin. Cream the butter and sugar together in an electric mixer and add the beaten egg. Sift together the flour and baking powder, add the spices and salt. Add the dry ingredients to the butter and sugar alternately with the bananas. Stir in the nuts or raisins. Pour the batter into the tin. Bake for 50 minutes to 1 hour, until the top is golden and the loaf is shrinking from the sides of the tin. The bread will be ready when a skewer inserted in the centre comes out clean. Stand the tin on a wire rack for 10 minutes before turning out the loaf to cool completely.

Apple and date muffins

For 12 muffins	50g caster sugar	1 egg
250g plain white flour	80g dates, stoned and chopped	200ml apple juice or milk
1 tsp baking powder		
1 tsp baking soda	2 apples, peeled, cored and chopped	100g melted butter
½ tsp salt		

Heat the oven to 200°C, 400°F, gas 6. Grease the muffin tins or use paper cases. Sift the flour, baking powder and baking soda into a bowl and add the salt and sugar. Stir in the dates and coat them lightly with the flour to prevent them sticking together. Then stir in the apples. Whisk the egg, stir in the apple juice or milk and the melted butter. Make a well in the dry ingredients, pour in the egg mixture and mix to a batter. It will probably look lumpy. Divide the batter between the tins or cases and bake for 15 minutes. Cool in the tins for 5–10 minutes then turn the muffins out onto a wire rack. Muffins are best eaten the day they are made.

Variations

Apricot and nut muffins Replace the dates and apples with 100g semi-dried apricots, chopped, and 60g pecans or walnuts, also chopped. Use milk rather than apple juice.

Blueberry muffins Replace the dates and apples with 170g blueberries and use milk rather than apple juice.

Cakes, pastry and batters

Baking is different from cooking and is often considered too daunting to try. Cooking can be done intuitively, adapting recipes, using ingredients to hand. Baking requires precision, and practice soon develops skills and demystifies the process. Accurately measured ingredients, attention to techniques, oven temperatures and timing are essential to turning out good cakes and pastry. Recipes need to be followed carefully. You can, however, take a more relaxed approach to batters for pancakes, puddings and fritters for they are less demanding.

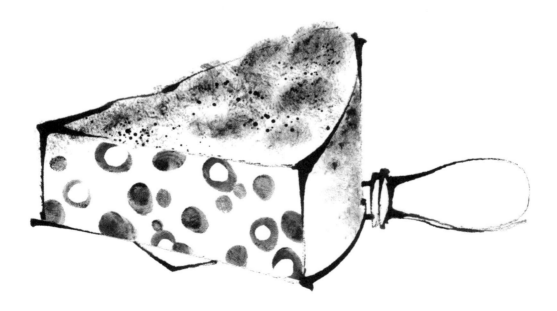

Cakes

To make a successful cake is one of the most pleasurable and satisfying aspects of cooking. If you are a beginner start with something simple like scones, brownies or coconut and rum cake and as your expertise and confidence increase, move on to fruit cakes and Victoria sponges before tackling the more difficult genoese sponge cakes and fragile nut cakes.

The essentials of cake making

In cake making, the proportions of the different ingredients and the baking time are important, so weigh and measure carefully and set a timer while the cake is in the oven. Ovens vary somewhat in their ability to sustain a given temperature; the times given for each recipe have worked for me and other testers, but check by one of the methods suggested below that your cake is ready before taking it from the oven.

Plain flour is the basis of most of the following recipes, sometimes mixed with potato or cornflour. I find it preferable to self-raising flour because the amount of raising agent, in the form of baking powder or a mixture of baking soda and cream of tartar, can be added to suit each recipe. For more detailed notes on flours, *see* p. 440.

Caster or granulated sugar, soft brown sugar, golden syrup or maple syrup, honey and treacle provide the sweetening. Fine caster sugar dissolves more quickly than granulated sugar and is best for creaming with butter and for meringues. Granulated sugar is good for mixtures such as scones, where the butter is rubbed into the dry ingredients. Soft brown sugar keeps cakes moist and gives them a distinctive flavour. Syrups, honey and treacle produce a close texture desirable in chocolate cakes and gingerbread.

I am not a fan of margarine, because it contributes nothing in flavour, and use unsalted butter or occasionally olive oil in cakes.

Eggs must be fresh. Medium-sized eggs are used in all the recipes unless otherwise specified. See p. 49 in the Egg chapter for notes on beating and whisking eggs.

Have all the ingredients at room temperature before starting to bake.

Tins and trays for baking

Non-stick equipment gives the best results. Choose cake tins with a loose base, or spring-form tins from which the sides can be released. There are now some on the market that are not scratched by knives so you can leave the cake on the base plate to serve it. For tarts, choose tins with a loose base. Small cakes can be made in shaped trays or in paper cases.

Tins should be greased with butter or a flavourless oil; even non-stick can stick occasionally. For plain cakes and sponges, it is best to grease and flour the tin. For some cakes, a lining of greaseproof or baking paper on the base of the tin will ensure that it turns out easily. For rich fruit cakes that are baked for a long time, it is best to line the whole tin. Grease the tin so the lining paper sticks to it.

To line the bottom, put the tin on the sheet of paper, draw round it, cut out and fit the paper into the tin and grease it. To line the sides, cut a strip of paper slightly longer and 1cm higher than the circumference of the tin. Fold up 1cm along one long side and cut slits at regular right angles to the edge at 1cm intervals along the folded side. Press the lining round the tin so that the slit edges lie flat on the bottom. Fit the base lining paper over the edges of the side lining and grease both.

A re-usable cooking tray liner is useful for lining baking trays for biscuits and meringues.

Equipment for mixing cakes

An electric mixer gives good results when creaming butter, whisking whole eggs or whites, or beating eggs and sugar, and saves a great deal of time. Use the recommended tools and speed for specific tasks.

A food processor can be used for sifting dry ingredients, whisking eggs or egg whites, creaming butter and sugar, and for making cakes like honey and spice cake when the liquids can be poured down the feed tube onto the dry ingredients. Use the appropriate fitting and don't run the machine for too long or at too high a speed.

Egg whites whisked in an electric mixer or food processor will be less well aerated than whites whisked by hand.

Baking cakes and biscuits

Make sure the oven is at the right temperature before putting in a cake. Cakes containing raising agents must be baked as soon as they are mixed, so heat the oven 15 minutes or so before it is needed. If the oven is not hot enough the raising agents will not release the gas needed to burst the starch grains in the flour and the cake will be heavy. To get rid of air bubbles, tap the tin lightly on the work surface before putting it into the oven.

Most cakes are best cooked in the middle of the oven with room for air to circulate between the tins if you are baking more than one. Cakes that need to bake for longer than 40 minutes may need to be covered with lightly buttered baking paper or foil to prevent them getting too brown.

Do not open the oven until at least three-quarters of the baking time has elapsed and do it gently because a sudden draught may make the cake collapse. To determine whether a cake is ready, insert a thin skewer or toothpick in the centre: if it comes out clean the cake is done. Or touch the cake lightly: it will feel firm and spring back if it is ready. Another indication is that it will start to shrink from the sides of the tin. Leave the cake for 5–10 minutes in the tin on a wire rack to allow air to circulate around it, before removing it from the tin. Then leave to cool completely on the wire rack.

Problems that can occur when making cakes

- *Creaming mixture curdles:* eggs added too quickly or eggs and butter not at same temperature. Adding a spoonful of flour with the eggs can help prevent curdling.
- *Thick crust:* oven too hot or cake baked too long.
- *Heavy texture:* not enough creaming or overmixed; eggs and sugar not aerated enough.
- *Cake sinking:* too much baking powder, or not baked long enough.
- *Fruit sinking:* fruit used wet, or too much baking powder or liquid; the mixture does not have enough strength to support the fruit.
- *Uneven rising:* cake baked too fast, oven temperature uneven or flour not well blended into a sponge cake.
- *Top cracked or raised in the centre:* oven too hot.

Storing cakes and biscuits

Store cakes and biscuits in airtight tins or well wrapped in foil, except cakes filled with cream or fresh fruit which should be kept in the refrigerator and eaten soon after making.

Creaming method

Soften but don't melt butter and beat it with sugar until it becomes pale and fluffy. This is hard work with a wooden spoon but can be done more quickly in a mixer or food processor. Sift the flour two or three times with the raising agent to ensure they are well mixed. You can use a sieve, which aerates as well as mixing, or just stir together well or pulse in a food processor. Beat whole eggs or egg yolks, depending on the recipe, one by one into the butter and sugar, then fold in the flour. Mixtures can sometimes curdle when the eggs are added, but if you stir in a little of the flour after each egg, this can be avoided. Retain as much air as possible in the mixture. If you have separated the eggs, beat the whites to peaks and fold them in (p. 49).

Victoria sponge

A Victoria sponge is usually sandwiched with raspberry jam, but use the jam you prefer. Just make sure it has a good flavour. Butter cream (p. 485) can also be used.

For 1 cake using 2 20cm sandwich tins	170g caster sugar	2–3 tbs milk
	3 eggs	raspberry jam
170g butter	170g self-raising flour	icing sugar

Heat the oven to 190°C, 375°F, gas 5. Grease the two sandwich tins and line the bases with paper (p. 461). Beat together the butter and sugar until light and creamy. Beat in the eggs, one at a time, adding a little flour if the mixture shows signs of curdling. Sift the flour over the mixture and fold it in together with the milk to give the mixture a soft consistency. Spoon half of the mixture into each tin and bake for 25–30 minutes until golden brown and springy to the touch. Turn the cakes out onto a wire rack and leave to cool. Remove the lining paper. Sandwich the cakes with jam or butter cream and sieve icing sugar over the top.

Variations

Marbled chocolate or coffee cake Make a Victoria sponge mixture. Grease and base-line an 18cm tin. Put half the mixture into the prepared tin and mix 2 tbs cocoa powder or 2 tbs instant coffee powder into the remainder. Add this mixture to the tin and pull a fork through the whole to create the marbled effect. Smooth the top with a spatula and bake at 180°C, 350°F, gas 4 for 45–50 minutes. If the cake is getting too brown, cover it loosely with buttered foil after 30 minutes. Insert a thin skewer in the centre: if it comes out clean, the cake is ready. Leave the tin on a rack for 10 minutes, then turn it out and leave to cool completely. If you have a kugelhopf mould, use it for this version, as they do in Austria. Bake as above. Ice with a glacé icing (p. 485).

Apricot cake Replace the milk in the basic recipe by 4 tbs fresh orange juice, and add this juice and the grated rind of 1 unwaxed orange when the eggs are added to the butter and sugar mixture. Grease and base-line an 18cm cake tin, pour in the mixture and cover the top with 400g halved and stoned apricots packed closely together. Sprinkle with water. Bake as marbled chocolate cake (*see* above). While the cake is cooling, spoon 2 tbs honey over the fruit.

Orange cake This is a wonderfully sticky, syrupy cake. Make a Victoria sponge mixture with the addition of the grated rind of 1 unwaxed orange, and replacing the milk by fresh orange juice. Bake in a greased and base-lined tin as above. When the cake has cooled, stand it on a plate and make holes all over it with a toothpick or thin skewer.

While the cake is baking make a syrup with the juice of 1 orange and ½ lemon, 100g caster sugar and flavour it if you wish with 3 bruised cardamom pods*. Heat gently until the sugar dissolves, then simmer for 4–5 minutes. Put the cake on a plate, spoon some of the syrup over it to be absorbed through the holes. Repeat until all the syrup is used.

If you prefer, add 2 tbs of an orange liqueur such as Grand Marnier to the cooling syrup instead of the cardamom flavouring.

Cherry and almond cake

This is a recipe developed by Marion Burdenuik, an expert cake maker who for many years made the birthday cakes for my two daughters, as well as imaginatively decorated Christmas cakes and vast quantities of brownies (p. 480). She tested many of the recipes in this section.

For 1 cake using a 20cm cake tin	120g butter	50g self-raising flour
	150g caster sugar	100g ground almonds
120g glacé cherries	3 eggs	1 tsp vanilla extract

Heat the oven to 180°C, 350°F, gas 4. Grease the tin and dust with flour. Rinse and dry the cherries if they are sticky and chop them. Beat the butter until it becomes creamy, then beat in the sugar. When the mixture is soft and light in colour, beat in the eggs one at a time with a spoonful of flour. Lightly beat in the rest of the flour and the almonds. Fold in the cherries and vanilla extract. Bake for 1 hour or until a skewer inserted in the centre comes out clean. Transfer the tin to a rack to cool for 10 minutes, then turn out the cake and leave to cool completely.

Marzipan and poppy seed cake

For 1 cake using a 1kg loaf tin	100ml soured cream or use single cream mixed with 2 tbs lemon juice	150g plain flour
150g butter		2 tsp baking powder
150g caster sugar	200g marzipan, chilled in the freezer for 30 minutes and grated	pinch salt
3 eggs, separated		100g poppy seeds
2 tbs rum		

Heat the oven to 180°C, 350°F, gas 4 and grease and base-line a 1kg loaf tin (p. 461). Beat together the butter and sugar until pale and fluffy. Add the egg yolks, one at a time, beating well to incorporate them, then add the rum and cream. Stir in the grated marzipan. Sift the flour, baking powder and salt together two or three times. Add the poppy seeds. Whisk the egg whites until they stand in peaks. Mix the flour into the batter, then 2–3 tbs egg whites to loosen it, and fold in the rest with a large metal spoon or spatula (p. 49). Turn into the tin and bake for about 1 hour until a skewer pushed into the centre comes out clean. Put the tin on a wire cooling rack for 10 minutes, then remove the cake and leave to cool on the rack.

Sponge or biscuit method

A true sponge is a mixture of beaten eggs, sugar, flour and flavourings. Occasionally, butter is added. The combined weight of the flour and sugar should equal the weight of the eggs in their shells. Weigh the eggs, crack them into a bowl and whisk lightly to combine. If the eggs weighed more than 200g, take out a little. Sift the flour two or three times with the raising agent to ensure they are well mixed. A sponge depends for its open texture and lightness on the air beaten in with the eggs. Beat the eggs with a wooden spoon in a bowl standing over (but not in) hot water, or more easily and quickly beat them in a mixer which will take 6–8 minutes. When the eggs are fluffy, beat in the sugar and keep beating until the mixture has expanded considerably and is thick and creamy. When you withdraw the beater it will leave a trail on the surface if the mixture has reached the right consistency. Fold in the sifted flour with a metal spoon, without losing air from the mixture. It should still be thick enough to pour but to spread slowly.

No-fat sponge cake

For 1 cake using 2 20cm sandwich tins	100g caster sugar	raspberry jam or fresh fruit for filling (optional)
100g plain flour	150ml whipped cream (p. 486)	
3–4 eggs (200g)		

Heat the oven to 180°C, 350°F, gas 4. Grease the tins and shake a little caster sugar all over them. Sift the flour thoroughly, two or three times. Warm the bowl of an electric mixer and beat the eggs and sugar on high speed for about 5 minutes, or until tripled in volume. Alternatively, put them in a mixing bowl over simmering water and whisk for about 10 minutes until the mixture is pale and very thick, and the whisk leaves a trail across the surface when it is removed. Fold in the flour with a metal spoon, retaining as much air as possible. Divide the mixture between the tins and bake for about 25–30 minutes. Cool the sponges on a wire rack. When they are cold, sandwich them with plain or flavoured whipped cream, and jam or fresh fruit if you wish. Once filled, refrigerate the cake.

This sponge is best eaten the day it is made, but it can also be frozen successfully.

Genoese sponge cake

This is a basic sponge with added butter, and greater keeping qualities.

For 1 cake using 2 20cm sandwich tins or a 20–22cm spring-form cake tin	4 eggs (200g)	150ml whipped cream (p. 486)
	100g caster sugar	icing sugar
100g plain flour	50g melted butter	
	fresh fruit	

Heat the oven to 180°C, 350°F, gas 4. Grease and base-line (p. 461), the tin or tins. Make the cake mix as described in the previous recipe, adding the butter last. Fill the tin or tins and bake for about 25–30 minutes. When the sponge is baked, cool on a rack.

Once cool, the cake can be sliced into 2 or 3 layers, filled with fresh fruits such as strawberries, raspberries, blueberries, sliced peaches or nectarines and plain or flavoured whipped cream. Sift icing sugar over the top.

Melting method

This method is used for moist cakes. Honey or syrup is heated with butter and sugar until the sugar dissolves and all is melted. The warm mixture is then stirred into the dry ingredients with the eggs. The method is easy and reliable for beginners.

Honey and spice cake

For 1 cake using a 25cm cake tin	½ tsp ground coriander	1 tsp baking soda
	¼ tsp ground cloves	1 tbs milk
500g honey	4 eggs	80g walnuts, chopped
125g butter	500g plain flour	80g candied orange peel, chopped
125g brown sugar	1 tsp baking powder	
1 tsp cinnamon		

Heat the oven to 180°C, 350°F, gas 4. Grease the cake tin, dust well with flour and shake out the excess. Heat together gently the honey, butter and sugar. When the sugar has dissolved, remove the pan from the heat and stir in the spices. Leave to cool a little, then beat in the eggs, one by one. Sift the flour and baking powder together. Dissolve the baking soda in the milk. Combine the honey and flour mixtures, beating well until smooth, and stir in the baking soda and milk. Add the walnuts and candied peel, making sure they are evenly distributed throughout the mixture.

Pour the cake batter into the tin and bake for 1 hour or until a skewer inserted in the cake comes out clean. Stand the tin on a wire rack for 5–10 minutes, then turn out the cake and leave it to cool completely.

Gingerbread

For about 18 pieces, using a 30x20x3cm tin	1 tsp mixed spice	125g butter
250g plain flour	50g soft brown sugar	150g black treacle or golden syrup
1 tsp baking soda	75g chopped almonds	2 eggs, beaten
2 tsp ground ginger	75g chopped preserved ginger or mixed peel	125ml milk

Heat the oven to 180°C, 350°F, gas 4. Grease and base-line the tin (p. 461). Sift together the flour, baking soda and spices two or three times in a large bowl, stir in the sugar, almonds and ginger or mixed peel. Melt the butter and treacle or syrup gently. As soon as the butter is liquid, stir the mixture into the dry ingredients together with the beaten eggs and milk. Pour the mixture into the tin and bake for 35–45 minutes, then cool on a wire rack in the tin for 15 minutes before turning it out to cool completely. Cut into squares for serving.

All-in-one method

To make cakes by this method, it is best to use an electric mixer or food processor which does the mixing quickly and efficiently. Mixing all the ingredients at once by hand is heavy work. It is another method that is easy for beginners.

Coconut and rum cake

For 1 cake using a 26cm ring mould	75g cornflour	For the icing
	150g plain flour	150g icing sugar
200g butter	3 tsp baking powder	3–4 tbs rum
200g sugar	100g desiccated coconut	
1 tsp vanilla extract		
3 eggs	2 tbs rum	

Heat the oven to 180°C, 350°F, gas 4. Grease and flour the ring mould. Combine all the cake ingredients in a large bowl and whisk for 2 minutes with an electric hand whisk. Turn the mixture into the mould and bake for 1 hour. Leave to cool in the tin for 10 minutes on a wire rack, then turn out the cake and leave to cool completely.

For the icing, mix together the icing sugar and rum, and coat the cake with it.

Mango streusel cake

The German word *streusel* corresponds, roughly, to our own 'crumble'.

For 1 cake using a 20–22cm spring-form cake tin	grated rind of $\frac{1}{2}$ unwaxed lemon	For the streusel
	2 eggs	80g butter
1–2 ripe mangoes (about 350g)	100g plain flour	60g plain flour
100g butter	40g cornflour or potato flour	60g cornflour or potato flour
100g caster sugar	1 tsp baking powder	100g demerara sugar
	2–3 tbs milk	½ tsp cinnamon

Heat the oven to 180°C, 350°F, gas 4. Grease and flour the tin. Peel the mangoes, slice the flesh away from the stone, and chop finely. Rub the streusel ingredients together with your fingertips or mix with a fork. Put the remaining ingredients into an electric mixer bowl and beat for 2 minutes, or whiz in a food processor. Turn this mixture into the tin; it will cover the base quite thinly. Spread the mango over the cake, leaving behind any excess juice, and top with the streusel. Bake for about 40 minutes, until a skewer inserted into the cake comes out clean. Put the tin to cool on a rack for 10 minutes before removing the sides of the tin and leaving the cake to cool completely.

Variation

· Replace the mangoes with papayas. Peel the papayas, remove the seeds, slice thinly and sprinkle with 1 tbs lemon juice. Leave to stand for 10 minutes before adding the slices to the cake. Top with the streusel as above.

Carrot and apple cake

This moist, lightly spiced cake also comes from Marion Burdenuik.

For 1 cake using a 20cm cake tin	125g carrots	For the topping
250g self-raising flour	2 eating apples	90g cream cheese or ricotta
2 tsp baking powder	60g pecan nuts or walnuts, chopped	90g butter
1 tsp cinnamon	2 eggs	180g icing sugar
150g soft brown sugar	150g sunflower oil	grated rind of 1 unwaxed orange
		pecan or walnut pieces

Heat the oven to 180°C, 350°F, gas 4. Grease and base-line the tin (p. 461). Sift the flour, baking powder and cinnamon together two or three times, then mix in the sugar. Make sure all is well blended. Peel and grate the carrots; peel, core and grate the apples. Mix them and the nuts into the flour and sugar, then make a well in the centre. Beat the eggs and pour them into the fruit and flour mixture with the oil, and beat well. When everything is well blended turn the mixture into the tin. Smooth the top. Bake for about 1 hour, until a skewer inserted in the middle comes out clean and the cake is beginning to shrink away from the sides of the tin. Remove the tin to a wire rack for 10 minutes, then turn out the cake and leave it on the rack to cool completely.

To make the topping, drain the ricotta well if you are using it, and put the butter to soften, but don't let it melt. Combine the cream cheese or ricotta and butter, then beat in the icing sugar and orange rind. Spread the mixture on the top of the cake and roughen it with a fork. Decorate with the nuts.

Rubbing-in method

This method is used for mixtures where the weight of fat is less than half the weight of flour. Rub the butter into the dry ingredients until the mixture resembles fine breadcrumbs. Add sugar, fruit, beaten eggs and other liquids.

Scones

For 12 scones

250g plain flour

½ tsp salt

1 tbs baking powder (or ½ tsp baking soda and 1 tsp cream of tartar)

50g butter

50g caster sugar

50g raisins or sultanas (optional)

1 egg mixed with milk to make 150ml

1 beaten egg for glazing

Sift the flour into a large bowl and add the salt and baking powder. Rub in the butter until the mixture resembles breadcrumbs. Stir in the sugar and the raisins if you are using them. Make a well in the centre and pour in the egg and milk. Use a knife or a fork to mix quickly to a dough. It should be soft but not wet.

Heat the oven to 220°C, 425°F, gas 7. Turn the mixture out onto a floured surface and knead gently to a flat round. Either press it with your knuckles or roll it lightly to a thickness of 1cm. Dip a 5cm pastry cutter in flour and cut the scones from the dough. Put the scones on a floured baking sheet. Brush the tops with the beaten egg and bake for 10–12 minutes. The sides will feel springy when they are ready. Cool on a rack.

Nut cakes

Nuts not only add variety of flavour and texture to cakes, they can replace flour, which is useful for people who are allergic to gluten; in addition, the fat in the nuts can replace butter, a bonus for cholesterol watchers. Many of the best recipes come from Austria and Hungary and from the Middle East.

Austrian almond and chocolate cake

Make this cake in a loose-bottomed tin because it is fragile and difficult to turn out.
It may be best to leave it on the base plate for serving.

For 1 cake using a 14–16cm cake tin	75g almonds in their skins	3 eggs, separated
	75g plain chocolate	75g icing sugar, sieved

Heat the oven to 180°C, 350°F, gas 4. Grease and flour the tin. Grind the almonds in
a nut or food mill or chop them finely in a food processor. Grate the chocolate or
chop it finely, and mix it with the almonds. Whisk the egg yolks with 60g sugar
until they are thick and pale, and the whisk leaves a trail across the surface when it
is raised. Whisk the egg whites until they stand in peaks, fold in the remaining
sugar and whisk again. Fold the chocolate and nuts into the yolk mixture
alternately with the egg whites. Turn the mixture into the tin and bake for 45
minutes. Leave in the tin on a rack for 10 minutes before turning the cake out.

The cake can be served alone or with a dollop of whipped cream for dessert.

Honey and hazelnut cake

This recipe comes from an old French book, *La bonne cuisine du Périgord* by La
Mazille. It makes a deliciously moist cake.

For 1 cake using an 18–20cm cake tin	3 large eggs, separated	100g hazelnuts, roasted, peeled (p. 488) and finely chopped
200ml clear honey	100g plain flour	4–6 tbs double cream

Heat the oven to 180°C, 350°F, gas 4 and grease the tin. Heat the honey in a jar or
jug in a pan of simmering water until it is quite liquid. Whisk the egg yolks until
pale and thick, then pour in the honey and mix well. Add the flour and hazelnuts
alternately to the eggs and honey, and stir in the cream. Whisk the egg whites to
peaks and fold them into the mixture. Pour the mixture into the tin and bake for
35–40 minutes. Leave the cake to cool in its tin on a wire rack. It is best left for a
day before cutting.

Chocolate cakes

Use very good plain chocolate with a high percentage of cocoa butter for baking (p. 524). Occasionally cocoa powder is used instead of chocolate, as in the torrone molle recipe; be sure to buy good quality cocoa or the cake will lack flavour.

Rich chocolate cake

For 1 cake using a 23cm cake tin	250g butter	120g self-raising flour
250g plain chocolate, broken into small pieces	4 eggs, separated	90g ground almonds
	100g caster sugar	

Heat the oven to 180°C, 350°F, gas 4. Grease and base-line the cake tin (p. 461). Melt the chocolate and butter together over low heat, stirring from time to time to ensure the mixture is smooth. Beat the egg yolks with 75g sugar until pale and fluffy, which will take about 6–8 minutes in an electric mixer. Fold in the chocolate mixture and the flour and almonds. Whisk the egg whites until stiff, add the rest of the sugar and whisk it in. Stir 2 tbs of the egg whites into the chocolate mixture to loosen it, then fold in the rest (p. 49). Pour the mixture into the tin and bake for about 40 minutes, until a skewer inserted in the middle comes out clean. Leave in the tin on a wire rack for 10 minutes before turning out.

Coat with chocolate icing (p. 485) or serve with whipped cream or flavoured crème fraîche (p. 486).

Light chocolate cake

This cake is made with potato flour which gives it a light texture and creamy taste.

For 1 cake using a 20cm cake tin	175g plain chocolate, broken into pieces	125g caster sugar
	175g butter	125g potato flour
		4 eggs, separated

Heat the oven to 190°C, 375°F, gas 5 and grease the cake tin. Melt the chocolate in a bowl over a pan of simmering water. Cream the butter and sugar until pale and fluffy, and stir in the chocolate. Add the potato flour and egg yolks, alternately, beating well. Whisk the egg whites until stiff and fold them in (p. 49). Pour the mixture into the tin and bake for 30–35 minutes. The cake will form a crust and will shrink from the sides of the tin but will appear uncooked if tested with a skewer because it gets firmer as it cools. Transfer the tin to a cooling rack for 10 minutes, then turn out the cake to cool completely.

The cake is fairly dry and so is best covered with whipped cream or served with a dollop of whipped cream (p. 486) and half a juicy pear for a dessert.

Torrone molle

This simple recipe for an Italian uncooked chocolate cake is adapted from the recipe in Elizabeth David's *Italian Food*; in this version, the mixture is prepared in a food processor. It can be made in a shallow square or oblong tin or in a ring mould for a more elegant presentation. The torrone molle goes very well with coffee after dinner instead of a dessert.

For 1 cake using a 25 x 25cm tin	180g ground almonds	180g unsweetened cocoa
180g petit beurre or other plain biscuits	180g caster sugar	1 egg
	180g butter	1 egg yolk

Lightly oil the tin or mould. Put the biscuits in a food processor and chop them coarsely. Do not let them turn into crumbs. Add the almonds to the processor and pulse to mix them with the biscuits. Put the sugar and butter in a pan and heat gently until melted. Take the pan from the heat and stir in the cocoa, then the whole egg and the yolk. Mix well and pour the mixture down the feed tube with the processor running slowly. Pulse until well mixed. Turn the mixture into the tin or ring mould and smooth the surface. Put it in the refrigerator and leave for several hours before turning out to serve.

Torrone molle is better if made the day before it is to be eaten. Cut it into squares, or into slices if you have used a ring mould.

Chocolate and chestnut cake

For 1 cake using a 20cm spring-form cake tin	50g butter	120g caster sugar
150g plain chocolate, broken into small pieces	250g canned unsweetened chestnut purée	icing sugar
	4 eggs, separated	

Heat the oven to 180°C, 350°F, gas 4. Grease and base-line (p. 461) the tin. Melt the chocolate and butter in a small pan over low heat. Stir occasionally so that they blend smoothly. Transfer the mixture to a bowl and sieve the chestnut purée into it. Whisk the egg yolks with 90g sugar until light and thick; this will take about 6–8 minutes in an electric mixer. Stir the egg mixture into the chocolate and chestnut mixture. Whisk the egg whites to peaks, add the remaining sugar and whisk again to incorporate it well. Stir 2–3 tbs whites into the chocolate mixture to loosen it, then quickly fold in the rest (p. 49). Turn the mixture into the tin and bake for about 50 minutes, until a skewer pushed into the centre comes out clean. Put the tin on a wire rack to cool for 10 minutes before turning out the cake onto the rack to cool completely.

Dust the top with icing sugar before serving. Crème fraîche or whipped cream (p. 486) makes a good accompaniment.

Fruit cakes

Fruit cakes keep very well and mellow with keeping; the more fruit they have the longer they will keep. They also benefit from being laced with alcohol: rum, whisky and brandy are the most usual. More can be spooned over the cake while it is being kept.

Rich fruit cake

This is the recipe we have used for our Christmas cake for several years, and for our daughter's wedding cake. Very easy to make, it is not solid and heavy, and it keeps well. It is a good idea to line the whole tin because the lining provides extra protection for the cake during the long baking period. Cover the top of the cake with foil if it is getting too brown during the cooking.

For 1 cake using a loose-bottomed 18cm tin	125g hazelnuts, skinned (p. 488) and chopped	250g butter
125g sultanas	125g pecan nuts, chopped	125g soft brown sugar
125g glacé pineapple, chopped		4 eggs
125g crystallized ginger, chopped	grated rind and juice of 1 unwaxed lemon	180g plain flour
180g glacé cherries, chopped	grated rind and juice of 1 unwaxed orange	pinch salt
	3 tbs Grand Marnier or other orange liqueur	125g ground almonds
		2 tbs golden syrup

Put the sultanas, pineapple, ginger, cherries, hazelnuts and pecan nuts in a bowl with the lemon and orange rind, the juices and the Grand Marnier and leave to macerate overnight.

Heat the oven to 180°C, 350°F, gas 4. Grease and line the cake tin (p. 461). Cream the butter and sugar until pale and fluffy. Beat in the eggs, one at a time, with 1 tbs flour. Sift the rest of the flour and salt together two or three times. Stir the flour, ground almonds and syrup into the mixture and then fold in the fruit and nuts. Turn the mixture into the tin and bake for 1½ hours, then lower the heat to 140°C, 275°F, gas 1 and bake for another hour. If the top is getting brown too quickly cover it with buttered baking paper or foil. When a skewer inserted in the centre of the cake comes out clean the cake is ready. Put the tin on a wire rack and leave the cake to cool in the tin.

To keep the cake, wrap it in greaseproof paper and again in foil or put it in an airtight tin.

No-fat fruit cake

This cake uses a fruit purée as its base rather than butter, and is rich with fruit and nuts. Whole candied peel tastes better than ready-chopped, and the cake keeps for a long time.

For 1 large cake using a deep 22–24cm tin		
100g ready-to-eat dried apricots, coarsely chopped	¼ tsp grated nutmeg	100g candied peel, chopped
	¼ tsp ground cloves	
	½ tsp mixed spice	90g pecan nuts, coarsely chopped
100ml water	180g glacé pineapple or cherries	
80ml fresh orange juice		90g pistachio nuts, coarsely chopped
	250g sultanas	
100g caster sugar	250g raisins	90g hazelnuts, skinned (p. 488) and coarsely chopped
3 eggs	100g currants	
250g plain flour	100g dates, stoned and chopped	3 tbs brandy
1 tsp ground cinnamon		

Heat the oven to 150°C, 300°F, gas 2. Grease and line the cake tin (p. 461). Blend the apricots and half the water in a food processor, then add the remaining water and the orange juice to make a smooth purée. Transfer the purée to a bowl and whisk together with the sugar and eggs until thick. Sift the flour and spices two or three times. If the pineapple or cherries are sticky, rinse and dry them, then chop. Mix all the fruit and nuts in a bowl and coat them with a tablespoon of flour. Fold the rest of the flour into the egg mixture with a large metal spoon. Fold in the fruit and nuts. Turn the mixture into the tin and smooth the top. Bake for 2–2¼ hours, until a skewer inserted in the middle comes out clean. Transfer the tin to a rack and leave the cake to cool in the tin for 1 hour before turning it out onto the rack. Do not remove the lining paper until the cake is completely cold. Prick the top with a large needle or fine skewer and pour the brandy over it.

To keep the cake, wrap it in greaseproof paper and wrap again in foil or put it in an airtight tin.

New Zealand fruit cake

The unusual ingredient in this cake is the pumpkin, which gives it a pleasant, moist texture.

For 1 cake using a 20cm cake tin	180g caster sugar	125g self-raising flour
180g butter	2 eggs	500g mixed dried fruit
	125g plain flour	200g cooked pumpkin

Heat the oven to 170°C, 325°F, gas 3. Grease and line the tin (p. 461). Cream the butter and sugar until pale, beat in the eggs and add all the other ingredients in the order listed. Turn the mixture into the tin. Bake for 1½ hours or a little longer, until a skewer inserted in the middle comes out clean. If the top is starting to brown too much, cover it with foil halfway through the cooking time.

Transfer the tin to a wire rack and leave the cake to cool in the tin.

Meringues

Meringue is a mixture of stiffly whisked egg white and caster sugar. The egg whites must be fresh and at room temperature. The bowl and whisk for making meringues must be scrupulously clean because the slightest speck of grease will prevent the eggs from rising. Take care when cracking the eggs that none of the yolk breaks into the whites. Use a metal or glass bowl, not plastic: egg whites will not whisk properly in plastic.

Problems that can occur when making meringues

- *Egg whites take a long time to become stiff:* whites contain grease (probably a speck of egg yolk); too much sugar; eggs not lifted enough when whisking to incorporate air.
- *The cooked meringue is cracked and discoloured:* oven too hot; not enough sugar.
- *Syrup leaks out of meringues:* moisture in the oven or on the tray; meringue mixture stood too long before going into the oven; granulated sugar used.
- If the meringue has stuck to the paper because syrup has leaked in the oven, rub a damp cloth under the paper and then it will peel off.

Basic meringue

Basic proportions for a crisp dry meringue are 50g caster sugar to 1 egg white (about 30g). A softer meringue, suitable for toppings, requires less sugar.

For a 20–22cm large meringue or 14 small meringues, use 100g caster sugar and 2 egg whites.

For a 24–26cm large meringue or 20 small meringues, use 150g caster sugar and 3 egg whites.

Whisk the egg whites until they have a firm texture. Gradually add half the sugar while still beating lightly to retain air. The mixture will start to look satiny. Spread some of the remaining sugar over the mixture and fold it in with a large metal spoon, making sure it is well blended. Continue until all the sugar is used.

Meringues are dried rather than baked in a very cool oven, 110°–120°C, 225°–235°F, gas ½. It is best to line the baking tray with a re-usable cooking liner or silicone-coated paper which needs no greasing, or with foil or greaseproof paper, both of which need to be brushed lightly with oil.

Small meringues Use 2 spoons to shape the mixture and place the rounds on the lined tray. To make nests, hollow out the centre and roughen the sides with a fork. Meringues can also be piped to a variety of shapes using a 10-mm piping tube. To eat at once, small meringues can be sandwiched with plain or flavoured whipped cream (p. **???**). Nests can be filled with fresh fruit, a fruit purée or fool (pp. 388–9).

Large meringues Draw a circle of the appropriate size on the lining paper or completely line a loose-bottomed shallow tin with paper. Either spread the meringue across the paper and push it into shape with a metal spatula, or spread it to fill the tin. It can also be piped using a large plain nozzle: make a spiral starting from the centre. The meringue should be about 2cm in depth.

Meringues take from 2–3 hours to dry, depending on their size. They should remain a very pale creamy colour. To check if the meringues are ready, pick one up carefully and gently tap on the bottom with your knuckle; it will sound hollow if it is ready. If necessary, leave them in the oven a little longer. Take the meringues from the oven and remove them from the paper. Take care because they are fragile. They can be stored in an airtight tin for several weeks.

Soplillos

These little nut meringues come from the Spanish province of Granada.

For about 16 pieces	200g caster sugar	150g blanched almonds, dry-roasted*, slivered or chopped
3 egg whites	grated rind of 1 unwaxed lemon	

Heat the oven to 150°C, 300°F, gas 2. Cover a large baking sheet with a re-usable cooking liner or silicone paper or greased greaseproof paper. Whisk the egg whites until stiff then beat in the sugar a little at a time. Fold in the lemon rind and the almonds. Spoon the mixture onto the baking sheet, leaving space for the meringues to spread somewhat, and bake for 1½ hours. Turn off the oven and leave the meringues until they have cooled completely.

Pavlova

Assemble the cake an hour or so before you will serve it.

For a 20–22cm meringue	200ml whipped cream (p. 486)	400g fresh fruit – sliced peaches or nectarines, raspberries, strawberries, sliced kiwi fruit
1 large meringue, *see* p. 477		

Flavour the cream with Cointreau, Grand Marnier, kirsch, rum or a liqueur of your choice. Spread the meringue with the cream and top with the fruit.

Variation

Vacherin A vacherin is a tiered meringue cake filled with flavoured whipped cream and decorated with chocolate or nuts or fresh fruit. Prepare 3 large meringues of the same size and sandwich them as in the pavlova. Assemble the vacherin an hour or two before it will be served to give the flavours time to blend.

Pineapple meringue cake

This cake comes from Costa Rica where there are many pineapple plantations. The deliciously sweet fruits are on sale in every village market and shop, and pineapple juice is available in every café and juice bar.

For 1 cake using a 24–26cm spring-form cake tin	3 egg yolks	For the meringue
100g butter	40g cornflour	½ medium pineapple (300g)
100g caster sugar	100g plain flour	3 egg whites
1 tsp vanilla extract	3 tsp cocoa powder	180g caster sugar
	2 tsp baking powder	2 tsp lemon juice

Heat the oven to 180°C, 350°F, gas 4. Grease and flour the tin. Combine butter, sugar, vanilla, egg yolks and the four dry ingredients in a bowl and whisk with an electric hand whisk for 2 minutes. Turn the mixture into the tin, it will make a thin layer, and bake for 25 minutes.

While the cake is baking, prepare the meringue. Peel the pineapple, remove the core, cut the flesh into small pieces and simmer it in water for 5 minutes. Drain well. Whisk the egg whites to peaks, then beat in half the sugar. Gradually add the rest of the sugar, folding it in with a large metal spoon. Fold in the lemon juice and pineapple pieces without any juice.

Spread the meringue over the cake and bake for a further 30–40 minutes. Place the tin on a rack for 15 minutes, then take out the cake and leave to cool completely. Some of the juice from the pineapple will seep into the cake base, making it moist.

Eat within a few hours of baking: this type of soft meringue does not keep well.

Small cakes and biscuits

Madeleines

You will need to have special shell-shaped moulds to make these light little cakes.

For 12 madeleines	100g plain flour	pinch of salt
1 egg	½ tsp baking powder	grated rind of 1 unwaxed lemon
80g caster sugar	1 tsp cornflour	
80g butter		

Heat the oven to 200°C, 400°F, gas 6. Butter and flour the madeleine moulds. Cream the egg and sugar together with an electric whisk for about 5 minutes until thick. Melt the butter over gentle heat and put aside. Sift the flour, baking powder, cornflour and salt together and add a little at a time to the egg mixture. Add the lemon rind and dribble in the melted butter, beating all together well with the electric whisk. It should take no longer than 1 minute. Spoon the mixture into the moulds and bake for 10–12 minutes.

Remove the madeleines from the tray as soon as they are ready. They are best eaten warm.

Flapjacks

For about 18 pieces using a 20 x 20 x 2cm tin	180g butter	250g rolled oats
	180g demerara sugar	pinch salt

Heat the oven to 190°C, 375°F, gas 5. Cream the butter, combine the other ingredients thoroughly and stir them into the butter, making sure all is well mixed. Turn the mixture into a well-greased shallow tin and smooth the top. Bake for about 30 minutes and cool in the tin on a wire rack for 10 minutes, then mark into fingers or squares with a knife. Wait until the mixture is completely cold before cutting the flapjacks and taking them out of the tin.

Brownies

Another recipe from Marion Burdenuik. These brownies are hugely and deservedly popular with everyone who has tasted them.

For 12–16 pieces	30g unsweetened cocoa powder	2 tbs milk
125g butter	½ tsp baking powder	30g butter
250g caster sugar	125g walnuts, chopped	1 tsp instant coffee
2 eggs	1 tbs milk	1 tbs boiling water
1 tsp vanilla extract	**For the topping**	180g icing sugar
60g plain flour	90g plain chocolate	

Heat the oven to 180°C, 350°F, gas 4. Grease and line a 26 x 16 x 2cm baking tin. Cream the butter and sugar until pale, then beat in the eggs one at a time. Stir in the vanilla extract. Sift the flour, cocoa and baking powder together two or three times and fold them into the creamed mixture with the walnuts and milk. Turn the mixture into the tin and smooth the top. Bake in the centre of the oven for 40 minutes, then cool in the tin on a wire rack.

For the topping, melt the chocolate in a bowl over a pan of hot (not boiling) water. Add the milk, the butter, and the coffee dissolved in the boiling water. Stir in the sifted icing sugar, and beat until smooth. Spread the icing over the cooled cake and leave to set. If you put the cake in the refrigerator for an hour or two the icing will set better. Cut in squares to serve.

Shortbread

For about 16 pieces	50g vanilla sugar* or caster sugar	250g plain flour
125g butter		pinch of salt

Heat the oven to 170°C, 325°F, gas 3. Grease a 26 x 16 x 2cm baking tin. Cream the butter and sugar until light and fluffy. Gradually mix in the flour and salt to make a light, crumbly mixture. Press the mixture into the tin and smooth the top. Mark fingers, but don't cut through. Bake for 25–30 minutes. Cool in the tin on a rack.

Variation

Pistachio shortbread Replace 90g flour by 90g shelled pistachios. Toast them in the oven at 200°C, 400°F, gas 6 for 5–6 minutes until they are just turning brown. Remove them from the oven and when cool grind them finely. Stir them into the flour and continue with the method described above.

Cinnamon biscuits

For about 36 biscuits	150g soft brown sugar	50g golden syrup
300g plain flour	90g butter	1 tsp milk (optional)
2 tsp ground cinnamon	1 egg	blanched almonds
1 tsp baking powder		

Heat the oven to 180°C, 350°F, gas 4. Sift the flour, cinnamon and baking powder into a bowl and stir in the sugar. Cut the butter into cubes and rub these into the flour with your fingertips until the mixture looks like breadcrumbs. Beat the egg, add the golden syrup and beat until smooth. Make a well in the centre of the mixture and add the egg and syrup. Mix the dough to a smooth ball; if it seems too stiff add 1 tsp milk. Wrap it in clingfilm and chill for 30 minutes.

Roll the dough out on a lightly floured surface to 5mm thick and cut into 4–5cm rounds with a biscuit cutter. Put a blanched almond in the centre of each biscuit.

Transfer the biscuits to a baking sheet and bake for about 12 minutes. They will still feel soft but harden on cooling. Cool on a rack.

Chocolate chip cookies

For about 16 cookies	50g soft brown sugar	½ tsp baking soda
125g butter	1 egg	pinch of salt
50g vanilla sugar*	125g plain flour	125g plain chocolate chips

Heat the oven to 190°C, 375°F, gas 5. Cream the butter and sugars until pale, then beat in the egg. Sift in the flour, baking soda and salt and mix well. Stir in the chocolate chips. Drop teaspoonfuls onto a baking sheet, leaving room for the cookies to spread. Bake for 8–10 minutes and take the cookies from the oven while the centres are still slightly soft. Leave them on the baking sheet for 5 minutes before removing them to a wire rack to cool.

Almond tuiles

Tuiles have the slightly curved shape of old French roof tiles. The batter is a fairly fluid one, to make light crisp biscuits. As soon as they are baked they must be shaped around a rolling pin or pressed into the bottom of a ring mould to give them their characteristic form. You will also need a wide thin spatula to lift the biscuits from the baking tray.

For about 20 biscuits	90g plain flour, sifted	90g melted and cooled butter
90g flaked almonds	2 egg whites	
90g icing sugar		

Heat the oven to 180°C, 350°F, gas 4, and grease two baking sheets thoroughly. Put 80g almonds, the sugar and flour into a bowl. Beat the egg whites lightly with a fork until frothy. Stir them gently into the dry ingredients with the melted butter, leaving behind in the pan any white residue from the butter. Drop ½ tbs batter onto the baking sheet and spread it lightly with the back of the spoon. Repeat, leaving room for the biscuits to spread during cooking. Scatter the remaining flaked almonds over the biscuits. Bake for 6–8 minutes then remove the tray from the oven. Lift each biscuit with a spatula and lightly press it over a rolling pin or into a ring mould for 2–3 minutes before cooling on a wire rack.

It is best to bake one sheet of biscuits at a time. Have the second tray ready to go into the oven as the first comes out. If you bake two at the same time you will not be able to work fast enough to shape all the biscuits. Before re-using a baking sheet, let it cool and then grease it thoroughly again.

Florentines

For 28–30 small biscuits	50g ground almonds	25g angelica or glacé cherries, chopped
125ml double cream	50g flaked almonds	25g plain flour
50g caster sugar	50g candied orange peel, chopped finely	pinch of salt
		100g plain chocolate

Heat the oven to 180°C, 350°F, gas 4. Line a baking sheet with baking parchment. Heat the cream and sugar gently until the sugar melts, then stir in both sorts of almonds, orange peel, angelica or cherries in that order. Remove the pan from the heat and sift in the flour and salt. Drop teaspoons of the mixture onto the tray and flatten them a little. Leave room for the biscuits to spread. Bake for about 12 minutes, then remove the tray from the oven. Leave the florentines to cool slightly before transferring them to a wire rack to cool completely.

Melt the chocolate in a bowl over simmering water and let it cool to lukewarm. Spread chocolate over the bottom of each florentine with a palette knife, and replace, chocolate side up, on the wire rack. When the chocolate is almost dry, draw wavy lines through the chocolate with a fork.

Note
If you have rice paper, line the baking sheet with rice paper, trim it around the biscuits when they are cooked and spread the chocolate over the rice paper.

Parmesan biscuits

For 25–30 biscuits	large pinch salt	2–3 tbs cream
100g butter	250g Parmesan, grated	1 yolk to glaze the biscuits
200g plain flour	3 egg yolks	

Combine the butter, flour, salt, Parmesan and egg yolks and mix to a dough with a grainy texture. If it seems too dry, add an extra egg yolk. Stir in the cream. Roll the dough into a ball, wrap in clingfilm and refrigerate for 30 minutes.

Heat the oven to 180°C, 350°F, gas 4. Butter a baking sheet. Roll out the dough to a thickness of 5mm on a floured surface and cut in rounds with a 4–5cm biscuit cutter. Put the biscuits on the sheet, brush with the lightly beaten remaining egg yolk and bake for about 15 minutes until golden. Transfer to a wire rack to cool.

Cheese straws

Makes about 24 straws	60g plain flour, sifted	60g butter
50g Parmesan, grated	1 tsp baking powder	1 egg yolk
50g Cheddar, grated	½ tsp paprika	

Heat the oven to 220°C, 425°F, gas 7. Put the cheeses, flour, baking powder and paprika into a mixing bowl and stir well to blend. Cut the butter into small pieces and rub it into the mixture. Add the egg yolk and mix to a stiff dough.

Turn the dough out onto a floured surface and cut it in half. Roll or shape each piece into an oblong, cut the oblongs in half and then into strips. Put them on ungreased baking sheets and bake until golden brown, 8–12 minutes. Put the baking sheet on a wire rack and leave the straws on the sheet until cold.

Salt and caraway straws

The dough for these straws is quickly made in a food processor.

For about 26 straws	large pinch salt	1 egg yolk
125g plain flour	60g butter	caraway seeds
¼ tsp paprika	2 tbs soured cream	coarse salt

Put the flour, paprika and salt into a food processor and pulse to sift. Add the butter, cut in cubes, and blend until the mixture resembles breadcrumbs. Add the cream and pulse to a ball of soft dough. To make by hand, rub the cubes of butter into the flour mixture until the texture is crumbly, then use the cream to bind it to a dough. Form into a ball, wrap in clingfilm and chill for 30 minutes.

Heat the oven to 200°C, 400°F, gas 6. Put the dough on a floured surface, cut it in two, and roll out each piece to a thinnish oblong. Cut the oblong in half and then into sticks. Transfer the straws to an ungreased baking sheet. Brush them with the lightly beaten egg yolk and sprinkle with caraway seeds and salt. Bake for 10–12 minutes, then remove the baking sheet to a wire rack and leave the straws to cool.

Icings, fillings and decorations

Here are a few simple ideas for decorating and filling cakes. Icings range from a basic mixture of sugar and water to enriched versions made with butter or chocolate which can also be used as fillings. Pastry cream and frangipane make well-flavoured bases for fruit tarts.

Glacé icing

Glacé icing is sieved icing sugar mixed with very little water: 250g icing sugar to 2–3 tbs hot water. Add the water gradually, stirring until all the sugar has dissolved and the mixture is smooth. It should just coat the back of a spoon. Stand the cake on a rack over a large plate. Pour the icing over the cake. Dip a palette knife in hot water and run it round the sides of the cake to spread the icing as it runs down and give a smooth finish. If too much runs off, scrape it up from the plate and re-use it.
  Glacé icing hardens as it dries.

Flavourings Add flavourings sparingly until you have a good flavour and colour. Use orange or lemon juice, strong black coffee, diluted rum or liqueur instead of water. For chocolate glacé icing, melt 50g chocolate with a little water, stir until smooth and mix it into the sieved icing sugar. Add a knob of butter to give it a good gloss.

Butter cream or icing

Butter cream can be used as a filling and on top of a cake. Cream together butter and icing sugar in the proportions of 100g butter to 150–200g icing sugar. To fill and cover a 20cm cake you will need 125g butter and 250g icing sugar.

Flavourings Add vanilla extract, unwaxed orange or lemon rind, cinnamon, rum, brandy or a liqueur, melted and cooled chocolate, strong black coffee.
  For a filling, add toasted and ground nuts (p. 488), praline (p. 487) or chopped preserved ginger.

Chocolate icing

A rich icing for chocolate cakes.

150g plain chocolate	5 tbs water	80g butter
6 tsp caster sugar		

Melt the chocolate, sugar and water together in a bowl over simmering water and stir until smooth, then remove the bowl from the heat and beat in the butter. Keep beating until the mixture cools, then use immediately. Smooth it over the cake with a palette knife dipped in hot water.

Chocolate caraque

Melt 60g plain chocolate in a bowl over simmering water. Pour it onto a marble slab or laminated surface and spread thinly with a palette knife. Leave until set, then with a long, sharp knife scrape off thin curling layers from the chocolate. Use to decorate the top of a cake.

Decoration for fruit cakes

Brush the top of the cake with 3–4 tbs warm honey or maple syrup and decorate it with roughly chopped walnuts, blanched almonds, toasted hazelnuts, glacé fruits, ready-to-eat dried fruits.

Simple cream fillings

The simplest filling is whipped cream (crème Chantilly) or crème fraîche sweetened with caster sugar (about 60g sugar to 500ml cream), to which you can add chopped toasted nuts, praline (p. 487), grated chocolate, a dash of strong black coffee, orange flower or rose-water (p. 398), a liqueur or a splash of rum.

Yogurt cream Use half double or whipping cream and half thick yogurt, with sugar and flavourings as above.

Pastry cream

Pastry cream (crème patissière) is a cooked custard-type cream often used as the base for fruit tarts and the filling for cakes, éclairs and choux buns.

This quantity is enough to fill one 26cm tart tin	60g caster sugar	300ml milk
	40g plain flour	vanilla pod
2 egg yolks		

Whisk the egg yolks, adding the sugar gradually, until they are pale, at least double in volume and the whisk leaves a trail on the surface when it is lifted. Sift and beat in the flour. Bring the milk to the boil with the vanilla pod. Remove the pod (rinse, dry and use again). While still beating, pour the milk onto the yolks. Return the mixture to the pan, stir continuously with a wooden spoon, and bring to the boil to ensure that the flour is cooked and the cream is smooth. It will thicken and detach itself from the sides of the pan. Turn the cream into a bowl, sprinkle caster sugar over the surface to prevent a skin forming and cover. Pastry cream will keep in the refrigerator for 2–3 days.

Variations
- To make a chocolate cream, stir in 90g melted plain chocolate while the cream is still warm.
- For a lemon or orange flavouring, omit the vanilla pod and add the grated rind of 1 unwaxed lemon or orange at the end.
- Omit the vanilla pod and stir in 1–2 tbs strong black coffee, rose-water, orange flower water, rum or liqueur, or 2–3 tbs praline (below) at the end.
- If stiffened with beaten egg whites, pastry cream can be used as a filling for éclairs and choux buns.

Frangipane cream

This almond filling is mostly used for fruit flans, pastry-based gâteaux and Bakewell tart.

This quantity will fill one 24cm tart tin	2 eggs	flavouring – lemon juice, orange flower water, rose-water (p. 398), kirsch, rum
125g butter	125g ground almonds	
125g caster sugar	30g plain flour, sifted	

Cream the butter and sugar until light and soft. Add the eggs, one at a time, beating well. Work in the almonds and flour, and flavour sparingly. The cream will keep for 3–4 days in the refrigerator.

Praline

This powder of ground nuts and sugar is easy to make and a useful flavouring for creams, ice creams, and as a decoration for cakes and pastries. It will keep well if stored in an airtight jar.

150g almonds, unblanched	150g caster sugar

Put the almonds and sugar into a pan and heat gently until the sugar melts. When it turns pale brown, stir with a metal spoon. When the sugar has caramelised to a golden brown, turn the mixture onto an oiled baking tray and leave to cool. Break the praline into pieces, then crush or grind to a powder in a blender or food processor.

Variations

· Use toasted blanched almonds instead of whole almonds.
· Use toasted, rubbed hazelnuts instead of almonds (*see* below).

To roast and peel hazelnuts Put the nuts on a baking sheet in an oven heated to 180°C, 350°F, gas 4. Leave them for 8–10 minutes, but stir them once or twice. The brown skins will darken and start to split. Take the nuts from the oven and put them on a clean tea towel. Fold the other end of the towel over and rub the nuts to loosen the skins. Shake them in a coarse sieve.

Pastry

Included here are instructions for making shortcrust (French pâte brisée) and choux pastry. Puff pastry and filo are a hassle to make and best bought fresh or frozen. For notes on using filo pastry, *see* p. 493.

Making shortcrust pastry

Shortcrust is the pastry most commonly used for savoury and sweet open tarts and covered pies.

Pastry dough must be mixed quickly and worked as little as possible to achieve a light crisp result when baked. If pastry is worked too much, or if too much water is added, the gluten in the flour will develop, making the pastry difficult to roll and chewy to eat. Pastry can be made in an electric mixer or a food processor, but use the pulse action of the latter rather than letting the machine run. Over-working will make the mixture oily. Take out the dough as soon as it starts to form a ball and work quickly by hand until supple. Allow pastry dough to relax for at least 30 minutes in the refrigerator before using it.

Plain flour is best for pastry making because it develops less gluten. Unsalted butter is the best fat because it gives the pastry a wonderful flavour; margarine will make a light pastry, but it doesn't add anything to the flavour. Lard gives a good texture for savoury pies, but it has a very high cholesterol content.

Use fat straight from the refrigerator. Egg, iced water or a combination of the two may be used for blending the pastry. Egg makes pastry richer. The exact amount of liquid needed depends on the absorbency of the flour, the type of fat and how well the two have been blended.

If the pastry is for sweet tarts add a little caster sugar to the flour.

Uncooked shortcrust pastry can be kept in the refrigerator for 2–3 days.

Rolling pastry

If the pastry has been chilled for longer than 30 minutes, leave it at room temperature for 10–15 minutes to become pliable before rolling it, otherwise it is likely to crack. Roll pastry on a floured surface with light, decisive movements and even pressure. The less pastry is handled, the lighter it will be. Don't lean on the rolling pin or you will crush the pastry; the aim is to extend it to the right size and shape as quickly as possible.

Flatten the pastry a little with your hand. Dust the pin lightly with flour and roll it away from you across the pastry with a long stroke. Turn the pastry ninety degrees and roll away from you again. Repeat the turning and rolling, checking that there is still enough flour under the pastry to stop it sticking. Roll the pastry a little larger than you need and trim it. Pastry that is too small cannot be stretched, it shrinks back during baking. Re-rolling toughens the pastry, so try to get it right first time.

Problems that can occur when making shortcrust pastry

- *Tough, hard pastry:* not enough fat or too much liquid; over-worked.
- *Crumbly pastry:* too much fat or not enough liquid to bind the pastry.
- *Pastry shrinks during cooking:* insufficient rest time; pastry stretched when rolled.

Lining a tart tin

Use a metal flan tin with a removable base; the tart can be unmoulded by slipping off the ring. To transfer the pastry to the tin, roll it loosely around the pin. Hold the pin over the centre of the tin and lower the pastry carefully into it. Press the pastry lightly into the base and edges before moving up the sides of the tin. Roll the rolling pin over the top of the tin to cut off overhanging pastry. Chill the pastry for 15–30 minutes to allow it to recover from handling.

Covering a pie

Roll out the pastry larger than the dish. From the edge, cut a strip the width of the rim of the pie dish. Wet the rim with a little water, press the strip of pastry onto it, then brush the strip with a little water. Fill the pie dish, putting a pie funnel or inverted egg cup in the middle to hold up the pastry if the contents are likely to shrink during cooking. Lift the pastry on to the rolling pin, and spread it from the centre of the dish, being careful not to stretch it. Press around the rim to seal the two layers of pastry together. Trim off excess pastry. Press all the way around the rim with the back of a fork to seal it well and to decorate the edge. Make a slit in the top so that steam can escape during baking.

Making a double-crust tart

Use a baking tin, sandwich tin or a fairly deep pie plate. Line the base as described for lining a tart tin. Add enough filling to come to the top of the tin, or mound it up slightly if it is likely to cook down. Roll the pastry for the top 2–3cm larger than the tin. Brush the pastry on the rim with a little water. Lift the pastry for the top and ease it over the filling. Press the edges together, letting the excess pastry hang over the sides. Trim the edges and seal the rim with the back of a fork. Make a slit in the top to allow steam to escape.

Baking blind

Pastry cases to be baked unfilled need to be weighted so that they keep in shape. Prick the base to stop it bubbling up during baking. Cut a piece of greaseproof paper big enough to line the tin and leave 4cm protruding above the rim. Fit it into the pastry case, pressing it into the edges of the tin. Fill it two-thirds full with dried beans or raw rice or ceramic baking beans. Bake in the oven preheated to 200°C, 400°F, gas 6, for 10 minutes, then lower the heat to 180°C, 350°F, gas 4, and bake for a further 5–6 minutes. Remove the paper and beans. This gives a partially baked case which can be filled after the base is sealed with a glaze (*see* below) and baked further.

To bake the case completely, bake for about 12 minutes after lowering the temperature of the oven. Let it cool for a few minutes in the tin on a rack before unmoulding it.

To bake tartlet shells blind, either fill them with beans as above or fit a second tin inside the pastry-lined tin, press it in gently and bake for 8 minutes. Remove the inner tin and bake for another 3–4 minutes at the lower temperature for a completely cooked case.

Glazing

Brush pastry lids with lightly beaten egg or milk before baking.

Tarts and flans that are to hold uncooked fillings are best glazed with egg yolk to prevent them going soggy. For cooked fillings melted butter or melted jam can be used (p. 423).

Shortcrust pastry

For a 20–22cm tin making 8–10 tartlets	For a 24–26cm tin making 12–14 tartlets	For a 28–30cm tin making 15–16 tartlets
150g plain flour	200g plain flour	250g plain flour
pinch of salt	¼ tsp salt	½ tsp salt
1½ tsp caster sugar (for sweet pastry)	2 tsp caster sugar (for sweet pastry)	2 tsp caster sugar (for sweet pastry)
75g butter	100g butter	125g butter
1 egg yolk (optional)	1 egg yolk (optional)	1 egg yolk (optional)
2 tbs iced water (more if needed)	3–4 tbs iced water (more if needed)	5–6 tbs iced water (more if needed)

Sift the flour with the salt. Mix in the sugar if you are using it. Cut the butter into small pieces and rub it into the flour with your fingertips until the mixture has the consistency of fine crumbs. Make a well in the centre, put in the lightly beaten egg yolk or a little iced water and mix quickly to a dough with a knife. Add more water gradually if necessary. Bring the dough together with your fingers, knead gently for 1–2 minutes on a lightly floured board until it is smooth. Shape the pastry into a ball, wrap in clingfilm and refrigerate for at least 30 minutes.

Using a food processor Pulse flour, salt (and sugar) to sift. Add the butter in small pieces and pulse for 5–10 seconds. Add the egg yolk if you're using one, and pulse again. Sprinkle over iced water, using half the amount stated above, pulse once or twice and add a little more water gradually if needed. Pastry made in a processor requires less liquid than pastry made by hand. As soon as the pastry starts to form a ball, take it out, work briefly by hand until smooth and supple, then wrap and refrigerate for 30 minutes.

Making choux pastry

Choux pastry is used for éclairs, profiteroles and other cream puffs and for savoury small buns such as cheese-flavoured gougères. Choux paste is first cooked on the top of the stove and then piped or shaped with a spoon onto baking trays, or deep-fried to make beignets. Use choux pastry within a few hours of making it.

Problems that can occur when making choux pastry
· *Cooked buns heavy:* too much fat, not enough eggs or not enough beating.
· *Buns collapse after baking:* oven too hot.

Choux pastry

For 18 or 20 medium buns	For 25 medium buns
80g butter	100g butter
180ml water	250ml water
120g plain flour	150g plain flour
½ tsp salt	½ tsp salt
1 tsp caster sugar (for sweet pastry)	1 tsp caster sugar (for sweet pastry)
3 eggs + 1 egg for glazing	4 eggs + 1 egg for glazing

Cut the butter in pieces and heat it gently with the water in a pan until the butter melts. Sift the flour, stir in the salt, and the sugar if it is to be used. Increase the heat and bring the butter and water to the boil, take the pan from the heat and tip in the flour, salt and sugar all at once. Beat rapidly with a wooden spoon until a dough is formed. Put the pan back over low heat and beat until the paste is smooth and leaves the sides of the pan – it will only take a minute or so. Leave to cool slightly, then beat in the eggs, one at a time, to make a glossy paste soft enough to fall from the spoon. This last part can be done in a food processor if you wish.

The pastry is now ready for use. Heat the oven to 200°C, 400°F, gas 6. Grease two baking trays or line with baking paper. Fill the mixture into a piping bag with a plain 1–1.25cm tube and pipe or shape rounds of 6–8cm with a spoon onto the trays. Leave space between them for the pastry to puff up and expand. Beat 1 egg lightly and brush the tops of the buns to glaze them. Bake for 20–25 minutes. The buns should be golden and crisp.

Cool them on a rack away from draughts. Split them with the tip of a knife to release steam. Fill them with pastry cream (p. 486) when cold, or with whipped double cream as in profiteroles (p. 427).

Variation

Gougères are made with cheese choux pastry. Add 50–60g grated Gruyère or Emmenthal when you add the last egg. Form buns as described above, paint the tops with beaten egg and sprinkle over another 10–15g grated cheese, then bake.

Using filo pastry

If you buy frozen filo pastry, thaw it in the refrigerator. When working with it, take out one sheet at a time and keep the remainder covered with a tea towel or a piece of clingfilm so that they do not dry out. Each sheet of filo is lightly brushed with melted butter, olive or sunflower oil before being used further.

Large pies

For large pies, filo is usually used in shallow oblong dishes or tins, such as a Swiss roll tin. The one I use most often is 20x30x3cm. The tin must be brushed with melted butter or oil before the pastry sheets are spread in it and buttered or oiled in their turn. Cut or fold the pastry to fit the tin and layer the sheets one on top of the other. If you are making a vegetable or meat pie, such as the aubergine filo pie (p. 108), you will need only a few sheets of pastry before putting in the filling, and a few sheets more to cover it. This pastry stays crisp after baking. For sweet pastries like the baklava (p. 426), the quantity of pastry is much greater and although the pastry is crisp when it comes from the oven the cold syrup poured over it softens it somewhat and melds it with the nut filling.

Filo parcels and rolls

To make these, start with 2 oiled or buttered sheets stacked (*see* above). Cut them lengthways into 3 or 4 strips. Put a teaspoon of filling about 5cm from the end nearest to you, leaving a border on each side. Fold the end over the filling, fold again, then fold in the sides. Continue folding to make a parcel. Alternatively, roll the strips around the filling, but again fold in the sides halfway through to seal the edges. *See* variation to aubergine filo pie (p. 108).

Triangular parcels

These are made from 2 sheets, stacked and cut into 3 strips. Place the filling near the end of a strip; bring the top of the strip diagonally over to meet the long side, forming a triangle. Continue folding in the same manner until the strip is used up. *See* variation to aubergine filo pie (p. 108).

Parcels to be fried should be brushed lightly with water to seal the edges.

Strudels

These are made with overlapping sheets of filo with a filling placed at one end and rolled up with the aid of a tea towel. The method is explained in detail in the recipe for cherry strudel (p. 426).

Batters

Batters are mixtures of milk or other liquids, eggs and flour, that are fluid enough to pour. They are used to make a variety of pancakes and griddle cakes, waffles, fritters and batter puddings. Different flours are used – wheat, buckwheat, rice, chick pea – in different parts of the world. Plain wheat flour is preferable for a light dough to make thin pancakes or crêpes; self-raising flour or batter in which baking powder is used will make thicker pancakes. Some pancakes are made with a yeast batter, for which strong plain flour can be used. Milk (or buttermilk or cream) makes richer batter than water. The eggs also contribute richness and elasticity. Salt is usually the only flavouring for savoury pancakes, although spices and herbs may be added to the mixture. Sugar and liqueurs are used for sweet batters. Oil or butter may be added to the mixture to help prevent it sticking to the pan.

Mixing batters

How the batter is mixed is generally less important than the consistency. The ingredients are simply mixed together: either whisked by hand or whizzed on high speed in a blender or food processor. Yeast batters should be well beaten to develop gluten, as when kneading dough. Most batters benefit from standing to allow the starches to expand. Batter thickens while resting, so it may be necessary to add more liquid before using it. English pancakes, French crêpes and batter puddings require a thin batter; fritters, waffles and griddle cakes need a firmer one.

Pancakes

This is a basic pancake batter recipe.

For 10–12 medium-sized pancakes	pinch salt	300ml milk
125g plain flour	1 egg	15g butter, melted or
	1 egg yolk	1 tbs oil (optional)

Sift the flour and salt into a bowl, make a well in the centre, put in the egg, egg yolk and some of the milk. Whisk, drawing in the flour from the sides of the bowl until all is well mixed. When the batter starts to thicken, whisk in the rest of the liquid and keep whisking until you have a smooth, quite thin cream. Stir in the butter or oil, if you are using it, at the end. To make the batter in a blender or food processor, put all the ingredients into the container and whiz until smooth. Let the batter rest for 30 minutes or longer. Heat the oven to 150°C, 300°C, gas 2.

Use a frying pan or omelette pan with a heavy base. It is useful if it is non-stick, too. I prefer to use a light oil such as sunflower oil to grease the pan because it burns less easily than butter. If you prefer butter, use clarified butter*.

Heat the pan and add 2 tbs oil. Swirl it around to coat the base and sides, and pour any excess into a small bowl. Stir the batter and put a small ladleful into the centre of the pan, rotate and tilt the pan to spread it evenly over the base. If you put in too much batter, the pancake will be thick; too little will result in holes. Fry for 1–2 minutes until the underside is a light golden brown and the top is set, then flip the pancake over and cook for about another minute until the bottom has small dark blisters. Use a palette knife or spatula to lift and turn the pancake; you don't have to toss it. Transfer the pancake to a plate. Lightly oil the pan, make sure it is hot enough, and cook the next pancake. Don't worry if the first one is a mess, it often is. Once you get the heat and the amount of batter right, the production line runs smoothly.

To keep pancakes hot once they are made, pile the cooked pancakes on top of each other on a heatproof plate so that they stay moist. Cover them with foil and put in the oven. They will keep for 20 minutes or so.

Pancakes can also be made in advance, stacked with sheets of kitchen paper or greaseproof paper between each, covered with clingfilm or put in a plastic bag and refrigerated for 2–3 days.

Recipes using pancakes occur on pp. 31–4 in First Courses and Light Dishes, and on p. 428 and p. 433 in Desserts.

Variations

Buckwheat pancakes Replace 60g plain flour by 60g buckwheat flour, and follow the basic recipe.

Herb pancakes Add 4–5 tbs chopped mixed fresh herbs to the batter.

Lemon pancakes Add the grated rind of 1 unwaxed lemon to the batter.

Sweet pancakes Add 1 tbs sugar with the flour.

Lacy crêpes Add 50g cooled melted butter with the milk and egg.

Yorkshire pudding

A traditional accompaniment to roast beef (p. 318) along with horseradish sauce, Yorkshire pudding is wonderful when well risen, light and crisp. It is important to have the fat very hot or the batter will absorb it and become soggy.

For 4–6	1 egg	300ml milk
125g plain flour	1 egg yolk	dripping or oil
½ tsp salt		

Heat the oven to 220°C, 425°F, gas 7. Whisk all the ingredients, except the dripping or oil, until well blended. Melt some dripping or heat 3 tbs oil in a shallow baking tin, 20 x 25cm, and when it is smoking pour in the batter. Put it into the oven at once and cook for 30–40 minutes until it is well risen, crisp and browned. If you prefer, make individual Yorkshire puddings in small deep patty tins and bake for 20–30 minutes.

Toad-in-the-hole

Fry whole sausages in the fat in the baking tin for 5 minutes before adding the batter made as above.

Fritters (Beignets)

This is a basic fritter batter recipe that can be used with vegetables and fruit.

Enough to coat about 500g food	¼ tsp freshly ground pepper or 1 tsp sugar	150ml beer, carbonated water or milk
125g plain flour	1 egg	
½ tsp salt	1 tbs melted butter	

Sift the flour and salt into a large bowl and stir in the pepper or sugar, depending on whether you are making savoury or sweet fritters. Make a well in the centre, add the egg, butter and beer, water or milk and mix to a thick batter. Alternatively, whiz all the ingredients in a blender or food processor until smooth. Leave to rest for 30 minutes.

Fritters can be shallow- or deep-fried. Make sure the fat is hot enough; the correct temperature for deep frying is 190°C, 375°F. A little batter dropped into the pan will sizzle and rise to the surface when the temperature is right. If you deep-fry, lower the fritters into the fat in a basket or on a wire scoop. Do not fry too many pieces at a time and make sure the fat is hot enough before frying another batch.

Fry fritters until crisp and golden; they will take 3–4 minutes if deep-fried, 2–4 minutes each side if shallow-fried. If they are soggy, the fat was not hot enough.

Drain fritters on kitchen paper before serving.

See vegetable fritters, p. 6, and fruit fritters, p. 428.

Variations

· For a lighter batter, whisk an additional egg white until stiff and fold it into the batter just before using it.
· For additional flavour, add ½ tsp turmeric or chilli powder to the batter.

Italian batter. *See* fritto misto, p. 426.

Tempura batter

This light Japanese batter is very good for fish and vegetables which are to be deep-fried. You can buy good prepared boxes of tempura batter made with Japanese flour, but it only takes a little time to make your own. Even though you use English flour, it will still taste good.

Makes enough to coat about 400g food	1 egg yolk	125g plain flour, sifted
	250ml iced water	

Gently mix the egg yolk with the water then tip in the flour. Stir lightly with a fork, the mixture should remain lumpy with bits of flour in it. If you over-mix it will be heavy. Tempura batter should be just thick enough to coat the food and must be used as soon as it is made, so have the fish or vegetables ready prepared and about 6cm oil heated in a wok or wide pan. Dip the food in flour and shake off the excess before coating in the batter and frying.

Jams and other preserves

Preserving food for winter supplies is no longer vitally important, but home-made jams, pickles and chutneys add variety to the store cupboard throughout the year. They are economical to make, and surveying a shelf of your own preserves is very rewarding. Good-quality fruit and vegetables are the basis of good preserves, whether sweet or savoury. For kitchen gardeners with seasonal gluts, or for an abundance of soft fruits from the local pick-your-own farm, preserves are a perfect answer.

Equipment

For all preserves, use a large heavy wide pan; a preserving pan with sloping sides is useful but not essential. A heavy base will prevent sticking and a pan wider than it is deep encourages evaporation. When making jam do not have the pan more than half full because the jam will bubble up and spit as it boils. Do not use unlined copper or brass when using vinegar in a recipe because it will react with the metal. You will also need a long-handled wooden spoon, a slotted spoon for skimming, nylon or plastic sieves (metal can leave an unpleasant taste), a jug or ladle for filling jars – an inexpensive jam funnel is helpful here, too – and a sugar thermometer can be useful but is not essential.

Make sure jars and bottles are not chipped or cracked. They must be sterilised before use: wash well in soapy water, rinse thoroughly in hot water and put them in a low oven (130°C, 250°F, gas ½) for 30 minutes. Screw-top lids are good, but they must be vinegar-proof or have a vinegar-proof lining if they are to be used for chutneys and pickles. Vinegar causes metal to corrode. Screw-top lids and corks should be boiled for 10 minutes then left to drain.

Packs of waxed papers, transparent discs and labels needed for covering and storing are available in kitchen shops and supermarkets.

Filling, covering and storing

Use warm jars when filling with hot preserves to prevent the jars cracking; leave the jars to cool before filling with cold preserves. Fill jars to the top and, while still very hot, cover the preserve with a waxed paper disc, waxed side down, pressed onto the surface. Cover with a transparent disc and then the lid, or secure the disc (or a double layer of clingfilm) with string or elastic band.

If a preserve is not covered while hot, leave until quite cold before covering. If you cover a warm preserve, moisture may form and cause spoilage.

Once the jars or bottles are sealed, wipe well to remove any sticky patches and remember to label clearly. Preserves are best kept in a cool, dry, dark place.

Jams and marmalades

Jam is a mixture of fruit and sugar. It should be clear, bright, firmly set but not too stiff, and have a distinctive fruit flavour. The fruit should be very fresh and ideally slightly under-ripe. It can be difficult to get jam made with over-ripe fruit to set. Successful jam making depends on the correct balance of pectin, acid and sugar.

Pectin is a natural gum-like substance found in all fruits and extracted when they are boiled; it is most easily extracted in under-ripe fruit. Acid helps in the extraction of pectin and is also essential for a good set. Sugar is the preservative in jam making, but the points between which a jam is liable to ferment because it contains too little sugar or crystallize because it contains too much are rather small.

Some fruits (citrus fruits, apples, damsons, gooseberries, black and red currants) have a high pectin and acid content and will set easily when cooked with the right amount of sugar. Fruits like cherries, raspberries, peaches, mangoes, strawberries are low in pectin as well as acidity, so both must be added to make a preserve. The easiest form in which to add acid is lemon juice, while pectin can be increased by combining high and low pectin fruits or by adding commercial pectin. Follow the manufacturer's instructions for the latter.

Granulated sugar or preserving sugar are most widely used for jam making. Commercial jam sugar with added natural apple pectin is also available; follow the instructions on the bag. The usual proportions are 375–500g sugar to every 500g fruit. If the sugar is warmed in a very low oven for 15–20 minutes before being added to the fruit it will dissolve more quickly.

Testing for setting

Test the jam when it begins to thicken slightly. Take up a little on a wooden spoon, hold it horizontal over the pan for a few seconds, then tilt to pour the jam back into the pan. If it forms a flake on the edge of the spoon which then falls away slowly, it is ready. Another test is to put a little onto a cold saucer and push it with a finger after a few seconds; if the jam wrinkles it will set. If it is still runny, boil longer and re-test in a few minutes. A reading of 105°C, 220°F on a sugar thermometer indicates the setting point. When ready, remove any scum from the surface, stir to distribute the fruit evenly and pot.

Problems that can occur when making jam

- *If the jam has not set:* it can be re-boiled, or a little liquid pectin can be added to it.
- *If the jam crystallizes:* the jam was boiled too long or too fast before all the sugar had dissolved; too much sugar was used.
- *If the jam ferments:* the jam was boiled too little; too little sugar was used; the fruit may have been over-ripe and mushy.
- *If mould occurs:* the jam was not very hot nor quite cold when covered with the waxed disc; the jam was kept in warm or damp conditions.

Apricot and almond jam

Use ripe but firm apricots for this jam. It is worth taking the trouble to crack 5–6 apricot stones with a hammer or nutcracker, extract the kernels, blanch them for 2 minutes and remove the skins; they will enhance the flavour.

For about 1.6kg	juice of 2 lemons	30g blanched split almonds
1kg apricots, halved and stoned	150ml water	
	1kg sugar	

Put the apricot halves, with a few kernels if possible, into a large pan with the lemon juice and water. Bring slowly to the boil, reduce the heat and simmer gently until the fruit is soft and translucent, about 30–40 minutes. Warm the sugar in a low oven (opposite) while the fruit is cooking. Add the sugar and stir until it has dissolved. Stir in the almonds. Increase the heat and boil briskly, stirring occasionally, until the mixture begins to thicken slightly; it will take 10–12 minutes. Test for setting (opposite). Remove the pan from the heat, skim any scum from the surface and leave to stand for 5 minutes or so. Stir to distribute the fruit evenly and pour the jam into warm sterilized jars. Cover and seal.

Spiced blackberry jelly

For about 800g	½ tsp ground cinnamon	sugar (for quantity *see* below)
1kg blackberries	pinch of ground cloves	juice of 2 lemons
250ml water		

Put the blackberries, water and spices in a large pan, bring slowly to the boil then simmer for about 25 minutes until soft and pulpy. Squash the fruit with a potato masher or the back of a wooden spoon as it cooks. Line a large plastic or nylon sieve with a piece of muslin (p. 528), tip in the blackberries and their juice and leave to drip through. Don't press or the jelly will be cloudy. Measure the juice and for every 600ml add 500g sugar. Put the juice, sugar and lemon juice into a clean pan and heat gently until the sugar dissolves. Bring to the boil and boil until setting point (p. 500) is reached – about 5 minutes. Pour into warm, sterilized jars, cover and seal.

Black currant jam

The cloves are not essential to the jam, but give it a lightly spiced flavour. Omit them if you wish.

For about 1.5kg	3–4 cloves	1.5kg sugar
1kg black currants	800ml water	

Strip the black currants (run the stalks through a fork) and discard any small green currants. Put the fruit in a large pan with the cloves and water. Bring slowly to the boil, then simmer until the skins and fruit are soft and the fruit mixture has reduced by about one third; it can take 45–50 minutes. Warm the sugar in a low oven (p. 500) for the last 30 minutes of the cooking time. Add the sugar over medium heat and stir until it has dissolved. Increase the heat and boil fast, stirring occasionally, until the jam thickens and setting point (p. 500) is reached. Blackcurrant jam sets quite quickly so test frequently to ensure it is not overcooked. Take the pan from the heat, remove any scum, leave to stand for a few minutes, then stir to distribute the fruit and pour into warm sterilized jars. Cover and seal.

Damson and apple jam

For about 3.2kg	250ml water	2kg sugar
1kg damsons	1kg cooking apples	

Remove any stalks from the damsons, slit the fruits along one side and put them in a large pan with the water and simmer until soft, about 30–40 minutes. The stones will rise to the surface during cooking and can be removed. Peel, core and chop the apples and add to the pan. Simmer until the apple is soft, but don't let it disintegrate; the texture of the jam is improved by some pieces of apple. While the apple is cooking, warm the sugar in a low oven (p. 500). Add the sugar, and stir until it dissolves. Turn up the heat and boil briskly until the mixture thickens and setting point is reached (p. 500). Remove the pan from the heat, skim off any scum, stir and pour into warm, sterilized jars. Cover and seal.

Four fruit jam

This recipe originally appeared in *Canning, Preserving and Pickling* by Marion Harris Neil, published in the 1930s.

For about 2.5kg	500g gooseberries	250g raspberries
1kg cherries, stones removed and reserved	500g red or black currants	1.5kg sugar

Tie the stones from the cherries in a piece of muslin (p. 528). Top and tail the gooseberries. Put the fruit and sugar into a large pan, bring slowly to the boil, stirring from time to time to prevent sticking, and boil until the liquid evaporates and the mixture thickens. Test for setting (p. 500). When the jam is ready, remove the pan from the heat. Discard the cherry stones, skim off any scum and leave to stand for a few minutes. Stir to distribute the fruit, pour the jam into warm, sterilized jars, cover and seal.

Plum, rum and walnut jam

For about 1.5kg	200ml water	100g walnuts, chopped
1kg plums	900g sugar	4 tbs dark rum

Cut the plums in half and discard the stones. Put the fruit into a large pan with the water and slowly bring to the boil. Simmer, stirring from time to time, until the plums are tender, about 30–40 minutes. Warm the sugar in a low oven (p. 500) while the fruit is cooking, then add it to the pan. Stir until the sugar has dissolved. Increase the heat and bring the mixture to a brisk boil and boil until setting point is reached (p. 500), about 12–15 minutes. Remove the pan from the heat, skim off any scum and stir in the walnuts and rum. Pour the jam into warm, sterilized jars, cover and seal.

Peach and orange jam

For about 2kg	2 unwaxed oranges	150ml water
1.5kg peaches	2 unwaxed lemons	1.5kg sugar

Immerse the peaches in boiling water for 1 minute, then drain and remove the skins. Cut them in half, remove the stones and slice the flesh. Put the slices in a large pan with the grated rind of the oranges and lemons and the water and simmer for 20–25 minutes until the peaches are tender. While the fruit is cooking, put the sugar in a low oven to warm (p. 500). Cut the pith from the oranges and lemons and cut the fruit into pieces over a bowl to catch the juices. Discard the pips. Add the citrus fruit and juice to the peaches and stir in the sugar until it dissolves. Boil briskly until the mixture thickens and setting point is reached (p. 500), about 10–12 minutes. Remove the pan from the heat, stir to distribute the fruit and pour into warm, sterilized jars. Cover and seal.

Raspberry jam

This recipe is for an uncooked jam with a vibrant flavour. It will keep for up to 3 months.

| For about 1.6kg | 1kg raspberries | 1kg sugar |

Heat the oven to 180°C, 350°F, gas 4. Put the raspberries and sugar into separate ovenproof dishes and put them in the oven to get very hot. This takes 20–30 minutes. Add the sugar to the raspberries and mix them thoroughly, mashing the raspberries with the back of a wooden spoon or a potato masher and stirring until the sugar has dissolved. Pour into warm sterilized jars at once, cover and seal.

Eliza Acton's 'superlative red currant jelly'

This recipe from *Modern Cookery* of 1845 makes a beautifully clear, sharp jelly 'of the finest possible flavour'. It does not set very hard, but is firm enough to spoon out.

| For about 800g | 1kg red currants | 1kg sugar |

Put the currants (there is no need to remove the stalks) and sugar into a large pan and bring to the boil. Stir as you do so and crush the currants with the back of the spoon. Boil rapidly for exactly 8 minutes, stirring all the time and skimming off the abundant scum from the surface. Turn the preserve into a fine nylon or plastic sieve, pressing the skin and pips against the sides to extract as much pectin as possible. Pour at once into small, warm, sterilized jars, cover and seal.

Strawberry jam

For about 1.4kg | 750g sugar | juice of 1 large lemon
1.5kg strawberries

Hull the strawberries after washing them, drain well and cut them into pieces. Layer them in a large pan with the sugar, ending with a layer of sugar. Cover with a clean cloth and leave to macerate for 6 hours.

Put the pan over low heat and add half the lemon juice. Simmer for 30 minutes, stirring occasionally. Stir briskly, crushing the fruit with a potato masher or the back of a wooden spoon, then increase the heat, add the rest of the lemon juice and boil for 10–15 minutes. Test for setting (p. 500) as the mixture thickens. Pour the jam into warm, sterilized jars, cover and seal.

Seville orange marmalade

Seville oranges are in season during January and early February, and bitter oranges from the southern hemisphere come in briefly in October, so don't delay in buying them if you want to make marmalade. At other times of the year, you can make marmalade with other citrus fruits. This method of first cooking the whole oranges in the oven or in a closed pan produces a thick, chunky marmalade.

For about 1.8kg | 1kg Seville oranges | sugar (for quantity *see* below)

Heat the oven to 170°C, 325°F, gas 3. Wash the fruit and put it into a casserole, cover with boiling water, cover tightly and bake for about 3 hours, until the fruit is soft enough to pierce easily with a skewer. Alternatively put the oranges in a large pan, cover with boiling water and the lid and simmer gently for 1½–2 hours. Take the oranges from the casserole or pan, reserving the liquid. Cut up the fruit – it is best to do this on a plate because it will produce a great deal of liquid, and I find a knife and fork the most efficient way to do the job. Having removed the pips as you cut, now return them to the cooking liquid and boil for 5 minutes, then strain, again reserving the liquid.

Weigh the fruit pulp and for every 500g take 750g sugar and 450ml of the liquid. Put everything into a large pan and cook gently until the sugar dissolves, then boil rapidly until setting point is reached (p. 500), about 10 minutes. Skim and let the marmalade cool slightly to help distribute the peel. As soon as a skin forms on the surface, stir the marmalade and pour into warm, sterilized jars. Cover and seal.

Grapefruit, lemon and ginger marmalade

For about 2.2kg	2.5 litres water	150g crystallized ginger, chopped
2 unwaxed grapefruit	1.5kg sugar	
2 unwaxed lemons		

Wash the fruit, remove the peel and cut it into thin strips. Remove excess pith from the fruit, including the pithy centres of the grapefruit but do not throw away. Slice the fruit thinly, removing and retaining the pips. Put the pips and some of the pith in a piece of muslin (p. 528) and put the bag into a large pan with the fruit and peel. Pour over the water and simmer for 1½ hours. For the last half-hour of the cooking time, put the sugar to warm in a low oven (p. 500).

The contents of the pan should have reduced almost by half. Take out the bag of pips and squeeze it thoroughly over the pan, then discard. Add the warmed sugar and stir until it dissolves. Increase the heat and bring the pan to a fast boil, stir in the ginger and cook until setting point is reached (p. 500), about 10 minutes. Take off any scum and leave the marmalade to cool slightly. When a skin begins to form on the surface, stir the pan and pour the marmalade into warm, sterilized jars. Cover and seal.

Preserves

The main preserving agents for fruit and vegetables are sugar and vinegar: sugar or syrup for sweet preserves, vinegar for pickles, and both for chutney. Spices and herbs add depth of flavour and give an aromatic lift to oils and vinegars.

Sweet preserves

Lemon curd

Use lemon curd in cake and tart fillings, on scones or bread. Store it in the refrigerator where it will keep for 2 months.

For about 500g	75g butter	3 eggs
250g sugar	grated rind and juice of 3 unwaxed lemons	

Put the sugar, butter, lemon rind and juice in a bowl placed over a pan of simmering water. Heat gently until the butter has melted and the sugar dissolved. Beat the eggs lightly and strain them into the mixture. Cook gently until the mixture thickens enough to coat the back of the spoon. It will take 15–20 minutes. Stir occasionally at first and constantly as the mixture thickens towards the end of the cooking time. Make sure that the water does not boil, for if the curd boils it will curdle.

Pour the curd into warm, sterilized jars, cover and seal.

Mincemeat

For about 1.5kg	60g mixed peel	½ tsp grated nutmeg
200g tart apples	60g peeled, chopped almonds	seeds of 4 cardamom pods*, crushed
200g ready-to-eat dried apricots	200g sugar	grated rind and juice of 1 unwaxed lemon
200g raisins	150g beef or vegetarian suet	grated rind and juice of 1 unwaxed orange
200g currants	1 tsp ground cinnamon	80ml rum or brandy
200g sultanas		

Peel, core and chop the apples, chop the apricots quite finely. Thoroughly mix the apple and apricot with the rest of the ingredients in a large china or earthenware bowl. Cover and leave to stand for 24 hours. Put into sterilized jars, making sure there are no air pockets. Cover and seal as for jam.

Chutneys and pickles

Chutneys and pickles are a simple way of preserving fruits and vegetables and providing additional flavourings for the store cupboard to serve with a curry, grilled meats, rice dishes, a selection of cold meats or cheeses. Spices are an essential part of chutney and pickle making: cinnamon, coriander, nutmeg and mace provide mild flavours; allspice, cardamom* and cloves are more aromatic; chillies, cayenne, mustard, ginger, garam masala* and curry powder add heat. You can vary the spicing to suit your own taste. I prefer to use wine, cider or white vinegar because I find malt vinegar too potent, but the latter is cheaper. Use sea salt, not table salt which has additives to keep it free-flowing.

Keep chutneys and pickles in a cool, dark place. *See* the notes on p. 499, with particular reference to keeping vinegar-based preserves out of contact with metal.

Chutneys

These are made principally with fruits and some aromatic vegetables cooked slowly with vinegar and sugar, laced with herbs and spices to produce rich sweet-sour or hot relishes. The vinegar, sugar, salt and spices act as preserving agents. Slow cooking is essential to produce a mellow flavour, as is allowing the chutney to mature in the jar for several weeks before eating. In fact, some chutneys will mature over 3–4 years. If you are making only a small quantity, it would be sensible to cover the pan so that the mixture does not dry out before it is fully cooked.

Fruit and vegetables for chutney need not be at their best (windfalls come into their own here) but make sure to remove all bruised and blemished parts, and don't use fruit that is over-ripe or mouldy. Chutneys invite improvisation, so try other combinations of fruits and spices, according to what is available.

It is difficult to be precise about the yield of chutney recipes because it depends on the thickness of the chutney and how much liquid evaporates during cooking. I have given amounts but they should be treated as a guideline only.

The chutneys in this chapter are all cooked; uncooked chutneys are in the Sauces chapter on p. 382–3.

Pickles

These are whole or sliced vegetables, or sometimes fruits, preserved in spiced vinegar to keep their shape and appearance. Use firm, fresh, even-sized vegetables. Vegetables may be salted overnight or pickled immediately in spiced vinegar. Use whole spices for pickles because ground ones cloud the vinegar. It is important that vegetables are well covered by vinegar when put in jars because the vinegar may evaporate. If the pickles have a tendency to float, put a piece of crumpled greaseproof paper in the top of the jar; after a few weeks it can be removed. Add more vinegar if necessary at this stage so that the food is always covered.

Problems that can occur when making chutney and pickles

- *Chutney dried out and shrunk in the jar:* cover not airtight, or jar stored in warm conditions.
- *Chutney thin and watery:* under-cooked.
- *Chutney mouldy on top:* under-cooked; there is not enough vinegar in the jar or the vinegar is too weak; the jars were not sterilized before filling.
- *Pickles dried out:* jars not airtight allowing vinegar to evaporate.

- *Pickles soft and mushy:* stored for too long.
- *Pickles that do not keep well:* insufficient salt or vinegar; vinegar too weak.
- *Pickles mouldy on top:* not completely covered with vinegar before storing.

Note that rust will form on metal lids and cause contamination, so use other forms of lid.

Apricot and apple chutney

For about 1.2kg	150g raisins	1 tsp mustard seeds
500g dried apricots	450ml white wine vinegar	½ tsp ground ginger
2 green apples		½ tsp ground allspice
3 large onions	250g muscovado sugar	1½ tsp salt

Soak the apricots in hot water for 3–4 hours unless they are the ready-to-eat type. Drain and chop them. Peel, core and chop the apples, peel and slice the onions. Put all the ingredients into a large pan and simmer until the mixture has reduced and thickened. It will take about 40 minutes. Stir occasionally to prevent sticking. Put the chutney into jars, cover and seal while hot.

Red pepper chutney

This chutney comes from Escoffier's *Ma Cuisine* and was quoted by Elizabeth David in *Spices, Salt and Aromatics in the English Kitchen.* Perhaps better described as a relish rather than a chutney, it keeps for a month or so and is excellent with cold meats.

For about 2kg	850g tomatoes	1 tsp allspice
500g Spanish onions, peeled	1 garlic clove, peeled and crushed	500g sugar
100ml olive oil	1 tsp ground ginger	250g sultanas
1kg red peppers		300ml wine vinegar

Chop the onions and brown them lightly in the oil. Cut the peppers in strips, discarding the seeds and white membrane, and add them to the onions. Stew them together gently for 10–15 minutes. Peel, seed and chop the tomatoes, and add them to the pan with the garlic, spices, sugar and sultanas. Stir to mix all the ingredients and add the vinegar. Cover the pan and cook over very low heat, using a heat diffuser if necessary, for about 1½ hours until you have an iridescent golden mixture. Put into warm, sterilized jars, cover and seal.

Carrot and raisin chutney

This is a fairly dry Indian sweet and sour chutney that is ready to eat within a few days. Serve with your favourite curry, a dish of rice and lentils (p. 185) or just spread it on bread.

For about 1.5kg

300ml wine, cider or white vinegar	1kg carrots, peeled	1 tsp ground cumin
750g sugar	4cm ginger, peeled	2 tsp garam masala*
	2 garlic cloves, peeled	1 tsp salt
	2 tsp chilli powder	200g raisins

Heat the vinegar and sugar slowly until the sugar dissolves. Grate the carrots. Chop the ginger finely and crush the garlic. Add the carrots, ginger, garlic, spices and salt to the vinegar and simmer for about 20 minutes, until most of the liquid has evaporated. Stir in the raisins and continue to cook for another 5–10 minutes until the carrots are almost dry. Remove the pan from the heat and leave to cool. Put into sterilized jars and keep for 2–3 days before eating.

Plum and pear chutney

A good autumn chutney to make with the last fruits of the season. I have sometimes replaced some of the fruit by apples and used raisins or sultanas instead of dates.

For about 1.8kg

1kg plums	500g onions, peeled	1 tsp ground ginger
1kg pears	500ml herb vinegar (p. 516)	1 tsp ground allspice
200g dates, stoned	2 garlic cloves, peeled and crushed	½ tsp grated nutmeg
		250g muscovado sugar

Cut the plums in half and discard the stones. Peel and core the pears and cut them in chunks. Chop the dates and the onions. Put all the ingredients except the sugar into a large pan and simmer for 30–40 minutes, stirring occasionally, until tender. Add the sugar and stir until it has dissolved. Simmer gently until the chutney is thick and the vinegar has evaporated, about 40 minutes. Leave to cool, then put into sterilized jars, cover and seal.

Green tomato chutney

For about 900g	1 medium onion, peeled and chopped	200ml wine or cider vinegar
800g green tomatoes, chopped	150g raisins	2 tsp mustard seeds (p. 76)
2 tart apples, peeled, cored and chopped	1 tsp salt	1 tsp coriander seed
	200g muscovado sugar	2 dried chillies

Put all the fruits and vegetables into a large pan with the salt, sugar and vinegar. Tie the spices in a piece of muslin (p. 528) and add them to the pan. Bring to the boil, and simmer, stirring often for 25–30 minutes until the chutney has thickened. Discard the spices. Put into warm, sterilized pots, cover and seal.

Red tomato chutney

For about 700g	6 cloves	250ml wine vinegar
1kg very ripe tomatoes	4cm ginger	250g sugar
1 medium onion	1 tsp salt	¼ tsp ground chilli
2 garlic cloves		

Peel and quarter the tomatoes. Peel and chop the onion and garlic. Tie the cloves and ginger in a piece of muslin (p.528) and put with the vegetables, salt and vinegar into a large pan. Simmer gently until the tomatoes and onions are soft and pulpy. Remove the pan from the heat and stir in the sugar. When it has dissolved return the pan to the heat and simmer gently until the vinegar is absorbed and the chutney is thick and jam-like, about 45 minutes. Stir in the chilli. Put the chutney into warm, sterilized jars, cover and seal.

Pickled beetroot

This sweet-sour pickle is quite different from the sharp, vinegary English pickled beetroot and comes from the Republic of Georgia.

For about 900g	300ml wine vinegar	4 cloves
1kg beetroot of similar size	4 tbs sugar	6 black peppercorns
	2 tsp dried mint	

Put the washed and unpeeled beetroot in a large pan, pour over boiling water, cover and simmer until they are just tender, about 15 minutes for baby beets, up to 45 minutes for large ones. Drain the beetroot, reserving 250ml of the cooking liquid. Turn the beetroot into a bowl of cold water to arrest the cooking, peel and slice them. Put them into sterilized jars. Bring the reserved cooking liquid to the boil with the vinegar and other ingredients. Pour the pickling liquid over the beetroot, making sure they are fully immersed. Cover and keep for at least a week before using.

Pickled onion

This recipe comes from the Yucatán peninsula in southern Mexico where the onion is served with tortillas stuffed with beans and chicken. It is good with cold meats, too.

For about 400g	½ tsp ground allspice	3 garlic cloves, peeled and sliced thinly
500g red onions, peeled	½ tsp ground cumin	about 300ml wine or cider vinegar
salt	½ tsp coarsely ground black pepper	
2 tsp dried oregano, rubbed (p. 517)		

Slice the onions thinly and blanch them in boiling salted water for 1 minute. Drain well and put into a wide bowl. Mix together the oregano and spices and mix them into the onion with the garlic. The best way to make sure all the onion is coated with the spice mixture is to stir the mixture with your hands. Put the onion into a sterilized jar, pressing it down. Pour over the vinegar, making sure there is enough to cover the onion completely. Cover and refrigerate. The onion can be eaten within 24 hours but will keep and mature for up to 3 weeks in the refrigerator.

Spiced preserves

Preserved lemons

Preserved lemons can now be bought in some delicatessens and some supermarkets, but it is very easy to make your own, and their distinctive, slightly salty taste is useful in salads, in dressings and salsas, as well as to flavour meat and vegetables. Use unwaxed lemons or, if you can't find them, scrub the lemons very thoroughly.

Take 4 or 5 lemons, wash them well and cut almost into four, leaving the pieces attached at the stalk end. Sprinkle coarse sea salt – about 1 tbs per lemon – into the cuts, close up the lemons again and put them in a large jar. Press down well and put a weight (a clean heavy stone will do) on top. Close the jar. After 2–3 days the lemons will begin to release some of their juices. Pour over enough fresh lemon juice (from 3–4 lemons) to cover them completely and leave for 1 month.

A piece of lemon exposed to the air may develop a harmless white mould. Just wash it off. The lemons will keep for a year, and the flavour improves with keeping.

Chilli jam (Nam prik pad)

This Thai relish can be served as a condiment to accompany Thai dishes or stirred into soups, stir-fries and rice dishes. It will also pep up a yogurt dressing.

Shrimp paste is made from fermented prawns, and is widely used in south-east Asian cooking. It is very pungent, the aroma being reminiscent of meat extract. It is used with vegetable, meat and poultry dishes as well as fish, giving depth of flavour. Available in blocks from oriental shops, it may be sold under the names of *trassi* or *blachan*. Once opened, keep the block in a jar to contain its pungent smell.

Dried shrimps, available whole or shredded, are another staple flavouring throughout tropical Asia. They go whole into vegetable dishes; when chopped, they are combined with pork, or they can be ground and sprinkled over noodles and salads. Available from oriental shops.

For 1 small jar	10 garlic cloves, peeled and sliced	4 tbs dried shrimps
1 tsp shrimp paste		3 tbs vegetable oil
5 large red chillies, fresh or dried, seeds and stalk removed	10 shallots, peeled and sliced	2 tbs sugar
		3 tbs tamarind* water

Wrap the shrimp paste in a piece of foil, place it under a hot grill or in a preheated oven for a few minutes until it darkens in colour. Tear the chillies into pieces. Dry-roast the chillies, garlic and shallots separately. This can be done in a hot oven (200°C, 400°F, gas 6), putting them on a large baking tray, or one by one in a dry, heavy frying pan. When the garlic, shallots and chillies are soft, put them into a food processor or a large mortar with the shrimp paste and blend to a paste. Scrape down the sides to make sure everything is well blended. Pound the dried shrimps finely and add them to the mixture. Heat the oil in a wok or frying pan and fry the paste until it smells fragrant and cooked. Stir in the sugar and tamarind water and fry a little longer until everything is well mixed and slightly reduced. Cool and put into a sterilized jar. Cover, seal and put in the refrigerator where it will keep for a month or so, although this small amount may not get the chance to do so. If you like the preserve, you can easily increase the quantities to make a few jars at a time.

Sweet chilli sauce (Saus prik)

Another Thai recipe, this hot, sweet and garlicky sauce is served in many Thai restaurants. You can buy bottles of chilli sauce, but it is easy to make at home and tastes much better. You can determine the heat of the sauce by increasing or reducing the number of chillies. Small chillies are much hotter than large ones, and if you leave the seeds in the sauce they will contribute more heat still.

For about 600ml		
150g fresh red chillies, stalks and seeds removed	3cm ginger, peeled and cut in pieces	150ml rice or wine vinegar
6 garlic cloves, peeled	250g sultanas	1 tsp salt
	200g tinned tomatoes, drained	350g sugar
		150ml water

Put the chillies, garlic, ginger, sultanas, tomatoes and vinegar into a food processor or blender and blend to a purée. If necessary, scrape down the sides to ensure all the ingredients are well mixed. Tip the purée into a pan and add the remaining ingredients. Bring to the boil, stirring to ensure the sugar dissolves, then simmer gently for 15–20 minutes, stirring from time to time, until the sauce has thickened slightly. Let it cool, then pour into sterilized bottles or jars and seal. The sauce will keep in the refrigerator for up to 2 months.

Flavoured oils and vinegars

Oils

Oils infused with herbs, spices and other flavourings are quickly and easily made. Choose a fairly neutral oil such as sunflower, safflower or corn for pungent flavours and use olive or grapeseed oil for milder herbs. Flavoured oils can be used in marinades and dressings, for stir-frying, brushing over foods to be grilled or for tossing cooked vegetables.

Herb oil

Use fresh herbs, either a single herb or a mixture: 3–4 tbs or 4–6 sprigs of herb to 500ml oil is about the right amount. Use herbs before they flower for then they have a more pungent aroma. Put them into a sterilized glass jar, cover with the oil, close and leave in a cool place for 2 weeks. Strain the oil into a sterilized bottle. Add a new herb sprig for decoration and identification. Herb oils can be used straight away and will keep for 9–12 months if stored in a cool, dark place.

Suitable herbs Basil, dill, fennel, mint, oregano, rosemary, savory, tarragon, thyme.

Other flavourings To use on their own or with herbs: seeds of anise, dill, fennel, garlic, lemon grass*.

Chilli oil

You can temper the heat by reducing the amount of chillies and removing the chilli seeds. Even a very mildly flavoured chilli oil is an asset in the cupboard because it adds flavour to many dishes and can also replace chillies in a dish requiring chillies cooked in oil. Chillies vary greatly in heat, so taste the oil as it matures and if it is getting too hot for your taste, remove the chillies.

Use 8–12 red chillies, fresh or dried, to 500ml oil. Split the chillies, put them into a sterilized jar, cover with oil and leave for 10–14 days. Strain into a sterilized bottle, add a dried chilli for identification if you wish and store in a cool, dark place.

Vinegars

Vinegars flavoured with herbs, fruit or spices are easy to make and they extend the range of flavours available for dressings, sauces and marinades. Wine, cider or rice vinegar are the best for making flavoured vinegars. Use flavoured vinegars in marinades, sauces and dressings or add a dash to give a lift to a stew or soup.

Use bottles with cork or plastic-lined caps. Vinegars will keep for several years, becoming more mellow as they age.

Herb vinegar

For herb vinegars, select fresh herbs, preferably before they flower, for they have a stronger flavour. Flower sprigs can be put into the finished bottles for their decorative effect. The right proportion is about 60g herbs to 500ml vinegar. Crush the sprigs or leaves to bring out their flavour, put them into a large sterilized jar and cover with vinegar. Leave to steep for 3 weeks, then strain the vinegar into sterilized bottles. Put a fresh sprig of herb into each bottle to serve as identification. Seal the bottles. The vinegar is ready for use.

Suitable herbs Basil, borage, chives, dill, lavender, lemon balm, lemon verbena, mint, rosemary, savory, tarragon, thyme.

Spiced vinegar

For spiced vinegars, use whole spices in order not to cloud the vinegar. Spiced vinegar is often made to use for pickling fruits and vegetables, but it can also be used for vinaigrette dressings and in cooking.

For 1 litre	2 tsp cloves	4 dried chillies (optional)
2 sticks cinnamon	1 tbs black peppercorns	
1 tbs allspice	2 blades mace	1 litre red or white wine vinegar

Divide the spices between 2 sterilized bottles and pour in the vinegar. Seal them. Shake the bottles occasionally over 6–8 weeks in order to extract maximum flavour.

If you want spiced vinegar in a hurry, bring the spices and vinegar to the boil, then pour into bottles. It can be used within 2 days, but would benefit from keeping for a week or two.

If the flavours of the vinegar become too strong with keeping, discard the spices.

Other flavourings To use on their own, with herbs or with the more pungent spices: chillies, coriander seed, dill seed, fennel seed, garlic, lemon grass*, unwaxed lemon and orange peel.

Appendices

Essential stores

Everyone has their own ideas about essentials: my suggestions are primarily for foods with a long shelf life that are used in many of the recipes in this book. You could, if necessary, make a meal from combinations of them, but mostly they are used with fresh ingredients as accompaniments or to add flavour, improve texture or provide a shortcut.

Dried herbs and spices

Herbs

Only a few dried herbs are worth having; most are better used fresh. Bay leaves, dried mint, oregano, thyme and a mixture such as herbes de Provence are the essentials. They keep their aroma and flavour when dried, and should last for a year or so before they become stale. Rub small-leaved herbs between your fingers to crush them and remove any small twigs before using.

Small jars or tubes of herbs in oil can be useful when fresh herbs are hard to get, but use them sparingly, the flavours can be a bit harsh.

At times of plenty, herbs can be chopped and frozen and then stored in small containers. They lose their texture, though, and can only be used as ingredients, not garnishes.

Spices

These are best stored whole to keep their flavour. They can be ground in a coffee grinder and some are marketed in pots with a very efficient ceramic grinder on top; they are just as quick to use as spooning out ready-ground powders. For many oriental dishes the flavours of spices are enhanced by brief dry-roasting* in a frying pan before grinding. Grinding your own spices has the added benefit of the wonderful aromas released as they are ground, which you seldom get if you stick your nose into a jar of powdered spice.

Black peppercorns, cardamom, cinnamon, cloves, coriander, cumin, nutmeg or mace, saffron and vanilla beans are the spices to keep whole. A pepper mill is essential; cardamom, cinnamon, cloves, coriander, cumin and mace can all be ground easily; nutmeg is grated. Saffron, the most expensive spice, is used sparingly, crushed with a pestle and mortar, and soaked in a little liquid. Vanilla beans are used whole or split; whole beans can often be rinsed and dried afterwards and used again, which makes their high price more reasonable. An alternative is a small bottle of vanilla extract, but avoid vanilla essence because it is nasty.

Cayenne, paprika and turmeric are only available ground but should be on your shelf in small quantities. Replace ground spices regularly; once the aroma has gone, the flavour will also have deteriorated and the spice will contribute little to your dish. A few dried chillies and red pepper flakes would complete your stock of spices.

Other flavourings

Alcohol

Any table wine you have open can be used in cooking, but I wouldn't waste a grand Burgundy in a coq au vin. Use a wine you wouldn't mind drinking, not something dilute or harsh and tannic. It is useful to have a fortified wine or two (dry sherry, port, dry madeira, Marsala) on hand and for most things the everyday supermarket or off-licence brands are fine.

Brandy, rum and whisky are the most useful spirits in the kitchen. Dry cider can replace wine (and is less expensive) particularly with fish and pork. Beer and stout are useful for slow-cooked casseroles and stews.

Anchovies

Fillets in oil, whether in small tins or large jars, are the most convenient way to buy anchovies. Use them for salads, pizza, sauces and dressings. Small amounts of anchovy pounded with other ingredients give a subtle depth of flavour which is neither fishy nor excessively salty.

Chilli sauce

There are dozens to choose from, whether pure and fiery Tabasco, or a West Indian sauce enriched with onions and spices, or a thick, sweetened sauce in the Chinese style. A dash of chilli sauce will add dimension and depth to lots of dishes and can be used to replace chillies if necessary.

Fish sauce

This is a fermented amber-coloured sauce much used in south-east Asian dishes, dressings and dips. The cheesy smell is pungent, the flavour milder and salty. Thai *nam pla* is lighter in colour and milder than Vietnamese *nuoc mam*. A dash of fish sauce can be used instead of anchovy in a sauce.

Mustard

The best all-purpose mustard is Dijon, hot and aromatic, tempered by verjuice (juice of unripe grapes) or mild vinegar. Buy a small jar because the aromatics deteriorate quite quickly after opening. English mustard powder mixed with cold water will produce a sharp pungent paste.

Salt

Use sea salt, whether large crystals or finely ground. The flavour is much purer than that of table salt to which chemicals have been added to keep it free running.

Soy sauce

The essential ingredient of oriental cooking, soy sauce is fermented from soy bean meal, wheat and salt. It is used for marinades and sauces, stir-fries, soups and braised dishes. Dark soy sauce is aged longer than light and has added molasses. Use light soy with light dishes, dark with hearty casseroles and red meats.

Oils and vinegars

Olive oil

Extra virgin olive oil is the best oil for salads; it is low in acidity, aromatic and has a rich, fruity taste often with a slightly bitter note at the end. Prices vary greatly. Oils from individual estates can be very expensive, but top-quality oils have an unsurpassed intensity and purity of flavour. These oils are best used alone to dress salad leaves or to drizzle over a dish just before serving so that this aroma and flavour are not masked. Use a less expensive oil for vinaigrettes and to blend with other pronounced flavourings, as in a marinade, for example. Extra virgin oils from the big brands or supermarket own labels are blended to a style and are the cheapest, but they can be disappointingly flat and flavourless. However these oils can be used for marinades and for cooking, as can ordinary virgin olive oil, which is a grade down from extra virgin and slightly higher in acidity. All olive oils are high in mono-unsaturated fatty acids.

Sesame oil

Produced from toasted sesame seeds, it is deep amber in colour with a rich nutty flavour and aroma. It is useful for oriental cooking; a spoonful gives flavour to soups and stir-fries and to dressings for cold vegetable dishes. It should be used sparingly and is usually sprinkled over food just before serving.

Sunflower oil

High in polyunsaturated fatty acids, sunflower oil is light, virtually tasteless and a very good oil for cooking. It also blends well with other oils and can be used for dressings and sauces.

Alternative all-purpose oils are groundnut and rapeseed; both are low in saturated fats. Safflower oil is highest in polyunsaturated fats, but has a rather strong flavour. Corn oil is another good cooking oil but I find its texture heavy. Vegetable oil, obtained by blending several different and usually unspecified oils, may contain oils such as coconut or palm which are high in saturated fats, and is best avoided.

Walnut oil

Tasting just like walnuts, this oil gives a wonderful flavour to salads, but the flavour diminishes if it is heated. Walnut oil goes rancid quite quickly so buy in small quantities.

Balsamic vinegar

A fine aged vinegar from Italy, this is matured over many years in a solera system of barrels made from different types of wood. Deep in colour, with a syrupy consistency and a complex, full, sweet-sour taste, balsamic vinegar may be 10 years old or up to 100. Prices vary greatly: a tiny bottle of traditional balsamic vinegar from Modena costs a fortune, but you need only a few drops to appreciate its unctuous texture and concentrated lingering flavour.

Sherry vinegar

This is an excellent vinegar with a rich, nutty flavour. It is aged for several years in a solera system as is sherry, and the taste reminds one distinctly of sherry. It is smooth enough to use alone as a flavouring for cooked vegetables.

Wine vinegar

White is more useful than red as an everyday vinegar. The best ones are matured slowly in barrels and are well flavoured without excessive acidity. Cider vinegar has a sharper flavour but can replace wine vinegar in combination with other strongly flavoured ingredients.

Dry ingredients

Beans and chick peas

There are many to choose from: flageolets, small haricots and cannellini beans are my favourites for flavour and texture. Remember they need soaking for several hours. *See also* the notes on p. 111.

Flour

Plain flour is needed for pastry, cakes and biscuits; for flour-based sauces and occasionally for thickening. At a pinch, you can make a loaf of bread with it, too.

Gelatine

This comes in powdered and leaf form. Instructions for how much to use are on the packaging and in the recipes, but essentially 1 sachet (about 12g/3 tsp) powdered gelatine or 4 leaves (about 12g) leaf gelatine will set 600ml liquid.

Lentils

The best are the slate-coloured lentils from Puy in France, or green-brown ones from Castelluccio in Italy; small red lentils which disintegrate in cooking are good for soups and purées.
  See also the notes on p. 140.

Pasta and noodles

A packet of spaghetti or flat ribbons will always provide a quick meal if you have olive oil and garlic or butter and Parmesan.

Rice

Basmati is the best long grain rice for flavour and texture. Use it for steamed rice, fried rice, pilafs and salads. For risotto or paella use a short grain rice such as arborio or carnaroli. *See also* the notes on pp. 176–7.

Stock granules

Marigold Swiss bouillon powder is the best brand; vegetable, vegan and low-salt versions are available. *See also* p. 2.

Sugar

Apart from granulated sugar for everyday use, fine caster sugar is needed for baking and desserts. Light and dark muscovado sugar are unrefined cane sugars rich in molasses; light will be more useful for most cooking. Demerara sugar: these large crystals are also available unrefined, but cheaper demeraras are often made from refined sugar mixed with molasses.

Cans, jars and packets

Beans and chick peas

Cans of these are a great saving on soaking and cooking time when you are in a hurry. Drain and rinse well before using.

Chocolate

Good-quality plain chocolate with a high percentage (65% or more) of cocoa solids is what you need for cooking. It is expensive, but the flavour and texture are infinitely better than cheaper chocolate to which emulsifiers, fats and lots of sugar have been added. Chocolate will keep for several months in a cold place.

Coconut milk and creamed coconut

These are used for soups, vegetables, Thai curries and other south-east Asian dishes. Creamed coconut mixed with milk or water is more economical than a can of coconut milk when you only need a small amount.

Dried fruit

Apricots, prunes, raisins and sultanas are needed for baking and desserts, and for some stews.

Dried mushrooms

Ceps (porcini) or the more expensive morels provide a concentrated mushroom flavour for sauces, stews, a mushroom ragoût or risotto. They are expensive, but a little goes a very long way.

Honey

Choose your favourite clear honey.

Jam

Apricot jam and red currant jelly are used for glazes, and the jelly is also good in savoury sauces.

Nuts

Almonds keep best in their skins, but it is useful to have a small quantity of flaked and ground ones (don't keep them so long that they taste like sawdust). Pine nuts do not keep for long, so buy a small quantity. Use them for vegetable dishes, pilafs, in baking and for making pesto. Walnuts also go rancid quite quickly but provide richness in stews, meat and vegetable dishes, and can be ground to make sauces or used in baking.

Olives

Good quality green and black olives, unpitted, and packed in olive oil are the best. Large olives are good for cooking and the tiny ones for garnishes.

Tomatoes

Cans of plum tomatoes, jars of sun-dried tomatoes in oil, sun-dried tomato paste, tomato purée and passata (thick sieved tomato purée) have dozens of uses. You do not need to have them all; cans of chopped tomatoes are the most essential. Semi-dried tomatoes are now to be found in more shops and are well worth trying. *See also* p. 167.

Fresh ingredients

There are a few fresh ingredients which will keep for a couple of weeks or so, and therefore must be considered kitchen essentials: butter, eggs, garlic, fresh ginger, lemons, onions, shallots and Parmesan cheese. If you intend to use the peel of lemons or other citrus fruit, buy unwaxed or organic fruit; otherwise, scrub the skin well before using. With these and the more usual store cupboard ingredients above you will seldom be at a loss for making a meal.

Frozen ingredients

If you have a freezer, you could not only use it for gluts of herbs but also to keep small amounts of stock (pp. 4–6). Another good freezer stand-by is a pack of petits pois.

Equipment

You do not need a kitchen crammed full of pots and pans and gadgets to cook well. In fact, cluttered cupboards and drawers are a distraction rather than an advantage. What matters most is that you should buy the best you can afford. Good quality pans will last for twenty years or more and well-made practical tools will pay for themselves. When you go shopping for pans and roasting tins make sure they are suitable for your hob or will fit in your oven. Handle equipment before buying to be sure that you can work with it comfortably. Think through the purpose of a pan or tool: is it the right thing for the job and do you really need it? It is best to build up your equipment as your cooking develops.

Essentials

Pans

Weight and size are important when choosing pans. Stainless steel is durable and non-reactive with acids, but does not conduct heat well. The best stainless steel pans have a layer of aluminium or copper in the base to conduct heat evenly. Enamelled cast-iron pans, casseroles and oven dishes are very heavy, and best for slow cooking. Non-stick titanium pans are the best quality and very hard wearing as long as you do not scratch the surface. Non-stick coatings are easy to clean and mean the amount of fat needed for frying can be reduced. Lightweight pans burn quickly and do not always maintain a constant temperature; the coating on cheap non-stick pans soon scratches and comes off – a dubious economy.

Three saucepans of different sizes, with lids, form the basic kit. A little food cooked in too large a pan is likely to burn; if the pan is too small, the food may overflow. For cooking pasta or making stock you need a larger, tall pan.

A frying pan, preferably non-stick, a sauté pan with a lid, a wok and a ribbed, coated cast-iron griddle plate will take care of all types of frying and grilling. A roasting tin can be used to roast or braise meat or vegetables in the oven.

Knives

Choose knives that feel sturdy and balanced in the hand. Stainless steel knives are most commonly used in domestic kitchens; unfortunately they blunt quite quickly. Carbon steel knives stay sharp longer, but they rust and discolour when used on acidic foods and must be washed and dried straight after using. The best – and most expensive – are high-carbon stainless steel knives which have the advantages of both.

Ceramic blades are very efficient also and stay sharp, but they, too, are expensive.

The essential kit is a small paring knife for peeling vegetables; a cook's knife with an 18 or 20cm blade for chopping and slicing, crushing garlic or ginger; a serrated knife for bread and cakes and a carving knife with a broad, firm blade. You will also need a knife sharpener or steel. A steel takes practice to use, whereas a sharpener is easy to use, and is effective provided you insert the blade at the correct angle. Keep knives on a rack or in a block. If they rattle around in a drawer the points will soon be damaged.

Other equipment

Durability and practicality are important, but other equipment need not be as expensive as pans and knives. The basic kit consists of:

3 wooden spoons of different sizes	whisk
wooden fork for pasta and rice	pestle and mortar
2 rubber or plastic spatulas	pepper mill
large perforated spoon	colander
large metal spoon	sieve
pair kitchen scissors	salad spinner
potato peeler	1 or 2 wooden or plastic boards
palette knife	large and small mixing bowls
fish slice	measuring jug
pair kitchen tongs	set of scales
potato masher	timer
thin skewer	heat diffuser
4-sided grater	corkscrew

Time- and labour-saving tools

Food processors and blenders range from simple and cheap to highly sophisticated and expensive. They have become invaluable. Some models take up a great deal of space, so think about where one will fit in your kitchen. These are not machines to keep in the cupboard and bring out occasionally; you are likely to find you use a processor most days.

Non-essentials

Some equipment is specific to a particular type of cooking and only worth buying if you develop an interest in that branch of cookery. In this category are cake and tart tins, bread tins and baking sheets, a brush for greasing them, pastry cutters and a rolling pin, a wire cooling rack, an electric hand whisk and even a food mixer; *see also* the notes on p. 442 and pp. 460–1. Regular pasta makers will find a machine for rolling and cutting the dough invaluable. For ice cream making an electric machine that chills and churns saves much time and produces ice cream with a better texture. If you become enthusiastic about preserving, having a preserving pan with sloping sides is an advantage, *see also* p. 499. An electric deep-fryer with a thermostat is useful if you often deep-fry food, and if you like omelettes it is worth investing in an omelette pan (information on these is given with the omelette recipes on p. 57). A steamer can be electric and expensive, or consist of a small metal basket to fit inside a pan or a stack of Chinese bamboo baskets to fit on a pan or wok.

Damp muslin is used for finely straining sauce when a sieve would let through too many particles. You can buy it from kitchen departments and shops, but if you don't have any, use a pop sock, cut open, to line the sieve instead. Another alternative is to use a coffee filter but these tend to absorb too much liquid. Small squares of muslin are also used for tying up orange pips in marmalade making, or spices when pickling. A pop sock again makes a good substitute.

There are other non-essentials that are useful in everyday cooking, and not all of these are expensive:

> Ceramic or earthenware ovenproof casserole dishes
> Gratin dish (ceramic, earthenware or enamelled cast iron)
> Soufflé dishes
> Small frying pan for dry-roasting spices and nuts
> Filleting knife with a flexible blade
> Mandoline with adjustable cutting blades for cutting vegetables finely
> Soft mushroom brush
> Zester for shredding rind from citrus fruit

Glossary

Asafoetida: a resin-like substance used as a spice in Indian cooking. Its smell, as the name suggests, is fetid, stinking even. However, once a pinch is fried briefly in oil, the nastiness vanishes and the oil takes on a pleasant onion-like flavour and gives depth to dishes in which it is used. Available as a yellow powder in small pots from Indian shops; it will last a very long time. Use sparingly. If you don't have it to hand, your dish will lack some depth of flavour but still be good.

Bain-marie: a large pan of simmering water in which to place a smaller pan or dish containing a mixture that needs delicate cooking. It can also be used for keeping sauces warm.

Bouquet garni: a little bundle of herbs used to flavour slowly cooked dishes. Remove before serving. A bouquet garni typically includes bay leaf, parsley and thyme, but the flavourings can be varied according to the dish to be cooked. Easy to make up yourself and better tasting but also widely available in little bags.

Butter, clarified: butter from which impurities and sediment have been removed. To prepare it, heat a large piece of unsalted butter over low heat and let it melt. Simmer for 10 minutes until the surface is bubbling and the impurities rise to the top. Cool briefly and pour through a muslin-lined sieve (*see* opposite) into a jar. Refrigerate when cold and keep for cooking. It can be heated to a higher temperature than ordinary butter and does not stick. It also keeps longer because the elements that turn butter rancid have been removed.

Cardamom: green pods, containing sticky brown-black seeds with a mellow, warm aroma and flavour, backed by a hint of camphor. Whole pods or the seeds alone may be lightly bruised or crushed to release the essential oils, or seeds may be ground to a powder. A versatile spice, cardamom is used in a wide range of savoury and sweet dishes: in pilafs, stews, vegetable dishes, to flavour sauces and syrups, and in desserts and baking. Buy whole pods; they remain aromatic for up to a year in an airtight container. The flavour of ready-ground cardamom dissipates quickly. Available from supermarkets.

Chiffonade: ribbons of leaf vegetables. Roll several leaves tightly together and slice across finely.

Clarified butter: *see* **Butter, clarified**

Deglaze: to add liquid to a pan to dissolve cooking juices stuck to the bottom. Scraping and stirring will dislodge them and they enrich the liquid as it comes to the boil. Add to a sauce or use to make gravy.

Dry-roasting: putting spices or nuts into a heated frying pan without any fat and shaking or stirring them until they darken in colour and, in the case of spices, give off an aroma.

Galangal: a rhizome related to ginger, but different in colour and with a much denser flesh. It has peppery ginger flavours and a sourish note. The dried or powdered form is less flavourful than fresh. The latter is sometimes available from supermarkets, otherwise oriental shops sell both, often under the names *laos* or *khaa*. It is used in south-east Asian cooking.

Garam masala: the principal spice blend of north Indian cookery. A masala or spice mix may have 2 or 3 components or up to 15, depending on the dish and the cook. Garam masala is a warming mix but is not dependent on chillies. Available in supermarkets.

Ghee: *see* **Butter, clarified.** This is the Indian version.

Harissa: a fiery yet aromatic chilli-based sauce from North Africa that is used in cooking and as a table condiment with couscous and tagines. Available in small cans or jars from supermarkets, delicatessens and Middle Eastern shops.

Julienne: strips of vegetables of uniform length and thickness, prepared by slicing the vegetables, stacking the slices and cutting through them lengthways to make thin strips.

Lardons: strips of bacon, salt pork or pancetta* used with aromatic vegetables as the base for a stew.

Lemon grass: a tropical grass of which the bulbous base of the shoots is used as a flavouring in south-east Asia. It is fibrous, so only the bottom third should be used, the stems either being very finely sliced or left whole and bruised and removed from the dish before serving. The taste is refreshing and clean, similar to that of lemon peel. Available from oriental shops, greengrocers and the fresh herb cabinets of supermarkets.

Lime leaves: shiny evergreen leaves that grow in an unusual double form. Fresh leaves are intensely fragrant with citrus and floral notes. Used whole or shredded in soups, curry pastes, curries and other dishes of south-east Asia. Fresh leaves are available in supermarket herb cabinets and from oriental shops. They keep well in the refrigerator wrapped in plastic or can be frozen. Dried leaves lack flavour.

Mirin: a syrupy rice wine used in Japanese marinades and sauces, including the glaze for teriyaki steak. It is only used in cooking. Shaoxing is a similar Chinese rice wine, but this one can be drunk (it has an alcohol content similar to sherry). Available from oriental shops. Amontillado sherry can be used as a substitute.

Pancetta: Italian belly of pork cured in salt and spices and rolled up like a salami. Use in the same way as bacon or salt pork. Available from supermarkets and delicatessens.

Rice wine: *see* **Mirin**

Sambal: an Indonesian chilli relish used in cooking and as a table condiment. There are different types, with added vegetables, fruits or dried shrimp, and varying degrees of heat. Available from delicatessens, oriental shops and some supermarkets. Sambal is also the name used for freshly prepared chilli and vegetable table condiments, such as the cucumber and pineapple sambal and the tomato sambal on p. 384.

Star anise: a pretty, eight-pointed brown star, the fruit of a small magnolia native to southern China, this spice has a similar aroma and taste to anise and fennel, with more pronounced licorice notes and a slight sweetness. Used in Chinese cooking; in western cooking, try it with steamed and braised vegetables. Available from oriental shops and some supermarkets.

Sweat: to cook food, usually chopped vegetables, in a little fat over very low heat in a covered pan so that the food steams in the juices it releases. Usually done as the preliminary part of cooking a stew or sauce.

Tahini: a paste made from ground sesame seeds used in Middle Eastern cooking for dressings, to flavour vegetables and mixed with garlic and lemon juice as a purée or dip. Available in Middle Eastern shops, delicatessens and some supermarkets.

Tamarind: a bean-shaped pod from which the pulp encasing the seeds is used as a flavouring and souring ingredient in India and southern Asia. It has a sweet-sour, fruity flavour. Tamarind can be bought as a concentrate to be diluted to make a paste or, with more liquid, tamarind water. Available from Indian and oriental shops and some supermarkets.

Vanilla sugar: sugar flavoured with vanilla is often required in baking. It can be bought in expensive small sachets from supermarkets and delicatessens, but it is very easy to make your own. Fill a jar with caster sugar (this is the most useful sugar for baking) and put in a vanilla pod. Replenish the sugar as you use it; the vanilla pod can be used for years.

Conversion chart

These conversions from metric measures to cups (primarily used in Australia and the USA) for common ingredients are approximate, but should provide an adequate guide for the cook who is more familiar with measurements by volume than by weight.

1 cup (250 ml) is the close equivalent to the following measurements:

120g almonds & other nuts, chopped	140g flour, unsifted
120g almonds, flaked	150g hazelnuts
110g almonds & other nuts, ground	350g honey, golden syrup, treacle
150g almonds, whole	230g lentils
110g beans, cooked	120g pine nuts
220g beans, dried	150g raisins, currants
120g breadcrumbs, dry	150g rice, cooked
55g breadcrumbs, fresh	200g rice, uncooked
225g butter	225g sugar, caster or granulated
220g cheese, cream or curd	125g sugar, icing
120g cheese, grated	220g sugar, soft brown
115g flour, sifted	120g walnuts, pecans

The following measurements are close equivalents:

12g butter	1 level tbs
110g butter	1 stick
12g flour	1 level tbs
15g sugar, granulated or caster	1 level tbs

liquid measures

5ml	1 tsp
15ml	1 tbs
100ml	½ cup less 2 tbs
125ml	½ cup
250ml	1 cup
500ml/½ litre	2 cups/1 US pint (16 fl oz)

Bibliography

Acton, Eliza, *Modern Cookery,* Longman, London, 1845

Alexander, Stephanie, *The Cook's Companion,* Viking, London, 1996

Brissenden, Rosemary, *South East Asian Food,* Penguin Books, London, 1996

Brown, Lynda, *The Modern Cook's Handbook,* Penguin Books, London, 1998

Clarke, Sally, *Sally Clarke's Book,* Macmillan, London, 1999; Pan, London, 2000

David, Elizabeth, *English Bread and Yeast Cookery,* Allen Lane, London, 1977; Penguin Books, London, 1979

— *French Provincial Cooking,* Michael Joseph, London, 1960; Penguin Books, London, 1965

— *Italian Food,* Macdonald & Co, London, 1954; Penguin Books, London, 1963

— *An Omelette and a Glass of Wine,* Jill Norman, London, 1984; Penguin Books, London, 1985

— *Spices, Salt and Aromatics in the English Kitchen,* Penguin Books, London, 1970

— *Summer Cooking,* Museum Press, London, 1955; Penguin Books, London, 1965

Davidson, Alan, *The Oxford Companion to Food,* OUP, Oxford, 1999

Davis, Joy, *Noodles and Pasta,* Ryland, Peters & Small, London, 1999

Field, Carol, *The Italian Baker,* Harper & Row, New York, 1985

Grigson, Jane, *Fish Cookery,* The International Wine and Food Society, 1973; Penguin Books, London, 1975. Revised as *Jane Grigson's Fish Book,* Michael Joseph, London, 1993; Penguin Books, London, 1994

— *Jane Grigson's Vegetable Book,* Michael Joseph, London, 1978

Halici, Nevin, *Nevin Halici's Turkish Cookbook,* Dorling Kindersley, London, 1989

Hazelton, Nika, *From Nika Hazelton's Kitchen,* Viking, New York, 1985

Helou, Anissa, *Lebanese Cuisine,* Grub Street, London, 1994

Hopkinson, Simon, *Roast Chicken & Other Stories,* Ebury Press, London, 1994

Hosking, Richard, *A Dictionary of Japanese Food, Ingredients and Culture,* Prospect Books, London, 1996

Jaffrey, Madhur, *An Invitation to Indian Cooking,* Alfred A. Knopf, New York, 1973; Penguin Books, London, 1978

— *Madhur Jaffrey's World Vegetarian,* Elbury Press, London, 1998

Kafka, Barbara, *Microwave Gourmet,* Morrow, New York, 1987

Leith, Prue, *Prue Leith's Dinner Parties,* Dorling Kindersley, London, 1984

Manfield, Christine, *Spice,* Viking, London, 1999

McGee, Harold, *The Curious Cook,* HarperCollins, London, 1992

Norman, Jill, *The Complete Book of Spices,* Dorling Kindersley, London, 1990

Olney, Richard, *The Good Cook,* Time-Life Books, London, 1979–82

— *Lulu's Provençal Table,* HarperCollins, New York, 1994

— *Simple French Food,* Jill Norman, London, 1981; Penguin Books, London, 1983

Roden, Claudia, *The Book of Jewish Food,* Viking, London, 1997; Penguin Books, London, 1999

— *A New Book of Middle Eastern Food,* Viking, London, 1985; Penguin Books, London, 1987

— *Picnic,* Jill Norman, London, 1981; Penguin Books, London, 1982

Sahni, Julie, *Classic Indian Cooking,* Dorling Kindersley, London, 1986

— *Classic Indian Vegetarian Cooking,* Dorling Kindersley, London, 1987

Slater, Nigel, *Appetite,* Fourth Estate, London, 2000

— *Real Food,* Fourth Estate, London, 1998

Solomon, Charmaine, *Encyclopedia of Asian Food,* Heinemann, Melbourne, 1996

Stein, Rick, *Taste of the Sea,* BBC Books, London, 1995

Taruschio, Ann and Franco, *Leaves from The Walnut Tree,* Pavilion Books, London, 1993

Thomas, Anna, *The Vegetarian Epicure,* Alfred A. Knopf, New York, 1972; Penguin Books, London, 1975

Waters, Alice, *Chez Panisse Café Cookbook,* HarperCollins, New York, 1999

— *Chez Panisse Vegetables,* HarperCollins, New York, 1996

Willan, Anne, *Complete Guide to Cookery,* Dorling Kindersley, London, 1989

Bibliography

Index

Recipes are listed both under their title (*in italics*) and by main ingredient (**in bold**) 535
if that is not also the first word of the title.

Recipes suitable for vegetarians have the letter v after the page reference.

Recipes with vegetarian options are denoted with (v)

Techniques have their headings in SMALL CAPITALS

Index

Index

548

Index

Index

Index

Index